D1803423

OREMUS

Speaking with God

in the

Words of the Roman Rite

Translated by

Martin D. O'Keefe, S.J.

The Institute of Jesuit Sources
Saint Louis, 1993

© Copyright 1992 by Martin D. O'Keefe, S.J. All rights reserved.
Published with permission of Jesuit superiors.

The Institute of Jesuit Sources
3700 West Pine Boulevard
Saint Louis, Missouri, 63108-3386
TEL 314-652-5737
FAX 314-652-0810

Library of Congress Catalogue Card Number 93-061062
ISBN 1-880810-05-0

IN MEMORY OF

PAUL F. DISTLER, S.J.

(1911 - 1986)

Cuius insigni memoria

praeceptoris, collaboratoris, et amici

hoc opus aliquantulo sit dignum

PREFACE

The Latin word "oremus," by itself, means simply, "Let us pray." In the Roman rite of the Mass, however, it often has another, more specific meaning: it is frequently a call to the use of the three prayer formularies that are found in each day's Mass texts, i.e., the Collect, the Prayer over the Gifts, and the Prayer after Communion.

These three prayer formularies are remarkable in at least two senses: almost without exception, they are gems of Latin literature; and they are superb prayers. First, as Latin literature, they are part of the age-old treasure of the Catholic Church, and part of the cultural and religious heritage of every member of the Mystical Body. Not that all of them are themselves old: some are, and some are not. But all are part of an old and venerable tradition of how the Church prays. Next, as prayers, they are a marvelous balance between the individualistic and the communal: they can be (and ordinarily are) used in a public context, at Mass; but they can also be used by an individual who wishes to pray privately for the community of the faithful but still in a special sort of union with that community.

It is of course no secret that an active knowledge of Latin is quickly becoming a rarity in the Roman rite of the Church. One might regret that fact, but that does not much alter the situation. And at least one consequence of this eclipse of Latin is the danger that these prayers--and, to be sure, other elements of the Latin liturgy--may effectively be lost to those whose patrimony they rightfully are. That would be a shame.

Somewhat more than ten years ago, in an earlier, experimental version of the present volume, the late Father Paul F. Distler, S.J., and I undertook to make a translation of at least some of these prayers available to English-speaking readers who lack a background in Latin. The aim that we eventually set ourselves was to provide each of the approximately 1435 prayers with as accurate and as dignified an English version as possible, granting the inherent differences between the two languages. It sometimes proved impossible to retain the exact structure of the Latin prayers without getting into awkward English; Latin, with its full complement of inflections, can frequently sustain a much longer and more complex type of sentence than good English usage and style will permit. None the less, where the structure could easily be retained, we endeavored to do so. In all cases, we felt it important to say exactly what the Latin said, neither more nor less, to whatever extent that could be done.

Father Distler died in 1986; and the present volume is a reworking of our earlier joint effort. In addition to a revision of the prayer formularies, I have included a translation of the 5 Sequences, the 84 Prefaces, and the 4 Canons that are in common use in the Roman rite. In the case of the Sequences, I have attempted a poetic translation; thus in that section I have taken much greater liberties with the Latin text than is the case with any other part of the project.

"Traducere est tradere" ("to translate is to betray"), says an old Latin adage. And certainly it is true that, in translating a work of art such as the prayers, the sequences, the prefaces, and the canons, one necessarily ends up, from a literary standpoint, with a lesser product than the original. Perhaps, though, even through the barrier of a translation, readers might be able to catch a glimpse of the rare literary beauty that the original--those readers' heritage--possesses. Moreover, even in translation, these works' power *as prayers* can make itself felt, even if some of the literary qualities do not survive the change in languages.

The Latin text is printed along with the translations, and that quite deliberately. For one thing, readers who know Latin may well wish to have the original text available. For another, this translation is intended to be--among other things--a help in studying the prayers; and for this, the Latin seems necessary. Finally, nothing quite guarantees a translator's fidelity to his task in the way that the uncompromising presence of the original text can.

I ask that readers note that the translations in this volume are intended for private use only: study, reflection, personal prayer. They are not intended for public, liturgical use. There are two reasons for this. First, legitimate public use of these translations would require a special ecclesiastical permission which I have not sought for them. The Church has, I believe, every right to determine which translations are to be used in the liturgy; and I feel that that right ought to be respected. Secondly, had this volume been intended for oral proclamation rather than for private use, the translations themselves might well have been different in style (even if not in content).

Some thanks are in order. I am most grateful to Very Reverend E. Edward Kinerk, S.J., and to Very Reverend David L. Fleming, S.J., present and past provincials of the Missouri Province of the Society of Jesus, respectively; without their encouragement and tangible support, this volume would not exist. I am similarly grateful to Rev. John W. Padberg, S.J., Director of the Institute of Jesuit Sources; my debt to him for this and for many other things is vastly greater than can adequately be expressed here. My thanks go also to Charles B. Wilber, without whose gracious (but quite extraordinary) technical expertise the production of the book would have been out of the question. Finally, to Maestro Will Schwartz, conductor and musical director of the Fort Collins, Colorado, symphony orchestra, I extend my gratitude and appreciation: if to someone who knows the beauty of sound as well as he does these prayers have some appeal, then Paul Distler and I can rest well content.

Martin D. O'Keefe, S.J.
The Institute of Jesuit Sources
Saint Louis, Missouri
September 7, 1993.

CONTENTS

I.	THE COLLECTS THE PRAYERS OVER THE GIFTS THE PRAYERS AFTER COMMUNION	p. 1
	General Overview	2
	Overview of the Proper of the Saints	4
	The Season of Advent	7
	The Season of Christmas	19
	The Season of Lent	31
	The Season of Easter	59
	Ordinary Time	81
	Proper of the Saints	101
	Commons	183
	Ritual Masses	217
	Masses and Prayers for Various Needs	237
	Votive Masses	277
	Masses for the Dead	289
II.	THE SEQUENCES	315
	The Day of Wrathful Judgment *(Dies Irae)*	317
	Sing Praise, O Sion *(Lauda Sion)*	319
	The Mother Stayed Standing, in Sorrow Rent *(Stabat Mater)*	321
	Come, Most Holy Spirit of Love *(Veni Sancte Spiritus)*	323
	To the Paschal Victim *(Victimae Paschali)*	324
III.	THE PREFACES	325
	List of Prefaces	327
IV.	THE EUCHARISTIC PRAYERS	367
	Eucharistic Prayer I	369
	Eucharistic Prayer II	373
	Eucharistic Prayer III	376
	Eucharistic Prayer IV	379
	GENERAL INDEX	383

OREMUS

Speaking with God

in the

Words of the Roman Rite

I

The Collects
The Prayers over the Gifts
The Prayers after Communion

THE COLLECTS
THE PRAYERS OVER THE GIFTS
THE PRAYERS AFTER COMMUNION

THE SEASON OF ADVENT	P. 7
Sundays in Advent	9
Weekdays prior to December 16	11
December 17-24	14
THE SEASON OF CHRISTMAS	19
Christmas Masses	21
Holy Family	23
Days Within the Octave	23
Solemnity of BVM, Mother of God	25
Second Sunday after Christmas	25
Epiphany	26
Baptism of the Lord	26
Weekday Masses from January 2 to the Baptism of the Lord	27
THE SEASON OF LENT	31
Ash Wednesday	33
Weekdays after Ash Wednesday	34
First Week	35
Second Week	38
Third Week	41
Fourth Week	45
Fifth Week	48
Passion (Palm) Sunday	51
Weekdays of Holy Week	52
Holy Thursday	54
Good Friday	55
THE SEASON OF EASTER	59
Holy Saturday	61
Easter Sunday	65
Weekdays of Easter Week	65
Second Sunday of Easter	68
Third Sunday of Easter	68
Fourth Sunday of Easter	69
Fifth Sunday of Easter	69
Sixth Sunday of Easter	69
Ascension	70
Seventh Sunday of Easter	70
Pentecost	71
Weekdays after 2nd, 4th, and 6th Sundays of Easter	72
Weekdays after 3rd and 5th Sundays of Easter	76
Weekdays after 7th Sunday of Easter	78
ORDINARY TIME	81
Sundays in Ordinary Time, 1 - 33	83
Christ the King (34th Sunday)	98
Wednesdays of the 34th Week	98
Trinity Sunday	99
Corpus Christi	99
Sacred Heart	100
PROPER OF THE SAINTS (for detail, see pp. 4-6)	101
January	103
February	108
March	113
April	116
May	121
June	126
July	135
August	142
September	152
October	159
November	167
December	175
COMMONS	183
Dedication of a Church	185
Blessed Virgin Mary	186
Martyrs	190
Pastors	198
Doctors of the Church	205
Virgins	206
Holy Men and Women	208
RITUAL MASSES	217
Christian Initiation	219
Viaticum	224
Wedding Masses	224
Weddings	224
Anniversaries	229
Blessing of an Abbot or Abbess	230
Consecration to a Life of Virginity	231
Religious Profession	231
Dedication of a Church	235

MASSES FOR VARIOUS NEEDS	237
I. For the Church	239
For the Universal Church	239
For the Local Church	241
For the Pope	242
For the Bishop	243
For Election of a Pope or Bishop	244
For a Council or Synod	245
For Priests	245
For Ministers of the Church	248
For Priestly Vocations	248
For Religious	249
For Religious Vocations	250
For the Laity	250
For the Unity of Christians	251
For the Spread of the Gospel	253
For Persecuted Christians	255
For Pastoral/Spiritual Meetings	255
II. For Public Needs	256
For the Nation or State	256
For Those Who Govern the State	256
For a Meeting of National Leaders	257
For the Head of State	257
For the Development of Nations	257
For Preserving Peace and Justice	258
For Peace	259
For Reconciliation	259
In Time of War or Revolution	260
III. For Various Public Concerns	261
At the Start of the Civil Year	261
For Sanctifying Human Work	261
At Planting Time	262
After the Harvest	264
In Time of Famine	264
For Fugitives and Exiles	265
For Captives	266
For Prisoners	267
For the Sick	267
For the Dying	268
In Time of Earthquake	269
For Rain	269
For Good Weather	269
To Ward Off Storms	270
In Time of Any Need	270
In Thanksgiving to God	271
IV. For Certain Particular Needs	272
For Forgiveness of Sins	272
To Ask for Charity	273
To Foster Harmony	273
For the Family	274
For Relatives and Friends	274
For Those Who Injure Us	275
For the Grace of a Happy Death	276
VOTIVE MASSES	277
Holy Trinity	279
Mystery of the Holy Cross	279
Holy Eucharist	279
Holy Name of Jesus	280
Precious Blood	280
Sacred Heart	281
Holy Spirit	282
Blessed Virgin Mary	283
Mary the Mother of the Church	283
Holy Name of Mary	284
Holy Angels	284
Saint Joseph	285
All the Holy Apostles	285
Saints Peter and Paul	286
Saint Peter	286
Saint Paul	286
One Apostle	287
All the Saints	287
MASSES FOR THE DEAD	289
I. Funeral Masses	291
II. Anniversary Masses	293
III. Various Commemorations	296
For One Dead Person	296
For Several (or All the) Dead	297
IV. Prayers for the Dead	300
For a Pope	300
For a Diocesan Bishop	301
For Another Bishop	302
For a Priest	303
For a Deacon	304
For a Religious	304
For One Dead Person	305
For a Young Person	306
For One Who Worked in the Service of the Gospel	307
For One Who Suffered Long	307
For One Who Died Suddenly	307
For Several Dead Persons	308
For Married Persons	309
For Parents	310
For Relatives, Friends, Benefactors	310
V. Funerals of Children	311
For a Baptized Child	311
For an Unbaptized Child	312

PROPER OF THE SAINTS

(A=Apostle; AB=Abbot; B=Bishop; D=Doctor; M=Martyr; P=Pope; PR=Priest; R=Religious; V=Virgin)

JANUARY

02	Basil and Gregory (BB-DD)	103
07	Raymond of Pentafort (PR)	103
13	Hilary (B-D)	103
17	Anthony (AB)	104
20	Fabian and Sebastian (MM)	104
21	Agnes (V-M)	105
22	Vincent (Deacon-M)	105
24	Francis de Sales (B-D)	105
25	Paul the Apostle, Conversion	106
26	Timothy and Titus (BB)	106
27	Angela Merici (V)	107
28	Thomas Aquinas (PR-D)	107
31	John Bosco (PR)	107

FEBRUARY

02	Presentation of the Lord	108
03	Blase (B-M)	109
03	Ansgar (B)	109
05	Agatha (V-M)	109
06	Paul Miki and Companions (MM)	110
09	Jerome Emiliani	110
10	Scholastica (V)	110
11	B.V.M. of Lourdes	111
14	Cyril and Methodius (BB)	111
17	Seven Holy Founders of Servites	111
21	Peter Damien (B-D)	112
22	Chair of Saint Peter	112
23	Polycarp (B-M)	112

MARCH

04	Casimir	113
07	Perpetua and Felicity (MM)	113
08	John of God (R)	113
09	Frances of Rome (R)	114
17	Patrick (B)	114
18	Cyril of Jerusalem (B-D)	114
19	Joseph, Husband of Mary	115
23	Turibius of Mongrovejo (B)	115
25	Annunciation	115

APRIL

02	Francis of Paola (Hermit)	116
04	Isidore (B-D)	116
05	Vincent Ferrer (PR)	117
07	John Baptist de la Salle (PR)	117
11	Stanislaus (M)	117
13	Martin I (P-M)	118
21	Anselm (B-D)	118
23	George (M)	118
24	Fidelis of Sigmaringen (PR-M)	119
25	Mark (Evangelist)	119
28	Peter Chanel (PR-M)	119
29	Catherine of Sienna (V-D)	120
30	Pius V (P)	120

MAY

01	Joseph the Worker	121
02	Athanasius (B-D)	121
03	Philip and James (AA)	122
12	Nereus and Achilleus (MM)	122
12	Pancratius (M)	122
14	Matthias (A)	123
18	John I (P-M)	123
20	Bernadine of Sienna (PR)	123
25	Venerable Bede (PR-D)	124
25	Gregory VII (P)	124
25	Mary Magdalene de Pazzi (V)	124
26	Philip Neri (PR)	125
27	Augustine of Canterbury (B)	125
31	Visitation	125
	Immaculate Heart of Mary	126

JUNE

01	Justin (M)	126
02	Marcellinus and Peter (MM)	127
03	Charles Lwanga and Comp. (MM)	127
05	Boniface (B-M)	128
06	Norbert (B)	128
09	Ephraem (Deacon-D)	128
11	Barnabas (A)	129

13 Anthony of Padua (PR-D)	129	
19 Romuald (AB)	130	
21 Aloysius Gonzaga (R)	130	
22 Paulinus of Nola (B)	131	
22 John Fisher & Thomas More (MM)	131	
23 Vigil of John the Baptist	131	
24 Birth of John the Baptist	132	
27 Cyril of Alexandria (B-D)	132	
28 Irenaeus (B-M)	133	
28 Vigil of Peter and Paul	133	
29 Peter and Paul (AA)	134	
30 First Martyrs of Rome	134	

16 Stephen of Hungary	147	
19 John Eudes (PR)	147	
20 Bernard (AB-D)	148	
21 Pius X (P)	148	
22 Queenship of Mary	149	
23 Rose of Lima (V)	149	
24 Bartholomew (A)	150	
25 Louis of France	150	
25 Joseph Calasanz (PR)	150	
27 Monica	151	
28 Augustine (B-D)	151	
29 Beheading of John the Baptist	151	

JULY

03 Thomas (A)	135	
04 Elizabeth of Portugal	135	
05 Anthony Mary Zaccaria (PR)	135	
06 Maria Goretti (V-M)	136	
11 Benedict (AB)	136	
13 Henry	137	
14 Camillus de Lellis (PR)	137	
15 Bonaventure (B-D)	137	
16 Our Lady of Mt.Carmel	138	
17 Lawrence of Brindisi (PR-D)	138	
22 Mary Magdalene	138	
23 Bridget (R)	139	
25 James (A)	139	
26 Joachim and Ann	140	
29 Martha	140	
30 Peter Chrysologus (B-D)	141	
31 Ignatius of Loyola (PR)	141	

SEPTEMBER

03 Gregory the Great (P-D)	152	
08 Birth of the B.V.M.	153	
13 John Chrysostom (B-D)	153	
14 Triumph of the Holy Cross	154	
15 Our Lady of Sorrows	154	
16 Cornelius and Cyprian (MM)	155	
17 Robert Bellarmine (B-D)	155	
19 Januarius (B-M)	156	
21 Matthew (Evangelist-A)	156	
26 Cosmas and Damian (MM)	157	
27 Vincent de Paul (PR)	157	
28 Wenceslaus (M)	158	
29 Michael, Gabriel, Raphael	158	
30 Jerome (PR-D)	158	

OCTOBER

01 Theresa of the Child Jesus (V)	159	
02 Holy Guardian Angels	160	
04 Francis of Assisi (R)	160	

AUGUST

01 Alphonsus Liguori (B-D)	142	
02 Eusebius of Vercelli (B)	142	
04 John Mary Vianney (PR)	142	
05 Dedication of St. Mary Major	143	
06 Transfiguration	143	
07 Sixtus II and Companions (MM)	144	
07 Cajetan (PR)	144	
08 Dominic (PR)	144	
10 Lawrence (Deacon-M)	145	
11 Clare (V)	145	
13 Pontian and Hippolytus (MM)	146	
14 Vigil of the Assumption	146	
15 Assumption of the B.V.M.	146	

06 Bruno (PR)	161	
07 Our Lady of the Rosary	161	
09 Denis and Companions (MM)	161	
09 John Leonard (PR)	161	
14 Callistus I (P-M)	162	
15 Teresa of Avila (V-D)	162	
16 Hedwig (R)	163	
16 Margaret Mary Alacoque (V)	163	
17 Ignatius of Antioch (B-M)	163	
18 Luke (Evangelist)	164	
19 John de Brebeuf, Isaac Jogues, and Companions (MM)	165	
19 Paul of the Cross (PR)	165	

23	John of Capistrano (PR)	166
24	Anthony Mary Claret (B)	166
28	Simon and Jude (AA)	166

NOVEMBER

01	All Saints	167
02	All Souls	167
03	Martin de Porres (R)	169
04	Charles Borromeo (B)	169
10	Leo the Great (P-D)	170
11	Martin of Tours (B)	170
12	Josephat (B-M)	171
15	Albert the Great (B-D)	171
16	Margaret of Scotland	172
16	Gertrude (V)	172
17	Elizabeth of Hungary (R)	172
18	Dedication of Churches of Peter and Paul	173
21	Presentation of the B.V.M.	173
22	Cecelia (V-M)	173
23	Clement I (P-M)	174
23	Columban (AB)	174
30	Andrew (A)	174

DECEMBER

03	Francis Xavier (PR)	175
04	John Damascene (PR-D)	176
06	Nicholas (B)	176
07	Ambrose (B-D)	176
08	Immaculate Conception	177
11	Damasus I (P)	177
12	Jane Frances de Chantal (R)	178
13	Lucy (V-M)	178
14	John of the Cross (PR-D)	178
21	Peter Canisius (PR-D)	179
23	John of Kanty (PR)	179
26	Stephen the Protomartyr	179
27	John (Evangelist-A)	180
28	Holy Innocents (MM)	180
29	Thomas Becket (B-M)	181
31	Sylvester I (P)	181

THE SEASON OF

ADVENT

THE FIRST SUNDAY OF ADVENT

Collect

Da, quaesumus, omnipotens Deus, hanc tuis fidelibus voluntatem, ut Christo tuo venienti iustis operibus occurrentes, eius dexterae sociati, regnum mereamur possidere caeleste. Per Dominum.

Almighty God, we ask you to grant your faithful people what they here desire. With their good works, they hasten to meet your Christ as He comes; may they be privileged to be placed at his right hand and to possess the heavenly kingdom where he lives and reigns....

Prayer over the Gifts

Suscipe, quaesumus, Domine, munera quae de tuis offerimus collata beneficiis, et quod nostrae devotioni concedis effici temporali, tuae nobis fiat praemium redemptionis aeternae. Per Christum.

Lord, we ask you to receive the offerings we bring, taken from the gifts you have given us. May what you allow our devoted service to accomplish in this life become our assurance of your eternal redemption. We ask this through Christ our Lord.

Prayer after Communion

Prosint nobis, quaesumus, Domine, frequentata mysteria, quibus nos, inter praetereuntia ambulantes, iam nunc instituis amare caelestia et inhaerere mansuris. Per Christum.

Lord, even as we walk amidst what is passing away, you now teach us, through these mysteries, to love the things of heaven and to cling to what has no end. May our repeated celebration of these mysteries help us to seek the eternal. We ask this....

THE SECOND SUNDAY OF ADVENT

Collect

Omnipotens et misericors Deus, in tui occursum Filii festinantes nulla opera terreni actus impediant, sed sapientiae caelestis eruditio nos faciat eius esse consortes. Qui tecum....

Almighty and merciful God, as we hasten to meet your Son, may no earthly concerns hold us back. Rather, may the teachings of your heavenly wisdom make us the companions of Him who lives and reigns with You and the Holy Spirit, one God, for ever and ever.

Prayer over the Gifts

Placare, Domine, quaesumus, nostrae precibus humilitatis et hostiis, et, ubi nulla suppetunt suffragia meritorum, tuae nobis indulgentiae succurre praesidiis. Per Christum.

Be pleased, Lord, by our humble prayers and offerings. Since we cannot claim to deserve anything because of what we have done, aid us with the help of your free and gracious mercy. We ask this through Christ our Lord.

Prayer after Communion

Repleti cibo spiritualis alimoniae, supplices te, Domine, deprecamur, ut, huius participatione mysterii, doceas nos terrena sapienter perpendere, et caelestibus inhaerere. Per Christum.

Lord, we are refreshed by the food that sustains our spirits, and we humbly ask that, through our sharing in this mystery, you would teach us to evaluate earthly concerns wisely, and to give our allegiance to heavenly ones. We ask this....

THE THIRD SUNDAY OF ADVENT

Collect

Deus, qui conspicis populum tuum nativitatis dominicae festivitatem fideliter exspectare, praesta, quaesumus, ut valeamus ad tantae salutis gaudia pervenire, et ea votis solemnibus alacri semper laetitia celebrare. Per Dominum.

God our Father, you see that your people are waiting in faith for the feast of the Lord's birth. Please grant that we may arrive at the joys of our magnificent redemption and celebrate them with renewed dedication and in ever-eager joy. We ask this....

Prayer over the Gifts

Devotionis nostrae tibi, Domine, quaesumus, hostia iugiter immoletur, quae et sacri peragat instituta mysterii, et salutare tuum nobis potenter operetur. Per Christum.

Lord, we ask that this sacrifice of our love and dedication may be offered to you unceasingly. May it fulfill the plan of this sacred mystery, and powerfully bring about your salvation within us. We ask this....

Prayer after Communion

Tuam, Domine, clementiam imploramus, ut haec divina subsidia, a vitiis expiatos, ad festa ventura nos praeparent. Per Christum.

Lord, we earnestly ask for your mercy, so that the heavenly gifts we have received may cleanse us from sin and so prepare us for the celebration that is to come. We ask this....

THE FOURTH SUNDAY OF ADVENT

Collect

Gratiam tuam, quaesumus, Domine, mentibus nostris infunde, ut qui, Angelo nuntiante, Christi Filii tui incarnationem cognovimus, per passionem eius et crucem ad resurrectionis gloriam perducamur. Per Dominum.

Lord, we ask that you pour forth your grace into our hearts. By the Angel's message, we have come to know of the incarnation of Christ your Son; through his suffering and his cross, may we be led to the glory of his resurrection. We ask this....

Prayer over the Gifts

Altari tuo, Domine, superposita munera Spiritus ille sanctificet, qui beatae Mariae viscera sua virtute replevit. Per Christum.

Lord, may that same Spirit who filled the womb of Blessed Mary with his power also sanctify the gifts that are placed upon your altar. We ask this....

Prayer after Communion

Sumpto pignore redemptionis aeternae, quaesumus, omnipotens Deus, ut quanto magis dies salutiferae festivitatis accedit, tanto devotius proficiamus ad Filii tui digne nativitatis mysterium celebrandum. Per Christum.

Almighty God, we have received the pledge of our eternal redemption. We ask that, the nearer we come to the happy day of our salvation, the more we may grow in dedicated love, so that we may worthily celebrate the mystery of the birth of your Son. We ask this....

WEEKDAYS OF ADVENT PRIOR TO DECEMBER 16: MONDAYS

Collect: First Week

Fac nos, quaesumus, Domine Deus noster, adventum Christi Filii tui sollicitos exspectare, ut, dum venerit pulsans, orationibus vigilantes, et in suis inveniat laudibus exsultantes. Per Dominum.

Lord our God, make us eager to await the coming of Christ your Son. When he comes and knocks, may he find us watchful in our prayer and joyful in our praise of him. We ask this....

Collect: Second Week

Dirigatur, quaesumus, Domine, in conspectu tuo nostrae petitionis oratio, ut ad magnum incarnationis Unigeniti tui mysterium nostrae vota servitutis illibata puritate perveniant. Per Dominum....

Lord, may our prayer and petition be guided in your divine sight, so that our promise to serve you may arrive pure and unstained at the celebration of the great mystery of your Son's incarnation. We ask this....

Collect: Third Week

Voci nostrae, quaesumus, Domine, aures tuae pietatis accommoda, et cordis nostri tenebras gratia Filii tui nos visitantis illustra. Per Dominum....

Lord, in your faithful love, please turn your attention to our prayer, and brighten the darkness of our hearts by the grace of your Son as he comes among us. We ask this....

Prayer over the Gifts and Prayer after Communion:

as on the First
Sunday of Advent (p.9)

WEEKDAYS OF ADVENT PRIOR TO DECEMBER 16: TUESDAYS

Collect: First Week

Propitiare, Domine Deus, supplicationibus nostris, et tribulantibus, quaesumus, tuae concede pietatis auxilium, ut, de Filii tui venientis praesentia consolati, nullis iam polluamur contagiis vetustatis. Per Dominum.

Lord our God, we ask you to be pleased with our prayers, and to grant us the help of your faithful love in our troubles. May we thus be comforted by the presence of your Son who is coming, and be now untainted by the sins of our past. We ask this....

Collect: Second Week

Deus, qui salutare tuum cunctis terrae finibus declarasti, tribue, quaesumus, ut nativitatis eius gloriam laetanter praestolemur. Per Dominum.

God our Father, you have made known your salvation to the far corners of the earth. Please grant that we may joyfully await the glory of its birth. We ask this....

Collect: Third Week

Deus, qui novam creaturam per Unigenitum tuum nos esse fecisti, in opera misericordiae tuae propitius intuere, et in adventu Filii tui ab omnibus nos maculis vetustatis emunda. Per Dominum.

God our Father, you have made us into a new creation through your only Son. Look with kindness on the works of your mercy, and, at the coming of your Son, cleanse us from all stain of the past. We ask this....

Prayer over the Gifts and Prayer after Communion:

as on the Second
Sunday of Advent (p.9)

WEEKDAYS OF ADVENT PRIOR TO DECEMBER 16: WEDNESDAYS

Collect: First Week

Praepara, quaesumus, Domine Deus noster, corda nostra divina tua virtute, ut, veniente Christo Filio tuo, digni inveniamur aeternae vitae convivio, et cibum caelestem, ipso ministrante, percipere mereamur. Per Dominum.

Lord our God, we ask that you prepare our hearts with your divine power, so that, when Christ your Son comes, we may be found worthy of the banquet of eternal life and may be privileged to receive our heavenly food at his hands. We ask this....

Collect: Second Week

Omnipotens Deus, qui nos praecipis iter Christo Domino praeparare, concede propitius, ut nullis infirmitatibus fatigemur, qui caelestis medici consolantem praesentiam sustinemus. Per Dmn.

Almighty God, you command us to prepare the way for Christ our Lord. In your mercy, please grant that in doing so we may be neither weakened nor wearied, since we are given the comforting presence of the Divine Physician. We ask this....

Collect: Third Week

Praesta, quaesumus, omnipotens Deus, ut Filii tui ventura sollemnitas et praesentis nobis vitae remedia largiatur, et praemia aeterna concedat. Per Dominum.

Almighty God, please grant that the coming feast of your Son may heal our ills in this present life and bestow on us rewards for all eternity. We ask this....

Prayer over the Gifts and Prayer after Communion:
as on the Third
Sunday of Advent (p.10)

WEEKDAYS OF ADVENT PRIOR TO DECEMBER 16: THURSDAYS

Collect: First Week

Excita, Domine, potentiam tuam, et magna nobis virtute succure, ut, quod nostra peccata praepediunt, gratia tuae propitiationis acceleret. Per Dominum.

Lord, stir up your power, and aid us with your great strength. May your gift of reconciliation hasten the coming of what our sins obstruct. We ask this....

Collect: Second Week

Excita, Domine, corda nostra ad praeparandas Unigeniti tui vias, ut, per eius adventum, purificatis tibi mentibus servire mereamur. Per Dominum.

Lord, stir up our hearts to prepare the way for your only Son. Through his coming, may we be privileged to serve you with pure hearts. We ask this....

Collect: Third Week

Indignos, quaesumus, Domine, nos famulos tuos, quos actionis propriae culpa contristat, Unigeniti tui adventu salutari laetifica. Per Dominum.

Lord, although the blame that stems from our own actions saddens us and makes us unworthy servants, we ask that you gladden us by the salvific coming of your only Son. We ask this....

Prayer over the Gifts and Prayer after Communion:
as on the First
Sunday of Advent (p.9)

WEEKDAYS OF ADVENT PRIOR TO DECEMBER 16: FRIDAYS

Collect: First Week

Excita, quaesumus, Domine, potentiam tuam, et veni, ut, ab imminentibus peccatorum nostrorum periculis, te mereamur protegente eripi, te liberante salvari. Qui vivis.

Lord, we ask that you stir up your power and come. From the perils that threaten us because of our sins, may we be privileged to be rescued by your protection and to be rendered secure by your deliverance. We ask this....

Collect: Second Week

Concede, quaesumus, omnipotens Deus, plebi tuae adventum Unigeniti tui cum summa vigilantia exspectare, ut, sicut ipse docuit auctor nostrae salutis, accensis lampadibus in eius occursum vigilantes properemus. Per Dominum....

Almighty God, please grant that your people may watch most carefully for the coming of your only Son. As he himself, the author of our salvation, has taught us, may we be vigilant, with our lamps burning, and may we hasten to meet him when he comes. We ask this....

Collect: Third Week

Praeveniat nos, omnipotens Deus, tua gratia semper atque subsequatur, ut, qui adventum Unigeniti tui summo cordis desiderio sustinemus, et praesentis vitae subsidia et futurae pariter consequamur. Per Domninum....

Almighty God, may your grace always precede our actions and support them. As we await the coming of your only Son with eager and longing hearts, may we receive your help for our present life and for the life to come as well. We ask this....

Prayer over the Gifts and Prayer after Communion:

as on the Second Sunday of Advent (p.9)

WEEKDAYS OF ADVENT PRIOR TO DECEMBER 16: SATURDAYS

Collect: First Week

Deus, qui ad liberandum humanum genus a vetustatis condicione, Unigenitum tuum in hunc mundum misisti, largire devote exspectantibus supernae tuae gratiam pietatis, ut ad verae perveniamus praemium libertatis. Per Dominum.

God our Father, you sent your only Son into this world to free the human race from its ancient sinfulness. Grant to those who singleheartedly await Him the grace of your own divine fidelity, so that we may gain the reward of true freedom. We ask this....

Collect: Second Week

Oriatur, quaesumus, omnipotens Deus, in cordibus nostris splendor gloriae tuae, ut, omni noctis obscuritate sublata, filios nos esse lucis Unigeniti tui manifestet adventus. Per Dominum.

Almighty God, we ask that the brilliance of your glory may arise and shine forth in our hearts, so that all darkness of night may be taken away and the coming of your only Son may reveal that we are sons of light. We ask this....

Prayer over the Gifts and Prayer after Communion:

as on the Third Sunday of Advent (p.10)

DECEMBER 17

Collect

Deus, humanae conditor et redemptor naturae, qui Verbum tuum in utero perpetuae virginitatis carnem assumere voluisti, respice propitius ad preces nostras, ut Unigenitus tuus, nostra humanitate suscepta, nos divino consortio sociare dignetur. Per Dominum.

God our Father, you both established and redeemed human nature, and you decreed that your Word should take on human flesh in a womb marked by perpetual virginity. Look with kindness on our prayers. Now that your only Son has taken our humanity unto himself, grant that he may see fit to join us to his divinity. We ask this....

Prayer over the Gifts

Ecclesiae tuae, Domine, dona sanctifica, et concede ut, per haec veneranda mysteria, pane caelesti refici mereamur. Per Christum.

Lord, we ask you to make the gifts of your Church holy, and to grant that, by means of these awesome mysteries, we may be privileged to be refreshed with heavenly food. We ask this....

Prayer after Communion

Divino munere satiati, quaesumus, omnipotens Deus, hoc desiderio potiamur, ut, a tuo accensi Spiritu, ante conspectum venientis Christi tui, velut clara luminaria fulgeamus. Per Christum.

We are filled with your divine gift, almighty God, and we ask that we may gain the desire to be inflamed by your Spirit, so as to shine as brilliant lights in the sight of your Christ when he comes. We ask this....

DECEMBER 18

Collect

Concede, quaesumus, omnipotens Deus, ut, qui sub peccati iugo ex vetusta servitute deprimimur, exspectata Unigeniti tui nova nativitate liberemur. Per Dominum.

Almighty God, we are weighed down in age-old slavery beneath the yoke of sin. Please grant that we may be set free from it by the new birth of your only Son which we awaited. We ask this....

Prayer over the Gifts

Sacrificium tibi, Domine, celebrandum tuo nomini nos reddat acceptos, ut ipsius aeternitatis mereamur esse consortes, qui mortalitatem nostram sua mortalitate curavit. Per Christum.

May the sacrifice that is to be offered to your name make us acceptable to you, Lord, so that we may be privileged to share in the eternal life of him who revoked our liability to death by himself becoming subject to death. We ask this....

Prayer after Communion

Suscipiamus, Domine, misericordiam tuam in medio templi tui, et redemptionis nostrae ventura sollemnia congruis honoribus praecedamus. Per Christum.

Lord, may we receive your mercy as we live within your Church. With fitting praise, may we prepare for the solemn events of our redemption that are to come. We ask this....

DECEMBER 19

Collect

Deus, qui splendorem gloriae tuae per sacrae Virginis partum mundo dignatus es revelare, tribue, quaesumus, ut tantae incarnationis mysterium et fidei integritate colamus, et devoto semper obsequio frequentemus. Per Dominum.

God our Father, you were pleased to show the world the splendor of your glory by means of the child born of the holy Virgin. Grant, we ask, that we may cherish the mystery of this magnificent birth with complete faith, and ever celebrate it with loving allegiance. We ask this....

Prayer over the Gifts

Propitius intuere munera, Domine, quaesumus, quae tuis altaribus exhibemus, ut, quod nostra fragilitate defertur, tua virtute sacretur. Per Christum.

Lord, in your kindness please look upon the gifts which we place on your altar. May what we bring here in our weakness be made holy by means of your power. We ask this....

Prayer after Communion

Gratias de collatis muneribus referentes, fac nos propitius, omnipotens Deus, quae ventura sunt desiderare praestanda, ut nativitatem Salvatoris nostri purificatis suscipiamus mentibus honorandam. Per Christum.

As we give thanks for the gifts you have given us, almighty God, we ask that in your kindness you make us yearn for the wonderful events to come, so that we may welcome the birth of the Savior as an event to be reverenced with hearts purified of sin. We ask this....

DECEMBER 20

Collect

Deus, cuius ineffabile Verbum, Angelo nuntiante, Virgo immaculata suscepit, et, domus divinitatis effecta, Sancti Spiritus luce repletur, quaesumus, ut nos, eius exemplo, voluntati tuae humiliter adhaerere valeamus. Per Dominum.

God our Father, at the Angel's message the most pure Virgin received your unutterable Word within herself. She became the dwelling place of the Godhead, and was filled with the light of the Holy Spirit. We ask that we may follow her example and adhere humbly to your will. We ask this....

Prayer over the Gifts

Intende, quaesumus, Domine, sacrificium singulare, ut, huius participatione mysterii, quae speranda credimus, exspectata sumamus. Per Christum.

Lord, we ask that you look upon this unique sacrifice. By sharing in this mystery, may we receive, as something long awaited, the gifts for which faith commands us to hope. We ask this....

Prayer after Communion

Quos munere caelesti reficis, Domine, divino tuere praesidio, ut, tuis mysteriis perfruentes, in vera facias pace gaudere. Per Christum.

Lord, with your divine protection guard those whom you refresh with this heavenly gift. As they gladly celebrate your mysteries, make them rejoice in true peace. We ask this....

DECEMBER 21

Collect

Preces populi tui, quaesumus, Domine, clementer exaudi, ut, qui de Unigeniti tui in nostra carne adventu laetantur, cum venerit in sua maiestate, aeternae vitae praemium consequantur. Per Dominum.

Lord, in your mercy please hear the prayers of your people. They rejoice at the coming of your only Son in our human flesh; when he comes in the fullness of his divine majesty, may they attain the reward of eternal life. We ask this....

Prayer over the Gifts

Ecclesiae tuae, Domine, munera placatus assume, quae et misericors offerenda tribuisti, et in nostrae salutis potenter efficis transire mysterium. Per Christum.

Lord, be pleased to receive the gifts of your Church. In your mercy, you gave them to us to offer, and in your power you cause them to be transformed into the mystery of our salvation. We ask this....

Prayer after Communion

Sit plebi tuae, Domine, continuata defensio divini participatio mysterii, ut, maiestati tuae plena devotione subiecta, salvationem mentis et corporis affluenter accipiat. Per Christum.

Lord, may your people's participation in this divine mystery be a constant protection for them. May they thus live in full obedience to your divine majesty, and so receive complete salvation of mind and body. We ask this....

DECEMBER 22

Collect

Deus, qui, hominem delapsum in mortem conspiciens, Unigeniti tui adventu redimere voluisti, praesta, quaesumus, ut qui humili eius incarnationem devotione fatentur, ipsius etiam Redemptoris consortia mereantur. Per Dominum.

God our Father, you saw that the human race had fallen to a state of death, and you willed to redeem it by the coming of your only Son. Please grant that those who with humble dedication proclaim his incarnation may be privileged to be his companions in his work as Redeemer. We ask this....

Prayer over the Gifts

In tua pietate confidentes, Domine, cum muneribus ad altaria veneranda concurrimus, ut, tua purificante nos gratia, iisdem quibus famulamur mysteriis emundemur. Per Christum.

Lord, relying confidently on your loving faithfulness, we hasten to come together, carrying our gifts to your sacred altar. We ask that your grace may purify us and that we may be cleansed by the very mysteries in which we take part. We ask this....

Prayer after Communion

Roboret nos, Domine, tui sacramenti perceptio, ut venienti Salvatori mereamur cum dignis operibus obviare, et beatitudinis praemia mereri. Per Christum.

May our reception of your sacrament strengthen us, Lord, so that we may be privileged to meet the coming Savior with fitting deeds and be worthy of the rewards of eternal life. We ask this....

DECEMBER 23

Collect

Omnipotens sempiterne Deus, nativitatem Filii tui secundum carnem propinquare cernentes, quaesumus, ut nobis indignis famulis tuis misericordiam praestet Verbum, quod ex Virgine Maria dignatum est caro fieri, et habitare in nobis. Qui tecum.

Almighty and eternal God, we are aware that your only Son's birth according to the flesh is drawing near. We ask that your Word, who saw fit to become flesh of the Virgin Mary and to live among us, may grant mercy to us, your unworthy servants. We ask this....

Prayer over the Gifts

Haec oblatio, qua divini cultus nobis est indita plenitudo, sit tibi, Domine, perfecta placatio, ut nostri Redemptoris exordia purificatis mentibus celebremus. Per Christum.

Lord, may this offering, by which the fullness of divine worship is granted to us, be the perfect means of our atonement with you, so that we may celebrate the birth of our Redeemer with pure hearts. We ask this....

Prayer after Communion

Caelesti munere satiatis, Domine, pacem tuam propitius indulge, ut Filio tuo dilectissimo venienti accensis lampadibus digni praestolemur occursum. Per Christum.

Lord, we are filled with your divine gifts. In your mercy, grant us your peace, so that with lighted lamps we may worthily wait to meet your most beloved Son as he comes. We ask this....

DECEMBER 24

Collect

Festina, quaesumus, ne tardaveris, Domine Iesu, ut adventus tui consolationibus subleventur, qui in tua pietate confidunt. Qui vivis.

Please hasten, Lord Jesus, and do not delay, so that those who trust in your faithful love may be consoled by the comfort of your coming. We ask this....

Prayer over the Gifts

Oblata tibi, Domine, munera benignus assume, ut eorum perceptione expiemur a peccatis, et adventus Filii tui gloriam puris mereamur mentibus praestolari. Per Christum.

Lord, in your kindness accept the gifts we offer you. By their being received, may we be cleansed of sin, and be privileged to await with pure hearts the glory of your Son's coming. We ask this....

Prayer after Communion

Da nobis, Domine, hoc dono tuo mirabili recreatis, ut, sicut adoranda Filii tui natalicia praevenimus, sic eius munera capiamus sempiterna gaudentes. Per Christum.

Lord, we have been renewed by this marvelous gift of yours. Grant that, just as we await the sacred birthday of your Son, so may we receive his eternal gifts with joy. We ask this....

THE SEASON OF CHRISTMAS

CHRISTMAS VIGIL MASS

Collect

Deus, qui nos redemptionis nostrae annua exspectatione laetificas, praesta, ut Unigenitum tuum, quem laeti suscipimus Redemptorem, venientem quoque Iudicem securi videre mereamur. Per Dominum.

God our Father, each year you gladden us with the prospect of our redemption. As your only Son comes as our Redeemer, we receive him with joy; when he comes to be our Judge, grant that we may be privileged to look upon him with confidence. We ask this....

Prayer over the Gifts

Tanto nos, Domine, quaesumus, promptiore servitio haec praecurrere concede sollemnia, quanto in his constare principium nostrae redemptionis ostendis. Per Christum.

Lord, please grant that we may await this solemn feast with a service made all the more eager by the degree to which you show us that it contains the beginning of our redemption. We ask this....

Prayer after Communion

Da nobis, quaesumus, Domine, unigeniti Filii tui recensita nativitate vegetari, cuius caelesti mysterio pascimur et potamur. Per Christum.

Lord, from the divine mystery of your only Son we receive food and drink. Please grant that we may be given new strength by our remembrance of his birth. We ask this....

CHRISTMAS MIDNIGHT MASS

Collect

Deus, qui hanc sacratissimam noctem veri luminis fecisti illustratione clarescere, da, quaesumus, ut cuius in terra mysteria lucis agnovimus, eius quoque gaudiis perfruamur in caelo. Per Dominum.

God our Father, you have made this most holy night brilliant by the splendor of the true light. We have come to know the mystery of this light on earth; please grant that we may experience its joys in heaven. We ask this....

Prayer over the Gifts

Grata tibi sit, Domine, quaesumus, hodiernae festivitatis oblatio, ut, per haec sacrosancta commercia, in illius inveniamur forma, in quo tecum est nostra substantia. Per Christum.

Lord, we ask that our offering on this feast today may be pleasing to you. Through this most holy interaction, may we be found to be like him who joins our nature to yours. We ask this....

Prayer after Communion

Da nobis, quaesumus, Domine Deus noster, ut, qui nativitatem Redemptoris nostri frequentare gaudemus, dignis conversationibus ad eius mereamur pervenire consortium. Per Christum.

Lord our God, we rejoice in celebrating the birth of our Redeemer. Please grant that, by living worthy lives, we may be privileged to enjoy his friendship. We ask this....

CHRISTMAS MASS AT DAWN

Collect

Da, quaesumus, omnipotens Deus, ut dum nova incarnati Verbi tui luce perfundimur, hoc in nostro resplendeat opere, quod per fidem fulget in mente. Per Christum.

Almighty God, as we are bathed in the new light of your Son who is born among us, we ask that what faith makes resplendent in our hearts may shine forth in our deeds. We ask this....

Prayer over the Gifts

Munera nostra, quaesumus, Domine, nativitatis hodiernae mysteriis apta proveniant, ut sicut homo genitus idem praefulsit et Deus, sic nobis haec terrena substantia conferat quod divinum est. Per Christum.

Lord, we ask that our gifts may be appropriate to the mysteries of the birth we celebrate this day. Just as he who underwent human birth today also possessed the splendor of God, so may these earthly offerings bestow on us what is divine. We ask this....

Prayer after Communion

Da nobis, Domine, Filii tui nativitatem laeta devotione colentibus, huius arcana mysterii et plena fide cognoscere, et pleniore caritatis ardore diligere. Per Christum.

Lord, as we celebrate the birth of your Son with joyful dedication, grant that we may understand the secrets of this mystery with a lively faith and may treasure them with an even more ardent love. We ask this....

CHRISTMAS MASS DURING THE DAY

Collect

Deus, qui humanae substantiae dignitatem et mirabiliter condidisti, et mirabilius reformasti, da, quaesumus, nobis eius divinitatis esse consortes, qui humanitatis nostrae fieri dignatus est particeps. Qui tecum.

God our Father, in marvelous fashion you established the dignity of the human race, and even more marvelously renewed it. Please grant that we may share in the divinity of him who saw fit to share in our humanity. We ask this....

Prayer over the Gifts

Oblatio tibi sit, Domine, hodiernae sollemnitatis accepta, qua et nostrae reconciliationis processit perfecta placatio, et divini cultus nobis est indita plenitudo. Per Christum.

Lord, may what we offer you on the solemn feast we celebrate today be acceptable to you. Through this offering, the perfect atonement needed for our reconciliation to you has been furthered, and the fullness of divine worship has been given to us. We ask this....

Prayer after Communion

Praesta, misericors Deus, ut natus hodie Salvator mundi, sicut divinae nobis generationis est auctor, ita et immortalitatis sit ipse largitor. Qui vivit.

Merciful God, the Savior of the world has been born this day. Grant that, just as he has been the source of our divine rebirth, so may he grant us life everlasting. We ask this....

THE HOLY FAMILY

Collect

Deus, qui praeclara nobis sanctae Familiae dignatus es exempla praebere, concede propitius, ut, domesticis virtutibus caritatisque vinculis illam sectantes, in laetitia domus tuae praemiis fruamur aeternis. Per Dominum.

God our Father, you have seen fit to give us the marvelous example of the Holy Family. In your mercy, grant that we may imitate that family by the virtues that befit our home lives and by the ties of love, and so joyfully experience the eternal rewards of your home. We ask this....

Prayer over the Gifts

Hostiam tibi placationis offerimus, Domine, suppliciter deprecantes, ut Deiparae Virginis beatique Ioseph interveniente suffragio, familias nostras in tua gratia firmiter et pace constituas. Per Christum.

Lord, as we offer you the sacrifice of reconciliation, we humbly pray that, through the intercession of the Virgin who bore your Son and of Saint Joseph, you will solidly establish our own families in your grace and peace. We ask this....

Prayer after Communion

Quos caelestibus reficis sacramentis, fac, clementissime Pater, sanctae Familiae exempla iugiter imitari, ut, post aerumnas saeculi, eius consortium consequamur aeternum. Per Christum.

Most merciful Father, now that you have refreshed us by these heavenly sacraments, make us constantly imitate the example of the Holy Family, so that, after the troubles of this world, we may enjoy their company in heaven. We ask this....

DECEMBER 29: FIFTH DAY OF THE CHRISTMAS OCTAVE

Collect

Omnipotens et invisibilis Deus, qui tuae lucis adventu mundi tenebras effugasti, sereno vultu nos, quaesumus, intuere, ut magnificentiam nativitatis Unigeniti tui dignis praeconiis collaudemus. Qui tecum vivit.

Almighty and invisible God, by the coming of your light you have put the world's darkness to flight. We ask you to look upon us with peaceful gaze, so that we may worthily praise and proclaim the wonders of the birth of your only Son. We ask this....

Prayer over the Gifts

Suscipe, Domine, munera nostra, quibus exercentur commercia gloriosa, ut, offerentes quae dedisti, teipsum mereamur accipere. Per Christum.

Lord, receive the gifts by which a wondrous exchange takes place. As we offer what you yourself have given us, may we be privileged to receive your very self. We ask this....

Prayer after Communion

Da, quaesumus, omnipotens Deus, ut mysteriorum virtute sanctorum iugiter vita nostra firmetur. Per Christum.

Almighty God, please grant that our lives may constantly be strengthened by the power of your holy mysteries. We ask this....

DECEMBER 30: SIXTH DAY OF THE CHRISTMAS OCTAVE

Collect

Concede, quaesumus, omnipotens Deus, ut nos Unigeniti tui nova per carnem nativitas liberet, quos sub peccati iugo vetusta servitus tenet. Per Dominum.

Almighty God, please grant that the new birth of your only Son in human flesh may release us from the ancient slavery that holds us in the yoke of sin. We ask this....

Prayer over the Gifts

Munera, quaesumus, Domine, tuae plebis propitiatus assume, ut, quae fidei pietate profitentur, sacramentis caelestibus apprehendant. Per Christum.

Lord, in your forgiving mercy please accept the gifts of your people. Through your heavenly sacraments may they achieve what their faith confidently professes. We ask this....

Prayer after Communion

Deus, qui nos sacramenti tui participatione contingis, virtutis eius effectus in nostris cordibus operare, ut suscipiendo muneri tuo per ipsum munus aptemur. Per Christum.

God our Father, you touch our lives by our participation in your sacrament. Make its power effective in our hearts, so that by means of the gift itself we may be prepared to receive it. We ask this....

DECEMBER 31: SEVENTH DAY OF THE CHRISTMAS OCTAVE

Collect

Omnipotens sempiterne Deus, qui in Filii tui nativitate tribuisti totius religionis initium perfectionemque constare, da nobis, quaesumus, in eius portione censeri, in quo totius salutis humanae summa consistit. Per Dominum.

Almighty and eternal God, you established the source and the fulfillment of all religion in the birth of your Son. Please grant that we may be counted among those who follow him, for in him is embodied the whole of human salvation. We ask this....

Prayer over the Gifts

Deus, auctor sincerae devotionis et pacis, da, quaesumus, ut et maiestatem tuam convenienter hoc munere veneremur, et sacri participatione mysterii fideliter sensibus uniamur. Per Christum.

God our Father, you are the author of true consecration and peace. Please grant that we may fittingly worship your divine majesty by this gift, and, by our participation in this sacred mystery, may truly be made one in mind and heart. We ask this....

Prayer after Communion

Diversis plebs tua, Domine, gubernata subsidiis, et praesentia pietatis tuae remedia capiat et futura, ut, transeuntium rerum necessaria consolatione fovente, fiducialius ad aeterna contendat. Per Christum.

Lord, your people rely on the guidance of different kinds of help. May we receive the aid we need from your loving goodness both now and in time to come, so that, even as we use the necessary assistance of things that pass away, we may even more faithfully strive to attain the things that are eternal. We ask this....

JANUARY 1: SOLEMNITY OF THE BLESSED VIRGIN MARY, MOTHER OF GOD

Collect

Deus, qui salutis aeternae, beatae Mariae virginitate fecunda, humano generi praemia praestitisti, tribue, quaesumus, ut ipsam pro nobis intercedere sentiamus, per quam meruimus Filium tuum auctorem vitae suscipere. Qui tecum vivit.

God our Father, through the fruitful virginity of Blessed Mary, you have bestowed the rewards of eternal salvation upon the human race. Through her, we were privileged to receive your Son, the source of our life. Please grant that we may experience her intercession on our behalf. We ask this....

Prayer over the Gifts

Deus, qui bona cuncta inchoas benignus et perficis, da nobis, de sollemnitate sanctae Dei Genetricis laetantibus, sicut de initiis tuae gratiae gloriamur, ita de perfectione gaudere. Per Christum.

God our Father, in your kindness you begin all good things and bring them to perfection. As we rejoice in this solemnity of the holy Mother of God, grant that we may take delight in the fullness of your grace, just as we do in its beginnings. We ask this....

Prayer after Communion

Sumpsimus, Domine, laeti sacramenta caelestia: praesta, quaesumus, ut ad vitam nobis proficiant sempiternam, qui beatam semper Virginem Mariam Filii tui Genetricem et Ecclesiae Matrem profiteri gloriamur. Per Christum.

Lord, we have joyfully received your heavenly sacraments. Please grant that they may lead us to eternal life, as we rejoice in acknowledging the ever-blessed Virgin Mary as the Mother of your Son and as the Mother of the Church. We ask this....

SECOND SUNDAY AFTER CHRISTMAS

Collect
Omnipotens sempiterne Deus, fidelium splendor animarum, dignare mundum gloria tua implere benignus, et cunctis populis appare per tui luminis claritatem. Per Dominum.

Almighty and eternal God, you are the brilliant light that illumines your faithful ones. In your kindness, be pleased to fill the world with your glory. Make your presence known to all peoples by the splendor of your brightness. We ask this....

Prayer over the Gifts
Oblata, Domine, munera Unigeniti tui nativitate sanctifica, qua nobis et via ostenditur veritatis, et regni caelestis vita promittitur. Per Christum.

Lord, sanctify the gifts we offer by the birth of your only Son, through which your way of truth is made known to us and life in the kingdom of heaven is promised to us. We ask this....

Prayer after Communion
Domine Deus noster, suppliciter te rogamus, ut, huius operatione mysterii, vitia nostra purgentur, et iusta desideria compleantur. Per Christum.

Lord our God, we humbly ask that, by the action of this mystery, our faults may be wiped away and our just desires fulfilled. We ask this....

EPIPHANY

Collect

Deus, qui hodierna die Unigenitum tuum gentibus stella duce revelasti, concede propitius, ut qui iam te ex fide cognovimus, usque ad contemplandam speciem tuae celsitudinis perducamur. Per Dominum.

God our Father, on this day you revealed your only Son to the nations by the star which drew them on. We have now come to know you by faith; in your mercy, grant that we may even be brought to enjoy the actual sight of your greatness. We ask this....

Prayer over the Gifts

Ecclesiae tuae, quaesumus, Domine, dona propitius intuere, quibus non iam aurum, thus, et myrra profertur, sed quod eisdem muneribus declaratur, immolatur, et sumitur, Iesus Christus. Qui vivit.

Lord, we ask that you look graciously upon the gifts of your Church. It is not gold, frankincense, and myrrh that is offered in these gifts; rather, it is the one who is proclaimed, offered, and received in them: Jesus Christ. We ask this....

Prayer after Communion

Caelesti lumine, quaesumus, Domine, semper et ubique nos praeveni, ut mysterium, cuius nos participes esse voluisti, et puro cernamus intuitu, et digno percipiamus affectu. Per Christum.

Lord, please guide us always and everywhere with your divine light. May our vision be clear to see the mystery in which you have willed us to take part, and our love be fitting to receive it. We ask this....

BAPTISM OF THE LORD

Collect

Omnipotens sempiterne Deus, qui Christum, in Iordane flumine baptizatum, Spiritu Sancto super eum descendente, dilectum Filium tuum sollemniter declarasti, concede filiis adoptionis tuae, ex aqua et Spiritu Sancto renatis, ut in beneplacito tuo iugiter perseverent. Per Dominum.

Almighty and eternal God, after Christ had been baptized in the Jordan River and as the Holy Spirit was descending upon him, you solemnly declared that he was your beloved Son. Grant that those who are your adopted children, born anew by water and the Holy Spirit, may always do what is pleasing to you. We ask this....

Alternate Collect

Deus, cuius Unigenitus in substantia nostrae carnis apparuit, praesta, quaesumus, ut, per eum, quem similem nobis foris agnovimus, intus reformari mereamur. Qui tecum vivit.

God our Father, your only Son has appeared in our human nature. We have come to know that he is like us in external appearance; through him, please grant us the privilege of being refashioned in mind and heart. We ask this....

Prayer over the Gifts

Suscipe munera, Domine, in dilecti Filii tui revelatione delata, ut fidelium tuorum oblatio in eius sacrificium transeat, qui mundi voluit peccata miseratus abluere. Qui vivit.

Lord, receive the gifts which we bring here to celebrate the manifestation of your beloved Son. In his mercy, he willed to wash away the sins of the world; may the offering of your faithful people become one with his sacrifice. We ask this....

Prayer after Communion

Sacro munere satiati, clementiam tuam, Domine, suppliciter exoramus, ut, Unigenitum tuum fideliter audientes, filii tui vere nominemur et simus. Per Christum.

Lord, we are filled with your divine gift, and we humbly ask for your mercy. In listening faithfully to your only Son, may we truly be termed, and actually be, your children.

WEEKDAYS OF CHRISTMASTIME

FROM JANUARY 2 TO THE SATURDAY BEFORE THE BAPTISM OF THE LORD

MONDAY

Collect (before Epiphany)

Da, quaesumus, Domine, populo tuo inviolabilem fidei firmitatem, ut, qui Unigenitum tuum in tua tecum gloria sempiternum in veritate nostri corporis natum de Matre Virgine confitentur, et a praesentibus liberentur adversis, et mansuris gaudiis inserantur. Per Dominum.

Lord, please make your people unshakeable and steadfast in their faith. As they profess that your only Son, ever in glory with you, has been born in true human flesh of the Virgin Mother, may they both be freed from present troubles and be brought to eternal joys. We ask this....

Collect (after Epiphany)

Corda nostra, quaesumus, Domine, tuae maiestatis splendor illustret, quo per mundi huius tenebras transire valeamus, et perveniamus ad patriam claritatis aeternae. Per Dominum.

Lord, we ask that the brilliance of your divine majesty may illuminate our hearts. By this means, may we be able to pass through the darkness of this world and arrive at the homeland of eternal light. We ask this....

Prayer over the Gifts

(as on December 29, p.23)

Prayer after Communion

(as on December 29, p.23)

WEEKDAYS AFTER JANUARY 2: TUESDAY

Collect (before Epiphany)

Deus, qui, per beatum sacrae Virginis partum, Filii tui carnem humanis fecisti praeiudiciis non teneri, praesta, quaesumus, ut, huius creaturae novitate suscepti, vetustatis antiquae contagiis exuamur. Per Dominum.

God our Father, because the blessed Child was born of the holy Virgin, you have seen to it that the flesh of your Son was not bound by human sinfulness. Please grant that we who have been granted entry into this newness of creation may be freed from the stain of our former sinfulness. We ask this....

Collect (after Epiphany)

(as on the Feast of the Baptism of the Lord, p.26)

Prayer over the Gifts and Prayer after Communion:

(as on December 30, p.24)

WEEKDAYS AFTER JANUARY 2: WEDNESDAY

Collect (before Epiphany)

Concede nobis, omnipotens Deus, ut salutare tuum, quod ad redemptionem mundi luce nova caelorum processit, nostris semper cordibus oriatur. Per Dominum.

Almighty God, grant that your salvation, which came forth for the redemption of the world when the new star appeared in the heavens, may ever arise in our hearts. We ask this....

Collect (after Epiphany)

Deus, illuminator omnium gentium, da populis tuis perpetua pace gaudere, et illud cordibus nostris splendidum lumen infunde, quod patrum nostrorum mentibus aspersisti. Per Dominum.

God our Father, you are the light of all the nations. Grant that your people may enjoy uninterrupted peace, and pour forth into our hearts that magnificent light which you showered on the minds of our forebears. We ask this....

Prayer over the Gifts
(as on December 31, p.24)

Prayer after Communion
(as on December 31, p.24)

WEEKDAYS AFTER JANUARY 2: THURSDAY

Collect (before Epiphany)

Deus, qui populo tuo, Unigeniti tui nativitate, redemptionis effectum mirabiliter inchoasti, ita, quaesumus, fidei famulis tuis tribue firmitatem, ut usque ad promissum gloriae praemium, ipso gubernante, perveniant. Per Dominum.

God our Father, at the birth of your only Son you began the wondrous process of redemption for your people. Please grant to your servants such constancy in their faith that, under your Son's guidance, they may come to the promised reward of glory. We ask this....

Collect (after Epiphany)

Deus, qui per Filium tuum aeternitatis tuae lumen cunctis gentibus suscitasti, da plebi tuae fulgorem plenum sui Redemptoris agnoscere, ut ad perpetuam claritatem per eius incrementa perveniat. Per Dominum.

God our Father, by means of your Son you enkindled the light of your immortality for the entire human race. Grant that your people may recognize the full radiance of their Redeemer, so that, through his growth in them, they may come to eternal splendor. We ask this....

Prayer over the Gifts
(as on December 29, p.23)

Prayer after Communion
(as on December 29, p.23)

WEEKDAYS AFTER JANUARY 2: FRIDAY

Collect (Before Epiphany)

Fideles tuos, quaesumus, Domine, benignus illumina, et splendore gloriae tuae corda eorum semper accende, ut Salvatorem suum et incessanter agnoscant, et veraciter apprehendant. Per Dominum.

Lord, in your mercy please enlighten the minds of your faithful people, and constantly enkindle their hearts with the brilliance of your glory, so that they may always recognize their Savior and unreservedly accept him. We ask this....

Collect (after Epiphany)

Praesta, quaesumus, omnipotens Deus, ut Salvatoris mundi, stella duce, manifestata nativitas, mentibus nostris reveletur semper et crescat. Per Dominum.

Almighty God, the birth of the Savior of the world became known under the guidance of a star. Please grant that his birth may be constantly revealed to our hearts, and may continually increase within them. We ask this....

Prayer over the Gifts
(as on December 30, p.24)

Prayer after Communion
(as on December 30, p.24)

WEEKDAYS AFTER JANUARY 2: SATURDAY

Collect (before Epiphany)

Omnipotens sempiterne Deus, qui per adventum unigeniti Filii tui nova luce radiare dignatus es, concede nobis, ut, sicut eum per Virginis partum in forma nostri corporis meruimus habere participem, ita et in eius regno gratiae mereamur esse consortes. Per Dominum.

Almighty and eternal God, in the coming of your only Son you have seen fit to shine forth with a new brilliance. We have been privileged to have him share in our human nature by his birth from the Virgin; grant that we may also be privileged to share his grace in his kingdom. We ask this....

Collect (after Epiphany)

Omnipotens sempiterne Deus, qui per Unigenitum tuum novam creaturam nos tibi esse fecisti, praesta, quaesumus, ut per gratiam tuam in illius inveniamur forma, in quo tecum est nostra substantia. Per Dominum.

Almighty and eternal God, through your only Son you have made us into your own new creation. In him our nature is joined to you; please grant that through your grace we may come to share in his likeness. We ask this....

Prayer over the Gifts
(as on December 31, p.24)

Prayer after Communion
(as on December 31, p.24)

THE SEASON OF LENT

ASH WEDNESDAY

Collect

Concede nobis, Domine, praesidia militiae christianae sanctis inchoare ieiuniis, ut, contra spiritales nequitias pugnaturi, continentiae muniamur auxiliis. Per Dominum.

Lord, grant that we may begin our defense in Christian warfare with holy fasting. We are about to do battle against spiritual wickedness; may we be protected by the help of self-discipline. We ask this....

Blessing of Ashes

Deum Patrem, fratres carissimi, suppliciter deprecemur, ut hos cineres, quos paenitentiae causa capitibus nostris imponimus, ubertate gratiae suae benedicere dignetur.

Deus, qui humiliatione flecteris et satisfactione placaris, aurem tuae pietatis precibus nostris inclina, et super famulos tuos, horum cinerum aspersione contactos, gratiam tuae benedictionis + effunde propitius, ut, quadragesimalem observantiam prosequentes, ad Filii tui paschale mysterium celebrandum purificatis mentibus pervenire mereantur. Per Christum.

Beloved brothers and sisters, we place these ashes upon our heads as a sign of repentance. Let us humbly ask God the Father to deign to bless them with the richness of his grace.

God our Father, you are moved when we humble ourselves and you are pleased when we repent of our sins. In your mercy, listen to our prayers, and graciously pour forth the favor of your blessing + on your people who are marked with the sprinkling of these ashes. As they persevere in the observance of Lent, may they be privileged to come with purified hearts to the celebration of the paschal mystery of your Son. We ask this....

Alternate Prayer for the Blessing of Ashes

Deus, qui non mortem sed conversionem desideras peccatorum, preces nostras clementer exaudi, et hos cineres, quos capitibus nostris imponi decernimus, benedicere + pro tua pietate dignare, ut qui nos cinerem esse et in pulverem reversuros cognoscimus, quadragesimalis exercitationis studio, peccatorum veniam et novitatem vitae, ad imaginem Filii tui resurgentis, consequi valeamus. Per Christum.

God our Father, you desire not the death but the repentance of sinners. In your mercy, hear our prayers, and in your kindness deign to bless + these ashes, which we have resolved to have placed upon our heads. We recognize that we are ashes and will return to dust. By our careful observance of the discipline of Lent, may we be able to obtain the forgiveness of our sins and achieve a newness of life like that of your risen Son. We ask this....

Prayer over the Gifts

Sacrificium quadragesimalis initii sollemniter immolamus, te, Domine, deprecantes, ut per paenitentiae caritatisque labores a noxiis voluptatibus temperemus, et, a peccatis mundati, ad celebrandam Filii tui passionem mereamur esse devoti. Per Christum.

Lord, as we solemnly offer this sacrifice that marks the beginning of Lent, we beg that, through our works of penance and charity, we may refrain from harmful pleasures and, cleansed of our sins, be privileged to be intent upon faithfully celebrating the passion of your Son. We ask this....

Prayer after Communion

Percepta nobis, Domine, praebeant sacramenta subsidium, ut tibi grata sint nostra ieiunia, et nobis proficiant ad medelam. Per Christum.

Lord, may the sacraments we have received secure your help for us, so that our fasting may both please you and serve to heal us. We ask this....

THURSDAY AFTER ASH WEDNESDAY

Collect

Actiones nostras, quaesumus, Domine, aspirando praeveni et adiuvando prosequere, ut cuncta nostra operatio a te semper incipiat, et per te coepta finiatur. Per Dominum.

Lord, please guide our actions by your inspiration, and foster them by your assistance, so that everything we do may always begin from you and, once begun, be brought to completion by your help. We ask this....

Prayer over the Gifts

Hostias, quaesumus, Domine, propitius intende, quas sacris altaribus exhibemus, ut, nobis indulgentiam largiendo, tuo nomini dent honorem. Per Christum.

Lord, look with kindness on the offerings which we place on your sacred altar. By winning us your forgiveness, may they give glory to your name. We ask this....

Prayer after Communion

Caelestis doni benedictione percepta, supplices te, Deus omnipotens, deprecamur, ut hoc idem nobis semper et indulgentiae causa sit et salutis. Per Christum.

Father most powerful, we have received the blessing of your heavenly gift. We humbly ask that it may always be a source of forgiveness and salvation for us. We ask this....

FRIDAY AFTER ASH WEDNESDAY

Collect

Inchoata paenitentiae opera, quaesumus, Domine, benigno favore prosequere, ut observantiam, quam corporaliter exercemus, mentibus etiam valeamus implere sinceris. Per Dominum.

Lord, by your kind favor please further the works of penance we have begun. May we thus be able to fulfill with sincere hearts the observance which we are undergoing in our bodies. We ask this....

Prayer over the Gifts

Sacrificium, Domine, observantiae quadragesimalis offerimus, quod tibi, quaesumus, mentes nostras reddat acceptas, et continentiae promptioris nobis tribuat facultatem. Per Christum.

Lord, we offer the sacrifice of our Lenten observance. May it make our hearts pleasing to you, and enable us to discipline ourselves more willingly. We ask this....

Prayer after Communion

Quaesumus, omnipotens Deus, ut, huius participatione mysterii a delictis omnibus expiati, remediis tuae pietatis aptemur. Per Christum.

Almighty God, through our participation in this mystery, we ask that we may be cleansed from all our sins and be prepared for the healing power of your loving faithfulness. We ask this....

SATURDAY AFTER ASH WEDNESDAY

Collect

Omnipotens sempiterne Deus, infirmitatem nostram propitius respice, atque ad protegendum nos dexteram tuae maiestatis extende. Per Dominum.

Almighty and eternal God, in your kindness look upon our weakness, and stretch forth the right hand of your majesty to protect us. We ask this....

Prayer over the Gifts

Suscipe, quaesumus, Domine, sacrificium placationis et laudis, et praesta, ut, huius operatione mundati, beneplacitum tibi nostrae mentis offeramus affectum. Per Christum.

Lord, please receive our sacrifice of atonement and praise. Grant that, cleansed by its action, we may offer you the love in our hearts that will be pleasing to you. We ask this....

Prayer after Communion

Caelestis vitae munere vegetati, quaesumus, Domine, ut, quod est nobis in praesenti vita mysterium, fiat aeternitatis auxilium. Per Christum.

Lord, we have been strengthened by the gift of heavenly life. We ask that, what forms a mystery to us in our present state, may become a benefit for us in achieving eternal life. We ask this....

FIRST SUNDAY OF LENT

Collect

Concede nobis, omnipotens Deus, ut, per annua quadragesimalis exercitia sacramenti, et ad intelligendum Christi proficiamus arcanum, et effectus eius digna conversatione sectemur. Per Dominum....

Almighty God, through our annual celebration of the Lenten observance, grant that we may progress in our understanding of the mystery of Christ. By constantly striving to take part in that mystery, may we achieve what it seeks to bring about in us. We ask this....

Prayer over the Gifts

Fac nos, quaesumus, Domine, his muneribus offerendis convenienter aptari, quibus ipsius venerabilis sacramenti celebramus exordium. Per Christum.

Lord, please make us properly prepared to offer these gifts, for it is by means of them that we celebrate the origin of this holy sacrament. We ask this....

Prayer after Communion

Caelesti pane refecti, quo fides alitur, spes provehitur et caritas roboratur, quaesumus, Domine, ut ipsum, qui est panis vivus et verus, esurire discamus, et in omni verbo, quod procedit de ore tuo, vivere valeamus. Per Christum.

Lord, we are refreshed by the heavenly food by which faith is nourished, hope is fostered, and charity strengthened. We ask that we may learn to hunger for Him who is the true and living bread, and that we may be able to live by every word that comes forth from your mouth. We ask this....

MONDAY OF THE FIRST WEEK IN LENT

Collect

Converte nos, Deus, salutaris noster, et, ut nobis opus quadragesimale proficiat, mentes nostras caelestibus instrue disciplinis. Per Dominum.

God our Father and our salvation, make us turn to you. So that the obervance of Lent may benefit us, fill our minds with your heavenly teachings. We ask this....

Prayer over the Gifts

Accepta tibi sit, Domine, nostrae devotionis oblatio, quae et conversationem nostram, te operante, sanctificet, et indulgentiam nobis tuae propitiationis obtineat. Per Christum.

Lord, may the offering of our loving dedication be acceptable to you. Through your action, may it make our dealings with one another holy and obtain for us the grace of your forgiveness. We ask this....

Prayer after Communion

Sentiamus, Domine, quaesumus, tui perceptione sacramenti, subsidium mentis et corporis, ut, in utroque salvati, de caelestis remedii plenitudine gloriemur. Per Christum.

Lord, through our reception of your sacrament we ask to experience your help for our minds and our bodies, so that we may be healed in both and may rejoice in the abundance of your heavenly aid. We ask this....

TUESDAY OF THE FIRST WEEK IN LENT

Collect

Respice, Domine, familiam tuam, et praesta, ut apud te mens nostra tuo desiderio fulgeat, quae se corporalium moderatione castigat. Per Dominum.

Lord, look upon your servants, and grant that while we are in your presence our hearts may be inflamed with longing for you, even as we discipline ourselves with moderation in bodily things. We ask this....

Prayer over the Gifts

Suscipe, creator omnipotens Deus, quae de tuae munificentiae largitate deferimus, et temporalia nobis collata praesidia ad vitam converte propitiatus aeternam. Per Christum.

God our Father, Creator almighty, receive the offerings we make to you, taken from the blessings your abundant generosity has given us. In your forgiving kindness, change these gifts, granted to us as transitory, into life eternal. We ask this....

Prayer after Communion

His nobis, Domine, mysteriis conferatur, quo, terrena desideria mitigantes, discamus amare caelestia. Per Christum.

Lord, by these mysteries, give us the ability to restrain our earthly desires and learn to love the things of heaven. We ask this....

WEDNESDAY OF THE FIRST WEEK IN LENT

Collect

Devotionem populi tui, quaesumus, Domine, benignus intende, ut, qui per abstinentiam temperantur in corpore, per fructum boni operis reficiantur in mente. Per Dominum....

Lord, in your kind mercy, please look upon your devoted people. They moderate their bodily desires by penance; may they be renewed in heart as a result of their good work. We ask this....

Prayer over the Gifts

Offerimus tibi, Domine, quae dicanda tuo nomini tu dedisti, ut, sicut eadem nobis efficis sacramentum, ita fieri tribuas remedium sempiternum. Per Christum.

Lord, we offer you the gifts that you yourself gave us to dedicate to your holy name. Just as you make them a pledge for us, so also grant that they may be a means of healing us for ever. We ask this....

Prayer after Communion

Deus, qui nos sacramentis tuis pascere non desistis, tribue, ut eorum nobis indulta refectio vitam, quaesumus, conferat sempiternam. Per Christum.

Lord, you never cease to nourish us with your sacraments. Please grant that the healing they confer may also bestow eternal life upon us. We ask this....

THURSDAY OF THE FIRST WEEK IN LENT

Collect

Largire nobis, quaesumus, Domine, semper spiritum cogitandi quae recta sunt, promptius et agendi, ut, qui sine te esse non possumus, secundum te vivere valeamus. Per Dominum.

Lord, please grant us the abiding wisdom to know what is right, and the readiness to carry it into action without delay. We cannot exist without you; may we be able to live according to your will. We ask this....

Prayer over the Gifts

Supplicum votis, Domine, esto propitius, et, populi tui oblationibus precibusque susceptis, omnium nostrum ad te corda converte. Per Christum.

Lord, be pleased by the gifts of those who call upon you. Receive the offerings and prayers of your people, and turn the hearts of all of us to you. We ask this....

Prayer after Communion

Quaesumus, Domine Deus noster, ut sacrosancta mysteria, quae pro reparationis nostrae munimine contulisti, et praesens nobis remedium esse facias et futurum. Per Christum.

Lord our God, you have given us these most holy mysteries as a help to our repentance. Please grant that they may aid us now and in the future. We ask this....

FRIDAY OF THE FIRST WEEK IN LENT

Collect

Da, quaesumus, Domine, fidelibus tuis observationi paschali convenienter aptari, ut suscepta sollemniter castigatio corporalis cunctis ad fructum proficiat animarum. Per Dominum.

Lord, please grant that your faithful people may be properly prepared to celebrate the Easter mystery. May the yearly penance we have undertaken in our bodies benefit the souls of all of us. We ask this....

Prayer over the Gifts

Suscipe, Domine, propitiatus hostias, quibus et te placari voluisti, et nobis salutem potenti pietate restitui. Per Christum.

In your forgiving mercy, Lord, receive our gifts. It is by our offering them that you have decreed that we are to please you and are to regain salvation through your power and compassion. We ask this....

Prayer after Communion

Tui nos, Domine, sacramenti refectio sancta restauret, et, a vetustate purgatos, in mysterii salutaris faciat transire consortium. Per Christum.

Lord, may the holy restorative action of your sacrament renew us and make us, once cleansed of our old sinfulness, share in your saving mystery. We ask this....

SATURDAY OF THE FIRST WEEK IN LENT

Collect

Ad te corda nostra, Pater aeterne, converte, ut nos, unum necessarium semper quaerentes et opera caritatis exercentes, tuo cultui praestes esse dicatos. Per Dominum.

Eternal Father, turn our hearts to you. Make of us a people dedicated to worshipping you, ever seeking the one thing that is necessary and always occupied in works of charity. We ask this....

Prayer over the Gifts

Haec quae nos reparent, quaesumus, Domine, beata mysteria suo nos munere dignos efficiant. Per Christum.

Lord, your holy mysteries are such that they restore us. We ask that they may make us worthy of their own sacred character and function. We ask this....

Prayer after Communion

Perpetuo, Domine, favore prosequere, quos reficis divino mysterio, et, quos imbuisti caelestibus institutis, salutaribus comitare solaciis. Per Christum.

By means of your unceasing favor, Lord, assist those whom you renew with this divine mystery; and by means of your saving comforts be with those whom you have instructed in your heavenly teachings. We ask this....

SECOND SUNDAY OF LENT

Collect

Deus, qui nobis dilectum Filium tuum audire praecepisti, verbo tuo interius nos pascere digneris, ut, spiritali purificato intuitu, gloriae tuae laetemur aspectu. Per Dominum.

God our Father, you have told us to listen to your beloved Son. Feed our spirit with your word, so that our inner vision may be purified and we may then rejoice at the sight of your glory. We ask this....

Prayer over the Gifts

Haec hostia, Domine, quaesumus, emundet nostra delicta, et ad celebranda festa paschalia fidelium tuorum corpora mentesque sanctificet. Per Christum.

Lord, may this offering wash away our sins and sanctify the bodies and minds of your faithful people to prepare us to celebrate the paschal feast. We ask this....

Prayer after Communion

Percipientes, Domine, gloriosa mysteria, gratias tibi referre satagimus, quod, in terra positos, iam caelestium praestas esse participes. Per Christum.

Lord, as we receive these marvelous mysteries, we are hard pressed to thank you enough, for you now allow us to share in heavenly things even though we still dwell on earth. We make our prayer through....

MONDAY OF THE SECOND WEEK IN LENT

Collect

Deus, qui ob animarum medelam castigare corpora praecepisti, concede, ut ab omnibus possimus abstinere peccatis, et corda nostra pietatis tuae valeant exercere mandata. Per Dominum.

God our Father, you have commanded us to discipline our bodies in order to heal our souls. Grant that we may be able to refrain from all sin, and that our hearts may be able to carry out the commands that your faithful goodness has given us. We ask this....

Prayer over the Gifts

Preces nostras, Domine, propitiatus admitte, et a terrenis effice illecebris liberatos, quos caelestibus tribuis servire mysteriis. Per Christum.

Lord, in your forgiving kindness hear our prayers. Free from all earthly entanglements those whom you allow to take part in your heavenly mysteries. We ask this....

Prayer after Communion

Haec nos communio, Domine, purget a crimine, et caelestis gaudii faciat esse consortes. Per Christum.

Lord, may this communion cleanse us from sin and make us share in the joy of heaven. We ask this....

TUESDAY OF THE SECOND WEEK IN LENT

Collect

Custodi, Domine, quaesumus, Ecclesiam tuam propitiatione perpetua, et quia sine te labitur humana mortalitas, tuis semper auxiliis et abstrahatur a noxiis, et ad salutaria dirigatur. Per Christum.

Lord, please guard your Church with your constant mercy. Since human frailty falters without your assistance, may the Church always be sheltered from evil by your aid and guided toward things that will preserve it. We ask this....

Prayer over the Gifts

Sanctificationem tuam nobis, Domine, his mysteriis operare placatus, quae nos et a vitiis terrenis emundet, et ad caelestia dona perducat. Per Christum.

Lord, in your mercy, make us holy by these mysteries. May they cleanse us from earthly evils and lead us to your heavenly gifts. We ask this....

Prayer after Communion

Sacrae nobis, quaesumus, Domine, mensae refectio, et piae conversationis augmentum, et tuae propitiationis continuum praestet auxilium. Per Christum.

Lord, we ask that the renewal this sacred table gives us may make our dealings with one another more holy and may grant us the constant help of your mercy. We ask this....

WEDNESDAY OF THE SECOND WEEK IN LENT

Collect

Conserva, Domine, familiam tuam bonis semper operibus eruditam, et sic praesentibus consolare praesidiis, ut propitius ad superna dona perducas. Per Dominum.

Lord, your servants are always being taught by your sacred works. Preserve us, and console us by those aids of yours which we have at hand, so that in your mercy you may lead us to your heavenly gifts. We ask this....

Prayer over the Gifts

Hostias, Domine, quas tibi offerimus, propitius intuere, et, per haec sancta commercia, vincula peccatorum nostrorum absolve. Per Christum.

Lord, in your kindness, look upon the gifts which we offer you; and, by this sacred interchange, loose the bonds of our sins. We ask this....

Prayer after Communion

Quaesumus, Domine Deus noster, ut, quod nobis ad immortalitatis pignus esse voluisti, ad salutis aeternae tribuas provenire suffragium. Per Christum.

Lord our God, you have willed to give us the pledge of eternal life. We ask you to grant that it may help and support us in achieving our eternal salvation. We ask this....

THURSDAY OF THE SECOND WEEK IN LENT

Collect

Deus, innocentiae restitutor et amator, dirige ad te tuorum corda fidelium, ut, Spiritus tui fervore concepto, et in fide inveniantur stabiles, et in opere efficaces. Per Dominum.

God our Father, you love sinlessness and you restore it when it has been lost. Guide the hearts of your servants toward you, so that, inflamed by your Spirit, they may be found firm in their faith and fruitful in their works. We ask this....

Prayer over the Gifts

Praesenti sacrificio, quaesumus, Domine, observantiam nostram sanctifica, ut, quod quadragesimalis exercitatio profitetur exterius, interius operetur effectu. Per Christum.

Lord, please make our penitential practice holy by means of this sacrifice. May the discipline of Lent thus make what we externally profess truly reflect what it brings about in our hearts. We ask this....

Prayer after Communion

Haec in nobis sacrificia, Deus, et actione permaneant, et operatione firmentur. Per Christum.

God our Father, may the effects of this sacrifice remain within our hearts and be confirmed by our deeds. We ask this....

FRIDAY OF THE SECOND WEEK IN LENT

Collect

Da, quaesumus, omnipotens Deus, ut, sacro nos purificante paenitentiae studio, sinceris mentibus ad sancta ventura facias pervenire. Per Dominum.

Almighty God, as the sacred practice of penance cleanses us, please grant that our hearts may be pure when we arrive at the holy events to come. We ask this....

Prayer over the Gifts

Miseratio tua, Deus, ad haec peragenda mysteria, famulos tuos, quaesumus, et praeveniat competenter, et devota conversatione perducat. Per Christum.

God our Father, may your mercy fully prepare your servants to celebrate these mysteries and bring them to do so by the lives of loving dedication it prompts them to lead. We ask this....

Prayer after Communion

Accepto, Domine, pignore salutis aeternae, fac nos, quaesumus, sic tendere congruenter, ut ad eam pervenire possimus. Per Christum.

Lord, we have received the promise of eternal salvation. We ask you to make us strive to live in such a way that we may be able to achieve the fulfillment of that promise. We ask this....

SATURDAY OF THE SECOND WEEK IN LENT

Collect

Deus, qui nos gloriosis remediis in terris adhuc positos iam caelestium rerum facis esse consortes, tu, quaesumus, in ista qua vivimus nos vita guberna, ut ad illam, in qua ipse es, lucem perducas. Per Dominum.

God our Father, even while we still dwell on earth, you heal us wonderfully and make us share in your heavenly gifts. We ask that you yourself may guide us in the life we now live, and thus lead us to that light in which you dwell. We ask this....

Prayer over the Gifts

Per haec veniat, quaesumus, Domine, sacramenta nostrae redemptionis effectus, qui nos et ab humanis retrahat semper excessibus, et ad salutaria dona perducat. Per Christum.

Lord, may our redemption be worked out through these sacraments. May it always restrain us from human excesses and lead us to your saving gifts. We ask this....

Prayer after Communion

Sacramenti tui, Domine, divina perceptio penetralia nostri cordis infundat, et sui nos participes potenter efficiat. Per Christum.

Lord, may the reception of your heavenly sacrament fill the inmost recesses of our hearts, and by its power make us share in your divine life. We ask this....

THIRD SUNDAY OF LENT

Collect

Deus, omnium misericordiarum et totius bonitatis auctor, qui peccatorum remedia in ieiuniis, orationibus, et eleemosynis demonstrasti, hanc humilitatis nostrae confessionem propitius intuere, ut, qui inclinamur conscientia nostra, tua semper misericordia sublevemur. Per Dominum.

God our Father, source of all mercy and all goodness, you have shown us that sin is healed by fasting, prayer, and almsgiving. In your kindness, look upon our acknowledgement of our lowliness. We are bowed down by the recognition of our own sinfulness; may we constantly be raised up by the help of your mercy. We ask this....

Prayer over the Gifts

His sacrificiis, Domine, concede placatus, ut, qui propriis oramus absolvi delictis, fraterna dimittere studeamus. Per Christum.

Lord, be pleased with this sacrifice and grant that we who seek to be forgiven our own sins may strive to forgive those of our own brothers and sisters. We ask this....

Prayer after Communion

Sumentes pignus caelestis arcani, et in terra positi iam superno pane satiati, te, Domine, supplices deprecamur, ut quod in nobis mysterio geritur, opere impleatur. Per Christum.

Lord, we receive your pledge of heavenly mysteries; and, though still on earth, we are filled with heavenly food. We humbly ask that by our actions we may bring to fulfillment what this mystery has accomplished in us. We ask this....

MONDAY OF THE THIRD WEEK IN LENT

Collect

Ecclesiam tuam, Domine, miseratio continua mundet et muniat, et quia sine te non potest salva consistere, tuo semper munere gubernetur. Per Dominum.

Lord, may your continued mercy cleanse and guard your Church. Since it cannot remain safe without you, may it always be governed by the gift of your care. We ask this....

Prayer over the Gifts

Munus quod tibi, Domine, nostrae servitutis offerimus, tu salutare nobis perfice sacramentum. Per Christum.

Lord, we offer you the gift of our love and dedication. Make that gift become a life-giving sacrament for us. We ask this....

Prayer after Communion

Tui nobis, quaesumus, Domine, communio sacramenti et purificationem conferat, et tribuat unitatem. Per Christum.

Lord, may our reception of your sacrament cleanse us from sin and bring us together in unity. We ask this....

TUESDAY OF THE THIRD WEEK IN LENT

Collect

Gratia tua ne nos, quaesumus, Domine, derelinquat, quae et sacrae nos deditos faciat servituti, et tuam nobis opem semper acquirat. Per Dominum.

Lord, may your grace not abandon us; rather, may it make us dedicated to your holy service and gain your constant help for us. We ask this....

Prayer over the Gifts

Concede nobis, quaesumus, Domine, ut haec hostia salutaris nostrorum fiat purgatio delictorum, et tuae propitiatio potestatis. Per Christum.

Lord, please grant that these gifts may cleanse and save us from our sins and be an offering that is pleasing and acceptable to your almighty power. We ask this....

Prayer after Communion

Vivificet nos, quaesumus, Domine, huius participatio sancta mysterii, et pariter nobis expiationem tribuat et munimen. Per Christum.

Lord, please grant that our holy participation in this mystery may bring us life and bestow on us both your forgiveness and your protection. We ask this....

WEDNESDAY OF THE THIRD WEEK IN LENT

Collect

Praesta, quaesumus, Domine, ut, per quadragesimalem observantiam eruditi et tuo verbo nutriti, sancta continentia tibi simus toto corde devoti, et in oratione tua semper efficiamur concordes. Per Dominum.

Lord, please grant that, trained by our observance of Lent and nourished by your word, we may be wholeheartedly dedicated to you in holy self-denial and ever united to you in prayer. We ask this....

Prayer over the Gifts

Suscipe, quaesumus, Domine, preces populi tui cum oblationibus hostiarum, et tua mysteria celebrantes ab omnibus nos defende periculis. Per Christum.

Lord, please receive the prayers of your people and their offerings. Ward off all danger from those of us who take part in your mysteries. We ask this....

Prayer after Communion

Sanctificet nos, Domine, qua pasti sumus, mensa caelestis, et, a cunctis erroribus expiatos, supernis promissionibus reddat acceptos. Per Christum.

Lord, may this heavenly table at which we are fed make us holy, cleanse us of all our errors, and make us worthy of your divine promises. We ask this....

THURSDAY OF THE THIRD WEEK IN LENT

Collect

Maiestatem tuam, Domine, suppliciter imploramus, ut, quanto magis dies salutiferae festivitatis accedit, tanto devotius ad eius celebrandum proficiamus paschale mysterium. Per Dominum.

Lord, we humbly ask your divine majesty that, the closer the day of our redemption's feast comes, the more intent we may become on celebrating its paschal mystery. We ask this....

Prayer over the Gifts

Ut tibi grata sint, Domine, munera populi tui, ab omni, quaesumus, eum contagio perversitatis emunda, nec falsis gaudiis inhaerere patiaris, quem ad veritatis tuae praemia venire promittis. Per Christum.

Lord, so that the gifts of your people may be acceptable to you, please cleanse us from all stain of evil and do not allow us to cling to false joys, for you promise that we are coming to the true rewards that you give. We ask this....

Prayer after Communion

Quos reficis, Domine, sacramentis, attolle benignus auxiliis, ut tuae salvationis effectum et mysteriis capiamus et moribus. Per Christum.

Lord, in your kindness, lift up and assist those whom you renew with these sacraments, so that your salvation may be wrought within us both by means of these mysteries and by our way of life. We ask this....

FRIDAY OF THE THIRD WEEK IN LENT

Collect

Cordibus nostris, quaesumus, Domine, gratiam tuam benignus infunde, ut ab humanis semper retrahamur excessibus, et monitis inhaerere valeamus, te largiente, caelestibus. Per Dominum.

Lord, in your kindness please pour out your grace into our hearts, so that we may always be restrained from human indulgences and, because of your generosity, may always abide by your heavenly commands. We ask this....

Prayer over the Gifts

Respice, quaesumus, Domine, propitius ad munera quae sacramus, ut tibi grata reddantur, et nobis salutaria semper exsistant. Per Christum.

Lord, please look with kindness upon the gifts which we dedicate to you. May they thus please you, and ever be a source of salvation to us. We ask this....

Prayer after Communion

Mentes nostras et corpora, Domine, quaesumus, operatio tuae virtutis infundat, ut, quod participatione sumpsimus, plena redemptione capiamus. Per Christum.

Lord, may your active power fill our minds and our bodies, so that we may attain in the fullness of redemption what we have received by our participation in this mystery. We ask this....

SATURDAY OF THE THIRD WEEK IN LENT

Collect

Observationis huius annua celebritate laetantes, quaesumus, Domine, ut, paschalibus sacramentis inhaerentes, plenis eorum effectibus gaudeamus. Per Dominum.

Lord, we are gladdened by the annual celebration of this Lenten observance, and we ask that we may remain faithful to the Easter sacraments and rejoice in their full effectiveness. We ask this....

Prayer over the Gifts

Deus, de cuius gratia venit ut ad mysteria tua purgatis sensibus accedamus, praesta, quaesumus, ut, in eorum traditione sollemniter honoranda, competens deferamus obsequium. Per Christum.

God our Father, it is by your favor that we come to your mysteries with purified hearts. Please grant that in solemnly honoring what they teach us we may worthily serve you. We ask this....

Prayer after Communion

Da nobis, quaesumus, misericors Deus, ut sancta tua, quibus incessanter explemur, sinceris tractemus obsequiis, et fideli semper mente sumamus. Per Christum.

Merciful God, we are constantly filled with your holy gifts. Please grant that we may always regard them with heartfelt reverence and receive them with ever-faithful hearts. We ask this....

FOURTH SUNDAY OF LENT

Collect

Deus, qui per Verbum tuum humani generis reconciliationem mirabiliter operaris, praesta, quaesumus, ut populus christianus prompta devotione et alacri fide ad ventura sollemnia valeat festinare. Per Dominum.

God our Father, through your Word you marvelously bring about the reconciliation of the human race to yourself. Please grant that your Christian people may be enabled to hasten to the coming solemn feasts with eager sincerity and deep faith. We ask this....

Prayer over the Gifts

Remedii sempiterni munera, Domine, laetantes offerimus, suppliciter exorantes, ut eadem nos et fideliter venerari, et pro salute mundi congruenter exhibere perficias. Per Christum.

Lord, we rejoice as we offer the gifts that heal us for all eternity. We humbly ask you to make us reverence them in faith and present them properly for the salvation of the world. We ask this....

Prayer after Communion

Deus, qui illuminas omnem hominem venientem in hunc mundum, illumina, quaesumus, corda nostra gratiae tuae splendore, ut digna et placita maiestati tuae cogitare semper, et te sincere diligere valeamus. Per Christum.

God our Father, you enlighten every human who comes into this world. Please enlighten our hearts with the brightness of your grace, so that our thoughts may always be worthy of you and pleasing to your divine majesty, and our love for you may always be genuine. We ask this....

MONDAY OF THE FOURTH WEEK IN LENT

Collect

Deus, qui ineffabilibus mundum renovas sacramentis, praesta, quaesumus, ut Ecclesia tua et aeternis proficiat institutis, et temporalibus non destituatur auxiliis. Per Dominum.

God our Father, you renew the world with your indescribable sacraments. Please grant that your Church may profit from your heavenly instruction, and also may not be bereft of your earthly assistance. We ask this....

Prayer over the Gifts

Dicatae tibi, Domine, quaesumus, capiamus oblationis effectum, ut, a terrenae vetustatis conversatione mundati, caelestis vitae profectibus innovemur. Per Christum.

Lord, we ask that we may achieve the results of the offering we have made to you. May we thus be cleansed from our former worldly associations and be renewed by an increase of divine life. We ask this....

Prayer after Communion

Sancta tua nos, Domine, quaesumus, et renovando vivificent, et sanctificando ad aeterna perducant. Per Christum.

Lord, we ask that your sacred mysteries may renew us and so give us life, and may make us holy and so lead us to eternal happiness. We ask this....

TUESDAY OF THE FOURTH WEEK IN LENT

Collect

Exercitatio veneranda sanctae devotionis, Domine, tuorum fidelium corda disponat, ut et dignis mentibus suscipiant paschale mysterium, et salvationis tuae nuntient praeconium. Per Dominum.

Lord, may the sacred practice of our holy religion predispose the hearts of your faithful people to receive the paschal mystery worthily within their hearts, and to make known the message of salvation you bring. We ask this....

Prayer over the Gifts

Offerimus tibi, Domine, munera quae dedisti, ut et creationis tuae circa mortalitatem nostram testificentur auxilium, et remedium nobis immortalitatis operentur. Per Christum.

Lord, we offer you the gifts which you yourself have given us. May they proclaim the sustaining power of your creative action regarding our mortal life, and bring about for us the healing reward of eternal life. We ask this....

Prayer after Communion

Purifica, quaesumus, Domine, mentes nostras benignus, et renova caelestibus sacramentis, ut consequenter et corporum praesens pariter et futurum capiamus auxilium. Per Christum.

Lord, in your mercy please purify our minds and renew them with your heavenly sacraments, with the result that we also receive help for our bodies as well, both now and in time to come. We ask this....

WEDNESDAY OF THE FOURTH WEEK IN LENT

Collect

Deus, qui et iustis praemia meritorum et peccatoribus veniam per paenitentiam praebes, tuis supplicibus miserere, ut reatus nostri confessio indulgentiam valeat percipere delictorum. Per Dominum.

God our Father, through penance you give your faithful people the rewards of their holy works, and you give sinners forgiveness. Have pity on those who call upon you. May the confession of our own guilt win for us the forgiveness of our sins. We ask this....

Prayer over the Gifts

Huius sacrificii potentia, Domine, quaesumus, et vetustatem nostram clementer abstergat, et novitatem nobis augeat et salutem. Per Christum.

Lord, we ask that the power of this sacrifice may mercifully wash away our old sinfulness and increase our new life and salvation. We ask this....

Prayer after Communion

Caelestia dona capientibus, quaesumus, Domine, non ad iudicium provenire patiaris, quae fidelibus tuis ad remedium providisti. Per Christum.

Lord, you have given your heavenly gifts to your faithful people as an aid to salvation. Please do not allow those who receive your gifts to come to judgment. We ask this....

THURSDAY OF THE FOURTH WEEK IN LENT

Collect

Clementiam tuam, Domine, supplici voto deposcimus, ut nos famulos tuos, paenitentia emendatos et bonis operibus eruditos, in mandatis tuis facias perseverare sinceros, et ad paschalia festa pervenire illaesos. Per Dominum.

Lord, in humble prayer we earnestly ask for your mercy. Corrected by penance and instructed by the good works we do, may we who are your servants sincerely keep your commandments and come unsullied to the paschal feast. We ask this....

Prayer over the Gifts

Concede, quaesumus, omnipotens Deus, ut huius sacrificii munus oblatum fragilitatem nostram ab omni malo purget semper et muniat. Per Christum.

Almighty God, please grant that the gifts we offer in this sacrifice may ever cleanse and safeguard our weak natures from every evil. We ask this....

Prayer after Communion

Purificent nos, quaesumus, Domine, sacramenta quae sumpsimus, et famulos tuos ab omni culpa liberos esse concede, ut, qui conscientiae reatu constringuntur, caelestis remedii plenitudine glorientur. Per Christum.

Lord, we ask that the sacraments we have received may cleanse us. Grant that your servants may be freed from all guilt, so that those who are bound by conscience's reproach may rejoice in the fullness of your divine healing. We ask this....

FRIDAY OF THE FOURTH WEEK IN LENT

Collect

Deus, qui fragilitati nostrae congrua subsidia praeparasti, concede, quaesumus, ut suae reparationis effectum et cum exsultatione suscipiat, et pia conversatione recenseat. Per Dominum.

God our Father, you have prepared fitting helps for our weakness. Please grant that our frail nature may receive your healing power with joy, and in loyal love may proclaim it to others. We ask this....

Prayer over the Gifts

Haec sacrificia nos, omnipotens Deus, potenti virtute mundatos, ad suum faciant puriores venire principium. Per Christum.

Almighty God, may these sacrificial offerings cleanse us by their mighty power and make us come with purer hearts to you, their source. We ask this....

Prayer after Communion

Praesta, quaesumus, Domine, ut, sicut de praeteritis ad nova transimus, ita, vetustate deposita, sanctificatis mentibus innovemur. Per Christum.

Lord, as we pass from what has been to what is to be, please grant that we may put our old ways behind us and with purified hearts lead a new life. We ask this....

SATURDAY OF THE FOURTH WEEK IN LENT

Collect

Dirigat corda nostra, quaesumus, Domine, tuae miserationis operatio, quia tibi sine te placere non possumus. Per Dominum.

Lord, we ask that your merciful action guide our hearts, for without your help we cannot please you. We ask this....

Prayer over the Gifts

Oblationibus nostris, quaesumus, Domine, placare susceptis, et ad te nostras etiam rebelles compelle propitius voluntates. Per Christum.

Lord, be pleased by the gifts we have offered and you have accepted. Even though our wills are rebellious, in your mercy make them turn to you. We ask this....

Prayer after Communion

Tua nos, quaesumus, Domine, sancta purificent, et operatione sua tibi placitos esse perficiant. Per Christum.

Lord, we beg that your holy gifts may cleanse us. By their action, may they make us pleasing to you. We ask this....

FIFTH SUNDAY OF LENT

Collect

Quaesumus, Domine Deus noster, ut in illa caritate, qua Filius tuus diligens mundum morti se tradidit, inveniamur ipsi, te opitulante, alacriter ambulantes. Per Dominum.

Lord our God, your Son handed himself over to death out of love for the world. Through your generous gift, please grant that we too may find ourselves walking eagerly in that same love. We ask this....

Prayer over the Gifts

Exaudi nos, omnipotens Deus, et famulos tuos, quos fidei christianae eruditionibus imbuisti, huius sacrificii tribuas operatione mundari. Per Christum.

Almighty God, you have instructed your faithful people in the teachings of the Christian faith. Hear our prayers, and grant that we may be cleansed by this sacrificial action. We ask this....

Prayer after Communion

Quaesumus, omnipotens Deus, ut inter eius membra semper numeremur, cuius Corpori communicamus et Sanguini. Per Christum.

Almighty God, please grant that we may always be counted among the members of Him whose Body and Blood we receive in Holy Communion. We ask this....

MONDAY OF THE FIFTH WEEK IN LENT

Collect

Deus, per cuius ineffabilem gratiam omni benedictione ditamur, praesta nobis, ita in novitatem a vetustate transire, ut regni caelestis gloriae praeparemur. Per Dominum.

God our Father, by your inestimable grace we are enriched with every blessing. Grant that we may pass from our old sinfulness into a new life in such a way that we may be made ready for the glory of your heavenly kingdom. We ask this....

Prayer over the Gifts

Concede nobis, Domine, quaesumus, ut, celebraturi sancta mysteria, tamquam paenitentiae corporalis fructum, laetam tibi exhibeamus mentium puritatem. Per Christum.

Lord, as we prepare to celebrate your sacred mysteries, please grant that, as a result of our bodily penance, we may display a purity of heart that will be pleasing to you. We ask this....

Prayer after Communion

Sacramentorum tuorum benedictione roborati, quaesumus, Domine, ut per haec semper emundemur a vitiis, et per sequelam Christi ad te festinanter gradiamur. Per Christum.

Lord, we are strengthened by the blessing of your sacraments. Through them, please grant that we may ever be cleansed of our sins; and, through our following of Christ, grant that we may come quickly to you. We ask this....

TUESDAY OF THE FIFTH WEEK IN LENT

Collect

Da nobis, quaesumus, Domine, perseverantem in tua voluntate famulatum, ut in diebus nostris et merito et numero populus tibi serviens augeatur. Per Dominum.

Lord, please grant us a constant obedience to your will, so that in our day there may be an increase in both how many people serve you and how well they do so. We ask this....

Prayer over the Gifts

Hostias tibi, Domine, placationis offerimus, ut et delicta nostra miseratus absolvas, et nutantia corda tu dirigas. Per Christum.

Lord, we offer you our sacrifice of atonement. In your mercy, please forgive our sins and personally guide our faltering hearts. We ask this....

Prayer after Communion

Da, quaesumus, omnipotens Deus, ut, quae divina sunt iugiter ambientes, donis semper mereamur caelestibus propinquare. Per Christum.

Almighty God, we are continually privileged to associate with things that are divine. As we do so, please grant that we may draw closer to your heavenly gifts. We ask this....

WEDNESDAY OF THE FIFTH WEEK IN LENT

Collect

Sanctificata per paenitentiam tuorum corda fidelium, Deus miserator, illustra, et, quibus praestas devotionis affectum, praebe supplicantibus pium benignus auditum. Per Dominum.

God of mercy, the hearts of your faithful people have been made holy through penance. Grant us your light. You give us the spirit of faithful dedication; in your mercy, grant a loving answer to our prayers as well. We ask this....

Prayer over the Gifts

Tibi, Domine, sacrificia dicata reddantur, quae sic ad honorem nominis tui deferenda tribuisti, ut eadem remedia fieri nostra praestares. Per Christum.

Lord, grant that this sacrifice may be wholly consecrated to you, for you have given it to us, to be offered for the honor of your holy name, in such a way that you might return it to us in order to heal us. We ask this....

Prayer after Communion

Caelestem nobis, Domine, praebeant sumpta mysteria medicinam, ut et vitia nostri cordis expurgent, et sempiterna nos protectione confirment. Per Christum.

Lord, may the mysteries we have received provide us with a heavenly cure. May they cleanse the sinfulness of our hearts and strengthen us by your constant protection. We ask this....

THURSDAY OF THE FIFTH WEEK IN LENT

Collect

Adesto, Domine supplicibus tuis, et spem suam in tua misericordia collocantes tuere propitius, ut, a peccatorum labe mundati, in sancta conversatione permaneant, et promissionis tuae perficiantur heredes. Per Dominum.

Lord, be present to those who call upon you, and in your kindness look upon them as they place their hope in your mercy. May they be cleansed from the stain of their sins, and may they continue to lead holy lives and become ever more prepared to be heirs of your promise. We ask this....

Prayer over the Gifts

Sacrificiis praesentibus, quaesumus, Domine, placatus intende, ut et conversioni nostrae proficiant et totius mundi saluti. Per Christum.

Lord, in your kind mercy please look upon the sacrifices we offer. May they help bring about our own repentance and the salvation of the entire world. We ask this....

Prayer after Communion

Satiati munere salutari, tuam, Domine, misericordiam deprecamur, ut hoc eodem sacramento, quo nos temporaliter vegetas, efficias perpetuae vitae participes. Per Christum.

Lord, we have been filled with your saving gift, and we ask for your mercy. Through this same sacrament by which you now give us life on earth, may you make us share in the life that has no end. We ask this....

FRIDAY OF THE FIFTH WEEK IN LENT

Collect

Absolve, quaesumus, Domine, tuorum delicta populorum, ut a peccatorum nexibus, quae pro nostra fragilitate contraximus, tua benignitate liberemur. Per Dominum.

Lord, please forgive the failings of your people. By our weakness, we have fallen into the bonds of sin; may we be freed from them by your generous kindness. We ask this....

Prayer over the Gifts

Praesta nobis, misericors Deus, ut digne tuis servire semper altaribus mereamur, et eorum perpetua participatione salvari. Per Christum.

Merciful God, grant that we may always be privileged to serve worthily at your altar and to attain salvation through our constant sharing in your gifts. We ask this....

Prayer after Communion

Sumpti sacrificii, Domine, perpetua nos tuitio non relinquat, et noxia semper a nobis cuncta depellat. Per Christum.

Lord, may the constant protection of the sacrifice we have received never desert us, and may it always shield us from everything that is harmful. We ask this....

SATURDAY OF THE FIFTH WEEK IN LENT

Collect

Deus, qui, licet salutem hominum semper operaris, nunc tamen populum tuum gratia abundantiore laetificas, respice propitius ad electionem tuam, ut piae protectionis auxilium et regenerandos muniat et renatos. Per Dominum.

God our Father, it is true that you are always at work, bringing about the salvation of the human race. But now you gladden your people with an even greater grace. In your kind mercy, look upon those whom you have chosen, so that the help of your loving protection may strengthen those who are to be reborn in baptism as well as those who have already been given new life. We ask this....

Prayer over the Gifts

Omnipotens sempiterne Deus, qui nos ad aeternam vitam in confessione tui nominis baptismatis reparas sacramento, suscipe tuorum munera et vota famulorum, ut in te sperantium et desideria iubeas perfici et peccata deleri. Per Christum.

Almighty, eternal God, by the sacrament of baptism you restore us to eternal life in the profession of your holy name. Receive the gifts and prayers of your servants, and command that the desires of those who hope in you may be fulfilled and their sins be washed away. We ask this....

Prayer after Communion

Maiestatem tuam, Domine, suppliciter deprecamur, ut, sicut nos Corporis et Sanguinis sacrosancti pascis alimento, ita divinae naturae facias esse consortes. Per Christum.

Lord, we humbly beg the favor of your divine majesty. Just as you nourish us with the food of your most sacred Body and Blood, so may you make us share in your divine nature. We ask this....

PASSION (PALM) SUNDAY

Prayer at the Procession (A)

Omnipotens sempiterne Deus, hos palmites tua benedictione + sanctifica, ut nos, qui Christum Regem exsultando prosequimur, per ipsum valeamus ad aeternam Ierusalem pervenire. Qui vivit et regnat.

Almighty and eternal God, sanctify + these palm branches with your blessing. We joyfully follow Christ our King; through his aid, may we be enabled to come to the eternal Jerusalem. We ask this....

Prayer at the Procession (B)

Auge fidem in te sperantium, Deus, et supplicum preces clementer exaudi, ut, qui hodie Christo triumphanti palmites exhibemus, in ipso fructus tibi bonorum operum afferamus. Qui vivit.

God our Father, increase the faith of those who hope in you, and in your mercy listen to the prayers of those who call upon you. Today we carry branches of palm in tribute to Christ in his triumph. May we bring to you the results of the good works we do as we live in him. We ask this....

Collect

Omnipotens sempiterne Deus, qui humano generi, ad imitandum humilitatis exemplum, Salvatorem nostrum carnem sumere, et crucem subire fecisti, concede propitius, ut et patientiae ipsius habere documenta et resurrectionis consortia mereamur. Per Dominum.

Almighty and eternal God, for the sake of the human race, you willed that our Savior should take human flesh upon himself and undergo the cross, in order to give us an example of the humility we should imitate. In your kindness, grant us the privilege both of keeping before us the example of his suffering and of enjoying his companionship in the resurrection. We ask this....

Prayer over the Gifts

Per Unigeniti tui passionem placatio tua nobis, Domine, sit propinqua, quam, etsi nostris operibus non meremur, interveniente sacrificio singulari, tua percipiamus miseratione praeveni. Per Christum.

Through the passion of your only Son, Lord, may your forgiveness draw near to us. Although we do not deserve it by our works, nonetheless through the workings of this unique sacrifice may we look forward to being reconciled to you because of your mercy. We ask this....

Prayer after Communion

Sacro munere satiati, supplices te, Domine, deprecamur, ut, qui fecisti nos morte Filii tui sperare quod credimus, facias nos, eodem resurgente, pervenire quo tendimus. Per Christum.

Lord, we are filled with your sacred gift, and we humbly come to you with our prayer. Through the death of your Son you made us hope for what we believe; through his resurrection may you make us arrive at the goal for which we are striving. We ask this....

MONDAY OF HOLY WEEK

Collect

Da, quaesumus, omnipotens Deus, ut, qui ex nostra infirmitate deficimus, intercedente unigeniti Filii tui passione, respiremus. Qui tecum.

Almighty God, please grant that we who fall through our own weakness may rise once again through the merits of your only Son's suffering and death. We ask this....

Prayer over the Gifts

Respice, Domine, propitius sacra mysteria quae gerimus, et, quod ad nostra evacuanda praeiudicia misericors praevidisti, vitam nobis tribue fructificare perpetuam. Per Christum.

Lord, in your kindness look upon the sacred mysteries which we offer. Since in your mercy you have made provision for revoking the sentence we deserved, grant that eternal life may flower forth for us. We ask this....

Prayer after Communion

Visita, quaesumus, Domine, plebem tuam, et corda sacris dicata mysteriis pietate tuere pervigili, ut remedia salutis aeternae, quae te miserante percipit, te protegente custodiat. Per Christum.

Lord, please come to your people, and with your ever-vigilant care guard the hearts of those who have been sanctified to you by these holy mysteries. Under your protection, may they safeguard the means to eternal salvation which they receive through your mercy. We ask this....

TUESDAY OF HOLY WEEK

Collect

Omnipotens sempiterne Deus, da nobis ita dominicae passionis sacramenta peragere, ut indulgentiam percipere mereamur. Per Dominum.

Almighty and eternal God, grant that we may celebrate the mystery of the Lord's passion in a way that will win us your forgiveness. We ask this....

Prayer over the Gifts

Hostias familiae tuae, quaesumus, Domine, placatus intende, et, quam sacris muneribus facis esse participem, tribuas ad eorum plenitudinem pervenire. Per Christum.

Lord, in your mercy, please look upon the sacrificial offerings of your servants. You allow us to take part in these sacred rites; so too, grant that we may share in their fulfillment. We ask this....

Prayer after Communion

Satiati munere salutari, tuam, Domine, misericordiam deprecamur, ut hoc eodem sacramento, quo nos voluisti temporaliter vegetari, perpetuae vitae facias esse participes. Per Christum.

Lord, we are filled with your saving gift, and we plead for your mercy. You have willed that we should be given life in this world through this sacrament. May you make us share in eternal life through it as well. We ask this....

WEDNESDAY OF HOLY WEEK

Collect

Deus, qui pro nobis Filium tuum crucis patibulum subire voluisti, ut inimici a nobis expelleres potestatem, concede nobis famulis tuis, ut resurrectionis gratiam consequamur. Per Dominum.

God our Father, it was your will that your Son should undergo the yoke of the Cross on our behalf, so that you might put to flight the power the enemy had over us. Grant that we, your servants, may attain the grace of the resurrection. We ask this....

Prayer over the Gifts

Suscipe, quaesumus, Domine, munus oblatum, et dignanter operare, ut, quod gerimus Filii tui mysterio passionis, piis effectibus consequamur. Per Christum.

Lord, please receive the gift we offer. In your kindness and mercy, see to it that we achieve the holy results of what we do in celebrating the mystery of the passion of your Son. We ask this....

Prayer after Communion

Largire sensibus nostris, omnipotens Deus, ut per temporalem Filii tui mortem, quam mysteria veneranda testantur, vitam te nobis dedisse perpetuam confidamus. Per Christum.

Almighty God, these sacred mysteries attest to the death of your Son in this life. Please grant us confident knowledge that you have thereby given us eternal life. We ask this....

HOLY THURSDAY: CHRISM MASS

Collect

Deus, qui unigenitum Filium tuum unxisti Spiritu Sancto Christumque Dominum constituisti, concede propitius, ut, eiusdem consecrationis participes effecti, testes Redemptionis inveniamur in mundo. Per Dominum.

God our Father, you anointed your only Son with the Holy Spirit and established him as Christ the Lord. We have been made sharers in his consecration; in your kindness, please grant that, while we are in this world, we may also prove to be witnesses to his redemption. We ask this....

Prayer over the Gifts

Huius sacrificii potentia, Domine, quaesumus, et vetustatem nostram clementer abstergat, et novitatem nobis augeat et salutem. Per Christum.

Lord, we ask that the power of this sacrifice may mercifully wash away our old sinfulness and increase our new life and salvation. We ask this....

Prayer after Communion

Supplices te rogamus, omnipotens Deus, ut quos tuis reficis sacramentis, Christi bonus odor effici mereantur. Per Christum.

Almighty God, we humbly ask that those whom you renew with your sacraments may have the privilege of being transformed into the pleasing fragrance of Christ. We ask this....

HOLY THURSDAY: EVENING MASS OF THE LORD'S SUPPER

Collect

Sacratissimam, Deus, frequentantibus Cenam, in qua Unigenitus tuus, morti se traditurus, novum in saecula sacrificium dilectionisque suae convivium Ecclesiae commendavit, da nobis, quaesumus, ut ex tanto mysterio plenitudinem caritatis hauriamus et vitae. Per Dominum.

God our Father, as your only Son was about to hand himself over to death, he gave his Church a new sacrifice for the ages and a banquet of his own love. As we celebrate his most sacred supper, please grant that we may drink deep of the fullness of love and life from this magnificent mystery. We ask this....

Prayer over the Gifts

Concede nobis, quaesumus, Domine, haec digne frequentare mysteria, quia, quoties huius hostiae commemoratio celebratur, opus nostrae redemptionis exercetur. Per Christum.

Lord, please grant that we may take part in these mysteries worthily, for as often as the remembrance of this sacrifice is celebrated, the work of our redemption is carried on. We ask this....

Prayer after Communion

Concede nobis, omnipotens Deus, ut sicut Cena Filii tui reficimur temporali, ita satiari mereamur aeterna. Per Christum.

Almighty God, grant that, just as we are renewed in this life by the supper of your Son, so we may have the privilege of having that renewal find its fulfillment at his banquet in heaven. We ask this....

GOOD FRIDAY

Initial Prayer: (A)

Reminiscere miserationum tuarum, Domine, et famulos tuos aeterna protectione sanctifica, pro quibus Christus, Filius tuus, per suum cruorem instituit paschale mysterium. Qui vivit.

Lord, for the benefit of your people, Christ your Son inaugurated the paschal mystery by his own blood. Be mindful of your mercies, and in your everlasting providence make us holy. We ask this....

Initial Prayer: (B)

Deus, qui peccati veteris hereditariam mortem, in qua posteritatis genus omne succeserat, Christi Filii tui, Domini nostri, passione solvisti, da, ut conformes eidem facti, sicut imaginem terreni hominis naturae necessitate portavimus, ita imaginem caelestis gratiae sanctificatione portemus. Per Christum.

God our Father, each age of the human race had been subject to inherited death because of the ancient sin. You freed us from that by the passion of your Son, Christ our Lord. Grant that we may be made like him. We have carried with us the likeness of an earthly person because of what we are; because of what grace has made us, may we now carry with us the image of a heavenly one. We ask this....

General Intercessory Prayers

(1) Oremus, dilectissimi nobis, pro Ecclesia sancta Dei, ut eam Deus et Dominus noster pacificare, adunare et custodire dignetur toto orbe terrarum, detque nobis, quietam et tranquillam vitam degentibus, glorificare Deum Patrem omnipotentem.

Omnipotens sempiterne Deus, qui gloriam tuam omnibus in Christo gentibus revelasti: custodi opera misericordiae tuae, ut Ecclesia tua, toto orbe diffusa, stabili fide in confessione tui nominis perseveret. Per Christum.

(1) My dear friends, let us pray for the holy Church of God. May our God and Lord see fit to give it peace, unity, and protection throughout the world; and may he grant that we enjoy a quiet, peaceful life and that we glorify God the almighty Father.

Almighty, eternal God, you have revealed your glory to all the nations in Christ. Protect the work your mercy has begun, so that your Church may spread throughout the world and continually profess your name with firm faith. We ask this....

(2) Oremus et pro beatissimo Papa nostro N., ut Deus et Dominus noster, qui elegit eum in ordine episcopatus, salvum atque incolumem custodiat Ecclesiae suae sanctae, ad regendum populum sanctum Dei.

Omnipotens sempiterne Deus, cuius iudicio universa fundantur, respice propitius ad preces nostras, et electum nobis Antistitem tua pietate conserva, ut christiana plebs, quae te gubernatur auctore, sub ipso Pontifice, fidei suae meritis augeatur. Per Christum.

(2) Let us also pray for our Holy Father, Pope N. May our Lord and God, who chose him to be a bishop, keep him strong and safe for the benefit of the holy Church, so that he may govern the holy people of God.

Almighty and eternal God, your command is the basis for all things. In your kindness, look upon our prayers, and, in your love, guard the Pope you have chosen for us. It is by your authority that the Christian people are governed; under the Supreme Pontiff, may the strength of their faith ever increase. We ask this....

(3) Oremus et pro Episcopo nostro N., pro omnibus Episcopis, presbyteris, diaconis Ecclesiae et universa plebe fidelium.

Omnipotens sempiterne Deus, cuius Spiritu totum corpus Ecclesiae sanctificatur et regitur, exaudi nos pro ministris tuis supplicantes, ut, gratiae tuae munere, ab omnibus tibi fideliter serviatur. Per Christum.

(3) Let us also pray for our Bishop N., for all bishops, priests, and deacons of the Church, and for all the faithful.

Almighty and eternal God, by your Spirit the entire body of the Church is sanctified and governed. Hear us as we pray for your ministers. By the gift of your grace, may they all serve you faithfully. We ask this....

(4) Oremus et pro catechumenis (nostris), ut Deus et Dominus noster adaperiat aures praecordiorum ipsorum ianuamque misericordiae, ut, per lavacrum regenerationis accepta remissione omnium peccatorum, et ipsi inveniantur in Christo Iesu Domino nostro.

Omnipotens sempiterne Deus, qui Ecclesiam tuam nova semper prole fecundas, auge fidem et intellectum catechumenis (nostris), ut, renati fonte baptismatis, adoptionis tuae filiis aggregentur. Per Christum.

(4) Let us also pray for (our) catechumens. May our God and Lord open both the ears of their inmost hearts and the doorway of his mercy; once they have received the forgiveness of all their sins by the waters of rebirth, may they be found to live in Christ Jesus our Lord.

Almighty and eternal God, you always make your Church fruitful with new offspring. Increase the faith and understanding of (our) catechumens. After they have been reborn at the font of baptism, may they be added to the fold of your adopted children. We ask this....

(5) Oremus et pro universis fratribus in Christum credentibus, ut Deus et Dominus noster eos, veritatem facientes, in una Ecclesia sua congregare et custodire dignetur.

Omnipotens sempiterne Deus, qui dispersa congregas et congregata conservas, ad gregem Filii tui placatus intende, ut, quos unum baptisma sacravit, eos et fidei iungat integritas et vinculum societ caritatis. Per Christum.

(5) Let us also pray for all of our brothers and sisters who place their belief in Christ. May our God and Lord see fit to gather them together into his one Church and guard them, since they act with sincere hearts.

Almighty and eternal God, you gather together what is scattered, and you guard what you have gathered together. Be pleased to look upon your Son's flock. The one baptism has consecrated them; may their one faith join them together, and the bond of love unite them. We ask this....

(6) Oremus et pro Iudais, ut, ad quos prius locutus est Dominus Deus noster, eis tribuat in sui nominis amore et in sui foederis fidelitate proficere.

Omnipotens sempiterne Deus, qui promissiones tuas Abrahae eiusque semini contulisti, Ecclesiae tuae preces clementer exaudi, ut populus acquisitionis prioris ad redemptionis mereatur plenitudinem pervenire. Per Christum.

(6) Let us also pray for the Jews. They were the first people to whom the Lord our God spoke; may He grant them an increased love of his name and a greater faithfulness to his covenant.

Almighty and eternal God, you gave your promises to Abraham and his offspring. In your mercy, hear the prayers of your Church. May the people of your earlier possession be privileged to come to the fullness of redemption. We ask this....

(7) Oremus et pro iis qui in Christum non credunt, ut, luce Sancti Spiritus illustrati, viam salutis et ipsi valeant introire.
Omnipotens sempiterne Deus, fac ut qui Christum non confitentur, coram te sincero corde ambulantes, inveniant veritatem, nosque, mutuo proficientes semper amore et ad tuae vitae mysterium plenius percipiendum sollicitos, perfectiores effice tuae testes caritatis in mundo. Per Christum.

(7) Let us pray also for those who do not believe in Christ. May they too be illumined by the light of the Holy Spirit, and so be able to enter upon the way to salvation.

Almighty and eternal God, bring it about that those who do not believe in Christ may discover the truth, as they walk before you with sincere hearts. Make us always progress in love for one another, strive eagerly to understand more fully the mystery of your life, and thus be better witnesses to your love in the world. We ask this....

(8) Oremus et pro iis qui Deum non agnoscunt, ut, quae recta sunt sincero corde sectantes, ad ipsum Deum pervenire mereantur.
Omnipotens sempiterne Deus, qui cunctos homines condidisti, ut te semper desiderando quaererent et inveniendo requiescerent, praesta, quaesumus, ut inter noxia quaeque obstacula omnes, tuae signa pietatis et in te credentium testimonium bonorum operum percipientes, te solum verum Deum nostrique generis Patrem gaudeant confiteri. Per Christum.

(8) Let us pray also for those who do not believe in God. As they seek what is right with sincere hearts, may they be privileged to come to know God himself.

Almighty and eternal God, you made the entire human race such that all would seek you in their longings and, having found you, would achieve their peaceful rest. Please grant that, despite any harmful thing that stands in the way, all people may see the signs of your love and the testimony of the good works of those who believe in you, and so come joyfully to profess you as the only true God and Father of our race. We ask this....

(9) Oremus et pro omnibus rempublicam moderantibus, ut Deus et Dominus noster mentes et corda eorum secundum voluntatem suam dirigat ad veram omnium pacem et libertatem.
Omnipotens sempiterne Deus, in cuius manu sunt hominum corda et iura populorum, respice benignus ad eos, qui nos in potestate moderantur, ut ubique terrarum populorum prosperitas, pacis securitas et religionis libertas, te largiente, consistant. Per Christum.

(9) Let us pray also for all rulers of nations. May our God and Lord direct their minds and hearts, according to his will, toward what will lead to true peace and freedom for all people.

Almighty and eternal God, in your hands are the hearts of the human race and the rights of its peoples. In your kindness, look upon those who have the power to govern us, so that the well-being of people throughout the earth, their secure peace, and their freedom of religion may, by your gift, be firmly established. We ask this....

(10) Oremus, dilectissimi nobis, Deum Patrem omnipotentem, ut cunctis mundum purget erroribus, morbos auferat, famem depellat, aperiat carceres, vincula solvat, viatoribus securitatem, peregrinantibus reditum, infirmantibus sanitatem atque morientibus salutem indulgeat.
Omnipotens sempiterne Deus, maestorum consolatio, laborantium fortitudo, pervaniant ad te preces de quacumque tribulatione clamantium, ut omnes sibi in necessitatibus suis misericordiam tuam gaudeant affuisse. Per Christum.

(10) Beloved people, let us pray to God the Father almighty. May he cleanse the world of all errors, take away all diseases, drive out famine, open prisons, dissolve bonds; and may he grant safety to travelers, a safe return home to those in foreign countries, health to the sick, and salvation to the dying.

Almighty and eternal God, solace of the saddened and strength of the weary, hear the prayers of those who cry to you in whatever tribulation, so that all people may rejoice that your mercy has been present to them in their needs. We ask this....

Prayer after Communion

Omnipotens sempiterne Deus, qui nos Christi tui beata morte et resurrectione reparasti, conserva in nobis opus misericordiae tuae, ut huius mysterii participatione perpetua devotione vivamus. Per Christum.

Almighty and eternal God, you have restored us by the holy death and resurrection of your Christ. Preserve within us the work your mercy has begun. By sharing in this mystery, may we live in unending faithfulness to you. We ask this....

Prayer over the People

Super populum tuum, quaesumus, Domine, qui mortem Filii tui in spe suae resurectionis recoluit, benedictio copiosa descendat, indulgentia veniat, consolatio tribuatur, fides sancta succrescat, redemptio sempiterna firmetur. Per Christum.

Lord, your people have contemplated the death of your Son, and they hope for his resurrection. May your rich blessing come down upon them. May your forgiveness come to them, and your comfort be given them. May their holy faith increase, and their eternal redemption be secured. We ask this....

THE SEASON OF

EASTER

HOLY SATURDAY

Blessing of the Fire

Deus, qui per Filium tuum claritatis tuae ignem fidelibus contulisti, novum hunc ignem + sanctifica, et concede nobis, ita per haec festa paschalia caelestibus desideriis inflammari, ut ad perpetuae claritatis puris mentibus valeamus festa pertingere. Per Christum.

God our Father, you brought the pure flame of your splendor to your faithful people through your Son. Make this new fire + holy. Grant that these paschal feasts may so inflame us with heavenly desires that our hearts may be cleansed and we may be enabled to come to the festival of eternal light. We ask this....

Prayers after the Readings

(1A) Omnipotens sempiterne Deus, qui es in omnium operum tuorum dispensatione mirabilis, intelligant redempti tui, non fuisse excellentius, quod initio factus est mundus, quam quod in fine saeculorum Pascha nostrum immolatus est Christus. Qui vivit.

(1A) Almighty and eternal God, you are wonderful in how you order all your works. Grant that your redeemed people may realize that the offering of Christ as our paschal sacrifice at the end of many ages is even more magnificent than was the creation of the world at the beginning of time. We ask this....

(1B) Deus, qui mirabiliter creasti hominem et mirabilius redemisti, da nobis, quaesumus, contra oblectamenta peccati mentis ratione persistere, ut mereamur ad aeterna gaudia pervenire. Per Christum.

(1B) God our Father, wonderful was your work of creating the human race, still more wonderful your work of redeeming it. Please grant us firm hearts to resist whatever tempts us to sin, so that we may be privileged to come to eternal happiness. We ask this....

(2) Deus, Pater summe fidelium, qui promissionis tuae filios diffusa adoptionis gratia in toto terrarum orbe multiplicas, et per paschale sacramentum Abraham puerum tuum universarum, sicut iurasti, gentium efficis patrem, da populis tuis digne ad gratiam tuae vocationis intrare. Per Christum.

(2) God, supreme Father of the faithful, you increase the children of your promise by pouring out the grace of adoption throughout the world; and through the paschal sacrament you make Abraham, your son, the father of all races, as you have promised. Grant that your people may begin to respond worthily to the grace of your call. We ask this....

(3A) Deus, cuius antiqua miracula etiam nostris temporibus coruscare sentimus, dum, quod uni populo a persecutione Pharaonis liberando dexterae tuae potentia contulisti, id in salutem gentium per aquam regenerationis operaris, praesta, ut in Abrahae filios et in Israeliticam dignitatem totius mundi transeat plenitudo. Per Christum.

(3A) God our Father, we know that the marvelous works you did in ancient times shine forth even in our day. By the power of your right hand, you once rescued a single nation from the persecution of Pharaoh; now, by the water of rebirth, you come to the rescue of all races and peoples. Grant that the entire world may become children of Abraham and enjoy the inheritance of the Israelites. We ask this....

(3B) Deus, qui primis temporibus impleta miracula novi testamenti luce reserasti, ut et Mare Rubrum forma sacri fontis exsisteret, et plebs a servitute liberata christiani populi sacramenta

praeferret, da, ut omnes gentes, Israelis privilegium merito fidei consecutae, Spiritus tui participatione regenerentur. Per Christum.

(3B) God our Father, in early times you disclosed the miraculous events that were fulfilled in the light of the New Testament. And so, the Red Sea acted as a symbol of the sacred fountain of baptism and the people rescued from slavery prefigured the sacraments of the Christian people. Grant that all nations may achieve the privilege of Israel as a reward for their faith and may be reborn by sharing in your Spirit. We ask this....

(4) *Omnipotens sempiterne Deus, multiplica in honorem nominis tui quod patrum fidei spopondidisti, et promissionis filios sacra adoptione dilata, ut, quod priores sancti non dubitavereunt futurum, Ecclesia tam magna ex parte iam cognoscat impletum. Per Christum.*

(4) Almighty and eternal God, for the honor of your holy name, increase what you pledged to our ancestors because of their faith: through your holy adoption, make the number of the children of the promise grow, so that your Church may recognize that you have in such large part already fulfilled what the ancient holy ones had no doubt that you would do. We ask this....

(5) *Omnipotens sempiterne Deus, spes unica mundi, qui prophetarum tuorum praeconio praesentium temporum declarasti mysteria, auge populi tui vota placatus, quia in nullo fidelium nisi ex tua inspiratione proveniunt quarumlibet incrementa virtutum. Per Christum.*

(5) Almighty and eternal God, you are the sole hope of the world. Through the preaching of the prophets you have made known the mysteries we celebrate today. Be pleased to make the love and dedication of your people grow, for no increase in any virtue at all comes to any one of your faithful people except through your inspiration. We ask this....

(6) *Deus, qui Ecclesiam tuam semper gentium vocatione multiplicas, concede propitius, ut, quos aqua baptismatis abluis, continua protectione tuearis. Per Christum.*

(6) God our Father, you continually increase your Church by calling all nations to belief. In your kindness, keep safe under your continual protection those whom you wash clean by the water of baptism. We ask this....

(7A) *Deus, incommutabilis virtus et lumen aeternum, respice propitius ad totius Ecclesiae sacramentum, et opus salutis humanae perpetuae dispositionis effectu tranquillius operare; totusque mundus experiatur et videat deiecta erigi, inveterata renovari et per ipsum Christum redire omnia in integrum, a quo sumpsere principium. Qui vivit.*

(7A) God our Father, you are changeless strength and eternal light. Look with kindness upon the sacrament that is your whole Church, and accomplish ever more peacefully the work of human salvation by your all-present providence. May the entire world experience of the sight of the downcast being raised up, the old renewed, and all things brought back into unity through the same Christ who is their source. We ask this....

(7B) *Deus, qui nos ad celebrandum paschale sacramentum utriusque Testamenti paginis instruis, da nobis intellegere misericordiam tuam, ut ex perceptione praesentium munerum firma sit exspectatio futurorum. Per Christum.*

(7B) God our Father, in the pages of both Testaments you teach us to celebrate the paschal sacrament. Grant that we may understand your mercy, so that by our awareness of the gifts you give us now, our hope in those yet to come may be made firm. We ask this....

Collect

Deus, qui hanc sacratissimam noctem gloria dominicae resurrectionis illustras, excita in Ecclesia tua adoptionis spiritum, ut, corpore et mente renovati, puram tibi exhibeamus servitutem. Per Dominum.

God our Father, you make this most sacred night brilliant by the glory of the Lord's resurrection. Stir up in your Church a sense of its adoption, so that we may be renewed in mind and body and may serve you with all our hearts. We ask this....

Prayer after the Litanies
(when candidates for baptism are present)

Omnipotens sempiterne Deus, adesto magnae pietatis tuae sacramentis, et ad recreandos novos populos, quos tibi fons baptismatis parturit, spiritum adoptionis emitte, ut, quod nostrae humilitatis gerendum est ministerio, virtutis tuae impleatur effectu. Per Christum.

Almighty and eternal God, be present in the sacraments of your great love, and send forth the Spirit of adoption to bring about the rebirth of a new people, whom the water of baptism bears for you. May what we are to do in our lowly ministry be brought to fulfillment by your mighty power. We ask this....

Blessing of the Water
(when candidates for baptism are present)

Deus, qui invisibili potentia per sacramentorum signa mirabilem operaris effectum, et creaturam aquae multis modis praeparasti, ut baptismi gratiam demonstraret; Deus, cuius Spiritus super aquas inter ipsa mundi primordia ferebatur, ut iam tunc virtutem sanctificandi aquarum natura conciperet; Deus, qui regenerationis speciem in ipsa diluvii effusione signasti, ut unius eiusdemque elementi mysterio et finis esset vitiis et origo virtutum; Deus, qui Abrahae filios per Mare Rubrum sicco vestigio transire fecisti, ut plebs, a Pharaonis servitute liberata, populum baptizorum praefiguraret; Deus, cuius Filius, in aqua Iordanis a Ioanne baptizatus, Sancto Spiritu est inunctus, et, in cruce pendens, una cum sanguine aquam de latere suo produxit, ac, post resurrectionem suam, discipulis iussit: "Ite, docete omnes gentes, baptizantes eos in nomine Patris, et Filii, et Spiritus Sancti": respice in faciem Ecclesiae tuae, eique dignare fontem baptismatis aperire. Sumat haec aqua Unigeniti tui gratiam de Spiritu Sancto, ut homo, ad imaginem tuam conditus, sacramento baptismatis a cunctis squaloribus vetustatis ablutus, in novam infantiam ex aqua et Spiritu Sancto resurgere mereatur. Descendat, quaesumus, Domine, in hanc plenitudinem fontis per Filium tuum virtus Spiritus Sancti, ut omnes, cum Christo consepulti per baptismum in mortem, ad vitam cum ipso resurgant. Per Christum.

God our Father, by your invisible power you work marvelous deeds by means of the signs that are the sacraments. You have prepared the creature that is water in myriad ways so that it might show forth the grace of baptism. Father, your Spirit moved over the waters at the very beginnings of the world, so that even then water might receive the power of sanctifying as part of its nature. Father, you made the very outpouring of the great flood a symbol of rebirth, so that in the mystery of one and the same element there should be both the end of vice and the beginning of virtue. Father, you made the children of Abraham pass through the Red Sea dry shod, so that a nation might be freed from slavery to Pharaoh and thus might prefigure the people of the baptized. Father, your Son was anointed with the Holy Spirit when he was baptized by John in the water of the Jordan. As he was hanging on the cross, water as well as blood flowed from his side; and, after his resurrection, he bade his disciples, "Go, teach all nations, baptizing them in the name of the Father, and of the Son, and of the Holy Spirit." God our Father, look upon the face of your Church, and open for her the font of baptism. May this water receive the grace of your only Son from the Holy Spirit, so that men and women, made in your image and washed clean of their old sinfulness by the sacrament of baptism, may be privileged to rise to a new birth by means of water and the Holy Spirit. Lord, through your Son may the power of the Holy Spirit come down upon this brimming font, so that all who have been buried with Christ through baptism into his death may rise to life with him. We ask this....

Blessing of the Water
(when no candidates for baptism are present)

Domine Deus noster, populo tuo hac nocte sacratissima vigilanti adesto propitius: et nobis, mirabile nostrae creationis opus, sed et redemptionis nostrae mirabilius, memorantibus, hanc aquam benedicere tu dignare. Ipsam enim tu fecisti, ut et arva fecunditate donaret, et levamen corporibus nostris munditiamque praeberet. Aquam etiam tuae ministram misericordiae condidisti: nam per ipsam solvisti tui populi servitutem illiusque sitim in deserto sedasti; per ipsam novum foedus nuntiaverunt prophetae, quod eras cum hominibus initurus; per ipsam denique, quam Christus in Iordane sacravit, corruptam naturae nostrae substantiam in regenerationis lavacro renovasti. Sit igitur haec aqua nobis suscepti baptismatis memoria, et cum fratribus nostris, qui sunt in Paschate baptizati, gaudia nos tribuas sociare. Per Christum.

Lord our God, in your mercy be present to your people as they keep vigil on this most sacred night. Graciously bless this water for us as we recall the wonderful work of our creation and the still more wonderful work of our redemption. For you have created water to give fruitfulness to our fields and to provide refreshment and cleansing for our bodies. You have also made water an instrument of your mercy, for by means of it you released your people from slavery and slaked their thirst in the desert; by means of it, the prophets announced the new covenant which you were about to make with humankind. Finally, by water, which Christ consecrated in the Jordan, you have renewed our tainted nature in the bath of rebirth. May this water therefore be a reminder for us of the baptism that we have received; and grant that we may share our joy with our brothers and sisters who have been baptized on this paschal feast. We ask this....

Prayer over the Gifts

Suscipe, quaesumus, Domine, preces populi tui cum oblationibus hostiarum, ut, paschalibus initiata mysteriis, ad aeternitatis nobis medelam, te operante, proficiant. Per Christum.

Lord, please receive the prayers and sacrificial offerings of your people. They have been introduced into the paschal mysteries; by your power, may they progress to the haven of eternity you have provided for them. We ask this....

Prayer after Communion

Spiritum nobis, Domine, tuae caritatis infunde, ut, quos sacramentis paschalibus satiasti, tua facias pietate concordes. Per Christum.

Lord, pour forth the Spirit of your love into us. You have filled us with the paschal sacraments; may we live in harmony with one another because of your faithful love. We ask this....

EASTER SUNDAY

Collect

Deus, qui hodierna die, per Unigenitum tuum, aeternitatis nobis aditum, devicta morte, reserasti, da nobis, quaesumus, ut, qui resurrectionis dominicae sollemnia colimus, per innovationem tui Spiritus in lumine vitae resurgamus. Per Dominum.

God our Father, on this day you have conquered death and given us access to eternity through your only Son. As we celebrate the solemn feast of the Lord's resurrection, please grant that, by the renewal your Spirit causes within us, we may rise one day in the light of life. We ask this....

Prayer over the Gifts

Sacrificia, Domine, paschalibus gaudiis exsultantes offerimus, quibus Ecclesia tua mirabiliter renascitur et nutritur. Per Christum.

Lord, we are gladdened with Easter joy, and we offer the sacrifice by which your Church is marvelously reborn and nourished. We make our prayer through....

Prayer after Communion

Perpetuo, Deus, Ecclesiam tuam pio favore tuere, ut, paschalibus renovata mysteriis, ad resurrectionis perveniat claritatem. Per Christum.

God our Father, guard your Church with you constant loving favor. May it be renewed by the Easter mysteries, and so attain the brilliance of the resurrection. We ask this....

EASTER MONDAY

Collect

Deus, qui Ecclesiam tuam nova semper prole multiplicas, concede famulis tuis, ut sacramentum vivendo teneant, quod fide perceperunt. Per Dominum.

God our Father, you continually increase your Church with new offspring. Grant that, in their daily lives, your servants may live in accord with that sacrament which they have received in faith. We ask this....

Prayer over the Gifts

Suscipe, quaesumus, Domine, munera tuorum propitius populorum, ut, confessione tui nominis et baptismate renovati, sempiternam beatitudinem consequantur. Per Christum.

Lord, in your kindness, please receive the gifts of your people, so that, renewed by their profession of your name and by baptism, they may attain eternal happiness. We ask this....

Prayer after Communion

Exuberet, quaesumus, Domine, mentibus nostris paschalis gratia sacramenti, ut, quos viam fecisti perpetuae salutis intrare, donis tuis dignos efficias. Per Christum.

Lord, we ask that the grace of this Easter sacrament may abound in our hearts. You have set us upon the way to eternal salvation; may you make us worthy of your gifts. We ask this....

EASTER TUESDAY

Collect

Deus, qui paschalia nobis remedia contulisti, populum tuum caelesti dono prosequere, ut, perfectam libertatem assecutus, in caelis gaudeat, unde nunc in terris exsultat. Per Dominum.

God our Father, you have given us the gift of your healing grace at Easter. Continue to give your people your heavenly gifts, so that they may achieve perfect freedom. They now find joy on earth in your gift; may they rejoice in its complete possession in heaven. We ask this....

Prayer over the Gifts

Oblationes familiae tuae, quaesumus, Domine, suscipe miseratus, ut, sub tuae protectionis auxilio, et collata non perdat, et ad aeterna dona perveniat. Per Christum.

Lord, in your mercy please accept the offerings of your servants. Under the help of your protection, may they not lose the gifts they have received, and may they arrive at the eternal ones you promise. We ask this....

Prayer after Communion

Exaudi nos, omnipotens Deus, et familiae tuae corda, cui perfectam baptismatis gratiam contulisti, ad promerendam beatitudinem aptes aeternam. Per Christum.

Almighty God, you have given the perfect grace of baptism to your servants. Hear us, and make the hearts of your servants fit to attain eternal happiness. We ask this....

EASTER WEDNESDAY

Collect

Deus, qui nos resurrectionis dominicae annua sollemnitate laetificas, concede propitius, ut, per temporalia festa quae agimus, pervenire ad gaudia aeterna mereamur. Per Dominum.

God our Father, you gladden us by the yearly celebration of the Lord's resurrection. Through the festivals we celebrate in our present life, mercifully grant us the privilege of arriving at eternal joy. We ask this....

Prayer over the Gifts

Suscipe, quaesumus, Domine, hostias redemptionis humanae, et salutem nobis mentis et corporis operare placatus. Per Christum.

Lord, please receive the sacrificial offerings that redeemed the human race. In your forgiving mercy, bring about the salvation of our minds and our bodies. We ask this....

Prayer after Communion

Ab omni nos, quaesumus, Domine, vetustate purgatos, sacramenti Filii tui veneranda perceptio in novam transferat creaturam. Per Christum.

Lord, may the holy reception of the sacrament of your Son cleanse us from all our ancient sinfulness and transform us into a new creation. We ask this....

EASTER THURSDAY

Collect

Deus, qui diversitatem gentium in confessione tui nominis adunasti, da, ut renatis fonte baptismatis una sit fides mentium et pietas actionum. Per Dominum.

God our Father, you have gathered together a variety of peoples in the profession of your name. For those who have been reborn at the font of baptism, grant that there may be but one faith in their hearts and one love in their deeds. We ask this....

Prayer over the Gifts

Hostias, quaesumus, Domine, placatus assume, quas et pro renatis gratanter deferimus, et pro acceleratione caelestis auxilii. Per Christum.

Lord, in your forgiving mercy, please accept the offerings which we bring in thanksgiving for those who have been reborn and in petition for the swift help of your divine protection. We ask this....

Prayer after Communion

Exaudi, Domine, preces nostras, ut redemptionis nostrae sacrosancta commercia et vitae nobis conferant praesentis auxilium et gaudia sempiterna concilient. Per Christum.

Lord, hear our prayers. May your most sacred action of redeeming us bring us your help in this present life and gain for us the joys of eternity. We ask this....

EASTER FRIDAY

Collect

Omnipotens sempiterne Deus, qui paschale sacramentum in reconciliationis humanae foedere contulisti, da mentibus nostris, ut, quod professione celebramus, imitemur effectu. Per Dominum.

Almighty and eternal God, you brought us the Easter sacrament as a covenant that would lead to human redemption. Give us the resolve to have our deeds testify to what we celebrate in faith. We ask this....

Prayer over the Gifts

Perfice, Domine, benignus in nobis paschalium munerum votiva commercia, ut a terrenis affectibus ad caeleste desiderium transferamur. Per Christum.

In your mercy, Lord, bring to completion in us this holy exchange of Easter gifts, so that we may be transformed from a love of earthly things to a desire for what is heavenly. We ask this....

Prayer after Communion

Continua, quaesumus, Domine, quos salvasti pietate custodi, ut, qui Filii tui passione sunt redempti, eius resurrectione laetentur. Per Christum.

Lord, with your constant love please guard those whom you have rescued. May those who have been redeemed by the passion of your Son thus be gladdened by his resurrection. We ask this....

EASTER SATURDAY

Collect

Deus, qui credentes in te populos gratiae tuae largitate multiplicas, ad electionem tuam propitius intuere, ut, qui sacramento baptismatis sunt renati, beata facias immortalitate vestiri. Per Dominum.

God our Father, by the generous outpouring of your grace you increase the number of those who believe in you. Look kindly upon the people you have chosen, and grant that those who have been reborn in the sacrament of baptism may be clothed in a blessed immortality. We ask this....

Prayer over the Gifts

Concede, quaesumus, Domine, semper nos per haec mysteria paschalia gratulari, ut continua nostrae reparationis operatio perpetuae nobis fiat causa laetitiae. Per Christum.

Lord, please grant that we may always rejoice because of these Easter mysteries. The work of our renewal goes on constantly; may this be a cause of unending joy for us. We ask this....

Prayer after Communion

Populum tuum, quaesumus, Domine, intuere benignus, et, quem aeternis dignatus es renovare mysteriis, ad incorruptibilem glorificandae carnis resurrectionem pervenire concede. Per Christum.

Lord, please look upon your people with kindness. You have seen fit to renew them with your eternal mysteries; grant that they may arrive at the deathless resurrection of a glorified body. We ask this....

SECOND SUNDAY OF EASTER

Collect

Deus misericordiae sempiternae, qui in ipso paschalis festi recursu fidem sacratae tibi plebis accendis, auge gratiam quam dedisti, ut digna omnes intelligentia comprehendant, quo lavacro abluti, quo spiritu regenerati, quo sanguine sunt redempti. Per Dominum.

God of everlasting mercy, by this annual Easter feast you enkindle the faith of the people consecrated to you. Increase the grace you have given them, so that they may all, with grateful awareness, realize what bath it is that has washed them clean, what spirit that has given them new birth, what blood that has redeemed them. We ask this....

Prayer over the Gifts

Suscipe, quaesumus, Domine, plebis tuae (et tuorum renatorum) oblationes, ut, confessione tui nominis et baptismate renovati, sempiternam beatitudinem consequantur. Per Christum.

Lord, please receive the offerings of your people (and of your newly baptized). May they be renewed by their profession of your name and by baptism, and so attain eternal happiness. We ask this....

Prayer after Communion

Concede, quaesumus, omnipotens Deus, ut paschalis perceptio sacramenti continua in nostris mentibus perseveret. Per Christum.

Almighty God, please grant that our reception of this Easter sacrament may have lasting effect on our hearts. We ask this....

THIRD SUNDAY OF EASTER

Collect

Semper exsultet populus tuus, Deus, renovata animae iuventute, ut, qui nunc laetatur in adoptionis se gloriam restitutum, resurrectionis diem spe certae gratulationis exspectet. Per Dominum.

God our Father, may your people always rejoice, for you have restored the youth of their souls. They are gladdened because they have been restored to the joy of their adoption as your sons and daughters. May they look forward to the day of the resurrection with confident hope in eternal happiness. We ask this....

Prayer over the Gifts

Suscipe munera, Domine, quaesumus, exsultantis Ecclesiae, et cui causam tanti gaudii praestitisti, perpetuae fructum concede laetitiae. Per Christum.

Lord, please receive the gifts of your joyous Church. You have given it reason for great gladness; grant it also the reward of eternal happiness. We ask this....

Prayer after Communion
(as on Easter Saturday, p.67)

FOURTH SUNDAY OF EASTER

Collect

Omnipotens sempiterne Deus, deduc nos ad societatem caelestium gaudiorum, ut eo perveniat humilitas gregis, quo processit fortitudo pastoris. Per Dominum.

Almighty and eternal God, guide us to a share in your heavenly joys, so that the lowly flock may follow to the place where its mighty Shepherd has already gone. We ask this....

Prayer over the Gifts
(As on Easter Saturday, p.67)

Prayer after Communion

Gregem tuum, Pastor bone, placatus intende, et oves, quas pretioso Filii tui sanguine redemisti, in aeternis pascuis collocare digneris. Per Christum.

Good Shepherd, you have redeemed your sheep by the precious blood of your Son. In your forgiving mercy, please look upon the members of your flock and guide them into eternal pastures. We ask this....

FIFTH SUNDAY OF EASTER

Collect

Deus, per quem nobis et redemptio venit et praestatur adoptio, filios dilectionis tuae benignus intende, ut in Christo credentibus et vera tribuatur libertas et hereditas aeterna. Per Dominum.

God our Father, through you redemption comes to us and we are granted adoption as your children. Look with kindness upon the sons and daughters of your love. May true freedom and an eternal inheritance be granted to those who believe in Christ. We ask this....

Prayer over the Gifts

Deus qui nos, per huius sacrificii veneranda commercia, unius summaeque divinitatis participes effecisti, praesta, quaesumus, ut, sicut tuam cognovimus veritatem, sic eam dignis moribus assequamur. Per Christum.

God our Father, through the sacred action of this sacrifice you have made us share in the one supreme divinity. We have come to know your truth; please grant that we may attain it by living worthily. We ask this....

Prayer after Communion

Populo tuo, quaesumus, Domine, adesto propitius, et, quem mysteriis caelestibus imbuisti, fac ad novitatem vitae de vetustate transire. Per Christum.

Lord, in your kindness be present to your people. You have filled them with your heavenly mysteries; make them pass from their old sinfulness to a new life. We ask this....

SIXTH SUNDAY OF EASTER

Collect

Fac nos, omnipotens Deus, hos laetitiae dies, quos in honorem Domini resurgentis exsequimur, affectu sedulo celebrare, ut quod recordatione percurrimus semper in opere teneamus. Per Dominum.

Almighty God, we keep these days of joy in honor of the risen Lord. Grant that we may celebrate them with a steadfast love, so that we may always show in our deeds what we recall in our grateful hearts. We ask this....

Prayer over the Gifts

Ascendant ad te, Domine, preces nostrae cum oblationibus hostiarum, ut, tua dignatione mundati, sacramentis magnae pietatis aptemur. Per Christum.

Lord, may our prayers and offerings rise before you. In your generous kindness, may we thus be cleansed and made fit to receive the sacraments of your great love. We ask this....

Prayer after Communion

Omnipotens sempiterne Deus, qui ad aeternam vitam in Christi resurrectione nos reparas, fructum in nobis paschalis multiplica sacramenti, et fortitudinem cibi salutaris nostris infunde pectoribus. Per Christum.

Almighty and eternal God, you restore us to eternal life by the resurrection of Christ. Increase the effect of the Easter sacrament in us, and pour forth into our hearts the steadfast courage that comes from the bread of salvation. We ask this....

Prayer over the Gifts

Sacrificium, Domine, pro Filii tui supplices venerabili nunc ascensione deferimus: praesta, quaesumus, ut his commerciis sacrosanctis ad caelestia consurgamus. Per Christum.

Lord, on this holy feast of the ascension of your Son, we now bring you our sacrifice and our prayerful plea. Through this most holy exchange of gifts please grant that we too may rise to heavenly joys. We ask this....

Prayer after Communion

Omnipotens sempiterne Deus, qui in terra constitutos divina tractare concedis, praesta, quaesumus, ut illuc tendat christianae devotionis affectus, quo tecum est nostra substantia. Per Christum.

Almighty and eternal God, although we dwell on earth you allow us to take part in your heavenly mysteries. Please grant that Christian love and faithfulness may lead us toward where our true life is found with you. We ask this....

ASCENSION

Collect

Fac nos, omnipotens Deus, sanctis exsultare gaudiis, et pia gratiarum actione laetari, quia Christi Filii tui ascensio est nostra provectio, et quo processit gloria capitis, eo spes vocatur et corporis. Per Dominum.

Almighty God, make us rejoice with holy gladness and give you thanks with overflowing hearts, for the ascension of Christ your Son is a sign of our own elevation, and our hope as members of his body is directed to the place where our head has preceded us in glory. We ask this....

SEVENTH SUNDAY OF EASTER

Collect

Supplicationibus nostris, Domine, adesto propitius, ut, sicut humani generis Salvatorem tecum in tua credimus maiestate, ita eum usque ad consummationem saeculi manere nobiscum, sicut ipse promisit, sentiamus. Per Dominum.

Lord, in your mercy hear our prayers. We believe that the Savior of the human race is now present with you in your divine glory; in like manner may we realize that, as he promised, he also remains with us until the end of time. We ask this....

Prayer over the Gifts

Suscipe, Domine, fidelium preces cum oblationibus hostiarum, ut, per haec piae devotionis officia, ad caelestem gloriam transeamus. Per Christum.

Lord, receive the prayers of your faithful people and their gifts. Through this offering of our love and dedication to you, may we come to heavenly glory. We ask this....

Prayer after Communion

Exaudi nos, Deus, salutaris noster, ut per haec sacrosancta mysteria in totius Ecclesiae confidamus corpore faciendum, quod eius praecessit in capite. Per Christum.

God our Father, you are our salvation. Hear us, and, through these most sacred mysteries, grant us confidence that what has already taken place for the Church's Head must also occur for all the members of his body. We ask this....

PENTECOST
VIGIL MASS

Collect

Omnipotens sempiterne Deus, qui paschale sacramentum quinquaginta dierum voluisti mysterio contineri, praesta, ut, gentium facta dispersione, divisiones linguarum ad unam confessionem tui nominis caelesti munere congregentur. Per Dominum.

Almighty and eternal God, you willed that the Easter sacrament should take place within the holy period of fifty days. Even though your people are scattered over all the earth, grant us the divine gift that the differences among our languages may be unified into the single profession of your name. We ask this....

Alternate Collect

Praesta, quaesumus, omnipotens Deus, ut claritatis tuae super nos splendor effulgeat, et lux tuae lucis corda eorum, qui per tuam gratiam sunt renati, Sancti Spiritus illustratione confirmet. Per Dominum.

Almighty God, please grant that the brilliance of your splendor may shine forth upon us. By the enlightenment of the Holy Spirit, may the radiance of your light strengthen the hearts of those who have been reborn through your grace. We ask this....

Prayer over the Gifts

Praesentia munera, quaesumus, Domine, Spiritus tui benedictione perfunde, ut per ipsa Ecclesiae tuae ea dilectio tribuatur, per quam salutaris mysterii toto mundo veritas enitescat. Per Christum.

Lord, please pour forth the blessing of your Spirit on these gifts of ours. Through them, may your Church be given that love which will make the truth of the mystery of salvation shine forth throughout the whole world. We ask this....

Prayer after Communion

Haec nobis, Domine, munera sumpta proficiant, ut illo iugiter Spiritu ferveamus, quem Apostolis tuis ineffabiliter infudisti. Per Christum.

Lord, may these gifts we have received benefit us. May we thus be constantly inflamed with that Spirit which, in indescribable fashion, you poured forth upon your Apostles. We ask this....

PENTECOST
MASS DURING THE DAY

Collect

Deus, qui sacramento festivitatis hodiernae universam Ecclesiam tuam in omni gente et natione sanctificas, in totam mundi latitudinem Spiritus Sancti dona defunde, et, quod inter ipsa evangelicae praedicationis exordia operata est divina dignatio, nunc quoque per credentium corda perfunde. Per Dominum.

God our Father, by the sacred event we celebrate in today's feast, you make your entire Church holy throughout every people and land. Pour down the gifts of the Holy Spirit on the length and breadth of the world. In our day as well, pour forth into the hearts of those who believe in you the things which your divine kindness accomplished when the Gospel first began to be preached. We ask this....

Prayer over the Gifts

Praesta, quaesumus, Domine, ut, secundum promissionem Filii tui, Spiritus Sanctus huius nobis sacrificii copiosius revelet arcanum, et omnem propitius reseret veritatem. Per Christum.

Lord, please grant that, as your Son promised, the Holy Spirit may make the hidden meaning of this sacrifice more fully known to us, and may, in his mercy, give us an understanding of all truth. We ask this....

Prayer after Communion

Deus, qui Ecclesiae tuae caelestia dona largiris, custodi gratiam quam dedisti, ut Spiritus Sancti vigeat semper munus infusum, et ad aeternae redemptionis augmentum spiritalis esca proficiat. Per Christum.

God our Father, you give your heavenly gifts to the Church. Protect the favor that you have given, so that the infused gift of the Holy Spirit may always flourish among us, and the food we have received for our souls may help us achieve the fullness of eternal redemption. We ask this....

WEEKDAYS
AFTER THE 2nd, 4th, and 6th SUNDAYS OF EASTER

MONDAYS

Collect (Week 2)

Omnipotens sempiterne Deus, quem paterno nomine invocare praesumimus, perfice in cordibus nostris spiritum adoptionis filiorum, ut promissam hereditatem ingredi mereamur. Per Dominum.

Almighty and eternal God, we dare to use the term Father as we call upon you. Bring to perfection within our hearts that spirit of adoption we have as your sons and daughters, so that we may be privileged to enter into our promised inheritance. We ask this....

Collect (Week 4)

Deus, qui in Filii tui humilitate iacentem mundum erexisti, fidelibus tuis sanctam concede laetitiam, ut, quos eripuisti a servitute peccati, gaudiis facias perfrui sempiternis. Per Dominum.

God our Father, by the obedience of your Son you raised up a prostrate world. Grant your faithful people a holy joy. You have rescued them from the slavery of sin; give them a happiness to enjoy that has no end. We ask this....

Collect (Week 6)

Concede, misericors Deus, ut, quod paschalibus exsequimur institutis, fructiferum nobis omni tempore sentiamus. Per Dominum.

Merciful God, grant that we may find fruitful in our lives throughout the entire year what we now celebrate in these paschal mysteries. We ask this....

Prayer over the Gifts
(as on the Third Sunday of Easter, p.68)

Prayer after Communion
(as on the Third Sunday of Easter, p.68)

TUESDAYS

Collect (Week 2)

Fac nos, quaesumus, omnipotens Deus, Domini resurgentis praedicare virtutem, ut, cuius muneris pignus accepimus, manifesta dona comprehendere valeamus. Per Dominum.

Almighty God, please grant that we may proclaim the power of the Lord in his resurrection. We have received the promise of his gifts; may we be able to understand them when they are made known to us. We ask this....

Collect (Week 4)

Praesta, quaesumus, omnipotens Deus, ut, qui resurrectionis dominicae mysteria colimus, redemptionis nostrae suscipere laetitiam mereamur. Per Dominum.

Almighty God, as we celebrate the mysteries of the resurrection of the Lord, please grant that we may be privileged to receive the joy of our redemption. We ask this....

Collect (Week 6)
(as on the Third Sunday of Easter, p.68)

Prayer over the Gifts
(as on Easter Saturday, p.67, and on the Fourth Sunday of Easter, p.69)

Prayer after Communion
(as on Easter Thursday, p.66)

WEDNESDAYS

Collect (Week 2)

Annua recolentes mysteria, quibus per renovatam originis dignitatem humana substantia spem resurrectionis accepit, clementiam tuam, Domine, suppliciter exoramus, ut, quod fide recolimus, perpetua dilectione capiamus. Per Dominum.

Lord, each year we recall the mysteries through which our human nature was restored to its original condition and so received the hope of resurrection. We humbly ask for your mercy, so that we may receive in neverfailing love what we here relive in faith. We ask this....

Collect (Week 4)

Deus, vita fidelium, gloria humilium, beatitudo iustorum, ad preces supplicum benignus intende, ut, qui promissa tuae sitiunt largitatis, de tua semper abundantia repleantur. Per Dominum.

God our Father, you are life for the faithful, exaltation for the lowly, and joy for the just. In your kindness listen to the prayers of those who call upon you. May they who thirst for the promises you have generously made ever be filled with your riches. We ask this....

Collect (Week 6)

Annue nobis, quaesumus, Domine, ut, quemadmodum mysterio resurrectionis Filii tui sollemnia colimus, ita et in adventu eius gaudere cum Sanctis omnibus mereamur. Per Dominum.

Lord, please hear our prayer. Just as we celebrate the solemn rites of the mystery of the resurrection of your Son, so may we also be privileged to rejoice with all his saints when he comes again in glory. We ask this....

Prayer over the Gifts
(as on the Fifth Sunday of Easter, p.69)

Prayer after Communion
(as on the Fifth Sunday of Easter, p.69)

THURSDAYS

Collect (Week 2)
(as on Monday after the Sixth Sunday of Easter, p.72)

Collect (Week 4)

Deus, qui humanam naturam supra primae originis reparas dignitatem, respice ad pietatis tuae ineffabile sacramentum, ut, quos regenerationis mysterio dignatus es innovare, in his dona tuae perpetuae gratiae benedictionisque conserves. Per Dominum.

God our Father, you restore our human nature to a dignity loftier than it had when first you created it. Look upon the indescribable pledge which your faithful love has made. Preserve the gifts of your everlasting favor and blessing in the hearts of those whom you have seen fit to make new by the mystery of rebirth. We ask this....

Collect (Week 6)
(where Ascension is celebrated on the following Sunday)

Deus, qui populum tuum tuae fecisti redemptionis participem, concede nobis, quaesumus, ut de resurrectione dominica perpetuo gratulemur. Per Dominum.

God our Father, you have made your people partakers in your redemption. Please grant that we may always rejoice in gratitude for the Lord's resurrection. We ask this....

Prayer over the Gifts
(as on the Sixth Sunday of Easter, p.69)

Prayer after Communion
(as on the Sixth Sunday of Easter, p.69)

FRIDAYS

Collect (Week 2)
(as on Wednesday of Holy Week, p.53)

Collect (Week 4)

Deus, qui et libertatis nostrae auctor es et salutis, exaudi supplicantium voces, et, quos sanguinis Filii tui effusione redemisti, fac, ut per te vivere et perpetua in te valeant incolumitate gaudere. Per Dominum.

God our Father, source of our freedom and our salvation, hear the prayers of those who call upon you. You have redeemed them by the shedding of your Son's blood; grant that through you they may have life, and in you they may rejoice in endless freedom from harm. We ask this....

Collect (Week 6)

Deus, qui ad aeternam vitam in Christi resurrectione nos reparas, erige nos ad consedentem in dextera tua nostrae salutis auctorem, ut, cum in maiestate sua Salvator noster advenerit, quos fecisti baptismo renasci, facias beata immortalitate vestiri. Per Dominum.

God our Father, you restore us to eternal life by the resurrection of Christ. Lift us up to the author of our salvation who sits at your right hand. When our Savior comes again in majestic glory, may you clothe in blessed immortality those whom you have caused to be reborn in baptism. We ask this....

Collect (Week 6)
(where Ascension is celebrated on the Seventh Sunday of Easter)

Exaudi, Domine, preces nostras, ut, quod tui Verbi sanctificatione promissum est, evangelico ubique compleatur effectu, et plenitudo adoptionis obtineat quod praedixit testificatio veritatis. Per Dominum.

Lord, hear our prayers. May the action of the Gospel everywhere bring to fulfillment what was promised by the holy action of your Word; and may the fullness of adoption achieve what the testimony of your Truth foretold. We ask this....

Prayer over the Gifts
(as on Easter Tuesday, p.65)

Prayer after Communion
(as on Easter Friday, p.67)

SATURDAYS

Collect (Week 2)
(as on the Fifth Sunday of Easter, p.69)

Collect (Week 4)

Omnipotens sempiterne Deus, semper in nobis paschale perfice sacramentum, ut, quos sacro baptismate dignatus es renovare, sub tuae protectionis auxilio multos fructus afferant, et ad aeternae vitae gaudia pervenire concedas. Per Dominum.

Almighty and eternal God, bring the Easter sacrament to constant fulfillment within us. You have seen fit to give us new life by holy baptism; by the help of your protection, grant that we may bear much fruit and come to the joys of eternal life. We ask this....

Collect (Week 6)

Deus, cuius Filius ad caelos ascendens Apostolis Sanctum Spiritum dignatus est polliceri, praesta, quaesumus, ut sicut illi multifaria doctrinae caelestis munera perceperunt, ita nobis quoque spiritalia dona concedas. Per Dominum.

God our Father, as your Son was ascending into heaven he saw fit to promise the Holy Spirit to the apostles. They received manifold gifts of heavenly learning; so too, please grant your spiritual gifts to us as well. We ask this....

Collect (Week 6)
(where Ascension is celebrated on the 7th Sunday of Easter)

Mentes nostras, quaesumus, Domine, bonis operibus semper informa, ut, ad meliora iugiter contendentes, paschale mysterium studeamus habere perpetuum. Per Dominum.

Lord, please form our hearts constantly with good works. May we ever strive after better things and seek to make the Easter mystery our own for ever. We ask this....

Prayer over the Gifts

Propitius, Domine, quaesumus, haec dona sanctifica, et, hostiae spiritalis oblatione suscepta, nosmetipsos tibi perfice munus aeternum. Per Christum.

Lord, in your kind mercy please make these gifts holy, and, by accepting the offering of our spiritual sacrifice, make of us an eternal oblation to yourself. We ask this....

Prayer after Communion

Sumpsimus, Domine, sacri dona mysterii, humiliter deprecantes, ut, quae in sui commemorationem nos Filius tuus facere praecepit, in nostrae proficiant caritatis augmentum. Per Christum.

Lord, we have received the gifts of your sacred mystery, and we bring you our humble prayer. May what your Son told us to do in his memory serve to increase our love. We ask this....

WEEKDAYS AFTER THE 3rd AND 5th SUNDAYS OF EASTER

MONDAYS

Collect (Week 3)

Deus, qui errantibus, ut in viam possint redire, veritatis tuae lumen ostendis, da cunctis, qui christiana professione censentur, et illa respuere, quae huic inimica sunt nomini, et ea quae sunt apta sectari. Per Dominum.

God our Father, you show the light of your truth to those who stray, so that they may return to the right path. Grant that all who are numbered among the Christian faithful may reject whatever is foreign to the name of Christian, and seek whatever is in accord with it. We ask this....

Collect (Week 5)

Deus, qui fidelium mentes unius efficis voluntatis, da populis tuis id amare quod praecipis, id desiderare quod promittis, ut, inter mundanas varietates, ibi nostra fixa sint corda, ubi vera sunt gaudia. Per Dominum.

God our Father, you see to it that the hearts of your faithful people are united into a single purpose. Grant your people the grace to love what you command and to desire what you promise, so that, amidst the uncertainties of this world, their hearts may be fixed on that place where true joys reside. We ask this....

Prayer over the Gifts
and
Prayer after Communion
(as on the Sixth Sunday of Easter, p.69)

TUESDAYS

Collect (Week 3)

Deus, qui renatis ex aqua et Spiritu Sancto caelestis regni pandis introitum, auge super famulos tuos gratiam quam dedisti, ut, qui ab omnibus sunt purgati peccatis, nullis priventur tua pietate promissis. Per Dominum.

God our Father, you throw open the gates of the kingdom of heaven to those who have been born anew by water and the Holy Spirit. Increase among your people the grace you have given, so that those who have been cleansed of all their sins may be deprived of none of the things which, in your trustworthy love, you have promised. We ask this....

Collect (Week 5)

Deus, qui ad aeternam vitam in Christi resurrectione nos reparas, da populo tuo fidei speique constantiam, ut non dubitemus implenda, quae te novimus auctore promissa. Per Dominum.

God our Father, you restore us to eternal life in the resurrection of Christ. Grant to your people a firm faith and hope, so that we may have no doubt about the fulfillment of those promises of which we know you are the author. We ask this....

Prayer over the Gifts
and
Prayer after Communion
(as on the Third Sunday of Easter, p.68)

WEDNESDAYS

Collect (Week 3)

Adesto, quaesumus, Domine, familiae tuae, et dignanter impende, ut, quibus fidei gratiam contulisti, in resurrectione Unigeniti tui portionem largiaris aeternam. Per Dominum.

Lord, please hear the prayers of your devoted people. You have given them the gift of faith; in your gracious mercy, grant also that they may share for all eternity in the resurrection of your only Son. We ask this....

Collect (Week 5)

Deus, innocentiae restitutor et amator, dirige ad te tuorum corda famulorum, ut, quos de incredulitatis tenebris liberasti, numquam a tuae veritatis luce discedant. Per Dominum.

God our Father, you restore integrity to your faithful people and you cherish it in them. Direct their hearts toward you. You have freed them from the darkness of unbelief; may they never depart from the light of your truth. We ask this....

Prayer over the Gifts
(as on the Fourth Sunday of Easter, p.69)

Prayer after Communion
(as on Easter Thursday, p.66)

THURSDAYS

Collect (Week 3)

Omnipotens sempiterne Deus, propensius his diebus tuam pietatem consequamur, quibus eam plenius te largiente cognovimus, ut, quos ab erroris caligine liberasti, veritatis tuae firmius inhaerere facias documentis. Per Dominum.

Almighty and eternal God, may we gain your faithful love more readily now, for during these days we have come to recognize it more fully because of your generous mercy. You have freed us from the darkness of error; make us cling more fully to the evidence of your truth. We ask this....

Collect (Week 5)

Deus, cuius gratia iusti ex impiis et beati efficimur ex miseris, adesto operibus tuis, adesto muneribus, ut quibus inest fidei iustificatio non desit perseverantiae fortitudo. Per Dominum.

God our Father, by your favor we who were evil become just and we who were wretched become blessed. Be present in your works, be present in your gifts, so that those who possess the justification that faith gives may not lack the strength to persevere in it. We ask this....

Prayer over the Gifts
and
Prayer after Communion
(as on the Fifth Sunday of Easter, p.69)

FRIDAYS

Collect (Week 3)

Praesta, quaesumus, omnipotens Deus, ut, qui gratiam dominicae resurrectionis cognovimus, ipsi per amorem Spiritus in novitatem vitae resurgamus. Per Dominum.

Almighty God, we have come to know the gift of the Lord's resurrection. Through the love that the Holy Spirit gives, please grant that we may rise to a new life. We ask this....

Collect (Week 5)

Tribue nobis, quaesumus, Domine, mysteriis paschalibus convenienter aptari, ut quae laetanter exsequimur perpetua virtute nos tueantur et salvent. Per Dominum.

Lord, please grant that we may be fittingly prepared by these paschal mysteries, so that what we celebrate in joy may protect and save us by its everlasting power. We ask this....

Prayer over the Gifts
and
Prayer after Communion
(as on Saturday of the 2nd, 4th, and 6th Week after Easter, p.75)

SATURDAYS

Collect (Week 3)

Deus, qui credentes in te fonte baptismatis innovasti, hanc renatis in Christo concede custodiam, ut, omni erroris incursu devicto, gratiam tuae benedictionis fideliter servent. Per Dominum.

God our Father, through the font of baptism you have bestowed new life on those who believe in you. Grant this protection to those who have been reborn in Christ: may they overcome every attack of error and faithfully preserve the favor of your blessing. We ask this....

Collect (Week 5)

Omnipotens aeterne Deus, qui nobis regeneratione baptismatis caelestem vitam conferre dignatus es, praesta, quaesumus, ut, quos immortalitatis efficis iustificando capaces, usque ad plenitudinem gloriae, te moderante, perveniant. Per Dominum.

Almighty and eternal God, you have seen fit to bestow divine life on us through the rebirth of baptism. By your forgiveness, you make us capable of immortality; please grant that, under your guidance, we may arrive at the fullness of glory. We ask this....

Prayer over the Gifts
(as on Easter Tuesday, p.65)

Prayer after Communion
(as on Easter Friday, p.67)

THE SEVENTH WEEK OF EASTER

MONDAY

Collect

Adveniat nobis, quaesumus, Domine, virtus Spiritus Sancti, qua voluntatem tuam fideli mente retinere, et pia conversatione depromere valeamus. Per Dominum.

Lord, we ask that the power of the Holy Spirit may come upon us, so that through it we may always be able to know your holy will truly, and to carry it out by the holy lives we lead. We ask this....

Prayer over the Gifts

Sacrificia nos, Domine, immaculata purificent, et mentibus nostris supernae gratiae dent vigorem. Per Christum.

Lord, may this spotless sacrifice cleanse us and give to our hearts the strength of your heavenly grace. We ask this....

Prayer after Communion
(as on the Fifth Sunday of Easter, p.69)

TUESDAY

Collect

Praesta, quaesumus, omnipotens et misericors Deus, ut Spiritus Sanctus adveniens templum nos gloriae tuae dignanter inhabitando perficiat. Per Dominum.

Almighty and merciful God, as your Holy Spirit comes to us, please grant that, by dwelling in us, he may make us a fitting temple for his glory. We ask this....

Prayer over the Gifts

(as on the Seventh Sunday of Easter, p.70)

Prayer after Communion

(as on Saturday of the 2nd, 4th, and 6th Weeks After Easter, p.75)

WEDNESDAY

Collect

Ecclesiae tuae, misericors Deus, concede propitius, ut, Sancto Spiritu congregata, toto sit corde tibi devota, et pura voluntate concordet. Per Dominum.

Merciful God, in your kindness grant that your Church, brought together by the Holy Spirit, may be wholeheartedly dedicated to you and be of one mind in its purity of intention. We ask this....

Prayer over the Gifts

Suscipe, quaesumus, Domine, sacrificia tuis instituta praeceptis, et sacris mysteriis, quae debitae servitutis celebramus officio, sanctificationem tuae nobis redemptionis dignanter adimple. Per Christum.

Lord, please receive the sacrifice that was established at your command. We celebrate these sacred mysteries in order to fulfill the service we owe you. Through them, may you be pleased to bring to perfection the holiness your redemptive work intends for us. We ask this....

Prayer after Communion

Gratiam tuam nobis, Domine, semper accumulet divini participatio sacramenti, et, sua nos virtute mundando, tanti muneris capaces indesinenter efficiat. Per Christum.

Lord, may our participation in your heavenly sacrament always increase your grace in us. By cleansing us with its power, may it make us ever capable of receiving such a great gift. We ask this....

THURSDAY

Collect

Spiritus tuus, quaesumus, Domine, spiritalia nobis dona potenter infundat, ut det nobis mentem, quae tibi sit placita, et aptet nos tuae propitius voluntati. Per Dominum.

Lord, we ask that your Spirit powerfully pour out his spiritual gifts upon us. May he thus give us a heart that will be pleasing to you, and may he graciously make us eager to obey your commands. We ask this....

Prayer over the Gifts

(as on Saturday after the 2nd, 4th, and 6th Sundays after Easter, p.75)

Prayer after Communion

Percepta mysteria, quaesumus, Domine, et eruditione nos instruant et participatione restaurent, ut ad spiritalia mereamur munera pervenire. Per Christum.

Lord, we ask that the mysteries we have received may confer wisdom upon us. May our sharing in them give us new life, so that we may be privileged to attain to your spiritual gifts. We ask this....

FRIDAY

Collect

Deus, qui nobis aeternitatis aditum glorificatione Christi tui et Sancti Spiritus illuminatione reserasti, concede, quaesumus, ut, tanti doni particeps, devotio nostra proficiat, et ad fidei transferamur augmentum. Per Dominum.

God our Father, you have thrown open the gates of eternity to us by the exaltation of your Christ and the light of the Holy Spirit. Please grant that our love and dedication may be increased by participating in this great gift, and that we may advance to a greater faith. We ask this....

Prayer over the Gifts

Hostias populi tui, quaesumus, Domine, miseratus intende, et, ut tibi reddantur acceptae, conscientias nostras Sancti Spiritus emundet adventus. Per Christum.

Lord, in your mercy please look upon the offering of your people. May the coming of the Holy Spirit cleanse our consciences, so that this sacrifice may be acceptable to you. We ask this....

Prayer after Communion

Deus, cuius mysteriis mundamur et pascimur, tribue, quaesumus, ut eorum nobis indulta refectio vitam conferat sempiternam. Per Christum.

God our Father, we are cleansed and nourished by your mysteries. Please grant that the gracious restoration they bring may bestow eternal life on us. We ask this....

SATURDAY

Collect

Praesta, quaesumus, omnipotens Deus, ut, qui paschalia festa peregimus, haec, te largiente, moribus et vita teneamus. Per Dominum.

Almighty God, we have celebrated the festivals of Easter. Through your generous kindness, please grant that we may hold to them firmly in our conduct and in our lives. We ask this....

Prayer over the Gifts

Mentes nostras, quaesumus, Domine, Spiritus Sanctus adveniens divinis praeparet sacramentis, quia ipse est remissio omnium peccatorum. Per Christum.

Lord, as the Holy Spirit comes, we ask that He prepare our hearts for these heavenly sacraments, since He is the forgiveness of all sin. We ask this....

Prayer after Communion

Annue, Domine, nostris precibus miseratus, ut, sicut de praeteritis ad nova sumus sacramenta translati, ita, vetustate deposita, sanctificatis mentibus innovemur. Per Christum.

Lord, in your mercy, listen to our prayers. We have been brought from our former condition to your new dispensation; may we also put aside our old sinfulness and be renewed and sanctified in heart. We ask this....

ORDINARY

TIME

FIRST SUNDAY IN ORDINARY TIME

Collect

Vota, quaesumus, Domine, supplicantis populi caelesti pietate prosequere, ut et quae agenda sunt videant, et ad implenda quae viderint convalescant. Per Dominum.

Lord, may your divine compassion attend the prayers of your people as they cry out to you, so that they may see what must be done and have the strength to carry it out. We ask this....

Prayer over the Gifts

Grata tibi sit, quaesumus, Domine, tuae plebis oblatio, per quam et sanctificationem referat, et quae pie precatur obtineat. Per Christum.

Lord, we ask that the offering of your people may be pleasing to you. Through it, may they obtain holiness and gain what they trustingly petition. We ask this....

Prayer after Communion

Supplices te rogamus, omnipotens Deus, ut quos tuis reficis sacramentis, tibi etiam placitis moribus dignanter deservire concedas. Per Christum.

Almighty God, you renew us with your sacraments. We humbly ask you to allow us to serve you earnestly and worthily by leading lives that are pleasing to you. We ask this....

SECOND SUNDAY IN ORDINARY TIME

Collect

Omnipotens sempiterne Deus, qui caelestia simul et terrena moderaris, supplicationes populi tui clementer exaudi, et pacem tuam nostris concede temporibus. Per Dominum.

Almighty and eternal God, you guide whatever happens in the heavens and on the earth. In your mercy, hear the prayers of your people, and grant us your peace in our day. We ask this....

Prayer over the Gifts

Concede nobis, quaesumus, Domine, haec digne frequentare mysteria, quia, quoties huius hostiae commemoratio celebratur, opus nostrae redemptionis exercetur. Per Christum.

Lord, please grant that we may take part in these mysteries worthily, for as often as the remembrance of the offering of Christ is celebrated, the work of our redemption is carried on. We ask this....

Prayer after Communion

Spiritum nobis, Domine, tuae caritatis infunde, ut, quos uno caelesti pane satiasti, una facias pietate concordes. Per Christum.

Lord, pour into us the Spirit of your love. You have filled us with the one food; make us be one at heart in loving care for one another. We ask this....

THIRD SUNDAY IN ORDINARY TIME

Collect

Omnipotens sempiterne Deus, dirige actus nostros in beneplacito tuo, ut in nomine dilecti Filii tui mereamur bonis operibus abundare. Per Dominum.

Almighty and eternal God, direct our actions in accord with your gracious purpose, so that, in the name of your beloved Son, we may be privileged to abound in good works. We ask this....

Prayer over the Gifts

Munera nostra, Domine, suscipe placatus, quae sanctificando nobis, quaesumus, salutaria fore concede. Per Christum.

Lord, in your forgiving mercy receive our offerings. We ask that you allow them to make us holy and so become a means of salvation for us. We ask this....

Prayer after Communion

Praesta nobis, quaesumus, omnipotens Deus, ut, vivificationis tuae gratiam consequentes, in tuo semper munere gloriemur. Per Christum.

Almighty God, please grant that we may obtain the gift of your life-giving grace and may always rejoice in it. We ask this....

FOURTH SUNDAY IN ORDINARY TIME

Collect

Concede nobis, Domine Deus noster, ut te tota mente veneremur, et omnes homines rationabili diligamus affectu. Per Dominum.

Lord our God, grant that we may worship you with our whole heart, and that we may love all men and women in a way that is truly human. We ask this....

Prayer over the Gifts

Altaribus tuis, Domine, munera nostra servitutis inferimus, quae, placatus assumens, sacramentum nostrae redemptionis efficias. Per Christum.

Lord, we bring to your altar the offerings that mark our service to you. In your forgiving mercy, accept them and make them the sacrament of our salvation. We ask this....

Prayer after Communion

Redemptionis nostrae munere vegetati, quaesumus, Domine, ut hoc perpetuae salutis auxilio fides semper vera proficiat. Per Christum.

Lord, we are nourished by the gift of our redemption. It is a means to eternal salvation; through it, we ask that our faith may ever increase and be true. We ask this....

FIFTH SUNDAY IN ORDINARY TIME

Collect

Familiam tuam, quaesumus, Domine, continua pietate custodi, ut, quae in sola spe gratiae caelestis innititur, tua semper protectione muniatur. Per Dominum.

Lord, please protect your people with your constant loving care. They rely solely on the hope of your heavenly grace; may they always be guarded by your protection. We ask this....

Prayer over the Gifts

Domine Deus noster, qui has potius creaturas ad fragilitatis nostrae subsidium condidisti, tribue, quaesumus, ut etiam aeternitatis nobis fiant sacramentum. Per Christum.

Lord our God, you made these creatures especially to help us in our weakness. Please grant that they may also become the sacrament of eternal life for us. We ask this....

Prayer after Communion

Deus, qui nos de uno pane et de uno calice participes esse voluisti, da nobis, quaesumus, ita vivere, ut, unum in Christo effecti, fructum afferamus pro mundi salute gaudentes. Per Christum.

God our Father, you willed that we should share the one bread and the one cup. Please grant that we may live in such a way that we are made one in Christ, and may work joyfully and effectively for the salvation of the world. We ask this....

SIXTH SUNDAY IN ORDINARY TIME

Collect

Deus, qui te in rectis et sinceris manere pectoribus asseris, da nobis tua gratia tales exsistere, in quibus habitare digneris. Per Dominum.

God our Father, you tell us that you dwell in upright and sincere hearts. By your grace, grant that we may live in such a way that you will see fit to make your dwelling within us. We ask this....

Prayer over the Gifts

Haec nos oblatio, quaesumus, Domine, mundet et renovet, atque tuam exsequentibus voluntatem fiat causa remunerationis aeternae. Per Christum.

Lord, we ask that this offering may cleanse and renew us. May it be a source of eternal reward for those who carry out your will. We ask this....

Prayer after Communion

Caelestibus, Domine, pasti deliciis, quaesumus, ut semper eadem, per quae veraciter vivimus, appetamus. Per Christum.

Lord, we have been fed with your heavenly delights. We ask that we may always seek after them, for through them we truly live. We ask this....

SEVENTH SUNDAY IN ORDINARY TIME

Collect

Praesta, quaesumus, omnipotens Deus, ut, semper rationabilia meditantes, quae tibi sunt placita, et dictis exsequamur et factis. Per Dominum.

Almighty God, as we constantly reflect upon our human condition, please grant that we may carry out in both word and deed the things that are pleasing to you. We ask this....

Prayer over the Gifts

Mysteria tua, Domine, debitis servitiis exsequentes, supplices te rogamus, ut, quod ad honorem tuae maiestatis offerimus, nobis proficiat ad salutem. Per Christum.

Lord, we celebrate your mysteries to fulfill the duty of service we owe you. We humbly ask that what we offer in honor of your divine majesty may further the work of our salvation. We ask this....

Prayer after Communion

Praesta, quaesumus, omnipotens Deus ut illius salutis capiamus effectum, cuius per haec mysteria pignus accepimus. Per Christum.

Almighty God, please grant that we may receive the fullness of that salvation whose pledge we have received in these mysteries. We ask this....

EIGHTH SUNDAY IN ORDINARY TIME

Collect

Da nobis, quaesumus, Domine, ut et mundi cursus pacifico nobis tuo ordine dirigatur, et Ecclesia tua tranquilla devotione laetetur. Per Dominum.

Lord, please grant that the course of world events may be guided for us by your gentle providence, and that your Church may have the joy of serving you in peace. We ask this....

Prayer over the Gifts

Deus, qui offerenda tuo nomini tribuis, et oblata devotioni nostrae servitutis ascribis, quaesumus clementiam tuam, ut, quod praestas unde sit meritum, proficere nobis largiaris ad praemium. Per Christum.

God our Father, you provide us with gifts to be offered to your name, and you look upon our offerings as loving service. What you give us is the source of our merit; please grant that it will also become the source of our reward. We ask this....

Prayer after Communion

Satiati munere salutari, tuam, Domine, misericordiam deprecamur, ut, hoc eodem quo nos temporaliter vegetas sacramento, perpetuae vitae participes benignus efficias. Per Christum.

Lord, we are filled with your saving gift, and we beg for your mercy. By this sacrament you give us life in this world. By it too, may your generous kindness grant us a share in eternal life. We ask this....

NINTH SUNDAY IN ORDINARY TIME

Collect

Deus, cuius providentia in sui dispositione non fallitur, te supplices exoramus, ut noxia cuncta submoveas, et omnia nobis profutura concedas. Per Dominum.

God our Father, your watchful care does not fail in its purpose. We humbly ask you to take away from us everything that is harmful, and to grant us everything that will be of benefit. We ask this....

Prayer over the Gifts

In tua pietate confidentes, Domine, cum muneribus ad altaria veneranda concurrimus, ut, tua purificante nos gratia, iisdem quibus famulamur mysteriis emundemur. Per Christum.

Lord, relying on your faithful love, we hasten to your sacred altar with our gifts. Through your purifying grace may we be cleansed by the very mysteries in which we take part. We ask this....

Prayer after Communion

Rege nos Spiritu tuo, quaesumus, Domine, quos pascis Filii tui Corpore et Sanguine, ut te, non solum verbo neque lingua, sed opere et veritate confitentes, intrare mereamur in regnum caelorum. Per Christum.

Lord, you feed us with the Body and Blood of your Son. Please govern us by your Spirit as well, so that we may acknowledge you not only in the words we speak, but also with the sincerity of our deeds, and so be privileged to enter the kingdom of heaven. We ask this....

TENTH SUNDAY IN ORDINARY TIME

Collect

Deus, a quo bona cuncta procedunt, tuis largire supplicibus, ut cogitemus, te inspirante, quae recta sunt, et, te gubernante, eadem faciamus. Per Dominum.

God our Father, all good things come from you. Hear our prayers as we ask that, under your inspiration, we may think what is right and, under your guidance, carry it out in our deeds. We ask this....

Prayer over the Gifts

Respice, Domine, quaesumus, nostram propitius servitutem, ut quod offerimus sit tibi munus acceptum, et nostrae caritatis augmentum. Per Christum.

Lord, please look with kindness upon the service we render you. May the gift we offer be acceptable to you, and may it serve to increase our love. We ask this....

Prayer after Communion

Tua nos, Domine, medicinalis operatio, et a nostris perversitatibus clementer expediat, et ad ea quae sunt recta perducat. Per Christum.

Lord, may the action of your healing care mercifully free us from our wickedness and lead us to what is right. We ask this....

ELEVENTH SUNDAY IN ORDINARY TIME

Collect

Deus, in te sperantium fortitudo, invocationibus nostris adesto propitius, et, quia sine te nihil potest mortalis infirmitas, gratiae tuae praesta semper auxilium, ut, in exsequendis mandatis tuis, et voluntate tibi et actione placeamus. Per Dominum.

God our Father, you are the strength of those who hope in you. In your kindness, listen to our pleas. Since our human weakness can accomplish nothing without you, grant us the constant help of your grace, so that in carrying out your commands we may please you by what we intend and what we do. We ask this....

Prayer over the Gifts

Deus, qui humani generis utramque substantiam praesentium munerum et alimento vegetas et renovas sacramento, tribue, quaesumus, ut eorum et corporibus nostris subsidium non desit et mentibus. Per Christum.

God our Father, by the food and the sacrament that these gifts are, you nourish and renew both the physical and the spiritual dimensions of human nature. Please grant that the help of your gifts may never be lacking to either our bodies or our souls. We ask this....

Prayer after Communion

Haec tua, Domine, sumpta sacra communio, sicut fidelium in te unionem praesignat, sic in Ecclesia tua unitatis operetur effectum. Per Christum.

Lord, this sacred communion which we have received heralds the union of your faithful people with you. May it also bring about the fullness of unity in your Church. We ask this....

TWELFTH SUNDAY IN ORDINARY TIME

Collect

Sancti nominis tui, Domine, timorem pariter et amorem fac nos habere perpetuum, quia numquam tua gubernatione destituis, quos in soliditate tuae dilectionis instituis. Per Dominum.

Lord, give us a constant fear of your holy name, but an unceasing love of it as well, for in your watchful care you never cease to guide those whom you have firmly established in your love. We ask this....

Prayer over the Gifts

Suscipe, Domine, sacrificium placationis et laudis, et praesta, ut, huius operatione mundati, beneplacitum tibi nostrae mentis offeramus affectum. Per Christum.

Lord, receive the sacrifice of our repentance and praise. Grant that we may be cleansed by its action and may offer you a heartfelt love that will be pleasing to you. We ask this....

Prayer after Communion

Sacri Corporis et Sanguinis pretiosi alimonia renovati, quaesumus, Domine, clementiam tuam, ut, quod gerimus devotione frequenti, certa redemptione capiamus. Per Christum.

Lord, we have been renewed by the nourishment given by Christ's sacred Body and precious Blood. We ask for your mercy, so that what we do in our oft-renewed consecration to you may bring about the assurance of redemption for us. We ask this....

THIRTEENTH SUNDAY IN ORDINARY TIME

Collect

Deus, qui, per adoptionem gratiae, lucis nos esse filios voluisti, praesta, quaesumus, ut errorum non involvamur tenebris, sed in splendore veritatis semper maneamus conspicui. Per Dominum.

God our Father, by your adoptive grace you have willed that we should be children of the light. Please grant that we may not become entangled in the darkness of error, but rather always remain resplendent in the brightness of truth. We ask this....

Prayer over the Gifts

Deus, qui mysteriorum tuorum dignanter operaris effectus, praesta, quaesumus, ut sacris apta muneribus fiant nostra servitia. Per Christum.

God our Father, you see fit to bring about the effects of your mysteries within us. Please grant that the service we render may be made appropriate to the sacred gifts you bestow. We ask this....

Prayer after Communion

Vivificet nos, quaesumus, Domine, divina quam obtulimus et sumpsimus hostia, ut, perpetua tibi caritate coniuncti, fructum qui semper maneat afferamus. Per Christum.

Lord, we ask that the sacred sacrifice which we have offered and received may give us life, so that, joined to you in unending love, we may bear fruit that will always perdure. We ask this....

FOURTEENTH SUNDAY IN ORDINARY TIME

Collect
(as on Monday of the Fourth Week After Easter, p.72)

Prayer over the Gifts

Oblatio nos, Domine, tuo nomini dicata purificet, et de die in diem ad caelestis vitae transferat actionem. Per Christum.

Lord, may the offering we make to your name purify us and further our progress toward attaining eternal life with each passing day. We ask this....

Prayer after Communion

Tantis, Domine, repleti muneribus, praesta, quaesumus, ut et salutaria dona capiamus, et a tua numquam laude cessemus. Per Christum.

Lord, we are filled with your marvelous gifts. Please grant that we may receive your saving graces and never cease to praise you. We ask this....

FIFTEENTH SUNDAY IN ORDINARY TIME

Collect
(as on Monday of the Third Week After Easter, p.76)

Prayer over the Gifts

Respice, Domine, munera supplicantis Ecclesiae, et pro credentium sanctificationis incremento sumenda concede. Per Christum.

Lord, look upon the gifts your Church offers as it pours out its needs to you. Grant that what we are to receive will increase the holiness of your believing people. We ask this....

Prayer after Communion

Sumptis muneribus, quaesumus, Domine, ut, cum frequentatione mysterii, crescat nostrae salutis effectus. Per Christum.

Lord, we have received your gifts, and we ask that the work of our salvation may be furthered as we take part in this mystery. We ask this....

SIXTEENTH SUNDAY IN ORDINARY TIME

Collect

Propitiare, Domine, famulis tuis, et clementer gratiae tuae super eos dona multiplica, ut, spe, fide, et caritate ferventes, semper in mandatis tuis vigili custodia perseverent. Per Dominum.

Lord, look with kindness upon your people, and in your mercy increase the gifts of your grace among them, so that, inflamed with hope, faith, and love, they may always persevere in carefully obeying your commands. We ask this....

Prayer over the Gifts

Deus, qui legalium differentiam hostiarum unius sacrificii perfectione sanxisti, accipe sacrificium a devotis tibi famulis, et pari benedictione, sicut munera Abel, sanctifica, ut, quod singuli obtulerunt ad maiestatis tuae honorem, cunctis proficiat ad salutem. Per Christum.

God our Father, you have decreed that the multiplicity of sacrifices in the old law should be brought to perfection by the excellence of this one sacrifice. Receive the sacrifice of the people who love you, and bless it with the same blessing you gave to the offering of Abel, so that what each person has brought to honor your divine majesty may further the salvation of all. We ask this....

Prayer after Communion

Populo tuo, quaesumus, Domine, adesto propitius, et, quem mysteriis caelestibus imbuisti, fac ad novitatem vitae de vetustate transire. Per Christum.

Lord, in your mercy be present to your people. You have filled them with your heavenly mysteries; grant that they may pass from their old sinfulness to a new life. We ask this....

SEVENTEENTH SUNDAY IN ORDINARY TIME

Collect

Protector in te sperantium, Deus, sine quo nihil est validum, nihil sanctum, multiplica super nos misericordiam tuam, ut, te rectore, te duce, sic bonis transeuntibus nunc utamur, ut iam possimus inhaerere mansuris. Per Dominum.

God our Father, you are the guardian of all who hope in you; without you, nothing is worth while, nothing is holy. Increase your mercy toward us. Under your governance and leadership, may we use transient goods in this life in such a way that even now we will be able to cling to those which are permanent. We ask this....

Prayer over the Gifts

Suscipe, quaesumus, Domine, munera, quae tibi de tua largitate deferimus, ut haec sacrosancta mysteria, gratiae tuae operante virtute, et praesentis vitae nos conversatione sanctificent, et ad gaudia sempiterna perducant. Per Christum.

Lord, please receive the gifts which we bring to you as the fruits of your own goodness to us. By the powerful action of your grace, may these most sacred mysteries make us holy in how we live our present lives and also lead us to eternal joys. We ask this....

Prayer after Communion

Sumpsimus, Domine, divinum sacramentum, passionis Filii tui memoriale perpetuum; tribue, quaesumus, ut ad nostram salutem hoc munus proficiat, quod ineffabili nobis caritate ipse donavit. Qui vivit.

Lord, we have received your heavenly sacrament, the lasting memorial of the passion of your Son. In his unspeakable love he himself gave us this gift; please grant that it may further our salvation. We ask this....

EIGHTEENTH SUNDAY IN ORDINARY TIME

Collect

Adesto, Domine, famulis tuis, et perpetuam benignitatem largire poscentibus, ut his, qui te auctorem et gubernatorem gloriantur habere, et grata restaures, et restaurata conserves. Per Dominum.

Lord, be present to your faithful people, and grant your unending kindness to whose who earnestly seek it. May you restore your favor and preserve it once it is restored for those who take pride in acknowledging you as their creator and ruler. We ask this....

Prayer over the Gifts

Propitius, Domine, quaesumus, haec dona sanctifica, et, hostiae spiritalis oblatione suscepta, nosmetipsos tibi perfice munus aeternum. Per Christum.

Lord, in your kindness please make these gifts holy. Receive our spiritual sacrifice, and make of us an eternal offering to yourself. We ask this....

Prayer after Communion

Quos caelesti recreas munere, perpetuo, Domine, comitare praesidio, et, quos fovere non desinis, dignos fieri sempiterna redemptione concede. Per Christum.

Lord, you renew us with your heavenly gift. Accompany our lives with your continual protection, and grant that those whom you ceaselessly cherish may become worthy of eternal salvation. We ask this....

NINETEENTH SUNDAY IN ORDINARY TIME

Collect

(as on Monday of the Second Week After Easter, p.72)

Prayer over the Gifts

Ecclesiae tuae, Domine, munera placatus assume, quae et misericors offerenda tribuisti, et in nostrae salutis potenter efficis transire mysterium. Per Christum.

Lord, be pleased to accept your Church's offering. In your mercy, you have given us what we are to offer you; by your power, you make it become the mystery of our salvation. We ask this....

Prayer after Communion

Sacramentorum tuorum, Domine, communio sumpta nos salvet, et in tuae veritatis luce confirmet. Per Christum.

Lord, may our reception of your sacraments in Holy Communion bring us salvation, and may it strengthen us in living in the light of your truth. We ask this....

TWENTIETH SUNDAY IN ORDINARY TIME

Collect

Deus, qui diligentibus te bona invisibilia praeparasti, infunde cordibus nostris tui amoris affectum, ut, te in omnibus et super omnia diligentes, promissiones tuas, quae omne desiderium superant, consequamur. Per Dominum.

God our Father, for those who love you you have prepared gifts which the eye cannot see. Pour into our hearts the fullness of your love, so that we may love you in all things and above all things, and may come to possess what you have promised, which surpasses anything we could desire. We ask this....

Prayer over the Gifts

(as on December 29, the Fifth Day of the Christmas Octave, p.23)

Prayer after Communion

Per haec sacramenta, Domine, Christi participes effecti, clementiam tuam humiliter imploramus, ut, eius imaginis conformes in terris, et eius consortes in caelis fieri mereamur. Per Christum.

Lord, through these sacraments we have been made sharers in Christ himself. We humbly ask that in your mercy we may become like him on earth, and thus deserve to become his companions in heaven. We ask this....

TWENTY-FIRST SUNDAY IN ORDINARY TIME

Collect
(as on Monday of the Fifth
Week after Easter, p.76)

Prayer over the Gifts

Qui una semel hostia, Domine, adoptionis tibi populum acquisisti, unitatis et pacis in Ecclesia tua propitius nobis dona concedas. Per Christum.

Lord, you gained your adopted people by a single sacrifice offered but once. In your kindness, grant to us who are members of your Church the gifts of unity and peace. We ask this....

Prayer after Communion

Plenum, quaesumus, Domine, in nobis remedium tuae miserationis operare, ac tales nos esse perfice propitius et sic foveri, ut tibi in omnibus placere valeamus. Per Christum.

Lord, please bring about in us the full healing that your mercy causes. In your kindness, cherish us and make us the sort of people who will be able to please you in all things. We ask this....

TWENTY-SECOND SUNDAY IN ORDINARY TIME

Collect

Deus virtutum, cuius est totum quod est optimum, insere pectoribus nostris tui nominis amorem, et praesta, ut in nobis, religionis augmento, quae sunt bona nutrias, ac, vigilanti studio, quae sunt nutrita custodias. Per Dominum.

God of power, everything that is best is yours. Implant in our hearts a love of your name. By increasing our faithfulness to you, please foster what is good in us, and by your constant care guard what you have fostered. We ask this....

Prayer over the Gifts

Benedictionem nobis, Domine, conferat salutarem sacra semper oblatio, ut, quod agit mysterio, virtute perficiat. Peer Christum.

Lord, may these holy gifts always bring us your saving blessing, so that our offering may accomplish in power what it undertakes in mystery. We ask this....

Prayer after Communion

Pane mensae caelestis refecti, te, Domine, deprecamur, ut hoc nutrimentum caritatis corda nostra confirmet, quatenus ad tibi ministrandum in fratribus excitemur. Per Christum.

Lord, we have been refreshed with bread from your heavenly table, and we ask that this nourishment of love may strengthen us to the point that we may be moved to serve you in our brothers and sisters. We ask this....

TWENTY-THIRD SUNDAY IN ORDINARY TIME

Collect
(as on the Fifth Sunday of Easter, p.69)

Prayer over the Gifts

Deus, auctor sincerae devotionis et pacis, da, quaesumus, ut et maiestatem tuam convenienter hoc munere veneremur, et sacri participatione mysterii fideliter sensibus uniamur. Per Christum.

God our Father, you are the source of true dedication and peace. Please grant that we may fittingly reverence your divine majesty with this gift, and, by sharing in this sacred mystery, may truly be united in heart. We ask this....

Prayer after Communion

Da fidelibus tuis, Domine, quos et verbi tui et caelesti sacramenti pabulo nutris et vivificas, ita dilecti Filii tui tantis muneribus proficere, ut eius vitae semper consortes effici mereamur. Per Christum.

Lord, you nourish and give life to your faithful people by the sacred food of your word and your sacrament. Grant that we may profit from the great gifts of your beloved Son in such a way as to be privileged to share ceaselessly in his life. We ask this....

TWENTY-FOURTH SUNDAY IN ORDINARY TIME

Collect

Respice nos, rerum omnium Deus creator et rector, et, ut tuae propitiationis sentiamus effectum, toto nos tribue tibi corde servire. Per Dominum.

God our Father, creator and ruler of all things, look upon us, and grant that we may serve you with our whole heart, so that we may experience the fullness of your forgiveness. We ask this....

Prayer over the Gifts

Propitiare, Domine, supplicationibus nostris, et has oblationes famulorum tuorum benignus assume, ut, quod singuli ad honorem tui nominis obtulerunt, cunctis proficiat ad salutem. Per Christum.

Lord, be pleased with our prayers, and in your kindness receive these gifts of your faithful people, so that what each of us offers to the honor of your name may advance the salvation of us all. We ask this....

Prayer after Communion

Mentes nostras et corpora possideat, quaesumus, Domine, doni caelestis operatio, ut non noster sensus in nobis, sed eius praeveniat semper effectus. Per Christum.

Lord, we ask that the action of your heavenly gift may take possession of our minds and bodies. May the effects of that gift, rather than our own inclinations, always prevail in us. We ask this....

TWENTY-FIFTH SUNDAY IN ORDINARY TIME

Collect

Deus, qui sacrae legis omnia constituta in tua et proximi dilectione posuisti, da nobis, ut, tua praecepta servantes, ad vitam mereamur pervenire perpetuam. Per Dominum.

God our Father, you centered the whole of your divine law around love of you and love of our neighbor. Grant that, by observing your commands, we may be privileged to come to eternal life. We ask this....

Prayer over the Gifts

Munera, quaesumus, Domine, tuae plebis propitiatus assume, ut, quae fidei pietate profitentur, sacramentis caelestibus apprehendant. Per Christum.

Lord, in your kindness please receive the gifts of your people. In your heavenly sacraments may they receive those things which they profess with firm faith. We ask this....

Prayer after Communion

Quos tuis, Domine, reficis sacramentis, continuis attolle benignus auxiliis, ut redemptionis effectum et mysteriis capiamus et moribus. Per Christum.

Lord, you renew us by your sacraments. By your constant help lift us up, so that we may receive the fullness of redemption in these mysteries and in our lives. We ask this....

TWENTY-SIXTH SUNDAY IN ORDINARY TIME

Collect

Deus, qui omnipotentiam tuam parcendo maxime et miserando manifestas, gratiam tuam super nos indesinenter infunde, ut, ad tua promissa currentes, caelestium bonorum facias esse consortes. Per Dominum.

God our Father, you make your limitless power most clearly known through your forgiveness and mercy. Pour out your grace on us unceasingly, and thus make us hasten to receive your promises and share in your heavenly gifts. We ask this....

Prayer over the Gifts

Concede nobis, misericors Deus, ut haec nostra tibi oblatio sit accepta, et per eam nobis fons omnis benedictionis aperiatur. Per Christum.

Merciful Father, grant that this offering of ours may be acceptable to you. Through it, may the source of all blessings be opened to us. We ask this....

Prayer after Communion

Sit nobis, Domine, reparatio mentis et corporis caeleste mysterium, ut simus eius in gloria coheredes, cui, mortem ipsius annuntiando, compatimur. Qui vivit.

Lord, may this heavenly mystery restore our minds and bodies, so that we who share in Christ's death by proclaiming it may also share in his inheritance in glory. We ask this....

TWENTY-SEVENTH SUNDAY IN ORDINARY TIME

Collect

Omnipotens sempiterne Deus, qui abundantia pietatis tuae et meritum supplicum excedis et vota, effunde super nos misericordiam tuam, ut dimittas quae conscientia metuit, et adicias quod oratio non praesumit. Per Dominum.

Almighty and eternal God, in your generous love you go far beyond what your prayerful people deserve and what they ask for. Pour out your mercy upon us. Forgive the sins that our consciences dread, and grant what our prayers dare not petition. We ask this....

Prayer over the Gifts
(as on Wednesday of the Seventh Sunday of Easter, p.79)

Prayer after Communion

Concede nobis, omnipotens Deus, ut de perceptis sacramentis inebriemur atque pascamur, quatenus in id quod sumimus transeamus. Per Christum.

Almighty God, grant that we may be exhilarated and nourished with the sacraments we have been given, even to the extent that we may actually become what we receive.

TWENTY-EIGHTH SUNDAY IN ORDINARY TIME

Collect

Tua nos, quaesumus, Domine, gratia semper et praeveniat et sequatur, ac bonis operibus iugiter praestet esse intentos. Per Dominum.

Lord God, we ask that your grace may always anticipate our needs and ever be with us; may it make us constant in our dedication to good works. We ask this....

Prayer over the Gifts
(as on the Seventh Sunday of Easter, p.70)

Prayer after Communion
(as on Saturday of the Fifth Week of Lent, p.51)

TWENTY-NINTH SUNDAY IN ORDINARY TIME

Collect

Omnipotens sempiterne Deus, fac nos tibi semper et devotam gerere voluntatem, et maiestati tuae sincero corde servire. Per Dominum.

Almighty and eternal God, grant that our will may ever be dedicated to you, and make us always serve your divine majesty with sincere hearts. We ask this....

Prayer over the Gifts

Tribue nos, Domine, quaesumus, donis tuis libera mente servire, ut, tua purificante nos gratia, iisdem quibus famulamur mysteriis emundemur. Per Christum.

Lord, please grant that we may serve you with freedom of heart in our use of your gifts, so that, through the grace you give to cleanse us, we may be purified by these very mysteries in which we share. We ask this....

Prayer after Communion

Fac nos, quaesumus, Domine, caelestium rerum frequentatione proficere, ut et temporalibus beneficiis adiuvemur, et erudiamur aeternis. Per Christum.

Lord, please grant that we may make progress by our sharing in these heavenly gifts. May we thereby be aided by the blessings of this life and be instructed by those of eternity. We ask this....

THIRTIETH SUNDAY IN ORDINARY TIME

Collect

Omnipotens sempiterne Deus, da nobis fidei, spei, et caritatis augmentum, et, ut mereamur assequi quod promittis, fac nos amare quod praecipis. Per Dominum.

Almighty and eternal God, grant us greater faith, hope, and love. Make us love what you command, so that we may be privileged to attain what you promise. We ask this....

Prayer over the Gifts

Respice, quaesumus, Domine, munera quae tuae offerimus maiestati, ut, quod nostro servitio geritur, ad tuam gloriam potius dirigatur. Per Christum.

Lord, please look with kindness upon the gifts which we offer to your divine majesty, so that whatever is done in the name of our service to you may be more surely directed to your glory. We ask this....

Prayer after Communion

Perficiant in nobis, Domine, quaesumus, tua sacramenta quod continent, ut, quae nunc specie gerimus, rerum veritate capiamus. Per Christum.

Lord, we ask that your sacraments may bring to perfection within us that which they contain within themselves, so that we may come to possess in its full reality what we now touch by symbol and sign. We ask this....

THIRTY-FIRST SUNDAY IN ORDINARY TIME

Collect

Omnipotens et misericors Deus, de cuius munere venit, ut tibi a fidelibus tuis digne et laudabiliter serviatur, tribue, quaesumus, nobis, ut ad promissiones tuas sine offensione curramus. Per Dominum.

Almighty and merciful God, it is by your gift that your faithful people serve you in a way that is proper and praiseworthy. Please grant that we may be blameless as we hasten to the fulfillment of your promises. We ask this....

Prayer over the Gifts

Fiat hoc sacrificium, Domine, oblatio tibi munda, et nobis misericordiae tuae sancta largitio. Per Christum.

Lord, may this sacrifice become a pure offering to you and cause your sacred mercy to be poured out upon us. We ask this....

Prayer after Communion

Augeatur in nobis, quaesumus, Domine, tuae virtutis operatio, ut, refecti caelestibus sacramentis, ad eorum promissa capienda tuo munere praeparemur. Per Christum.

Lord, we ask that your powerful influence upon us may increase, so that, renewed by your heavenly sacraments, we may, through your gift, be prepared to receive what those sacraments promise. We ask this....

THIRTY-SECOND SUNDAY IN ORDINARY TIME

Collect

Omnipotens et misericors Deus, universa nobis adversantia propitiatus exclude, ut, mente et corpore pariter expediti, quae tua sunt liberis mentibus exsequamur. Per Dominum.

Almighty and merciful God, in your kindness ward off everything that would be harmful to us, so that, with minds and bodies freed from fear, we may be able to carry out your work with unencumbered hearts. We ask this....

Prayer over the Gifts

Sacrificiis praesentibus, Domine, quaesumus, intende placatus, ut, quod passionis Filii tui mysterio gerimus, pio consequamur affectu. Per Christum.

Lord, in your kindness and mercy, please look upon this sacrifice of ours. May we attain in dutiful love what we recall in this mystery of the passion of your Son. We ask this....

Prayer after Communion

Gratias tibi, Domine, referimus sacro munere vegetati, tuam clementiam implorantes, ut, per infusionem Spiritus tui, in quibus caelestis virtus introivit, sinceritatis gratia perseveret. Per Christum.

Lord, we thank you for giving us life by your sacred gift. We beg for your mercy and ask that, through the outpouring of your Spirit, the grace of faithful service may perdure among those into whom your divine power has entered. We ask this....

THIRTY-THIRD SUNDAY IN ORDINARY TIME

Collect

Da nobis, quaesumus, Domine Deus noster, in tua semper devotione gaudere, quia perpetua est et plena felicitas, si bonorum omnium iugiter serviamus auctori. Per Dominum.

Lord our God, please grant that we may always be gladdened by your love, for our joy will be lasting and complete if we constantly serve the author of all good. We ask this....

Prayer over the Gifts

Concede, quaesumus, Domine, ut oculis tuae maiestatis munus oblatum et gratiam nobis devotionis obtineat, et effectum beatae perennitatis acquirat. Per Christum.

Lord, please grant that the gift we offer in the sight of your divine majesty may obtain for us the grace of devoted service to you and result in our gaining a blessed eternity. We ask this....

Prayer after Communion

Sumpsimus, Domine, sacri dona mysterii, humiliter deprecantes, ut, quae in sui commemorationem nos Filius tuus facere praecepit, in nostrae proficiant caritatis augmentum. Per Christum.

Lord, we have received the gifts of your sacred mystery, and we humbly ask that what your Son commanded us to do in memory of him may bring about an increase in our love. We ask this....

CHRIST THE KING

THIRTY-FOURTH AND LAST SUNDAY IN ORDINARY TIME

Collect

Omnipotens sempiterne Deus, qui in dilecto Filio tuo, universorum Rege, omnia instaurare voluisti, concede propitius, ut tota creatura, a servitute liberata, tuae maiestati deserviat ac te sine fine collaudet. Per Dominum.

Almighty and eternal God, you willed to restore all things in your beloved Son, the King of the universe. In your kindness, grant that the whole of creation may be freed from the yoke of sin, and may serve your divine majesty and praise you unceasingly. We ask this....

Prayer over the Gifts

Hostiam tibi, Domine, humanae reconciliationis offerentes, suppliciter deprecamur, ut ipse Filius tuus cunctis gentibus unitatis et pacis dona concedat. Qui vivit.

Lord, we offer you the sacrifice that brings about the redemption of the human race, and we humbly ask that your Son himself may grant to all nations the gifts of unity and peace. We ask this....

Prayer after Communion

Immortalitatis alimoniam consecuti, quaesumus, Domine, ut, qui Christi Regis universorum gloriamur oboedire mandatis, cum ipso in caelesti regno sine fine vivere valeamus. Per Christum.

Lord, we have received the food of immortality, and we ask that we who rejoice in obeying the commands of Christ the King of the universe may be enabled to live with him in his kingdom forever. We ask this....

WEEKDAYS OF THE THIRTY-FOURTH WEEK IN ORDINARY TIME

Collect

Excita, quaesumus, Domine, tuorum fidelium voluntates, ut, divini operis fructum propensius exsequentes, pietatis tuae remedia maiora percipiant. Per Dominum.

Lord, please stir up the wills of your faithful people, so that they may give greater evidence of your divine work within them, and may receive a greater share of the healing power of your divine goodness. We ask this....

Prayer over the Gifts

Suscipe, Domine, sacra munera, quae tuo nomini iussisti dicanda, et, ut per ea tuae pietati reddamur accepti, fac nos tuis semper oboedire mandatis. Per Christum.

Lord, receive these sacred gifts which you have commanded us to offer to your holy name. Make us always obedient to your commands, so that through these gifts we may be made acceptable to your loving goodness. We ask this....

Prayer after Communion

Quaesumus, omnipotens Deus, ut, quos divina tribuis participatione gaudere, a te numquam separari permittas. Per Christum.

Almighty God, we pray that you never permit those to be separated from you whom you allow to rejoice in sharing these divine mysteries. We ask this....

TRINITY SUNDAY
FIRST SUNDAY AFTER PENTECOST

Collect

Deus Pater, qui, Verbum veritatis et Spiritum sanctificationis mittens in mundum, admirabile mysterium tuum hominibus declarasti, da nobis, in confessione verae fidei, aeternae gloriam Trinitatis agnoscere, et Unitatem adorare in potentia maiestatis. Per Dominum.

God our Father, in sending your Word of truth and your Spirit of holiness into the world, you have revealed to the human race the marvelous mystery that is you yourself. Grant that, in our profession of the true faith, we may proclaim the glory of your everlasting Trinity, and adore your Unity in its majestic power. We ask this....

Prayer over the Gifts

Sanctifica, quaesumus, Domine Deus noster, per tui nominis invocationem, haec munera nostrae servitutis, et per ea nosmetipsos tibi perfice munus aeternum. Per Christum.

Lord our God, by our invocation of your sacred name, please make holy these offerings, which mark our service to you. Through them, make us an everlasting gift to yourself. We ask this....

Prayer after Communion

Proficiat nobis ad salutem corporis et animae, Domine Deus noster, huius sacramenti susceptio, et sempiternae sanctae Trinitatis eiusdemque individuae Unitatis confessio. Per Christum.

Lord our God, may we benefit in both body and soul by our reception of this sacrament and by our profession of your holy and eternal Trinity and your undivided Unity. We ask this....

CORPUS CHRISTI
THURSDAY AFTER TRINITY SUNDAY

Collect

Deus, qui nobis sub sacramento mirabili passionis tuae memoriam reliquisti, tribue, quaesumus, ita nos Corporis et Sanguinis tui sacra mysteria venerari, ut redemptionis tuae fructum in nobis iugiter sentiamus. Qui vivis.

Lord Jesus Christ, you left us a remembrance of your passion in this marvelous sacrament. Grant that we may reverence the sacred mysteries of your Body and Blood in such a way that we may constantly experience within ourselves the effects of your redemption. We ask this....

Prayer over the Gifts

Ecclesiae tuae, quaesumus, Domine, unitatis et pacis propitius dona concede, quae sub oblatis muneribus mystice designantur. Per Christum.

Lord our God, in your kindness please grant to your Church the gifts of unity and peace, which are mystically portrayed in the gifts we have offered. We ask this....

Prayer after Communion

Fac nos, quaesumus, Domine, divinitatis tuae sempiterna fruitione repleri, quam pretiosi Corporis et Sanguinis tui temporalis perceptio praefigurat. Qui vivis.

Lord, please fill us with the endless enjoyment of your divinity, as foreshadowed by our reception of your precious Body and Blood here on earth. We ask this....

SACRED HEART

FRIDAY AFTER THE SECOND SUNDAY AFTER PENTECOST

Collect

Concede, quaesumus, omnipotens Deus, ut qui, dilecti Filii tui Corde gloriantes, eius praecipua in nos beneficia recolimus caritatis, de illo donorum fonte caelesti supereffluentem gratiam mereamur accipere. Per Dominum.

Almighty God, we take joy in the Heart of your beloved Son and call to mind the special favors we have received from his love. Please grant that we may be privileged to receive abundant grace from that heavenly fountain of gifts. We ask this....

Alternate Collect

Deus, qui nobis in corde Filii tui, nostris vulnerato peccatis, infinitos dilectionis thesauros misericorditer largiri dignaris, concede, quaesumus, ut, illi devotum pietatis nostrae praestantes obsequium, dignae quoque satisfactionis exhibeamus officium. Per Dominum.

God our Father, in your mercy you have seen fit to grant us a limitless treasure of love in the heart of your Son, wounded as it was by our sins. Please grant that we may bring to him the devoted service of our love, and also offer him fitting reparation. We ask this....

Prayer over the Gifts

Respice, quaesumus, Domine, ad ineffabilem Cordis dilecti Filii tui caritatem, ut quod offerimus sit tibi munus acceptum et nostrorum expiatio delictorum. Per Christum.

Lord, please look upon the unspeakable love of the Heart of your beloved Son, so that what we offer may be an acceptable gift to you and an atonement for our sins. We ask this....

Prayer after Communion

Sacramentum caritatis, Domine, sancta nos faciat dilectione fervere, qua, ad Filium tuum semper attracti, ipsum in fratribus agnoscere discamus. Per Christum.

Lord, may this sacrament, which symbolizes your love, inflame us with a holy charity which will ever draw us to your Son. Through it, may we learn to recognize him in our brothers and sisters. We ask this....

PROPER OF THE SAINTS

JANUARY 2

SAINTS BASIL THE GREAT and GREGORY NAZIANZEN

BISHOPS AND DOCTORS OF THE CHURCH

Collect

Deus, qui Ecclesiam tuam beatorum Basilii et Gregorii exemplis et doctrinis dignatus es illustrare, concede, quaesumus, ut tuam discamus in humilitate veritatem et eam in caritate fideliter operemur. Per Dominum.

God our Father, you have seen fit to enlighten the Church by the lives and teaching of Saints Basil and Gregory. Please grant that we may be docile in learning your truth, and faithful in putting what we have learned into loving practice. We ask this....

Prayer over the Gifts and Prayer after Communion:
Cf. Common of Pastors (for Bishops), p. 199,
or
Common of Doctors of the Church, p. 205.

JANUARY 7

SAINT RAYMOND OF PEÑAFORT

PRIEST

Collect

Deus, qui beatum Raimundum presbyterum insignis in peccatores misericordiae virtute decorasti, eius nobis intercessione concede, ut, a peccati servitute soluti, quae tibi sunt placita liberis mentibus exsequamur. Per Dominum.

God our Father, you made your priest Saint Raymond renowned for the virtue of outstanding compassion toward sinners. Through his intercession, grant that we may be freed from our enslavement to sin and, with unencumbered hearts, may do what is pleasing to you. We ask this....

Prayer over the Gifts and Prayer after Communion:
Cf. Common of Pastors, p. 200.

JANUARY 13

SAINT HILARY

BISHOP AND DOCTOR OF THE CHURCH

Collect

Praesta, quaesumus, omnipotens Deus, ut divinitatem Filii tui, quam beatus Hilarius episcopus constanter asseruit, et convenienter intellegere valeamus, et veraciter profiteri. Per Dominum.

Almighty God, your bishop Saint Hilary unflaggingly upheld the divinity of your Son. Please grant that we too may properly understand it and faithfully profess it. We ask this....

Prayer over the Gifts and Prayer after Communion:
Cf. Common of Pastors (for Bishops), p. 199,
or
Common of Doctors of the Church, p. 205.

JANUARY 17
SAINT ANTHONY
ABBOT

Collect

Deus, qui beato Antonio abbati tribuisti mira tibi in deserto conversatione servire, eius nobis interventione concede, ut, abnegantes nosmetipsos, te iugiter super omnia diligamus. Per Dominum.

God our Father, you granted to Saint Anthony the Abbot the favor of being wonderfully close to you in serving you in the desert. Through his intercession, grant that we may practice self-denial and constantly love you above all things. We ask this....

Prayer over the Gifts

Accepta tibi sint, Domine, quaesumus, munera nostrae servitutis, pro beati Antonii commemoratione altari tuo proposita, et concede, ut, a terrenis impedimentis absoluti, te solo divites efficiamur. Per Christum.

Lord, we ask that the gifts that mark our service to you may be acceptable as we place them on your altar in honor of Saint Anthony. Grant that we may be freed from whatever would bind us to earth and be made wealthy in the possession of you alone. We ask this....

Prayer after Communion

Sacramentis tuis, Domine, salubriter enutritos, cunctas fac nos semper insidias inimici superare, qui beato Antonio dedisti contra potestates tenebrarum claras referre victorias. Per Christum.

Lord, you have granted us the saving nourishment of your sacraments. Make us always overcome every snare of the enemy, just as you gave Saint Anthony the strength to win decisive victories in fighting the powers of darkness. We ask this....

JANUARY 20
SAINT FABIAN
POPE AND MARTYR

SAINT SEBASTIAN
MARTYR

Collect (Saint Fabian)

Deus, tuorum gloria sacerdotum, praesta, quaesumus, ut, beati Fabiani martyris tui interveniente suffragio, eiusdem proficiamus fidei consortio dignoque servitio. Per Dominum.

God our Father, you are the glory of your priests. Through the intercession of your martyr Saint Fabian, please grant that we may progress in sharing his faith and in serving you worthily. We ask this....

Collect (Saint Sebastian)

Praesta nobis, quaesumus, Domine, spiritum fortitudinis, ut, glorioso exemplo beati Sebastiani martyris tui edocti, tibi magis quam hominibus oboedire discamus. Per Dominum.

Lord, we have been taught by the magnificent example of your martyr Saint Sebastian. Please grant us true courage, so that we may learn to give our obedience to you rather than to mere humans. We ask this....

Prayer over the Gifts and Prayer after Communion:

St. Fabian: Common of Martyrs, p. 193,
or
Common of Pastors (for Popes), p. 198.

St. Sebastian: Common of Martyrs, p.193.

JANUARY 21
SAINT AGNES

VIRGIN AND MARTYR

Collect

Omnipotens sempiterne Deus, qui infirma mundi eligis ut fortia quaeque confundas, concede propitius, ut, qui beatae Agnetis martyris tuae natalicia celebramus, eius in fide constantiam subsequamur. Per Dominum.

Almighty and eternal God, you choose the weak things of the world in order to confound the strong. As we celebrate the birth of your martyr Saint Agnes, grant in your mercy that we may imitate her unshakeable faith. We ask this....

Prayer over the Gifts and Prayer after Communion:
Cf. Common of Martyrs, p. 193,
or
Common of Virgins, p. 206.

JANUARY 22
SAINT VINCENT

DEACON AND MARTYR

Collect

Omnipotens sempiterne Deus, tuum in nobis Spiritum clementer infunde, ut corda nostra ea dilectione valida potiantur, per quam sanctus martyr Vincentius omnia corporis tormenta devicit. Per Dominum.

Almighty and eternal God, in your mercy pour out your Spirit upon us, so that our hearts may attain that strong love through which your holy martyr Saint Vincent overcame all his bodily torments. We ask this....

Prayer over the Gifts and Prayer after Communion:
Cf. Common of Martyrs, p. 193.

JANUARY 24
SAINT FRANCIS DE SALES

BISHOP AND DOCTOR OF THE CHURCH

Collect

Deus, qui ad animarum salutem beatum Franciscum episcopum omnibus omnia factum esse voluisti, concede propitius, ut, eius exemplo, tuae mansuetudinem caritatis in fratrum servitio semper ostendamus. Per Dominum.

God our Father, you willed that your bishop Saint Francis should become all things to all people, so that the salvation of souls could be achieved. In your mercy, grant that we may follow his example and always exhibit your own gentle love in the service of our brothers and sisters. We ask this....

Prayer over the Gifts

Per hanc salutarem hostiam quam offerimus tibi, Domine, cor nostrum divino illo Sancti Spiritus igne succende, quo mitissimum beati Francisci animum mirabiliter inflammasti. Per Christum.

Through this saving offering which we make to you, Lord, set our hearts on fire with that same divine flame of the Holy Spirit by which you so marvelously enkindled the gentle heart of Saint Francis. We ask this....

Prayer after Communion

Concede, quaesumus, omnipotens Deus, ut, per sacramenta quae sumpsimus, beati Francisci caritatem et mansuetudinem imitantes in terris, gloriam quoque consequamur in caelis. Per Christum.

Almighty God, through the sacraments we have received, grant that we may imitate the gentle love of Saint Francis on earth, and so attain heavenly glory. We ask this....

JANUARY 25
THE CONVERSION OF SAINT PAUL THE APOSTLE

Collect

Deus, qui universum mundum beati Pauli apostoli praedicatione docuisti, da nobis, quaesumus, ut, cuius conversionem hodie celebramus, per eius ad te exempla gradientes, tuae simus mundo testes veritatis. Per Dominum.

God our Father, you instructed the entire world through the preaching of your apostle Saint Paul. As we celebrate his conversion today, please grant, through his example, that we may come near to you and be witnesses of your truth to the world. We ask this....

Prayer over the Gifts

Illo nos, quaesumus, Domine, divina tractantes, fidei lumine Spiritus perfundat, quo beatum Paulum apostolum ad gloriae tuae propagationem iugiter collustravit. Per Christum.

Lord, as we take part in these sacred rites, we beg of you that the Holy Spirit may fill us with the same light of faith by which He constantly illuminated Saint Paul the Apostle for the spread of your glory. We ask this....

Prayer after Communion

Sacramenta quae sumpsimus, Domine Deus noster, in nobis foveant caritatis ardorem, quo beatus apostolus Paulus vehementer accensus, omnium pertulit sollicitudinem Ecclesiarum. Per Christum.

Lord our God, may the sacraments which we have received foster within us that burning love which so strongly inflamed your apostle Paul that he bore within himself a solicitous care for all the churches. We ask this....

JANUARY 26
SAINTS TIMOTHY AND TITUS

BISHOPS

Collect

Deus, qui beatos Timotheum et Titum apostolicis virtutibus decorasti, utriusque intercessione concede, ut, iuste et pie viventes in hoc saeculo, ad caelestem mereamur patriam pervenire. Per Dominum.

God our Father, you adorned Saints Timothy and Titus with the virtues of the apostles. Through the intercession of them both, grant that we may live just and holy lives in this world and be privileged to come safely to our heavenly homeland. We ask this....

Prayer over the Gifts and Prayer after Communion:
Cf. *Common of Pastors (for Bishops)*, p. 199.

JANUARY 27
SAINT ANGELA MERICI

VIRGIN

Collect

Pietati tuae, quaesumus, Domine, nos beata virgo Angela commendare non desinat, ut, eius caritatis et prudentiae documenta sectantes, tuam valeamus doctrinam custodire et moribus profiteri. Per Dominum.

Lord, we ask that your virgin Saint Angela may never cease to recommend us to your faithful love, so that, following the example of her charity and prudence, we may be able to safeguard your teachings and profess them by how we live. We ask this....

Prayer over the Gifts and Prayer after Communion:
Cf. Common of Virgins, p. 206,
or
Common of Holy Men and Women (for Teachers), p. 213.

JANUARY 28
SAINT THOMAS AQUINAS

PRIEST AND DOCTOR OF THE CHURCH

Collect

Deus, qui beatum Thomam sanctitatis zelo ac sacrae doctrinae studio conspicuum effecisti, da nobis, quaesumus, et quae docuit intellectu conspicere, et quae gessit imitatione complere. Per Dominum.

God our Father, you made Saint Thomas Aquinas outstanding in his zeal for the pursuit of holiness and in his dedication to sacred learning. Please grant that we may comprehend with our minds the truths that he taught and, by imitating him, may bring to fulfillment the deeds he performed. We ask this....

Prayer over the Gifts and Prayer after Communion:
Cf. Common of Doctors of the Church, p. 205,
or
Common of Pastors, p. 200,
or
Common of Holy Men and Women (for Religious), p. 211.

JANUARY 31
SAINT JOHN BOSCO

PRIEST

Collect

Deus, qui beatum Ioannem presbyterum adulescentium patrem et magistrum excitasti, concede, quaesumus, ut, eodem caritatis igne succensi, animas quaerere tibique soli servire valeamus. Per Dominum.

God our Father, you raised up your priest Saint John Bosco to be a father and a teacher for young people. Please grant that we too, inflamed by the same fiery love as he, may be enabled to pursue the salvation of souls and the service of you alone. We ask this....

Prayer over the Gifts and Prayer after Communion:
Cf. Common of Pastors, p. 200,
or
Common of Holy Men and Women (for Teachers), p. 213.

FEBRUARY 2
PRESENTATION OF THE LORD

Allocution

Fratres carissimi: ante dies quadraginta celebravimus cum gaudio festum Nativitatis Domini. Hodie vero occurrit dies ille beatus, quo Iesus a Maria et Ioseph praesentatus est in templo, exterius quidem legem implens, rerum veritate autem occurrens populo suo credenti. Spiritu Sancto impulsi, in templum venerunt beati illi senes et cognoverunt Dominum eodem Spiritu illuminati, et confessi sunt eum in exsultatione. Ita et nos, congregati in unum per Spiritum Sanctum, procedamus ad domum Dei obviam Christo. Inveniemus eum et cognoscemus in fractione panis, donec veniat manifestus in gloria.

Dear brothers and sisters: forty days ago we joyfully celebrated the feast of the birth of the Lord. Now that blessed day is at hand on which Jesus was presented in the temple by Mary and Joseph, fulfilling the law, indeed, as far as external actions are concerned, but in reality beginning to meet his believing people. For, moved by the Holy Spirit, those holy and elderly people came into the temple; enlightened by the same Spirit, they recognized the Lord and acknowledged him with joy. In the same way, as we are gathered together into one body by the same Holy Spirit, let us too go forward to the house of God to meet Christ. We shall find him and recognize him in the breaking of the bread, until the time when he comes resplendent in his glory.

Blessing of the Candles:
First Formula

Deus, omnis luminis fons et origo, qui iusto Simeoni Lumen ad revelationem gentium hodie demonstrasti, te supplices deprecamur, ut hos cereos sanctificare tua + benedictione digneris, tuae plebis vota suscipiens, quae ad tui nominis laudem eos gestatura concurrit, quatenus per virtutum semitam ad lucem indeficientem pervenire mereamur. Per Christum.

God our Father, you are the cause and source of all brightness; and on this day you showed to blessed Simeon a Light to be revealed to the nations. We humbly ask you to make these candles holy + with your blessing. Your people come here to carry these candles to the glory of your name. Receive their prayers so that they may walk in the path of virtue, and thus may be privileged to arrive at the unfailing light. We ask this....

Blessing of the Candles:
Alternate Formula

Deus, lumen verum, aeternae lucis propagator et auctor, cordibus infunde fidelium perpetui luminis claritatem, ut, quicumque in templo sancto tuo splendore praesentium luminum adornantur, ad lumen gloriae tuae feliciter valeant pervenire. Per Christum.

God our Father, you are the true light; eternal brilliance comes forth from you and radiates outward from you. Pour out the brightness of your unfailing light into the hearts of the faithful, so that whoever is bathed by the glow of these candles in your holy temple may be enabled to arrive in joy at the radiance of your glory. We ask this....

Collect

Omnipotens sempiterne Deus, maiestatem tuam supplices exoramus, ut, sicut unigenitus Filius tuus hodierna die cum nostrae carnis substantia in templo est praesentatus, ita nos facias purificatis tibi mentibus praesentari. Per Dominum.

Almighty and eternal God, your only Son was today presented in the temple in the human flesh he shared with us. We humbly ask your divine majesty to allow us, in like manner, to be presented to you with purified hearts. We ask this....

Prayer over the Gifts

Gratum tibi sit, Domine, quaesumus, exsultantis Ecclesiae munus oblatum, qui unigenitum Filium tuum voluisti Agnum immaculatum tibi offerri pro saeculi vita. Per Christum.

Lord, you willed that your only Son should be offered to you as a spotless Lamb for the life of the world. We ask that the gift offered by your joyful Church may be pleasing to you. We ask this....

Prayer after Communion

Per haec sancta quae sumpsimus, Domine, perfice in nobis gratiam tuam, qui exspectationem Simeonis implesti, ut, sicut ille mortem non vidit nisi prius Christum suscipere mereretur, ita et nos, in occursum Domini procedentes, vitam obtineamus aeternam. Per Christum.

Lord, through the holy sacraments which we have received, bring your grace to completion within us, as you fulfilled the hope of Simeon. He did not see death without first being privileged to welcome Christ; so also, may we obtain eternal life as we go forward to meet the Lord. We ask this....

FEBRUARY 3

SAINT BLASE
BISHOP AND MARTYR

SAINT ANSGAR
BISHOP

Collect: Saint Blase

Exaudi, Domine, populum tuum, cum beati Blasii martyris patricinio supplicantem, et ut temporalis vitae nos tribuas pace gaudere, et aeternae reperire subsidium. Per Dominum.

Lord, listen to your people as we pray to you under the patronage of your martyr Saint Blase. Grant that we may rejoice in a peaceful life on earth, and may find help in the prospect of an eternal life in heaven. We ask this....

Collect: Saint Ansgar

Deus, qui ad multas illuminandas gentes beatum Ansgarium episcopum mittere voluisti, eius nobis intercessione concede, ut in tuae veritatis luce iugiter ambulemus. Per Dominum.

God our Father, you willed to send your bishop Saint Ansgar to instruct the peoples of many lands. Through his intercession, grant that we too may ever walk in the light of your truth. We ask this....

Prayer over the Gifts and Prayer after Communion:
St. Blase: Common of Martyrs, p. 193, or Common of Pastors (for Bishops), p. 199.
St. Ansgar: Common of Pastors (for Missionaries), p.203, or Common of Pastors (for Bishops), p. 199.

FEBRUARY 5
SAINT AGATHA

VIRGIN AND MARTYR

Collect

Indulgentiam nobis, quaesumus, Domine, beata Agatha virgo et martyr imploret, quae tibi grata semper exstitit et virtute martyrii et merito castitatis. Per Dominum.

Lord, your virgin and martyr Saint Agatha was always pleasing to you because of her courageous martyrdom and her steadfast purity. We beg that she may implore you to grant forgiveness to us. We ask this....

*Prayer over the Gifts
and
Prayer after Communion:*
Cf. *Common of Martyrs*, p. 193 or *Common of Virgins*, p. 206.

FEBRUARY 6
SAINTS PAUL MIKI AND COMPANIONS

MARTYRS

Collect

Deus, omnium fortitudo sanctorum, qui beatos martyres Paulum eiusque socios per crucem ad vitam vocare dignatus es, praesta, quaesumus, ut, eorum intercessione, fidem quam profitemur usque ad mortem fortiter teneamus. Per Dominum.

God our Father, you are the strength of all your saints; and you saw fit to call your blessed martyrs Paul and his companions to life without end by means of death on a cross. Through their intercession, please grant that, to the end of our lives, we may have the courage to hold fast to the faith we profess. We ask this....

*Prayer over the Gifts and
Prayer after Communion:*
Cf. *Common of Martyrs*, p. 190.

FEBRUARY 9
SAINT JEROME EMILIANI

Collect

Deus, Pater misericordiarum, qui beatum Hieronymum adiutorem et patrem orphanis providisti, eius nobis intercessione concede, ut spiritum adoptionis, quo filii tui nominamur et sumus, fideliter custodiamus. Per Dominum.

God, Father of mercy, you sent Saint Jerome to be a friend and father to orphans. Through his intercession, grant that we may faithfully preserve the spirit of adoption by which we are known as and truly are your children. We ask this....

*Prayer over the Gifts
and
Prayer after Communion:*
Cf. *Common of Holy Men and Women (for Teachers)*, p. 213.

FEBRUARY 10
SAINT SCHOLASTICA

VIRGIN

Collect

Beatae Scholasticae virginis memoriam recolentes, quaesumus, Domine, ut, eius exemplo, tibi intemerata caritate serviamus et felices obtineamus tuae dilectionis effectus. Per Dominum.

As we call to mind the memory of your holy virgin Scholastica, Lord, we ask that, through her example, we may serve you with undefiled charity and successfully attain the reward of your love for us. We ask this....

Prayer over the Gifts and Prayer after Communion:
Cf. Common of Virgins, p. 206, or Common of Holy Men and Women (for Religious), p. 211.

FEBRUARY 11
OUR LADY OF LOURDES

Collect

Concede, misericors Deus, fragilitati nostrae praesidium, ut, qui immaculatae Dei Genetricis memoriam agimus, intercessionis eius auxilio, a nostris iniquitatibus resurgamus. Per Dominum.

Merciful God, grant that your strength may bolster our weakness, so that, as we call to mind the immaculate Mother of God, we may rise from our sinfulness through the help of her intercession. We ask this....

Prayer over the Gifts and Prayer after Communion:
Cf. Common of the Blessed Virgin, p. 186.

FEBRUARY 14
SAINTS CYRIL
AND METHODIUS

BISHOPS

Collect

Deus, qui per beatos fratres Cyrillum et Methodium Slavoniae gentes illuminasti, da cordibus nostris tuae doctrinae verba percipere, nosque perfice populum in vera fide et recta confessione concordem. Per Dominum.

God our Father, you brought your light to the Slavic races through the holy brothers Cyril and Methodius. Grant that we may receive the words of your teaching in our hearts, and make of us a people truly at one in the profession of the true faith and in its fervent proclamation. We ask this....

Prayer over the Gifts and Prayer after Communion:
Cf. Common of Pastors (for Founders of Churches), p. 202, or Common of Pastors (for Missionaries), p. 203, or Common of Holy Men and Women, p. 208.

FEBRUARY 17
SEVEN HOLY FOUNDERS
OF THE ORDER OF SERVITES
OF THE BLESSED VIRGIN MARY

Collect

Beatorum fratrum, Domine, pietatem nobis benignus infunde, qua et Dei Genetricem sunt devotissime venerati, et tuum ad te populum provexerunt. Per Dominum.

Lord, in your kindness pour forth upon us that same loving dedication that the seven holy brothers had, whereby they honored the Mother of God most ardently and advanced your people in their progress toward you. We ask this....

Prayer over the Gifts and Prayer after Communion:
Cf. Common of Holy Men and Women (for Religious), p. 211.

FEBRUARY 21
SAINT PETER DAMIEN

BISHOP AND DOCTOR OF THE CHURCH

Collect

Concede nos, quaesumus, omnipotens Deus, beati Petri episcopi monita et exempla sectari, ut, Christo nihil praeponentes et Ecclesiae tuae servitio semper intenti, ad aeternae lucis gaudia perducamur. Per Dominum.

Almighty God, grant that we may heed the teaching and example of Saint Peter Damien. May we place nothing ahead of our service of Christ, and may we always be intent upon the service of your Church, and so be led to the joys of eternal light. We ask this....

Prayer over the Gifts and Prayer after Communion:

Cf. Common of Pastors (for a Bishop), p. 199 or Common of Doctors of the Church, p. 205 or Common of Holy Men and Women (for Religious), p. 211.

FEBRUARY 22
CHAIR OF SAINT PETER

Collect

Praesta, quaesumus, omnipotens Deus, ut nullis nos permittas perturbationibus concuti, quos in apostolicae confessionis petra solidasti. Per Dominum.

Almighty God, you have grounded us firmly on the rock of the apostolic profession of faith. Please grant that we may never be assaulted by anxious cares. We ask this....

Prayer over the Gifts

Ecclesiae tuae, quaesumus, Domine, preces et hostias benignus admitte, ut, beato Petro pastore, ad aeternam perveniat hereditatem, quo docente fidei tenet integritatem. Per Christum.

In your kindness, Lord, please accept the prayers and offerings of your Church. May it arrive at its eternal inheritance, for Saint Pater is its shepherd, and by his teachings it posseses the fullness of faith. We ask this....

Prayer after Communion

Deus, qui nos, beati Petri apostoli festivitatem celebrantes, Christi Corporis et Sanguinis communione vegetasti, praesta, quaesumus, ut hoc redemptionis commercium sit sacramentum nobis unitatis et pacis. Per Christum.

God our Father, in our celebration of the feast of Saint Peter your apostle, you have given us life by our reception of the Body and Blood of Christ. Please grant that this sacred act of our redemption may also be a sacrament of unity and peace for us. We ask this....

FEBRUARY 23
SAINT POLYCARP

BISHOP AND MARTYR

Collect

Deus universae creaturae, qui beatum Polycarpum episcopum in numero martyrum dignatus es aggregare, eius nobis intercessione concede, ut cum illo partem calicis Christi capientes, in vitam resurgamus aeternam. Per Dominum.

God of the entire universe, you saw fit to join your bishop Saint Polycarp to the number of your martyrs. By his intercession, grant that we may take part with him in the cup of Christ, and so rise to eternal life. We ask this....

Prayer over the Gifts and
Prayer after Communion:
Cf. Common of Martyrs, p. 193, or Common of Pastors (for a Bishop), p. 199.

MARCH 4
SAINT CASIMIR

Collect

Deus omnipotens, cui servire regnare est, concede nobis, beati Casimiri intercedente suffragio, tibi in sanctitate et iustitia perpetuo famulari. Per Dominum.

Almighty God, to serve you is to reign. Through the intercession of Saint Casimir, grant that we may always serve you in holiness and justice. We ask this....

Prayer over the Gifts and
Prayer after Communion:
Cf. Common of Holy Men and Women, p. 208.

MARCH 7
SAINTS PERPETUA AND FELICITY

MARTYRS

Collect

Deus, cuius urgente caritate beatae martyres Perpetua et Felicitas tormentum mortis, contempto persecutore, vicerunt, da nobis, quaesumus, earum precibus, ut in tua semper dilectione crescamus. Per Dominum.

God our Father, your holy martyrs Perpetua and Felicity were prompted by an impelling love for you to disdain their persecutor and so to overcome the torment of death. Through their prayers, please grant that we may always grow in our love of you. We ask this....

Prayer over the Gifts and
Prayer after Communion:
Cf. Common of Martyrs, p. 190, or Common of Holy Men and Women, p. 208.

MARCH 8
SAINT JOHN OF GOD

RELIGIOUS

Collect

Deus, qui beatum Ioannem misericordiae spiritu perfudisti, da, quaesumus, ut, caritatis opera exercentes, inter electos in regno tuo inveniri mereamur. Per Dominum.

God our Father, you poured out the spirit of mercifulness upon Saint John of God. Please grant that we too may perform works of charity and so be privileged to be found among your elect in your kingdom. We ask this....

Prayer over the Gifts and
Prayer after Communion:
Cf. Common of Holy Men and Women (for Religious), p. 211, or Common of Holy Men and Women (for Those Who Performed Works of Mercy), p. 213.

MARCH 9
SAINT FRANCES OF ROME

RELIGIOUS

Collect

Deus, qui nobis in beata Francisca singulare dedisti coniugalis et monasticae conversationis exemplar, fac nos tibi perseveranter deservire, ut in omnibus vitae adiunctis te conspicere et sequi valeamus. Per Dominum.

God our Father, in Saint Frances of Rome you gave us an outstanding model of both married life and the religious vocation. Make us serve you faithfully, so that we may be able to know and do your will in all the circumstances of life. We ask this....

Prayer over the Gifts and Prayer after Communion:
Cf. Common of Holy Men and Women (for Religious), p. 211.

MARCH 17
SAINT PATRICK

BISHOP

Collect

Deus, qui ad praedicandam Hiberniae populis gloriam tuam beatum Patricium episcopum providisti, eius meritis et intercessione concede, ut, qui christiano nomine gloriantur, tua mirabilia hominibus iugiter annuntient. Per Dominum.

God our Father, you raised up your bishop Saint Patrick to make your glory known to the people of Ireland. Through his merits and prayers, grant that all who rejoice in being known as Christians may constantly proclaim your wonderful deeds to all men and women. We ask this....

Prayer over the Gifts and Prayer after Communion:
Cf. Common of Pastors (for Missionaries), p.203, or Common of Pastors (for a Bishop), p. 199.

MARCH 18
SAINT CYRIL OF JERUSALEM

BISHOP AND DOCTOR OF THE CHURCH

Collect

Deus, qui Ecclesiam tuam per beatum Cyrillum episcopum ad mysteria salutis profundius attingenda mirabiliter adduxisti, da nobis, eius intercessione, Filium tuum ita agnoscere, ut vitam abundantius habeamus. Per Dominum.

God our Father, through your bishop Saint Cyril of Jerusalem you marvelously brought your Church into a more profound understanding of the mysteries of salvation. Through his intercession grant that we may come to know your Son in such a way that we may have life more fully. We ask this....

Prayer over the Gifts and Prayer after Communion:
Cf. Common of Pastors (for a Bishop), p. 199 or Common of Pastors (for a Doctor of the Church), p. 205.

MARCH 19
SAINT JOSEPH, HUSBAND OF MARY

Collect

Praesta, quaesumus, omnipotens Deus, ut humanae salutis mysteria, cuius primordia beati Ioseph fideli custodiae commisisti, Ecclesia tua, ipso intercedente, iugiter servet implenda. Per Dominum.

Almighty God, you entrusted the beginnings of the mysteries of human salvation to the faithful care of Saint Joseph. Through his intercession, please grant that your Church may constantly strive for the fulfillment of those mysteries. We ask this....

Prayer over the Gifts

Quaesumus, Domine, ut, sicut beatus Ioseph Unigenito tuo, nato de Maria Virgine, pia devotione deserviit, ita et nos mundo corde tuis altaribus mereamur ministrare. Per Christum.

Lord, just as Saint Joseph carefully and lovingly served your only Son, who was born of the Virgin Mary, so too please grant that we may be privileged to assist at your altar with pure hearts. We ask this....

Prayer after Communion

Familiam tuam, quaesumus, Domine, quam de beati Ioseph sollemnitate laetantem ex huius altaris alimonia satiasti, perpetua protectione defendi, et tua in ea propitiatus dona custodi. Per Christum.

Lord, with food from your altar you have fed your faithful people as they rejoice on this feast of Saint Joseph. Please guard them with your unfailing protection, and in your mercy preserve your gifts within them. We ask this....

MARCH 23
SAINT TURIBIUS OF MONGROVEJO

BISHOP

Collect

Deus, qui Ecclesiam tuam beati Turibii episcopi apostolicis curis zeloque veritatis auxisti, concede, ut populus tibi sacratus fidei et sanctitatis nova semper incrementa suscipiat. Per Dominum.

God our Father, your made your Church grow through the pastoral care that Bishop Saint Turibius exercised and the concern for truth that he showed. Grant that the people who are consecrated to you may ever receive an increased faith and holiness. We ask this....

Prayer over the Gifts and Prayer after Communion:
Cf. Common of Pastors (for a Bishop), p. 199.

MARCH 25
ANNUNCIATION

Collect

Deus, qui Verbum tuum in utero Virginis Mariae veritatem carnis humanae suscipere voluisti, concede, quaesumus, ut, qui Redemptorem nostrum Deum et hominem confitemur, ipsius etiam divinae naturae mereamur esse consortes. Per Dominum.

God our Father, you willed that your Word should take on the reality of human flesh in the womb of the Virgin Mary. Please grant that we who acknowledge our Redeemer to be both divine and human may be privileged to share also in his nature as God. We ask this....

Prayer over the Gifts

Ecclesiae tuae munus, omnipotens Deus, dignare suscipere, ut, quae in Unigeniti tui incarnatione primordia sua constare cognoscit, ipsius gaudeat hac sollemnitate celebrare mysteria. Per Christum.

All-powerful God, be pleased to receive the gift of your Church. It recognizes that its own beginnings arise from the incarnation of your only Son; grant that it may rejoice in celebrating that mystery on this feast. We ask this....

Prayer after Communion

In mentibus nostris, quaesumus, Domine, verae fidei sacramenta confirma, ut, qui conceptum de Virgine Deum verum et hominem confitemur, per eius salutiferae resurrectionis potentiam, ad aeternam mereamur pervenire laetitiam. Per Christum.

Lord, please strengthen the workings of the true faith within our hearts, so that we who profess that He who was conceived by the Virgin is both truly God and truly human may, through the power of his life-giving resurrection, be privileged to come to eternal joy. We ask this....

APRIL 2
SAINT FRANCIS OF PAOLA

HERMIT

Collect

Deus, humilium celsitudo, qui beatum Franciscum sanctorum tuorum gloria sublimasti, tribue, quaesumus, ut, eius meritis et exemplo, promissa humilibus praemia feliciter consequamur. Per Dominum.

God our Father, you are the exaltation of the lowly. You raised up Saint Francis of Paola by giving him the glory of your saints; through his merits and example, please grant that we may joyfully attain the rewards you have promised to the humble of heart. We ask this....

Prayer over the Gifts and Prayer after Communion:
Cf. Common of Holy Men and Women (for Religious), p. 211.

APRIL 4
SAINT ISIDORE

BISHOP AND DOCTOR OF THE CHURCH

Collect

Exaudi, quaesumus, Domine, preces nostras, quas in beati Isidori commemoratione deferimus, ut Ecclesia tua eius intercessionibus adiuvetur, cuius caelestibus instruitur disciplinis. Per Dominum.

Lord, we ask you to hear the prayers which we offer in memory of Saint Isidore. Your Church is instructed by his heavenly teachings; may it also be aided by his intercession. We ask this....

Prayer over the Gifts and Prayer after Communion:
*Cf. Common of Pastors (for a Bishop), p. 199
or
Common of Doctors of the Church, p. 205.*

APRIL 5
SAINT VINCENT FERRER

PRIEST

Collect

Deus, qui beatum Vincentium presbyterum ministrum praedicationis evangelicae suscitasti, praesta, quaesumus, ut, quem venturum iudicem nuntiavit in terris, beati videamus regnantem in caelis. Per Dominum.

God our Father, you raised up your priest Saint Vincent Ferrer for the ministry of preaching the Gospel. Please grant that we may joyfully see reigning in heaven the One whom Saint Vincent proclaimed to be coming as our judge on earth. We ask this....

Prayer over the Gifts and Prayer after Communion:

Cf. Common of Pastors (for Missionaries), p. 203, or Common of Holy Men and Women (for Religious), p. 211.

APRIL 7
SAINT JOHN BAPTIST DE LA SALLE

PRIEST

Collect

Deus, qui ad christianam iuventutem educandam beatum Ioannem Baptistam elegisti, excita in Ecclesia tua institutores, qui humanae et christianae iuvenum disciplinae toto corde sese devoveant. Per Dominum.

God our Father, you chose Saint John Baptist de la Salle to educate Christian youth. Raise up teachers within your Church who will wholeheartedly devote themselves to the human and Christian training of young people. We ask this....

Prayer over the Gifts and Prayer after Communion:

Cf. Common of Pastors, p. 200, or Common of Holy Men and Women (for Teachers), p. 213.

APRIL 11
SAINT STANISLAUS

BISHOP AND MARTYR

Collect

Deus, pro cuius honore beatus episcopus Stanislaus gladiis persecutorum occubuit, praesta, quaesumus, ut fortes in fide usque ad mortem perseverare valeamus. Per Dominum.

God our Father, for your honor your bishop Saint Stanislaus fell by the swords of persecutors. Please grant that we may be able to remain firm in our faith until we die. We ask this....

Prayer over the Gifts and Prayer after Communion:

Cf. Common of Martyrs, p. 193 or p. 196, or Common of Pastors (for a Bishop), p. 199.

APRIL 13
SAINT MARTIN I

POPE AND MARTYR

Collect

Da nobis, quaesumus, omnipotens Deus, adversa mundi invicta mentis constantia tolerare, qui beatum Martinum papam et martyrem nec minis terreri nec poenis passus es superari. Per Dominum.

Almighty God, you did not allow Saint Martin, your pope and martyr, to be terrified by threats or to be overcome by sufferings. Please grant that we too may bear the opposition of the world with firm hearts. We ask this....

Prayer over the Gifts and Prayer after Communion:
Cf. Common of Martyrs, p. 193 or p. 196, or Common of Pastors (for a Pope), p. 198.

APRIL 21
SAINT ANSELM

BISHOP AND DOCTOR OF THE CHURCH

Collect

Deus, qui beato Anselmo episcopo dedisti alta sapientiae tuae quaerere et docere, fac ita fidem tuam intellectui nostro subvenire, ut cordi dulce sapiant quae nobis credenda mandasti. Per Dominum.

God our Father, you granted your bishop Saint Anselm the gift of pursuing and teaching the very heights of your own wisdom. Make our faith in you assist our intellect in such a way that together they may savor the sweet solace for the heart that is the truths you have commanded us to believe. We ask this....

Prayer over the Gifts and Prayer after Communion:
Cf. Common of Pastors (for a Bishop), p.199, or Common of Doctors of the Church, p. 205, or Common of Holy Men and Women (for Religious), p. 211.

APRIL 23
SAINT GEORGE

MARTYR

Collect

Magnificantes, Domine, potentiam tuam, supplices exoramus, ut, sicut sanctus Georgius dominicae fuit passionis imitator, ita sit fragilitatis nostrae promptus adiutor. Per Dominum.

Extolling your power, Lord, we humbly pray that, in the same fashion as he imitated the sufferings and death of Christ, Saint George may be swift to assist our weakness. We ask this....

Prayer over the Gifts and Prayer after Communion:
Cf. Common of Martyrs, p. 193 or p. 196.

APRIL 24
SAINT FIDELIS OF SIGMARINGEN

PRIEST AND MARTYR

Collect

Deus, qui beatum Fidelem, amore tuo succensum, in fidei propagatione martyrii palma decorare dignatus es, ipso interveniente, concede, ut, in caritate fundati, cum illo resurrectionis Christi virtutem cognoscere mereamur. Per Dominum.

God our Father, you saw fit to crown Saint Fidelis of Sigmaringen with the palm of martyrdom while he was inflamed with love of you and so was working to spread the faith. Through his intercession grant that we may be gounded in love and, along with him, be privileged to understand the power of the resurrection of Christ. We ask this....

Prayer over the Gifts and Prayer after Communion:
Cf. Common of Martyrs, p. 193 or p. 196, or Common of Pastors, p. 200.

APRIL 25
SAINT MARK

EVANGELIST

Collect

Deus, qui beatum Marcum evangelistam tuum evangelicae praedicationis gratia sublimasti, tribue, quaesumus, eius nos eruditione ita proficere, ut vestigia Christi fideliter sequamur. Per Dominum.

God our Father, you greatly honored your evangelist Saint Mark by giving him the grace to proclaim the Gospel. Please grant that we may so come to understand what he taught that we may faithfully follow the footsteps of Christ. We ask this....

Prayer over the Gifts

Gloriam beati Marci venerantes, tibi, Domine, hostias laudis offerimus, teque suppliciter deprecamur, ut evangelica praedicatio in Ecclesia tua iugiter perseveret. Per Christum.

Lord, as we honor the glorious memory of Saint Mark and offer you our sacrifice of praise, we humbly ask that the Gospel may ever continue to be proclaimed within your Church. We ask this....

Prayer after Communion

Praesta, quaesumus, omnipotens Deus, ut, quod de sancto altari tuo accepimus, nos sanctificet, et in fide Evangelii, quod beatus Marcus praedicavit, fortes efficiat. Per Christum.

Almighty God, please grant that what we have received from your sacred altar may make us holy; and may it make us strong in our belief in the Gospel which Saint Mark proclaimed. We ask this....

APRIL 28
SAINT PETER CHANEL

PRIEST AND MARTYR

Collect

Deus, qui ad dilatandam Ecclesiam tuam beatum Petrum martyrio coronasti, da nobis, in his paschalibus gaudiis, ita Christi mortui et resurgentis mysteria frequentare, ut novitatis vitae testes esse mereamur. Per Dominum.

God our Father, you crowned Saint Peter Chanel with martyrdom in order to increase your Church. As we celebrate these paschal joys, grant that we may take part in the mysteries of Christ's death and resurrection in such a way that we may be privileged to be witnesses to his new life. We ask this....

Prayer over the Gifts and Prayer after Communion:
Cf. Common of Martyrs, p. 196, or Common of Pastors (for Missionaries), p. 203.

APRIL 29
SAINT CATHERINE OF SIENA

VIRGIN AND DOCTOR OF THE CHURCH

Collect

Deus, qui beatam Catharinam in contemplatione dominicae passionis et in Ecclesiae tuae servitio divino amore flagrare fecisti, ipsius intercessione concede, ut populus tuus, Christi mysterio sociatus, in eius gloriae revelatione semper exsultet. Per Dominum.

God our Father, you set Saint Catherine of Sienna on fire with divine love in contemplating the Lord's passion and in serving the Church. Your people are together joined to the mystery of Christ; through Saint Catherine's intercession, grant that they may always rejoice in the revelation of his glory. We ask this....

Prayer over the Gifts

Suscipe, Domine, quam in beatae Catharinae commemoratione offerimus hostiam salutarem, ut, illius monitis eruditi, tibi vero Deo fereventius gratias agere valeamus. Per Christum.

Lord, receive the saving offering which we bring to you in memory of Saint Catherine, so that we may be taught by her counsels and be able to give more fervent thanks to you, the true God. We ask this....

Prayer after Communion

Aeternitatem nobis, Domine, conferat, qua pasti sumus, mensa caelestis, quae beatae Catherinae vitam etiam aluit temporalem. Per Christum.

Lord, may the heavenly banquet with which we are nourished bestow eternal life upon us, just as it sustained even the earthly life of Saint Catherine. We ask this....

APRIL 30
SAINT PIUS V

POPE

Collect

Deus, qui in Ecclesia tua beatum Pium papam ad fidem tuendam ac te dignius colendum providus excitasti, da nobis, ipso intercedente, vivida fide ac fructuosa caritate mysteriorum tuorum esse participes. Per Dominum.

God our Father, in your provident care you raised up Pope Saint Pius V within your Church to guard the faith and to foster a more fitting worship of your divine majesty. Through his intercessio3n grant that we may participate in your holy mysteries with a strong faith and an effective love. We ask this....

Prayer over the Gifts and Prayer after Communion:
Cf. Common of Pastors (for a Pope), p. 198.

MAY 1
SAINT JOSEPH THE WORKER

Collect

Rerum conditor, Deus, qui legem laboris humano generi statuisti, concede propitius, ut, Sancti Ioseph exemplo et patrocinio, opera perficiamus quae praecipis, et praemia consequamur quae promittis. Per Dominum.

God our Father, creator of all things, you decreed the law of work for the human race. Through the example and prayers of Saint Joseph, grant in your mercy that we may do the works which you command and attain the reward which you promise. We ask this....

Prayer over the Gifts

Fons totius misericordiae, Deus, respice ad munera nostra, quae in commemoratione beati Ioseph maiestati tuae deferimus, et concede propitius, ut oblata dona fiant praesidia supplicantium. Per Christum.

God our Father, source of all mercy, look upon the offerings which we bring to your divine majesty as we honor Saint Joseph. In your kindness, grant that the gifts we present may become the strength of those who seek your protection. We ask this....

Prayer after Communion

Caelestibus, Domine, pasti deliciis, supplices te rogamus, ut, exemplo beati Ioseph, caritatis tuae in cordibus nostris testimonia gerentes, perpetuae pacis fructu iugiter perfruamur. Per Christum.

Lord, we have been fed with your heavenly gifts. Through the example of Saint Joseph, we humbly ask that we may bear witness to your love in our hearts and may always enjoy the benefits of everlasting peace. We ask this....

MAY 2
SAINT ATHANASIUS
BISHOP AND DOCTOR OF THE CHURCH

Collect

Omnipotens sempiterne Deus, qui beatum Athanasium episcopum divinitatis Filii tui propugnatorem eximium suscitasti, concede propitius, ut, eius doctrina et protectione gaudentes, in tui cognitione et amore sine intermissione crescamus. Per Dominum.

Almighty and eternal God, you raised up your bishop Saint Athanasius as an outstanding defender of your Son's divinity. In your mercy, grant that we may rejoice in his teaching and in his protection, and may constantly grow in our knowledge and love of you. We ask this....

Prayer over the Gifts

Respice, Domine, munera quae tibi in commemoratione sancti Athanasii perhibemus, eiusque fidem profitentibus illibatam tuae testificatio veritatis prosit ad salutem. Per Christum.

Lord, look upon the gifts that we present you in memory of Saint Athanasius. May his proclamation of your truth lead to the salvation of those who profess his untainted faith. We ask this....

Prayer after Communion

Da nobis, quaesumus, omnipotens Deus, ut Unigeniti tui vera divinitas, quam cum beato Athanasio firmiter confitemur, per hoc sacramentum vivificet nos semper et muniat. Per Christum.

Almighty God, please grant that the true divinity of your only Son, which we along with Saint Athanasius firmly profess, may always animate and protect us through the sacrament we have received. We ask this....

MAY 3
SAINTS PHILIP AND JAMES

APOSTLES

Collect

Deus, qui nos annua apostolorum Philippi et Iacobi festivitate laetificas, da nobis, ipsorum precibus, in Unigeniti tui passione et resurrectione consortium, ut ad perpetuam tui visionem pervenire mereamur. Per Dominum.

God our Father, you give us joy by the annual celebration of the feast of your apostles Philip and James. Through their prayers, grant that we may share in the passion and resurrection of your only Son, and so be privileged to come to the eternal vision of your divine majesty. We ask this....

Prayer over the Gifts

Suscipe, Domine, munera quae pro apostolorum Philippi et Iacobi festivitate deferimus, et immaculatam nobis religionem mundamque largire. Per Christum.

Lord, receive the gifts which we bring in honor of the feast of your apostles Philip and James, and grant that our service of you may be pure and spotless. We ask this....

Prayer after Communion

Purifica, quaesumus, Domine, mentes nostras per haec sancta quae sumpsimus, ut, cum apostolis Philippo et Iacobo te in Filio contemplantes, vitam habere mereamur aeternam. Per Christum.

Lord, please cleanse our hearts through the sacred communion we have received, so that, in company with your apostles Philip and James, we may contemplate you in your Son, and thus be privileged to possess eternal life. We ask this....

MAY 12
SAINTS NEREUS AND ACHILLEUS

MARTYRS

SAINT PANCRATIUS

MARTYR

Collect
(Sts. Nereus and Achilleus)

Praesta, quaesumus, omnipotens Deus, ut, qui gloriosos martyres Nereum et Achilleum fortes in sua confessione cognovimus, pios apud te in nostra intercessione sentiamus. Per Dominum.

Almighty God, we have come to know blessed Nereus and Achilleus as martyrs steadfast in their profession of faith. Please grant that we may also experience them as constant in their intercession for us in your presence. We ask this....

Prayer over the Gifts and Prayer after Communion:
Cf. Common of Martyrs, p. 194.

Collect
(St. Pancratius)

Laetetur Ecclesia tua, Deus, beati Pancratii martyris confisa suffragiis, atque, eius precibus gloriosis, et devota permaneat, et secura consistat. Per Dominum.

God our Father, may your Church rejoice in its reliance on the patronage of your martyr Saint Pancratius. By his holy prayers, may it remain steadfast and live without fear. We ask this....

*Prayer over the Gifts and
Prayer after Communion:*
Cf. *Common of Martyrs, p. 196.*

MAY 14
SAINT MATTHIAS

APOSTLE

Collect

Deus, qui beatum Matthiam Apostolorum collegio sociasti, eius nobis interventione concede, ut, dilectionis tuae sorte gaudentes, cum electis numerari mereamur. Per Dominum.

God our Father, you joined Saint Matthias to the company of the Apostles. Through his intercession grant that we too may rejoice in the selection that your love makes, and may be privileged to be numbered among your elect. We ask this....

Prayer over the Gifts

Ecclesiae tuae, Domine, munera pro festo beati Matthiae reverenter oblata suscipias, et per ea nos gratiae tuae virtute confirma. Per Christum.

Lord, receive the gifts which your Church reverently offers on this feast of Saint Matthias. Through them, strengthen us by the power of your grace. We ask this....

Prayer after Communion

Familiam tuam, Domine, divinis ne cesses replere muneribus, ut, beato Matthia pro nobis intercedente, in partem sortis sanctorum in lumine nos digneris accipere. Per Christum.

Lord, do not cease to fill your chosen people with heavenly gifts. Through the intercession of Saint Matthias on our behalf, may you see fit to allot us a share in the reward of the saints in glory. We ask this....

MAY 18
SAINT JOHN I

POPE AND MARTYR

Collect

Deus, fidelium remunerator animarum, qui hunc diem beati Ioannis papae martyrio consecrasti, exaudi preces populi tui, et praesta, ut, qui eius merita veneramur, fidei constantiam imitemur. Per Dominum.

God our Father, you reward your faithful people, and you have sanctified this day by the martyrdom of your pope, Saint John I. Hear the prayers of your people and grant that, as we honor his merits, we may also imitate his steadfast faith. We ask this....

*Prayer over the Gifts and
Prayer after Communion:*
Cf. *Common of Martyrs, p. 196, or Common of Pastors (for a Pope), p. 198.*

MAY 20
SAINT BERNARDINE
OF SIENA

PRIEST

Collect

Deus, qui beato Bernadino presbytero sancti nominis Iesu amorem eximium tribuisti, eius meritis precibusque concede, ut Spiritus nos semper tuae dilectionis accendat. Per Dominum.

God our Father, you gave your priest Saint Bernadine of Sienna a great love for the holy name of Jesus. Through his merits and prayers grant that we may ever be inflamed with the Spirit of your love. We ask this....

*Prayer over the Gifts and
Prayer after Communion:*

Cf. Common of Pastors (for Missionaries), p. 203, or Common of Holy Men and Women (for Religious), p. 211.

MAY 25

VENERABLE BEDE
PRIEST AND DOCTOR OF THE CHURCH

SAINT GREGORY VII
POPE

SAINT MARY MAGDALENE DE PAZZI
VIRGIN

Collect (Venerable Bede)

Deus, qui Ecclesiam tuam beati Bedae presbyteri eruditione clarificas, famulis tuis concede propitius, et eius semper illustrari sapientia, et meritis adiuvari. Per Dominum.

God our Father, you continue to make your Church renowned by the learning of your priest Saint Bede. In your mercy, grant that your faithful people may always be enlightened by his wisdom and aided by his merits. We ask this....

*Prayer over the Gifts and
Prayer after Communion:*
Cf. Common of Doctors of the Church, p. 205,
or
Common of Holy Men and Women (for Religious), p. 211.

Collect (St. Gregory VII)

Da Ecclesiae tuae, quaesumus, Domine, spiritum fortitudinis zelumque iustitiae, quibus beatum Gregorium papam clarescere voluisti, ut, iniquitatem reprobans, quaecumque recta sunt libera exerceat caritate. Per Dominum.

Lord, you willed that your pope Saint Gregory VII should be outstanding for his spirit of courage and his thirst for justice. Please grant these virtues to your Church as well, so that it may shun evil and do whatever is right with freedom and love. We ask this....

*Prayer over the Gifts and
Prayer after Communion:*
Cf. Common of Pastors (for a Pope), p. 198.

*Collect
(Saint Mary Magdalene de Pazzi)*

Deus, virginitatis amator, qui beatam Mariam Magdalenam virginem, tuo amore succensam, donis caelestibus decorasti, da ut, quam hodie veneramur, eius puritatis caritatisque imitemur exempla. Per Dominum.

God our Father, you love virginity, and you adorned your virgin Saint Mary Magdalene de Pazzi with heavenly gifts because of her great love for you. Grant that we may imitate the example of the purity and love of this saint whom we honor today. We ask this....

*Prayer over the Gifts and
Prayer after Communion:*
Cf. Common of Virgins, p. 206.

MAY 26
SAINT PHILIP NERI

PRIEST

Collect

Deus, qui fideles tibi servos sanctitatis gloria sublimare non desistis, concede propitius, ut illo nos igne Spiritus Sanctus inflammet, quo beati Philippi cor mirabiliter penetravit. Per Dominum.

God our Father, you never cease to raise your faithful servants to great heights of holiness. In your mercy, grant that the Holy Spirit may set us on fire with that flame of love with which he so wonderfully permeated the heart of Saint Philip Neri. We ask this....

Prayer over the Gifts

Hostiam tibi laudis offerentes, quaesumus, Domine, ut, beati Philippi exemplo, ad tui nominis gloriam proximique servitium hilares nos semper praestemus. Per Christum.

Lord, we bring you our sacrifice of praise. Through the example of Saint Philip, please grant that we may offer ourselves joyfully for the glory of your name and for the service of our neighbor. We ask this....

Prayer after Communion

Caelestibus, Domine, pasti deliciis, quaesumus, ut, beati Philippi imitatione, semper eadem, per quae veraciter vivimus, appetamus. Per Christum.

Lord, we have been nourished with your heavenly food, and we ask that, in imitation of Saint Philip, we may ever seek those things which give us true life. We ask this....

MAY 27
SAINT AUGUSTINE OF CANTERBURY

BISHOP

Collect

Deus, qui beati Augustini episcopi praedicatione Anglorum gentes ad Evangelium perduxisti, tribue, quaesumus, ut eius laborum fructus in Ecclesia tua perenni fecunditate persistant. Per Dominum.

God our Father, through the preaching of your bishop Saint Augustine of Canterbury you led the English people to your Gospel. Please grant that the results of his labors may be continually fruitful within your Church. We ask this....

Prayer over the Gifts and Prayer after Communion:

Cf. Common of Pastors (for Missionaries), p.203, or Common of Pastors (for Bishops), p.199.

MAY 31
VISITATION

Collect

Omnipotens sempiterne Deus, qui beatam Virginem Mariam, Filium tuum gestantem, ad visitandam Elizabeth inspirasti, praesta, quaesumus, ut, afflanti Spiritui obsequentes, cum ipsa te semper magnificare possimus. Per Dominum.

Almighty and eternal God, while the Blessed Virgin Mary bore your Son, you inspired her to visit Saint Elizabeth. Please grant that we may be obedient to the Spirit who inspires us, and, in the company of Mary, be enabled to praise you unceasingly. We ask this....

Prayer over the Gifts

Maiestati tuae, Domine, hoc nostrum gratum sit sacrificium salutare, sicut beatissimae Unigeniti tui Matris habuisti acceptabilem caritatem. Per Christum.

Lord, you judged acceptable the love of the holy Mother of your only Son. In the same way, may this saving sacrifice of ours be pleasing to your divine majesty. We ask this....

Prayer after Communion

Magnificet te, Deus, Ecclesia tua qui tuis fecisti magna fidelibus, et, quem latentem beatus Ioannes cum exsultatione praesensit, eundem semper viventem cum laetitia in hoc percipiat sacramento. Per Christum.

God our Father, may your Church glorify you, for you have performed marvelous deeds for your faithful people. Saint John the Baptist joyfully acknowledged Christ, even hidden as he was in Mary's womb. In this sacrament, may the Church rejoice in recognizing that same ever-living Lord. We ask this....

SATURDAY AFTER THE SECOND SUNDAY AFTER PENTECOST: IMMACULATE HEART OF MARY

Collect

Deus, qui in corde beatae Mariae Virginis dignum Sancti Spiritus habitaculum praeparasti, concede propitius, ut, eiusdem Virginis intercessione, tuae gloriae templum inveniri mereamur. Per Christum.

God our Father, in the heart of the Blessed Virgin Mary you prepared a worthy dwelling place for the Holy Spirit. In your mercy and through the intercession of the same holy Virgin, grant that we may be privileged to be found to be a temple of your glory. We ask this....

Prayer over the Gifts

Preces, Domine, tuorum respice oblationesque fidelium in beatae Mariae Dei Genetricis commemoratione delatas, ut tibi gratae sint, et nobis conferant tuae propitiationis auxilium. Per Christum.

Lord, look upon the prayers and offerings that your faithful people bring to you in remembrance of Blessed Mary, the Mother of God. May they be acceptable to you and bring us your forgiving assistance. We ask this....

Prayer after Communion

Redemptionis aeternae participes effecti, quaesumus, Domine, ut, qui Genetricis Filii tui memoriam agimus, et de gratiae tuae plenitudine gloriemur, et salvationis continuum sentiamus augmentum. Per Christum.

Lord, we have been granted a share in your eternal redemption. As we commemorate the Mother of your Son, we ask that we may rejoice in the fullness of your grace and experience a continual growth in the work of salvation within us. We ask this....

JUNE 1
SAINT JUSTIN

MARTYR

Collect

Deus, qui per stultitiam crucis eminentem Iesu Christi scientiam beatum Iustinum martyrem mirabiliter docuisti, eius nobis intercessione concede, ut, errorum circumventione depulsa, fidei firmitatem consequamur. Per Dominum.

God our Father, through the foolishness of the Cross you marvelously instructed your martyr Saint Justin in the profound wisdom of Jesus Christ. Through your saint's intercession, grant that we may shun the fraud of error and attain an unshakeable faith. We ask this....

Prayer over the Gifts

Concede nobis, quaesumus, Domine, haec digne frequentare mysteria, quae beatus Iustinus strenua virtute defendit. Per Christum.

Lord, please grant that we may worthily take part in these mysteries, which Saint Justin defended with such vigorous courage. We ask this....

Prayer after Communion

Caelesti alimonia refecti, supplices te, Domine, deprecamur, ut, beati Iustini martyris monitis obsequentes, de acceptis donis semper in gratiarum actione maneamus. Per Christum.

Lord, we have been refreshed with your heavenly food, and we humbly ask that we may follow the counsels of your martyr Saint Justin and ever be grateful for the gifts we have received. We ask this....

JUNE 2
SAINTS MARCELLINUS AND PETER

MARTYRS

Collect

Deus, qui nos sanctorum martyrum Marcellini et Petri confessione gloriosa circumdas et protegis, praesta nobis ex eorum imitatione proficere, et oratione fulciri. Per Dominum.

God our Father, you guard and protect us by the magnificent profession of faith of your holy martyrs Marcellinus and Peter. Grant that we may benefit by imitating them and may be supported by their prayers. We ask this....

Prayer over the Gifts and Prayer after Communion:
Cf. Common of Martyrs, p. 190.

JUNE 3
SAINTS CHARLES LWANGA AND COMPANIONS

MARTYRS

Collect

Deus, qui sanguinem martyrum semen christianorum esse fecisti, concede propitius, ut tuae ager Ecclesiae, qui est beatorum Caroli eiusque sociorum cruore rigatus, in amplam tibi messem iugiter fecundetur. Per Dominum.

God our Father, you turned the blood of martyrs into the seed of Christians. The field that is your Church was watered by the blood of Saints Charles Lwanga and his companions; in your mercy, grant that it may always bring forth a rich harvest for you. We ask this....

Prayer over the Gifts

Hostias tibi, Domine, offerimus, suppliciter exorantes, ut, sicut beatis martyribus magis mori quam peccare tribuisti, ita nos facias, tibi soli deditos, altari tuo ministrare. Per Christum.

Lord, we bring you our offerings and our humble prayers. You granted your holy martyrs the grace to die rather than sin. May you ensure that we are dedicated solely to you in our service at your altar. We ask this....

Prayer after Communion

Sumpsimus, Domine, divina sacramenta, sanctorum martyrum tuorum victoriam recolentes: quaesumus, ut, quae ipsis ad perferenda supplicia contulerunt, ea nobis inter adversa praebeant fidei caritatisque constantiam. Per Christum.

Lord, we have received your heavenly sacraments while recalling the victory of your holy martyrs. These sacraments enabled them to endure their sufferings; please grant that they may also provide us with a firm faith and love in the midst of the adversities that we endure. We ask this....

JUNE 5
SAINT BONIFACE

BISHOP AND MARTYR

Collect

Sanctus martyr, Domine, Bonifatius pro nobis interventor exsistat, ut fidem, quam ore docuit et sanguine consignavit, firmiter teneamus, et operibus profiteamur confidenter. Per Dominum.

Lord, may your holy martyr Boniface intercede for us, so that our hearts may firmly retain and our deeds confidently profess the faith that he taught by his words and sealed with his blood. We ask this....

Prayer over the Gifts and Prayer after Communion:
Cf. Common of Martyrs, p. 193, or Common of Pastors (for Missionaries), p. 203.

JUNE 6
SAINT NORBERT

BISHOP

Collect

Deus, qui beatum Norbertum episcopum Ecclesiae tuae oratione ac pastorali zelo ministrum eximium effecisti, praesta, quaesumus, ut, eius interveniente suffragio, fidelium grex pastores iuxta cor tuum et salutaria pascua semper inveniat. Per Dominum.

God our Father, you made your bishop Saint Norbert an outstanding servant of your Church in his prayer and pastoral care. Through his intercession, please grant that your faithful flock may always find shepherds modeled after your own heart and pastures that will lead them to salvation. We ask this....

Prayer over the Gifts and Prayer after Communion:
Cf. Common of Pastors (for Bishops), p. 199, or Common of Holy Men and Women (for Religious), p. 211.

JUNE 9
SAINT EPHREM

DEACON AND DOCTOR OF THE CHURCH

Collect

Cordibus nostris, quaesumus, Domine, Spiritum Sanctum benignus infunde, cuius afflatu beatus Ephraem diaconus in tuis mysteriis decantandis exsultavit, eiusque virtute tibi soli deserviit. Per Dominum.

Lord, in your kindness please pour forth your Holy Spirit into our hearts. By His inspiration your deacon Saint Ephraem delighted in proclaiming your mysteries in song, and by His power the saint devoted himself to you alone. We ask this....

Prayer over the Gifts and Prayer after Communion:

Cf. *Common of Doctors of the Church, p. 205.*

JUNE 11
SAINT BARNABAS

APOSTLE

Collect

Deus, qui beatum Barnabam, plenum fide et Spiritu Sancto, ad gentium conversionem segregare praecepisti, concede, ut Evangelium Christi, quod strenue praedicavit, ore et opere fideliter nuntietur. Per Dominum.

God our Father, you ordered Saint Barnabas, filled with faith and the Holy Spirit, to set himself apart for the conversion of the gentiles. Grant that the Gospel of Christ, which he tirelessly proclaimed, may be faithfully announced in both word and deed. We ask this....

Prayer over the Gifts

Oblata munera, quaesumus, Domine, tua benedictione sanctifica, quae, te donante, nos flamma tuae dilectionis accendant, per quam beatus Barnabas lumen Evangelii gentibus apportavit. Per Christum.

Lord, please bless the offerings we have brought and make them holy. They are your gift to us; may they set us on fire with the flame of your love, which drove Saint Barnabas to bring the light of the Gospel to the nations. We ask this....

Prayer after Communion

Aeternae pignus vitae capientes, te, Domine, humiliter imploramus, ut, quod pro beati Barnabae apostoli memoria in imagine gerimus sacramenti, manifesta perceptione sumamus. Per Christum.

Lord, we have received the pledge of eternal life. We have offered our gift in memory of your holy apostle Barnabas, and we humbly ask that we may perceive with clear understanding what we now offer under the appearance of a sacrament. We ask this....

JUNE 13
SAINT ANTHONY
OF PADUA

PRIEST AND DOCTOR
OF THE CHURCH

Collect

Omnipotens sempiterne Deus, qui populo tuo beatum Antonium praedicatorem insignem dedisti, eumque in necessitatibus intercessorem, concede, ut, eius auxilio, christianae vitae documenta sectantes, in omnibus adversitatibus te subvenientem sentiamus. Per Dominum.

Almighty and eternal God, you gave Saint Anthony of Padua to your people as an outstanding preacher as well as an advocate for their needs. Through his assistance, grant that we may follow his example of the Christian life and experience your help in every adversity. We ask this....

Prayer over the Gifts and Prayer after Communion:

Cf. *Common of Pastors, p. 200, or Common of Doctors of the Church, p. 205, or Common of Holy Men and Women (for Religious), p. 211.*

JUNE 19
SAINT ROMUALD

ABBOT

Collect

Deus, qui per beatum Romualdum in Ecclesia tua eremiticam vitam renovasti, concede, ut, nosmetipsos abnegantes et Christum sequentes, feliciter ad caelestia regna mereamur ascendere. Per Dominum.

God our Father, through Saint Romuald you renewed the life of the religious hermit within your Church. Grant that we may practice self-denial and follow Christ, and thus be privileged to attain the happiness of ascending into your heavenly kingdom. We ask this....

Prayer over the Gifts and Prayer after Communion:
Cf. Common of Holy Men and Women (for Religious), p. 211.

JUNE 21
SAINT ALOYSIUS GONZAGA

RELIGIOUS

Collect

Deus, caelestium auctor donorum, qui in beato Aloisio miram vitae innocentiam cum paenitentia sociasti, eius meritis et intercessione concede, ut, innocentem non secuti, paenitentem imitemur. Per Dominum.

God our Father, source of all heavenly gifts, in Saint Aloysius you joined a wonderous innocence to a life of penance. Through his merits and intercession, grant that we who have not followed him in his innocence may imitate him in his penance. We ask this....

Prayer over the Gifts

Caelesti convivio fac nos, Domine, exemplo sancti Aloisii, nuptiali veste semper indutos accumbere, ut ex huius participatione mysterii gratia tua divites efficiamur. Per Christum.

Lord, through this heavenly banquet and by the example of Saint Aloysius, make us always recline at your heavenly table, robed in wedding garments. By our sharing in this mystery may we be made rich in your grace. We ask this....

Prayer after Communion

Angelorum esca nutritos, fac nos, Domine, pura tibi conversatione servire, et, eius quem hodie colimus exemplo, in gratiarum semper actione manere. Per Christum.

Lord, we are nourished by the food of angels. Today we honor the memory of Saint Aloysius; following his example, may we always serve you with unsullied devotion and ever give grateful thanks to you. We ask this....

JUNE 22
SAINT PAULINUS OF NOLA

BISHOP

SAINTS JOHN FISHER AND THOMAS MORE

MARTYRS

Collect
(Saint Paulinus of Nola)

Deus, qui beatum Paulinum episcopum paupertatis amore et pastorali sollicitudine clarescere voluisti, concede propitius, ut, cuius merita celebramus, caritatis imitemur exempla. Per Dominum.

God our Father, you wished your bishop Saint Paulinus of Nola to be outstanding in his love for poverty and his care for your people. In your kindness, grant that we may imitate the charity of this saint whose good deeds we celebrate today. We ask this....

Prayer over the Gifts and Prayer after Communion:
Cf. Common of Pastors (for Bishops), p. 199.

Collect
(Sts. John Fisher and Thomas More)

Deus, qui verae fidei formam in martyrio consummasti, concede propitius, ut, sanctorum Ioannis et Thomae intercessione roborati, fidem, quam ore profitemur, testimonio vitae confirmemus. Per Dominum.

God our Father, you bring the true faith to perfection in martyrdom. In your mercy, grant that we may be strengthened by the intercession of Saints John Fisher and Thomas More; may we, by the testimony of our lives, affirm the faith that we profess in our words. We ask this....

Prayer over the Gifts and Prayer after Communion:
Cf. Common of Martyrs, p. 190.

JUNE 23
VIGIL OF SAINT JOHN THE BAPTIST

Collect

Praesta, quaesumus, omnipotens Deus, ut familia tua per viam salutis incedat, et, beati Ioannis Praecursoris hortamenta sectando, ad eum quem praedixit secura perveniat, Dominum nostrum Iesum Christum. Qui tecum vivit.

Almighty God, please grant that your faithful people may advance along the path to salvation. By following the counsels of the Precursor Saint John, may they come safely to Him whom Saint John foretold, our Lord Jesus Christ, who lives and reigns....

Prayer over the Gifts

Munera populi tui, Domine, propitius intende, in beati Ioannis Baptistae sollemnitate delata, et praesta, ut, quae mysterio gerimus, debitae servitutis actione sectemur. Per Christum.

Lord, in your kindness look upon the gifts that your people bring on this feast of Saint John the Baptist. Grant that we may serve you with fitting deeds, and so carry out what we celebrate here in mystery. We ask this....

Prayer after Communion

Sacris dapibus satiatos, Beati Ioannis Baptistae nos, Domine, praeclara comitetur oratio, et, quem Agnum nostra ablaturum crimina nuntiavit, ipsum

Filium tuum poscat nobis fore placatum. Qui vivit.

Lord, we have been filled with your sacred gifts, and we ask that the powerful prayers of Saint John the Baptist may be with us. He proclaimed that the Lamb of God would take away our sins; may he pray that that same Lamb of God, your Son, be pleased with us. We ask this....

JUNE 24
BIRTH OF SAINT JOHN THE BAPTIST

Collect

Deus, qui beatum Ioannem Baptistam suscitasti, ut perfectam plebem Christo Domino praepararet, da populis tuis spiritualium gratiam gaudiorum, et omnium fidelium mentes dirige in viam salutis et pacis. Per Dominum.

God our Father, you raised up Saint John the Baptist in order to make ready a perfect people for Christ the Lord. Grant to your people the grace of spiritual joy, and direct the hearts of all your faithful ones into the way of salvation and peace. We ask this....

Prayer over the Gifts

Tua, Domine, muneribus altaria cumulamus, illius nativitatem honore debito celebrantes, qui Salvatorem mundi et cecinit affaturum, et adesse monstravit. Qui vivit.

Lord, we fill your altar with our gifts as we pay due honor to the birth of Saint John the Baptist. He foretold that the Savior of the World was coming, and pointed him out when he came. We make our prayer through....

Prayer after Communion

Caelestis Agni convivio refecti, quaesumus, Domine, ut Ecclesia tua, sumens de beati Ioannis Baptistae generatione laetitiam, quem ille praenuntiavit venturum, suae regenerationis cognoscat auctorem. Per Christum.

Lord, we have been refreshed by the banquet of the Lamb of God. Your Church rejoices in the birth of Saint John the Baptist; we ask that it may recognize the author of its own new life in him whom John foretold would come. We ask this....

JUNE 27
SAINT CYRIL OF ALEXANDRIA

BISHOP AND DOCTOR OF THE CHURCH

Collect

Deus, qui beatum Cyrillum episcopum divinae maternitatis beatissimae Virginis Mariae assertorem invictum effecisti, concede, ut, qui vere eam Genetricem Dei credimus, per incarnationem Christi Filii tui salvemur. Qui tecum vivit et regnat....

God our Father, you made your bishop Saint Cyril of Alexandria a staunch defender of the sacred motherhood of the Blessed Virgin Mary. Grant that we who believe that she is truly the Mother of God may come to salvation through the incarnation of Christ your Son, who lives and reigns....

Prayer over the Gifts and Prayer after Communion:
Cf. Common of Pastors (for Bishops), p. 199,
or
Common of Doctors of the Church, p. 205.

JUNE 28
SAINT IRENAEUS

BISHOP AND MARTYR

Collect

Deus, qui beato Irenaeo episcopo tribuisti, ut veritatem doctrinae pacemque Ecclesiae feliciter confirmaret, concede, quaesumus, eius intercessione, ut nos, fide et caritate renovati, ad unitatem concordiamque fovendam semper simus intenti. Per Dominum.

God our Father, you gave your bishop Saint Irenaeus the happy gift of strengthening both true doctrine and tranquillity within the Church. Through his intercession, please grant that we too, renewed in our own faith and love, may always strive to foster unity and harmony. We ask this....

Prayer over the Gifts

Gloriam tibi, Domine, conferat sacrificium, quod in natali beati Irenaei tibi laetanter offerimus, et praebeat nobis diligere veritatem, ut et inviolatam Ecclesiae fidem teneamus, et stabilem unitatem. Per Christum.

Lord, may this sacrifice, which we joyfully offer you on the feast of Saint Irenaeus, give glory to you and gain for us a love of truth, so that we may retain the full purity of the Church's faith and its unshakeable unity. We ask this....

Prayer after Communion

Per haec sacra mysteria, quaesumus, Domine, da nobis fidei miseratus augmentum, ut, quae sanctum Irenaeum episcopum usque ad mortem retenta glorificat, nos etiam iustificet veraciter hanc sequentes. Per Christum.

Lord, through these sacred mysteries, please have pity on us and grant us an increase in faith. Holding to the faith firmly until death brought your bishop Saint Irenaeus eternal glory; may that same faith bring us to salvation as we live it in truth. We ask this....

JUNE 28
(EVENING)

VIGIL OF SAINTS
PETER AND PAUL

Collect

Da nobis, quaesumus, Domine Deus noster, beatorum apostolorum Petri et Pauli intercessionibus sublevari, ut per quos Ecclesiae tuae superni muneris rudimenta donasti, per eos subsidia perpetuae salutis impendas. Per Dominum.

Lord our God, please grant that we may be aided by the intercession of your holy apostles Peter and Paul. Through them, grant us help on our way to eternal life, just as you gave your Church the beginnings of your heavenly gift through them. We ask this....

Prayer over the Gifts

Munera, Domine, tuis altaribus adhibemus, de beatorum apostolorum Petri et Pauli sollemnitatibus gloriantes, ut quantum sumus de nostro merito formidantes, tantum de tua benignitate gloriemur salvandi. Per Christum.

Lord, we bring our gifts to your altar as we joyfully celebrate the feast of your holy apostles Peter and Paul. From your gracious desire to bring us to salvation may we derive a joyous hope as intense as the dread we feel at what we deserve through our own merits. We ask this....

Prayer after Communion

Caelestibus sacramentis, quaesumus, Domine, fideles tuos corrobora, quos Apostolorum doctrina illuminasti. Per Christum.

Lord, by means of your heavenly sacraments please strengthen your people, whom you have enlightened by the teachings of the Apostles. We ask this....

JUNE 29
SAINTS PETER AND PAUL

APOSTLES

Collect

Deus, qui huius diei venerandam sanctamque laetitiam in apostolorum Petri et Pauli sollemnitate tribuisti, da Ecclesiae tuae eorum in omnibus sequi praeceptum, per quos religionis sumpsit exordium. Per Dominum.

God our Father, you have given us a reverent and holy joy in the celebration of today's feast of your apostles Peter and Paul. Grant that your Church may follow their teaching in all things, for it is through them that it received the beginnings of the faith. We ask this....

Prayer over the Gifts

Hostiam, Domine, quam nomini tuo exhibemus sacrandam, apostolica prosequatur oratio, nosque tibi reddat in sacrificio celebrando devotos. Per Christum.

Lord, may the prayers of your apostles accompany the sacrifice which we bring to be consecrated to your name, and may they make us devoted to you in the offering of that sacrifice. We ask this....

Prayer after Communion

Da nobis, Domine, hoc sacramento refectis, ita in Ecclesia conversari, ut, perseverantes in fractione panis Apostolorumque doctrina, cor unum simus et anima una, tua caritate firmati. Per Christum.

Lord, grant that we who have been renewed by this sacrament may so live in your Church that we remain constant in the breaking of the bread and the teaching of the Apostles. May we be strengthened by your love, and be of one heart and one mind. We ask this....

JUNE 30
FIRST MARTYRS OF THE CHURCH OF ROME

Collect

Deus, qui Romanae Ecclesiae copiosa primordia martyrum sanguine consecrasti, concede, quaesumus, ut firma virtute de tanti agone certaminis solidemur, et pia semper victoria gaudeamus. Per Dominum.

God our Father, you consecrated the fertile beginnings of the Church of Rome with the blood of martyrs. Please grant that we may be strengthened by the steadfast courage they showed in the midst of their great struggle, and always rejoice in their holy victory. We ask this....

Prayer over the Gifts and Prayer after Communion:
Cf. Common of Martyrs, p. 190.

JULY 3
SAINT THOMAS
APOSTLE

Collect

Da nobis, omnipotens Deus, beati Thomae apostoli festivitate gloriari, ut eius semper et patrociniis sublevemur, et vitam credentes habeamus in nomine eius, quem ipse Dominum agnovit, Iesum Christum Filium tuum. Qui tecum vivit.

Almighty God, grant that we may rejoice on this feast of your apostle Saint Thomas. May we always be aided by his intercession; as believers, may we possess life in the name of him whom Saint Thomas himself acknowledged as Lord: Jesus Christ, your Son, who lives and reigns with you....

Prayer over the Gifts

Debitum tibi, Domine, nostrae reddimus servitutis, suppliciter exorantes, ut in nobis tua munera tuearis, qui in confessione beati Thomae apostoli laudis tibi hostias immolamus. Per Christum.

Lord, we bring you the service that we owe you, and we offer you our sacrifice of praise as we recall the profession of faith your apostle Saint Thomas made. We humbly ask that you guard the gifts you have given us. We ask this....

Prayer after Communion

Deus, cuius Unigeniti Corpus in hoc veraciter suscipimus sacramento, praesta, quaesumus, ut, quem Dominum Deumque nostrum cum apostolo Thoma fide cognoscimus, ipsum opere quoque profiteamur et vita. Per Christum.

God our Father, we truly receive the Body of your only Son in this sacrament. In company with your apostle Saint Thomas we recognize him in faith as our Lord and our God. Please grant that we may also proclaim him in our lives and in our deeds. We ask this....

JULY 4
SAINT ELIZABETH
OF PORTUGAL

Collect

Deus, auctor pacis et amator caritatis, qui beatam Elizabeth mira dissidentes componendi gratia decorasti, da nobis, eius intercessione, pacis opera exercere, ut filii Dei nominari possimus. Per Dominum.

God our Father, you are the source of peace, and you love charity. You blessed Saint Elizabeth of Portugal with the marvelous gift of reconciling people who were in conflict with one another; through her intercession, grant that we may carry out the works of peace, so that we can be called children of God. We ask this....

Prayer over the Gifts and Prayer after Communion:
Cf. Common of Holy Men and Women (For Those Who Performed Works of Mercy), p. 213.

JULY 5
SAINT ANTHONY
MARY ZACCARIA
PRIEST

Collect

Da nobis, Domine, ut supereminentem Iesu Christi scientiam spiritu Pauli Apostoli prosequamur, qua beatus Antonius Maria eruditus verbum salutis in Ecclesia tua iugiter praedicavit. Per Dominum.

Lord, grant that, in imitation of the spirit of Paul the Apostle, we may earnestly pursue the surpassing knowledge of Jesus Christ, which taught Saint Anthony Mary Zaccaria ever to preach the word of salvation within your Church. We ask this....

Prayer over the Gifts and Prayer after Communion:
Cf. Common of Pastors, p. 200, or Common of Holy Men and Women (for Teachers), p. 213, or Common of Holy Men and Women (for Religious), p. 211.

JULY 6
SAINT MARIA GORETTI
VIRGIN AND MARTYR

Collect

Deus, innocentiae auctor et castitatis amator, qui famulae tuae Mariae iuvenili aetate martyrii gratiam contulisti, da nobis, quaesumus, eius intercessione, in tuis mandatis constantiam, qui dedisti certanti virgini coronam. Per Dominum.

God our Father, source of innocence and lover of chastity, you granted your servant Saint Maria Goretti the grace of martyrdom when she was but a young girl. You gave her the crown of victory in her struggle for her virginity; through her intercession, grant that we may be faithful in our struggle to keep your commandments. We ask this....

Prayer over the Gifts and Prayer after Communion:
Cf. Common of Martyrs, p. 193, or Common of Virgins, p. 206.

JULY 11
SAINT BENEDICT
ABBOT

Collect

Deus, qui beatum Benedictum abbatem in schola divini servitii praeclarum constituisti magistrum, tribue, quaesumus, ut, amori tuo nihil praeponentes, viam mandatorum tuorum dilatato corde curramus. Per Dominum.

God our Father, you made the holy abbot Saint Benedict an outstanding master in teaching men and women to serve you. Please grant that we may place nothing ahead of your love, and may run with uplifted spirits along the path of your commandments. We ask this....

Prayer over the Gifts

Haec sancta, Domine, quae in beati Benedicti celebritate deferimus, respice benignus, et praesta, ut nos, eius exemplis te quaerentes, unitatis in tuo servitio pacisque dona consequi mereamur. Per Christum.

Lord, in your kindness, look upon these holy gifts which we offer on this feast of Saint Benedict. Through the example he gave, grant that we may seek you always and be made worthy to attain the gifts of unity and peace in your service. We ask this....

Prayer after Communion

Accepto pignore vitae aeternae, te, Domine, suppliciter deprecamur, ut, beati Benedicti monitis obsequentes, operi tuo fideliter serviamus, et fratres ferventi diligamus caritate. Per Christum.

Lord, we have received the pledge of eternal life, and we humbly ask that, in obedience to the counsels of Saint Benedict, we may faithfully give ourselves to your work and may love our brothers and sisters with an ardent charity. We ask this....

JULY 13
SAINT HENRY

Collect

Deus, qui beatum Henricum, gratiae tuae ubertate praeventum, e terreni cura regiminis ad superna mirabiliter erexisti, eius nobis intercessione largire, ut inter mundanas varietates puris ad te mentibus festinemus. Per Dominum.

God our Father, with the riches of your grace you prepared Saint Henry ahead of time, and wondrously raised him from the cares of an earthly kingdom to the joys of a heavenly one. Through his intercession grant that, in the midst of earthly cares, we may hasten to you with pure hearts. We ask this....

Prayer over the Gifts and Prayer after Communion:
Cf. Common of Holy Men and Women, p. 208.

JULY 14
SAINT CAMILLUS DE LELLIS
PRIEST

Collect

Deus, qui sanctum Camillum presbyterum caritatis in infirmos singulari gratia decorasti, eius meritis, Spiritum nobis tuae dilectionis infunde, ut, tibi in fratribus servientes, ad te, hora exitus nostri, securi transire possimus. Per Dominum.

God our Father, you adorned your priest Saint Camillus de Lellis with the gift of a unique love for the sick. Through his merits, pour into us the Spirit of your love, so that we may serve you in our brothers and sisters and, at the hour of our death, be able to pass safely to you. We ask this....

Prayer over the Gifts and Prayer after Communion:
Cf. Common of Holy Men and Women (for Those Who Performed Works of Mercy), p. 213.

JULY 15
SAINT BONAVENTURE

BISHOP AND DOCTOR OF THE CHURCH

Collect

Da, quaesumus, omnipotens Deus, ut, beati Bonaventurae episcopi natalicia celebrantes, et ipsius proficiamus eruditione praeclara, et caritatis ardorem iugiter aemulemur. Per Dominum.

Almighty God, please grant that we who celebrate the heavenly birth of your bishop Saint Bonaventure may benefit from his outstanding wisdom and ever imitate the ardor of his love. We ask this....

Prayer over the Gifts and Prayer after Communion:
Cf. Common of Pastors (for Bishops), p. 199, or Common of Doctors of the Church, p. 205.

JULY 16
OUR LADY OF MOUNT CARMEL

Collect

Adiuvet nos, quaesumus, Domine, gloriosae Virginis Mariae intercessio veneranda, ut, eius muniti praesidiis, ad montem, qui Christus est, pervenire valeamus. Qui tecum vivit.

Lord, we ask that the holy intercession of the Blessed Virgin Mary may aid us, so that, guarded by her help, we may be able to arrive at the mountain which is Christ. We ask this....

Prayer over the Gifts and Prayer after Communion:
Cf. Common of the Blessed Virgin Mary, p. 186.

JULY 21
SAINT LAWRENCE OF BRINDISI

PRIEST AND DOCTOR OF THE CHURCH

Collect

Deus, qui pro nominis tui gloria et animarum salute beato Laurentio presbytero spiritum consilii et fortitudinis contulisti, da nobis, in eodem spiritu, et agenda cognoscere, et cognita, eius intercessione, perficere. Per Dominum.

God our Father, to foster the glory of your name and the salvation of souls you gave your priest Saint Lawrence of Brindisi the Spirit's gifts of counsel and fortitude. Grant that we, under the guidance of that same Spirit, may know what we should do and, through Saint Lawrence's intercession, may carry that knowledge into action. We ask this....

Prayer over the Gifts and Prayer after Communion:
Cf. Common of Pastors, p. 200, or Common of Doctors of the Church, p. 205.

JULY 22
SAINT MARY MAGDALENE

Collect

Deus, cuius Unigenitus Mariae Magdalenae ante omnes gaudium nuntiandum paschale commisit, praesta, quaesumus, ut, eius intercessione et exemplo, Christum viventem praedicemus, et in gloria tua regnantem videamus. Qui tecum vivit.

God our Father, your only Son entrusted to Mary Magdalene before anyone else the happy task of announcing the Easter joy. Through her intercession and example, please grant that we may proclaim that Christ lives, and see him reigning in your glorious kingdom. We ask this....

Prayer over the Gifts

Suscipe, Domine, munera in beatae Mariae Magdalenae commemoratione exhibita, cuius caritatis obsequium unigenitus Filius tuus clementer suscepit impensum. Qui vivit.

Lord God, your only Son mercifully saw fit to accept the service of Saint Mary Magdalene when she so lavishly expended it. Please receive the gifts which we offer to you in her memory. We ask this....

Prayer after Communion

Mysteriorum tuorum, Domine, sancta perceptio perseverantem illum nobis amorem infundat, quo beata Maria Magdalena Christo magistro suo indesinenter adhaesit. Qui vivit.

Lord, may our holy reception of your mysteries pour into us that lasting love which made Saint Mary Magdalene ceaselessly cling to Christ her teacher. We ask this....

JULY 23
SAINT BRIDGET

RELIGIOUS

Collect

Domine Deus noster, qui beatae Birgittae, Filii tui passionem meditanti, secreta caelestia revelasti, da nobis famulis tuis, in revelatione gloriae tuae gaudere laetantes. Per Dominum.

Lord our God, you made heavenly secrets known to Saint Bridget as she contemplated the passion of your Son. Grant that we, your faithful people, may rejoice with great happiness in the revelation of your glory. We ask this....

Prayer over the Gifts and Prayer after Communion:
Cf. *Common of Holy Men and Women (for Religious), p. 211.*

JULY 25
SAINT JAMES THE GREATER

APOSTLE

Collect

Omnipotens sempiterne Deus, qui Apostolorum tuorum primitias beati Iacobi sanguine dedicasti, da, quaesumus, Ecclesiae tuae ipsius confessione firmari, et iugiter patrociniis confoveri. Per Dominum.

Almighty and eternal God, you consecrated the beginnings of the work of your Apostles by the blood of Saint James. Please grant that your Church may be strengthened by his profession of faith and ever be fostered by his protection. We ask this....

Prayer over the Gifts

Munda nos, Domine, passionis Filii tui baptismate salutari, ut in festo sancti Iacobi, quem primum inter Apostolos calicis eius participem esse voluisti, beneplacitum tibi sacrificium offeramus. Per Christum.

Lord, wash us by the saving cleansing of your Son's passion. You willed that Saint James should be the first among the Apostles to partake of the Lord's cup of suffering. On this, his feast day, may we offer you a sacrifice that will please you. We ask this....

Prayer after Communion

Beati apostoli Iacobi, quaesumus, Domine, intercessione nos adiuva, pro cuius festivitate percepimus tua sancta laetantes. Per Christum.

Lord, please help us by the intercession of your holy apostle Saint James, on whose feast we have joyfully

JULY 26
SAINTS JOACHIM AND ANN
PARENTS OF THE BLESSED VIRGIN MARY

Collect

Domine, Deus patrum nostrorum, qui beatis Ioachim et Annae hanc gratiam contulisti ut ex eis incarnati Filii tui Mater nasceretur, utriusque precibus concede, ut salutem tuo promissam populo consequamur. Per Dominum.

Lord God of our Fathers, you granted to Saints Joachim and Ann the grace of being the parents of the mother of your incarnate Son. Through the prayers of both of these saints, grant that we may attain the salvation you have promised to your people. We ask this....

Prayer over the Gifts

Suscipe, quaesumus, Domine, munera nostrae devotionis, et praesta, ut eiusdem benedictionis, quam Abrahae et eius semini promisisti, mereamur esse participes. Per Christum.

Lord, please receive the gifts that mark our dedication to you, and grant that we may be privileged to share in the same blessing which you promised to Abraham and his descendants. We ask this....

Prayer after Communion

Deus, qui Unigenitum tuum ex hominibus nasci voluisti, ut homines ex te mirabili mysterio renascerentur, quaesumus, ut, quos filiorum pane satiasti, adoptionis spiritu benignitate tua sanctifices. Per Christum.

God our Father, you willed that your only Son should be born of the human race, so that humans might be reborn at your hands in mysterious and marvelous fashion. We ask that, in your kindness, you sanctify with the spirit of adoption those whom you have filled with the food that is reserved for sons and daughters. We ask this....

JULY 29
SAINT MARTHA

Collect

Omnipotens sempiterne Deus, cuius Filius in domo beatae Marthae dignatus est hospitari, da, quaesumus, ut, eiusdem intercessione, Christo in fratribus nostris fideliter ministrantes, in aede caelesti a te recipi mereamur. Per Dominum.

Almighty and eternal God, your Son saw fit to be a guest in the home of Saint Martha. Through her intercession, please grant that we may faithfully serve Christ in our brothers and sisters, and thus be privileged to be welcomed by you into your heavenly home. We ask this....

Prayer over the Gifts

In beata Martha te, Domine, mirabilem praedicantes, maiestatem tuam suppliciter exoramus, ut, sicut eius tibi gratum exstitit caritatis obsequium, sic nostrae servitutis accepta reddantur officia. Per Christum.

Lord, we proclaim your goodness as it was shown in Saint Martha. Her works of love proved pleasing to you; we humbly ask your divine majesty that the offering of our worship may also be acceptable to you. We ask this....

Prayer after Communion

Corporis et Sanguinis Unigeniti tui sacra perceptio, Domine, ab omnibus nos caducis rebus avertat, ut, exemplo beatae Marthae, valeamus tibi et sincera in terris caritate proficere, et tui perpetua in caelis visione gaudere. Per Christum.

Lord, may the sacred reception of the Body and Blood of your only Son turn us away from everything that is destined to perish. Through the example of Saint Martha, may we be able to serve you by growing in sincere charity on earth, and so rejoice in the unending vision of your glory in heaven. We ask this....

JULY 30
SAINT PETER CHRYSOLOGUS

BISHOP AND DOCTOR OF THE CHURCH

Collect

Deus, qui beatum Petrum Chrysologum episcopum Verbi tui incarnati praeconem egregium effecisti, eius nobis intercessione concede, ut tuae salutis mysteria et iugiter scrutemur in corde, et fideliter significemus in opere. Per Dominum.

God our Father, you made your bishop Saint Peter Chrysologus outstanding in his proclamation of your incarnate Word. Through his intercession, grant that we may constantly meditate upon the mysteries of your salvation within our hearts, and faithfully make them known by our deeds. We ask this....

Prayer over the Gifts and Prayer after Communion:
Cf. Common of Pastors (for Bishops), p. 199, or Common of Doctors of the Church, 205.

JULY 31
SAINT IGNATIUS OF LOYOLA

PRIEST

Collect

Deus, qui, ad maiorem tui nominis gloriam propagandam, beatum Ignatium in Ecclesia tua suscitasti, concede, ut, eius auxilio et imitatione certantes in terris, coronari cum ipso mereamur in caelis. Per Dominum.

God our Father, for the spread of the greater glory of your name, you raised up Saint Ignatius of Loyola within your Church. Grant that we may be privileged to be crowned in heaven with him, by whose help and example we engage in our struggle on earth. We ask this....

Prayer over the Gifts

Placeant, Domine Deus, oblationes in celebratione sancti Ignatii tibi delatae, et praesta, ut sacrosancta mysteria, in quibus omnis sanctitatis fontem constituisti, nos quoque in veritate sanctificent. Per Christum.

Lord God, may the offerings which we make to you on this feast of Saint Ignatius be pleasing to you. You have placed the source of all sanctity in these sacred mysteries; grant that they may make of us a people who are truly holy. We ask this....

Prayer after Communion

Laudis hostia, Domine, quam pro sancto Ignatio gratias agentes obtulimus, ad perpetuam nos maiestatis tuae laudationem perducat. Per Christum.

Lord, may this sacrifice of praise, which we have gratefully offered in honor of Saint Ignatius, lead us to the everlasting praise of your divine majesty. We ask this....

AUGUST 1
SAINT ALPHONSUS LIGUORI

BISHOP AND DOCTOR OF THE CHURCH

Collect

Deus, qui in Ecclesia tua nova semper instauras exempla virtutum, da nobis in zelo animarum beati Alphonsi Mariae episcopi ita vestigiis adhaerere, ut eius in caelis assequamur et praemia. Per Dominum.

God our Father, you constantly raise up new models of virtue within your Church. Grant that we may follow in the footsteps of your bishop Saint Alphonsus Mary Liguori in his zeal for souls, and so attain the same reward in heaven that he received. We ask this....

Prayer over the Gifts

Caelesti, Domine, Spiritus igne corda nostra clementer exure, qui beato Alfonso Mariae tribuisti et haec mysteria celebrare, et per eadem hostiam tibi sanctam seipsum exhibere. Per Christum.

Lord, you granted to Saint Alphonsus Mary the grace to celebrate these mysteries and, through them, to offer himself as a pure sacrifice to you. In your mercy, set our hearts on fire with the heavenly flame of your Spirit. We ask this....

Prayer after Communion

Deus, qui beatum Alfonsum Mariam fidelem dispensatorem et praeconem tanti mysterii providisti, concede, ut fideles tui illud frequenter percipiant, et, percipiendo, te sine fine collaudent. Per Christum.

God our Father, you gave us Saint Alphonsus Mary to proclaim this great mystery and to celebrate it faithfully. Grant that your faithful people may receive it often and, in receiving it, may ceaselessly praise you. We ask this....

AUGUST 2
SAINT EUSEBIUS OF VERCELLI

BISHOP

Collect

Fac nos, Domine Deus, in asserenda Filii tui divinitate, sancti Eusebii episcopi constantiam imitari, ut, fidem servantes quam ipse docuit, eiusdem Filii tui vitae participes esse mereamur. Per Dominum.

Lord our God, make us imitate the steadfastness of your bishop Saint Eusebius of Vercelli in proclaiming the divinity of your Son, so that we may guard the faith which he taught and be privileged to share the life of that self-same Son of yours, who lives and reigns....

Prayer over the Gifts and Prayer after Communion:
Cf. Common of Pastors (for Bishops), p.199.

AUGUST 4
SAINT JOHN MARY VIANNEY

PRIEST

Collect

Omnipotens et misericors Deus, qui sanctum Ioannem Mariam prebyterum pastorali studio mirabilem effecisti, da, quaesumus, ut, eius exemplo et intercessione, fratres in caritate Christi tibi lucremur, et cum eis aeternam gloriam consequi valeamus. Per Dominum.

Almighty and merciful God, you made your priest Saint John Mary Vianney exemplary in his exercise of pastoral care. Through his example and intercession, please grant that we may win for you those who are to be our brothers and sisters in the love of Christ and, along with them, be enabled to attain eternal glory. We ask this....

Prayer over the Gifts and Prayer after Communion:
Cf. Common of Pastors, p. 200.

AUGUST 5
DEDICATION OF THE BASILICA OF SAINT MARY MAJOR

Collect

Famulorum tuorum, quaesumus, Domine, delictis ignosce, ut, qui tibi placere de nostris actibus non valemus, Genetricis Filii tui intercessione salvemur. Per Dominum.

Lord, please forgive the sins of your faithful people, so that we who cannot please you by our own actions may reach salvation through the intercession of the Mother of your Son. We ask this....

Prayer over the Gifts and Prayer after Communion:
Cf. Common of the Blessed Virgin Mary, p. 186.

AUGUST 6
TRANSFIGURATION

Collect

Deus, qui fidei sacramenta in Unigeniti tui gloriosa Transfiguratione patrum testimonio roborasti, et adoptionem filiorum perfectam mirabiliter praesignasti, concede nobis famulis tuis, ut, ipsius dilecti Filii tui vocem audientes, eiusdem coheredes effici mereamur. Per Dominum.

God our Father, during the radiant Transfiguration of your only Son, you strengthened our belief in the mysteries of faith by the testimony of the patriarchs, and you marvelously foreshadowed the full adoption of your children. Grant that your faithful people may listen to the voice of your beloved Son and be privileged to be made co-heirs with him. We ask this....

Prayer over the Gifts

Oblata munera, quaesumus, Domine, gloriosa Unigeniti tui Transfiguratione sanctifica, nosque a peccatorum maculis, splendoribus ipsius illustrationis, emunda. Per Christum.

Lord, by means of the glorious Transfigfuration of your only Son, please make holy the gifts we have offered. By the radiance of that same vision, cleanse us from the stain of sin. We ask this....

Prayer after Communion

Caelestia, quaesumus, Domine, alimenta quae sumpsimus in eius nos transforment imaginem, cuius claritatem gloriosa Transfiguratione manifestare voluisti. Per Christum.

Lord, may the heavenly food we have received transform us into the likeness of him whose radiance you willed to make known in the glory of the Transfiguration. We ask this....

AUGUST 7
POPE SAINT SIXTUS II AND COMPANIONS

MARTYRS

SAINT CAJETAN

PRIEST

Collect
(Saints Sixtus and Companions)

Quaesumus, omnipotens Deus, ut nos, virtute Spiritus Sancti, et ad credendum dociles et ad confitendum fortes efficias, qui beato Xysto eiusque sociis, propter verbum tuum et testimonium Iesu, animas suas ponere tribuisti. Per Dominum.

Almighty God, you granted to Saint Sixtus and his companions the grace to lay down their lives in defending your word and in professing their belief in Jesus. Through the power of the Holy Spirit, please make us docile in believing and courageous in professing our faith. We ask this....

Prayer over the Gifts and Prayer after Communion:
Cf. Common of Martyrs, p. 190.

Collect
(Saint Cajetan)

Deus, qui beato Caietano presbytero apostolicam vivendi formam imitari tribuisti, eius nobis exemplo et intercessione concede in te semper confidere, et regnum tuum indesinenter quaerere. Per Dominum.

God our Father, you gave your priest Saint Cajetan the grace to imitate the Apostles' way of life. Through his example and intercession grant that we may ever put our trust in you and ceaselessly seek your kingdom. We ask this....

Prayer over the Gifts and Prayer after Communion:
Cf. Common of Pastors, p. 200, or Common of Holy Men and Women (for Religious), p. 211.

AUGUST 8
SAINT DOMINIC

PRIEST

Collect

Adiuvet Ecclesiam tuam, Domine, beatus Dominicus meritis et doctrinis, atque pro nobis efficiatur piissimus interventor, qui tuae veritatis exstitit praedicator eximius. Per Dominum.

Lord, may Saint Dominic help your Church by his merits and teachings. He was an outstanding preacher of your truth; may he also be a most faithful intercessor for us. We ask this....

Prayer over the Gifts

Preces, quas tibi, Domine, offerimus, intercedente beato Dominico, clementer intende, et, huius sacrificii virtute potenti, propugnatores fidei gratiae tuae protectione confirma. Per Christum.

Lord, through the intercession of Saint Dominic, graciously hear the prayers which we offer you. By the powerful action of this sacrament and through the protection of your grace, strengthen those who defend the faith. We ask this....

Prayer after Communion

Caelestis, Domine, virtutem sacramenti, quo in beati commemoratione Dominici pasti sumus, percipiat Ecclesia tua plenae devotionis affectu, et cuius praedicatione floruit, eius intercessione iuvetur. Per Christum.

Lord, we have been fed with your holy sacrament on this feast of Saint Dominic. May your Church experience the powerful effect of this heavenly sacrament in complete love for you. May it be aided by the intercession of this same saint through whose preaching it has benefited so greatly. We ask this....

AUGUST 10
SAINT LAWRENCE

DEACON AND MARTYR

Collect

Deus, cuius caritatis ardore beatus Laurentius servitio claruit fidelis et martyrio gloriosus, fac nos amare quod amavit, et opere exercere quod docuit. Per Dominum.

God our Father, in his intense love for you Saint Lawrence became outstanding for his faithful service to you and glorious in his martyrdom. Make us love what he loved, and carry out what he taught by the lives that we lead. We ask this....

Prayer over the Gifts

Suscipe propitius, Domine, munera in beati Laurentii celebritate laetanter oblata, et ad nostrae salutis auxilium provenire concede. Per Christum.

Lord, in your kindness receive the gifts that we joyfully offer on this feast of Saint Lawrence; grant that they may become a help to our salvation. We ask this....

Prayer after Communion

Sacro munere satiati, supplices te, Domine, deprecamur, ut, quod in festivitate sancti Laurentii debitae servitutis praestamus obsequium, salvationis tuae sentiamus augmentum. Per Christum.

Lord, we have been filled with your sacred gift, and we humbly pray to you. Since on this feast of Saint Lawrence we make the offering that fulfills the service we owe you, may we experience an increase in your saving grace. We ask this....

AUGUST 11
SAINT CLARE

VIRGIN

Collect

Deus, qui beatam Claram ad paupertatis amorem misericorditer adduxisti, eius nobis intercessione concede, ut, in paupertate spiritus Christum sequentes, ad tui contemplationem in caelesti regno mereamur. Per Dominum.

God our Father, in your mercy you called Saint Clare to a love of poverty. Through her intercession grant that we may follow Christ in poverty of spirit and attain the privilege of contemplating you in your heavenly kingdom. We ask this....

Prayer over the Gifts and Prayer after Communion:

Cf. Common of Virgins, p. 206, or Common of Holy Men and Women (for Religious), p. 211.

AUGUST 13
SAINTS PONTIAN AND HIPPOLYTUS

MARTYRS

Collect

Patientia pretiosa iustorum tuae nobis, Domine, quaesumus, affectum dilectionis accumulet, et in cordibus nostris sacrae fidei semper exerceat firmitatem. Per Dominum.

Lord, may the priceless patience of your holy ones increase our love for you and make your sacred faith ever firmer within our hearts. We ask this....

Prayer over the Gifts and Prayer after Communion:
Cf. Common of Martyrs, p. 190 or Common of Pastors (for a Pope), p. 198.

AUGUST 14
VIGIL OF THE ASSUMPTION

Collect

Deus, qui beatam Virginem Mariam, eius humilitatem respiciens, ad hanc gratiam evexisti, ut Unigenitus tuus ex ipsa secundum carnem nasceretur, et hodierna die superexcellenti gloria coronasti, eius nobis precibus concede, ut, redemptionis tuae mysterio salvati, a te exaltari mereamur. Per Dominum.

God our Father, you looked upon the lowliness of the Blessed Virgin Mary and called her to the pinnacle of grace wherein your only Son would be born of her according to the flesh; and you crowned her on this day with surpassing glory. Through the Virgin's prayers, grant that we too, who have been granted salvation through the mystery of redemption that you have wrought, may enjoy the privilege of being raised up by you. We ask this....

Prayer over the Gifts

Suscipe, quaesumus, Domine, sacrificium placationis et laudis, quod in sanctae Dei Genetricis Assumptione celebramus, ut ad veniam nos obtinendam perducat, et in perpetua gratiarum constituat actione. Per Christum.

Lord, please receive the sacrifice of atonement and praise which we offer on this feast of the Assumption of the holy Mother of God. We pray that it may help us attain your forgiveness and make us ever grateful to you. We ask this....

Prayer after Communion

Mensae caelestis participes effecti, imploramus clementiam tuam, Domine Deus noster, ut, qui Assumptionem Dei Genetricis colimus, a cunctis malis imminentibus liberemur. Per Christum.

Lord our God, we have been given a share in your heavenly banquet, and we beg for your mercy. May we who venerate the Assumption of the Mother of God be freed from all evils that threaten us. We ask this....

AUGUST 15
ASSUMPTION

Collect

Omnipotens sempiterne Deus, qui immaculatam Virginem Mariam, Filii tui Genetricem, corpore et anima ad caelestem gloriam assumpsisti, concede, quaesumus, ut, ad superna semper intenti, ipsius gloriae mereamur esse consortes. Per Dominum.

Almighty and eternal God, you raised the body and soul of the immaculate Virgin Mary, Mother of your Son, to heavenly glory. Please grant that we may ever be intent on heavenly things, and be privileged to share in her glory. We ask this....

Prayer over the Gifts

Ascendat ad te, Domine, nostrae devotionis oblatio, et, beatissima Virgine Maria in caelum assumpta intercedente, corda nostra, caritatis igne succensa, ad te iugiter aspirent. Per Christum.

Lord, may the offering of our dedication rise before you. The Blessed Virgin Mary was taken up into heaven; by her intercession, may our hearts be inflamed with the fire of love and ever seek after you. We ask this....

Prayer after Communion

Sumptis, Domine, salutaribus sacramentis, da, quaesumus, ut, intercessione beatae Mariae Virginis in caelum assumptae, ad resurrectionis gloriam perducamur. Per Christum.

Lord, we have received your saving sacraments. Through the intercession of the Blessed Virgin Mary, who was taken up into heaven, please grant that we may be led to the glory of the resurrection. We ask this....

AUGUST 16
SAINT STEPHEN
OF HUNGARY

Collect

Concede, quaesumus, Ecclesiae tuae, omnipotens Deus, ut beatum Stephanum, quem regnantem in terris propagatorem habuit, propugnatorem habere mereamur gloriosum in caelis. Per Dominum.

All-powerful God, while Saint Stephen of Hungary ruled on earth, your Church enjoyed his powerful influence in spreading the faith. Now that he lives gloriously in heaven, may we be privileged to have him as our protector. We ask this....

Prayer over the Gifts and
Prayer after Communion:
Cf. Common of Holy Men and Women, p. 208.

AUGUST 19
SAINT JOHN EUDES

PRIEST

Collect

Deus, qui beatum Ioannem presbyterum ad annuntiandum investigabiles Christi divitias mirabiliter elegisti, da nobis, eius exemplis et monitis, ut, in tua scientia crescentes, secundum Evangelii lumen fideliter conversemur. Per Dominum.

God our Father, in your wondrous care you chose your priest Saint John Eudes to preach the unfathomable riches of Christ. Through his example and teaching, grant that we may grow in our knowledge of you and faithfully live together according to the light of the Gospel. We ask this....

Prayer over the Gifts and
Prayer after Communion:
Cf. Common of Pastors, p. 200, or Common of Holy Men and Women (for Religious), p. 211.

AUGUST 20
SAINT BERNARD

ABBOT AND DOCTOR OF THE CHURCH

Collect

Deus, qui beatum Bernardum abbatem, zelo domus tuae succensum, in Ecclesia tua lucere simul et ardere fecisti, eius nobis intercessione concede, ut, eodem spiritu ferventes, tamquam filii lucis iugiter ambulemus. Per Dominum.

God our Father, you set your abbot Saint Bernard on fire with concern for your house, and you caused him to illuminate your Church and to burn with zeal within it. Through his intercession grant that we may be inflamed with that same spirit, and may ever walk as children of the light. We ask this....

Prayer over the Gifts

Maiestati tuae, Domine, unitatis et pacis offerimus sacramentum, sancti Bernardi abbatis memoriam recolentes, qui, verbo et opere praeclarus, Ecclesiae tuae ordinis concordiam strenue procuravit. Per Christum.

Lord, we offer to your divine majesty the sacrament of unity and peace as we celebrate the memory of your abbot Saint Bernard. He was outstanding in word and work, and he vigorously sought and attained harmony within the ranks of your Church. (We make our offering through Christ our Lord.)

Prayer after Communion

Cibus, quem sumpsimus, Domine, in celebratione beati Bernardi, suum in nobis operetur effectum, ut, eius exemplis roborati et monitis eruditi, Verbi tui incarnati rapiamur amore. Qui vivit.

Lord, may this food which we have received in honor of Saint Bernard work its effect in us, so that we may be strengthened by his example and instructed by his teaching, and thus be enraptured with love for your incarnate Word. We ask this....

AUGUST 21
SAINT PIUS X

POPE

Collect

Deus, qui, ad tuendam catholicam fidem et universa in Christo instauranda, sanctum Pium papam caelesti sapientia et apostolica fortitudine replevisti, concede propitius, ut, eius instituta et exempla sectantes, praemia consequamur aeterna. Per Dominum.

God our Father, to safeguard the Catholic faith and to restore all things in Christ, you filled Pope Saint Pius X with heavenly wisdom and apostolic courage. In your mercy grant that we may follow his teaching and example, and so attain our eternal reward. We ask this....

Prayer over the Gifts

Oblationibus nostris, Domine, benigne susceptis, da, quaesumus, ut haec divina mysteria, sancti Pii papae monita secuti, sinceris tractemus obsequiis, et fideli mente sumamus. Per Christum.

Lord, mercifully accept our offerings and please grant that, following the teachings of Pope Saint Pius X, we may treat these divine mysteries with sincere reverence and receive them with faithful hearts. We ask this....

Prayer after Communion

Memoriam sancti Pii papae celebrantes, quaesumus, Domine Deus noster, ut, virtute mensae caelestis, constantes efficiamur in fide, et in tua simus caritate concordes. Per Christum.

Lord our God, as we celebrate the memory of Pope Saint Pius X, we ask that through our participation in this heavenly banquet we may be made firm in faith and united in your love. We ask this....

Lord, we have received your heavenly sacraments, and we humbly pray that we who devoutly recall the memory of the Blessed Virgin Mary may be privileged to share in your eternal banquet. We ask this....

AUGUST 22
QUEENSHIP OF MARY

Collect

Deus, qui Filii tui Genetricem nostram constituisti Matrem atque Reginam, concede propitius, ut, ipsius intercessione suffulti, tuorum in regno caelesti consequamur gloriam filiorum. Per Dominum.

God our Father, you made the Mother of your Son our mother and queen. In your mercy, grant that we may be supported by her intercession and attain the glory that belongs to your children in your heavenly kingdom. We ask this....

Prayer over the Gifts

Memoriam recolentes beatae Virginis Mariae, tibi, Domine, munera nostra offerimus, deprecantes, ut eius nobis succurrat humanitas, qui tibi oblationem seipsum in cruce obtulit immaculatam. Qui vivit.

Lord, we celebrate the memory of the Blessed Virgin Mary, and we offer our gifts to you. We ask that we may be aided by the human nature of Him who sacrificed himself on the cross as a pure offering to you. We ask this....

Prayer after Communion

Sumptis, Domine, sacramentis caelestibus, te supplices deprecamur, ut, qui beatae Virginis Mariae memoriam venerando recolimus, aeterni convivii mereamur esse participes. Per Christum.

AUGUST 23
SAINT ROSE OF LIMA

VIRGIN

Collect

Deus, qui beatam Rosam, tuo amore succensam, mundum relinquere et tibi soli in austeritate paenitentiae vacare fecisti, da nobis, eius intercessione, ut, vias vitae sectantes in terris, torrente deliciarum tuarum perfruamur in caelis. Per Dominum.

God our Father, you set Saint Rose of Lima on fire with love for you, and made her abandon the world and spend her time for your sake alone in practicing austere penance. Through her intercession grant that, while we are on this earth, we may follow the path that leads to eternal life, and then enjoy the abundance of your delights in heaven. We ask this....

Prayer over the Gifts and Prayer after Communion:
Cf. Common of Virgins, p. 206, or Common of Holy Men and Women (for Religious), p. 211.

AUGUST 24
SAINT BARTHOLOMEW

APOSTLE

Collect

Robora in nobis, Domine, fidem, qua Filio tuo beatus Bartholomaeus apostolus sincero animo adhaesit, et praesta, ut, ipso deprecante, Ecclesia tua cunctis gentibus salutis fiat sacramentum. Per Dominum.

Lord, strengthen within us that faith which made your apostle Saint Bartholomew wholeheartedly cling to your Son. Through his prayers, grant that your Church may become the sacrament of salvation for all peoples. We ask this....

Prayer over the Gifts

Beati apostoli Bartholomaei festivitatem, Domine, recensentes, quaesumus, ut eius intercessione tua capiamus auxilia, in cuius honorem tibi laudis hostias immolamus. Per Christum.

Lord, we celebrate the feast of your apostle Saint Bartholomew. In his honor we offer you our sacrifice of praise; we ask that we may receive help from you through his intercession. We ask this....

Prayer after Communion

Sumpsimus, Domine, pignus salutis aeternae, festivitatem beati Bartholomaei apostoli celebrantes, quod sit nobis, quaesumus, vitae praesentis auxilium pariter et futurae. Per Christum.

Lord, we have received the pledge of eternal salvation as we celebrate the feast of your apostle Saint Bartholomew. We ask that it may help us in living our present life as well as in attaining the life to come. We ask this....

AUGUST 25
SAINT LOUIS

SAINT JOSEPH CALASANZ

PRIEST

Collect
(Saint Louis)

Deus, qui beatum Ludovicum e terreni regiminis cura ad caelestis regni gloriam transtulisti, eius, quaesumus, intercessione concede, ut, per munera temporalia quae gerimus, regnum tuum quaeramus aeternum. Per Dominum.

God our Father, you raised Saint Louis from the cares of an earthly kingdom to the glory of a heavenly one. Through his intervention, please grant that we may seek your eternal kingdom by carrying out our duties while we are on this earth. We ask this....

Prayer over the Gifts and Prayer after Communion:
Cf. Common of Holy Men and Women, p. 208.

Collect
(Saint Joseph Calasanz)

Deus, qui beatum Ioseph presbyterum tanta caritate et patientia decorasti, ut in pueris erudiendis omnique virtute exornandis constanter incumberet, concede, quaesumus, ut quem sapientiae praeceptorem colimus, veritatis cooperatorem iugiter imitemur. Per Dominum.

God our Father, you adorned your priest Saint Joseph Calasanz with such love and patience that he constantly devoted himself to educating youth and to instilling every virtue into them. Please grant that we may imitate the consistent docility to truth of this saint, whom we honor as a wise teacher. We ask this....

*Prayer over the Gifts and
Prayer after Communion:*
Cf. Common of Holy Men and Women (for Teachers), p. 213, or Common of Pastors, p. 200.

AUGUST 27
SAINT MONICA

Collect

Deus, maerentium consolator, qui beatae Monicae pias lacrimas in conversione filii sui Augustini misericorditer suscepisti, da nobis, utriusque interventu, peccata nostra deplorare, et gratiae tuae indulgentiam invenire. Per Dominum.

God our Father, you console those who grieve, and you mercifully granted the loving and tearful pleas of Saint Monica by converting her son Saint Augustine. Through the intercession of these two saints, grant that we may repent of our sins and discover your gracious forgiveness. We ask this....

*Prayer over the Gifts and
Prayer after Communion:*
Cf. Common of Holy Men and Women (for Holy Women), p. 214.

AUGUST 28
SAINT AUGUSTINE

BISHOP AND DOCTOR OF THE CHURCH

Collect

Innova, quaesumus, Domine, in Ecclesia tua spiritum quo beatum Augustinum episcopum imbuisti, ut, eodem nos repleti, te solum verae fontem sapientiae sitiamus, et superni amoris quaeramus auctorem. Per Dominum.

Lord, please renew within your Church the spirit with which you inspired your bishop Saint Augustine. Filled with that same spirit, may we thirst for you alone as the font of true wisdom and seek you alone as the source of divine love. We ask this....

Prayer over the Gifts

Salutis nostrae memoriale celebrantes, clementiam tuam, Domine, suppliciter exoramus, ut hoc sacramentum pietatis fiat nobis signum unitatis et vinculum caritatis. Per Christum.

Lord, as we celebrate this memorial of our redemption, we humbly ask for your mercy. May this sacrament of love be a sign of unity and a bond of charity for us. We ask this....

Prayer after Communion

Sanctificet nos, quaesumus, Domine, mensae Christi participatio, ut, eius membra effecti, simus quod accepimus. Per Christum.

Lord, we ask that our sharing in the banquet of Christ may make us holy, so that we may be made members of Christ and thus actually become what we have received. We ask this....

AUGUST 29
BEHEADING OF SAINT JOHN THE BAPTIST

Collect

Deus, qui beatum Ioannem Baptistam et nascentis et morientis Filii tui Praecursorem esse voluisti, concede, ut, sicut ille veritatis et iustitiae martyr occubuit, ita et nos pro tuae confessione doctrinae strenue certemus. Per Dominum.

God our Father, you willed that Saint John the Baptist should be the herald both of your Son's birth and of his death. Just as Saint John fell as a martyr for truth and justice, so too grant that we may earnestly strive to profess our faith in your teaching. We ask this....

Prayer over the Gifts

Da nobis, Domine per haec munera quae tibi offerimus, illam tuarum rectitudinem semitarum, quam beatus Ioannes, vox in deserto clamantis, edocuit, et, fuso sanguine, magna virtute signavit. Per Christum.

Lord, through the gifts which we offer you, grant us that straightness of your paths which Saint John, the voice of one crying in the wilderness, taught us and to which, by shedding his blood, he attested with such great courage. We ask this....

Prayer after Communion

Concede nobis, Domine, sancti Ioannis Baptistae natale recensentibus, ut et salutaria sacramenta quae sumpsimus significata veneremur, et in nobis potius edita gaudeamus. Per Christum.

Lord, as we recall the heavenly birth of Saint John the Baptist, grant that we may honor these saving sacraments which we have received and which have been announced to us, or rather that we may rejoice in them as they have come to fulfillment within us. We ask this....

SEPTEMBER 3
SAINT GREGORY
THE GREAT

POPE AND DOCTOR OF THE CHURCH

Collect

Deus, qui populis tuis indulgentia consulis et amore dominaris, da spiritum sapientiae, intercedente beato Gregorio papa, quibus dedisti regimen disciplinae, ut de profectu sanctarum ovium fiant gaudia aeterna pastorum. Per Dominum.

God our Father, you care for your people with tenderness and you rule over them with love. Through the intercession of Pope Saint Gregory the Great, grant the spirit of wisdom to those to whom you have given the power to rule, so that from the progress of your holy flock may come the eternal joy of its shepherds. We ask this....

Prayer over the Gifts

Annue nobis, quaesumus, Domine, ut, in celebratione beati Gregorii, haec nobis prosit oblatio, quam immolando totius mundi tribuisti relaxari delicta. Per Christum.

Lord, please hear our prayer on this feast of Saint Gregory, so that we may benefit from this sacrifice, upon whose offering you have made the forgiveness of the sins of the entire world depend. We ask this....

Prayer after Communion

Quos Christo reficis pane vivo, eosdem edoce, Domine, Christo magistro, ut in commemoratione beati Gregorii tuam discant veritatem, et eam in caritate operentur. Per Christum.

Lord, with Christ as their teacher, instruct those whom you nourish with Christ as their living food, so that on this feast of Saint Gregory, we may come to learn your truth and carry it out in works of love. We ask this....

SEPTEMBER 8
BIRTH OF THE BLESSED VIRGIN MARY

Collect

Famulis tuis, quaesumus, Domine, caelestis gratiae munus impertire, ut, quibus beatae Virginis partus exstitit salutis exordium, Nativitatis eius festivitas pacis tribuat incrementum. Per Dominum.

Lord, please grant your faithful people the gift of your heavenly grace. May the feast of the Blessed Virgin's birth bestow even greater peace upon those for whom her Son's birth was the beginning of salvation. We ask this....

Prayer over the Gifts

Unigeniti tui, Domine, nobis succurrat humanitas, ut, qui natus de Virgine Matris integritatem non minuit, sed sacravit, a nostris nos piaculis exuens, oblationem nostram tibi reddat acceptam. Qui vivit.

Lord, may the fact that your only Son took on human nature come to our aid. In being born of the Virgin, he did not lessen his mother's chastity but rather consecrated it; may he strip us of our sins and render our offering acceptable to you. We ask this....

Prayer after Communion

Exsultet Ecclesia tua, Domine, quam sacris mysteriis refecisti, de beatae Mariae Virginis Nativitate congaudens, quae universo mundo spes fuit et aurora salutis. Per Christum.

Lord, may your Church, which you have renewed by these sacred mysteries, be filled with gladness as it rejoices on the feast of the birth of the Blessed Virgin Mary, who was the hope of the entire world and the dawn of salvation. We ask this....

SEPTEMBER 13
SAINT JOHN CHRYSOSTOM

BISHOP AND DOCTOR OF THE CHURCH

Collect

Deus, in te sperantium fortitudo, qui beatum Ioannem Chrysostomum episcopum mira eloquentia et tribulationis experimento clarescere voluisti, da nobis, quaesumus, ut, eius doctrinis eruditi, invictae patientiae roboremur exemplo. Per Dominum.

God our Father, you are the strength of those who hope in you. You willed that your bishop Saint John Chrysostom should be renowned for his wonderful eloquence and for the sufferings he experienced. Please grant that we may be instructed by his teachings and strengthened by the example of his dauntless patience. We ask this....

Prayer over the Gifts

Sacrificium tibi placeat, Deus, in commemoratione beati Ioannis Chrysostomi libenter exhibitum, quo monente, nos etiam totos tibi reddimus collaudantes. Per Christum.

God our Father, because of the teaching of Saint John Chrysostom we too surrender ourselves completely to your praise. May the sacrifice we willingly offer you in his memory please you. We ask this....

Prayer after Communion

Concede, misericors Deus, ut mysteria, quae pro beati Ioannis Chrysostomi commemoratione sumpsimus, nos in tua caritate confirment, et tuae fideles confessores veritatis efficiant. Per Christum.

Merciful God, grant that the mysteries we have received in memory of Saint John Chrysostom may strengthen us in our love for you and make us faithfully profess your truth. We ask this....

SEPTEMBER 14
TRIUMPH OF THE
HOLY CROSS

Collect

Deus, qui Unigenitum tuum crucem subire voluisti, ut salvum faceret genus humanum, praesta, quaesumus, ut, cuius mysterium in terra cognovimus, eius redemptionis praemia in caelo consequi mereamur. Per Dominum.

God our Father, you willed that your only Son should undergo the Cross in order to rescue the human race. While on earth, we have come to know the mystery of the Cross; please grant that we may be privileged to attain its rewards in heaven. We ask this....

Prayer over the Gifts

Haec oblatio, Domine, quaesumus, ab omnibus nos purget offensis, quae in ara crucis totius mundi tulit offensam. Per Christum.

Lord, this offering took away the sins of the entire world on the altar of the Cross. We pray that it may cleanse us from all our sins. We ask this....

Prayer after Communion

Refectione tua sancta enutriti, Domine Iesu Christe, supplices deprecamur, ut, quos per lignum crucis vivificae redemisti, ad resurrectionis gloriam perducas. Qui vivis.

Lord Jesus Christ, we have been nourished by your holy banquet, and we humbly ask that you lead to the glory of the resurrection those whom you have redeemed by the wood of the life-giving Cross. We ask this....

SEPTEMBER 15
OUR LADY OF SORROWS

Collect

Deus, qui Filio tuo in cruce exaltato compatientem Matrem astare voluisti, da Ecclesiae tuae, ut, Christi passionis cum ipsa consors effecta, eiusdem resurrectionis particeps esse mereatur. Per Dominum.

God our Father, you willed that your Son's Mother should stand next to him and suffer with him as he was raised up on the Cross. Grant that your Church may be her companion in the passion of Christ, and so be privileged to share in his resurrection. We ask this....

Prayer over the Gifts

Suscipe, misericors Deus, ad tui nominis laudem preces hostiasque in veneratione beatae Mariae Virginis exhibitas, quam, stantem iuxta crucem Iesu, clementer nobis Matrem piissimam providisti. Per Christum.

Merciful God, in your loving kindness you gave us the Blessed Virgin Mary as a most loving mother when she stood beside the cross of Jesus. Receive the prayers and gifts which we offer in her honor to the glory of your holy name. We ask this....

Prayer after Communion

Sumptis, Domine, sacramentis redemptionis aeternae, supplices deprecamur, ut, compassionem beatae Mariae Virginis recolentes, ea in nobis pro Ecclesia adimpleamus, quae desunt Christi passionum. Per Christum.

Lord, we have received the sacrament of eternal salvation. As we keep in mind the suffering the Blessed Virgin Mary bore with her Son, we humbly ask that, on behalf of the Church, we may fill up in our own lives whatever is lacking in the sufferings of Christ. We ask this....

SEPTEMBER 16
POPE SAINT CORNELIUS AND SAINT CYPRIAN

MARTYRS

Collect

Deus, qui populo tuo beatos Cornelium et Cyprianum sedulos pastores et invictos martyres praestitisti, concede ut, eorum intercessione, fide et constantia roboremur, et pro Ecclesiae unitate operam tribuamus impense. Per Dominum.

God our Father, you gave your people Saints Cornelius and Cyprian as zealous shepherds and invincible martyrs. Through their intercession, grant that we may be strengthened in our faith and loyalty to you, and may work earnestly for the unity of the Church. We ask this....

Prayer over the Gifts

Suscipe, quaesumus, Domine, munera populi tui pro martyrum tuorum passionibus dicata sanctorum, et quae beatis Cornelio et Cypriano in persecutione fortitudinem ministrarunt, nobis quoque praebeant inter adversa constantiam. Per Christum.

Lord, please receive the gifts that your people offer in honor of the sufferings of your holy martyrs. May what provided Saints Cornelius and Cyprian with courage in their suffering also give us strength in the midst of our trials. We ask this....

Prayer after Communion

Per haec mysteria quae sumpsimus, Domine, supplices exoramus, ut, sanctorum martyrum Cornelii et Cypriani exemplo, spiritus tui fortitudine confirmati, evangelicae veritati possimus testimonium perhibere. Per Christum.

Lord, through these mysteries which we have received and by means of the example of the holy martyrs Cornelius and Cyprian, we humbly ask that we may be strengthened by the power of your Spirit and so be able to bear witness to the truth of the Gospel. We ask this....

SEPTEMBER 17
SAINT ROBERT BELLARMINE

BISHOP AND DOCTOR OF THE CHURCH

Collect

Deus, qui, ad tuae fidem Ecclesiae vindicandam, beatum Robertum episcopum mira eruditione et virtute decorasti, eius intercessione concede, ut populus tuus eiusdem fidei semper integritate laetetur. Per Dominum.

God our Father, to make evident the truthfulness of your Church's faith, you endowed your bishop Saint Robert Bellarmine with outstanding learning and holiness. Through his intercession, grant that your people may always rejoice in the purity and entirety of that same faith. We ask this....

*Prayer over the Gifts and
Prayer after Communion:*
Cf. Common of Pastors (for Bishops), p. 199, or Common of Doctors of the Church, p. 205.

SEPTEMBER 19
SAINT JANUARIUS

BISHOP AND MARTYR

Collect

Deus, qui nos concedis beati Ianuarii martyris memoriam venerari, da nobis in aeterna beatitudine de eius societate gaudere. Per Dominum.

God our Father, you allow us to honor the memory of your martyr Saint Januarius. Grant that we may enjoy his company in the eternal blessedness of heaven. We ask this....

*Prayer over the Gifts and
Prayer after Communion:*
Cf. Common of Martyrs, p. 193, or Common of Pastors (for Bishops), p. 199.

SEPTEMBER 21
SAINT MATTHEW

APOSTLE AND EVANGELIST

Collect

Deus, qui ineffabili misericordia beatum Matthaeum ex publicano Apostolum es dignatus eligere, da nobis, eius exemplo et intercessione suffultis, ut, te sequentes, tibi firmiter adhaerere mereamur. Per Dominum.

God our Father, in your unspeakable mercy you saw fit to choose the publican Saint Matthew to be your apostle. Grant that, strengthened by his example and intercession, we too may follow you and be privileged to put our full trust in you. We ask this....

Prayer over the Gifts

Memoriam beati Matthaei recensentes, preces et hostias tibi, Domine, deferimus, suppliciter exorantes, ut Ecclesiam tuam benignus aspicias, cuius fidem Apostolorum praedicationibus nutrivisti. Per Christum.

Lord, we are mindful of the memory of Saint Matthew as we bring our prayers and gifts to you. We humbly ask that you look with kindness upon your Church, whose faith you have nourished by the preaching of the Apostles. We ask this....

Prayer after Communion

Salutaris gaudii participes, Domine, quo laetus Salvatorem in domo sua convivam sanctus Matthaeus excepit, da, ut cibo semper reficiamur illius, qui non iustos sed peccatores vocare venit ad salutem. Qui vivit.

Lord, we share in the joy of the salvation which gladdened Saint Matthew as he received the Savior as a guest in his home. Grant that we may always be refreshed by the food of Him who came to call not the self-righteous but rather sinners to salvation. We ask this....

SEPTEMBER 26
SAINTS COSMAS AND DAMIAN

MARTYRS

Collect

Magnificet te, Domine, sanctorum tuorum Cosmae et Damiani veneranda memoria, quia et illis gloriam sempiternam, et opem nobis ineffabili providentia contulisti. Per Dominum.

Lord, may the holy memory of your saints Cosmas and Damian glorify you, for in your unspeakable providence you have given them eternal glory and us the grace of your assistance. We ask this....

Prayer over the Gifts

In tuorum, Domine, pretiosa morte iustorum, sacrificium illud offerimus, de quo martyrium sumpsit omne principium. Per Christum.

Lord, in honor of the priceless death of your holy ones we offer this sacrifice from which suffering for the faith derives all its meaning. We make our prayer through....

Prayer after Communion

Conserva in nobis, Domine, munus tuum, et quod, te donante, pro commemoratione beatorum martyrum Cosmae et Damiani percepimus, salutem nobis praestet et pacem. Per Christum.

Lord, preserve your gift within us. May what we have received from your generous hand in remembrance of the holy martyrs Cosmas and Damian bring us salvation and peace. We ask this....

SEPTEMBER 27
SAINT VINCENT DE PAUL

PRIEST

Collect

Deus, qui ad salutem pauperum et cleri institutionem beatum Vincentium presbyterum virtutibus apostolicis imbuisti, praesta, quaesumus, ut, eodem spiritu ferventes, et amemus quod amavit, et quod docuit operemur. Per Dominum.

God our Father, for the salvation of the poor and the training of the clergy, you endowed your priest Saint Vincent de Paul with apostolic virtues. Please grant that, inflamed by that same spirit, we may love what he loved and put into practice what he taught. We ask this....

Prayer over the Gifts

Deus, qui beato Vincentio divina celebranti mysteria tribuisti quod tractabat imitari, concede, ut, huius sacrificii virtute, ipsi quoque in oblationem tibi acceptabilem transeamus. Per Christum.

God our Father, when Saint Vincent offered the holy mysteries you gave him the grace to imitate what he celebrated. By the power of this sacrifice, grant that we too may become an offering that is acceptable to you. We ask this....

Prayer after Communion

Caelestibus, Domine, refecti sacramentis, supplices deprecamur, ut ad imitandum Filium tuum pauperibus evangelizantem, sicut exemplis beati Vincentii provocamur, ita et patrociniis adiuvemur. Per Christum.

Lord, we have been renewed by your heavenly sacraments. In order to imitate your Son, who brought the Good News to the poor, we humbly ask that we may be aided by the patronage of Saint Vincent, just as we are inspired by his example. We ask this....

SEPTEMBER 28
SAINT WENCESLAUS

MARTYR

Collect

Deus, qui beatum martyrem Venceslaum caelesti regno terrenum postponere docuisti, eius precibus concede, ut, nosmetipsos abnegantes, tibi toto corde adhaerere valeamus. Per Dominum.

God our Father, you taught your holy martyr Saint Wenceslaus to value a heavenly kingdom above an earthly one. By his prayers grant that we may deny ourselves and be able to cling to you with our whole hearts. We ask this....

Prayer over the Gifts and Prayer after Communion:
Cf. Common of Martyrs, p. 193.

SEPTEMBER 29
SAINTS MICHAEL, GABRIEL, AND RAPHAEL

ARCHANGELS

Collect

Deus, qui miro ordine Angelorum ministeria hominumque dispensas, concede propitius, ut, a quibus tibi ministrantibus in caelo semper assistitur, ab his in terra vita nostra muniatur. Per Dominum.

God our Father, in wondrous fashion you direct the works of Angels and humans. In your mercy, grant that our life on earth may be protected by those who, as ministering spirits, ever stand before you in heaven. We ask this....

Prayer over the Gifts

Hostias tibi, Domine, laudis offerimus, suppliciter deprecantes, ut easdem, angelico ministerio in conspectum tuae maiestatis delatas, et placatus accipias, et ad salutem nostram provenire concedas. Per Christum.

Lord, as we offer you our sacrifice of praise, we humbly ask that, when it is carried into the presence of your divine majesty by the hands of the Angels, you will be pleased to accept it and will grant that it may be an aid to our salvation. We ask this....

Prayer after Communion

Pane caelesti refecti, supplices te, Domine, deprecamur, ut, eius fortitudine roborati, sub Angelorum tuorum fideli custodia, fortes, salutis progrediamur in via. Per Christum.

Lord, we have been fed with your heavenly food, and we humbly ask that, strengthened by its power and through the faithful protection of your Angels, we may progress with courage in the way of salvation. We ask this....

SEPTEMBER 30
SAINT JEROME

PRIEST AND DOCTOR OF THE CHURCH

Collect

Deus, qui beato Hieronymo presbytero suavem et vivum Scripturae Sacrae affectum tribuisti, da, ut populus tuus verbo tuo uberius alatur, et in eo fontem vitae inveniat. Per Dominum.

God our Father, you gave your priest Saint Jerome a pleasing and vibrant love for Sacred Scripture. Grant that your people may be more richly nourished by your word, and find in it the fountain of life. We ask this....

Prayer over the Gifts

Tribue nobis, Domine, ut, exemplo beati Hieronymi, verbum tuum meditati, ad salutarem hostiam maiestati tuae offerendam promptius accedamus. Per Christum.

Lord, grant that we may follow the example of Saint Jerome in pondering your word, and so more readily come to offer the sacrifice of salvation to your divine majesty. We ask this....

Prayer after Communion

Sancta tua quae sumpsimus, Domine, de beati Hieronymi celebritate laetantes, tuorum excitent corda fidelium, ut, sacris intenta doctrinis, intellegant quod sequantur, et sequendo vitam obtineant sempiternam. Per Christum.

Lord, as we rejoice in this celebration honoring Saint Jerome, we have received your holy sacrament. May it stir up the hearts of your faithful people, so that they may be intent upon your sacred teachings, understand the doctrine they follow, and, by following it, attain everlasting life. We ask this....

OCTOBER 1
SAINT THERESA OF THE CHILD JESUS

VIRGIN

Collect

Deus, qui regnum tuum humilibus parvulisque disponis, fac nos beatae Teresiae tramitem prosequi confidenter, ut, eius intercessione, gloria tua nobis reveletur aeterna. Per Dominum.

God our Father, you give your kingdom to the humble and the childlike. Make us confidently follow the way of life that Saint Theresa of the Child Jesus pursued, so that, through her intercession, your eternal glory may be made known to us. We ask this....

Prayer over the Gifts

In beata Teresia te, Domine, mirabilem praedicantes, maiestatem tuam suppliciter exoramus, ut, sicut eius tibi grata sunt merita, sic nostrae servitutis accepta reddantur officia. Per Christum.

Lord, we proclaim your magnificence because of Saint Theresa. We humbly ask your divine majesty that, just as her holy life is pleasing to you, so may these offerings of our service be made acceptable to you. We ask this....

Prayer after Communion

Sacramenta quae sumpsimus, Domine, illius in nobis vim amoris accendant, quo beata Teresia se tibi addixit, tuamque cupiit miserationem pro omnibus impetrare. Per Christum.

Lord, may the sacraments that we have received stir up within us the power of that love by which Saint Theresa consecrated herself to you and sought to beg your mercy for all people. We ask this....

OCTOBER 2
HOLY GUARDIAN ANGELS

Collect

Deus, qui ineffabili providentia sanctos Angelos tuos ad nostram custodiam mittere dignaris, largire supplicibus tuis, et eorum semper protectione defendi, et aeterna societate gaudere. Per Dominum.

God our Father, in your mysterious providence you see fit to send your holy Angels to be our guardians. Grant that your people may ever be defended by the Angels' protection and may enjoy their unending company in heaven. We ask this....

Prayer over the Gifts

Suscipe, Domine, munera, quae pro sanctorum Angelorum tuorum veneratione deferimus, et concede propitius, ut, perpetuis eorum praesidiis, a praesentibus periculis liberemur, et ad vitam feliciter perveniamus aeternam. Per Christum.

Lord, receive the gifts which we bring in honor of your holy angels. In your mercy and through the angels' ceaseless protection, grant that we may be freed from present dangers and joyfully come to eternal life. We ask this....

Prayer after Communion

Quos tantis, Domine, in vitam aeternam dignaris pascere sacramentis, angelico ministerio dirige in viam salutis et pacis. Per Christum.

Lord, through the ministry of the angels, guide into the path of salvation and peace those whom you see fit to nourish with these great sacraments that lead to eternal life. We ask this....

OCTOBER 4
SAINT FRANCIS OF ASSISI

RELIGIOUS

Collect

Deus, qui beato Francisco paupertate et humilitate Christo configurari tribuisti, concede, ut per illius semitas gradientes, Filium tuum sequi et tibi coniungi laeta valeamus caritate. Per Dominum.

God our Father, you gave Saint Francis the privilege of being made like Christ in poverty and lowliness. Grant that, treading the same path as he, we may be enabled to follow your Son and be united with you in joyful love. We ask this....

Prayer over the Gifts

Munera tibi, Domine, offerentes, quaesumus, ut ad mysterium crucis celebrandum convenienter aptemur, cui beatus Franciscus tam ardenter adhaesit. Per Christum.

Lord, as we offer you our gifts, we ask that we may be properly prepared to celebrate the mystery of the Cross, to which Saint Francis was so ardently attached. We ask this....

Prayer after Communion

Da nobis, quaesumus, Domine, per haec sancta quae sumpsimus, ut, beati Francisci caritatem zelumque apostolicum imitantes, tuae dilectionis effectus percipiamus et in salutem omnium effundamus. Per Christum.

Lord, through the holy sacraments which we have received, please grant that we may imitate the apostolic charity and zeal of Saint Francis: may we experience the effect of your love and devote ourselves completely to the salvation of all men and women. We ask this....

OCTOBER 6
SAINT BRUNO

PRIEST

Collect

Deus, qui sanctum Brunonem ad serviendum tibi in solitudine vocasti, eius nobis intercessione concede, ut, per huius mundi varietates, tibi iugiter vacemus. Per Dominum.

God our Father, you called Saint Bruno to serve you in a life of solitude. Through his intercession grant that, amid the changeable circumstances in which we live, we may be constant in our fidelity to you. We ask this....

Prayer over the Gifts and Prayer after Communion:
Cf. Common of Pastors, p. 200, or Common of Holy Men and Women (for Religious), p. 211.

OCTOBER 7
OUR LADY
OF THE ROSARY

Collect

Gratiam tuam, quaesumus, Domine, mentibus nostris infunde, ut qui, Angelo nuntiante, Christi Filii tui incarnationem cognovimus, beata Maria Virgine intercedente, per passionem eius et crucem ad resurrectionis gloriam perducamur. Per Dominum.

Lord, we ask you to pour forth your grace into our hearts. Through the angel's message we have come to know about the incarnation of Christ your Son; through the intercession of the Blessed Virgin Mary, lead us by means of his passion and cross to the glory of the resurrection. We ask this....

Prayer over the Gifts

Fac nos, quaesumus, Domine, his muneribus oblatis convenienter aptari, et Unigeniti tui mysteria ita recolere, ut eius digni promissionibus effici mereamur. Per Christum.

Lord, please grant that our lives may be fittingly conformed to these gifts we have offered. Make us recall the mysteries of your only Son in such a way that we may be privileged to become worthy of his promises. We ask this....

Prayer after Communion

Quaesumus, Domine Deus noster, ut, qui in hoc sacramento Filii tui mortem et resurrectionem annuntiamus, eius socii passionum effecti, consolationis etiam ac gloriae mereamur esse participes. Per Christum.

Lord our God, we ask that we who proclaim the death and resurrection of your Son in this sacrament may become companions in his sufferings and so be privileged to share in his joy and glory as well. We ask this....

OCTOBER 9
SAINT DENIS
AND COMPANIONS

MARTYRS

SAINT JOHN LEONARD

PRIEST

Collect
(Saint Denis and Companions)

Deus, qui beatum Dionysium eiusque socios ad praedicandam gentibus gloriam tuam misisti, eosque virtute constantiae in passione roborasti, tribue nobis, quaesumus, ex eorum imitatione prospera mundi despicere, et nulla eius adversa formidare. Per Dominum.

God our Father, you sent Saint Denis and his companions to proclaim your wonders to the nations, and you strengthened them with the virtue of perseverance in the midst of suffering. Please grant that, in imitation of them, we may spurn the riches of the world and fear none of its enmity. We ask this....

Prayer over the Gifts and Prayer after Communion:
Cf. Common of Martyrs, p. 190.

Collect
(Saint John Leonard)

Bonorum omnium largitor, Deus, qui per beatum Ioannem presbyterum populis Evangelium nuntiari fecisti, eius intercessione concede, ut fides vera semper et ubique proficiat. Per Dominum.

God our Father, you are the giver of all good gifts. Through your priest Saint John Leonard you brought about the preaching of the Gospel to the nations; through his intercession grant that the true faith may flourish everywhere and at all times. We ask this....

Prayer over the Gifts and Prayer after Communion:
Cf. Common of Pastors (for Missionaries), p.203, or Common of Holy Men and Women (for Those Who Performed Works of Mercy), p. 213.

OCTOBER 14
SAINT CALLISTUS I

POPE AND MARTYR

Collect

Preces populi tui, quaesumus, Domine, clementer exaudi, ut beati Callisti papae meritis adiuvemur, cuius passione laetamur. Per Dominum.

Lord, in your mercy please hear the prayers of your people, so that we may be helped by the merits of Pope Saint Callistus, whose sufferings we joyfully commemorate. We ask this....

Prayer over the Gifts and Prayer after Communion:
Cf. Common of Martyrs, p. 193, or Common of Pastors (for a Pope), p. 198.

OCTOBER 15
SAINT TERESA OF AVILA

VIRGIN AND DOCTOR OF THE CHURCH

Collect

Deus, qui per Spiritum tuum beatam Teresiam suscitasti, ut requirendae perfectionis semitam Ecclesiae manifestaret, da nobis et caelestis eius doctrinae pabulo semper nutriri, et verae sanctitatis desiderio accendi. Per Dominum.

God our Father, through your Spirit you raised up Saint Teresa of Avila to show the Church the path to follow in seeking perfection. Grant that we may always be nourished by the food of her heavenly teaching and inflamed with the desire for true holiness. We ask this....

Prayer over the Gifts

Munera nostra, Domine, tuae sint accepta maiestati, cui beatae Teresiae tantopere placuit devotionis obsequium. Per Christum.

Lord, the loving service of Saint Teresa pleased you greatly. In the same way, may our offerings too be acceptable to your divine majesty. We ask this....

Prayer after Communion

Subdita tibi familia, Domine Deus noster, quam caelesti pane satiasti, fac ut, exemplo beatae Teresiae, misericordias tuas in aeternum cantare laetetur. Per Christum.

Lord our God, with heavenly food you have filled the faithful people who are under your care. Through the example of Saint Teresa make us joyfully sing of your mercies for all ages to come. We ask this....

OCTOBER 16
SAINT HEDWIG

RELIGIOUS

SAINT MARGARET MARY ALACOQUE

VIRGIN

Collect
(Saint Hedwig)

Concede, quaesumus, omnipotens Deus, ut veneranda nobis beatae Hedvigis intercessio tribuat caeleste subsidium, cuius vita mirabilis omnibus humilitatis praestat exemplum. Per Dominum.

Almighty God, the marvelous life of Saint Hedwig provides all of us with an example of humility. Please grant that her holy prayers may obtain heavenly help for us. We ask this....

Prayer over the Gifts and Prayer after Communion:
Cf. Common of Holy Men and Women (for Religious), p. 211.

Collect
(Saint Margaret Mary Alacoque)

Effunde super nos, quaesumus, Domine, spiritum quo beatam Margaritam Mariam singulariter ditasti, ut scire valeamus supereminentem scientiae caritatem Christi, et impleamur in omnem plenitudinem Dei. Per Dominum.

Lord, please pour forth upon us the spirit with which you so uniquely enriched Saint Margaret Mary Alacoque, so that we may be able to know the love of Christ which surpasses all understanding and be filled with the fullness of God himself. We ask this....

Prayer over the Gifts and Prayer after Communion:
Cf. Common of Virgins, p. 206, or Common of Holy Men and Women (for Religious), p. 211.

OCTOBER 17
SAINT IGNATIUS
OF ANTIOCH

BISHOP AND MARTYR

Collect

Omnipotens sempiterne Deus, qui sanctorum martyrum confessionibus Ecclesiae tuae sacrum corpus exornas, concede, quaesumus, ut hodierna gloria passionis, sicut beato Ignatio magnificentiam tribuit sempiternam, ita nobis perpetuum munimen operetur. Per Dominum.

Almighty and eternal God, you adorn the holy body of your Church with the testimony of your holy martyrs. The glory of the sufferings we commemorate today brought Saint Ignatius of Antioch eternal splendor; please grant that it may also bring us your unending aid. We ask this....

Prayer over the Gifts

Grata tibi sit, Domine, nostrae devotionis oblatio, qui beatum Ignatium, frumentum Christi, per martyrii passionem panem mundum suscepisti. Per Christum.

Lord, you accepted the sacrifice of Saint Ignatius, the wheat of Christ who was made into pure bread by the sufferings of his martyrdom. May the offerings of our dedicated service also be pleasing to you. We ask this....

Prayer after Communion

Reficiat nos, Domine, panis caelestis, quem in beati Ignatii natali suscepimus, ac tribuat nos nomine et opere esse christianos. Per Christum.

Lord, may the heavenly bread, which we have received on this feast of Saint Ignatius's birth into eternal life, renew us and enable us to be Christians both in name and in deed. We ask this....

OCTOBER 18
SAINT LUKE

EVANGELIST

Collect

Domine Deus, qui beatum Lucam elegisti, ut praedicatione et scriptis mysterium tuae in paupe-res dilectionis revelaret, concede, ut, qui tuo iam nomine glorientur, cor unum et anima una esse perseverent, et omnes gentes tuam mereantur videre salutem. Per Dominum.

Lord our God, you chose Saint Luke to be the preacher and writer who would make known the mystery of your love for the poor. Grant that those who already glory in your name may continue to be of one heart and one mind, and that all peoples may be privileged to behold your salvation. We ask this....

Prayer over the Gifts

Donis caelestibus, da nobis, quaesumus, Domine, libera tibi mente servire, ut munera, quae in festivitate beati Lucae deferimus, et medelam nobis operentur et gloriam. Per Christum.

Lord, through your heavenly gifts please grant that we may serve you freely, so that the gifts which we bring on this feast of Saint Luke may heal our sinfulness and bring us to heavenly glory. We ask this....

Prayer after Communion

Praesta, quaesumus, omnipotens Deus, ut, quod de sancto altari tuo accepimus, nos sanctificet, et in fide Evangelii, quod sanctus Lucas praedicavit, fortes efficiat. Per Christum.

Almighty God, please grant that what we have received from your sacred altar may make us holy and render us strong in our belief in the Gospel which Saint Luke proclaimed. We ask this....

OCTOBER 19

SAINTS ISAAC JOGUES, JOHN DE BREBEUF, AND COMPANIONS

MARTYRS

SAINT PAUL OF THE CROSS

PRIEST

Collect
(Sts. John, Isaac, and Companions)

Deus, qui primitias fidei in borealibus Americae regionibus sanctorum Ioannis et Isaac eorumque sociorum praedicatione et sanguine consecrasti, concede propitius, ut, eorum intercessione, florida christianorum seges ubique in dies augeatur. Per Dominum.

God our Father, you consecrated the first fruits of the faith in the territory of North America by the preaching and martyrdom of Saints John de Brebeuf, Isaac Jogues, and their companions. Through their intercession, mercifully grant that the harvest of Christians may everywhere increase and ripen with each passing day. We ask this....

Prayer over the Gifts and Prayer after Communion:
Cf. Common of Martyrs, p. 190, or Common of Pastors (for Missionaries), p. 203.

Collect
(Saint Paul of the Cross)

Impetret nobis, Domine, gratiam tuam sanctus presbyter Paulus, qui unico crucem amore dilexit, ut, eius exemplo vividius incitati, crucem nostram fortiter amplectamur. Per Dominum.

Lord, may your priest Saint Paul, who loved the Cross with a singular love, obtain your grace for us, so that we may be more ardently inflamed by his example and thus embrace our own cross with courage. We ask this....

Prayer over the Gifts
(Saint Paul)

Respice quas offerimus hostias, omnipotens Deus, in commemoratione beati Pauli, et praesta, ut, qui dominicae passionis mysteria celebramus, imitemur quod agimus. Per Christum.

Almighty God, look upon the sacrifice we offer in remembrance of Saint Paul, and grant that we who celebrate the mysteries of the Lord's passion may imitate what we celebrate. We ask this....

Prayer after Communion
(Saint Paul)

Deus, qui crucis mysterium in beato Paulo mirabiliter illustrasti, concede propitius, ut, ex hoc sacrificio roborati, Christo fideles haereamus, et in Ecclesia ad salutem omnium operemur. Per Christum.

God our Father, in marvelous fashion you showed forth the mystery of the Cross in the life of Saint Paul. In your mercy grant that, strengthened by this sacrifice, we may faithfully remain close to Christ and work within the Church for the salvation of all people. We ask this....

OCTOBER 23
SAINT JOHN OF CAPISTRANO

PRIEST

Collect

Deus, qui, ad populum fidelem in angustiis confortandum, beatum Ioannem suscitasti, praesta, quaesumus, ut nos in tuae protectionis securitate constituas, et Ecclesiam tuam perpetua pace custodias. Per Dominum.

God our Father, you raised up Saint John of Capistrano to comfort your faithful people in their trials. Please grant us the security of your protection and preserve your Church in unending peace. We ask this....

Prayer over the Gifts and Prayer after Communion:
Cf. Common of Pastors (for Missionaries), p. 203

OCTOBER 24
SAINT ANTHONY MARY CLARET

BISHOP

Collect

Deus, qui in evangelizandis populis beatum Antonium Mariam episcopum mira caritate et patientia roborasti, eius nobis intercessione concede, ut, quae tua sunt quaerentes, enixe in Christo lucrandis fratribus incumbamus. Per Dominum.

God our Father, you strengthened your bishop Saint Anthony Mary Claret with wonderful charity and patience in the task of preaching the Gospel to the nations. Through his intercession grant that we may seek the things that belong to you and work earnestly to gain brothers and sisters in Christ. We ask this....

Prayer over the Gifts and Prayer after Communion:
Cf. Common of Pastors (for Bishops), p. 199, or Common of Pastors (for Missionaries), p. 203, or Common of Holy Men and Women (for Religious), p. 211.

OCTOBER 28
SAINTS SIMON AND JUDE

APOSTLES

Collect

Deus, qui nos per beatos Apostolos ad agnitionem tui nominis venire tribuisti, intercedentibus sanctis Simone et Iuda, concede propitius, ut semper augeatur Ecclesia incrementis in te credentium populorum. Per Dominum.

God our Father, you ordained that we should come to the knowledge of your name through your holy apostles. Through the intercession of Saints Simon and Jude, mercifully grant that the Church may always be increased by the growing number of people who believe in you. We ask this....

Prayer over the Gifts

Gloriam, Domine, sanctorum apostolorum Simonis et Iudae perpetuam venerantes, quaesumus, ut vota nostra suscipias et ad sacra mysteria celebranda nos digne perducas. Per Christum.

Lord, as we honor the eternal glory of your holy apostles Simon and Jude, we ask you to receive our prayers and lead us to a worthy celebration of these sacred mysteries. We ask this....

Prayer after Communion

Perceptis, Domine, sacramentis, supplices in Spiritu Sancto deprecamur, ut, quae pro apostolorum Simonis et Iudae veneranda gerimus passione, nos in tua dilectione conservent. Per Christum.

Lord, now that we have received your sacraments, we humbly pray in the Holy Spirit that what we do in honoring the sufferings of your apostles Simon and Jude may preserve us in your love. We ask this....

NOVEMBER 1
ALL SAINTS

Collect

Omnipotens sempiterne Deus, qui nos omnium Sanctorum tuorum merita sub una tribuisti celebritate venerari, quaesumus, ut desideratam nobis tuae propitiationis abundantiam, multiplicatis intercessoribus, largiaris. Per Dominum.

Almighty and eternal God, you have given us the opportunity to honor the meritorious lives of all your saints in a single celebration. Since there are so many saints to intercede for us, please grant us the fullness of your mercy which we so eagerly desire. We ask this....

Prayer over the Gifts

Grata tibi sint, Domine, munera, quae pro cunctorum offerimus honore Sanctorum, et concede, ut, quos iam credimus de sua immortalitate securos, sentiamus de nostra salute sollicitos. Per Christum.

Lord, may the offering which we make in honor of all your saints be pleasing to you. We believe that they are already assured of their own eternal reward; grant that we may experience their concern for our salvation. We ask this....

Prayer after Communion

Mirabilem te, Deus, et unum Sanctum in omnibus Sanctis tuis adorantes, tuam gratiam imploramus, qua, sanctificationem in tui amoris plenitudine consummantes, ex hac mensa peregrinantium ad caelestis patriae convivium transeamus. Per Christum.

God our Father, we adore your glory as it is manifested in the number of your saints, for you are marvelous, you alone are holy. We beg for your grace; by means of it, may we complete our period of sanctification in the fullness of your love and pass from this altar of wayfarers to the banquet of our heavenly home. We ask this....

NOVEMBER 2
ALL SOULS

FIRST MASS

Collect

Preces nostras, quaesumus, Domine, benignus exaudi, ut, dum attollitur nostra fides in Filio tuo a mortuis suscitato, in famulorum tuorum praestolanda resurrectione spes quoque nostra firmetur. Per Dominum.

Lord, in your mercy please hear our prayers. As our faith is strengthened in your Son, who was raised from the dead, so too may our hope be made firm as we wait for the resurrection of your faithful ones. We ask this....

Prayer over the Gifts

Nostris, Domine, propitiare muneribus, ut famuli tui defuncti assumantur in gloriam cum Filio tuo, cuius magno pietatis iungimur sacramento. Per Christum.

Lord, be pleased by our gifts, so that your faithful people who have died may be taken into glory with your Son, by whose great sacrament of love we are made one. We ask this....

Prayer after Communion

Praesta, quaesumus, Domine, ut famuli tui defuncti in mansionem lucis transeant et pacis, pro quibus paschale celebravimus sacramentum. Per Christum.

Lord, please grant that your sons and daughters who have died and on whose behalf we have offered this Easter sacrifice may pass to an eternal home of light and peace. We ask this....

SECOND MASS

Collect

Deus, gloria fidelium et vita iustorum, cuius Filii morte et resurrectione redempti sumus, propitiare famulis tuis defunctis, ut, qui resurrectionis nostrae mysterium agnoverunt, aeternae beatitudinis gaudia percipere mereantur. Per Dominum.

God our Father, you are the glory of those who believe in you and the life of those who are just. By your Son's death and resurrection we have been redeemed. Look with forgiveness upon your sons and daughters who have died, so that just as they have come to know the mystery of our resurrection, so too they may be privileged to receive the joys of eternal happiness. We ask this....

Prayer over the Gifts

Omnipotens et misericors Deus, his sacrificiis ablue, quaesumus, famulos tuos defunctos a peccatis eorum in sanguine Christi, ut, quos mundasti aqua baptismatis, indesinenter purifices indulgentia pietatis. Per Christum.

Almighty and merciful God, through this sacrifice please wash your faithful departed in the blood of Christ and free them from their sins. With your forgiving love, ceaselessly purify those whom you have cleansed in the water of baptism. We ask this....

Prayer after Communion

Sumpto sacramento Unigeniti tui, qui pro nobis immolatus resurrexit in gloria, te, Domine, suppliciter exoramus pro famulis tuis defunctis, ut, paschalibus mysteriis mundati, futurae resurrectionis munere glorientur. Per Christum.

Lord, we have received the sacrament of your only Son, who was sacrificed for us and rose again in glory. We humbly pray to you on behalf of your sons and daughters who have died, asking that they may be cleansed by these Easter mysteries and rejoice in the gift of the resurrection to come. We ask this....

THIRD MASS

Collect

Deus, qui Unigenitum tuum, devicta morte, ad caelestia transire fecisti, concede famulis tuis defunctis, ut, huius vitae mortalitate devicta, te conditorem et redemptorem possint perpetuo contemplari. Per Dominum.

God our Father, you caused your only Son to ascend into heaven after he had conquered death. Grant that your faithful departed ones, having overcome the frailness of this life, may be able to look upon you, their creator and redeemer, for ever and ever. We ask this....

Prayer over the Gifts

Pro omnibus famulis tuis in Christo dormientibus hostiam, Domine, suscipe benignus oblatam, ut, per hoc sacrificium singulare vinculis mortis exuti, vitam mereamur aeternam. Per Christum.

Lord, in your mercy receive these gifts, offered for all your sons and daughters who sleep in Christ. Through this unique sacrifice may they be freed from the bonds of death and be privileged to possess eternal life. We ask this....

Prayer after Communion

Multiplica, Domine, his sacrificiis susceptis, super famulos tuos defunctos misericordiam tuam, et, quibus donasti baptismi gratiam, da eis aeternorum plenitudinem gaudiorum. Per Christum.

Lord, receive this sacrifice and pour out your mercy on your sons and daughters who have died. You gave them the grace of baptism; grant them also the fullness of eternal happiness. We ask this....

NOVEMBER 3
SAINT MARTIN DE PORRES

RELIGIOUS

Collect

Deus, qui beatum Martinum per humilitatis iter ad caelestem gloriam perduxisti, tribue nobis eius ita nunc persequi exempla praeclara, ut exaltari cum ipso mereamur in caelis. Per Dominum.

God our Father, by means of the pathway of humility you led Saint Martin de Porres to heavenly glory. Grant that in this life we may follow his shining example in such a way that we may be privileged to be glorified with him in heaven. We ask this....

Prayer over the Gifts and Prayer after Communion:
Cf. Common of Holy Men and Women (for Religious), p. 211.

NOVEMBER 4
SAINT CHARLES BORROMEO

BISHOP

Collect

Custodi, quaesumus, Domine, in populo tuo spiritum, quo beatum Carolum episcopum implevisti, ut Ecclesia indesinenter renovetur, et, Christi se imagini conformans, ipsius vultum mundo valeat ostendere. Per Dominum.

Lord, please preserve among your people that spirit with which you filled your bishop Saint Charles Borromeo, so that the Church may be constantly renewed and, molding itself to the image of Christ, may be able to show his countenance to the world. We ask this....

Prayer over the Gifts

Intende munera, Domine, altaribus tuis pro beati Caroli commemoratione proposita, et huius sacrificii virtute concede, ut, sicut illum pastoralis officii vigilantia et praeclaris virtutum meritis sublimasti, ita nos facias sinceris operum fructibus abundare. Per Christum.

Lord, look upon the gifts placed on your altar in memory of Saint Charles. You made him exemplary in his watchful care over his pastoral charge and in the shining merits of his virtues. By the power of this sacrifice, grant that we too may be rich in the true fruits of our good works. We ask this....

Prayer after Communion

Praestent nobis, quaesumus, Domine, sacra mysteria quae sumpsimus eam animi fortitudinem, quae beatum Carolum reddidit in ministerio fidelem et in caritate ferventem. Per Christum.

Lord, we pray that the sacred mysteries we have received may provide us with that strength of soul which made Saint Charles so faithful in his office and so ardent in his love. We ask this....

NOVEMBER 10
SAINT LEO THE GREAT

POPE AND DOCTOR OF THE CHURCH

Collect

Deus, qui adversus Ecclesiam tuam, in apostolicae petrae soliditate fundatam, portas inferi numquam praevalere permittis, da ei, quaesumus, ut, intercedente beato Leone papa, in tua veritate consistens, pace continua muniatur. Per Dominum.

God our Father, you never permit the gates of hell to prevail against your Church, founded as it is on the solid rock of the Apostles. Through the intercession of Pope Saint Leo the Great, grant that it may remain firm in your truth and be safe in unending peace. We ask this....

Prayer over the Gifts

Oblatis muneribus, quaesumus, Domine, Ecclesiam tuam benignus illumina, ut et gregis tui proficiat ubique successus, et grati fiant nomini tuo, te gubernante, pastores. Per Christum.

Lord, through the gifts we have offered, please enlighten your Church, so that the growth of your flock may everywhere be fostered and its shepherds, under your guidance, may be pleasing to you. We ask this....

Prayer after Communion

Refectione sancta enutritam guberna, quaesumus, Domine, tuam placatus Ecclesiam, ut, potenti moderatione directa, et incrementa libertatis accipiat, et in religionis integritate persistat. Per Christum.

Lord, in your mercy please govern your Church, which you have fed with sacred food. Guided by your powerful hand, may it experience an increase in freedom and stand firm in the fullness of its life of faith. We ask this....

NOVEMBER 11
SAINT MARTIN OF TOURS

BISHOP

Collect

Deus, qui in beato Martino episcopo sive per vitam sive per mortem magnificatus es, innova gratiae tuae mirabilia in cordibus nostris, ut neque mors neque vita separare nos possit a caritate tua. Per Dominum.

God our Father, in the life and the death of your bishop Saint Martin of Tours you were equally glorified. Renew the wonders of your grace in our hearts, so that neither death nor life can separate us from your love. We ask this....

Prayer over the Gifts

Sanctifica, quaesumus, Domine Deus, haec munera, quae in honorem sancti Martini laetanter offerimus, ut per ea vita nostra inter adversa et prospera semper dirigatur. Per Christum.

Lord God, please make these gifts holy. We offer them joyfully in honor of Saint Martin, so that through them our lives may find guidance both in good times and in bad. We ask this....

Prayer after Communion

Da nobis, Domine, unitatis sacramento refectis, perfectam in omnibus cum tua voluntate concordiam, ut, sicut beatus Martinus totum se tibi subiecit, ita et nos esse tui veraciter gloriemur. Per Christum.

Lord, we have been renewed by the sacrament of unity. Grant us a complete conformity to your divine will in all things, so that just as Saint Martin surrendered himself wholly to you, so we too may truthfully glory in belonging to you. We ask this....

NOVEMBER 12
SAINT JOSAPHAT

BISHOP AND MARTYR

Collect

Excita, quaesumus, Domine, in Ecclesia tua Spiritum, quo repletus beatus Iosaphat animam suam pro ovibus posuit, ut, eo intercedente, nos quoque eodem Spiritu roborati, animam nostram pro fratribus ponere non vereamur. Per Dominum.

Lord, please stir up within your Church that Spirit which filled Saint Josaphat and inspired him to give his life for his flock. Through his holy prayers, may we too be strengthened by that same Spirit, and not be afraid to lay down our lives for our brothers and sisters. We ask this....

Prayer over the Gifts

Clementissime Deus, munera haec tua benedictione perfunde, et nos in tua fide confirma, quam sanctus Iosaphat effuso sanguine asseruit. Per Christum.

Most merciful God, pour forth your blessing on these gifts, and strengthen us in that faith in you which Saint Josephat proclaimed by the shedding of his blood. We ask this....

Prayer after Communion

Spiritum, Domine, fortitudinis et pacis haec nobis tribuat mensa caelestis, ut, sancti Iosaphat exemplo, vitam nostram ad honorem et unitatem Ecclesiae libenter impendamus. Per Christum.

Lord, may this heavenly banquet confer on us the spirit of courage and peace, so that, following the example of Saint Josephat, we may gladly spend our lives for the honor and unity of the Church. We ask this....

NOVEMBER 15
SAINT ALBERT THE GREAT

BISHOP AND DOCTOR
OF THE CHURCH

Collect

Deus, qui Albertum episcopum in humana sapientia cum divina fide componenda magnum effecisti, da nobis, quaesumus, ita eius magisterii inhaerere doctrinis, ut per scientiarum progressus ad profundiorem tui cognitionem et amorem perveniamus. Per Dominum.

God our Father, you made your bishop Saint Albert the Great renowned for his ability to reconcile human wisdom and divine faith. Please grant that we may be faithful to the truths he taught, and so, through a greater knowledge of the human sciences, come to a deeper knowledge and love of you. We ask this....

Prayer over the Gifts and Prayer after Communion:
Cf. Common of Pastors (for Bishops), p. 199, or Common of Doctors of the Church, p. 205.

NOVEMBER 16
SAINT MARGARET OF SCOTLAND

SAINT GERTRUDE

VIRGIN

Collect
(Saint Margaret)

Deus, qui beatam Margaritam eximia in pauperes caritate mirabilem effecisti, da ut, eius intercessione et exemplo, imaginem bonitatis tuae inter homines referamus. Per Dominum.

God our Father, you made Saint Margaret of Scotland outstanding in her great love for the poor. Through her intercession and exaxmple, grant that we may spread the image of your goodness among men and women. We ask this....

Prayer over the Gifts and Prayer after Communion:
Cf. Common of Holy Men and Women (for Those Who Performed Works of Mercy), p. 213.

Collect
(Saint Gertrude)

Deus, qui iucundam tibi mansionem in corde beatae Gertrudis virginis praeparasti, ipsius intercessione, cordis nostri tenebras clementer illustra, ut te in nobis praesentem et operantem laetanter experiamur. Per Dominum.

God our Father, you prepared a most pleasing dwelling place for yourself in the heart of your virgin Saint Gertrude. Through her intercession, mercifully enlighten the darkness of our hearts, so that we may have the joy of experiencing your presence and action within us. We ask this....

Prayer over the Gifts and Prayer after Communion:
Cf. Common of Virgins, p. 206, or Common of Holy Men and Women (for Religious), p. 211.

NOVEMBER 17
SAINT ELIZABETH OF HUNGARY

RELIGIOUS

Collect

Deus, qui beatae Elizabeth tribuisti in pauperibus Christum cognoscere ac venerari, da nobis, eius intercessione, egenis et tribulatis iugi caritate servire. Per Dominum.

God our Father, you gave Saint Elizabeth of Hungary the gift of recognizing and reverencing Christ in his poor. Through her intercession, grant that we may serve the needy and the troubled with unfailing love. We ask this....

*Prayer over the Gifts and
Prayer after Communion:*
Cf. Common of Holy Men and Women (for Those Who Performed Works of Mercy), p. 213, or Common of Holy Men and Women (for Religious), p. 211.

NOVEMBER 18
DEDICATION OF THE CHURCHES OF PETER AND PAUL

Collect

Ecclesiam tuam, Domine, apostolicis defende praesidiis, ut, per quos initium divinae cognitionis accepit, per eos usque in finem saeculi capiat gratiae caelestis augmentum. Per Dominum.

Lord, defend your Church with the vigilant strength of the Apostles. Through the aid of those from whom it received the beginnings of its knowledge of you, may it receive an increase of heavenly grace from now until the end of time. We ask this....

Prayer over the Gifts

Servitutis nostrae tibi, Domine, munus offerentes, tuam deprecamur clementiam, ut tradita nobis apostolorum Petri et Pauli ministerio veritas in cordibus nostris illibata perseveret. Per Christum.

Lord, as we offer you the gift that marks our service to you, we humbly beg for your mercy, asking that the truth given us by the ministry of the apostles Peter and Paul may remain unsullied in our hearts. We ask this....

Prayer after Communion

Populus tuus, quaesumus, Domine, caelesti pane refectus, apostolorum Petri et Pauli commemoratione laetetur, quem eorum donasti patrocinio gubernari. Per Christum.

Lord, may your people, refreshed with your heavenly food, rejoice on this feast of the apostles Peter and Paul, for you have given us the gift of being guided by their intercession. We ask this....

NOVEMBER 21
PRESENTATION OF THE BLESSED VIRGIN MARY

Collect

Sanctissimae venerantibus Virginis Mariae memoriam gloriosam, ipsius nobis, quaesumus, Domine, intercessione concede, ut de plenitudine gratiae tuae nos quoque mereamur accipere. Per Dominum.

Lord, as we honor the glorious memory of the most holy Virgin Mary, we ask that, through her intercession, we too may be privileged to receive of the fullness of your grace. We ask this....

*Prayer over the Gifts and
Prayer after Communion:*
Cf. Common of the Blessed Virgin, p. 186.

NOVEMBER 22
SAINT CECELIA

VIRGIN AND MARTYR

Collect

Supplicationibus nostris, Domine, adesto propitius, et, beatae Ceceliae intercessione, preces nostras dignanter exaudi. Per Dominum.

Lord, in your kindness listen to our pleas and, through the intercession of Saint Cecelia, mercifully hear our prayers. We ask this....

Prayer over the Gifts and Prayer after Communion:
Cf. Common of Martyrs, p. 193, or Common of Virgins, p. 206.

NOVEMBER 23
SAINT CLEMENT I

POPE AND MARTYR

SAINT COLUMBAN

ABBOT

Collect
(Saint Clement I)

Omnipotens sempiterne Deus, qui in omnium sanctorum tuorum es virtute mirabilis, da nobis in beati Clementis annua commemoratione laetari, qui, Filii tui sacerdos et martyr, quod mysterio gessit, testimonio comprobavit, et quod praedicavit ore, confirmavit exemplo. Per Dominum.

Almighty and eternal God, you are wonderful in the goodness and strength of all your saints. Grant that we may rejoice in this yearly celebration in honor of Pope Saint Clement I, who, as a priest and martyr of your Son, affirmed by his martyrdom what he celebrated at the altar and confirmed by his deeds what he preached in words. We ask this....

Prayer over the Gifts and Prayer after Communion:
Cf. Common of Martyrs, p. 193, or Common of Pastors (for a Pope), p. 198.

Collect
(Saint Columban)

Deus, qui in beato Columbano evangelizandi munus et monasticae vitae studium mirabiliter coniunxisti, praesta, quaesumus, ut, eius intercessione et exemplo, te super omnia quaerere et credentium populum augere studeamus. Per Dominum.

God our Father, in Saint Columban you joined in marvelous fashion the work of preaching the Gospel with the pursuit of the monastic life. By his intercession and example, please grant that we may strive to seek you above all things and to increase the number of those who believe in you. We ask this....

Prayer over the Gifts and Prayer after Communion:
Cf. Common of Pastors (for Missionaries), p. 203, or Common of Holy Men and Women (for Religious), p. 211.

NOVEMBER 30
SAINT ANDREW

APOSTLE

Collect

Maiestatem tuam, Domine, suppliciter exoramus, ut, sicut Ecclesiae tuae beatus Andreas apostolus exstitit praedicator et rector, ita apud te sit pro nobis perpetuus intercessor. Per Dominum.

Lord, your apostle Saint Andrew was both preacher and ruler in your Church on earth. We humbly beg your divine majesty to grant that he may likewise be our unceasing advocate in your presence in heaven. We ask this....

Prayer over the Gifts

Concede nobis, omnipotens Deus, ut his muneribus, quae in beati Andreae festivitate deferimus, et tibi placeamus exhibitis, et vivificemur acceptis. Per Christum.

Almighty God, we bring these gifts on this feast of Saint Andrew. Grant that we may please you by offering them and be granted divine life by your accepting them. We ask this....

Prayer after Communion

Roboret nos, Domine, sacramenti tui communio, ut, exemplo beati Andreae apostoli, Christi mortificationem ferentes, cum ipso vivere mereamur in gloria. Per Christum.

Lord, may our reception of your sacrament strengthen us, so that, through the example of your apostle Saint Andrew, we may carry about with us the death of Christ and so be privileged to live with him in glory. We ask this....

DECEMBER 3
SAINT FRANCIS XAVIER

PRIEST

Collect

Deus, qui beati Francisci praedicatione multos tibi populos acquisisti, da ut fidelium animi eodem fidei zelo ferveant, et uberrima ubique prole Ecclesia sancta laetetur. Per Dominum.

God our Father, through the preaching of Saint Francis Xavier you won many peoples to your name. Grant that the hearts of your faithful may be inflamed with the same zeal for the faith that he had, and that your holy Church may everywhere rejoice in the large number of her children. We ask this....

Prayer over the Gifts

Suscipe, Domine, munera, quae tibi in beati Francisci commemoratione deferimus, et praesta ut, sicut ille desiderio salutis hominum ad terras longinquas est progressus, ita et nos, testimonium Evangelio efficaciter perhibentes, ad te cum fratribus properare festinemus. Per Christum.

Lord, receive the gifts which we bring in memory of Saint Francis. He journeyed to far-off lands in his longing for the salvation of men and women; grant that we too may bear effective witness to the Gospel and, along with our brothers and sisters, may hasten to come quickly to you. We ask this....

Prayer after Communion

Mysteria tua, Deus, eum in nobis accendant caritatis ardorem, quo beatus Franciscus pro animarum salute flagravit, ut, vocatione nostra dignius ambulantes, promissum bonis operariis praemium cum eo consequamur. Per Christum.

Lord, may your sacred mysteries enkindle in us that burning love with which Saint Francis was inflamed in seeking the salvation of souls. May we live in a manner more worthy of our calling and, with Saint Francis, receive the reward you have promised to those who labor faithfully. We ask this....

DECEMBER 4
SAINT JOHN OF DAMASCUS

PRIEST AND DOCTOR OF THE CHURCH

Collect

Praesta nobis, quaesumus, Domine, sancti Ioannis presbyteri precibus adiuvari, ut vera fides, quam ille excellenter docuit, sit semper lux et fortitudo nostra. Per Dominum.

Lord, please grant that we may be helped by the prayers of your priest Saint John Damascene, so that the true faith, which he taught so expertly, may ever be our light and our strength. We ask this....

Prayer over the Gifts and Prayer after Communion:
Cf. Common of Pastors, p. 200, or Common of Doctors of the Church, p. 205.

DECEMBER 6
SAINT NICHOLAS

BISHOP

Collect

Misericordiam tuam, Domine, supplices imploramus, et, beati Nicolai episcopi interveniente suffragio, nos in omnibus custodi periculis, ut via salutis nobis pateat expedita. Per Dominum.

Lord, we humbly ask for your mercy. Through the intercessory prayers of your bishop Saint Nicholas, guard us in the midst of every danger, so that the path of salvation may readily lie open to us. We ask this....

Prayer over the Gifts and Prayer after Communion
Cf. Common of Pastors (for Bishops), p. 199.

DECEMBER 7
SAINT AMBROSE

BISHOP AND DOCTOR OF THE CHURCH

Collect

Deus, qui beatum Ambrosium episcopum catholicae fidei doctorem et apostolicae fortitudinis exemplum effecisti, excita in Ecclesia tua viros secundum cor tuum, qui eam fortiter et sapienter gubernent. Per Dominum.

God our Father, you made your bishop Saint Ambrose a renowned teacher of the Catholic faith and a model of apostolic courage. Raise up in your Church men after your own heart to govern it with courage and wisdom. We ask this....

Prayer over the Gifts

Illa nos, quaesumus, Domine, divina tractantes, Spiritus Sanctus fidei luce perfundat, qua beatum Ambrosium ad gloriae tuae propagationem iugiter collustravit. Per Christum.

Lord, as we celebrate your divine mysteries, we ask that the Holy Spirit may pour forth upon us that same light of faith with which he constantly illumined Saint Ambrose in order to spread your glory. We ask this....

Prayer after Communion

Huius sacramenti, Domine, virtute roboratos, fac nos beati Ambrosi documentis ita proficere, ut, viriliter per tuas semitas festinantes, ad aeterni suavitatem convivii praeparemur. Per Christum.

Lord, we are strengthened by the power of this sacrament. Make us so progress in the teachings of Saint Ambrose that we may run courageously along your paths and be made ready for the delights of your eternal banquet. We ask this....

DECEMBER 8
IMMACULATE CONCEPTION

Collect

Deus, qui per immaculatam Virginis Conceptionem dignum Filio tuo habitaculum praeparasti, quaesumus, ut, qui ex morte eiusdem Filii tui praevisa, eam ab omni labe praeservasti, nos quoque mundos, eius intercessione, ad te pervenire concedas. Per Dominum.

God our Father, through the Immaculate Conception of the Blessed Virgin you prepared a worthy dwelling-place for your Son. You preserved her from all stain because of the death you foresaw your Son would suffer. We ask that, through her intercession, you cleanse us from sin and allow us to come to you in heaven. We ask this....

Prayer over the Gifts

Salutarem hostiam, quam in sollemnitate immaculatae Conceptionis beatae Virginis Mariae tibi, Domine, offerimus, suscipe dignanter, et praesta, ut, sicut illam tua gratia praeveniente ab omni labe profitemur immunem, ita, eius intercessione, a culpis omnibus liberemur. Per Christum.

Lord, mercifully receive the saving gift which we offer you on this feast of the Immaculate Conception of the Blessed Virgin Mary. We proclaim that through your anticipatory grace she was kept free of all stain; through her intercession, grant that we too may be freed from all our faults. We ask this....

Prayer after Communion

Sacramenta quae sumpsimus, Domine Deus noster, illius in nobis culpae vulnera reparent, a qua immaculatam beatae Mariae Conceptionem singulariter praeservasti. Per Christum.

Lord our God, may the sacrament we have received heal within us the wounds of that guilt from which, in a unique way, you preserved the Immaculate Conception of the Blessed Virgin Mary. We ask this....

DECEMBER 11
SAINT DAMASUS I

POPE

Collect

Praesta, quaesumus, Domine, ut martyrum tuorum iugiter merita celebremus, quorum exstitit beatus Damasus papa cultor et amator. Per Dominum.

Lord, please grant that we may ever celebrate the meritorious lives of your martyrs, whom Pope Saint Damasus so notably venerated and loved. We ask this....

Prayer over the Gifts and Prayer after Communion:
Cf. *Common of Pastors (for a Pope)*, p. 198.

DECEMBER 12
SAINT JANE FRANCES DE CHANTAL

RELIGIOUS

Collect

Deus, qui beatam Ioannam Franciscam per varias vitae semitas praeclaris meritis illustrasti, ipsius nobis intercessione concede, ut, in vocatione nostra fideliter ambulantes, lucis exempla iugiter ostendamus. Per Dominum.

God our Father, you made Saint Jane Frances de Chantal renowned for her outstanding merits in two different walks of life. Through her intercession grant that we may walk faithfully in our calling and ever provide an example of your inspiration. We ask this....

Prayer over the Gifts and Prayer after Communion:
Cf. Common of Holy Men and Women (for Religious), p. 211.

DECEMBER 13
SAINT LUCY

VIRGIN AND MARTYR

Collect

Intercessio nos, quaesumus, Domine, sanctae Luciae virginis et martyris gloriosa confoveat, ut eius natalicia et temporaliter frequentemus, et conspiciamus aeterna. Per Dominum.

Lord, we ask that the heavenly intercession of your virgin and martyr Saint Lucy may always encourage us, so that we may celebrate her birth while we are here on earth, and at the same time look forward to a heavenly birth. We ask this....

Prayer over the Gifts and Prayer after Communion:
Cf. Common of Martyrs, p. 193, or Common of Virgins, p. 206.

DECEMBER 14
SAINT JOHN OF THE CROSS

PRIEST AND DOCTOR OF THE CHURCH

Collect

Deus, qui sanctum Ioannem presbyterum perfectae sui abnegationis et crucis amatorem eximium effecisti, concede ut, eius imitationi iugiter inhaerentes, ad contemplationem gloriae tuae perveniamus aeternam. Per Dominum.

God our Father, you gave your priest Saint John of the Cross an exemplary love of complete self-denial and the Cross. Grant that we may always persevere in imitating him, and so come to the eternal vision of your glory. We ask this....

Prayer over the Gifts

Respice quas offerimus hostias, omnipotens Deus, in commemoratione beati Ioannis, et praesta, ut, qui dominicae passionis mysteria celebramus, imitemur quod agimus. Per Christum.

Almighty God, look upon the gifts we offer in memory of Saint John, and grant that we who celebrate the mysteries of the Lord's passion may imitate that in which we take part. We ask this....

Prayer after Communion

Deus, qui crucis mysterium in beato Ioanne mirabiliter illustrasti, concede propitius, ut, ex hoc sacrificio roborati, Christo fideles haereamus, et in Ecclesia ad salutem omnium operemur. Per Christum.

God our Father, in the life of Saint John you wondrously exemplified the mystery of the Cross. In your mercy, grant that, strengthened by this sacrifice, we may faithfully cling to Christ and work within the Church for the salvation of all. We ask this....

DECEMBER 21
SAINT PETER CANISIUS

PRIEST AND DOCTOR
OF THE CHURCH

Collect

Deus, qui ad tuendam catholicam fidem virtute et doctrina beatum Petrum presbyterum roborasti, eius intercessione concede, ut, qui veritatem quaerunt, te Deum gaudenter inveniant, et in tua confessione populus credentium perseveret. Per Dominum.

God our Father, in order to safeguard the Catholic faith, you strengthened your priest Saint Peter Canisius with virtue and learning. Through his intercession, grant that those who seek the truth may joyfully discover you, the one God; grant also that the people who already believe in you may remain firm in their faith. We ask this....

*Prayer over the Gifts and
Prayer after Communion:*
Cf. Common of Pastors, p. 200, or Common of Doctors of the Church, p. 205.

DECEMBER 23
SAINT JOHN OF KANTY

PRIEST

Collect

Da, quaesumus, omnipotens Deus, ut, exemplo sancti Ioannis presbyteri, in sanctorum scientia procedamus, atque, misericordiam omnibus exhibentes, apud te indulgentiam consequamur. Per Dominum.

Almighty God, please grant that, through the example of your priest Saint John of Kanty, we may progress in the wisdom of the saints and, by showing mercy to everyone, may ourselves attain your forgiveness. We ask this....

*Prayer over the Gifts and
Prayer after Communion:*
Cf. Common of Pastors, p. 200, or Common of Holy Men and Women (for Those Who Performed Works of Mercy), p. 213.

DECEMBER 26
SAINT STEPHEN,
THE FIRST MARTYR

Collect

Da nobis, quaesumus, Domine, imitari quod colimus, ut discamus et inimicos diligere, quia eius natalicia celebramus, qui novit etiam pro persecutoribus exorare. Per Dominum.

Lord, we celebrate today the birth into eternal life of one who knew how to pray even for his persecutors. Please grant that we may imitate what we celebrate, so that we too may learn to love even our enemies. We ask this....

Prayer over the Gifts

Munera, quaesumus, Domine, tibi sint hodiernae devotionis accepta, quae beati Stephani martyris commemoratio gloriosa depromit. Per Christum.

Lord, we ask that these gifts, which we bring today in token of our homage and which the blessed feast of your martyr Saint Stephen prompts us to offer, may be acceptable to you. We ask this....

Prayer after Communion

Gratias agimus, Domine, multiplicatis circa nos miserationibus tuis, qui et Filii tui nativitate nos salvas, et beati martyris Stephani celebratione laetificas. Per Christum.

Lord, we thank you for your countless mercies to us, for you grant us salvation by the birth of your Son and you fill us with joy on this feast of your martyr Saint Stephen. We make our prayer through....

DECEMBER 27
SAINT JOHN
THE EVANGELIST

APOSTLE

Collect

Deus, qui per beatum apostolum Ioannem Verbi tui nobis arcana reserasti, praesta, quaesumus, ut, quod ille nostris auribus excellenter infudit, intelligentiae competentis eruditione capiamus. Per Dominum.

God our Father, through your apostle Saint John you made the mystery of your Word known to us. Please grant that our minds may be sufficiently prepared to receive what Saint John so wondrously proclaimed to us. We ask this....

Prayer over the Gifts

Munera, quaesumus, Domine, oblata sanctifica, et praesta, ut ex huius cenae convivio aeterni Verbi secreta hauriamus, quae ex eodem fonte apostolo tuo Ioanni revelasti. Per Christum.

Lord, please make holy these gifts we have offered. From the banquet that is this supper you revealed the mysteries of your eternal Word to your apostle John. Grant that, from that same source, we too may drink deeply of those mysteries. We ask this....

Prayer after Communion

Praesta, quaesumus, omnipotens Deus, ut Verbum caro factum, quod beatus Ioannes apostolus praedicavit, per hoc mysterium quod celebravimus habitet semper in nobis. Per Christum.

Almighty God, please grant that the Word made flesh, whom your apostle Saint John proclaimed, may always dwell in us through the power of the mystery that we have celebrated. We ask this....

DECEMBER 28
HOLY INNOCENTS

MARTYRS

Collect

Deus, cuius hodierna die praeconium Innocentes martyres non loquendo sed moriendo confessi sunt, da, quaesumus, ut fidem tuam, quam lingua nostra loquitur, etiam moribus vita fateatur. Per Dominum.

God our Father, your holy innocent martyrs today made their proclamation of faith not by speech but by death. Please grant that, by how we live our lives, we may bear witness to the faith in you which our voices declare. We ask this....

Prayer over the Gifts

Suscipe, Domine, quaesumus, devotorum munera famulorum, et eos tuis purifica servientes pietate mysteriis, quibus etiam iustificas ignorantes. Per Christum.

Lord, please receive the gifts of your children who love you. Purify them as they faithfully honor the mysteries of your love by which you bring them to holiness even before they come to know you. We ask this....

Prayer after Communion

Salvationis abundantiam tribue, Domine, fidelibus in eorum festivitate tua sancta sumentibus, qui, Filium tuum humana necdum voce profitentes, caelesti sunt gratia pro eius nativitate coronati. Per Christum.

Lord, grant the fullness of salvation to your faithful people as they receive your holy gifts on the feast of those who, though they could not yet profess their belief in your Son by means of human speech, were none the less crowned with heavenly favor because of his birth. We ask this....

DECEMBER 29
SAINT THOMAS BECKET

BISHOP AND MARTYR

Collect

Deus, qui beato Thomae martyri pro iustitia magno animo vitam profundere tribuisti, da nobis, eius intercessione, nostram pro Christo vitam in hoc saeculo abnegare, ut eam in caelo invenire possimus. Per Dominum.

God our Father, you gave your martyr Saint Thomas Becket the grace to pour out his life with great generosity for the sake of justice. Through his intercession, grant that we may renounce our lives in this world for the sake of Christ, so that we may be able to find them in heaven. We ask this....

Prayer over the Gifts and Prayer after Communion:
Cf. Common of Martyrs, p. 193, or Common of Pastors (for Bishops), p. 199.

DECEMBER 31
SAINT SYLVESTER I

POPE

Collect

Auxiliare, Domine, populo tuo, beati Sylvestri papae intercessione suffulto, ut, praesentem vitam sub tua gubernatione transcurrens, mereatur feliciter invenire perpetuam. Per Christum.

Lord, grant your help to your people, who are sustained by the prayers of Pope Saint Sylvester, so that they may pass through this present life under your guidance and have the joyful privilege of finding life everlasting. We ask this....

Prayer over the Gifts and Prayer after Communion:
Cf. Common of Pastors (for a Pope), p. 198.

COMMONS

COMMON OF THE DEDICATION OF A CHURCH

ON THE ANNIVERSARY OF THE DEDICATION, IN THE CHURCH ITSELF

Collect

Deus, qui nobis per singulos annos huius sancti templi tui consecrationis reparas diem, exaudi preces populi tui, et praesta, ut fiat hic tibi semper purum servitium et nobis plena redemptio. Per Dominum.

God our Father, each year you bring back for us the day on which this holy church of yours was consecrated. Hear the prayers of your people, and grant that in this church our service of you may always be untainted and in it we may find the fullness of redemption. We ask this....

Prayer over the Gifts

Memores diei quo domum tuam, Domine, gloria dignatus es ac sanctitate replere, nosmetipsos, quaesumus, fac hostias tibi semper acceptas. Per Christum.

Lord, we are mindful of the day when you saw fit to fill this dwelling place of yours with your own glorious holiness. We ask that you make us into offerings that are always acceptable to you. We ask this....

Prayer after Communion

Benedictionis tuae, quaesumus, Domine, plebs tibi sacra fructus reportet et gaudium, ut, quod in huius festivitatis die corporali servitio exhibuit, spiritaliter se retulisse cognoscat. Per Christum.

Lord, we ask that your holy people receive the joyous benefit of your blessing, so that they may realize that they have received a spiritual return for the bodily service they have rendered on this feast day. We ask this....

COMMON OF THE DEDICATION OF A CHURCH

ON THE ANNIVERSARY OF THE DEDICATION, OUTSIDE OF THE CHURCH ITSELF

Collect

Deus, qui de vivis et electis lapidibus aeternum habitaculum tuae praeparas maiestati, multiplica in Ecclesia tua spiritum gratiae quem dedisti, ut fidelis tibi populus in caelestis aedificationem Ierusalem semper accrescat. Per Dominum.

God our Father, from living and chosen stones you make an eternal dwelling place for your divine majesty. Increase within your Church the spirit of grace which you have bestowed, so that your faithful people may ever increase, for the building up of the heavenly Jerusalem. We ask this....

Alternate Collect

Deus, qui populum tuum Ecclesiam vocare dignatus es, da, ut plebs in nomine tuo congregata te timeat, te diligat, te sequatur, et ad caelestia promissa, te ducente, perveniat. Per Dominum.

God our Father, you saw fit to call your people the Church. Grant that the people who are gathered in your name may fear you, love you, follow you, and, under your guidance, arrive at the heavenly rewards you have promised. We ask this....

Prayer over the Gifts

Suscipe, quaesumus, Domine, munus oblatum, et poscentibus concede, ut hic sacramentorum virtus et votorum obtineatur effectus. Per Christum.

Lord, please receive the gift we offer, and grant the plea of your people: within this church, may they experience the power of the sacraments and obtain the answers to their prayers. We ask this....

Prayer after Communion

Deus, qui nobis supernam Ierusalem per temporale Ecclesiae tuae signum adumbrare voluisti, da, quaesumus, ut, huius participatione sacramenti, nos tuae gratiae templum efficias, et habitationem gloriae tuae ingredi concedas. Per Christum.

God our Father, you willed to prefigure the heavenly Jerusalem for us by means of the earthly symbol of your Church. Please grant our prayer that, through our sharing in this sacrament, you will make us a temple of your grace and will allow us to enter the place where your glory dwells. We ask this....

COMMON OF THE BLESSED VIRGIN MARY: #1

Collect

Concede nos famulos tuos, quaesumus, Domine Deus, perpetua mentis et corporis sanitate gaudere, et, gloriosa beatae Mariae semper Virginis intercessione, a praesenti liberari tristitia, et aeterna perfrui laetitia. Per Dominum.

Lord God, please grant that we, your people, may enjoy unending health of mind and body. Through the glorious prayers of blessed Mary, ever Virgin, grant that we may be delivered from present sadness and enjoy eternal happiness. We ask this....

Alternate Collect

Famulorum tuorum, quaesumus, Domine, delictis ignosce, ut, qui tibi placere de actibus nostris non valemus, Genetricis Filii tui Domini nostri intercessione salvemur. Per Dominum.

Lord, we ask you to forgive the sins of your people, so that we who cannot please you by our own actions may be brought to salvation by the prayers of the Mother of your Son our Lord. We ask this....

Prayer over the Gifts

Unigeniti tui, Domine, nobis succurrat humanitas, ut, qui natus de Virgine Matris integritatem non minuit sed sacravit, a nostris nos piaculis exuens, oblationem nostram tibi reddat acceptam. Per Christum.

Lord, may the fact that your only Son took on human nature come to our aid. In being born of the Virgin, he did not lessen his mother's chastity but rather consecrated it; may he strip us of our sins and render our offering acceptable to you. We ask this....

Prayer after Communion

Sumentes, Domine, caelestia sacramenta, quaesumus clementiam tuam, ut, qui de beatae Virginis Mariae festivitate laetamur, eiusdem Virginis imitatione, redemptionis nostrae mysterio digne valeamus famulari. Per Christum.

Lord, as we receive your heavenly sacraments, we ask for your mercy. We rejoice on this feast of the Blessed Virgin Mary; in imitation of her, may we be able to take part worthily in the mystery of our redemption. We ask this....

COMMON OF THE BLESSED VIRGIN MARY: #2

Collect

Concede, misericors Deus, fragilitati nostrae praesidium, ut, qui sanctae Dei Genetricis memoriam agimus, intercessionis eius auxilio a nostris iniquitatibus resurgamus. Per Dominum.

Merciful God, grant your strength to our weakness, so that we who are mindful of the holy Mother of God may, through the help of her prayers, rise from our sins. We ask this....

Alternate Collect

Adiuvet nos, quaesumus, Domine, beatae Mariae semper Virginis intercessio veneranda, et a cunctis periculis absolutos in tua faciat pace gaudere. Per Dominum.

Lord, we ask that the holy prayers of blessed Mary, ever Virgin, may come to our aid, free us from all dangers, and make us rejoice in your peace. We ask this....

Prayer over the Gifts

Genetricis Filii tui memoriam venerantes, quaesumus, Domine, ut sacrificii huius oblatio nosmetipsos, gratia tua largiente, tibi perficiat munus aeternum. Per Christum.

Lord, as we honor the memory of the Mother of your Son, we pray that, through the generous outpouring of your grace, the offering of this sacrifice may make us an everlasting gift to you. We ask this....

Prayer after Communion

Redemptionis aeternae participes effecti, quaesumus, Domine, ut, qui Genetricis Filii tui memoriam agimus, et de gratiae tuae plenitudine gloriemur, et salvationis continuum sentiamus augmentum. Per Christum.

Lord, we have been given a share in eternal redemption. As we call to mind the memory of the Mother of your Son, we ask that we may rejoice in the fullness of your grace and experience constant progress toward salvation. We ask this....

COMMON OF THE BLESSED VIRGIN MARY: #3

Collect

Sanctissimae venerantibus Virginis Mariae memoriam gloriosam, ipsius nobis, quaesumus, Domine, intercessione concede, ut de plenitudine gratiae tuae nos quoque mereamur accipere. Per Dominum.

Lord, as we honor the glorious memory of the most holy Virgin Mary, please grant that, through her intercession, we too may be privileged to receive of the fullness of your grace. We ask this....

Alternate Collect

Domine Iesu, qui virginalem aulam beatae Mariae, in qua habitares, eligere dignatus es, da, quaesumus, ut, sua nos defensione munitos, iucundos facias suae interesse festivitati. Qui vivis.

Lord Jesus, you saw fit to choose the Virgin Mary as an unsullied home in which to dwell. Please grant that we may be guarded by her protection and make us happily take part in her festival. We ask this....

Prayer over the Gifts

Laudis tibi, Domine, hostias offerimus, de Genetricis Filii tui festivitate laetantes; praesta, quaesumus, ut per haec sacrosancta commercia ad redemptionis aeternae proficiamus augmentum. Per Christum.

Lord, as we rejoice on this feast of the Mother of your Son, we bring you our offering of praise. Please grant that through this sacred exchange we may achieve progress toward our eternal salvation. We ask this....

Prayer after Communion

Sumptis, Domine, sacramentis caelestibus, te supplices deprecamur, ut, qui beatae Mariae Virgi-

nis memoriam venerando recolimus, aeterni convivii mereamur esse participes. Per Christum.

Lord, as we who have received your heavenly sacraments reverently recall the memory of the Blessed Virgin Mary, we humbly ask that we may be privileged to share in your eternal banquet. We ask this....

COMMON OF THE BLESSED VIRGIN MARY #4 (ADVENT)

Collect

Deus, qui de beatae Mariae Virginis utero Verbum tuum, Angelo nuntiante, carnem suscipere voluisti, praesta supplicibus tuis, ut, qui vere eam Dei Genetricem credimus, eius apud te intercessionibus adiuvemur. Per Dominum.

God our Father, you willed that, at the angel's announcement, your Word should take on human flesh in the womb of the Blessed Virgin Mary. We believe that she is truly the Mother of God. Grant to your suppliant people that we may be aided by her intercession with you. We ask this....

Prayer over the Gifts

Altari tuo, Domine, superposita munera Spiritus ille sanctificet, qui beatae Mariae viscera sua virtute replevit. Per Christum.

Lord, may the gifts we have placed on your altar be made holy by the same Spirit who filled the womb of blessed Mary with his power. We ask this....

Prayer after Communion

Mysteria quae sumpsimus, Domine Deus noster, misericordiam tuam in nobis semper ostendant, ut Filii tui incarnatione salvemur, qui Genetricis eius memoriam fideli mente celebramus. Per Christum.

Lord our God, may the mysteries we have received always show forth your mercy toward us. May we thus be granted salvation by the incarnation of your Son, whose mother's memory we honor with faithful hearts. We ask this....

COMMON OF THE BLESSED VIRGIN MARY #5 (CHRISTMAS)

Collect

Deus, qui salutis aeternae, beatae Mariae virginitate fecunda, humano generi praemia praestitisti, tribue, quaesumus, ut ipsam pro nobis intercedere sentiamus, per quam meruimus Filium tuum auctorem vitae suscipere. Qui tecum vivit.

God our Father, you gave the rewards of eternal salvation to the human race through the life-bearing virginity of blessed Mary. Through her we were privileged to receive your Son, the author of life; please grant that we may experience her intercession on our behalf. We ask this....

Prayer over the Gifts

Suscipe, Domine, munera quae tibi offerimus, et praesta, ut corda nostra, Sancti Spiritus luce irradiata, exemplo beatae Virginis Mariae, tua semper valeant perquirere et conservare. Per Christum.

Lord, receive the gifts we offer you, and, through the example of the Blessed Virgin Mary, grant that, with hearts illumined by the light of the Holy Spirit, we may ever be enabled to seek diligently after what is yours and guard it when we have found it. We ask this....

Prayer after Communion

Incarnati Verbi tui Corpore et Sanguine refecti, quaesumus, Domine, ut haec divina mysteria, quae in festivitate beatae Virginis Mariae laetanter accepimus, eiusdem Filii tui divinitatis participes nos semper efficiant. Per Christum.

Lord, we have been fed with the Body and Blood of your Word Made Flesh. On this feast of the Blessed Virgin Mary, we have joyfully received these sacred sacraments; we pray that they may ever make us sharers in the divinity of your Son. We ask this....

COMMON OF THE BLESSED VIRGIN MARY #6 (EASTER SEASON)

Collect

Deus, qui, per resurrectionem Filii tui Domini nostri Iesu Christi, mundum laetificare dignatus es, praesta, quaesumus, ut, per eius Genetricem Virginem Mariam, perpetuae capiamus gaudia vitae. Per Dominum.

God our Father, by the resurrection of your Son, our Lord Jesus Christ, you saw fit to gladden the world. Through the intercession of his Virgin Mother Mary, please grant that we may receive the joys of eternal life. We ask this....

Alternate Collect

Deus, qui Apostolis tuis, cum Maria Matre Iesu orantibus, Sanctum dedisti Spiritum, da nobis, ut, ipsa intercedente, maiestati tuae fideliter servire et nominis tui gloriam verbo et exemplo diffundere valeamus. Per Dominum.

God our Father, you gave the Holy Spirit to your Apostles while they were at prayer in the company of Mary, the Mother of Jesus. Through her intercession, grant that we may faithfully serve your divine majesty and be enabled to spread the glory of your name by what we say and do. We ask this....

Prayer over the Gifts

Festivitatem recolentes beatae Virginis Mariae, tibi, Domine, munera nostra offerimus, deprecantes, ut eius nobis succurrat humanitas, qui tibi oblationem seipsum in cruce obtulit immaculatam. Qui vivit.

Lord, as we commemorate this feast of the Blessed Virgin Mary, we bring our gifts to you and ask that we may be aided by the human nature of Him who offered himself to you on the cross as a spotless victim. We ask this....

Prayer after Communion

In mentibus nostris, quaesumus, Domine, verae fidei sacramenta confirma, ut, qui conceptum de Virgine Deum verum et hominem confitemur, per eius salutiferae resurrectionis potentiam, ad aeternam mereamur pervenire laetitiam. Per Christum.

Lord, please make the mysteries of the true faith steadfast in our hearts. We profess our belief that He who was born of the Virgin is truly God and truly human; by the power of his life-giving resurrection, may we be privileged to arrive at eternal joy. We ask this....

COMMON OF THE BLESSED VIRGIN MARY: OTHER PRAYERS

Collect

Concede, quaesumus, omnipotens Deus, ut fideles tui, qui sub sanctissimae Virginis Mariae patrocinio laetantur, eius pia intercessione a cunctis malis liberentur in terris, et ad gaudia aeterna pervenire mereantur in caelis. Per Dominum.

Almighty God, your faithful people rejoice in the protection of the most holy Virgin Mary. Through her loving intercession, grant that we may be freed from every evil on earth and be privileged to come to eternal joy in heaven. We ask this....

Prayer over the Gifts

Preces, Domine, tuorum respice oblationesque fidelium, in beatae Mariae Dei Genetricis commemoratione delatas, ut tibi gratae sint, et nobis conferant tuae propitiationis auxilium. Per Christum.

Lord, look upon the prayers and gifts of your faithful people, offered on this feast of blessed Mary, the Mother of God. May they be acceptable to you and win for us your forgiveness and help. We ask this....

Prayer after Communion

Salutaribus refecti sacramentis, supplices te, Domine, deprecamur, ut, qui festivitatem beatae Virginis Dei Genetricis Mariae venerando egimus, redemptionis tuae fructum perpetuo experiri mereamur. Per Christum.

Lord, we have been renewed by your saving sacraments, and we have reverently celebrated this feast of the Blessed Virgin Mary, Mother of God. We humbly ask that we may be privileged to experience the ceaseless effects of your redemption. We ask this....

COMMON OF MARTYRS: #1, SEVERAL MARTYRS, OUTSIDE OF THE EASTER SEASON

Collect

Praesta, Domine, precibus nostris cum exsultatione proventum, ut sanctorum martyrum N. et N., quorum diem passionis annua devotione recolimus, etiam fidei constantiam subsequamur. Per Dominum.

Lord, grant a joyful fulfillment to our prayers, so that we who annually celebrate the day on which your holy martyrs N. and N. suffered may also follow the example of their unshakeable faith. We ask this....

Prayer over the Gifts

Suscipe, sancte Pater, munera quae in sanctorum martyrum commemoratione deferimus, et nobis famulis tuis concede, ut in confessione tui nominis inveniri stabiles mereamur. Per Christum.

Holy Father, receive the gifts we offer in memory of your holy martyrs. Grant that we, your chosen people, may be privileged to be found constant in the profession of your name. We ask this....

Prayer after Communion

Deus, qui crucis mysterium in sanctis martyribus tuis mirabiliter illustrasti, concede propitius, ut, ex hoc sacrificio roborati, Christo fideliter haereamus, et in Ecclesia ad salutem omnium operemur. Per Christum.

God our Father, in your holy martyrs you wondrously show forth the mystery of the Cross. In your kindness please grant that, strengthened by this sacrifice, we may remain faithful and loyal to Christ and work within the Church for the salvation of all men and women. We ask this....

COMMON OF MARTYRS: #2, SEVERAL MARTYRS, OUTSIDE OF THE EASTER SEASON

Collect

Omnipotens sempiterne Deus, qui sanctis N. et N. pro Christo pati donasti, nostrae quoque fragilitati divinum praetende subsidium, ut sicut illi pro te mori non dubitarunt, ita nos fortes in tua confessione vivere valeamus. Per Dominum.

Almighty and eternal God, you gave Saints N. and N. the gift of suffering for Christ. Extend your heavenly aid to our weakness as well; just as the martyrs did not hesitate to die for your sake, so in our lifetime may we be able to profess your name with courage. We ask this....

Prayer over the Gifts

Fiat tibi, quaesumus, Domine, hostia sacranda placabilis pretiosi celebritate martyrii, quae et peccata nostra purificet, et tuorum tibi vota conciliet famulorum. Per Christum.

Lord, we pray that you may be pleased by this gift, which we bring to be sanctified on this feast of a martyrdom which we hold dear. May it wash away our sins and make the prayers of your chosen people acceptable to you. We ask this....

Prayer after Communion

Pane caelesti nutritos et in Christo unum corpus effectos, da nos, quaesumus, Domine, ab eius caritate numquam separari et, sanctorum martyrum tuorum N. et N. exemplo, propter eum qui dilexit nos omnia fortiter superare. Per Christum.

Lord, we are fed with heavenly food and made into one body in Christ. Please grant that we may never be separated from His love but rather, following the example of your holy martyrs N. and N., may bravely surmount all obstacles for the sake of Him who loved us. We ask this....

COMMON OF MARTYRS: #3, SEVERAL MARTYRS, OUTSIDE OF THE EASTER SEASON

Collect

Fraterna nos, Domine, martyrum tuorum corona laetificet, quae et fidei nostrae praebeat incrementa virtutum, et multiplici nos suffragio consoletur. Per Dominum.

Lord, may the heavenly crown of our brothers and sisters, your martyrs, gladden us. May it provide an increase of virtue in our lives of faith, and may it console us by the number of intercessors we have. We ask this....

Alternate Collect

Beatorum martyrum N. et N., quaesumus, Domine, tibi nos oratio grata commendet, et in tuae veritatis professione confirmet. Per Dominum.

Lord, the prayer of your holy martyrs N. and N. is pleasing to you. May it recommend us to you and strengthen us in our proclamation of your truth. We ask this....

Prayer over the Gifts

Suscipe, quaesumus, Domine, munera populi tui pro martyrum tuorum passionibus dicata sanctorum, et, quae beatis N. et N. in persecutione fortitudinem ministrarunt, nobis quoque praebeant inter adversa constantiam. Per Christum.

Lord, please receive the gifts of your people, offered in honor of the sufferings of your holy martyrs. May what furnished Saints N. and N. with strength in the midst of persecution also make us faithful in the midst of our difficulties. We ask this....

Prayer after Communion

Conserva in nos, Domine, munus tuum, et quod, te donante, pro festivitate beatorum martyrum N. et N. percepimus, et salutem nobis praestet et pacem. Per Christum.

Lord, preserve your gift within us. May what we have received from your generous hand on this feast of the holy martyrs N. and N. bring us salvation and peace. We ask this....

COMMON OF MARTYRS: #4, SEVERAL MARTYRS, OUTSIDE OF THE EASTER SEASON

Collect

Deus, qui nos annua sanctorum N. et N. festivitate laetificas, concede propitius, ut, quorum natalicia colimus, virtutem quoque passionis imitemur. Per Dominum.

God our Father, you gladden us by the yearly feast of Saints N. and N. We celebrate their birth into eternal life; in your mercy, grant that we may also imitate the strength they had in the midst of suffering. We ask this....

Alternate Collect

Deus, qui sanctis N. et N. ad hanc gloriam veniendi copiosam munus gratiae contulisti, da famulis tuis, martyrum intercedentibus meritis, veniam peccatorum, et concede, ut ab omnibus adversitatibus liberentur. Per Dominum.

God our Father, you gave your saints N. and N. the gift of your grace so that they might come to the rich state of glory they now enjoy. Through the merits and prayers of your martyrs, grant your faithful people the forgiveness of their sins, and grant that they may be freed from all their troubles. We ask this....

Prayer over the Gifts

Hostias tibi, Domine, pro commemoratione beatorum N. et N. offerimus, suppliciter deprecantes, ut, sicut illis praebuisti sacrae fidei claritatem, sic nobis indulgentiam largiaris et pacem. Per Christum.

Lord, we offer you our gifts in memory of Saints N. and N. We humbly ask that, just as you gave them the clear light of the holy faith, so also will you grant us forgiveness and peace. We ask this....

Prayer after Communion

Concede nobis, Domine, per haec sacramenta caelestia, gratiam in beatorum martyrum N. et N. celebritate multiplicem, ut de tanti agone certaminis discamus et firma solidari patientia, et pia exsultare victoria. Per Christum.

Lord, through these heavenly sacraments, grant us your many graces on this feast of your holy martyrs N. and N., so that from their great struggle we may learn to be rooted in steadfast patience and to rejoice in a holy victory. We ask this....

COMMON OF MARTYRS: #5, SEVERAL MARTYRS, OUTSIDE OF THE EASTER SEASON

Collect

Da nobis, quaesumus, Domine, fidei miseratus augmentum, ut, quos sanctos martyres tuos N. et N. usque ad sanguinem retenta glorificat, nos etiam iustificet, veraciter hanc sequentes. Per Dominum.

Lord, in your mercy please grant us an increase in faith. Your holy martyrs N. and N. had a firm grasp on that faith and it made them illustrious even to death; may it bring us holiness as we try to live it in truth. We ask this....

Prayer over the Gifts

Sacrificiis praesentibus, Domine, quaesumus, intende placatus, ut, quod passionis Filii tui mysterio gerimus, beatorum N. et N. exemplis, pio consequamur affectu. Per Christum.

Lord, in your mercy please look upon the sacrifices we offer and be appeased by them, so that, following the example of Saints N. and N., we may with loving hearts achieve the effect of what we celebrate in the mystery of the passion of your Son. We ask this....

Alternate Prayer over the Gifts

Haec hostia, Domine, quam in beatorum N. et N. triumpho deferimus, corda nostra tui amoris igne iugiter inflammet, et ad promissa perseverantibus praemia disponat. Per Christum.

Lord, may this offering, which we bring to you in honor of the victory of Saints N. and N., ever inflame our hearts with the fire of your love, and prepare us for the rewards you have promised to those who faithfully persevere. We ask this....

Prayer after Communion

Pasti, Domine, pretioso Corpore et Sanguine unigeniti Filii tui, da, quaesumus, in commemoratione beatorum martyrum tuorum N. et N., perseveranti caritate in te manere, de te vivere, et ad te moveri. Per Christum.

Lord, we have been nourished with the priceless Body and Blood of your only Son. On this feast of your holy martyrs N. and N., please grant that, with unflagging love, we may remain in you, draw life from you, and be drawn toward you. We ask this....

COMMON OF MARTYRS: #6, ONE MARTYR, OUTSIDE OF THE EASTER SEASON

Collect

Omnipotens et misericors Deus, qui martyrem tuum N. passionis suae tormenta superare fecisti, concede, ut, qui eius triumphi diem celebramus, insuperabiles tua protectione ab hostis insidiis maneamus. Per Dominum.

Almighty and merciful God, you made your martyr N. overcome the torments of his suffering. Grant that we who celebrate the day of his victory may, through your protection, remain unconquerable by the snares of the enemy. We ask this....

Prayer over the Gifts

Oblata munera, quaesumus, Domine, tua benedictione sanctifica, quae, te donante, nos illa flamma tuae dilectionis accendat, per quam sanctus N. tormenta sui corporis universa devicit. Per Christum.

Lord, with your blessing please make holy the gifts we have offered. By your generous gift, may that blessing inflame us with the same fire of love through which Saint N. overcame all the torments inflicted on his body. We ask this....

Alternate Prayer over the Gifts

Accepta tibi sint, quaesumus, Domine, munera, quae in commemoratione beati martyris tui N. deferimus, ut eo maiestati tuae sint placita, sicut illius effusio sanguinis apud te exstitit pretiosa. Per Christum.

Lord, we ask that our gifts, which we offer in memory of your holy martyr N., may be acceptable to you, so that they may be pleasing to your divine majesty in the same way that the outpouring of his blood was precious in your eyes. We ask this....

Prayer after Communion

Praestent nobis, quaesumus, Domine, sacra mysteria quae sumpsimus eam animi fortitudinem, quae beatum N. martyrem tuum reddidit in tuo servitio fidelem et in passione victorem. Per Christum.

Lord, we ask that the sacred mysteries which we have received may provide us with the same strength of soul which made your holy martyr N. faithful in your service and victorious in his sufferings. We ask this....

COMMON OF MARTYRS: #7, ONE MARTYR, OUTSIDE OF THE EASTER SEASON

Collect

Omnipotens sempiterne Deus, qui beato N. usque ad mortem pro iustitia certare tribuisti, fac nos, eius intercessione, pro amore tuo omnia adversa tolerare et ad te, qui solus es vita, tota virtute properare. Per Dominum.

Almighty and everlasting God, you gave Saint N. the grace to struggle for justice even to the point of dying for it. Through his intercession, grant that we may bear all our difficulties out of love for you, and hasten toward you with all our strength, for you alone are our life. We ask this....

Prayer over the Gifts

Clementissime Deus, munera haec tua benedictione perfunde et nos in fide confirma, quam beatus N. effuso sanguine asseruit. Per Christum.

Most merciful God, pour out your blessing on these gifts, and strengthen us in that faith which Saint N. proclaimed by the shedding of his blood. We ask this....

Alternate Prayer over the Gifts

Hostias tibi, Domine, pro commemoratione beati martyris tui N. offerimus, quem a tui corporis unitate nulla tentatio separavit. Per Christum.

Lord, we offer our gifts to you in memory of your holy martyr Saint N., whom no temptation succeeded in separating from the unity of your mystical body. We make our prayer through....

Prayer after Communion

Sacris, Domine, recreati mysteriis, quaesumus, ut, miram beati N. constantiam aemulantes, patientiae praemium consequi mereamur aeternum. Per Christum.

Lord, we have been renewed by your sacred mysteries; and we ask that, in imitation of the exemplary fidelity of Saint N., we may be privileged to attain the eternal reward promised to patient endurance. We ask this....

COMMON OF MARTYRS: #8, SEVERAL MARTYRS, WITHIN THE EASTER SEASON

Collect

Quaesumus, omnipotens Deus, ut nos, virtute Spiritus Sancti, et ad credendum dociles et ad confitendum fortes efficias, qui beatis martyribus

N. et N. propter verbum tuum et testimonium Iesu animas ponere tribuisti. Per Dominum.

Almighty and eternal God, you gave your holy martyrs N. and N. the grace to lay down their lives because of your word and in witness to Jesus. By the power of the Holy Spirit, please make us receptive to what we should believe and strong in professing our faith in it. We ask this....

Alternate Collect

Deus, a quo constantiam fides, et virtutem sumit infirmitas, tribue nobis, martyrum N. et N. exemplo et precibus, in Unigeniti tui passione et resurrectione consortium, ut cum eis apud te gaudium perfectum consequamur. Per Dominum.

God our Father, faith acquires its firmness from you and weakness its strength. Through the example and prayers of the martyrs N. and N., grant us a share in the passion and resurrection of your only Son, so that along with the martyrs we may attain perfect joy in your sight. We ask this....

Prayer over the Gifts

In tuorum, Domine, pretiosa morte iustorum, sacrificium illud offerimus, de quo martyrium sumpsit omne principium. Per Christum.

Lord, in memory of the precious death of your holy ones we offer that sacrifice from which every martyrdom has derived its origin and meaning. We make our prayer through....

Prayer after Communion

Beatorum martyrum N. et N. caelestem victoriam divino convivio celebrantes, te, Domine, deposcimus, ut panem vitae hic edentes, des vincere, et vincentes des edere de ligno vitae in paradiso. Per Christum.

Lord, in this sacred banquet we rejoice at the heavenly triumph of your holy martyrs N. and N. We beg that, as we eat the bread of life here on earth, you will grant us victory over sin, and will grant to the victorious the privilege of eating from the tree of life in Paradise. We ask this....

COMMON OF MARTYRS: #9, SEVERAL MARTYRS, WITHIN THE EASTER SEASON

Collect

Laetificet nos, quaesumus, Domine, beatorum martyrum tuorum N. et N. gloriosa festivitas, quos, Unigeniti tui passionem et resurrectionem voce libera confitentes, pretiosum sanguinem gloriosa morte fundere fecisti. Per Dominum.

Lord, we ask that this radiant feast of your holy martyrs N. and N. may fill our hearts with joy. They freely chose to voice their belief in the passion and resurrection of your only Son, and you granted them the grace of pouring out their life's blood in a magnificent death. We ask this....

Prayer over the Gifts

Praesentia munera, quaesumus, Domine, ita serena pietate intuere, ut Sancti Spiritus perfundantur benedictione, et in nostris cordibus eam dilectionem validam operentur, per quam sancti martyres N. et N. omnia corporis tormenta devicerunt. Per Christum.

Lord, in your tranquil love be pleased to look upon the gifts we bring in such a way that they may be filled with the blessing of the Holy Spirit, and may stir up in our hearts that strong love through which your holy martyrs N. and N. overcame all their physical torments. We ask this....

Prayer after Communion

Unius panis alimonia refecti, in commemoratione beatorum martyrum N. et N. suppliciter te, Domine, deprecamur, ut nos in tua iugiter caritate confirmes, et in novitate vitae concedas ambulare. Per Christum.

Lord, on this feast of the holy martyrs N. and N. we are refreshed by the food of this one bread, and we humbly ask you to strengthen us always in your love and to grant us the gift of walking in newness of life. We ask this....

COMMON OF MARTYRS: #10, ONE MARTYR, WITHIN THE EASTER SEASON

Collect

Deus, qui ad illustrandam Ecclesiam tuam beatum N. martyrii victoria decorare dignatus es, concede propitius, ut, sicut ipse dominicae passionis imitator fuit, ita nos, per eius vestigia gradientes, ad gaudia sempiterna pervenire mereamur. Per Dominum.

God our Father, you saw fit to adorn Saint N. with the palm of martyrdom in order to exalt the Church. He imitated the passion of the Lord; in your mercy, grant that we too may be privileged to follow in his footsteps and arrive at eternal happiness. We ask this....

Prayer over the Gifts

Suscipe, Domine, sacrificium placationis et laudis, quod in commemoratione beati martyris N. tuae offerimus maiestati, ut nos perducat ad veniam, et in perpetua gratiarum constituat actione. Per Christum.

Lord, receive this sacrifice of atonement and praise, which we offer to your divine majesty in memory of your martyr Saint N. May it lead us to your forgiveness and make us ever give thanks to you. We ask this....

Prayer after Communion

Tua, Domine, sumpsimus dona caelestia de hodierna festivitate laetantes; praesta, quaesumus, ut, qui in hoc divino convivio mortem Filii tui annuntiamus, eiusdem resurrectionis et gloriae cum sanctis martyribus participes esse mereamur. Per Christum.

Lord, we have received your heavenly gifts as we joyfully celebrate today's feast. Please grant that we who have proclaimed the death of your Son in this sacred banquet may, along with the holy martyrs, be privileged to share in his resurrection and glory. We ask this....

COMMON OF MARTYRS: OTHER PRAYERS FOR MARTYRS: FOR MARTYRS WHO WERE MISSIONARIES

Collect

Maiestatis tuae clementiam suppliciter deprecamur, omnipotens et misericors Deus, ut, sicut Unigeniti tui agnitionem per beatorum martyrum N. et N. praedicationem populorum cordibus infudisti, ita, eorum intercessione, fidei stabilitate firmentur. Per Dominum.

Almighty and compassionate God, we humbly plead for your sovereign mercy. You filled the minds and hearts of the peoples of foreign lands with a knowledge of your only Son by means of the preaching of your holy martyrs N. and N.; through their intercession, may those same peoples be confirmed in the sureness of their faith. We ask this....

Prayer over the Gifts

Martyrum tuorum N. et N. passionem venerantes, fac nos, Domine, hoc sacrificio mortem Unigeniti tui digne annuntiare, cui parum fuit hortari martyres verbo, nisi firmaret exemplo. Per Christum.

Lord, make us who honor the sufferings of your martyrs N. and N. properly proclaim, by means of this sacrifice, the death of your only Son, for whom it was not enough to encourage the martyrs by word alone without also strengthening them by the example of his own suffering and death. We ask this....

Prayer after Communion

Caelestibus, Domine, pasti deliciis, supplices te rogamus, ut, exemplo beatorum N. et N., caritatis et passionis Filii tui in mentibus nostris signa feramus, et perpetuae pacis fructu iugiter perfruamur. Per Christum.

Lord, we have been fed with your heavenly delights and, through the example of Saints N. and N., we humbly ask that we may bear within our hearts the signs of the love and sufferings of your Son, and may always enjoy the reward of everlasting peace. We ask this....

COMMON OF MARTYRS: OTHER PRAYERS FOR MARTYRS: FOR A VIRGIN MARTYR

Collect

Deus, qui nos hodie beatae N. annua commemoratione laetificas, concede propitius, ut eius adiuvemur meritis, cuius castitatis et fortitudinis irradiamur exemplis. Per Dominum.

God our Father, every year on this day you give us the joy of celebrating the feast of Saint N. We are inspired by the shining examples of her purity and courage; in your mercy, grant that we may also be aided by her merits. We ask this....

Prayer over the Gifts

Munera, quaesumus, Domine, quae in celebritate beatae N. deferimus, ita gratiae tuae efficiantur accepta, sicut eius tibi placitum exstitit passionis certamen. Per Christum.

Lord, we ask that the gifts which we bring on this feast of Saint N. may be made acceptable to you in the same way that her struggle and suffering were pleasing to you. We ask this....

Prayer after Communion

Deus, qui beatam N. pro gemina virginitatis et martyrii victoria inter Sanctos coronasti, da, quaesumus, per huius virtutem sacramenti, ut, omne malum fortiter superantes, caelestem gloriam consequamur. Per Christum.

God our Father, you placed Saint N. among the ranks of your saints because of her double triumph in being both a virgin and a martyr. Through the power of this sacrament, please grant that we may courageously overcome all evil and attain heavenly glory. We ask this....

COMMON OF MARTYRS: OTHER PRAYERS FOR MARTYRS: FOR A HOLY WOMAN MARTYR

Collect

Deus, cuius munere virtus in infirmitate perficitur, da omnibus beatae N. gloriam recolen-

tibus, ut, quae abs te sumpsit robur ut vinceret, abs te quoque vincendi nobis gratiam semper obtineat. Per Dominum.

God our Father, by your gracious gift virtue is made perfect in weakness. Grant to all who celebrate the triumph of Saint N. that, just as she drew from you the strength to overcome her torments, so also she may ever obtain from you the grace for us to conquer sin. We ask this....

Prayer over the Gifts

Hodiernum, Domine, sacrificium laetanter offerimus, quo, beatae N. caelestem victoriam recensentes, et tua magnalia praedicamus, et nos acquisisse gaudemus suffragia gloriosa. Per Christum.

Lord, with joy we offer you today's sacrifice, in which, calling to mind the heavenly victory of Saint N., we both proclaim your great deeds and rejoice that we have come to possess such glorious intercessors. We make our prayer through....

Prayer after Communion

Sumentes, Domine, gaudia sempiterna de participatione sacramenti, et de memoria beatae N., suppliciter deprecamur, ut, quae sedula servitute, donante te, gerimus, dignis sensibus tuo munere capiamus. Per Christum.

Lord, we partake of everlasting joy by sharing in this sacrament and by remembering Saint N. Through your gracious gift, we humbly ask that we may receive with fitting gratitude what your generosity enables us to do in careful service to you. We ask this....

COMMON OF PASTORS: #1, FOR POPES OR BISHOPS

Collect (for Popes)

Omnipotens sempiterne Deus, qui beatum N. cuncto populo tuo praeesse, ac verbo et exemplo prodesse voluisti, eodem intercedente, pastores Ecclesiae tuae cum gregibus sibi commissis custodi et dirige in viam salutis aeternae. Per Dominum.

Almighty and eternal God, you willed that Saint N. should shepherd your entire people and benefit them by his word and example. Through his intercession, guard all the shepherds of your Church along with the sheep committed to their care; and guide them into the way that leads to salvation. We ask this....

Collect (for Bishops)

Deus, qui Ecclesiae tuae in beato N. boni pastoris exemplum providere dignatus es, concede propitius, ut, eius intercessione, in loco pascuae tuae perpetuo collocari mereamur. Per Dominum.

God our Father, you saw fit to give your Church a model of a good shepherd in the person of Saint N. Through his intercession, grant that we may be privileged to live forever in the place of your heavenly pasture. We ask this....

Prayer over the Gifts

Laudis tibi, Domine, hostias offerimus in tuorum commemoratione Sanctorum, quibus nos et praesentibus exui malis confidimus, et futuris. Per Christum.

Lord, we offer you our gift of praise in memory of your saints, through whose help we trust that we may be delivered from present evils, and future ones as well. We make our prayer through....

Prayer after Communion

Sacramenta quae sumpsimus, Domine Deus noster, in nobis foveant caritatis ardorem, quo beatus N. vehementer accensus pro Ecclesia tua se iugiter impendebat. Per Christum.

Lord our God, may the sacraments which we have received foster within us the fire of that love which so powerfully inspired Saint N. to spend himself ceaselessly on behalf of your Church. We ask this....

COMMON OF PASTORS: #2, FOR POPES OR BISHOPS

Collect (for Popes)

Deus, qui beatum N., quem totius Ecclesiae praestitisti esse pastorem, miro virtutis et doctrinae splendore coruscare fecisti, da nobis talis episcopi merita venerantibus, ut per bona opera lucere coram hominibus et per amorem ardere coram te valeamus. Per Dominum.

God our Father, you caused Saint N. to be the shepherd of the universal Church, and you made him stand out as a brilliant example of virtue and learning. As we reverence the life and deeds of this great bishop, grant that in the eyes of all men and women we may shine forth because of our good deeds, and in your own eyes we may be on fire with love for you. We ask this....

Collect (for Bishops)

Da nobis, quaesumus, omnipotens Deus, beati N. episcopi digne memoriam venerari, et, sicut illum quibus praeerat, verbo et exemplo prodesse voluisti, ita ipsius apud te semper intercessionis suffragia sentiamus. Per Dominum.

Almighty God, please grant that we may fittingly celebrate the memory of your bishop Saint N. You willed that by his word and example he should benefit those who were in his care; may we too experience the benefit of his intercession in your sight. We ask this....

Prayer over the Gifts

Annue nobis, quaesumus, Domine, ut, in hac festivitate beati N., haec nobis prosit oblatio, quam immolando totius mundi tribuisti relaxari delicta. Per Christum.

Lord, we ask that you look upon us favorably, so that on this feast of Saint N. this sacrifice may benefit us, for you have made the loosening of the bonds of the whole world's sins depend on its being offered. We ask this....

Prayer after Communion

Acceptorum munerum virtus, Domine Deus, in hac festivitate beati N. nobis effectus impleat, ut simul et mortalis vitae subsidium conferat, et gaudium perpetuae felicitatis obtineat. Per Christum.

Lord God, may the power of the gifts we have received on this feast of Saint N. have this effect on us, that at one and the same time it provide strength for us in our earthly life and win for us the joy of eternal happiness. We ask this....

COMMON OF PASTORS: #3, FOR BISHOPS

Collect

Omnipotens sempiterne Deus, qui beatum N. episcopum plebi tuae sanctae praeesse voluisti, quaesumus, ut, eius suffragantibus meritis, pietatis tuae gratiam largiaris. Per Dominum.

Almighty and eternal God, you willed that your bishop Saint N.

should have charge of your holy people. Through his merits and prayers, please grant us the favor of your loving kindness. We ask this....

Prayer over the Gifts

Hostias, quaesumus, Domine, quas in festivitate beati N. sacris altaribus exhibemus, propitius respice, ut, nobis indulgentiam largiendo, tuo nomini dent honorem. Per Christum.

Lord, please look with favor upon the gifts we present at your holy altar on this feast of Saint N. By winning the gift of your compassion for us may they give glory to your name. We ask this....

Prayer after Communion

Refecti sacris mysteriis, Deomine, suppliciter deprecamur, ut, beati N. exemplo, studeamus confiteri quod credidit, et opere exercere quod docuit. Per Christum.

Lord, we who have been renewed by your holy mysteries humbly ask that, through the example of Saint N., we may strive to profess what he believed and to carry out in action what he taught. We ask this....

COMMON OF PASTORS: #4, FOR BISHOPS

Collect

Deus, qui beatum N. divine caritate flagrantem, fideque, quae vincit mundum, insignem, sanctis Pastoribus mirabiliter aggregasti, praesta, quaesumus, ut, ipso intercedente, nos quoque, in fide et caritate perseverantes, eius gloriae consortes fieri mereamur. Per Dominum.

God our Father, in wondrous fashion you added Saint N., afire with love of you and noted for that faith which overcomes the world, to the number of your holy shepherds. Through his intercession, please grant that we too may stand firm in faith and love, and be privileged to share in his glory. We ask this....

Prayer over the Gifts

Suscipe, Domine, haec munera populi tui, quae tibi in beati N. festivitate offerimus, ut per eadem, sicut confidimus, tuae pietatis sentiamus auxilium. Per Christum.

Lord, receive the gifts of your people, which we offer you on this feast of Saint N. Through them, as we confidently trust, may we experience the help of your love. We ask this....

Prayer after Communion

Corporis sacri et pretiosi Sanguinis alimonia repleti, quaesumus, Domine Deus noster, ut, quod pia devotione gerimus, certa redemptione capiamus. Per Christum.

Lord our God, we are filled with the food of the sacred Body of Christ and his precious Blood, and we ask that we may receive in the certainty of redemption what we offer in loving dedication. We ask this....

COMMON OF PASTORS: #5, FOR PASTORS

Collect

Deus, fidelium lumen et pastor animarum, qui beatum N. (episcopum) in Ecclesia posuisti, ut oves tuas verbo pasceret et informaret exemplo, da nobis, eius intercessione, et fidem servare, quam verbo docuit, et viam sequi, quam exemplo monstravit. Per Dominum.

God our Father, you are the light of your faithful people and the shepherd of their souls. You placed (your bishop) Saint N. in your Church to feed your flock by his preaching and to form them by his example. Through his intercession grant that we may both remain true to the faith which he taught by his words, and follow the way of life which he showed by his actions. We ask this....

Prayer over the Gifts

Maiestatem tuam suppliciter imploramus, omnipotens Deus, ut, sicut gloriam divinae potentiae munera pro Sanctis oblata testantur, sic nobis effectum tuae salvationis impendant. Per Christum.

Almighty God, the gifts offered in honor of the saints bear witness to the awesomeness of your divine power. We humbly ask your divine majesty that, in the same way, they may result in redemption for us. We ask this....

Prayer after Communion

Sumpta mysteria, quaesumus, Domine, aeternis nos praeparent gaudiis, quae beatus N. fideli dispensatione promeruit. Per Christum.

Lord, we ask that the mysteries we have received may prepare us for the everlasting joys that Saint N. gained by the faithful performance of his office. We ask this....

Alternate Prayer after Communion

Refectione sacra enutritos, fac nos, omnipotens Deus, exempla beati N. iugiter sequentes, te perpeti devotione colere, et indefessa omnibus caritate proficere. Per Christum.

Almighty God, we have been fed at your sacred banquet. Make us always follow the example of Saint N. by worshipping you through unfailing service and by developing a tireless love for all men and women. We ask this....

COMMON OF PASTORS: #6, FOR PASTORS

Collect

Deus, qui beatos (episcopos) N. et N. ad pascendum populum tuum spiritu veritatis et dilectionis implevisti, praesta, ut, quorum festivitatem venerando agimus, eorum imitatione proficiamus, et intercessione sublevemur. Per Dominum.

God our Father, you filled (your bishops) Saints N. and N. with the spirit of truth and love so that they could feed your flock. Grant that we who reverently celebrate their feast may make progress in imitating them and be strengthened by the help of their prayers. We ask this....

Prayer over the Gifts

Suscipe, quaesumus, Domine, hoc sacrificium populi tui, ut, quod tibi in honore beatorum N. et N. offertur ad gloriam, nobis tribuas ad salutem perpetuam. Per Christum.

Lord, please receive the sacrifice of your people. May you return to us as an aid to our eternal salvation the gift which, in honor of Saints N. and N., we now offer in order to glorify you. We ask this....

Prayer after Communion

Sumpsimus, Domine, sanctorum tuorum N. et N. memoriam celebrantes, sacramenta caelestia; praesta, quaesumus, ut, quod temporaliter gerimus, aeternis gaudiis consequamur. Per Christum.

Lord, we have received your heavenly sacraments in memory of your saints N. and N. Please grant that, in the joys of eternity, we may come to possess what we now celebrate on earth. We ask this....

COMMON OF PASTORS: #7, FOR PASTORS

Collect

Supplices te rogamus, omnipotens Deus, ut, intercedentibus sanctis tuis N. et N., et tua in nobis dona multiplices, et tempora nostra in pace disponas. Per Dominum.

Almighty God, through the intercession of your saints N. and N., we humbly ask that you increase your gifts to us and make us pass all our days in peace. We ask this....

Prayer over the Gifts

Praetende munera, quaesumus, Domine, altaribus tuis pro beatorum tuorum N. et N. commemoratione proposita, ut, sicut per haec beata mysteria illis gloriam contulisti, ita nobis indulgentiam largiaris. Per Christum.

Lord, we ask you to look kindly upon the gifts we have placed on your altar in memory of your saints N. and N., so that, just as through these sacred mysteries you brought heavenly glory to them, so also you may grant your forgiveness to us. We ask this....

Prayer after Communion

Mensa caelestis, omnipotens Deus, in omnibus festivitatem beatorum N. et N. celebrantibus supernas vires firmet et augeat, ut et fidei donum integrum custodiamus, et per ostensum salutis tramitem ambulemus. Per Christum.

Lord, may this sacred meal make your heavenly strength surer and greater for all of us who celebrate the feast of Saints N. and N, so that we may guard the integrity of the gift of faith and walk along the path of salvation which you have shown to us. We ask this....

COMMON OF PASTORS: #8, FOR FOUNDERS OF CHURCHES

Collect

Omnipotens et misericors Deus, qui beati N. praedicatione patres nostros illuminare dignatus es, concede nobis, quaesumus, ut, qui christiano gloriamur nomine, fidem quam profitemur iugiter operibus ostendamus. Per Dominum.

Almighty and eternal God, by the preaching of Saint N. you saw fit to enlighten our forefathers. Please grant that, by our deeds, we who rejoice in being called Christians may always give evidence of the faith that we profess. We ask this....

Alternate Collect

Respice, Domine, familiam tuam, quam beatus N. (episcopus) genuit verbo veritatis, et vitae aluit sacramento, ut, quos gratia tua fecit illius ministerio fideles, faciat eiusdem precibus in caritate ferventes. Per Dominum.

Lord, look upon your chosen people whom (your bishop) Saint N. brought to birth by his preaching of the truth and nourished with the sacrament of eternal life. Through his prayers, may your grace make your people ardent in loving you, just as through his life and work it has made them faithful to you. We ask this....

Prayer over the Gifts

Annue, quaesumus, omnipotens Deus, ut haec sacrificia populi tui, quae tibi in commemoratione beati N. offerimus, donis caelestibus propitiatus immisceas. Per Christum.

Almighty God, look favorably upon us. In your mercy, unite these sacrifices of your people, which we offer in honor of Saint N., with your heavenly gifts. We ask this....

Prayer after Communion

Sumpsimus, Domine, pignus redemptionis aeternae, beati N. festivitate laetantes, quod sit nobis, quaesumus, vitae praesentis auxilium pariter et futurae. Per Christum.

Lord, as we rejoice on the feast of Saint N., we have received the pledge of eternal salvation. May it aid us both for our present life and for the life to come. We ask this....

COMMON OF PASTORS: #9, FOR FOUNDERS OF CHURCHES

Collect

Respice, quaesumus, Domine, ad tuam benignus Ecclesiam N., et, cui per apostolicam sanctorum N. et N. sollicitudinem religionis exordium donasti, per eorum intercessionem, tribue continuum christianae pietatis affectum. Per Dominum.

Lord, in your kindness look upon your church at N. You gave it a beginning in your holy faith through the apostolic care of Saints N. and N.; through their intercession, grant it a continuing sense of Christian love. We ask this....

Alternate Collect

Deus, qui beati N. (episcopi) praedicatione patres nostros vocasti in admirabile Evangelii lumen, fac, ut, eius intercessione, crescamus in gratia et cognitione Domini nostri Iesu Christi, Filii tui. Qui tecum.

God our Father, you called our forefathers into the wonderful light of your Gospel through the preaching of (your bishop) Saint N. Through his intercession, make us grow in your grace and in our knowledge of your Son, our Lord Jesus Christ, who lives and reigns....

Prayer over the Gifts

Suscipe, quaesumus, Domine, munera populi tui, pro sanctorum tuorum N. et N. festivitate delata, et sincero nos corde perfice benignus acceptos. Per Christum.

Lord, please receive the gifts of your people, which we offer on this feast of your saints N. and N. In your mercy, make us pleasing to you by rendering our hearts sincere. We ask this....

Prayer after Communion

Laetificet nos acceptum de altari salutare tuum, Domine, in sanctorum N. et N. festivitate, qua, de tuis beneficiis solliciti, pretiosa fidei nostrae initia veneramur, et te in Sanctis tuis mirabilem praedicamus. Per Christum.

Lord, may your saving grace, which we have received from this altar on the feast of Saints N. and N., fill us with joy. As we seek your favors on this feast, we honor the priceless beginnings of our faith and proclaim that you are marvelous in your saints. We ask this....

COMMON OF PASTORS: #10, FOR MISSIONARIES

Collect

Deus, qui per beatum N. (episcopum) infideles populos de tenebris ad lucem veritatis venire tribuisti, da nobis, eius intercessione, in fidei stabilitate consistere, et in spe Evangelii, quod praedicavit, constantes permanere. Per Dominum.

God our Father, through (your bishop) Saint N. you granted unbelieving people the gift of emerging from their darkness into the light of truth. Through his intercession, grant that we may be solidly rooted in the faith and may firmly persevere in our hope in the Gospel which he preached. We ask this....

COMMON OF PASTORS: #11, FOR MISSIONARIES

Alternate Collect

Omnipotens sempiterne Deus, qui huius diei laetitiam in beati N. glorificatione consecrasti, concede propitius, ut fidem illam, quam inexplebili studio semper asseruit, iugiter retinere et opere complere studeamus. Per Dominum.

Almighty and everlasting God, you made this day's joy holy by the exaltation of Saint N. He always proclaimed the faith with insatiable zeal; in your mercy, please grant that we may always strive to preserve that faith and bring it to fulfillment by our works. We ask this....

Collect

Deus, qui Ecclesiam tuam beati N. religionis zelo et apostolicis curis amplificasti, eius intercessione concede, ut fidei et sanctitatis nova semper incrementa suscipiat. Per Dominum.

God our Father, you increased your Church through Saint N's zeal for the faith and his apostolic concern and efforts. Through his intercession grant that it may always increase anew in faith and holiness. We ask this....

Prayer over the Gifts

Respice quas offerimus hostias, omnipotens Deus, in beati N. festivitate, et praesta, ut, qui dominicae passionis mysteria celebramus, imitemur quod agimus. Per Christum.

Almighty God, look upon the gifts we offer on this feast of Saint N. As we commemorate the mysteries of the Lord's passion, grant that we may imitate what we celebrate. We ask this....

Prayer over the Gifts

Propitiare, Domine, supplicationibus nostris, et ab omni culpa liberos esse concede, ut, purificante nos gratia tua, iisdem quibus famulamur mysteriis emundemur. Per Christum.

Lord, graciously be pleased by our prayers, and grant that we may be freed from every fault. And so, may your grace purify us, and may we be cleansed by the very mysteries in which we take part. We ask this....

Prayer after Communion

Huius mysterii virtute, confirma, Domine, famulos tuos in fide veritatis, ut eam ubique ore et opere confiteantur, pro qua beatus N. laborare non destitit et vitam suam impendit. Per Christum.

Lord, by the power of this mystery, strengthen your chosen people's faith in your truth. By word and work may they everywhere profess the faith for which Saint N. never ceased to labor and for which he spent his entire life. We ask this....

Prayer after Communion

Sacramenta quae sumpsimus, Domine Deus noster, illam nobis fidem innutriant, quam et apostolica docuit praedicatio, et beati N. sollicitudo custodivit. Per Christum.

Lord our God, may the sacraments that we have received nurture within us that faith which the preaching of the Apostles first taught and which the care of Saint N. kept safe. We ask this....

COMMON OF PASTORS: #12, FOR MISSIONARIES

Collect

Deus, cuius ineffabili misericordia beatus N. evangelizavit investigabiles divitias Christi, da nos, eius intercessione, crescere in scientia tua, et, in omni opere bono fructificantes, secundum Evangelii veritatem coram te fideliter ambulare. Per Dominum.

God our Father, because of your ineffable mercy toward us, Saint N. announced the good news of the unfathomable riches of Christ. Through his intercession, grant that we may grow in our knowledge of you and, bearing fruit in every good work, may faithfully walk in your presence according to the truth of the Gospel. We ask this....

Alternate Collect for Missionary Martyrs

Praesta, quaesumus, omnipotens Deus, ut beatorum N. et N. fidem congrua devotione sectemur, qui pro eiusdem dilatatione coronam martyrii meruerunt. Per Christum.

Almighty God, for their work in spreading the faith, Saints N. and N. were privileged to be given the crown of martyrdom. Please grant that, with fitting love, we may participate in their faith. We ask this....

Prayer over the Gifts

Beati N. memoriam recensentes, quaesumus, Domine, ut his muneribus tibi oblatis benedictionem effundas de caelis, quo, ex eis sumentes, et omnibus careamus culpis et caelestibus repleamur eduliis. Per Christum.

Lord, we are mindful of Saint N., and we ask that you pour forth your blessing from heaven upon these gifts which we offer you. As we take part in these offerings, may we be delivered from every fault and be filled with your heavenly food. We ask this....

Prayer after Communion

Sancta tua nos, Domine, sumpta vivificent, ut, qui beati N. commemoratione gaudemus, eius quoque apostolicae virtutis proficiamus exemplo. Per Christum.

Lord, may your holy gifts, which we have received, give us life, so that we who rejoice on this feast of Saint N. may also benefit from the example of his apostolic virtue. We ask this....

COMMON OF DOCTORS OF THE CHURCH: #1

Collect

Omnipotens aeterne Deus, qui beatum N. (episcopum) Ecclesiae tuae doctorem dedisti, praesta, ut, quod ille divino affatus spiritu docuit, nostris iugiter stabiliatur in cordibus, et quem patronum, te donante, amplectimur, eum apud tuam misericordiam defensorem habeamus. Per Dominum.

Almighty and eternal God, you gave (your bishop) Saint N. to your Church as its teacher. Grant that what he taught, as he spoke through the prompting of the Holy Spirit, may always remain fixed in our hearts, and that we may have him as our protector in the sight of your divine mercy, just as we embrace him as the patron whom you have given us. We ask this....

Prayer over the Gifts

Sacrificium tibi placeat, Deus, in festivitate beati N. libenter exhibitum, quo monente, nos etiam totos tibi reddimus collaudantes. Per Christum.

Lord, may our sacrifice please you as we joyfully offer it on this feast of Saint N., at whose urging we also offer you our entire selves as a gift of praise. We ask this....

Prayer after Communion

Quos Christo reficis pane vivo, eosdem edoce, Domine, Christe magistro, ut in festivitate beati N. tuam discant veritatem, et eam in caritate operentur. Per Christum.

Lord, with Christ as their teacher, instruct your people, whom you renew with Christ as their living bread, so that on this feast of Saint N. they may come to know your truth and carry it out in works of love. We ask this....

COMMON OF DOCTORS OF THE CHURCH: #2

Collect

Domine Deus, qui beatum N. caelesti doctrina imbuere dignatus es, da nobis, ipsius interventu, eandem doctrinam fideliter custodire, et moribus profiteri. Per Dominum.

Lord God, you saw fit to endow Saint N. with heavenly wisdom. Through his intercession, grant that we may carefully guard that same wisdom and profess it by how we live. We ask this....

Prayer over the Gifts

Illa nos, quaesumus, Domine, divina tractantes, Spiritus Sanctus fidei luce perfundat, qua beatum N. ad gloriae tuae propagationem iugiter collustravit. Per Christum.

Lord, as we take part in these sacred mysteries, we pray that the Holy Spirit may pour forth upon us that light of faith through which he constantly inspired Saint N. to spread your glory. We ask this....

Prayer after Communion

Caelesti alimonia refecti, supplices te, Domine, deprecamur, ut, beati N. monitis, de acceptis donis semper in gratiarum actione maneamus. Per Christum.

Lord, we are renewed with heavenly food, and we humbly ask that, through the teaching of Saint N., we may ever be grateful for the gifts we have received. We ask this....

COMMON OF VIRGINS: #1

Collect

Exaudi nos, Deus, salutaris noster, ut, sicut de beatae N. virginis commemoratione gaudemus, ita piae devotionis erudiamur affectu. Per Dominum.

God our salvation, hear our prayers. As we rejoice at the memory of your virgin Saint N., may we benefit from the example of her faithful and devoted love. We ask this....

Prayer over the Gifts

In beata virgine N. te, Domine, mirabilem praedicantes, maiestatem tuam suppliciter exoramus, ut, sicut eius tibi grata sunt merita, sic nostrae servitutis accepta reddantur officia. Per Christum.

Lord, as we proclaim your greatness in the person of your virgin Saint N., we humbly ask your divine majesty that, just as her life and works were pleasing to you, so may the offering of our service to you be acceptable in your sight. We ask this....

Prayer after Communion

Divini muneris participatione refecti, quaesumus, Domine Deus noster, ut, exemplo beatae N., mortificationem Iesu in corpore nostro circumferentes, tibi soli adhaerere studeamus. Per Christum.

Lord our God, we are renewed by our sharing in your sacred gift, and we ask that, through the example of Saint N., we may carry about in our bodies the death of Jesus and ever strive for allegiance to you alone. We ask this....

COMMON OF VIRGINS: #2

Collect

Domine Deus, qui beatam N. virginem caelestibus donis cumulasti, tribue, quaesumus, ut, eius virtutes aemulantes in terris, gaudiis cum ipsa perfruamur aeternis. Per Dominum.

Lord our God, you enriched your virgin Saint N. with many heavenly gifts. Please grant that we may imitate her virtues while we are still on earth, and enjoy eternal happiness with her in heaven. We ask this....

Alternate Collect for a Virgin and Foundress

Fac, Domine Deus noster, ut beata virgo N., sponsa tibi fidelis, divinae caritatis flammam excitet in cordibus nostris, quam, ad perennem Ecclesiae tuae gloriam, aliis virginibus inseruit. Per Dominum.

Lord our God, grant that the virgin Saint N., your faithful spouse, may enkindle in our hearts that fire of divine love which she inspired in her followers, to the endless exaltation of your Church. We ask this....

Prayer over the Gifts

Dicatae, quaesumus, Domine, capiamus oblationis effectum, ut, beatae N. exemplo, terrenae vetustatis conversatione mundati, caelestis vitae profectibus innovemur. Per Christum.

Lord, we ask that we may receive the reward of the offering we bring, so that, through the example of Saint N., we may be cleansed of our old way of living on earth and be renewed by an increase in your divine life. We ask this....

Prayer after Communion

Corporis et Sanguinis Unigeniti tui sacra perceptio, Domine, ab omnibus nos caducis rebus avertat, ut exemplo beatae N. valeamus tui et sincera in terris caritate proficere, et perpetua in caelis visione gaudere. Per Christum.

Lord, may the sacred reception of the Body and Blood of your only Son turn us away from whatever is transitory. By the example of Saint N., may we be able to progress in our unfeigned love for you while on earth, and rejoice in the endless vision of you in heaven. We ask this....

COMMON OF VIRGINS: #3

Collect

Deus, qui te in puris manere cordibus asseris, da nobis, beatae N. virginis intercessione, per gratiam tuam tales exsistere, in quibus habitare digneris. Per Dominum.

God our Father, you tell us that you live in hearts that are unstained. By the intercession of your virgin Saint N. and through your gracious gift, may we live in such a way that you will see fit to dwell in us. We ask this....

Alternate Collect

Exaudi, quaesumus, Domine, preces nostras, ut, qui beatae N. virginis virtutem devote recolimus, in tui amore permanere et usque in finem semper crescere mereamur. Per Dominum.

Lord, please hear our prayers, so that we who lovingly recall the virtuous life of your virgin Saint N. may be privileged to remain in your love and to grow in it always, until the very end of our lives. We ask this....

Prayer over the Gifts

Suscipe, Domine, obsequium humilitatis nostrae, quod tibi in commemoratione beatae N. virginis exhibemus, et nos, per immaculatam hostiam, da iugiter in tuo conspectu pio sanctoque amore flagrare. Per Christum.

Lord, receive the offering of our lowliness, which we bring you in memory of your virgin Saint N. Through this spotless gift, grant that we may ever be afire with a love that is faithful and holy in your sight. We ask this....

Prayer after Communion

Caelesti pane refecti, humiliter deprecamur clementiam tuam, Domine, ut, qui de beatae N. commemoratione gaudemus, veniam delictorum, sospitatem corporum, gratiamque et gloriam aeternam consequamur animarum. Per Christum.

Lord, we are renewed with your heavenly food, and we humbly ask for your mercy. May we who rejoice on this feast of Saint N. attain forgiveness for our sins, health for our bodies, and your eternal grace and glory for our souls. We ask this....

COMMON OF VIRGINS: #4

Collect

Multiplica super nos, quaesumus, Domine, misericordiam tuam, ut, sicut in beatarum virginum N. et N. festivitate pia devotione laetamur, ita earum perpetua societate, te largiente, fruamur. Per Dominum.

Lord, please pour out your many mercies upon us, so that we who rejoice in loving dedication on this feast of your holy virgins N. and N. may, through your gracious gift, enjoy their unending company in heaven. We ask this....

Prayer over the Gifts

In sanctarum virginum N. et N. commemoratione te, Domine, mirabilem praedicantes, munera votiva deferimus; praesta, quaesumus, ut, sicut earum tibi grata sunt merita, sic nostrae servitutis accepta reddantur officia. Per Christum.

Lord, we proclaim your greatness and we bring you our prayerful gifts on this feast of your holy virgins N. and N. Please grant that, just as their lives and works are pleasing to you, so also these offerings of our service may be made acceptable to you. We ask this....

Prayer after Communion

Sumpta mysteria, quaesumus, Domine, in hac festivitate beatarum virginum N. et N., incitent nos iugiter et illustrent, ut digne adventum Filii tui praestolemur, et ad supernas eius nuptias admittamur. Per Christum.

Lord, we ask that the mysteries which we have received on this feast of the holy virgins N. and N. may ever encourage and enlighten us, so that we may fittingly await the coming of your Son and be admitted to his wedding feast in heaven. We ask this....

COMMON OF HOLY MEN AND WOMEN: #1

Collect

Omnipotens sempiterne Deus, qui per glorificationem Sanctorum novissima dilectionis tuae argumenta largiris, concede propitius, ut, ad Unigenitum tuum fideliter imitandum, et ipsorum intercessione commendemur, et incitemur exemplo. Per Dominum.

Almighty and eternal God, in exalting the saints you give us a most persuasive proof of your love. In your mercy, grant that we may be favored by their intercession and spurred on by their example, so that we may faithfully imitate your only Son. We ask this....

Prayer over the Gifts

Preces nostras, Domine, quaesumus, propitiatus admitte, et, ut digne tuis famulemur altaribus, Sanctorum tuorum nos intercessione custodi. Per Christum.

Lord, in your mercy please accept our prayers and, by the intercession of the saints, keep a watchful care over us, so that we may worthily assist at your altar. We ask this....

Prayer after Communion

Omnipotens sempiterne Deus, Pater totius consolationis et pacis, praesta familiae tuae in celebritate Sanctorum ad laudem tui nominis congregatae, ut, per Unigeniti tui sumpta mysteria, pignus accipiat redemptionis aeternae. Per Christum.

Almighty and eternal God, source of all consolation and peace, on this festival of the saints your chosen people have come together for the praise of your name. Through these mysteries of your only Son which they have received, grant that they may receive the pledge of eternal redemption. We ask this....

COMMON OF HOLY MEN AND WOMEN: #2

Collect

Deus, qui solus es sanctus, et sine quo nullus est bonus, intercessione beati N. iube nos tales fieri, qui non debeamus tua gloria privari. Per Dominum.

God our Father, you alone are holy; without you, no one can be called good. Through the intercession of Saint N., make us become such that there will be no cause for us to be separated from your glory. We ask this....

Prayer over the Gifts

Praesta nobis, quaesumus, omnipotens Deus, ut nostrae humilitatis oblatio et pro tuorum tibi grata sit honore Sanctorum, et nos corpore pariter et mente purificet. Per Christum.

Almighty God, please grant that our humble offering may, for the honor of the saints, please you and purify us in body as well as in mind. We ask this....

Prayer after Communion

In nataliciis Sanctorum quaesumus, Domine, ut, sacramenti munere vegetati, bonis, quibus per tuam gratiam nunc fovemur, perfruamur aeternis. Per Christum.

Lord, on this feast, which celebrates the entrance of your saints into heaven, we ask that we may be granted life by the gift of this sacrament and may come to enjoy that eternal reward which, through your grace, now encourages us. We ask this....

COMMON OF HOLY MEN AND WOMEN: #3

Collect

Deus, qui infirmitati nostrae, ad terendam salutis viam, in Sanctis tuis exemplum et praesidium collocasti, concede propitius, ut, qui beati N. natalicia colimus, per eius ad te exempla gradiamur. Per Dominum.

God our Father, in the person of your saints you have established an example and an aid for our weakness, so as to make smooth the way to salvation. In your mercy, grant that we who honor the birth into heaven of Saint N. may come near to you by following his (her) example. We ask this....

Prayer over the Gifts

Praesenti oblatione, Domine, in beati N. commemoratione delata, fidelibus tuis, quaesumus, pacis et unitatis dona largire. Per Christum.

Lord, through the offering we now present on the feast of Saint N., please grant to your faithful people the gifts of peace and unity. We ask this....

Prayer after Communion

Sacramenta quae sumpsimus, Domine, in commemoratione beati N. mentes et corda nostra sanctificent, ut divinae consortes naturae effici mereamur. Per Christum.

Lord, may the sacraments that we have received in memory of Saint N. make our minds and hearts holy, so that we may be privileged to be given a share in your divine nature. We ask this....

COMMON OF HOLY MEN AND WOMEN: #4

Collect

Deus, qui nos conspicis ex nostra infirmitate deficere, ad amorem tuum nos misericorditer per Sanctorum tuorum exempla restaura. Per Dominum.

God our Father, you see that we fail because of our weakness. Through the example of your saints, mercifully restore us to your love. We ask this....

Prayer over the Gifts

Sacrificia, Domine, quae in hac festivitate sancti N. tuae offerimus maiestati, nobis sint ad salutem efficacia, et tuae placita pietati. Per Christum.

Lord, may the sacrifice we offer your divine majesty on this feast of Saint N. be effective in helping us reach salvation and pleasing to you who are loving and faithful. We ask this....

Prayer after Communion

Sacro munere satiati, supplices te, Domine, deprecamur, ut, quod debitae servitutis celebramus officio, salvationis tuae sentiamus augmentum. Per Christum.

Lord, we have been filled with your sacred gift, and we humbly beg to experience as an increase in your saving grace the very gift which we offer in fulfillment of our duty of worship and service. We ask this....

COMMON OF HOLY MEN AND WOMEN: #5

Collect

Impetret, quaesumus, Domine, fidelibus tuis auxilium oratio iusta Sanctorum, et, in quorum sunt celebritate devoti, fiant in eorum perpetua sorte participes. Per Dominum.

Lord, we ask that the holy prayers of the saints may win help for your faithful people. May we share in the endless happiness of those whose feast we devoutly celebrate. We ask this....

Prayer over the Gifts

Hostias ad altare tuum offerentibus, Domine, da nobis illum pietatis affectum, quem beato N. infudisti, ut pura mente ac fervido corde rei sacrae attendamus, et sacrificium tibi placitum nobisque proficuum celebremus. Per Christum.

Lord, as we bring our offerings to your altar, give us that spirit of loving faithfulness which you poured into the heart of Saint N., so that we may take part in this sacred action with pure minds and zealous hearts, and may offer a sacrifice that will be pleasing to you and beneficial to us. We ask this....

Prayer after Communion

Sacramentorum tuorum, Domine, communio sumpta nos salvet, et in tuae veritatis luce confirmet. Per Christum.

Lord, may our reception of your sacraments bring us salvation and strengthen us in the light of your truth. We ask this....

COMMON OF HOLY MEN AND WOMEN: #6

Collect

Concede, quaesumus, omnipotens Deus, ut ad meliorem vitam Sanctorum tuorum exempla nos provocent, quatenus beati N., cuius memoriam celebramus, etiam actus incessanter imitemur. Per Dominum.

Almighty God, please grant that the example of your saints may so incite us to a better way of life that we may always imitate even the very actions of Saint N., whose memory we celebrate. We ask this....

Prayer over the Gifts

Munera nostra, Domine, sacris altaribus offerentes, in hac festivitate Sanctorum tuorum, quaesumus clementiam tuam, ut eadem et supremam tibi gloriam operentur, et uberrimam nobis gratiam assequantur. Per Christum.

Lord, as we offer our gifts upon your altar on this feast of your saints, we ask for your mercy, so that these gifts may give you the greatest possible honor and win for us your most generous favor. We ask this....

Prayer after Communion

Quaesumus, Domine Deus noster, ut divina mysteria, quae in tuorum commemoratione Sanctorum frequentamus, salutem et pacem in nobis operentur aeternam. Per Christum.

Lord our God, we ask that these sacred mysteries, in which we take part on this feast of your saints, may bring us eternal salvation and peace. We ask this....

COMMON OF HOLY MEN AND WOMEN: #7, FOR RELIGIOUS

Collect

Deus, cuius munere beatus N. Christum pauperem et humilem perseveravit imitari, concede nobis, ipso intercedente, ut, in vocatione nostra fideliter ambulantes, ad eam perfectionem, quam nobis in Filio tuo proposuisti, pervenire valeamus. Per Dominum.

God our Father, by your gracious gift Saint N. continually imitated the poor and humble Christ. Through this saint's prayers, grant that we may walk faithfully in the path to which we are called, and be enabled to arrive at that state of perfection which you have modeled for us in the person of your Son. We ask this....

Alternate Collect for an Abbot

Da nobis, quaesumus, Domine, inter mundi huius varietates toto corde rebus caelestibus adhaerere, qui per beatum N. abbatem evangelicae nobis perfectionis documenta donasti. Per Dominum.

Lord, through your abbot Saint N. you have given us an example of evangelical perfection. Please grant that we may wholeheartedly cling to the things of eternity even though we are in the midst of the transitory things of this world. We ask this....

Prayer over the Gifts

Clementissime Deus, qui, vetere homine consumpto, novum secundum te in beato N. creare dignatus es, concede propitius, ut nos pariter renovati hanc placationis hostiam tibi acceptabilem offeramus. Per Christum.

Most merciful God, in Saint N. you saw fit to do away with human sinfulness and make a new creature according to your own desire. Mercifully grant that we too may be renewed, and that we may offer in this sacrifice of atonement a gift that will be pleasing to you. We ask this....

Prayer after Communion

Quaesumus, omnipotens Deus, ut, qui huius sacramenti muniamur virtute, exemplo beati N. discamus te super omnia semper inquirere, et novi hominis formam in hoc saeculo portare. Per Christum.

Almighty God, we ask that we who are strengthened by the power of this sacrament may learn, from the example of Saint N., ever to seek you above all else and to carry within us the image of your new creation while we are in this world. We ask this....

COMMON OF HOLY MEN AND WOMEN: #8, FOR RELIGIOUS

Collect

Deus, qui beatum N. ad tuum regnum in hoc saeculo perquirendum per caritatis perfectae prosecutionem vocasti, concede, ut, eius intercessione roborati, in dilectionis via spiritu gaudentes progrediamur. Per Dominum.

God our Father, you called Saint N. to the task of seeking your kingdom in this world by striving to attain perfect charity. Grant that we may be strengthened by his (her) intercession and, with joyful hearts, may progress in the way of love. We ask this....

Prayer over the Gifts

Accepta tibi sint, quaesumus, Domine, munera nostrae servitutis pro beati N. commemoratione altari tuo proposita, et concede, ut, a terrenis impedimentis absoluti, te solo divites efficiamur. Per Christum.

Father, we ask that these gifts we owe you as Lord may be pleasing to you as we place them on your altar in memory of Saint N. Grant that we may be freed from earthly hindrances and may find our riches in you alone. We ask this....

Prayer after Communion

Per huius virtutem sacramenti, quaesumus, Domine, beati N. exemplo, deduc nos iugiter in tua dilectione, et opus bonum quod coepisti in nobis perfice usque in diem Christi Iesu. Qui vivit.

Lord, by the power of this sacrament and through the example of Saint N., please lead us always in the way of your love, and bring to perfection, even unto the day of the coming of Christ Jesus, the good work that you have begun in us. We ask this....

COMMON OF HOLY MEN AND WOMEN: #9, FOR THOSE WHO PERFORMED WORKS OF MERCY

Collect

Deus, qui Ecclesiam tuam in dilectione tuae divinitatis et proximi cuncta servare caelestia mandata docuisti, da nobis, ut, beati N. exemplo caritatis opera exercentes, inter benedictos regni tui connumerari mereamur. Per Dominum.

God our Father, you taught your Church how to fulfill all your divine commands through love for your divine majesty and for our neighbor. Through the example of Saint N., grant that we may perform works of charity and be privileged to be counted among the blessed in your kingdom. We ask this....

Prayer over the Gifts

Suscipe, Domine, munera populi tui, et praesta, ut, qui Filii tui immensae caritatis opus recolimus, in tui et proximi dilectione, Sanctorum tuorum exemplo, confirmemur. Per Christum.

Lord, receive the gifts of your people. As we commemorate the labor of immense love that your Son performed, grant that, by the example of your saints, we may be strengthened in our love for you and for our neighbor. We ask this....

Prayer after Communion

Sacris mysteriis refectos, da nos, quaesumus, Domine, beati N. exempla sectari, qui te indefessa pietate coluit, et populo tuo immensa profuit caritate. Per Christum.

Lord, we have been renewed by your sacred mysteries, and we ask you to grant us the grace of following the example of Saint N., who worshipped you with tireless fidelity and benefited your people with his (her) intense love. We ask this....

Alternate Prayer after Communion

Sacramenti salutaris, Domine, pasti deliciis, tuam supplices deprecamur pietatem, ut, sancti N. caritatis imitatores effecti, consortes simus et gloriae. Per Christum.

Lord, we have been fed with the delights of your saving sacrament, and we humbly ask for your loving mercy. May we become imitators of Saint N.'s charity, and thus become sharers in his (her) heavenly glory. We ask this....

COMMON OF HOLY MEN AND WOMEN: #10, FOR TEACHERS

Collect

Deus, qui in Ecclesia tua beatum N. suscitasti, ut proximis viam salutis monstraret, da nobis, eius exemplo, Christum magistrum ita sequi, ut ad te cum fratribus nostris pervenire valeamus. Per Dominum.

God our Father, you raised up Saint N. within your Church to show those around him (her) the way to salvation. Through his (her) example, grant that we may follow Christ our teacher in such a way that, in company with our brothers and sisters, we may be able to come to you. We ask this....

Prayer over the Gifts

Accepta tibi sit, quaesumus, Domine, sacratae plebis oblatio pro tuorum commemoratione Sanctorum, et praesta, ut, ex huius participatione mysterii, exempla tuae caritatis referamus. Per Christum.

Lord, we ask that the offering your holy people make in remembrance of your saints may please you. Since we have shared in this mystery, please grant that we may become examples of your love. We ask this....

Prayer after Communion

Tribuat nobis, omnipotens Deus, refectio sancta subsidium, ut, exemplo Sanctorum tuorum, et fraternitatis caritatem et lumen veritatis in corde exhibeamus et opere. Per Christum.

Almighty God, may this holy banquet provide us with your help. Through the example of your saints, may we display love for our brothers and sisters and manifest the light of your truth in our hearts and in our deeds. We ask this....

COMMON OF HOLY MEN AND WOMEN: #11, FOR HOLY WOMEN

Collect
(for One Holy Woman)

Deus, qui nos annua beatae N. festivitate laetificas, da, quaesumus, ut, quam veneramur officio, etiam piae conversationis sequamur exemplo. Per Dominum.

God our Father, you gladden us by the yearly feast of Saint N. We honor her for the service she rendered; may we also follow the example of her holy life. We ask this....

Alternate Collect
(for Several Holy Women)

Concede, quaesumus, omnipotens Deus, ut veneranda nobis beatarum N. et N. intercessio tribuat caeleste subsidium, quarum vita mirabilis omnibus salutare praestat exemplum. Per Dominum.

Almighty God, the marvelous lives of Saints N. and N. give a salutary example to everyone. Please grant that their holy prayers may obtain divine help for us. We ask this....

Prayer over the Gifts

Hostias tibi, Domine, pro sanctae N. commemoratione deferimus, suppliciter deprecantes, ut indulgentiam nobis pariter conferant et salutem. Per Christum.

Lord, we bring our gifts to you in memory of Saint N., and we humbly ask that they may obtain for us both your forgiveness and your salvation. We ask this....

Prayer after Communion

Divini operatio sacramenti, omnipotens Deus, in hac festivitate beatae N. illuminet nos pariter et inflammet, ut et sanctis iugiter desideriis ferveamus, et bonis operibus abundemus. Per Christum.

Almighty God, may the action of this heavenly sacrament enlighten our minds and inflame our hearts on this feast of Saint N., so that we may always be on fire with holy desires and be rich in good works. We ask this....

COMMON OF HOLY MEN AND WOMEN: #12, FOR HOLY WOMEN

Collect

Deus, humilium celsitudo, qui beatam N. caritatis et patientiae decore excellere disposuisti, eius meritis et intercessione concede, ut, crucem nostram iugiter ferentes, te semper diligere valeamus. Per Dominum.

God our Father, you are the exaltation of the lowly, and you made Saint N. eminent by the splendor of her charity and patience. By her merits and prayers grant that we may be able to carry our cross unfailingly and love you unceasingly. We ask this....

Alternate Collect

Effunde super nos, Domine, spiritum agnitionis et dilectionis tuae, quo ancillam tuam N. implevisti, ut, sedula eius imitatione tibi sincere obsequentes, fide et opere placeamus. Per Dominum.

Lord, pour forth upon us that spirit of the knowledge and love of you with which you filled your servant Saint N., so that we may follow you sincerely, in careful imitation of your saint, and be pleasing to you in our faith and in our works. We ask this....

Prayer over the Gifts

Hostias, Domine, tuae plebis intende, et, quas in honore Sanctorum tuorum devota mente celebrat, proficere sibi sentiat ad salutem. Per Christum.

Lord, look upon the offerings of your people. May they come to experience as a help toward salvation the gifts which, with loving heart, they bring to your altar in honor of your saints. We ask this....

Prayer after Communion

Repleti sumus, Domine, muneribus tuis, quae in celebritate beatae N. percepimus; tribue, quaesumus, ut eorum et mundemur effectu, et muniamur auxilio. Per Christum.

Lord, we are filled with your gifts, which we have received on the feast of Saint N. Please grant that we may be cleansed by the action they perform and strengthened by the help they bring. We ask this....

RITUAL

MASSES

I. CHRISTIAN INITIATION #1, ELECTION, OR ENROLLMENT OF NAMES

Collect

Deus, qui, licet salutem hominum semper operaris, nunc tamen populum tuum gratia abundantiore laetificas, respice propitius ad electionem tuam, ut piae protectionis auxilium et regenerandos muniat et renatos. Per Dominum.

God our Father, it is true that you are always working to bring about the salvation of the human race. But now you gladden your people with an even more bountiful grace. In your mercy, look upon the choice you have made, so that the help of your loving protection may safeguard both those who are to be reborn and those who already have been. We ask this....

Prayer over the Gifts

Omnipotens sempiterne Deus, qui nos ad aeternam vitam in confessione tui nominis baptismatis reparas sacramento, suscipe tuorum munera et vota famulorum, ut in te sperantium et desideria iubeas perfici et peccata deleri. Per Christum.

Almighty and eternal God, by the sacrament of baptism you restore us to eternal life in the profession of your name. Receive the offerings and prayers of your chosen people, and command that the hopes of those who trust in you be fulfilled and their sins washed away. We ask this....

Prayer after Communion

Purificent nos, quaesumus, Domine, sacramenta quae sumpsimus, et famulos tuos ab omni culpa liberos esse concede, ut, qui conscientiae reatu constringuntur, caelestis remedii plenitudine glorientur. Per Christum.

Lord, we ask that the sacraments we have received may cleanse us. Grant that your chosen people may be free from every fault, so that they who are bound by the reproach of conscience may rejoice in the fullness of your heavenly cure. We ask this....

I. CHRISTIAN INITIATION #2, THE SCRUTINIES

Collect (First Scrutiny)

Da, quaesumus, Domine, electis nostris digne atque sapienter ad confessionem tuae laudis accedere, ut dignitate pristina, quam originali transgressione perdiderunt, per tuam gloriam reformentur. Per Dominum.

Lord, please grant that our chosen brothers and sisters may come forward worthily and wisely to profess their praise of you. Through your glorious power, may they be remade into that former state of innocence which they lost by original sin. We ask this....

Collect (Second Scrutiny)

Omnipotens sempiterne Deus, Ecclesiam tuam spiritali iucunditate multiplica, ut, qui sunt generatione terreni, fiant regeneratione caelestes. Per Dominum.

Almighty and eternal God, increase your Church by giving it the spiritual joy of seeing those who are citizens of this world by birth become citizens of heaven by rebirth. We ask this....

Collect (Third Scrutiny)

Concede, Domine, electis nostris, ut, sanctis edocti mysteriis, et renoventur fonte baptismatis et inter Ecclesiae tuae membra numerentur. Per Dominum.

Lord, grant that our chosen brothers and sisters, who have been instructed in the sacred mysteries, may be renewed by the waters of baptism and be enrolled among the members of your Church. We ask this....

Prayer over the Gifts
(First Scrutiny)

Miseratio tua, Deus, ad haec percipienda mysteria famulos tuos, quaesumus, et praeveniat competenter et devota conversatione perducat. Per Christum.

God our Father, we ask that your mercy may properly prepare your chosen people to receive these mysteries, and may guide them through those mysteries in devout participation. We ask this....

Prayer over the Gifts
(Second Scrutiny)

Remedii sempiterni munera, Domine, laetantes offerimus, suppliciter exorantes, ut eadem nos et digne venerari et pro salvandis congruenter exhibere perficias. Per Christum.

Lord, in joy we offer the gifts that mark our eternal healing, and we humbly ask that you make us honor those gifts worthily and offer them properly on behalf of those who are to be saved. We ask this....

Prayer over the Gifts
(Third Scrutiny)

Exaudi nos, omnipotens Deus, et famulos tuos, quos fidei christianae primitiis imbuisti, huius sacrificii tribuas operatione mundari. Per Christum.

Almighty God, you have filled your chosen ones with the beginnings of the Christian faith. Hear us, and grant that they may be cleansed by the action of this sacrifice. We ask this....

Prayer after Communion
(First Scrutiny)

Adesto, Domine, quaesumus, redemptionis effectibus, ut, quos sacramentis aeternitatis instituenes, eosdem protegas dignanter aptando. Per Christum.

Lord, be present to us in your efficacious work of redemption. By preparing them fittingly, protect those whom you will initiate into the sacraments of eternity. We ask this....

Prayer after Communion
(Second Scrutiny)

Tu semper, quaesumus, Domine, tuam attolle benignus familiam, tu dispone correctam, tu propitius tuere subiectam, tu guberna perpetua bonitate salvandam. Per Christum.

Lord, in your mercy please lift up your chosen people unceasingly. Correct and guide them; mercifully place them under your care and protect them. Govern them, for it is by your ceaseless goodness that they are to be saved. We ask this....

Prayer after Communion
(Third Scrutiny)

Concurrat, Domine, quaesumus, populus tuus et toto tibi corde subiectus obtineat, ut, ab omni perturbatione securus, et salvationis suae gaudia promptus exerceat et pro regenerandis benignus exoret. Per Christum.

Lord, we ask that your people may come together in unity and continue their service to you with all their hearts. May they be freed from every fear, readily enjoy the happiness of their own redemption, and lovingly pray for those who are to be reborn. We ask this....

I. CHRISTIAN INITIATION
#3, BAPTISM (#A)

Collect

Deus, qui nos facis passionis et resurrectionis Filii tui participare mysterium, praesta, quaesumus, ut, adoptionis filiorum Spiritu roborati, in novitate vitae iugiter ambulemus. Per Dominum.

God our Father, you make us share in the mystery of your Son's suffering and resurrection. Please grant that we may be strengthened by the spirit of adoption we have received as sons and daughters, and may ever walk in newness of life. We ask this....

Prayer over the Gifts

Quos Filio tuo conformatos (et chrismatis signaculo perfectos) populo sacerdotali propitius aggregasti, rogamus, Domine, ut in acceptabiles hostias computare digneris, et una cum oblationibus Ecclesiae tuae benignus accipias. Per Christum.

Lord, these sons and daughters of yours have been made like your Son (and have been perfected by being signed with chrism), and in your mercy you have numbered them among your priestly people. We ask that you see fit to count them among the offerings that are pleasing to you, and that in your kindness you receive them as you receive the offerings of your Church. We ask this....

Prayer after Communion

Praesta, quaesumus, Domine, ut, carnis et sanguinis Filii tui praediti sacramento, in communione Spiritus eius fratrumque dilectione ita crescamus, quatenus ad plenam corporis Christi mensuram caritate vivida dilatemur. Per Christum.

Lord, we have been gifted with the sacrament of your Son's flesh and blood. Please grant that we may grow in our union with his Spirit and in our love for one another to the point that in the intensity of our love we arrive at the full measure of the body of Christ. We ask this....

I. CHRISTIAN INITIATION
#3, BAPTISM (#B)

Collect

Deus, qui nos regeneras verbo vitae, da, ut, corde sincero illud accipientes, veritatem alacres faciamus, et fraternae afferamus fructus plurimos caritatis. Per Dominum.

God our Father, you bring us to birth anew by your word of life. Grant that we may receive that word with sincere hearts, eagerly live according to your truth, and bear abundant fruit in our love for our brothers and sisters. We ask this....

Prayer over the Gifts

Ad paratum panem accedentibus vinumque commixtum ianuam, Domine, resera cenae tuae, ut, caeleste cum gaudiis convivium celebrantes, inter sanctorum cives tuosque domesticos censeamur. Per Christum.

Lord, as we come to the bread that has been prepared and the the wine that has been poured, open the door that leads to your banquet. As we celebrate this heavenly meal in joy, may we be considered to be fellow-citizens with your saints and members of your household. We ask this....

Prayer after Communion

Praeclarum, Domine, mortis et resurrectionis Filii tui mysterium, quod annuntiavimus, celebrando, fac, ut, per huius sacramenti virtutem, etiam vivendo fateamur. Per Christum.

Lord, through our celebration of the magnificent mystery of the death and resurrection of your Son, which we have proclaimed, and by means of the power of this sacrament, we ask you to make us also bear witness to that mystery by means of how we live. We ask this....

I. CHRISTIAN INITIATION #4, CONFIRMATION (#A)

Collect

Praesta, quaesumus, omnipotens et misericors Deus, ut Spiritus Sanctus adveniens templum nos gloriae suae dignanter inhabitando perficiat. Per Dominum.

Almighty and merciful God, please grant that your Holy Spirit may come upon us and, in his mercy, dwell in us, and so make of us a temple of his glory. We ask this....

Alternate Collect

Promissionem tuam, quaesumus, Domine, super nos propitiatus adimple, ut Spiritus Sanctus adveniens nos coram mundo testes efficiat Evangelii Domini nostri Iesu Christi. Qui tecum.

Lord, we ask that, in your kindness, you fulfill the promise you made to us. Let the Holy Spirit come and make us witnesses of the Gospel of our Lord Jesus Christ throughout the world. We ask this....

Prayer over the Gifts

Famulorum tuorum, quaesumus, Domine, suscipe vota clementer, et praesta, ut, Filio tuo perfectius configurati, in testimonium eius indesinenter accrescant, memoriale participantes redemptionis eius, qua Spiritum tuum nobis ipse promeruit. Qui tecum.

Lord, in your mercy please receive the prayers of your servants. Grant that they may ever be made more like your Son and may continually grow in bearing witness to him, since they share in this remembrance of that redemption by which he himself earned for us the gift of your Spirit. We ask this....

Prayer after Communion

Spiritu Sancto, Domine, perunctos tuique Filii sacramento nutritos tua in posterum benedictione prosequere, ut, omnibus adversitatibus superatis, Ecclesiam tuam sanctitate laetificent, eiusque in mundo incrementa suis operibus et caritate promoveant. Per Christum.

Lord, with your blessing for their future guard those who have been anointed with the Holy Spirit and fed with the sacrament of your Son, that they may overcome all obstacles, gladden your Church by their holiness, and foster its growth throughout the world by their works and their love. We ask this....

I. CHRISTIAN INITIATION #4, CONFIRMATION (#B)

Collect

Spiritum Sanctum tuum, quaesumus, Domine, super nos dignanter effunde, ut omnes, in unitate fidei ambulantes, et caritatis eius fortitudine roborati, ad mensuram aetatis plenitudinis Christi occurramus. Per Dominum.

Lord, in your mercy please pour forth your Holy Spirit upon us, so that all of us may walk together in the one faith and, fortified by the strength of Christ's love, may hasten to come to his full and mature stature. We ask this....

Prayer over the Gifts

Hos famulos tuos, Domine, una cum Unigenito tuo benignus admitte, ut, qui eius cruce spiritalique sunt unctione signati, se tibi cum ipso iugiter offerentes, largiorem in dies effusionem tui Spiritus mereantur. Per Christum.

Lord, in your kindness, receive these sons and daughters of yours along with your only Son. They have been marked with the sign of his cross and with this spiritual anointing; may they ever offer themselves to you in his company, and be privileged to be given a more abundant outpouring of your Spirit with each passing day. We ask this....

Prayer after Communion

Quos tui Spiritus, Domine, cumulasti muneribus, tuique auxisti Unigeniti nutrimento, fac etiam in plenitudine legis instructos, ut coram mundo tuae libertatem adoptionis iugiter manifestent, et propheticum tui populi munus sua valeant sanctitate praebere. Per Christum.

Lord, you have enriched these sons and daughters of yours with the gifts of your Spirit, and you have made them grow with the food of your only Son. Make them also wise in the full knowledge of your law, so that they may ever exemplify for the world the freedom of your children of adoption, and may by their holiness be enabled to show forth the prophetic role of your people. We ask this....

I. CHRISTIAN INITIATION
#4, CONFIRMATION (#C)

Collect

Mentes nostras, quaesumus, Domine, Paraclitus qui a te procedit illuminet, et inducat in omnem, sicut tuus promisit Filius, veritatem. Qui tecum.

Lord, we ask that the Advocate who comes forth from you may enlighten our minds and, as your Son promised, may lead us to all truth. We ask this....

Prayer over the Gifts

Suscipe, quaesumus, Domine, oblationem familiae tuae, ut, qui donum Spiritus Sancti susceperunt, et collata custodiant, et ad aeterna praemia perveniant. Per Christum.

Lord, please receive the offerings of your chosen people, so that those who have received the gift of the Holy Spirit may guard what has been given to them and may arrive at the reward of eternal life. We ask this....

Prayer after Communion

Spiritum nobis, Domine, tuae caritatis infunde, ut, quos uno pane caelesti satiasti, una facias pietate concordes. Per Christum.

Lord, pour forth the Spirit of your love. You have filled us with the one bread of heaven; may you also unite us in a single spirit of dedication. We ask this....

III. VIATICUM

Collect

Deus, cuius Filius nobis est via, veritas, et vita, respice clementer famulum tuum N. et praesta, ut, tuis promissionibus se committens, et Corpore Filii tui recreatus, ad regnum tuum progrediatur in pace. Per Dominum.

God our Father, your Son is our way, our truth, and our life. Look mercifully on your servant N. As he (she) entrusts himself (herself) to your promises and has been renewed by the body of your Son, grant that he (she) may go forth into your heavenly kingdom in peace. We ask this....

Prayer over the Gifts

Sacrificium nostrum, Pater sancte, intuere benignus, ut Agnum tibi paschalem repraesentet, cuius passio paradisi ianuas reseravit, et famulum tuum N. in aeternum munus per gratiam tuam introducat. Per Christum.

Holy Father, in your kindness look upon our sacrifice. In your sight, may it portray the Paschal Lamb, whose suffering opened the gates of heaven; and by your gracious gift may it lead your servant N. to his (her) eternal reward. We ask this....

Prayer after Communion

Domine, qui es salus aeterna in te credentium, praesta, quaesumus, ut famulus tuus N., caelesti pane potuque refectus, in regnum luminis et vitae securus perveniat. Per Christum.

Lord, you are the eternal salvation of those who believe in you. Please grant that your servant N., who has been renewed by your heavenly food and drink, may come safely into the kingdom of light and life. We ask this....

IV. WEDDING MASS
#1. FOR THE CELEBRATION OF MARRIAGE (#A)

Collect

Deus, qui tam excellenti mysterio coniugale vinculum consecrasti, ut Christi et Ecclesiae sacramentum praesignares in foedere nuptiarum, praesta, quaesumus, his famulis tuis, ut, quod fide percipiunt, opere persequantur. Per Dominum.

God our Father, you have sanctified the bonds of matrimony in a marvelous and mysterious fashion: in the covenant of marriage you symbolize the sacrament of Christ and his Church. Please grant that these servants of yours may fulfill what they receive in faith by the kind of life they lead. We ask this....

Alternate Collect

Deus, qui in humano genere creando, unitatem inter virum et mulierem esse voluisti, famulos tuos, qui coniugali copulandi sunt foedere, unius vinculo dilectionis astringe, ut, quos in caritate fructificare largiris, ipsius caritatis testes esse concedas. Per Dominum.

God our Father, when you created the human race you willed that man and woman should be united into one. Bind together with a single love these servants of yours who are to be joined in the marriage covenant. You give them a gift of love that flourishes; grant that they may bear witness to that love. We ask this....

Prayer over the Gifts

Suscipe, quaesumus, Domine, pro sacra connubii lege munus oblatum, et cuius largitor es operis, esto dispositor. Per Christum.

Lord, please receive the gift we offer in honor of your sacred law of matrimony. You are the author of the sacrament that is marriage; be also its guardian. We ask this....

Prayer over the Husband and Wife

Dominum, fratres carissimi, suppliciter deprecemur, ut super hanc familiam suam, quae huic sponso nupsit in Christo, benedictionem gratiae suae clementer effundat, et quos foedere sancto coniunxit (Christi Corporis et Sanguinis sacramento) una faciat caritate concordes.

Deus, qui potestate virtutis tuae de nihilo cuncta fecisti, qui, dispositis universitatis exordiis et homine ad imaginem tuam facto, inseparabile viro mulieris adiutorium condidisti, ut iam non duo essent, sed una caro, docens quod unum placuisset institui numquam licet disiungi:

Deus, qui tam excellenti mysterio coniugalem copulam consecrasti, ut Christi et Ecclesiae sacramentum praesignares in foedere nuptiarum:

Deus, per quem mulier iungitur viro, et societas, principaliter ordinata, ea benedictione donatur, quae sola nec per originalis peccati poenam nec per diluvii est ablata sententiam:

Respice propitius super hanc familiam tuam, quae, maritali iuncta consortio, tua se expetit benedictione muniri: sit in ea gratia dilectionis et pacis, imitatrixque sanctarum permaneat feminarum, quarum in Scripturis laudes praedicantur.

Confidat in ea cor viri sui, qui, parem sociam et gratiae vitae coheredem agnoscens, eam honore debito prosequatur eoque diligat semper amore, quo Christus suam dilexit Ecclesiam.

Et nunc te, Domine, deprecamur, ut hi famuli tui nexi fidei mandatisque permaneant, et, uni thoro iuncti, morum sint integritate conspicui; Evangelii robore communiti, bonum Christi testimonium omnibus manifestent; (in sobole sint fecundi, sint parentes virtutibus comprobati; videant ambo filios filiorum suorum) et, optatam demum senectutem adepti, ad beatorum vitam et ad caelestia regna perveniant. Per Christum.

Dear brothers and sisters, let us humbly ask the Lord in his mercy to pour out the blessing of his gracious favor on this servant of his, now married in Christ to her husband. He has joined this couple in this holy union (and in the sacrament of the Body and Blood of Christ); may he unite them in a single love.

God our Father, by your mighty power you created everything out of nothing. After the foundations of the universe had been laid and the human race created in your image and likeness, you made woman as an inseparable helpmate for man, so that they should not longer be two, but one flesh; and you taught thereby that no one may ever legitimately separate what you have been pleased to unite.

God our Father, in this marvelous mystery you have sanctified the union of marriage, so that in the marital covenant you might symbolize the sacrament that is Christ and the Church.

God our Father, it is through you that woman is united to man, and their union, firmly established, is endowed with the one blessing that was neither taken away in punishment for original sin nor cancelled by the judgment that you rendered at the time of the flood.

In your mercy, look upon your servant, who has been joined in the union of marriage and now asks to be strengthened with your blessing. May she enjoy the gifts of love and peace, and may she steadfastly imitate those holy women whose praises are proclaimed in the Holy Scriptures.

May the heart of her husband put its trust in her. May he recognize her as his co-equal companion and his fellow-heir in the life of grace; and may he accord her the honor that is due her. May he always love her with that love with which Christ has loved his Church.

And now, Lord, we ask that these servants of yours may ever remain bound to the faith and to the commandments. May they live in perfect fidelity to each other, and may they be noted for the upright lives they lead. May they be fortified with the strength of the Gospel, and stand out as faithful witnesses to Christ in the presence of all. (May they be fruitful in having children, and be parents admired for their virtue; and may they both see their children's children.) Finally, after they have at last attained a happy old age, may they come to the life of the blessed and to your heavenly kingdom. We ask this....

Prayer after Communion

Huius, Domine, sacrificii virtute, instituta providentiae tuae pio favore comitare, ut, quos sancta societate iunxisti (et uno pane unoque calice satiasti) una etiam facias caritate concordes. Per Christum.

Lord, by the power of this sacrament accompany with loving care what your providence has begun, so that those whom you have joined in this holy union (and have filled with the one bread and the one cup) may also be one at heart in their love for each other. We ask this....

IV. WEDDING MASS #1, FOR THE CELEBRATION OF MARRIAGE (#B)

Collect

Adesto, Domine, supplicationibus nostris, et super hos famulos tuos gratiam tuam benignus effunde, ut qui apud tua coniunguntur altaria in mutua caritate firmentur. Per Dominum.

Lord, listen to our prayers, and mercifully pour forth your gracious favor on these servants of yours. They are being joined together in marriage before your altar; may they be strengthened in their mutual love for each other. We ask this....

Prayer over the Gifts

Munera, quae tibi, Domine, laetantes offerimus, benignus assume, et, quos sacramenti foedere coniunxisti, paterna pietate custodi. Per Christum.

Lord, in your mercy accept the gifts we joyfully offer you. In your fatherly love, guard those whom you have joined together in this sacramental union. We ask this....

Prayer over the Husband and Wife

Super hos sponsos, qui, matrimonium ineuntes, ad altare accedunt, ut (Christi Corporis Sanguinisque participes) mutua semper dilectione nectantur, Dominum deprecemur.

Pater sancte, qui hominem ad imaginem tuam conditum masculum creasti et feminam, ut vir et mulier, in carnis et cordis unitate coniuncti, munus suum in mundo adimplerent:

Deus, qui, ad amoris tui consilium revelandum, in mutua dilectione sponsorum foedus illud adumbrari voluisti, quod ipse cum populo tuo inire dignatus es, ut, sacramenti significatione completa, in fidelium tuorum coniugali consortio Christi et Ecclesiae nuptiale pateret mysterium: super hos famulos tuos (N. et N.) dexteram tuam, quaesumus, propitiatus extende.

Praesta, Domine, ut, in huius quod ineunt sacramenti consortio, inter se amoris tui dona communicent, et, praesentiae tuae signum invicem ostendentes, cor unum fiant et anima una. Da etiam, Domine, ut domum, quam aedificant, opere quoque sustentent, filiosque suos, evangelica disciplina formatos, caelesti familiae tuae praeparent cooptandos.

Hanc familiam tuam N. tuis digneris benedictionibus cumulare, ut, uxoris ac matris munera complens, casta suam domum dilectione refoveat, et gratia decoret affabili. Hunc etiam famulum tuum N. caelesti, Domine, benedictione prosequere, ut mariti fidelis officia digne persolvat et providi patris.

Concede, Pater sancte, ut, qui coram te coniugio copulati ad mensam tuam accedere cupiunt, caeleste aliquando convivium participare laetentur. Per Christum.

Let us pray to the Lord on behalf of this bride and groom who come to the altar of God as they begin their married life, so that, (sharing as they do in the Body and Blood of Christ,) they may always be bound together by their love for each other.

Father most holy, you established the human race in your own likeness and divided it into male and female, so that man and woman might be joined in one flesh and one spirit and might carry out the task assigned them in the world.

God our Father, to make known the plan your love devised, you willed that the mutual love of husbands and wives should foreshadow that covenant which you saw fit to enter into with your people. In that way, once marriage's sacramental character was added, the bridal mystery of Christ and the Church would be clearly shown in the marriage union of your faithful people. We ask that you stretch out your hand in kindly mercy over these servants of yours (N. and N.).

Grant, Lord, that in this union upon which they have entered through this sacrament, they may share with each other the gifts of your love, may show each other the evidence of your presence to them, and become one heart and one spirit. Grant too, Lord, that through their labor they may maintain the home they build together, and that they may train their children in the precepts of the Gospel and prepare them to be made part of your heavenly family.

Graciously give your generous blessings to this servant of yours N., that she may fulfill her duties as wife and mother, and may build up her home with her chaste love and adorn it with her gracious kindliness. Grant your heavenly blessing to your servant N. as well, Lord, that he may worthily carry out the task of being a faithful husband and a provident father.

Father most holy, grant that those who have been joined together in marriage in your presence and who now seek to approach your holy table may some day have the joy of sharing in your heavenly banquet. We ask this....

Prayer after Communion

Mensae tuae participes effecti, quaesumus, Domine, ut, qui nuptiarum iunguntur sacramento, tibi semper adhaereant, et tuum hominibus nomen annuntient. Per Christum.

Lord, we who have been allowed to share in your banquet ask that those who are joined in the sacrament of marriage may always remain faithful to you and make your name known to men and women everywhere. We ask this....

IV. WEDDING MASS #1, FOR THE CELEBRATION OF MARRIAGE (#C)

Collect

Praesta, quaesumus, omnipotens Deus, ut hi famuli tui, nuptiarum sacramento iungendi, in fide quam profitentur accrescant, et sobole fideli tuam ditent Ecclesiam. Per Dominum.

Almighty God, please grant that these servants of yours who are to be joined together in the sacrament of matrimony may grow in the faith they profess and may enrich your Church with children who share that faith. We ask this....

Prayer over the Gifts

Propitiare, Domine, supplicationibus nostris, et has oblationes, quas tibi pro his famulis tuis sancto foedere copulatis offerimus, benigno suscipe vultu, ut per haec mysteria in mutua caritate tuoque amore firmentur. Per Christum.

Lord, mercifully hear our prayers. Look with kindness upon these gifts and receive them, as we offer them on behalf of these servants of yours who have been joined together in this sacred covenant. By these mysteries may they be strengthened in their affection for each other and their love for you. We ask this....

Prayer over the Husband and Wife

Precibus nostris, fratres carissimi, super hos sponsos, Dei benedictionem supplices invocemus, ut ipse suo foveat benignus auxilio, quos ditavit connubii sacramento.

Pater sancte, mundi conditor universi, qui virum atque mulierem ad imaginem tuam creasti, eorumque societatem tua voluisti benedictione cumulari, te pro hac sponsa humiliter deprecamur, quae hodie viro suo nuptiarum iungitur sacramento.

Super eam, Domine, eiusque vitae consortem benedictio tua copiosa descendat, ut, dum mutuo connubii dono fruuntur, familiam ornent filiis, ditent Ecclesiam.

Laeti te laudent, Domine, te maesti requirant; te in laboribus sibi gaudeant adesse ut faveas, te sentiant in necessitatibus astare ut lenias; te in coetu sancto precentur, tuos in mundo se testes ostendant; et, adepti prosperam senectutem cum hac qua circumdantur amicorum corona, ad caelestia regna perveniant. Per Christum.

By our own prayers, my brothers and sisters, let us earnestly call down God's blessing upon this couple, that God in his mercy may favor them with his aid as he has enriched them with the sacrament of marriage.

Father most holy, creator of the entire world, you made man and woman in your own likeness, and willed that their union should be enriched with your blessing.

We humbly pray on behalf of this bride who is today joined to her husband in the sacrament of marriage. May your bountiful blessing come down upon her and upon him who now shares her life. As they rejoice in the mutual gift of marriage, may they ennoble their home with children and through them enrich your Church.

May they praise you in times of joy, Lord, and seek your aid in times of sorrow. May they be gladdened in the midst of their toils by knowing that you are with them to aid them, and may they realize that you are present in the midst of their needs to lighten their burden. May they call upon you in the holy assembly, and show themselves to be witnesses to you amidst the world. And, after they attain a happy old age, may they come to the heavenly kingdom along with the circle of friends who surround them. We ask this....

Prayer after Communion

Concede, quaesumus, omnipotens Deus, ut accepti virtus sacramenti in his famulis tuis sumat augmentum, et hostiae quam obtulimus a nobis omnibus percipiatur effectus. Per Christum.

Almighty God, please grant that the power of the sacrament these servants of yours have received may increase its effects in them, and that the fruits of the offering we have made may be felt by all of us. We ask this....

IV. WEDDING MASS #2, ON THE ANNIVERSARY OF MARRIAGE (#A)

Collect

Deus, creator omnium, qui virum et feminam in principio condidisti, ut vinculum constitueret coniugale, unionem famulorum tuorum N. et N. benedic et confirma, ut coniunctionis Christi cum Ecclesia imaginem semper perfectiorem exhibeant. Per Dominum.

God our Father, creator of all things, in the beginning you made man and woman so that they would fashion the marriage bond. Bless and strengthen the union of your servants N. and N., that they may ever show forth a more perfect image of the union between Christ and his Church. We ask this....

Prayer over the Gifts

Deus, qui ex latere Christi sanguinem et aquam manare fecisti ad humanae regenerationis significanda mysteria, munera nostra in gratiarum actionem pro famulis tuis N. et N. dignare suscipere, et eorum coniugium tuis donis omnibus munerari. Per Christum.

God our Father, you made blood and water flow forth from the side of Christ so as to symbolize the mystery of human rebirth. Graciously accept the gifts we offer in thanksgiving on behalf of your servants N. and N., and bestow all of your gifts upon their union. We ask this....

Prayer after Communion

Superno cibo potuque refectis, Domine, his famulis tuis in gaudio et caritate corda dilata, ut sit eorum domus sedes honestatis et pacis, et omnibus ad consolationes pateat caritatis. Per Christum.

Lord, your servants have been refreshed with heavenly food and drink. Expand their hearts in joy and love, so that their home may be a center of honor and peace, and be open to all as a place to enjoy the comforts of love. We ask this....

IV. WEDDING MASS #2, FOR ANNIVERSARIES OF MARRIAGE (#B, ON THE 25TH ANNIVERSARY)

Collect

Domine, qui hos famulos tuos N. et N. indissolubili matrimonii nexu coniunxisti, et animorum communione dignatus es inter labores et gaudia sustentare, eorum, quaesumus, auge et purifica caritatem, ut mutua (cum prole sua) sanctificatione laetentur. Per Dominum.

Lord, you joined these servants of yours N. and N. together in the indestructible union of marriage, and you have seen fit to sustain them throughout their difficulties and their joys by the unity of hearts you gave them. We ask that you increase and purify their love, so that (, in the company of their children,) they may rejoice in each other's growth in holiness. We ask this....

Prayer over the Gifts

Haec munera, Deus, in gratiarum actione pro famulis N. et N. dignanter assume, ut exinde pacem et gaudium abundanter exhauriant. Per Christum.

Lord, in your kindness, receive these gifts on behalf of your servants N. and N., so that from this offering they may draw generous amounts of peace and joy. We ask this....

Prayer after Communion

Deus, qui ad mensam familiae tuae hos coniuges N. et N. (cum liberis et amicis) propitius admisisti, da eis fortiter et alacriter in mutuam communionem sic progredi, ut usque ad caeleste convivium, tuo munere, coniungantur. Per Christum.

God our Father, in your mercy you have granted this husband and wife N. and N. (along with their children and friends) access to the table of your chosen people. Grant that they may unreservedly and eagerly grow toward mutual union with each other, so that, through your gift, they may even be joined together at your heavenly banquet. We ask this....

IV. WEDDING MASS #2, FOR ANNIVERSARIES OF MARRIAGE (#C, ON THE 50TH ANNIVERSARY)

Collect

Deus pater omnipotens, hos coniuges N. et N. clementer aspicias (cum sobole sua, quam ad vitam fidemque genuerunt), pro bonis longaevae conversationis operibus, et eorum fructiferam benedic senectutem, sicut eorum caritatis primitias sacramento mirabili confirmasti. Per Dominum.

God, Father most powerful, in view of the good works they have done during their long life together, look mercifully on this husband and wife N. and N. (and upon their children, to whom they have given both the life of the body and the life of faith). Make their remaining years rich in blessings, just as through the great sacrament of marriage you strengthened their love when it began long ago. We ask this....

Prayer over the Gifts

Haec munera, Deus, in gratiarum actionem pro famulis tuis N. et N. dignanter assume, qui tot annos una simul fide sincera vixerunt, et omnia bona unitatis et pacis a tua postulant largitate. Per Christum.

God our Father, in your kindness receive these gifts, which we bring in thanksgiving for your servants N. and N. They have lived for so many years together in trusting faith, and they seek from your generosity all the blessings that come from unity and peace. We ask this....

Prayer after Communion

Mensae tuae pasti deliciis, te, Domine, deprecamur, ut hos coniuges N. et N. in sancta senectuite custodias, donec ambos, plenos dierum, ad tuum admittas caeleste convivium. Per Christum.

Fed by the goodness of your banquet, Lord, we ask that you guard this married couple N. and N. throughout their remaining holy years, until you choose to admit both of them, filled with length of days, to your heavenly banquet. We ask this....

V. BLESSING OF AN ABBOT OR ABBESS

Collect

Concede, quaesumus, Domine, famulo tuo N., quem huius communitatis N. abbatem elegisti, ut factis et doctrina ad ea quae recta sunt fratrum suorum animos instruat, quatenus aeternae remunerationis mercedem a te, Pastore piissimo, una cum ipsis laetus percipiat. Per Dominum.

Lord, you have chosen your servant N. to be abbot (abbess) of this community at N. Please grant that in his (her) example and teachings he (she) may inspire the hearts of his brothers (her sisters) toward righteousness until the day when, along with them, he (she) rejoices in receiving the gift of an everlasting reward from you, the most loving of all shepherds. We ask this....

Prayer over the Gifts

Suscipe, quaesumus, Domine, munera famulorum tuorum et praesta, ut, seipsos in spiritalem hostiam offerentes, vera humilitate, obedientia et pace iugiter repleantur. Per Christum.

Lord, please receive the gifts of your people, and grant that, in offering themselves as a spiritual sacrifice, they may ever be filled with true humility, obedience, and peace. We ask this....

Prayer after Communion

Familiam tuam, Domine, respice propitius, et nos, qui mysterium fidei celebravimus, fac per semitas Evangelii indesinenter currere, in omnibus te glorificantes. Per Christum.

Lord, in your mercy, look upon your people. We have celebrated the Mystery of our faith; make us follow the paths of the Gospel swiftly and without fail, giving glory to you in all things. We ask this....

VI. CONSECRATION TO A LIFE OF VIRGINITY

Collect

Da, quaesumus, Domine, his famulabus tuis, quibus virginale infudisti propositum, inchoati operis consummatum effectum, et, ut perfectam tibi offerant plenitudinem, initia sua perducere mereantur ad finem. Per Dominum.

Lord, please grant to these servants of yours, whom you have inspired with the desire to live in holy virginity, the fullness of the state they have chosen to enter. So that they may offer you their gift in perfect fulfillment, we ask too that they may be privileged to carry through to its completion the work they have begun. We ask this....

Prayer over the Gifts

Oblatis hostiis, quaesumus, Domine, his famulabus tuis perseverantiam suscepti propositi benignus accommoda, ut, apertis ianuis, summi Regis adventu, regnum caeleste cum laetitia mereantur intrare. Per Christum.

Lord, through the gifts we have offered, we ask that in your mercy you enable these servants of yours to carry through the resolve they have made, so that, when the doors are opened at the coming of the King of Kings, they may have the joyful privilege of entering into the kingdom of heaven. We ask this....

Prayer after Communion

Repleti, Domine, muneribus sacris, supplices deprecamur, ut famularum tuarum N. et N. conversatio et humanae societatis profectui constanter faveat, et ad Ecclesiae incrementum indesinenter proficiat. Per Christum.

Lord, we are filled with your sacred gifts, and we humbly ask that the daily lives of your servants N. and N. will always foster the progress of the human family and will ceaselessly aid the growth of the Church. We ask this....

VII. RELIGIOUS PROFESSION
#1, FIRST PROFESSION

Collect

Concede, quaesumus, Domine, his fratribus nostris, quibus Christum pressius sectandi propositum inspirasti, incepti itineris felicem exitum, ut perfectum devotionis munus tibi mereantur offerre. Per Dominum.

Lord, please grant to these brothers (sisters) of ours, whom you have inspired with the desire to follow Christ more closely, a happy ending to the journey they have undertaken, so that it may be their privilege to offer you a perfect gift of love. We ask this....

Prayer over the Gifts

Suscipe, Domine, quaesumus, oblationes et preces, quas tibi offerimus celebrantes professionis religiosae primordia, et praesta, ut famulorum tuorum primitiae, tua fovente gratia, in fructus uberrimos convertantur. Per Christum.

Lord, please receive the gifts and prayers we offer you as we celebrate the beginnings of the religious life of your servants. Through the loving care of your grace, grant that the first fruits of their religious lives may grow into a most abundant harvest. We ask this....

Prayer after Communion

Laetificent nos, Domine, sumpta mysteria et praesta, ut, eorum virtute, hi famuli tui inchoata religionis munera fideliter adimpleant et liberam tibi exhibeant servitutem. Per Christum.

Lord, may the mysteries we have received bring us joy. Through their power grant that these servants of yours may faithfully fulfill the duties of the religious life they have undertaken, and offer you their service in freedom. We ask this....

VII. RELIGIOUS PROFESSION
#2, PERPETUAL PROFESSION (#A)

Collect

Deus, qui in his famulis tuis baptismatis gratiam tanta voluisti frondere virtute, ut Filii tui vestigia pressius sequi contenderent, concede, ut ipsi, evangelicam perfectionem iugiter sectantes, Ecclesiae sanctitatem adaugeant eiusque apostolicum confirment vigorem. Per Dominum.

God our Father, you have willed that the grace of baptism should flower to such a degree of strength in the lives of these servants of yours that they strive to follow the footsteps of your Son more closely. Grant that, in constantly following the way of evangelical perfection, they may increase your Church's holiness and strengthen its apostolic zeal. We ask this....

Prayer over the Gifts

Servorum tuorum, Domine, munera et vota benignus assume, et evangelica profitentes consilia tua caritate confirma. Per Christum.

Lord, in your mercy accept the gifts and vows of your servants, and strength them by the power of your love as they profess the evangelical counsels. We ask this....

Prayer after Communion

Divinis mysteriis veneranter assumptis, te, Domine, supplices deprecamur, ut hos famulos tuos, sacra tibi oblatione devinctos, et Sancti Spiritus igne succendas et Filio tuo perenni iungas consortio. Qui tecum.

Lord, having reverently received your sacred mysteries, we humbly ask that, with the fire of the Holy Spirit, you inflame the hearts of these servants of yours who are bound to you by their holy vows, and that you join them to your Son in eternal friendship. We ask this....

VII. RELIGIOUS PROFESSION
#2, PERPETUAL PROFESSION (#B)

Collect

Domine, sancte Pater, servorum tuorum N. et N. propositum confirma benignus, et fac ut baptismatis gratia, quam novis cupiunt nexibus roborari, plenum in eis sumat effectum, quo tuae maiestati debitum cultum retribuant, et Christi regnum apostolico dilatent ardore. Per Dominum.

Lord, Father most holy, in your mercy strengthen the resolve of your servants N. and N. They desire that the grace of their baptism should be strengthened by new ties to you. Make that grace achieve its full effect in them, so that they may pay proper homage to your divine majesty and enlarge the kingdom of Christ by their apostolic fervor. We ask this....

Prayer over the Gifts

Oblationes famulorum tuorum, Domine, clementer assume, easque in sacramentum redemptionis converte, et, quos ad Filium tuum pressius imitandum paterna voluisti dispensatione vocare, Sancti Spiritus reple muneribus. Per Christum.

Lord, mercifully receive your servants' offerings, and transform them into the sacrament of salvation. Fill with the gifts of the Holy Spirit those whom in your fatherly care you have willed to call to a closer following of your Son. We ask this....

Prayer after Communion

Laetificet nos, Domine, confirmati propositi hodierna sollemnitas ac divini sacramenti veneranda perceptio, et concede propitius, ut geminatum devotionis munus famulorum tuorum pectora in Ecclesiae hominumque servitium vehementi caritate compellat. Per Christum.

Lord, may today's solemnization of a confirmed resolve, as well as the holy reception of your divine sacrament, bring us joy. In your mercy, grant that this two-fold gift of dedication may urge on the hearts of your servants in vigorous love to serve the Church and their fellow men and women. We ask this....

VII. RELIGIOUS PROFESSION
#3: RENEWAL OF VOWS

Collect

Deus, rerum ordinator hominumque rector, respice super hos filios tuos, qui oblationem sui cupiunt confirmare, et praesta, ut, in dies, Ecclesiae mysterio arctius coniungantur, et humanae familiae bono devoveantur impensius. Per Dominum.

God our Father, guide of all things and ruler of the human race, look upon these sons (daughters) of yours who wish to re-affirm the offering of themselves they have made. Grant that day by day they may be joined ever more closely to the mystery of the Church and may dedicate themselves more ardently to the good of the human family. We ask this....

Prayer over the Gifts

Populi tui, quaesumus, Domine, munera propitius intuere, quae hi fratres nostri castitatis, paupertatis, obedientiae renovata augent oblatione, et temporalia dona in sacramentum aeternitatis converte, et offerentium mentes ad Filii tui conforma imaginem. Per Christum.

Lord, please look mercifully upon your people's gifts, which these brothers (sisters) of ours increase by offering once again their pledge of chastity, poverty, and obedience. Turn these earthly gifts into the sacrament of eternity and form the minds of those offering them into the likeness of your Son. We ask this....

Prayer after Communion

Sumptis, Domine, caelestibus sacramentis, supplices te rogamus, ut hi famuli tui, qui, superna gratia tantum confisi, ardua renovarunt proposita, Christi virtute roborentur et Sancti Spiritus muniantur praesidio. Per Christum.

Lord, we have received your heavenly sacraments, and we humbly ask that these servants of yours, who have relied solely on your divine grace as they renewed their difficult resolve, may be strengthened by the power of Christ and guarded by the protection of the Holy Spirit. We ask this....

VII. RELIGIOUS PROFESSION #4, 25TH AND 50TH ANNIVERSARIES

Collect

Domine, Deus fidelis, da nobis, quaesumus, gratias tibi referre pro tua erga fratrem nostrum N. benignitate, qui acceptum a te donum hodie renovare contendit; robora in eo spiritum perfectae caritatis, ut gloriae tuae et operi salutis in dies valeat ferventius inservire. Per Dominum.

Lord, God most faithful, please grant that we may give you thanks for your goodness to our brother (sister) N., who today seeks to renew the gift he (she) received from you. Strengthen in him (her) the spirit of perfect charity, so that with each passing day he (she) may be able to work more fervently for your glory and for the task of human salvation. We ask this....

Prayer over the Gifts

Suscipe, Domine, una cum muneribus oblationem sui, quam hodie frater noster N. confirmare desiderat, et per virtutem Sancti Spiritus imagini dilecti Filii tui amplius eum conformare digneris. Qui vivit.

Lord, along with our gifts receive the offering of himself (herself) which our brother (sister) N. wishes to reaffirm today. Through the power of the Holy Spirit, mercifully form him (her) yet more into the likeness of your beloved Son. We ask this....

Prayer after Communion

Sumpsimus, Domine, Corpus et Sanguinem Filii tui, quae in iucunda celebratione huius anniversarii contulisti; concede, quaesumus, ut frater noster N., caelesti pane potuque refectus, incepti itineris ad te ducentis felicem progressum obtineat. Per Christum.

Lord, we have received the Body and Blood of your Son, which you have given us as we joyfully celebrate this anniversary. Please grant that our brother (sister) N., who has been refreshed with heavenly food and drink, may make joyful progress in that journey leading to you which he (she) has begun. We ask this....

VIII. DEDICATION OF A CHURCH: #1, ON THE DAY OF DEDICATION

Collect

Omnipotens sempiterne Deus, effunde super hunc locum gratiam tuam, et omnibus te invocantibus auxilii tui munus impende, ut hic verbi tui et sacramentorum virtus omnium fidelium corda confirmet. Per Dominum.

Almighty and eternal God, pour forth your favor upon this place, and grant the gift of your help to all who call upon you, so that the power of your word and your sacraments may here strengthen the hearts of all your faithful people. We ask this....

Prayer over the Gifts

Accepta tibi sint, Domine, munera laetantis Ecclesiae, ut populus tuus, in hanc domum sanctam conveniens, per haec mysteria salutem perpetuam consequatur. Per Christum.

Lord, may the gifts of your joyful Church be pleasing to you, so that your people, as they come together to your holy dwelling-place, may attain eternal salvation through these mysteries. We ask this....

Prayer after Communion

Multiplica, Domine, quaesumus, per haec sancta quae sumpsimus, veritatem tuam in mentibus nostris, ut te in templo sancto iugiter adoremus, et in conspectu tuo cum omnibus Sanctis gloriemur. Per Christum.

Lord, through these sacred gifts which we have received, please increase our knowledge of your truth, so that we may always worship you in your holy temple and exult at being in your sight in the company of all the saints. We ask this....

VIII. DEDICATION OF A CHURCH: #2, DEDICATION OF AN ALTAR

Collect

Deus, qui ad Filium tuum in ara crucis exaltatum omnia attrahere voluisti, caelesti gratia perfunde fideles tuos hanc tibi dicantes altaris mensam, ad quam eos, in unum congregatos, provide nutries Spirituque effuso, in dies constitues plebem tibi sacratam. Per Dominum.

God our Father, you willed to draw all things to your Son after He had been raised on the altar of the Cross. Fill your faithful people with your heavenly grace as they consecrate this altar table to you. It is here that in your fatherly care you will unite them together and feed them, and, by the outpouring of the Spirit, will make them a people sacred to yourself. We ask this....

Prayer over the Gifts

Descendat, quaesumus, Domine Deus noster, Spiritus tuus Sanctus super hoc altare, qui et dona populi tui sanctificet, et sumentium corda dignanter emundet. Per Christum.

Lord our God, we ask that your Holy Spirit come down upon this altar to make the gifts of your people holy and, in his mercy, to cleanse the hearts of those who receive your gifts. We ask this....

Prayer after Communion

Da nobis, Domine, tuis semper altaribus inhaerere, ubi sacrificii sacramentum celebratur, ut, fide et caritate coniuncti, dum Christo reficimur in Christum transformemur. Qui vivit.

Lord, please grant that we may always be faithful to your altar, where the sacramental sacrifice is offered. Joined together in faith and love, may we be transformed into Christ while we are being renewed by Him. We ask this....

MASSES FOR VARIOUS NEEDS

I. FOR THE CHURCH
#1, FOR THE
UNIVERSAL CHURCH (#A)

Collect

Deus, qui regnum Christi ubique terrarum dilatari providentia mirabili disposuisti, et omnes homines salutaris effici redemptionis participes, praesta, quaesumus, ut Ecclesia tua universalis sit salutis sacramentum, et tuae in homines caritatis manifestet et operetur mysterium. Per Dominum.

God our Father, in your marvelous providence you arranged that the kingdom of Christ should be extended throughout the whole earth, and that the entire human race should be made to share in your saving redemption. Please grant that your Church may be a sacrament of salvation throughout the world, and that it may both reveal and bring about the mystery of your love for men and women. We ask this....

Prayer over the Gifts

Plebis tuae sacratae respice munera, misericors Deus, et per huius sacramenti virtutem concede, ut credentium in te multitudo genus electum, regale sacerdotium, gens sancta, populus acquisitionis tibi iugiter efficiatur. Per Christum.

Merciful God, look upon the gifts offered by the people who are consecrated to you, and through the power of this sacrament grant that the entire number of those who believe in you may ever be made into a chosen race, a royal priesthood, a holy nation, a people you have obtained for yourself. We ask this....

Prayer after Communion

Deus, qui tuis Ecclesiam iugiter pascis et roboras sacramentis, concede nobis mensa caelesti refectis, ut, caritatis tuae documentis obsequendo, fermentum vivificans et salutis instrumentum humano efficiamur consortio. Per Christum.

God our Father, you constantly nourish and strengthen the Church with your sacraments. Grant that we who have been renewed by your heavenly banquet may give heed to the evidence of your love and so become a life-giving leaven and an instrument of salvation for the entire human family. We ask this....

I. FOR THE CHURCH
#1, FOR THE
UNIVERSAL CHURCH (#B)

Collect

Deus, qui in Christi tui testamento ex omnibus gentibus populum tibi congregare non desinis, in Spiritu ad unitatem coalescentem, concede, ut Ecclesia tua, missioni sibi creditae fidelis, cum hominum familia iugiter incedat, et tamquam fermentum et veluti anima societatis humanae in Christo renovandae et in familiam Dei transformandae semper exsistat. Per Dominum.

God our Father, in the new covenant of your Christ you ceaselessly gather unto yourself, from all parts of the human race, a people which grows toward unity in the Holy Spirit. Grant that your Church, in fidelity to the mission entrusted to it, may ever move about among the human family, and be present to it as both its leaven and its soul as our human society is renewed in Christ and transformed into the household of God. We ask this....

Prayer over the Gifts

Munera quae tibi offerimus, Domine, suscipe benignus, et praesta, ut Ecclesia tua, de latere Christi in cruce dormientis exorta, ex huius participatione mysterii suam iugiter hauriat sanctitatem, qua semper vivat suoque digne respondeat auctori. Per Christum.

Lord, in your mercy receive the gifts we offer you, and grant that your Church, born from the side of Christ as he slept upon the cross, may always draw its holiness from participating in this holy mystery. In that holiness may the Church ever live, and out of that holiness may it ever respond worthily to its Founder. We ask this....

Prayer after Communion

Sacramento Filii tui recreati, te, Domine, deprecamur, ut Ecclesiae tuae operationem fecundes, qua salutaris mysterii plenitudinem pauperibus continuo revelas, quos ad tui regni praecipuam vocasti portionem. Per Christum.

Lord, we are renewed by the sacrament of your Son, and we ask that you make the work of the Church successful. Through that work you continually make the fullness of salvation's mystery known to the poor, whom you have summoned to a special place in your kingdom. We ask this....

I. FOR THE CHURCH
#1, FOR THE
UNIVERSAL CHURCH (#C)

Collect

Concede, quaesumus, omnipotens Deus, ut Ecclesia tua semper ea plebs sancta permaneat de unitate Patris et Filii et Spiritus Sancti adunata, quae tuae sanctitatis et unitatis sacramentum mundo manifestet, et ipsum ad perfectionem tuae conducat caritatis. Per Dominum.

Almighty God, please grant that your Church may ever be true to its role as the holy people made one by the unity of the Father, Son, and Holy Spirit, a people who make the sign of your holiness and unity known to the world and who lead the world to the fullness of your love. We ask this....

Prayer over the Gifts

Immensae Filii tui caritatis memoriale celebrantes, te, Domine, suppliciter exoramus, ut eiusdem salutaris operis fructus, per Ecclesiae tuae ministerium, ad totius mundi proficiat salutem. Per Christum.

Lord, as we celebrate this remembrance of your Son's fathomless love, we humbly ask that, through the ministry of your Church, the effect of this same salvific sacrifice may advance the salvation of the entire world. We ask this....

Prayer after Communion

Deus, qui mirabili sacramento Ecclesiae fortitudinem tribuis et solamen, da populo tuo per haec sancta Christo adhaerere, ut, temporalibus muneribus quae gerit, tuum in libertate regnum aedificet aeternum. Per Christum.

God our Father, by this wonderful sacrament you give your Church strength and comfort. Through these sacred mysteries, grant that your people may be faithful to Christ, so that through the earthly functions they perform they may freely build up your eternal kingdom. We ask this....

I. FOR THE CHURCH
#1, FOR THE
UNIVERSAL CHURCH (#D)

Collect

Omnipotens sempiterne Deus, qui gloriam tuam omnibus in Christo gentibus revelasti, custodi opera misericordiae tuae, ut Ecclesia sancta, toto orbe diffusa, stabili fide in confessione tui nominis perseveret. Per Dominum.

Almighty and eternal God, in Christ you have made your glory known to all peoples. Watch over your merciful deeds, so that your Church, spread throughout the world, may continue to profess your name with unshaken faith. We ask this....

Prayer over the Gifts

Deus, qui eodem sacrificio Ecclesiam tuam iugiter sanctificas, quo eam mundasti, da, ut, capiti suo Christo unita, cum eo se tibi offerat, et pura tibi voluntate concordet. Per Christum.

God our Father, you constantly make your Church holy by the same sacrifice with which you cleansed it. Grant that, in union with Christ its head, it may offer itself to you along with Him and may be of one mind with you in the purity of its desires. We ask this....

Prayer after Communion

Refectione sancta enutritam, guberna, quaesumus, Domine, tuam placatus Ecclesiam, ut, potenti moderatione directa, et incrementa libertatis accipiat, et in religionis integritate persistat. Per Christum.

Lord, in your forgiving mercy, govern your Church, which you have nourished with this holy meal, so that, guided by your powerful direction, it may receive the gift of greater freedom and may stand firm in the purity of its faith. We ask this....

I. FOR THE CHURCH
#1, FOR THE LOCAL CHURCH (#E)

Collect

Deus, qui in singulis Ecclesiis per orbem peregrinis unam, sanctam, catholicam, et apostolicam manifestas Ecclesiam, plebi tuae concede benignus ita pastori suo adunari atque per Evangelium et Eucharistiam congregari in Spiritu Sancto, ut universitatem populi tui digne valeat repraesentare, et signum fiat atque praesentiae Christi in mundo instrumentum. Per Dominum.

God our Father, in each local church scattered throughout the world, you show forth the one, holy, catholic, and apostolic Church. In your mercy grant your people such unity with their shepherd and, through the Gospel and the Eucharist, such community in the Holy Spirit that they will be able to portray worthily the universality of your people and will be able to be both the sign and the means of Christ's presence in the world. We ask this....

Prayer over the Gifts

Immensae Filii tui caritatis memoriale celebrantes, te, Domine, suppliciter exoramus, ut eiusdem salutaris operis fructus, per Ecclesiae tuae ministerium, ad totius mundi proficiat salutem. Per Christum.

Lord, as we celebrate this remembrance of your Son's fathomless love, we humbly ask that, through the ministry of your Church, the effect of this same salvific sacrifice may advance the salvation of the entire world. We ask this....

Prayer after Communion

Vigeat in hac Ecclesia tua, Domine, et usque in finem perseveret fidei integritas, morum sanctitas, fraterna caritas et munda religio, et, quam Filii tui corpore et verbo tuo pascere non desinis, eam quoque tuis non cesses gubernare praesidiis. Per Christum.

Lord, may purity of faith, holiness of conduct, mutual love, and a spotless religion flourish now in this, your Church, and remain there until the end of time. You never cease to nourish your Church with the Body of your Son and with your Word; so also, may you never cease to guide and protect it. We ask this....

I. FOR THE CHURCH
#2, FOR THE POPE (#A)

Collect

Deus, qui providentiae tuae consilio super beatum Petrum, ceteris Apostolis praepositum, Ecclesiam tuam aedificari voluisti, respice propitius ad Papam nostrum N., et concede, ut, quem Petri constituisti successorem, populo tuo visibile sit unitatis fidei et communionis principium et fundamentum. Per Dominum.

God our Father, in the plan of your divine providence you willed that your Church should be built upon Saint Peter, the head of the Apostles. In your mercy, look upon our Pope, N. You made him the successor of Peter; grant that he may be the visible source and basis of your people's oneness in belief and of their unity with one another. We ask this....

Alternate Collect

Deus, omnium fidelium pastor et rector, famulum tuum N., quem pastorem Ecclesiae tuae praeesse voluisti, propitius respice; da ei, quaesumus, verbo et exemplo, quibus praeest proficere, ut ad vitam, una cum grege sibi credito, perveniat sempiternam. Per Dominum.

God our Father, shepherd and ruler of all the faithful, look with kindness upon your servant N., whom you have willed should preside as shepherd over your Church. Please grant that, in both word and example, he may benefit those over whom he has charge, so that he, along with the flock committed to his care, may come to eternal life. We ask this....

Prayer over the Gifts

Oblatis, quaesumus, Domine, placare muneribus, et Ecclesiam tuam sanctam, una cum Papa nostro N., quem ipsi constituisti pastorem, assidua protectione guberna. Per Christum.

Lord, we ask that you be pleased with the gifts we have offered, and that, with your constant protection, you guard your holy Church, along with our Pope N., whom you have named its shepherd. We ask this....

Prayer after Communion

Mensae caelestis participes effecti, supplices te, Domine, deprecamur, ut, huius virtute mysterii, Ecclesiam tuam in unitate et caritate confirmes, et famulum tuum N., cui pastorale munus tradidisti, una cum commisso sibi grege salves semper et munias. Per Christum.

Lord, we have been made to share in your heavenly meal, and we humbly ask that, by the power of this mystery, you strengthen your Church's unity and love. May you always preserve and protect your servant N., to whom you have assigned the office of chief shepherd, and the flock committed to his care. We ask this....

I. FOR THE CHURCH
#2, FOR THE POPE (#B)

Collect

Deus, qui in apostoli Petri successione famulum tuum N. elegisti totius gregis esse pastorem, supplicantem populum intuere propitius, et praesta, ut, qui Christi vices gerit in terris, fratres confirmet, et omnis Ecclesia cum ipso communicet in vinculo unitatis, amoris, et pacis, quatenus in te, animarum pastore, omnes veritatem et vitam assequantur aeternam. Per Dominum.

God our Father, you chose your servant N. as a successor of the apostle Peter to be the shepherd of your entire flock. Look mercifully upon your people as they pray to you, and grant that Christ's vicar on earth may strengthen his brothers and sisters. Grant too that the entire Church may be united with him in a bond of unity, love, and peace, until that time when they all obtain in you, the shepherd of their souls, eternal truth and life. We ask this....

1. FOR THE CHURCH
#3, FOR THE BISHOP (#A)

Collect

Deus, pastor aeterne fidelium, qui Ecclesiae tuae multiplici dispensatione praees et amore dominaris, da, quaesumus, famulo tuo N., quem plebi tuae praefecisti, ut gregi, cuius est pastor, Christi vice praesideat, et fidelis sit doctrinae magister, sacri cultus sacerdos et gubernationis minister. Per Dominum.

God our Father, eternal shepherd of the faithful, you oversee your Church in manifold ways, and you rule it with your love. Please grant that your servant N., whom you have placed over your people, may in Christ's stead watch over the flock for which he is the shepherd. May he be faithful as a teacher for sacred doctrine, a priest for sacred worship, and an assistant to you for the governance of the Church. We ask this....

Alternate Collect

Deus, omnium fidelium pastor et rector, famulum tuum N., quem pastorem Ecclesiae N. praeesse voluisti, propitius respice; da ei, quaesumus, verbo et exemplo, quibus praeest proficere, ut ad vitam, una cum grege sibi credito, perveniat sempiternam. Per Dominum.

God our Father, shepherd and ruler of all the faithful, look with kindness upon your servant N., whom you have willed should preside as shepherd over your Church at N. Please grant that, in both word and example, he may benefit those over whom he has charge, so that he, along with the flock committed to his care, may come to eternal life. We ask this....

Prayer over the Gifts

Haec oblatio, Domine, pro famulo tuo N. delata sit tibi munus acceptum, et, quem sacerdotem magnum in tuo populo suscitasti, apostolicarum virtutum muneribus, ad gregis profectum, exorna. Per Christum.

Lord, may this offering, which we bring on behalf of your servant N., be a gift that pleases you. You have raised him up to be chief priest among your people. Adorn him with your gifts of apostolic virtues for the benefit of his flock. We ask this....

Prayer after Communion

Huius, Domine, virtute mysterii, in famulo tuo N. episcopo nostro gratiae tuae dona multiplica, ut et tibi digne persolvat pastorale ministerium, et fidelis dispensationis aeterna praemia consequatur. Per Christum.

Lord, by the power of this mystery, increase the gifts of your grace toward your servant and our bishop N., so that he may carry out his pastoral charge in a way that is worthy of you and may attain the eternal reward of his faithful stewardship. We ask this....

God our Father, as its eternal shepherd, you govern your flock with your constant protection. In your limitless goodness grant your Church the sort of shepherd who will please you by his holiness and benefit us by his watchful care. We ask this....

I. FOR THE CHURCH
#3, FOR THE BISHOP (#B)

Collect

Da, quaesumus, Domine, famulo tuo N., quem pascendo gregi tuo in Apostolorum successione praefecisti, spiritum consilii et fortitudinis, spiritum scientiae et pietatis, ut, populum sibi creditum fideliter gubernans, Ecclesiae aedificet in mundo sacramentum. Per Dominum.

Lord, you have placed your servant N. over your flock to feed it as a successor of the Apostles. Please grant him the spirit of counsel and courage, the spirit of knowledge and of dedication, so that in faithfully governing the people entrusted to him he may build up the sacrament that is the Church in the world. We ask this....

Prayer over the Gifts

Tuae nobis, Domine, abundantia pietatis indulgeat, ut, per sacra munera quae tibi reverenter offerimus, gratum maiestati tuae pastorem Ecclesiae sanctae praeesse gaudeamus. Per Christum.

Lord, through the sacred gifts which we reverently offer you, may the richness of your faithful love grant us the favor of rejoicing in knowing that there rules over your holy Church a shepherd who is pleasing to your divine majesty. We ask this....

I. FOR THE CHURCH
#4, FOR THE ELECTION
OF A POPE OR BISHOP

Collect

Deus, qui, pastor aeternus, gregem tuum assidua custodia gubernas, eum immensa tua pietate concedas Ecclesiae pastorem, qui tibi sanctitate placeat, et vigili nobis sollicitudine prosit. Per Dominum.

Prayer after Communion

Refectos, Domine, Corporis et Sanguinis Unigeniti tui saluberrimo sacramento, nos mirifica tuae maiestatis gratia de illius pastoris concessione laetificet, qui et plebem tuam virtutibus instruat, et fidelium mentes evangelica veritate perfundat. Per Christum.

Lord, we have been renewed by the most saving sacrament of the Body and Blood of your only Son. May the marvelous favor of your divine majesty gladden us by giving us the kind of shepherd who will build up your people in virtue and will steep the minds of your faithful ones in the truth of the Gospel. We ask this....

I. FOR THE CHURCH
#5, FOR A COUNCIL OR SYNOD

Collect

Ecclesiae tuae, Domine, rector et custos, infunde, quaesumus, famulis tuis spiritum intelligentiae, veritatis et pacis, ut, quae tibi placita sunt, toto corde cognoscant et, agnita, tota virtute sectentur. Per Dominum.

Lord, ruler and guardian of your Church, please pour into the hearts of your faithful people the spirit of understanding, truth, and peace, so that with their whole heart they may understand what is pleasing to you and, having understood it, may pursue it with all their strength. We ask this....

Alternate Collect

Deus, qui populis tuis indulgentia consulis et amore dominaris, da spiritum sapientiae quibus dedisti regimen disciplinae, ut plebs tua ad veritatis agnitionem pleniorem et sanctitatis tibi acceptum ducatur augmentum. Per Dominum.

God our Father, by your mercy you take thought for your people's future, and by your love you rule over them. Give the spirit of wisdom to those to whom you have given the office of governing us, so that your people may be led to a fuller understanding of your truth and to an increase in holiness that will please you. We ask this....

Prayer over the Gifts

Respice, clementissime Deus, munera servorum tuorum, et gratiam tui luminis illis impende, ut quae recta sunt in oculis tuis veraciter intellegant, et fiducialiter exsequantur. Per Christum.

Most merciful God, look upon the gifts of your servants and grant them the grace of your inspiration, so that they may truly understand what is good in your sight and confidently pursue it. We ask this....

Prayer after Communion

Da, quaesumus, misericors Deus, ut sancta quae sumpsimus famulos tuos in veritate confirment, et honorem tui nominis illos faciant exquirere. Per Christum.

Merciful God, please grant that the holy mysteries we have received may confirm your servants in the truth and make them seek the honor of your name. We ask this....

I. FOR THE CHURCH
#6, FOR PRIESTS

Collect

Deus, qui Unigenitum tuum summum aeternumque constituisti sacerdotem, praesta, ut quos ministros tuorumque mysteriorum dispensatores elegit, in accepto ministerio adimplendo fideles inveniantur. Per Dominum.

God our Father, you established your only Son as supreme and eternal priest. Grant that those whom He has chosen to assist at and administer your mysteries may be found faithful in fulfilling the office they have received. We ask this....

Alternate Collect

Domine Deus noster, qui in regendo populo tuo ministerio uteris sacerdotum, tribue illis perseverantem in tua voluntate famulatum, ut ministerio atque vita tuam valeant in Christo gloriam procurare. Per Dominum.

Lord our God, in governing your people you make use of the ministry of priests. Grant that they may ever serve your holy will, so that in their work and in their lives they may be able to attend to your glory in Christ. We ask this....

Prayer over the Gifts

Deus, qui sacerdotes tuos sacris altaribus tuoque populo ministrare voluisti, per huius sacrificii virtutem concede propitius, ut eorum servitium tibi iugiter placeat, et fructum qui semper maneat in Ecclesia tua valeat afferre. Per Christum.

God our Father, you willed that your priests should serve at your sacred altar and minister to your people. Through the power of this sacrifice, mercifully grant that their service may always be pleasing to you, and may bear within your Church that fruit which lasts for ever. We ask this....

Prayer after Communion

Sacerdotes tuos, Domine, et omnes famulos tuos vivificet divina, quam obtulimus et sumpsimus, hostia, ut, perpetua tibi caritate coniuncti, digne famulari tuae mereantur maiestati. Per Christum.

Lord, may the heavenly sacrifice we have offered and received give life to your priests and to all your servants, so that, united to you in everlasting love, they may be privileged to serve your divine majesty worthily. We ask this....

I. FOR THE CHURCH
#7, FOR THE PRIEST HIMSELF (#A)

Collect

Deus, qui non propriis suffragentibus meritis, sed sola ineffabilis gratiae tuae largitate, me familiae tuae praeesse voluisti, tribue me tibi digne persolvere ministerium sacerdotalis officii, plebemque commissam, te in omnibus gubernante, dirigere concede. Per Dominum.

God our Father, it was not because of any merit of mine which recommended me, but rather solely because of the generosity of your mysterious grace that you willed that I should preside over your people. Grant that I may fulfill the office of priest in a way that is worthy of you; and grant that, with the help of your guidance in all things, I may direct the people committed to my care. We ask this....

Prayer over the Gifts

Deus, dierum temporumque potens et benigne moderator, collatis in me per gratiam tuam propitiare muneribus, et, praesentis oblationis virtute, in hunc affectum dirige cor plebis et sacerdotis, ut nec pastori oboedientia gregis, nec gregi desit cura pastoris. Per Christum.

God our Father, powerful and kindly ruler of the days and seasons, look with favor on the gifts that have been given to me by your grace. By the power of this gift we now offer, direct the hearts of your people and of your priest, so that they strive that neither the obedience of the flock to its shepherd, nor the care of the shepherd for his flock, be found lacking. We ask this....

Prayer after Communion

Omnipotens sempiterne Deus, origo cunctarum perfectioque virtutum, da mihi, quaesumus, huius participatione mysterii, et exercere quae recta sunt et praedicare quae vera, ut instructionem gratiae tuae fidelibus et agendo praebeam et docendo. Per Christum.

Almighty and eternal God, source and supreme example of all virtue, please grant that, by sharing in this mystery, I may both do what is right and preach what is true, so that in both example and teaching I may make your grace known to your faithful people. We ask this....

I. FOR THE CHURCH #7, FOR THE PRIEST HIMSELF (#B)

Collect

Aures tuae pietatis, clementissime Deus, inclina precibus meis, et gratia Sancti Spiritus illumina cor meum, ut tuis mysteriis digne ministrare, Ecclesiae tuae fideliter servire, teque merear aeterna caritate diligere. Per Dominum.

Most merciful God, lend your loving ear to my prayers, and enlighten my heart with the grace of the Holy Spirit, that I may be privileged to preside at your mysteries worthily, serve your Church faithfully, and love you with a love that has no end. We ask this....

Prayer over the Gifts

Suscipe, Deus omnipotens, haec munera, quae tibi offerimus veneranter, et respiciens Christum tuum, sacerdotem simul et hostiam, da, ut, eius sacerdotii particeps effectus, oblationem spiritalem me tibi semper exhibeam placentem. Per Christum.

Almighty God, receive these gifts, which we reverently offer you. Look upon your Christ, who is at the same time both priest and victim; and grant that I, who have been made to share in his priesthood, may always offer myself to you as a spiritual oblation that is pleasing to you. We ask this....

Prayer after Communion

Pane caelesti confirmatum et novi testamenti calice congaudentem, fac me, Pater sancte, tibi servire fideliter, et in salutem hominum vitam fortiter devoteque consumere. Per Christum.

Father most holy, I am strengthened with the bread of heaven and I rejoice in the cup of the new covenant. Make me serve you faithfully and spend my life in working courageously and lovingly for the salvation of the human race. We ask this....

I. FOR THE CHURCH #7, FOR THE PRIEST HIMSELF (#C, ON THE ANNIVERSARY OF ORDINATION)

Collect

Pater sancte, qui me ad communionem cum aeterno Christi tui sacerdotio et ad Ecclesiae tuae ministerium nullis meis meritis elegisti, praesta, ut Evangelii strenuus ac mitis praedicator exsistam, et mysteriorum tuorum fidelis dispensator inveniar. Per Dominum.

Father most holy, through no merits of my own you chose me to share in the eternal priesthood of your Christ and to serve your Church. Grant that I may be both vigorous and gentle in preaching the Gospel, and be a faithful steward of your mysteries. We ask this....

Prayer over the Gifts

Pro nostrae servitutis augmento sacrificium tibi, Domine, laudis offerimus, ut, quod immeritis contulisti, propitius exsequaris. Per Christum.

Lord, we offer you this sacrifice of praise so that our service to you may be bettered; in your mercy and despite our unworthiness, may you bring to a happy conclusion the work you have given us. We ask this....

Prayer after Communion

Ad gloriam, Domine, tui nominis annua festa repetens sacerdotalis exordii, mysterium fidei laetanter celebravi, ut in veritate hoc sim, quod in sacrificio mystice tractavi. Per Christum.

Lord, each year, for the glory of your name, in remembering the happy day when my priesthood began I have joyfully celebrated the mystery of faith, so that I may truly be what I have performed in a mystical way in this sacrifice. We ask this....

I. FOR THE CHURCH
#8, FOR THE MINISTERS OF THE CHURCH

Collect

Deus, qui ministros Ecclesiae tuae docuisti non ministrari velle, sed fratribus ministrare, illis, quaesumus, concede et in actione sollertiam, et cum mansuetudine ministerii in oratione constantiam. Per Dominum.

God our Father, you instructed the ministers of your Church not to wish to be served, but rather to wish to serve their brothers and sisters. Please grant them both skill in their actions and perseverance in prayer, along with gentleness in the exercise of their office. We ask this....

Prayer over the Gifts

Pater sancte, cuius Filius discipulorum voluit lavare pedes, ut nobis praeberet exemplum, suscipe, quaesumus, nostrae munera servitutis, et praesta, ut, nosmetipsos in spiritalem hostiam offerentes, spiritu humilitatis et diligentiae repleamur. Per Christum.

Father most holy, your Son desired to wash the feet of his disciples so as to set an example for us. Please receive the gifts that mark our service to you, and grant that in offering ourselves as a spiritual oblation we may be filled with the spirit of humility and diligence. We ask this....

Prayer after Communion

Concede famulis tuis, Domine, caelesti cibo potuque repletis, ut, ad gloriam tuam et salutem credentium procurandam, fideles inveniantur Evangelii, sacramentorum caritatisque ministri. Per Christum.

Lord, your servants have been filled with heavenly food and drink. So that they may work for your glory and for the salvation of those who believe in you, grant that they may be found to be faithful ministers of the Gospel, of the sacraments, and of your love. We ask this....

I. FOR THE CHURCH
#9, FOR VOCATIONS TO THE PRIESTHOOD

Collect

Deus, qui pastores populo tuo providere voluisti, effunde in Ecclesia tua Spiritum pietatis et fortitudinis, qui dignos altaribus tuis excitet ministros, et Evangelii tui strenuos ac mites assertores efficiat. Per Dominum.

God our Father, you have willed to provide shepherds for your people. Pour forth into your Church the Spirit of devotedness and courage to raise up worthy ministers for your altar and to make them staunch and gentle defenders of the Gospel. We ask this....

Prayer over the Gifts

Plebis tuae, quaesumus, Domine, preces et munera benignus intende, ut dispensatores mysteriorum tuorum multiplicentur, et in amore tuo iugiter perseverent. Per Christum.

Lord, in your mercy look upon the prayers and gifts of your people, so that the stewards of your mysteries may increase in number and may ever persevere in your love. We ask this....

Prayer after Communion

Pane mensae caelestis refecti, te, Domine, deprecamur, ut, per hoc sacramentum caritatis, illa semina maturescant, quae magna in agrum Ecclesiae tuae largitate dispergis, quatenus multi sorte sibi eligant tibi in fratribus ministrare. Per Christum.

Renewed by bread from your heavenly table, Lord, we humbly ask that through this great sacrament of love, those seeds may ripen which in your great generosity you sow in the field that is the Church, until the day when many will make their allotted choice to serve you in their brothers and sisters. We ask this....

I. FOR THE CHURCH
#10, FOR RELIGIOUS

Collect

Deus, omnis boni propositi inspirator atque perfector, dirige famulos tuos in viam salutis aeternae, et, quos, relictis omnibus, tibi se totos devoverunt, fac, Christum sequentes et ea quae sunt saeculi abnegantes, in spiritu paupertatis et cordis humilitate tibi et fratribus suis fideliter deservire. Per Dominum.

God our Father, you inspire every good resolve and bring it to completion. Guide your servants into the path of eternal salvation. Bring it about that those who have left all things behind and have vowed themselves completely to you may, in following Christ and in rejecting whatever belongs merely to this world, live in the spirit of poverty and in humility of heart as they faithfully serve both you and their brothers and sisters. We ask this....

Prayer over the Gifts

Sanctifica, quaesumus, Domine, per haec sancta quae tibi offerimus, famulos tuos, quos in nomine tuo congregasti, ut, fideliter vota sua tibi reddentes, maiestati tuae sincero corde deserviant. Per Christum.

Lord, through these sacred gifts which we offer, please make holy these servants of yours whom you have gathered together in your name, so that in faithfully fulfilling their vows to you they may serve your divine majesty with sincere hearts. We ask this....

Prayer after Communion

Servos tuos, Domine, in amore tuo congregatos et de uno pane participantes, da unanimes considerare invicem in provocationem caritatis et bonorum operum, ut eorum sancta conversatione Christi testes veri ubique exhibeantur. Per Christum.

Lord, grant that your servants, gathered together in your love and sharing in the one bread, may with one heart be mindful of one another in fostering charity and good works, so that in their holy lives they may show themselves to be true witnesses to Christ wherever they are. We ask this....

I. FOR THE CHURCH
#11, FOR RELIGIOUS VOCATIONS

Collect

Pater sancte, qui, licet fideles omnes ad perfectionem caritatis invitas, multos tamen excitare non desinis, qui Filii tui vestigia pressius sequantur, concede, ut, quos tibi in sortem peculiarem elegeris, conversatione sua valeant regni tui signum ostendere Ecclesiae mundoque perspicuum. Per Dominum.

Father most holy, even though you call all of the faithful to perfect love, nevertheless you ceaselessly inspire many to follow more closely in the footsteps of your Son. Grant that those whom you have chosen for yourself to live in that special way may, through their holy lives among us, be enabled to provide both the Church and the world with a clear sign of your kingdom. We ask this....

Alternate Collect
(For Use by Religious Themselves)

Familiam tuam, quaesumus, Domine, propitius respice et nova prole semper amplifica, ut et filios suos ad propositam caritatis perfectionem adducere, et ad hominum salutem efficaciter valeat laborare. Per Dominum.

Lord, in your mercy please look upon your religious family and ever increase its numbers with new members, so that it may be enabled to lead its sons (daughters) to the perfection of love that is set before them, and to work effectively for the salvation of men and women. We ask this....

Prayer over the Gifts

Munera quae tibi offerimus, Pater sancte, suscipe miseratus, et omnibus, qui Filium tuum per arctam viam imitari laeta sibi mente proponunt, communionem concede fraternam et spiritalem libertatem. Per Christum.

Father most holy, in your mercy receive the gifts we offer you. To all those who joyfully resolve to imitate your Son by following the narrow path, grant union among themselves and freedom of spirit. We ask this....

Prayer after Communion

Famulos tuos, Domine, spiritali cibo potuque confirma ut, evangelicae semper vocationi fideles, vivam ubique Filii tui imaginem repraesentent. Per Christum.

Lord, strengthen your servants with this heavenly food and drink, so that in being ever faithful to their vocation of following the Gospel, they may present a living portrayal of your Son wherever they may be. We ask this....

Alternate Prayer after Communion
(for Use by Religious Themselves)

Huius, Domine, virtute sacramenti, da nobis, quaesumus, perseverantem in tua voluntate famulatum, ut tuam caritatem mundo testari et bona quae sola non amittuntur valeamus fortiter inquirere. Per Christuum.

Lord, by the power of this sacrament, please grant us a lasting obedience to your divine will, so that we may be able to witness to your love amid the world and with courage seek those goods which alone do not perish. We ask this....

I. FOR THE CHURCH
#12, FOR THE LAITY

Collect

Deus, qui Evangelii virtutem veluti fermentum in mundum misisti, concede fidelibus tuis, quos in medio mundi negotiorumque secularium vitam rium vitam agere vocasti, ut, spiritu christiano ferventes, per temporalia quae gerunt munera, regnum tuum iugiter instaurent. Per Dominum.

God our Father, you sent the power of the Gospel as a leaven into the world. Grant to your faithful people, whom you have called to live their lives engaged in secular pursuits in the midst of the world, that they may be on fire with the spirit of Christ and may ever build up your kingdom by means of the temporal tasks they perform. We ask this....

Prayer over the Gifts

Deus, qui Filii tui sacrificio cunctum voluisti mundum salvare, per huius oblationis virtutem concede, ut famuli tui, quos etiam in statu laicali ad apostolatum vocare non desinis, et mundum spiritu imbuant Christi, et eius sint sanctificationis fermentum. Per Christum.

God our Father, you willed to bring the entire world to salvation through the sacrifice of your Son. Through the power of this offering, grant that your servants, whom you ceaselessly call to the apostolate even as they live in the lay state, may fill the world with the spirit of Christ and be the leaven that makes it holy. We ask this....

Prayer after Communion

De plenitudine gratiae tuae sumentes, quaesumus, Domine, ut, eucharistici convivii fortitudine roborati, fideles tui, quos rebus saecularibus deditos esse voluisti, strenui sint evangelicae testes veritatis, et Ecclesiam tuam in rebus temporalibus praesentem iugiter reddant et actuosam. Per Christum.

Lord, as we receive of the fullness of your grace, we ask that your faithful people, who have been strengthened by the courage they derive from this eucharistic banquet and whom you have willed should devote themselves to secular pursuits, may be vigorous witnesses to the truth of the Gospel, and may constantly show your Church to be present and active in temporal concerns. We ask this....

I. FOR THE CHURCH
#13, FOR THE
UNITY OF CHRISTIANS (#A)

Collect

Omnipotens sempiterne Deus, qui dispersa congregas et congregata conservas, ad gregem Filii tui placatus intende, ut, quos unum sacravit baptisma, eos et fidei iungat integritas, et vinculum societ caritatis. Per Dominum.

Almighty and eternal God, you gather together what has been scattered, and you safeguard what you have gathered together. In your forgiving mercy, look upon the flock of your Son, so that an undiminished faith may unite those whom the one baptism has made holy, and the bond of love may hold them together as one. We ask this....

Alternate Collect

Supplices te rogamus, amator hominum, Domine: pleniorem Spiritus tui gratiam super nos effunde benignus, et praesta, ut, digne qua nos vocasti vocatione ambulantes, testimonium veritatis exhibeamus hominibus, et omnium credentium unitatem in vinculo pacis fidentes inquiramus. Per Dominum.

Lord, you love the human race. In your mercy, we humbly ask you to pour forth the grace of your Spirit upon us yet more abundantly. Grant that, by living in a way worthy of the vocation to which you have called us, we may bear witness to your truth among all men and women; and grant that with confidence we may seek a unity bonded by peace among all who believe in you. We ask this....

Prayer over the Gifts

Qui una semel hostia, Domine, adoptionis tibi populum acquisisti, unitatis et pacis in Ecclesia tua propitius nobis dona concedas. Per Christum.

Lord, by the one unique victim you have acquired an adopted people. In your mercy, grant us the gifts of unity and peace within your Church. We ask this....

Prayer after Communion

Haec tua, Domine, sumpta sacra communio, sicut fidelium in te unionem praesignat, sic in Ecclesia tua unitatis operetur effectum. Per Christum.

Lord, may our reception of your sacred communion bring about unity in your Church, just as it signifies in advance the union of all the faithful in you. We ask this....

I. FOR THE CHURCH
#13, FOF THE
UNITY OF CHRISTIANS (#B)

Collect

Deus, qui diversitatem gentium in confessione tui nominis adunasti, da nobis et velle et posse quae praecipis, ut populo ad regnum tuum vocato una sit fides mentium et pietas actionum. Per Dominum.

God our Father, you have made the various peoples of the world one in the profession of your name. Grant us the willingness and the ability to do what you command, so that, for the people who are called to your kingdom, there may be but one faith in their hearts and one love in their actions. We ask this....

Alternate Collect

Preces populi tui, quaesumus, Domine, placatus intende, et praesta, ut fidelium corda in tua laude et communi paenitentia iungantur, quatenus, christianorum divisione sublata, in perfecta Ecclesiae communione ad aeternum tuum regnum properemus laetantes. Per Dominum.

Lord, in your forgiving mercy please look upon the prayers of your people. Grant that the hearts of your faithful may be united in praise of you and in shared repentance, until the time when differences among Christians have been removed and we may hasten to your eternal kingdom in joy and in perfect union within your Church. We ask this....

Prayer over the Gifts

Salutaris nostrae memoriale celebrantes, clementiam tuam, Domine, suppliciter exoramus, ut hoc sacramentum pietatis fiat nobis signum unitatis et vinculum caritatis. Per Christum.

Lord, as we celebrate this memorial of our redemption, we humbly ask for your mercy, so that this sacrament of love may become a sign of unity and a bond of charity for us. We ask this....

Prayer after Communion

Spiritum nobis, Domine, tuae caritatis infunde, ut, huius sacrificii virtute, una facias in te credentes pietate concordes. Per Christum.

Lord, pour forth upon us the Spirit of your love, so that through the power of this sacrifice you may make those who believe in you one in heart through the one bond of religion. We ask this....

I. FOR THE CHURCH
#13, FOR THE
UNITY OF CHRISTIANS (#C)

Collect

Populum tuum, quaesumus, Domine, propitius respice, et Spiritus tui super ipsum dona clementer effunde, ut in veritatis iugiter amore succrescat, et perfectam christianorum unitatem studio perquirat et opere. Per Dominum.

Lord, in your mercy, please look upon your people, and graciously pour out the gifts of your Spirit upon them, so that they may always grow in their love of truth and, in both their thoughtful study and the works they perform, may seek diligently the complete unity of Christians. We ask this....

Alternate Collect

Ubertatem misericordiarum tuarum, Domine, revela super nos et, in virtute Spiritus tui, christianorum divisiones remove, ut Ecclesia tua signum inter nationes elevatum clarius appareat, et mundus, tuo Spiritu illustratus, in Christum credat quem misisti. Per Dominum.

Lord, open to us the richness of your mercy and, by the power of your Spirit, take away the divisions that exist among Christians. May your Church then stand out more clearly as a sign held up to the nations; and may the world be illumined by your Spirit and so come to believe in Christ whom you have sent. We ask this....

Prayer over the Gifts

Quam tibi, Domine, offerimus hostia et purificationem conferat, et omnes uno baptismate coniunctos eorundem mysteriorum tandem participes efficiat. Per Christum.

Lord, may the sacrifice we offer to you cleanse us and make all who are joined together by the one baptism share at long last in the same mysteries. We ask this....

Prayer after Communion

Sacramenta Christi tui sumentes, quaesumus, Domine, ut in Ecclesia tua sanctificationis gratiam renoves quam dedisti, et omnes qui christiano gloriantur nomine in unitate fidei tibi servire mereantur. Per Christum.

Lord, as we receive the sacraments of your Christ, we ask that you renew within your Church the grace of holiness which you have given. May all who are happy to be known as Christians be privileged to share one and the same faith while serving you. We ask this....

I. FOR THE CHURCH
#14, FOR THE
SPREAD OF THE GOSPEL (#A)

Collect

Deus, qui omnes homines vis salvos fieri et ad agnitionem veritatis venire, respice messem tuam multam et operarios in eam mitte dignanter, ut omni creaturae Evangelium praedicetur, et plebs tua, verbo vitae congregata et sacramentorum virtute suffulta, in via salutis et caritatis procedat. Per Dominum.

God our Father, you wish the entire human race to be saved and to come to a knowledge of the truth. Look upon your great harvest, and mercifully send laborers into it, so that the Gospel may be preached to every creature and so that your people, gathered together by the word of life and supported by the power of the sacraments, may go forward in the path of salvation and love. We ask this....

Alternate Collect

Deus, qui Filium tuum lumen verum in mundum misisti, effunde Spiritum promissionis, qui veritatis semina in cordibus hominum iugiter diffundat et fidei suscitet obsequium, ut omnes, per baptismum ad novam vitam generati, unum populum tuum ingredi mereantur. Per Dominum.

God our Father, you sent your Son into the world as its true light. Pour forth the Spirit whom he promised, so as ever to plant the seeds of truth in the hearts of men and women and to arouse in them the obedient response of faith. May all who have been born to a new life through baptism be privileged to take their places among your united people. We ask this....

Prayer over the Gifts

Respice, Domine, in faciem Christi tui, qui pro omnibus redemptionem tradidit semetipsum, ut per eum ab ortu solis usque ad occasum nomen tuum magnificetur in gentibus, et una ubique maiestati tuae exhibeatur oblatio. Per Christum.

Lord, look upon the face of your Christ, who gave himself as the price of redemption for all. Through him may your name then be glorified among the nations, from the rising of the sun to its setting; and may one and the same sacrifice then be offered everywhere to your divine majesty. We ask this....

Prayer after Communion

Redemptionis nostrae munere vegetati, quaesumus, Domine, ut, hoc perpetuae salutis auxilio, fides semper vera proficiat. Per Christum.

Lord, we are nourished with the gift of our redemption, and we ask that, through this aid to everlasting salvation, that faith which is ever true may increase and spread. We ask this....

I. FOR THE CHURCH
#14, FOR THE SPREAD OF THE GOSPEL (#B)

Collect

Deus, qui Ecclesiam tuam sacramentum salutis cunctis gentibus esse voluisti, ut Christi salutiferum opus usque in fines saeculorum perseveret, excita tuorum corda fidelium, et praesta, ut ad omnem creaturam salvandam urgentius vocari se sentiant, quatenus ex omnibus populis una familia unusque tibi populus exsurgat et crescat. Per Dominum.

God our Father, you willed that your Church should be the sign of salvation for all nations, so that the life-giving work of Christ would be carried on until the end of the ages. Stir up the hearts of your faithful, and grant that they may realize that they are called even more compellingly to work for the salvation of every creature, until the time comes when from every nation there shall arise and grow only one human family, one people dedicated to you. We ask this....

Prayer over the Gifts

Munera supplicantibus Ecclesiae, Domine, in conspectum maiestatis tuae ascendant accepta, cui pro totius mundi salute grata exstitit Filii tui passio gloriosa. Per Christum.

Lord, may the gifts your Church prayerfully offers be acceptable to you as they arise to the sight of your divine majesty, just as the glorious passion of your Son was so pleasing to you when he offered it for the salvation of the entire world. We ask this....

Prayer after Communion

Sanctificet nos, quaesumus, Domine, mensae tuae participatio, et praesta, ut, quam Unigenitus tuus in cruce operatus est salutem, omnes gentes per Ecclesiae tuae sacramentum gratanter accipiant. Per Christum.

Lord, we ask that our sharing in your banquet may make us holy. Grant that, through the sacrament of your Church, all nations may joyfully receive the salvation which your only Son brought about for them on the Cross. We ask this....

I. FOR THE CHURCH
#15, FOR CHRISTIANS UNDERGOING PERSECUTION

Collect

Deus, qui inscrutabili providentia passionibus Filii tui vis Ecclesiam sociari, praesta fidelibus tuis, in tribulatione propter nomen tuum versantibus, spiritum patientiae et caritatis, ut promissionum tuarum fidi inveniantur testes atque veraces. Per Dominum.

God our Father, in your mysterious providence you wish the Church to be joined to the sufferings of your Son. Grant to your faithful people, immersed in distress because of your name, the spirit of patience and love, so that they may be seen to be faithful and truthful witnesses of your promises. We ask this....

Prayer over the Gifts

Suscipe, quaesumus, Domine, humilitatis nostrae preces et hostias, et praesta, ut, qui, tibi fideliter servientes, hominum persecutiones patiuntur, gaudeant se Christi Filii tui sacrificio sociari, et sua sentiant inter electorum nomina scripta esse in caelis. Per Christum.

Lord, please receive our humble prayers and offerings, and grant that those who suffer persecution from their fellow men and women while striving to serve you faithfully may be gladdened by knowing that they are united with the sacrifice of Christ your Son, and may realize that their names are recorded among those of your chosen ones in heaven. We ask this....

Prayer after Communion

Per huius sacramenti virtutem famulos tuos, Domine, in veritate confirma, et fidelibus tuis in tribulatione positis concede, ut, crucem sibi post Filium tuum baiulantes, christiano nomine iugiter valeant inter adversa gloriari. Per Christum.

Lord, by the power of this sacrament strengthen your servants in your truth, and grant that your faithful people who are in distress, as they carry their cross behind your Son, may ever, even in the midst of adversity, be able to rejoice in being known as Christians. We ask this....

I. FOR THE CHURCH
#16, FOR PASTORAL OR SPIRITUAL MEETINGS

Collect

Infunde in nobis, quaesumus, Domine, spiritum intellegentiae, veritatis et pacis, ut quae tibi sunt placita toto corde noscamus, et, quae noverimus, unanimi voluntatum consensione sectemur. Per Dominum.

Lord, please pour forth upon us the spirit of understanding, truth, and peace, so that with all our hearts we may come to know what pleases you and, with single-minded intent, may seek to achieve what we have learned. We ask this....

Alternate Collect

Deus, cuius Filius omnibus in nomine suo congregatis promisit seipsum in medio eorum affuturum, praesta, quaesumus, ut illum praesentem nobiscum sentiamus, et abundare in cordibus nostris gratiam, misericordiam et pacem in veritate et caritate experiamur. Per Dominum.

God our Father, your Son promised that he would be present in the midst of all who are gathered together in his name. Please grant that we may realize that he is present among us, and, in truth and love, may experience his grace, mercy, and peace abounding in our hearts. We ask this....

Prayer over the Gifts

Respiciat, quaesumus, clementia tua, Domine, tuorum munera famulorum, ut, quae sunt in oculis tuis salutaria atque recta, et veraciter intellegant, et fiducialiter eloquantur. Per Christum.

Lord, we ask that your merciful gaze be upon the offerings of your servants, so that they may truly understand and faithfully proclaim what is, in your eyes, right and helpful toward salvation. We ask this....

Prayer after Communion

Da nobis, misericors Deus, ut sancta quae sumpsimus et nos in tua voluntate confirment, et testes ubique veritatis efficiant. Per Christum.

Merciful God, grant that the holy gifts we have received may strengthen our obedience to your will and make us witnesses to your truth wherever we may be. We ask this....

II. FOR PUBLIC NEEDS #17, FOR THE NATION OR STATE

Collect

Deus, qui mirabili consilio universa disponis, suscipe benignus quas pro patria nostra tibi fundimus preces, ut sapientia moderatorum et honestate civium concordia et iustitia firmentur atque fiat cum pace prosperitas perpetua. Per Dominum.

God our Father, in your wondrous plan you regulate all things. In your mercy, receive the prayers we pour forth on behalf of our country, so that, through the wisdom of those who govern and the character of those whom they govern, harmony and justice may be strengthened and there may be endless well-being and peace. We ask this....

II. FOR PUBLIC NEEDS #18, FOR THOSE WHO GOVERN THE STATE

Collect

Omnipotens sempiterne Deus, in cuius manu sunt hominum corda et iura populorum, respice benignus ad eos qui nos in potestate moderantur, ut ubique terrarum populorum prosperitas, pacis securitas et religionis libertas, te largiente, consistant. Per Dominum.

Almighty and eternal God, in your hands are human hearts and the rights of peoples. Look with kindness upon those who have authority to govern us, so that everywhere on earth, by your gracious gift, the well-being of people, the stability of peace, and the freedom of religion may be guaranteed. We ask this....

II. FOR PUBLIC NEEDS
#19, FOR A MEETING OF NATIONAL LEADERS

Collect

Deus, qui miro ordine universa disponas et ineffabiliter gubernas, respice propitius in congregatos moderatores nationum, eisque Spiritum tuae sapientiae clementer infunde, ut in communem salutem et pacem omnia disponant atque a voluntate tua numquam discedant. Per Dominum.

God our Father, in your wonderful design you regulate all things and in mysterious fashion you govern them. In your kindness, look upon the leaders of our nations who are gathered together, and mercifully fill them with the Spirit of your wisdom, so that they may decide all things for the common welfare and for peace, and never depart from what you command. We ask this....

II. FOR PUBLIC NEEDS
#20, FOR THE HEAD OF STATE

Collect

Deus, cui potestates humanae deserviunt, da famulo tuo (regi nostro) N. prosperum suae dignitatis effectum, in qua, te semper timens tibique placere contendens, populo sibi credito liberam ordinis tranquillitatem iugiter procuret et servet. Per Dominum.

God our Father, all human authority is subject to you. Give your servant (our king) N. a favorable outcome to his office of governance. May he always fear you and seek to please you, and may he ever strive to achieve and safeguard freedom and serenity of mind for the people entrusted to him. We ask this....

II. FOR PUBLIC NEEDS
#21, FOR THE DEVELOPMENT OF NATIONS

Collect

Deus, qui unam dedisti cunctis gentibus originem, et unam ex eis in te voluisti familiam congregare, tuae caritatis ardore omnium corda perfunde et fratrum suorum desiderio iustae progressionis accende, ut, per bona quae cunctis affluenter largiris, humana singulorum perficiatur persona, et aequitas atque iustitia, quavis divisione sublata, in hominum societate firmentur. Per Dominum.

God our Father, you gave a common origin to all the nations of the human race, and from them all you have willed to gather together a single family for yourself. Fill the hearts of all people with the fire of your love, and inflame them with the desire for the just advancement of their brothers and sisters, so that the human personality of everyone may be brought to perfection by means of the goods that you lavish upon all of us, and so that equality and justice may be established throughout human society, with all divisions among us taken away. We ask this....

Prayer over the Gifts

Preces ad te clamantium, Domine, propitiatus exaudi, et, Ecclesiae tuae oblatione suscepta, praesta, ut omnes homines spiritu filiorum Dei repleantur, quatenus, inaequalitatibus in caritate superatis, una fiat in tua pace populorum familia. Per Christum.

Lord, in your forgiving mercy, hear the prayers of those who call upon you. Receive the offering of your Church, and grant that all men and women may be filled with the spirit of the children of God, so that, with all inequality overcome in love, there may be but the one human family, living in your peace. We ask this....

Prayer after Communion

Uno pane refecti, quo humanam familiam iugiter instauras, quaesumus, Domine, ut, ex unitatis participatione sacramenti, validum et purum hauriamus amorem ad progredientes populos iuvandos, et ad opus iustitiae, inspirante caritate, perficiendum. Per Christum.

Lord, we have been renewed by the one bread with which you ceaselessly build up the human family. Through our sharing in the sacrament of unity, we ask that we may derive a strong and pure love for aiding developing peoples and for performing the work of justice under the inspiration of love. We ask this....

II. FOR PUBLIC NEEDS #22, FOR PRESERVING PEACE AND JUSTICE (#A)

Collect

Deus, qui pacificos revelasti filios tuos esse vocandos, praesta, quaesumus, ut illam instauremus sine intermissione iustitiam, quae sola firmam pacem spondeat et veracem. Per Dominum.

God our Father, you have told us that peacemakers should be called your children. Please grant that we may never cease to build up that type of justice which alone promises a firm and true peace. We ask this....

Alternate Collect

Deus, qui paternam curam omnium geris, concede propitius, ut homines, quibus unam originem dedisti, et unam in pace familiam constituant, et fraterno semper animo uniantur. Per Dominum.

Almighty God, you exercise your fatherly care over all. You gave all men and women a common origin; in your mercy, grant that they may form a single family living in peace, and be united by the love one finds among brothers and sisters. We ask this....

Prayer over the Gifts

Filii tui, pacifici Regis, sacrificium salutare, his sacamentorum signis oblatum, quibus pax et unitas designantur, quaesumus, Domine, ad concordiam proficiat inter omnes filios tuos confirmandam. Per Christum.

Lord, we ask that the saving sacrifice of your Son, the King of Peace, offered under these sacramental signs which symbolize peace and unity, may help strengthen harmony among all your children. We ask this....

Prayer after Communion

Largire nobis, quaesumus, Domine, spiritum caritatis, ut, Corpore et Sanguine Unigeniti tui vegetati, pacem inter omnes, quam ipse reliquit, efficaciter nutriamus. Per Christum.

Lord, please grant us the spirit of your love, so that, nourished by the Body and Blood of your only Son, we may effectively foster among the human family that peace which he himself gave to us. We ask this....

II. FOR PUBLIC NEEDS
#22, FOR PEACE (#B)

Collect

Deus, conditor mundi, sub cuius arbitrio omnium saeculorum ordo decurrit, adesto propitius invocationibus nostris et tranquillitatem pacis praesentibus concede temporibus, ut in laudibus misericordiae tuae incessabili exsultatione laetemur. Per Dominum.

God our Father, creator of the world, all the centuries march in order according to your will. In your kindness, hear our prayers and grant us a serene peace in our day, so that our joy may know no end as we praise your mercy. We ask this....

Alternate Collect

Deus pacis, immo pax ipsa, quem discordans animus non capit, quem mens cruenta non recipit, praesta, ut, qui concordes sunt, boni perseverantiam teneant, qui discordes sunt, mali oblivione sanentur. Per Dominum.

God of peace, yes, true Peace itself whom a disordered spirit cannot attain nor a bloodstained mind receive, grant that those who are at harmony with one another may always persevere in that good work, and that those who are at odds may, by forgetting the evil they plan, be healed. We ask this....

II. FOR PUBLIC NEEDS
#22 bis, FOR RECONCILIATION

Collect

Deus clementiae et reconciliationis, qui praecipuos dies salutis hominibus praebes ad te omnium Creatorem et Patrem agnoscendum, (per hoc acceptabile tempus) propitius nos adiuva, ut, libenter verbum pacis a te accipientes, omnia in Christo instaurandi tuae deserviamus voluntati. Per Dominum.

God of mercy and reconciliation, you grant your human children special days of saving grace so that they may come to know you, the Creator and Father of all. Mercifully help us (throughout this favorable time), so that we may willingly receive the word of peace which you speak, and dedicate ourselves to your desire to restore all things in Christ. We ask this....

Alternate Collect

Deus, verae libertatis auctor, qui omnes homines unum vis efformare populum a servitute solutum, (quique gratiae et benedictionis tempus nobis praebes,) concede, quaesumus, ut, incrementa libertatis accipiens, universale salutis sacramentum in mundum Ecclesia tua vividius appareat atque in homines caritatis manifestet et operetur mysterium. Per Dominum.

God our Father, author of true freedom, you wish all men and women to form a single people, free from any bondage, (and you give us a special season filled with your grace and blessing). Please grant that your Church may enjoy greater freedom, may more clearly show itself to the world as the sign of salvation for all, and may demonstrate and bring about the mystery of your love for men and women. We ask this....

Prayer over the Gifts

Memorare, Domine, Filium tuum, qui est pax et reconciliatio nostra, mundi peccatum suo sanguine delevisse, et munera Ecclesiae tuae propitius aspiciens, da ut, (gratiam huius temporis cum laetitia celebrantes,) libertatem Christi ad omnes possimus extendere. Qui vivit.

Lord, be mindful that your Son, who is our peace and reconciliation, has washed away the sins of the world by his blood. In your forgiving mercy, look upon the gifts of your Church, and grant that (as we joyfully celebrate this grace-filled season,) we may be able to offer the freedom of Christ to every man and woman. We ask this....

Prayer after Communion

Sacramentum Filii tui, quod sumpsimus, quaesumus, Domine, vires nostras adaugeat, ut, ex hoc unitatis mysterio, validum hauriamus amorem et ubique tuae pacis operatores efficiamur. Per Christum.

Lord, we have received the sacrament of your Son. We ask that it may increase our strength, and so enable us to derive a vigorous love from this mystery of unity and to strive for your peace everywhere. We ask this....

II. FOR PUBLIC NEEDS #23, IN TIME OF WAR OR REVOLUTION

Collect

Deus misericors et fortis, qui bella conteris deprimisque superbos, immanitates a nobis et lacrimas dignare festinanter arcere, ut omnes in veritate tui nominari filii mereamur. Per Dominum.

Merciful and powerful God, you destroy wars and bring down the proud. Hasten to ward off cruelty and sorrow from us, so that all of us may be privileged to be truly known as your children. We ask this....

Alternate Collect

Deus, auctor pacis et amator, quem nosse vivere, cui servire regnare est, protege ab omnibus impugnationibus supplices tuos, ut, qui in defensione tua confidimus, nullius hostilitatis arma timeamus. Per Dominum.

God our Father, author and lover of peace, to know you is to live, and to serve you is to reign. From all attack, defend those who cry to you, so that we who trust in your protection may need fear no enemy's weapons of war. We ask this....

Prayer over the Gifts

Memorare, Domine, Filium tuum, qui est ipse pax, odia nostra suo Sanguine peremisse, et, mala nostra propitiatus aspiciens, da, ut hominibus quos diligis pacem haec hostia cum tranquillitate restituat. Per Christum.

Lord, remember that your Son, who is Peace itself, has destroyed our hatreds by his blood. In your forgiving mercy, look upon the evils we suffer, and grant that this offering may restore peace and serenity to the men and women you love. We ask this....

Prayer after Communion

Uno pane, qui cor hominis confirmat, suaviter satiatis, da nobis, Domine, et belli furores superare feliciter, et tuam amoris ac iustitiae legem firmiter custodire. Per Christum.

Lord, we are delighted to be filled with the one bread which strengthens the human heart. Grant that we may successfully overcome the ravages of war and resolutely preserve your law of love and peace. We ask this....

III. FOR VARIOUS PUBLIC CONCERNS
#24, AT THE BEGINNING OF THE CIVIL YEAR

Collect

Deus, qui, sine initio et sine fine, totius es principium creaturae, da nobis ita hunc annum, cuius initia tibi dedicamus, transigere, ut et substantia abundemus, et sanctitatis operibus fulgeamus. Per Dominum.

God our Father, you are without beginning and without end, and you are the source of all creation. We dedicate the start of this year to you. Grant that we may progress through it in such a way that we have an abundance of the material things we need and are noteworthy for our works of holiness. We ask this....

Prayer over the Gifts

Sacrificia quae tibi offerimus ita tuis oculis, Domine, sint accepta, ut omnes, qui initia huius anni cum laetitia celebramus, reliquum excursum eius in tua mereamur transigere caritate. Per Christum.

Lord, may the sacrifices we offer be pleasing in your sight, so that all of us, who joyfully celebrate the beginning of this year, may be privileged to pass the remainder of its days in your love. We ask this....

Prayer after Communion

Adesto, Domine, populis, qui sacra mysteria contigerunt, ut in toto decursu huius anni nullis periculis affligantur, qui in tua semper protectione confidunt. Per Christum.

Lord, be present to your people who have touched upon your sacred mysteries. Throughout the entire course of this year may they not be imperiled by any dangers, for their constant trust is in your protection. We ask this....

III. FOR VARIOUS PUBLIC CONCERNS
#25, FOR THE SANCTIFICATION OF HUMAN WORK (#A)

Collect

Rerum conditor Deus, qui hominem iussisti laboris officia sustinere, da, ut opus quod incipimus huius vitae prosit incrementis, et regno Christi dilatando tua benignitate proficiat. Per Dominum.

God our Father, creator of all things, you have commanded the human race to undertake the obligation of working. Grant that the task we begin may benefit us by making our present life better, and that, through your kindness, it may aid in furthering the kingdom of Christ. We ask this....

Alternate Collect

Deus, qui humano labore immensum creationis opus iugiter perficis atque gubernas, exaudi preces populi supplicantis, et praesta, ut omnes homines digno potiantur labore, quo, suam conditionem honestantes, arctius coniuncti fratribus suis valeant inservire. Per Dominum.

God our Father, by means of human labor you are constantly perfecting and guiding the great work of creation. Hear the prayers of your people as they cry to you, and grant that all men and women may find fitting work by which they may bring honor to their state of life, and by which, united more closely with their brothers and sisters, they may be able to attend to one another's needs. We ask this....

Prayer over the Gifts

Deus, qui humanum genus praesentium munerum et alimento vegetas et renovas sacramento, tribue, quaesumus, ut eorum et corporibus nostris subsidium non desit et mentibus. Per Christum.

God our Father, you give life to men and women by the food from which come the gifts we offer, and you give life anew by the sacrament those gifts will become. Please grant that our bodies and minds may never lack the aid our offering provides. We ask this....

Prayer after Communion

Unitatis et caritatis mensae participes effecti, rogamus, Domine, clementiam tuam, ut, per opera quae nobis implenda commisisti, et vitam sustentemus terrenam, et regnum tuum aedificemus fidentes. Per Christum.

Lord, we have been privileged to share in the banquet of unity and love. We ask for your mercy, so that, through the tasks you have given us to fulfill, we may sustain our lives here on earth and may build up your kingdom in faith. We ask this....

III. FOR VARIOUS PUBLIC CONCERNS
#25, FOR THE SANCTIFICATION OF HUMAN WORK (#B)

Collect

Deus, qui naturalium rerum virtutes hominum labori subdere voluisti, concede propitius, ut, operibus nostris christiano spiritu intenti, sinceram caritatem cum fratribus exercere, et creationi divinae perficiendae sociam operam praestare mereamur. Per Dominum.

God our Father, it is your will that the powers of nature be subject to the influence of human work. In your mercy, grant that, devoting ourselves to our labors in a Christian way, we may be privileged to practice a sincere charity toward our brothers and sisters, and to perform our common task of completing your work of creation. We ask this....

Prayer over the Gifts

Suscipe, Domine, munera supplicantis Ecclesiae, et praesta, ut, per humanum quem tibi offerimus laborem, operi Christi redemptoris consociari mereamur. Per Christum.

Lord, receive the gifts of your Church as it cries to you, and grant that, through the human toil we offer you, we may be privileged to be joined to the work of Christ our Redeemer. We ask this....

Prayer after Communion

Guberna, quaesumus, Domine, temporalibus adiumentis quos dignaris aeternis recreare mysteriis. Per Christum.

Lord, we ask that, with the helps you give us on this earth, you will guide those whom you see fit to renew with your eternal mysteries. We ask this....

III. FOR VARIOUS PUBLIC CONCERNS
#26, AT PLANTING TIME (#A)

Collect

Deus, quo iuvante, semina terrae mandamus, tua multiplicanda virtute, concede, ut, quae nostris scimus deesse laboribus, per te, qui das solus incrementum, suppleantur abunde. Per Dominum.

God our Father, it is with your help that we place this seed in the earth, so that it can be made fruitful by your power. You alone give the increase;

may you supply in great abundance what we know our efforts cannot achieve. We ask this....

Prayer over the Gifts

Deus, qui verus es corporalium auctor fructuum et spiritalium summus agricola, da, quaesumus, laborum profectus nostrorum, ut fructus terrae abundanter capiamus, et, quae ab una providentia sumunt principium, ad tuam gloriam semper cooperentur. Per Christum.

God our Father, you are the true source of the food we need for our bodies, and the heavenly gardener who supplies our spiritual needs. Please grant a successful outcome to our work, so that we may reap a rich harvest. Grant also that all things that find their common origin in your one providence may always work together for your glory. We ask this....

Prayer after Communion

Qui tuis nos, Domine, reficis sacramentis, manuum nostrarum adesto laboribus, ut, qui in te vivimus, movemur, et sumus, terrae seminibus benedictione concessa de segetibus multiplicatis nutriamur. Per Christum.

Lord, you renew us with your sacraments. Be present to the work of our hands, so that we who live, move, and have our being in you may enjoy your blessing on the seeds we have placed in the earth and may find our nourishment in the rich harvest they will become. We ask this....

III. FOR VARIOUS PUBLIC CONCERNS
#26, AT PLANTING TIME (#B)

Collect

Benedictionem tuam, Domine Deus, super populum tuum propitiatus infunde, quatenus, dante te benignitatem, terra nostra proferat fructus suos, quibus ad honorem sancti tui nominis grata semper mente fruamur. Per Dominum.

Lord our God, in your forgiving mercy pour out your blessing on your people, until, through your generous kindness, our land produces its yield and we enjoy its fruits with ever-grateful hearts, to the glory of your holy name. We ask this....

Prayer over the Gifts

Nostris, Domine, adesto muneribus, ut, qui de granis frumenti deferimus tibi panem in tui Corpus Filii transmutandum, semini terrae committendo per te concessa benedictione laetemur. Per Christum.

Lord, receive our gifts, so that we who bring bread, made from grains of wheat, to be changed into the body of your Son may be made joyful by the gift of your blessing on this seed that is to be placed in the earth. We ask this....

Prayer after Communion

Concede fidelibus tuis, omnipotens Deus, congruam terrae fructuum largitatem, quibus temporaliter enutriti, spiritalibus quoque proficiant incrementis, ut, quorum in hoc sacramento pignus acceperunt, bona consequantur aeterna. Per Christum.

Almighty God, grant your faithful people a bountiful and suitable crop, so that, nourished in their earthly needs by it, they may progress in their spiritual growth as well, so as to attain the eternal goods whose promise they have received in this sacrament. We ask this....

III. FOR VARIOUS PUBLIC CONCERNS #27, AFTER THE HARVEST

Collect

Domine, Pater bone, qui terram homini providus tradidisti, concede, ut fructibus ex ea collectis vitam sustentare possimus, iisdemque ita semper utamur, ut laudi tuae et omnium utilitati, te opitulante, proficiant. Per Dominum.

Lord, good Father of us all, in your loving care you have given the earth to the human race. Grant that we may be able to sustain our lives from the fruits we gather from that earth, and that we may always use these in such a way that, with your help, they will promote your glory and be to the advantage of everyone. We ask this....

Alternate Collect

Gratias tibi referimus, Domine, pro fructibus, quos in salutem hominum terra produxit, quatenus, sicut illos summae tuae temperamentum providentiae comparavit, ita de terra cordis nostri germen iustitiae et fructus caritatis facias exoriri. Per Dominum.

Lord, for the fruits that the earth has brought forth for the good of the human race, we are grateful to you, even to the point of asking that, just as the wise judgment of your holy providence has brought these fruits to maturity, so also you may make the seed of justice and the fruit of charity spring forth in the field of our hearts. We ask this....

Prayer over the Gifts

Sanctifica, Domine, munera, quae tibi de terra fructificante cum gratiarum actione deferimus, et, qui nobis terrenarum frugum tribuis ubertatem, fac mentes nostras caelesti fertilitate fecundas. Per Christum.

Lord, make holy the gifts which we bring from the fruitful earth in thanksgiving to you. You give us the abundance of what grows on the land; so too, make our hearts rich in heavenly fruitfulness. We ask this....

Prayer after Communion

Da, quaesumus, Domine, ut de perceptis terrae fructibus hoc salutari mysterio tibi gratias exhibentes, eodem operante in nobis, bona potiora consequi mereamur. Per Christum.

Lord, please grant that we who in this saving mystery give you thanks for the fruits of the earth we have received may, by the action of that same mystery within us, be privileged to attain to higher goods. We ask this....

III. FOR VARIOUS PUBLIC CONCERNS #28, IN TIME OF FAMINE, OR FOR THOSE SUFFERING FROM FAMINE (#A)

Collect

Deus, qui bonus et omnipotens omnibus provides creaturis, efficacem da nobis dilectionem erga fratres ciborum inopiam patientes, ut, fame depulsa, libero ac securo corde tibi valeant deservire. Per Dominum.

God our Father, in your goodness and almighty power you see to the welfare of the whole of creation. Give us a practical love for our brothers and sisters who lack sufficient food, so that, with their hunger abated, they may be able to serve you with hearts that are free and safe from care. We ask this....

Prayer over the Gifts

Respice, Domine, oblationem, quam tibi de tuis datis optimis exhibemus, ut, quae divinae abundantiam vitae et unitatem in caritate significat, ad aequam nos partitionem mutuumque impellat fraternitatis officium. Per Christum.

Lord, look upon the offering we bring you, taken from the choicest of your gifts. It signifies the abundance of your divine life and our unity in your love; may it also urge us on to share your gifts fairly and to perform the task we all have to treat others as our brothers and sisters. We ask this....

Prayer after Communion

Deus, Pater omnipotens, supplices te rogamus, ut panis vivus, qui de caelo descendit, ad fratres inopes nos roboret sublevandos. Per Christum.

God, almighty Father, we humbly ask that the divine bread which comes down from heaven may strengthen us, so that we may help our brothers and sisters who are in need. We ask this....

III. FOR VARIOUS PUBLIC CONCERNS
#28, IN TIME OF FAMINE: FOR USE BY THOSE SUFFERING FROM FAMINE (#B)

Collect

Deus, qui mortem non fecisti, et escam praebes omni carni, tuorum famem famulorum miseratus expelle, ut laetius corda nostra et expeditius tibi valeant deservire. Per Dominum.

God our Father, death is not of your making. You grant food to every living creature; in your mercy, drive out the famine your servants are suffering, so that our hearts can serve you more joyfully and eagerly. We ask this....

Prayer over the Gifts

Tibi, Domine, de nostra egestate haec munera libenter offerimus, a tua benignitate suppliciter exorantes, ut tuae sint nobis largitionis primitiae salutaris. Per Christum.

Lord, we willingly offer you these gifts, taken from what we need, and we humbly ask of your kind mercy that we may enjoy the first fruits of your saving generosity. We ask this....

Prayer after Communion

Qui cibum caelestem, Domine, a tua largitate suscepimus, quaesumus, ut spem nobis et robur sic conferat ad laborem, ut efficaciter nostris fratrumque necessitatibus subvenire possimus. Per Christum.

Lord, we who have received heavenly food from your generous hand ask that it may give us hope and strength to work in such a way that we can effectively relieve our own needs and those of our brothers and sisters. We ask this....

III. FOR VARIOUS PUBLIC CONCERNS
#29, FOR FUGITIVES AND EXILES

Collect

Domine, cui nullus est alienus, nemo ab opitulatione longinquus, profugos et exsules, segregatos homines puerosque dispersos propitius intuere, ut illis reditus in patriam, nobis erga egenum et advenam a te benignitas tribuatur. Per Dominum.

Lord, no one is a stranger to you, no one is far removed from your help. In your mercy, look upon fugitives and exiles, men and women separated from their kin, children scattered from their homes. To them, grant a return to their homeland; and to us, grant the gift of showing kindness to the needy and the stranger. We ask this....

Prayer over the Gifts

Domine, qui tuum voluisti Filium ponere animam suam, ut in unum tuos dispersos filios congregaret, praesta, ut haec pacifica oblatio communionem obtineat animorum, et caritatem fraternitatis adaugeat. Per Christum.

Lord, you willed that your Son should lay down his life, so that he might gather together your scattered children into one. Grant that this offering, which establishes our peace, may bring us a union of hearts and increase the love we have for our brothers and sisters. We ask this....

Prayer after Communion

Domine, qui nos uno pane et uno calice refecisti, da nobis humanitatem in advenas ac derelictos sincero corde sectari, ut omnes in terra viventium congregari denique mereamur. Per Christum.

Lord, you have renewed us with the one bread and the one cup. Grant that with sincere hearts we may show kindness toward strangers and the abandoned, so that all of us may at length be privileged to be gathered together in the land of the living. We ask this....

III. FOR VARIOUS PUBLIC CONCERNS
#30, FOR CAPTIVES

Collect

Deus, cuius Filius, ad redimendum genus humanum a captivitate peccati, formam servi accipere dignatus est, da famulis tuis in vinculis constitutis, ut illa libertate potiantur, qua omnes homines, filios tuos, voluisti donari. Per Dominum.

God our Father, your Son saw fit to take upon himself the status of a slave in order to rescue the human race from its slavery to sin. Grant that your servants who are in captivity may come to possess the sort of freedom with which you have willed all human beings, as your children, to be endowed. We ask this....

Prayer over the Gifts

Per humanae redemptionis salutare sacramentum, quod tibi, Domine, offerimus, praesta, ut famuli tui a captivitate solvantur, et animae perpetua gaudeant libertate. Per Christum.

Lord, through the saving sacrament that brings about human redemption, we ask that your servants may be released from captivity and may rejoice in unending freedom of spirit. We ask this....

Prayer after Communion

Nostrae libertatis pretium recolentes, tuam, Domine, pro fratribus nostris imploramus clementiam, ut a vinculis solvantur, et servi fiant iustitiae tuae. Per Christum.

Lord, as we remember the price that was paid for our freedom, we beg for your mercy for our brothers and sisters, so that they may be released from their bonds and may work to foster your justice. We ask this....

III. FOR VARIOUS PUBLIC CONCERNS
#31, FOR PRISONERS

Collect

Omnipotens et misericors Deus, cui soli patent cordium secreta, qui iustum agnoscis et impium iustificare vales, exaudi preces nostras pro famulis tuis in carcere detentis, et praesta, ut per patientiam et spem in afflictione subleventur, et citius valeant sine offensione ad propria reverti. Per Dominum.

Almighty and merciful God, the secrets of human hearts are known to you alone; you know how to recognize an innocent person and you have the power to reconcile a sinner. Hear our prayers for your servants who are in prison, and grant that through patience and hope they may be consoled in the midst of their affliction, and be enabled to return to their homes swiftly and without hatred. We ask this....

Alternate Mass for Those Imprisoned for the Sake of the Gospel:
Cf. Mass for Christians Undergoing Persecution, p. 255.

III. FOR VARIOUS PUBLIC CONCERNS
#32, FOR THE SICK

Collect

Deus, qui languores nostros voluisti ab unigenito Filio tuo portari, ut infirmitatis et patientiae virtutem ostenderes humanae, preces nostras pro fratribus in aegritudine positis benignus exaudi, et praesta, ut, qui doloribus, aerumnis aliisve morbis premuntur, et inter eos qui beati praedicantur se sentiant electos, et Christo pro mundi salute patienti se sciant unitos. Per Dominum.

God our Father, you willed that your only Son should bear our weaknesses, so that you might show the power there is in human suffering and in patience. In your mercy, hear our prayers for our brothers and sisters who are ill, and grant that those who bear the heavy burden of pain, suffering, or other illness may recognize that they have been chosen to be numbered among those who are called blessed, and may know that they are united to Christ in his sufferings for the salvation of the world. We ask this....

Alternate Collect

Omnipotens sempiterne Deus, salus aeterna credentium, exaudi nos pro famulis tuis infirmis, pro quibus misericordiae tuae imploramus auxilium, ut, reddita sibi sanitate, gratiarum tibi in Ecclesia tua referant actiones. Per Dominum.

Almighty and eternal God, you are the endless well-being of those who believe in you. Hear our prayers for your servants who are ill and for whom we beg your merciful help, so that they may be restored to health and may give thanks to you in your Church. We ask this....

Prayer over the Gifts

Deus, cuius nutibus vitae nostrae momenta decurrunt, suscipe preces et hostias, quibus tuam pro fratribus aegrotantibus misericordiam imploramus, ut, de quorum periculo metuimus, de eorum salute laetemur. Per Christum.

God our Father, the moments of our life pass by according to your good pleasure. Accept the prayers and offerings by which we ask for your mercy for our ailing brothers and sisters. We now fear for them in the dangers they face; in time to come, may we rejoice in their well-being. We ask this....

Prayer after Communion

Deus, infirmitatis humanae singulare praesidium, auxilii tui super infirmos famulos tuos ostende virtutem, ut, ope misericordiae tuae adiuti, Ecclesiae tuae sanctae incolumes repraesentari mereantur. Per Christum.

God our Father, you alone sustain our human weakness. Show the power of your help to your ailing servants, so that, aided by your mercy, they may be privileged to be restored to your Church safe and sound. We ask this....

III. FOR VARIOUS PUBLIC CONCERNS
#33, FOR THE DYING

Collect

Omnipotens et misericors Deus, qui humano generi, per ipsum mortis institutum, aeternae vitae aditum misericorditer reserasti, respice propitius famulum tuum extremo agone laborantem, ut, consociatus Filii tui passioni et eius sanguine signatus, tibi valeat immaculatus praesentari. Per Dominum.

Almighty and eternal God, by death itself you have mercifully opened up the way to eternal life for the human race. Look with kindness upon your servant who is undergoing his (her) final struggle, so that, joined to the passion of your Son and sealed with his blood, he (she) may be able to enter into your presence cleansed of the stain of sin. We ask this....

Alternate Collect
(for Those Who Will Die Today)

Omnipotens et misericors Deus, qui amorem tuum creaturis omnibus ubique manifestas, audi benigne preces quas pro hodie morituris effundimus, ut, pretioso sanguine Filii tui redempti, absque peccati macula de hoc mundo valeant exire atque in sinu misericordiae tuae perenniter requiescere. Per Dominum.

Almighty and merciful God, you everywhere show your love for all creatures. In your kindness, hear the prayers which we pour forth for those who are to die today. Since they have been redeemed by the precious blood of your Son, may they be able to leave this world free from the stain of sin and find eternal rest in your merciful care. We ask this....

Prayer over the Gifts

Suscipe, Deus, hostiam, quam tibi pro famulo tuo in extremo vitae constituto fidenter offerimus, et da per eam universa illius delicta purgari, ut, qui tuae dispositionis aerumnis in hac vita premitur, in futura requiem consequatur aeternam. Per Christum.

Lord, receive the offering which we offer you in faith on behalf of your servant who is in his (her) last moments of life. Grant that through it he (she) may be cleansed of all sin. In your providence, he (she) now endures suffering in this life; may he (she) find eternal rest in the life to come. We ask this....

Prayer after Communion

Per huius, Domine, sacramenti virtutem, famulum tuum dignare clementer tua gratia sustinere, ut in hora mortis contra se inimicum praevalere non videat, sed cum Angelis tuis transitum habere mereatur ad vitam. Per Christum.

Lord, through the power of this sacrament, be pleased to sustain your servant by your gracious mercy, so that in the hour of his (her) death, he (she) may not see the enemy prevail over him (her), but rather may be privileged to pass to eternal life in the company of your holy Angels. We ask this....

III. FOR VARIOUS PUBLIC CONCERNS
#34, IN TIME OF EARTHQUAKE

Collect

Deus, qui fundasti terram super stabilitatem suam, parce metuentibus, propitiare supplicibus, ut, trementis terrae periculis penitus amotis, clementiam tuam iugiter sentiamus, et, tua protectione securi, tibi serviamus gratanter. Per Dominum.

God our Father, you are the one who set the earth firmly upon its foundations. Spare those who are afraid; be merciful to those who cry to you. After the dangers of earthquake have been completely removed from us, may we experience your constant mercy and, safe under your protection, then serve you with joy. We ask this....

III. FOR VARIOUS PUBLIC CONCERNS
#35, FOR RAIN

Collect

Deus, in quo vivimus, movemur, et sumus, pluviam nobis tribue congruentem, ut, praesentibus subsidiis sufficienter adiuti, sempiterna fiducialius appetamus. Per Dominum.

God our Father, in you we live, move, and have our being. Grant us the rain we need, so that we may have enough of the help we need now, and thus may more faithfully seek the things that are eternal. We ask this....

III. FOR VARIOUS PUBLIC CONCERNS
#36, FOR GOOD WEATHER

Collect

Omnipotens sempiterne Deus, qui nos et castigando sanas et ignoscendo conservas, praesta supplicibus tuis, ut optata aeris serenitate laetemur, et pietatis tuae donis ad gloriam nominis tui salutemque nostram semper utamur. Per Dominum.

Almighty and everlasting God, you heal us by your chastisements and you keep us safe by your forgiveness. Grant that we who call upon you may rejoice in the fair weather for which we hope, and grant that it may always be for the glory of your name and for our own salvation that we use the gifts that your faithful love gives us. We ask this....

III. FOR VARIOUS PUBLIC CONCERNS
#37, TO WARD OFF STORMS

Collect

Deus, cuius nutu universa oboediunt elementa, te supplices exoramus, ut, sedatis terrentibus procellis, in materiam transeat laudis comminatio potestatis. Per Dominum.

God our Father, all facets of nature obey your wishes. We humbly ask that the storms which terrify us may be calmed, and that our dread of your power may become a reason for us to praise you. We ask this....

Prayer over the Gifts

Suscipe, quaesumus, Domine, preces et oblationes nostras, ut, qui peccatorum nostrorum flagellis percutimur, miserationis tuae gratia liberemur. Per Christum.

Lord, please accept our prayers and gifts, so that we who suffer from the punishments our sins deserve may be delivered from them by your gracious mercy. We ask this....

Prayer after Communion

Tribulationem nostram, quaesumus, Domine, propitius respice, et iram tuae indignationis, quam pro peccatis iuste meremur, per passionem Filii tui, propitiatus averte. Per Christum.

Lord, in your kindness, please look upon our sufferings. In your forgiving mercy and through the passion of your Son, turn aside your anger and displeasure, which we have justly earned by our sins. We ask this....

III. FOR VARIOUS PUBLIC CONCERNS
#38, IN TIME OF ANY NEED (#A)

Collect

Deus, refugium nostrum in laboribus, virtus in languoribus, solamen in fletibus, parce populo tuo, ut, dignis flagellationibus castigatus, in tua miseratione denique respiret. Per Dominum.

God our Father, you are our rest amid our labors, our strength amid our weaknesses, our solace amid our sorrows. Spare your people, so that after they have suffered the punishment they deserve, they may at length be consoled by your mercy. We ask this....

III. FOR VARIOUS PUBLIC CONCERNS
#38, IN TIME OF ANY NEED (#B)

Collect

Omnipotens et misericors Deus, afflictionem nostram propitiatus intende, et ita filiorum tuorum onus alleva fidemque confirma, ut in paterna semper providentia tua sine dubitatione confidant. Per Dominum.

Almighty and merciful God, in your forgiving love look upon our sufferings. Lighten your children's burden and strengthen their faith in such a way that they may always trust unhesitatingly in your fatherly providence. We ask this....

Prayer over the Gifts

Suscipe, Domine, munera, quae tibi fidenter offerimus, et, quam maeroris amaritudinem sustinemus, fac ut in suavitatis sacrificium convertatur. Per Christum.

Lord, receive the gifts which we offer you in faith, and make the bitterness of the sorrow we bear change into an offering that will please you. We ask this....

Prayer after Communion

Te supplices, Domine, exoramus, ut, dapibus recreati munitique divinis, et futuros labores fortiter aggredi valeamus, et fratres in pressura positos impensius confirmemus. Per Christum.

Lord, since we have been refreshed and strengthened by your heavenly banquet, we humbly ask that we may be enabled to face our future tasks with courage and to strengthen our afflicted brothers and sisters more generously. We ask this....

III. FOR VARIOUS PUBLIC CONCERNS
#39, IN THANKSGIVING TO GOD (#A)

Collect

Deus, qui famulos tuos in tribulatione positos semper miseratus exaudis, pro benignitate tua gratias agentes, te supplices deprecamur, ut, liberi a malis omnibus, in gaudio tibi iugiter serviamus. Per Dominum.

God our Father, in your mercy you always hear the prayers of your servants who are in distress. We thank you for your generous kindness, and humbly ask to be freed from all evil and to serve you in joy forever. We ask this....

Prayer over the Gifts

Domine, qui Filium tuum dedisti nobis, ut nos a morte omnique malo benignus eriperet, quaesumus, ut hoc sacrificium clementer accipias, quod ab aerumnis liberi tibi in gratiarum offerimus actionem. Per Christum.

Lord, you gave us your Son so that, in his kindness, he might save us from death and from every evil. In your mercy, please accept this offering which we who have been freed from our troubles offer you in gratitude. We ask this....

Prayer after Communion

Omnipotens Deus, qui per hunc panem vitae famulos tuos et a peccati vinculo liberare et vires eorum dignaris tua pietate reficere, da nobis in spem gloriae sine intermissione proficere. Per Christum.

Almighty God, through this bread of life you see fit to free your servants from the bonds of sin and, in your loving faithfulness, to renew their strength. Grant that we may ceaselessly grow in our hope for heavenly glory. We ask this....

III. FOR VARIOUS PUBLIC CONCERNS
#39, IN THANKSGIVING TO GOD (#B)

Collect

Deus, Pater donorum omnium, a quo descendere confitemur quidquid habemus aut sumus, beneficia doce nos immensae tuae pietatis agnoscere, ac te sincero corde totaque nostra virtute diligere. Per Dominum.

God our Father, you are the source of all gifts, and we acknowledge that whatever we have or are comes from you. Teach us to recognize the blessings we receive from your great love and fidelity, and show us how to love you with sincere hearts and with our whole strength. We ask this....

Prayer over the Gifts

Pro collatis donis sacrificium tibi, Domine, laudis offerimus, suppliciter deprecantes, ut quod immeritis contulisti ad nominis tui gloriam referamus. Per Christum.

Lord, we offer you our sacrifice of praise for the favors you have bestowed upon us. We humbly ask that we may bring, as offerings to the glory of your holy name, the very gifts that, despite our unworthiness, you have given to us. We ask this....

Prayer after Communion

Deus, qui nobis in cibum spiritualem reddidisti Filii tui sacramentum salutare, quod tibi in actionem obtulimus gratiarum, da nobis ita virtutis et gaudii muneribus confirmari, ut tibi servire devotius, et nova beneficia consequi mereamur. Per Christum.

God our Father, you have given back to us, as heavenly food, the saving sacrifice of your Son which we gratefully offered you. Grant that we may be so strengthened by your gifts of courage and joy that we may be privileged to serve you more ardently and obtain yet other favors from you. We ask this....

IV. FOR CERTAIN PARTICULAR NEEDS
#40, FOR THE FORGIVENESS OF SINS

Collect

Supplicum preces, quaesumus, Domine, propitiatus exaudi, et confitentium tibi parce peccatis, ut pariter nobis indulgentiam tribuas benignus et pacem. Per Dominum.

Lord, in your forgiving mercy please hear the prayers of those who cry to you and forgive the sins of those who profess their repentance to you, so that in your kindness you may grant us pardon as well as peace. We ask this....

Alternate Collect

Propitiare, Domine, populo tuo, et ab omnibus absolve peccatis, ut, quod nostris offensionibus promeremur, tua indulgentia repellatur. Per Dominum.

Lord, be forgiving toward your people and free them from all their sins, so that the punishment we deserve for our transgressions may be kept away by your mercy. We ask this....

Prayer over the Gifts

Hostias tibi, Domine, placationis et laudis offerimus, ut et delicta nostra miseratus absolvas, et nutantia corda tu dirigas. Per Christum.

Lord, we offer you our sacrifice of atonement and praise, asking that you take pity on us, forgive our sins, and guide our straying hearts. We ask this....

Prayer after Communion

Praesta nobis, misericors Deus, ut, percipientes hoc munere veniam peccatorum, illa deinceps vitare tua gratia valeamus, et tibi sincero corde servire. Per Christum.

Merciful God, grant that, as we receive the forgiveness of our sins in this great gift, we may, by means of your grace, be enabled to avoid sin from now on and serve you wholeheartedly. We ask this....

IV. FOR CERTAIN PARTICULAR NEEDS
#41, TO ASK FOR CHARITY

Collect

Corda nostra, quaesumus, Domine, tuae Spiritu caritatis inflamma, ut tuae digna semper ac placita maiestati cogitare et te in fratribus sincere diligere valeamus. Per Dominum.

Lord, please enkindle our hearts with the Spirit of your love, so that we may always think thoughts that are worthy of your divine majesty and pleasing to you, and may sincerely love you in our brothers and sisters. We ask this....

Prayer over the Gifts

Propitius, Domine, quaesumus, haec dona sanctifica, et, hostiae spiritalis oblatione suscepta, concede, ut caritatem tuam ad omnes possimus extendere. Per Christum.

Lord, in your kind mercy, please make these gifts holy. Receive the offering of our spiritual sacrifice, and grant that we may be able to touch all men and women with your love. We ask this....

Prayer after Communion

Quos uno pane caelesti satiasti, quaesumus, Domine, ut Sancti Spiritus gratia perfundas, et abundanter reficias perfectae dulcedine caritatis. Per Christum.

Lord, please pour forth the gift of your Holy Spirit into those whom you have filled with the one heavenly bread, and refresh them fully with the sweet taste of perfect charity. We ask this....

IV. FOR CERTAIN PARTICULAR NEEDS
#42, TO FOSTER HARMONY

Collect

Deus, summa unitas et vera caritas, da fidelibus tuis cor unum et animam unam, ut Ecclesiae tuae corpus concordia vigeat, et, quae veritatis confessione nititur, stabili unitate firmetur. Per Dominum.

God our Father, unity finds its highest expression in you and charity its very essence. Give your faithful people one heart and one mind, so that the Mystical Body of your Church may grow strong in the harmony of its members. It draws its strength from its profession of truth; may it be made secure by an enduring unity. We ask this....

Prayer over the Gifts

Deus, qui nos ad imaginem tuam sacramentis renovas et praeceptis, gressus nostros in semitis tuis perfice miseratus, ut caritatis donum, quod a nobis sperari fecisti, per haec quae offerimus sacrificia tribuas apprehendi. Per Christum.

God our Father, with your sacraments and your commandments you remake us into your own likeness. In your mercy, guide our steps along your paths, so that, through this sacrifice we offer, you may allow us to obtain the gift of charity, which you have made an object of our hope. We ask this....

Prayer after Communion

Sumpsimus, Domine, sacramentum unitatis; praesta nobis, quaesumus, sancta unanimitate in domo tua viventibus, pacem habere quam tradimus, pacem servare quam sumimus. Per Christum.

Lord, we have received the sacrament of unity. As we live united in holiness within your house, please grant that we may possess the peace we give to others, and preserve the peace we receive. We ask this....

IV. FOR CERTAIN PARTICULAR NEEDS
#43, FOR THE FAMILY

Collect

Deus, cuius in ordinatione societas familiaris firmum suum habet fundamentum, respice famulorum tuorum preces miseratus, et praesta, ut, exempla sanctae Familiae Unigeniti tui domesticis virtutibus caritatisque obsequio sectantes, in laetitia domus tuae praemiis fruamur aeternis. Per Dominum.

God our Father, the community that is the family finds its firm basis in the ordered structure that you have assigned to it. Mercifully hear the prayers of your servants, and grant that we may follow the example of the Holy Family of your only Son in eagerly cultivating the virtues proper to our homes and in striving for what charity requires, and so may joyfully come to the enjoyment of the eternal rewards of your heavenly home. We ask this....

Prayer over the Gifts

Hostiam tibi placationis offerimus, Domine, suppliciter deprecantes, ut familias nostras in tua gratia firmiter et pace constituas. Per Christum.

Lord, we offer you our sacrifice of atonement and humbly ask that you establish our families firmly in your grace and in your peace. We ask this....

Prayer after Communion

Quos caelestibus reficis sacramentis, fac, clementissime Pater, sanctae Familiae Unigeniti tui exempla iugiter imitari, ut, post aerumnas saeculi, eius consortium consequantur aeternum. Per Christum.

Most merciful Father, make those whom you refresh with your heavenly sacraments ever imitate the example of the Holy Family of your only Son, so that, after the trials of this world, they may enjoy the Holy Family's company for all eternity. We ask this....

IV. FOR CERTAIN PARTICULAR NEEDS
#44, FOR RELATIVES AND FRIENDS

Collect

Deus, qui caritatis dona, per gratiam Sancti Spiritus, tuorum fidelium cordibus infudisti, da famulis tuis, pro quibus tuam deprecamur clementiam, salutem mentis et corporis, ut te tota virtute diligant, et, quae tibi sunt placita, tota dilectione perficiant. Per Dominum.

God our Father, through the grace of the Holy Spirit you have poured forth the gifts of charity into the hearts of your faithful people. Grant to your servants, for whom we beg your mercy, health of mind and body, so that they may love you with their whole strength and, in that complete love, may do the things that please you. We ask this....

Prayer over the Gifts

Miserere, Domine, famulis tuis, pro quibus hoc laudis sacrificium tuae offerimus maiestati, ut, per haec sancta, supernae benedictionis gratiam obtineant, et gloriam aeternae beatitudinis acquirant. Per Christum.

Lord, have mercy on your servants for whom we offer this sacrifice of praise to your divine majesty. Through these sacred mysteries, may they receive the grace of your heavenly blessing and obtain the glory of unending happiness. We ask this....

Prayer after Communion

Te, quaesumus, Domine, sumentes divina mysteria, ut famulis tuis, quibus dedisti in nos caritatem, indulgentiam tribuas peccatorum, consolationem vitae gubernationemque perpetuam, quatenus nos omnes, tibi unanimes servientes, ante faciem tuam congaudentes pervenire mereamur. Per Christum.

Lord, you have given your servants the love they have for us. As we receive your sacred mysteries, we ask you to grant them forgiveness of sins, satisfaction in life, and your unending guidance, until the time comes when all of us, at one in serving you, may have the joyful privilege of coming into your presence. We ask this....

IV. FOR CERTAIN PARTICULAR NEEDS
#45, FOR THOSE WHO INJURE US

Collect

Deus, qui caritatis tuae praecepto voluisti, ut nos affligentibus amorem impendamus sincerum, da nobis ita novae legis sequi mandata, ut bona pro malis reddere et alii aliorum onera portare studeamus. Per Dominum.

God our Father, in your commandment of charity you have willed that we should show a sincere love for those who injure us. Grant that we may follow the commands of the new law in such a way that we earnestly try to return good for evil and try to bear one another's burdens. We ask this....

Prayer over the Gifts

Pacem cum omnibus habere cupientes, tibi, Domine, pro his qui nobis adversantur hoc sacrificium offerimus, et Filii tui mortem commemoramus, per quam, cum inimici essemus, tibi reconciliati sumus. Per Christum.

Lord, in our desire to be at peace with everyone, we offer you this sacrifice for those who are opposed to us; and we recall the death of your Son, through which we were reconciled to you even though we had been at enmity with you. We make our prayer through....

Prayer after Communion

Per haec pacis nostrae mysteria, da nos, Deus, cum omnibus esse pacificos, et eos qui nobis adversantur tibi gratos efficere, nobisque placatos. Per Christum.

God our Father, through these mysteries from which comes our peace, grant that we may be at peace with everyone, and that those who are at odds with us may be pleasing to you and reconciled to us. We ask this....

IV. FOR CERTAIN PARTICULAR NEEDS #46, TO SEEK THE GRACE OF A HAPPY DEATH

Collect

Deus, qui nos ad imaginem tuam creasti, et pro nobis Filium tuum mortem subire voluisti, concede supplicibus tuis ita vigilare omni tempore orantes, ut absque peccati macula de hoc mundo exire, et in sinu misericordiae tuae cum exsultatione requiescere mereamur. Per Dominum.

God our Father, you created us in your own image and likeness, and you willed that your Son should undergo death for us. Grant that we who seek your help may be ever watchful in prayer in such a way that we may be privileged to depart from this world unsullied by the stain of sin and find joyful rest in the grasp of your merciful care. We ask this....

Prayer over the Gifts

Sicut mortem nostram occidisti, Domine, morte Unigeniti tui, ita eiusdem sacramenti virtute praesta, ut, voluntati tuae oboedientes usque ad mortem, cum pace et fiducia de hoc saeculo exire, et ipsius resurrectionis participes effici tuo munere valeamus. Per Christum.

You have destroyed our death by the death of your only Son, Lord. So also, by the power of His sacrament, grant that we may be obedient to your will until the end of our lives, may depart from this world in peace and confidence, and may, by your gracious gift, be enabled to share in His resurrection. We ask this....

Prayer after Communion

Immortalitatis pignora, Domine, per haec mysteria consecuti, pro nostrae mortis exitu pietatis tuae auxilium supplices imploramus, ut, inimici superatis insidiis, in sinu gloriae tuae reficiamur aeternae. Per Christum.

Lord, in these mysteries we have received the promise of eternal life. We humbly ask for the aid of your faithful love when we come to die, so that we may overcome the snares of the evil one and find repose in the embrace of your eternal glory. We ask this....

VOTIVE

MASSES

VOTIVE MASS #1:
OF THE HOLY TRINITY

*Cf. Mass for Trinity
Sunday, p. 99.*

VOTIVE MASS #2,
OF THE MYSTERY
OF THE HOLY CROSS

*Cf. Mass for the
Triumph of the
Holy Cross, p. 154.*

VOTIVE MASS #3,
OF THE
HOLY EUCHARIST (#A)

*Cf. Mass for
Corpus Christi,
p. 99, or Below.*

Collect

Deus, qui humanae redemptionis opus per Unigeniti tui paschale mysterium implevisti, concede propitius, ut, qui Christi mortem et resurrectionem in sacramentorum signis annuntiamus fidenter, salvationis tuae continuum experiamur augmentum. Per Dominum.

God our Father, you have completed the work of human redemption by the Easter mystery of your only Son. In your mercy, grant that we who confidently proclaim the death and resurrection of Christ in the external signs of the sacraments may experience a continual increase in your saving grace. We ask this....

Prayer over the Gifts

Salutaris nostrae memoriale celebrantes, clementiam tuam, Domine, suppliciter exoramus, ut hoc sacramentum pietatis fiat nobis signum unitatis et vinculum caritatis. Per Christum.

Lord, as we celebrate this memorial of our salvation, we humbly ask for your mercy, so that this sacrament of devoted love may become a symbol of unity and a bond of charity for us. We ask this....

Prayer after Communion

Sanctificet nos, quaesumus, Domine, mensae caelestis participatio, ut, per Corpus et Sanguinem Christi, fraternitas cuncta copuletur. Per Christum.

Lord, we ask that our sharing in your heavenly banquet may make us holy, so that, through the Body and Blood of Christ, the entire fellowship of human beings may be joined together in unity. We ask this....

VOTIVE MASS #3,
OF THE
HOLY EUCHARIST (#B)

Collect

Deus, qui ad gloriam tuam et generis humani salutem Christum voluisti summum aeternumque constituere sacerdotem, praesta, ut populus, quem sanguine suo tibi acquisivit, ex eius memorialis participatione, virtutem crucis ipsius capiat et resurrectionis. Per Dominum.

God our Father, for your own honor and for the salvation of the human race you chose to appoint Christ as the eternal high priest. Grant that the people he has acquired for you by his blood may, through their sharing in his commemoration, receive the saving power of his cross and resurrection. We ask this....

Prayer over the Gifts

Concede nobis, quaesumus, Domine, haec digne frequentare mysteria, quia, quoties huius hostiae commemoratio celebratur, opus nostrae redemptionis exercetur. Per Christum.

Lord, please grant that we may take part in these mysteries worthily, for as often as the remembrance of this sacrifice is celebrated, the work of our redemption is carried on. We ask this....

Prayer after Communion

Quaesumus, Domine, ut, huius participatione sacrificii, quod in sui commemorationem Filius tuus praecepit offerri, nosmetipsos cum illo oblationem facias tibi sempiternam. Per Christum.

Lord, by our sharing in this sacrifice which your Son commanded us to offer in his memory, please make us, in company with him, an everlasting offering to you. We ask this....

VOTIVE MASS #4, OF THE HOLY NAME OF JESUS

Collect

Sanctissimum Iesu nomen venerantibus, nobis, Domine, concede propitius, ut, eius in hac vita dulcedine perfruentes, sempiterno gaudio in patria repleamur. Per Dominum.

Lord, as we pay honor to the most holy name of Jesus, please grant that we who take pleasure in that name's sweetness in this life may be filled with everlasting joy in our true home. We ask this....

Prayer over the Gifts

In eius nomine, Pater omnipotens, munera nostra dignare suscipere, in quo quidquid petierimus nos certe consecuturos esse confidimus, ipso Filio tuo benignissime pollicente. Qui vivit.

Father most powerful, be pleased to receive our offerings in the name of Him in whom we trust that we will surely receive whatever we ask, as your Son himself most mercifully promises. We ask this....

Prayer after Communion

Tua nos, quaesumus, Domine, miseratione concede, ut in his sacris mysteriis Dominum Iesum dignis obsequiis veneremur, in cuius nomine voluisti omne genu flecti, omnesque homines invenire salutem. Per Christum.

Lord, in your mercy, please grant that in these holy mysteries we may honor the Lord Jesus worthily by the reverence we pay him, for you have willed that every knee should bend at his name and that all people should find salvation in it. We ask this....

VOTIVE MASS #5, OF THE PRECIOUS BLOOD OF OUR LORD JESUS CHRIST

Collect

Deus, qui pretioso Unigeniti tui Sanguine universos homines redemisti, conserva in nobis opus misericordiae tuae, ut, nostrae salutis mysterium iugiter recolentes, eiusdem fructum consequi mereamur. Per Dominum.

God our Father, you redeemed the entire human race by the precious blood of your only Son. Preserve within us the work of your mercy, so that, ever mindful of the mystery of our salvation, we may be privileged to attain its effects. We ask this....

Prayer over the Gifts

Maiestati tuae, Domine, oblationis nostrae munera proferentes, ad novi testamenti Mediatorem Iesum his mysteriis accedamus, eiusque aspersionem Sanguinis salutiferam innovemus. Qui vivit.

Lord, as we offer our sacrificial gifts to your divine majesty, may we in these mysteries draw near to Jesus, the Mediator of the New Covenant, and experience anew the life-giving sprinkling of his blood. We ask this....

Prayer after Communion

Cibo refecti, Domine, potuque salutis, Salvatoris nostri, quaesumus, semper Sanguine perfundamur, qui fons aquae nobis fiat in vitam salientis aeternam. Per Christum.

Lord, we who are renewed by the food and drink of salvation ask that we may ever be sprinkled with the blood of our Savior, and that it may become for us a fountain of water springing up unto eternal life. We ask this....

Alternate Prayer after Communion

Refecti cibo potuque caelesti, quaesumus, omnipotens Deus, ut ab hostium defendas formidine, quos pretioso Filii tui Sanguine redemisti. Qui vivit.

Almighty God, we who are renewed by heavenly food and drink ask that you protect from the fear of their enemies those whom you have redeemed by the precious blood of your Son. We ask this....

VOTIVE MASS #6, OF THE SACRED HEART OF JESUS

Cf. Mass for the Feast of the Sacred Heart, p. 100, or Below.

Collect

Fac nos, Domine Deus, Cordis Filii tui virtutibus indui et affectibus inflammari, ut, eius imagini conformes effecti, aeternae redemptionis mereamur esse participes. Per Dominum.

Lord our God, clothe us with the virtues of the Heart of your Son and set us on fire with his love, so that we may be remade in his likeness and be privileged to share in eternal redemption. We ask this....

Prayer over the Gifts

Deus, Pater misericordiarum, qui propter nimiam caritatem, qua dilexisti nos, Unigenitum tuum nobis ineffabili bonitate donasti, praesta, quaesumus, ut, cum ipso in unum consummati, dignum tibi offeramus obsequium. Per Christum.

God, Father of mercies, in your unspeakable goodness and because of the great love you have for us, you gave us your only Son. Please grant that we may be made perfect in union with him in this sacrifice and offer you worthy service. We ask this....

Prayer after Communion

Tui sacramenti caritatis participes effecti, clementiam tuam, Domine, suppliciter imploramus, ut Christo conformemur in terris, et eius gloriae consortes fieri mereamur in caelis. Per Christum.

Lord, we have been given a share in your sacrament of love, and we humbly ask for your mercy, so that we may become like Christ on earth and be privileged to become his companions in glory in heaven. We ask this....

VOTIVE MASS #7, OF THE HOLY SPIRIT (#A)

Collect

Deus, qui corda fidelium Sancti Spiritus illustratione docuisti, da nobis in eodem Spiritu recta sapere, et de eius semper consolatione gaudere. Per Dominum.

God our Father, you have instructed the hearts of your faithful people by the inspiration of the Holy Spirit. Grant that, in that same Spirit, we may always cherish what is right and ever rejoice in the comfort He gives. We ask this....

Prayer over the Gifts

Munera, quaesumus, Domine, oblata sanctifica, et corda nostra Sancti Spiritus illustratione emunda. Per Christum.

Lord, please bless the gifts we have offered, and cleanse our hearts through the enlightenment of the Holy Spirit. We ask this....

Prayer after Communion

Sancti Spiritus, Domine, corda nostra mundet infusio, et sui roris intima aspersione fecundet. Per Christum.

Lord, may the outpouring of the Holy Spirit cleanse our hearts and make them abound in good works by the penetrating dew of his grace. We ask this....

VOTIVE MASS #7, OF THE HOLY SPIRIT (#B)

Collect

Mentes nostras, quaesumus, Domine, Paraclitus qui a te procedit illuminet, et inducat in omnem, sicut tuus promisit Filius, veritatem. Qui tecum.

Lord, we ask that the Paraclete, who comes forth from you, may enlighten our minds and, as your Son promised, lead us to a knowledge of all truth. We ask this....

Alternate Collect

Deus, cui omne cor patet et omnis voluntas loquitur, et quem nullum latet secretum, purifica per infusionem Spiritus Sancti cogitationes cordis nostri, ut te perfecte diligere, et digne laudare mereamur. Per Dominum.

God our Father, every heart is open to you, every desire makes itself known to you; no secret is hidden from you. Through the outpouring of the Holy Spirit, cleanse the thoughts of our hearts, so that we may have the privilege of loving you completely and praising you worthily. We ask this....

Prayer over the Gifts

Intende, quaesumus, Domine, spiritalem hostiam altaribus tuis piae devotionis studio propositam, et da famulis tuis spiritum rectum, ut fides eorum haec dona tibi conciliet, et commendet humilitas. Per Christum.

Lord, please look upon the spiritual sacrifice that we place upon your altar in our desire to dedicate ourselves to you in love. Grant your servants the proper attitude of mind and heart so that their faith will make their gifts acceptable to you and their humility will make them pleasing to you. We ask this....

Prayer after Communion

Domine Deus noster, qui nos vegetare dignatus es caelestibus alimentis, suavitatem Spiritus tui penetralibus nostri cordis infunde, ut, quae temporali devotione percepimus, sempiterno munere capiamus. Per Christum.

Lord our God, you have seen fit to give us life through this heavenly food. Pour forth the delightful action of your

Holy Spirit into our inmost hearts, so that we may receive as a permanent gift in eternity what we have received with transitory love in this life. We ask this....

VOTIVE MASS #7, OF THE HOLY SPIRIT (#C)

Collect

Deus, qui universam Ecclesiam tuam in omni gente et natione sanctificas, in totam mundi latitudinem Spiritus tui dona defunde, ut, quod in ipsis evangelicae praedicationis exordiis tua est operata dignatio, nunc quoque per credentium corda diffundat. Per Dominum.

God our Father, you make your worldwide Church holy, in whatever people or nation it exists. Pour down the gifts of your Spirit upon the length and breadth of the world, so that what your gracious mercy brought about when the Gospel was first preached may be poured out upon the hearts of your believing people in the present time as well. We ask this....

Alternate Collect

Deus, cuius Spiritu regimur, cuius protectione servamur, praetende nobis misericordiam tuam, et exorabilis tuis esto supplicibus, ut in te credentium fides tuis semper beneficiis adiuvetur. Per Dominum.

God our Father, we are ruled by your Spirit and guarded by your protection. Stretch forth to us the arm of your mercy, and be moved by the prayers of your people who call to you, so that the faith of those who believe in you may ever be strengthened by the gifts they receive from you. We ask this....

Prayer over the Gifts

Sacrificia, Domine, tuis oblata conspectibus, ignis Spiritus sanctificet, qui discipulorum Filii tui corda succendit. Per Christum.

Lord, may the fire of the Holy Spirit, which inflamed the hearts of your Son's disciples, sanctify the offering we make in your sight. We ask this....

Prayer after Communion

Haec nobis, Domine, munera sumpta proficiant, ut illo iugiter Spiritu ferveamus, quem Apostolis tuis ineffabiliter infudisti. Per Christum.

Lord, may these gifts we have received help us ever to be inflamed by that Spirit whom you mysteriously poured out upon your Apostles. We ask this....

VOTIVE MASS #8, OF THE BLESSED VIRGIN MARY (#A)

Cf. Common of the Blessed Virgin Mary, pp. 186-190.

VOTIVE MASS #8, OF THE BLESSED VIRGIN MARY: #B, MARY THE MOTHER OF THE CHURCH

Collect

Deus, misericordiarum Pater, cuius Unigenitus, cruci affixus, beatam Mariam Virginem, Genetricem suam, Matrem quoque nostram constituit, concede, quaesumus, ut, eius cooperante caritate,

Ecclesia tua, in dies fecundior prolis sanctitate exsultet et in gremium suum cunctas attrahat familias populorum. Per Dominum.

God, Father of mercies, when your only Son was nailed to the Cross, He appointed his Mother, the Blessed Virgin Mary, to be our mother as well. Please grant that, with the aid of her sustaining love, your Church may daily bear more children, rejoice in the holiness of its offspring, and draw all of the families of nations into its loving embrace. We ask this....

Prayer over the Gifts

Suscipe, Domine, oblationes nostras et in mysterium salutis converte, cuius virtute et caritate Virginis Mariae, Ecclesiae Matris, inflammemur et operi redemptionis cum ea arctius sociari mereamur. Per Christum.

Lord, receive our offerings, and change them into the mystery of salvation. By its power, may we be inflamed by the love of the Virgin Mary, the Mother of the Church, and also be privileged to be united more closely to the work of salvation along with her. We ask this....

Prayer after Communion

Sumpto, Domine, pignore redemptionis et vitae, supplices adprecamur, ut Ecclesia tua, materna Virginis ope, et Evangelii praeconio universas gentes erudiat et Spiritus effusione orbem terrarum adimpleat. Per Christum.

Lord, we have received the pledge of redemption and of eternal life. We humbly pray that, through the motherly aid of the Virgin, your Church may enlighten all peoples through its preaching of the Gospel, and that, by the outpouring of the Holy Spirit, it may bring the entire earth to fulfillment. We ask this....

VOTIVE MASS #8, OF THE BLESSED VIRGIN MARY: #C, THE HOLY NAME OF MARY

Collect

Deus, cuius Filius in ara crucis exspirans beatissimam Virginem Mariam Matrem voluit esse nostram, quam suam elegerat, concede propitius, ut, qui sub eius praesidium secure confugimus, materno invocato nomine confortemur. Per Dominum.

God our Father, when your Son was dying on the altar of the Cross, he wished the Blessed Virgin Mary, whom He had chosen as his own mother, to be our mother as well. Please grant that we who confidently hasten to be sheltered by her protection may be strengthened by invoking her as our mother. We ask this....

Prayer over the Gifts
and
Prayer after Communion

Cf. Common of the Blessed Virgin Mary, pp. 186-190.

VOTIVE MASS #9, OF THE HOLY ANGELS

Cf. Feast of Saints Michael, Gabriel, and Raphael, p. 158,

or

Feast of the Holy Guardian Angels, p. 160.

VOTIVE MASS #10, OF SAINT JOSEPH

Collect

Deus, qui ineffabili providentia beatum Ioseph sanctissimae Genetricis Filii tui sponsum eligere dignatus es, praesta, quaesumus, ut, quem protectorem veneramur in terris, intercessorem habere mereamur in caelis. Per Dominum.

God our Father, in your mysterious providence you saw fit to choose Saint Joseph to be the husband of the most holy Mother of your Son. We honor him as our protector on earth; please grant us the privilege of having him as our intercessor in heaven. We ask this....

Prayer over the Gifts

Laudis hostiam immolaturi, Pater sancte, suppliciter postulamus, ut in ministerio nostro beati Ioseph precibus foveamur, cui dedisti Unigenitum tuum vice in terris custodire paterna. Per Christum.

Father most holy, as we prepare to offer you our sacrifice of praise, we humbly and earnestly ask that in carrying out our duties we may have the loving protection of the prayers of Saint Joseph, to whom you entrusted a father's role in the care of your only Son on earth. We ask this....

Prayer after Communion

His recreati, Domine, vivificis sacramentis, in iustitia tibi semper et sanctitate vivamus, beati Ioseph exemplo et intercessione, qui magnis tuis perficiendis mysteriis vir iustus et oboediens ministravit. Per Christum.

Lord, we are renewed by these life-giving sacraments. May we always live for you in justice and holiness, aided by the example and intercession of Saint Joseph who, as a just and obedient man, provided what was needed for the great mysteries that you were to perform. We ask this....

VOTIVE MASS #11, OF ALL THE HOLY APOSTLES

Collect

Beatorum Apostolorum honore continuo Ecclesia tua, Domine, semper exsultet, ut his praesulibus gubernetur, quorum doctrina gaudet et meritis. Per Dominum.

Lord, may your Church ever find joy in the continuous honor paid to your holy Apostles, so that it may be guided by those same leaders in whose teaching and holy lives it rejoices. We ask this....

Prayer over the Gifts

Effunde in nos, Domine, quem in Apostolos effudisti abunde, Spiritum Sanctum tuum, ut cognoscamus ea, quae per eos nobis donasti, et sacrificium laudis ad gloriam tuam rite offeramus. Per Christum.

Lord, pour down upon us your Holy Spirit whom you so lavishly poured down upon the Apostles, so that we may understand the gifts you have given us through them and properly offer our sacrifice of praise to your glory. We ask this....

Prayer after Communion

Fac nos, Deus, cum exsultatione et simplicitate cordis perseverare in doctrina Apostolorum, in fractione panis communicantes et orationibus. Per Christum.

God our Father, as we share with one another in the breaking of the bread and in prayer, make us joyful and singleminded in adhering to the teachings of the Apostles. We ask this....

VOTIVE MASS #12, OF SAINTS PETER AND PAUL

Cf. Mass for the Vigil of the Feast of Sts. Peter and Paul, p. 133.

VOTIVE MASS #13, OF SAINT PETER, APOSTLE

Collect

Deus, qui beato Petro apostolo tuo, collatis clavibus regni caelestis, ligandi atque solvendi pontificium tradidisti, concede, ut, intercessionis eius auxilio, a peccatorum nostrorum nexibus liberemur. Per Dominum.

God our Father, in giving your apostle Saint Peter the keys to the kingdom of heaven, you gave him the supreme power of binding and releasing. By the help of his intercession, grant that we may be freed from the bonds our sins have forged. We ask this....

Prayer over the Gifts

Oblationem populi tui, quaesumus, Domine, suscipe propitius in commemoratione beati Petri apostoli, quem ad confitendum te Deum vivum tuumque Filium secreta revelatione docuisti, et gloriosa fecisti passione Magistro suo testimonium perhibere. Per Christum.

Lord, in your kindness receive the offering of your people in remembrance of your apostle Saint Peter. By a mysterious revelation, you instructed him, so that he would acknowledge you, the living God, and your Son; and by his triumphant suffering and death you made him bear witness to Him who was his Master and Teacher. We ask this....

Prayer after Communion

Ad convivium, Domine, salutis admissi, beati Petri apostoli memoriam venerantes, gratanter exposcimus, ut Filio tuo, qui solus verba vitae habet, iugiter haereamus, quatenus oves gregis tui fideles ad pascua feliciter deducamur aeterna. Per Christum.

Lord, we have been granted access to the banquet of salvation. As we honor the memory of your apostle Saint Peter, we joyfully and earnestly ask that we may ever be loyal to your Son, who alone has the words of life, until, as the faithful sheep of your flock, we are led in happiness to our eternal pasture. We ask this....

VOTIVE MASS #14, OF SAINT PAUL, APOSTLE

Collect

Domine Deus, qui beatum Paulum apostolum ad praedicandum Evangelium mirabiliter designasti, da fide mundum universum imbui, quam ipse coram regibus gentibusque portavit, ut iugiter Ecclesia tua capiat augmentum. Per Dominum.

Lord our God, in miraculous fashion you chose your apostle Saint Paul to preach the Gospel. So that your Church may constantly increase, grant that the entire world may be filled with that faith which he bore amid kings and entire peoples. We ask this....

Prayer over the Gifts

Illo nos, quaesumus, Domine, divina tractantes, fidei lumine Spiritus perfundat, quo beatum Paulum apostolum ad gloriae tuae propagationem collustravit. Per Christum.

Lord, as we take part in these sacred mysteries, we ask that the Holy Spirit may pour down upon us that light of faith by which he enlightened your apostle Saint Paul in order to increase your glory. We ask this....

Prayer after Communion

Corporis et Sanguinis Filii tui, Domine, communione refectis, concede, ut ipse Christus sit nobis vivere, nihilque ab eius nos separet caritate, et, beato monente Apostolo, in dilectione cum fratribus ambulemus. Per Christum.

Lord, we are renewed by our communion in the Body and Blood of your Son. Grant that Christ himself may be our life, that nothing may separate us from his love, and, in keeping with the instruction of your holy apostle, that we may walk lovingly with our brothers and sisters. We ask this....

VOTIVE MASS #15, OF ONE APOSTLE

Collect

Robora in nobis, Domine, fidem, qua Filio tuo beatus N. apostolus sincero animo adhaesit, et praesta, ut, ipso deprecante, Ecclesia tua cunctis gentibus salutis fiat sacramentum. Per Dominum.

Lord, strengthen within us that faith by which your holy apostle Saint N. remained wholeheartedly faithful to your Son. Through his prayers, grant that your Church may become the sign of salvation to all peoples. We ask this....

Prayer over the Gifts

Beati N. apostoli commemoratione tibi munera deferentes, quaesumus, Domine, ut, eius exemplo, digne Evangelio Christi conversantes, fidei evangelicae collaboremus. Per Christum.

Lord, as we bring our gifts to you in remembrance of your holy apostle Saint N., please grant that, through his example, we may lead lives that are worthy of the Gospel of Christ, and may work together on behalf of that Gospel's faith. We ask this....

Prayer after Communion

Sumpsimus, Domine, pignus salutis aeternae, memoriam beati N. apostoli celebrantes, quod sit nobis, quaesumus, vitae praesentis auxilium pariter et futurae. Per Christum.

Lord, in celebrating the memory of your apostle Saint N., we have received the promise of eternal salvation. We pray that this pledge may help us in the present life as well as in the life to come. We ask this....

VOTIVE MASS #16, OF ALL THE SAINTS

Collect

Deus, omnis fons sanctitatis, fac nos in nostra unumquemque vocatione digne ambulare, intercedentibus Sanctis tuis, quibus divisiones gratiarum in terra et unam in caelo mercedem gloriosam contulisti. Per Dominum.

God our Father, you are the source of all holiness. You gave your Saints different gifts of grace while they were on earth, but the same glorious reward in heaven; through their intercession, grant that each of us may worthily walk the path to which we are called. We ask this....

Prayer over the Gifts

Grata tibi sint, Domine, munera, quae pro cunctorum offerimus honore Sanctorum, et concede, ut, quos iam credimus de sua immortalitate securos, sentiamus de nostra salute sollicitos. Per Christum.

Lord, may the gifts we offer in honor of all your Saints be pleasing to you. We believe that they are now in secure possession of endless life; grant that we may experience their care and concern for our salvation. We ask this....

Prayer after Communion

Deus, qui nos de uno pane reficis et una spe sustentas, tua nos partiter gratia corrobora, ut omnes, cum Sanctis tuis unum in Christo corpus et unus spiritus, ad gloriam cum ipso resurgamus. Per Christum.

God our Father, you renew us with the one bread and you sustain us with the one hope. In the same way, strengthen us with your grace, so that, along with your Saints, we may all be one body and one spirit in Christ and may rise to glory with him. We ask this....

MASSES FOR THE DEAD

MASSES FOR THE DEAD
I. FUNERAL MASS: #A, OUTSIDE OF EASTER SEASON

Collect

Deus, Pater omnipotens, cuius Filium mortuum fuisse et resurrexisse fides nostra fatetur, concede propitius, ut hoc mysterio famulus tuus N., qui in illo dormivit, per illum resurgere laetetur. Per Dominum.

God, Father most powerful, our faith proclaims that your Son died and rose again from the dead. Through this mystery, mercifully grant that your servant N., who has fallen asleep in Christ, may have the joy of rising by means of Him. We ask this....

Alternate Collect

Deus, cui proprium est misereri semper et parcere, te supplices exoramus pro famulo tuo N., quem (hodie) ad te migrare iussisti, ut, quia in te speravit et credidit, concedas eum ad veram patriam perduci, et gaudiis perfrui sempiternis. Per Dominum.

God our Father, unfailing pity and forbearance are characteristic of you. We humbly pray for your servant N., whom you have (today) commanded to come into your presence. Since he (she) hoped and believed in you, grant that he (she) may be escorted to his (her) true homeland and enjoy eternal happiness. We ask this....

Prayer over the Gifts

Pro famuli tui N. salute hostias tibi, Domine, suppliciter offerimus tuam clementiam deprecantes, ut, qui Filium tuum pium Salvatorem esse non dubitavit, misericordem Iudicem inveniat. Per Christum.

Lord, we humbly offer you our sacrifice for the eternal welfare of your servant N., and we pray for your mercy. May he (she) who had no doubt that your Son was his (her) loving Savior also find Him to be a merciful Judge. We ask this....

Prayer after Communion

Domine Deus, cuius Filius in sacramento Corporis sui viaticum nobis reliquit, concede propitius, ut per hoc frater noster N. ad ipsam Christi perveniat mensam aeternam. Per Christum.

Lord our God, in the sacrament of his Body, your Son left us the sacred food we need for a safe final journey. In your mercy, grant that through this sacrament our brother (sister) N. may come to Christ's eternal banquet. We ask this....

MASSES FOR THE DEAD
I. FUNERAL MASS: #B, OUTSIDE OF EASTER SEASON

Collect

Deus, misericordia peccatorum et tuorum beatitudo Sanctorum, da, quaesumus, famulo tuo N., cuius dispositionis (hodie) officia humanitatis persolvimus, cum electis tuis beati muneris portionem, ut eum, a mortalitatis nexibus absolutum, in die resurrectionis ante faciem tuam praesentari concedas. Per Dominum.

God our Father, you are the mercy that sinners need and the happiness that your Saints enjoy. As we celebrate (today) the rites marking the burial of your servant N.'s earthly body, please grant him (her) a share in the joyful status of the Saints. May you grant him (her) freedom from the bonds of human frailty and the gift of being escorted into your presence on that day when the dead shall rise again. We ask this....

Prayer over the Gifts

Adesto, Domine, quaesumus, pro famulo tuo N., cuius in die dispositionis hoc sacrificium tibi placationis offerimus, ut, si qua et peccati macula inhaesit aut vitium humanum infecit, dono tuae pietatis indulgeas et abstergeas. Per Christum.

Lord, please hear us as we pray for your servant N. We offer you our sacrifice of atonement on the day of his (her) funeral, so that by means of the gift that comes from your goodness you may forgive and wash away any blemish of sin that has clung to him (her) or any human fault that mars him (her). We ask this....

Prayer after Communion

Praesta, quaesumus, omnipotens Deus, ut famulus tuus N., qui (hodie) de hoc saeculo migravit, his sacrificiis purgatus et a peccatis expeditus, resurrectionis suscipiat gaudia sempiterna. Per Christum.

Almighty God, please grant that your servant N., who has gone forth from this world (today), may be cleansed and freed from his (her) sins by this sacrifice, and may receive the eternal joys of the resurrection. We ask this....

Lord, in your kindness hear our prayers. Our faith finds its basis in your Son's resurrection from the dead; so also, in the resurrection of your servant N. which we await, may our hope find its strength. We ask this....

Prayer over the Gifts

Nostris, Domine, propitiare muneribus, ut famulus tuus N. assumatur in gloriam cum Filio tuo, cuius magno pietatis iungimur sacramento. Per Christum.

Lord, be pleased with our gifts, so that your servant N. may be taken up into glory with your Son, by whose great sacrament of faithful love we are made into one people. We ask this....

Prayer after Communion

Praesta, quaesumus, Domine, ut famulus tuus N. in mansionem lucis transeat et pacis, pro quo paschale celebravimus sacramentum. Per Christum.

Lord, please grant that your servant N., for whom we have celebrated this Easter sacrament, may enter into an abode of light and peace. We ask this....

MASSES FOR THE DEAD
I. FUNERAL MASS: #C, DURING EASTER SEASON

Collect

Preces nostras, quaesumus, Domine, benignus exaudi, ut, dum extollitur nostra fides in Filio tuo a mortuis suscitato, in famuli tui N. praestolanda resurrectione spes quoque nostra firmetur. Per Dominum.

MASSES FOR THE DEAD
I. FUNERAL MASS: #D, OTHER PRAYERS FOR A FUNERAL MASS

Collect

Deus, cui soli competit vitam post mortem praestare, libera famulum tuum N. ab omnibus peccatis, ut, qui Christi tui resurrectionem credidit, tempore resurrectionis gloriosus tibi iungatur. Per Dominum.

God our Father, none but you can confer life after death. Free your servant N. from all sin, so that he (she) who put his (her) faith in the resurrection of your Christ may be gloriously united with you when the dead shall rise again. We ask this....

Prayer over the Gifts

Omnipotens et misericors Deus, his sacrificiis ablue, quaesumus, famulum tuum N. a peccatis suis in sanguine Christi, ut, quem mundasti aqua baptismatis, indesinenter purifices indulgentia pietatis. Per Christum.

Almighty and merciful God, through this sacrifice and in the blood of Christ cleanse your servant N. from his (her) sins, so that through your loving forgiveness you may eternally cleanse him (her) whom you have washed in the waters of baptism. We ask this....

Prayer after Communion

Sumpto sacramento Unigeniti tui, qui pro nobis immolatus resurrexit in gloria, te, Domine, suppliciter exoramus pro famulo tuo N., ut, paschalibus mysteriis mundatus, futurae resurrectionis munere glorietur. Per Christum.

Lord, we have received the sacrament of your only Son, who was sacrificed for us and rose again in glory. We humbly pray to you for your servant N., that he (she) may be cleansed by these Easter mysteries and may rejoice in the gift of the resurrection to come. We ask this....

MASSES FOR THE DEAD
II. ANNIVERSARY MASS: #A, OUTSIDE OF EASTER SEASON

Collect

Deus, gloria fidelium et vita iustorum, cuius Filii morte et resurrectione redempti sumus, propitiare famulo tuo N., ut, qui resurrectionis nostrae mysterium agnovit, aeternae beatitudinis gaudia percipere mereatur. Per Dominum.

God our Father, you are the glory of those who believe in you and the life of those who are just; and it is by the death and resurrection of your Son that we have been redeemed. Be merciful to your servant N. He (She) believed in the mystery of the resurrection; may he (she) be privileged to receive the rewards of eternal happiness. We ask this....

Prayer over the Gifts

Munera, quaesumus, Domine, quae tibi pro famulo tuo N. offerimus, placatus intende, ut, remediis purgatus caelestibus, in tua gloria semper vivus sit et beatus. Per Christum.

Lord, in your forgiving mercy, please look upon the gifts we offer for your servant N., so that he (she) may be cleansed by these heavenly cures and then forever live in the blessedness of your glory. We ask this....

Prayer after Communion

Sacris reparati mysteriis, te, Domine, suppliciter exoramus, ut famulus N., a delictis omnibus emundatus, aeterno resurrectionis munere ditari mereatur. Per Christum.

Lord, we are restored by these sacred mysteries, and we humbly pray that your servant N. may be cleansed from all stain of sin and be privileged to enjoy the rich and unending gift of rising from the dead. We ask this....

MASSES FOR THE DEAD
II. ANNIVERSARY MASS: #B, OUTSIDE OF EASTER SEASON

Collect

Quaesumus, Domine, ut famulo tuo N., cuius dispositionis diem commemoramus, rorem misericordiae tuae perennem infundas, et Sanctorum tuorum largiri digneris consortium. Per Dominum.

Lord, we call to mind the day on which your servant N. was buried; and we ask that you pour forth the constant freshness of your mercy upon him (her), and that you be pleased to grant him (her) admission to the company of your Saints. We ask this....

Prayer over the Gifts

Adesto, Domine, supplicationibus nostris pro famulo tuo N., cuius hodie annua dies agitur, ut, per hoc sacrificium propitiationis et laudis, eum Sanctorum tuorum consortio sociare digneris. Per Christum.

Lord, hear our prayers for your servant N., whose anniversary we celebrate today. Through this sacrifice of atonement and praise, may you see fit to add him (her) to the company of your Saints. We ask this....

Prayer after Communion

Precibus nostris et sacrificiis, Domine, pro famulo tuo N. benigne susceptis, te supplices deprecamur, ut, si quae ei maculae peccati adhaeserunt, remissionis tuae misericordia deleantur. Per Christum.

Lord, mercifully receive our prayers and sacrifices for your servant N. We humbly ask that any stains of sin which may yet cling to him (her) may be removed by your merciful forgiveness. We ask this....

MASSES FOR THE DEAD
II. ANNIVERSARY MASS: #C, DURING EASTER SEASON

Collect

Omnipotens et misericors Deus, cuius Filius voluntarie pro nobis carnis subiit mortem, concede propitius famulo tuo N. admirabili eius resurrectionis victoriae sociari. Per Dominum.

Almighty and merciful God, your Son freely chose to undergo bodily death on our behalf. In your kindness, grant that your servant N. may be given a share in the wonderful victory of your Son's resurrection. We ask this....

Prayer over the Gifts and Prayer after Communion:
Cf. Funeral Mass #D, p. 292.

MASSES FOR THE DEAD
II. ANNIVERSARY MASS: #D, OTHER PRAYERS FOR AN ANNIVERSARY

Collect

Concede, quaesumus, Domine, per beatam Filii tui passionem, famulo tuo N. remissionem, quam semper optavit, peccatorum, ut, te in veritate cognoscens, visione tua iugiter perfrui mereatur. Per Dominum.

Lord, through the sacred passion of your Son, please grant your servant N. that forgiveness of his (her) sins for which he (she) always hoped, so that he (she) may know you as you truly are and may be privileged to gaze upon you forever. We ask this....

Prayer over the Gifts

Sacrificium tibi, Domine, pro famulo tuo N. suppliciter offerimus, ut, qui te iam dono tuae illuminationis agnovit, tibi adhaerere perpetuo laetetur. Per Christum.

Lord, we humbly offer you our sacrifice on behalf of your servant N., asking that, as he (she) has already come to know you in this life by the gift of your revelation, so also may he (she) rejoice in being joined to you for ever. We ask this....

Prayer after Communion

Repleti alimonia reparationis et vitae, quaesumus, Domine, ut per eam frater noster N., ab omnibus peccatis emundatus, ad caeleste valeat transire consortium. Per Christum.

Lord, we are filled with the food that restores us and gives us life. Through it, we ask that our brother (sister) N. may be cleansed of all his (her) sins and be enabled to join the company of those who are in heaven. We ask this....

MASSES FOR THE DEAD
II. ANNIVERSARY MASS: #E, OTHER PRAYERS FOR AN ANNIVERSARY

Collect

Deus indulgentiarum, da famulo tuo N., cuius anniversarium depositionis diem celebramus, refrigerii sedem, quietis beatitudinem, et luminis claritatem. Per Dominum.

God of all mercies, we celebrate the anniversary of the burial of your servant N. Give him (her) a place of rest, a peaceful happiness, and the brilliance of your own light. We ask this....

Prayer over the Gifts

Supplicatio tibi nostra, Domine, et grata pariter exsistat oblatio, ut famulo tuo N., pro cuius salute defertur, plenitudinem tuae redemptionis acquirat. Per Christum.

Lord, may our prayer be pleasing to you, and our offering as well, so that they may obtain the fullness of your redemption for your servant N., for whose eternal salvation we offer them. We ask this....

Prayer after Communion

Praesta, quaesumus, omnipotens Deus, ut famulus tuus N., pro quo hoc sacrificium tuae obtulimus maiestati, per huius virtutem sacramenti a peccatis omnibus expiatus, lucis perpetuae, te miserante, recipiat beatitudinem. Per Christum.

Almighty God, please grant that your servant N., for whom we have offered this sacrifice to your divine majesty, may be cleansed from all his (her) sins by the power of this sacrament and may, through your merciful gift, receive the happiness of eternal light. We ask this....

MASSES FOR THE DEAD
III. VARIOUS COMMEMORATIONS: #A, FOR ONE DECEASED PERSON

Collect

Deus, Pater omnipotens, qui nos crucis mysterio confirmasti et Filii tui resurrectionis sacramento signasti, concede propitius famulo tuo N., ut, mortalitatis nexibus expeditus, electorum tuorum aggregetur consortio. Per Dominum.

God, Father most powerful, you have strengthened us by the mystery of the Cross and marked us by the sacrament of the resurrection of your Son. In your mercy, grant that your servant N., freed from the bonds of mortality, may be added to the number of your chosen ones in heaven. We ask this....

Alternate Collect

Inclina, Domine, aurem tuam ad preces nostras, quibus misericordiam tuam supplices deprecamur, ut famulum tuum N., quem in hoc saeculo tuo populo misericorditer aggregasti, in pacis et lucis regione constituas, et Sanctorum tuorum concedas esse consortem. Per Dominum.

Lord, grant a hearing to our prayers, in which we humbly beg for your mercy. In your kindness, you counted your servant N. among your people in this life; grant him (her) now a place of peace and light, and grant that he (she) may be a companion of your Saints. We ask this....

Prayer over the Gifts

Propitiare, quaesumus, Domine, famulo tuo N., pro quo hostiam tibi laudis immolamus, te suppliciter deprecantes, ut, per haec piae placationis officia, resurgere mereatur ad vitam. Per Christum.

Lord, please be merciful to your servant N., for whom we offer this sacrifice of praise. Through this offering that signifies our love and repentance, we humbly ask that he (she) may be privileged to rise to eternal life. We ask this....

Prayer after Communion

Vitalibus refecti sacramentis, quaesumus, Domine, ut frater noster N., quem testamenti tui participem effecisti, huius mysterii purificatus virtute, in pace Christi sine fine laetetur. Per Christum.

Lord, we are renewed with your life-giving sacraments. You saw to it that our brother (sister) N. shared in your covenant; we ask that he (she) may be cleansed by the power of this mystery and rejoice in the endless peace of Christ. We ask this....

MASSES FOR THE DEAD
III. VARIOUS COMMEMORATIONS: #B, FOR ONE DECEASED PERSON

Collect

Absolve, quaesumus, Domine, famulum tuum N. ab omni vinculo delictorum, ut, qui in hoc saeculo Christo meruit conformari, in resurrectionis gloria inter Sanctos tuos resuscitatus respiret. Per Dominum.

Lord, we ask you to release your servant N. from every bond of sin. In this world, he (she) was privileged to be made like Christ; may he (she) be raised from the dead and live once more among your Saints in the glory of the resurrection. We ask this....

Prayer over the Gifts

Annue nobis, quaesumus, Domine, ut famulo tuo N. haec prosit oblatio, quam immolando, totius mundi tribuisti relaxari delicta. Per Christum.

Lord, you have made the forgiveness of the sins of the whole world depend upon the offering of this sacrifice. Please grant our prayer that the offering of it now may benefit your servant N. We ask this....

Prayer after Communion

Prosit, quaesumus, Domine, famulo tuo N. sacrificium Ecclesiae tuae, ut, cum Sanctis, Christi consortium inveniat, cuius misericordiae consecutus est sacramentum. Per Christum.

Lord, we ask that the sacrifice of your Church may benefit your servant N., so that, in the company of the Saints, he (she) may find the companionship of Christ, whose sacrament of mercy he (she) has received. We ask this....

MASSES FOR THE DEAD
III. VARIOUS COMMEMORATIONS: #C, FOR SEVERAL (OR ALL THE) DECEASED

Collect

Deus, qui Unigenitum tuum, devicta morte, ad caelestia transire fecisti, concede famulis tuis (N. et N.), ut, huius vitae mortalitate devicta, te conditorem et redemptorem possint perpetuo contemplari. Per Dominum.

God our Father, you saw to it that your only Son rose to heaven after his victory over death. Grant that your servants (N. and N.) may overcome the death this present life entails and forever be able to contemplate you, their creator and redeemer. We ask this....

Alternate Collect

Fidelium, Deus, omnium conditor et redemptor, famulis tuis remissionem cunctorum tribue peccatorum, ut indulgentiam, quam semper optaverunt, piis supplicationibus consequantur. Per Dominum.

God our Father, creator and redeemer of all those who believe in you, grant your servants the forgiveness of all their sins, so that through our faithful prayers they may obtain that forgiveness for which they have always hoped. We ask this...

Prayer over the Gifts

Hostias, quaesumus, Domine, quas tibi pro famulis tuis offerimus, propitiatus intende, ut, quibus fidei christianae meritum contulisti, dones et praemium. Per Christum.

Lord, in your forgiving mercy, please look upon the offerings which we bring to you on behalf of your servants. You gave them the privilege of professing the Christian faith; grant them also its reward. We ask this....

Prayer after Communion

Multiplica, Domine, his sacrificiis susceptis, super famulos tuos defunctos misericordiam tuam, et, quibus donasti baptismi gratiam, da eis aeternorum plenitudinem gaudiorum. Per Christum.

Lord, receive these sacrifices and pour out your abundant mercy upon your servants who have died. You gave them the grace of baptism; grant them also the fullness of eternal joys. We ask this....

Alternate Prayer after Communion

Famulis tuis, quaesumus, Domine, oratio proficiat supplicantium, ut eos, his sacrificiis, et a peccatis omnibus exuas, et aeternae salvationis facias esse participes. Per Christum.

Lord, we ask that the prayers of your people who cry to you may help your servants. Through these sacrifices, free them from all their sins and allow them to share in eternal salvation. We ask this....

MASSES FOR THE DEAD
III. VARIOUS COMMEMORATIONS: #D, FOR SEVERAL (OR ALL THE) DECEASED

Collect

Omnipotens sempiterne Deus, vita mortalium et exsultatio Sanctorum, te supplices exoramus pro famulis tuis (N. et N.), ut, mortalitatis nexibus expediti, regnum tuum in gloria possideant sempiterna. Per Dominum.

Almighty and eternal God, you are the life of men and women on earth and the joy of your Saints in heaven. We humbly pray for your servants (N. and N.), so that they may be freed from the bonds of mortality and possess your kingdom in unending glory. We ask this....

Alternate Collect

Omnipotens sempiterne Deus, qui vivorum dominaris simul et defunctorum, omniumque miserereis, te suppliciter exoramus, ut, pro quibus effundimus preces, pietatis tuae clementia delictorum suorum veniam consequantur, et de te beati congaudeant ac te sine fine collaudent. Per Dominum.

Almighty and eternal God, you rule over the living as well as the dead, and you have mercy on them all. We humbly ask that those for whom we pray may attain the forgiveness of their sins through your loving mercy and, as saints in heaven, may together rejoice in you and praise you without end. We ask this....

Prayer over the Gifts

Pro famulis tuis N. et N. et omnibus in Christo dormientibus hostiam, Domine, suscipe benignus oblatam, ut, per hoc sacrificium singulare vinculis mortis exuti, vitam mereantur aeternam. Per Christum.

Lord, in your mercy, receive the sacrifice offered for your servants N. and N. and for all who sleep in Christ. Through this unique sacrifice may they be freed from the bonds of death and be privileged to receive eternal life. We ask this....

Prayer after Communion

Divina participantes mysteria, quaesumus, omnipotens Deus, ut haec eadem nobis proficiant ad salutem, et famulis tuis defunctis, pro quibus tuam deprecamur clementiam, prosint ad indulgentiam. Per Christum.

Almighty God, as we take part in your sacred mysteries, we ask that they may help us on our way to salvation. May they also help gain your forgiveness for your servants who have died and for whom we beg your mercy. We ask this....

MASSES FOR THE DEAD
III. VARIOUS COMMEMORATIONS: #E, FOR SEVERAL (OR ALL THE) DECEASED

Collect

Deus, cuius miseratione fideles requiescunt, famulis tuis N. et N. et omnibus in Christo quiescentibus da propitius veniam peccatorum, ut, a cunctis reatibus absoluti, Christi tui resurrectioni socientur. Qui tecum.

God our Father, in your mercy your faithful ones find rest. In your kindness, grant the forgiveness of their sins to your servants N. and N. and to all who sleep in Christ, so that they may be freed from all their guilt and be made to share in the resurrection of your Christ. We ask this....

Alternate Collect

Quaesumus, Domine, famulis tuis defunctis misericordiam concede perpetuam, ut eis proficiat in aeternum quod in te speraverunt et crediderunt. Per Dominum.

Lord, please grant your endless mercy to your servants who have died. May the hope and the belief they had in you help them to enter into eternal life. We ask this....

Prayer over the Gifts

Munera, Domine, quaesumus, quae pro tuorum requie famulorum offerimus, placatus intende, ut, per haec salutis humanae subsidia, tuorum numero redemptorum sorte perpetua censeantur. Per Christum.

Lord, in your forgiving mercy, look favorably upon the gifts we offer for the eternal rest of your servants. By this aid to human salvation, may they be counted among the number of those whom, by your eternal decree, you have redeemed. We ask this....

Prayer after Communion

Sumpsimus, Domine, redemptionis sacramenta, tuam clementiam obsecrantes, ut, te miserante, nobis viventibus tutelam obtineant, et defunctis nostris veniam sempiternam. Per Christum.

Lord, we have received the sacraments of our redemption, and we earnestly ask for your mercy. Through your pitying care, may these sacraments obtain protection for us who are still alive and eternal pardon for our dead. We ask this....

Alternate Prayer after Communion

Inveniant, quaesumus, Domine, famuli tui, omnesque in Christo quiescentes, lucis aeternae consortium, qui, in hac luce positi, tuum consecuti sunt sacramentum. Per Christum.

Lord, your servants, and all who sleep in Christ, received your sacrament while in the light of this life; we ask that they now find a share in eternal light. We ask this....

MASSES FOR THE DEAD
IV. PRAYERS FOR THE DEAD: #1A, FOR A POPE

Collect

Deus, fidelis remunerator animarum, praesta, ut famulus tuus Papa noster N., quem Petri constituisti vicarium et Ecclesiae tuae pastorem, gratiae et miserationis tuae mysteriis, quae fidenter dispensavit in terris, laetanter apud te perpetuo fruatur in caelis. Per Dominum.

God our Father, you faithfully reward souls that are true to you. Please grant that your servant and our Pope, N., whom you appointed vicar of Saint Peter and shepherd of your Church, may, in unending happiness in your presence in heaven, enjoy the mysteries of your grace and your mercy, which he faithfully distributed while he was on earth. We ask this....

Prayer over the Gifts

Quaesumus, Domine, ut, per haec piae placationis officia, famulum tuum Papam nostrum N. beata retributio comitetur, et misericordia tua nobis gratiae dona conciliet. Per Christum.

Lord, through these offerings that express our love and repentance, we ask that a blessed reward may attend your servant and our Pope, N., and that your mercy may provide us with the gifts of your grace. We ask this....

Prayer after Communion

Divinae tuae communionis refecti sacramentis, quaesumus, Domine, ut famulus tuus Papa noster N., quem Ecclesiae tuae visibile voluisti fundamentum unitatis in terris, beatitudini gregis tui feliciter aggregetur. Per Christum.

Lord, we are renewed by your sacrament of Holy Communion, and we ask that your servant, our Pope N., whom you chose to be the visible basis for the unity of your Church on earth, may have the joy and happiness of being added to your heavenly flock. We ask this....

MASSES FOR THE DEAD
IV. PRAYERS FOR THE DEAD: #1B, FOR A POPE

Collect

Deus, qui Ecclesiae tuae famulum tuum Papam nostrum N. ineffabili tua dispositione praeesse voluisti, praesta, quaesumus, ut, qui Filii tui vices gerebat in terris, ab ipso in gloria recipiatur aeterna. Per Dominum.

God our Father, in your mysterious decree, you willed that your servant, our Pope N., should have supreme charge of your Church. He was your Son's vicar on earth; please grant that he may be received by your Son into eternal glory. We ask this....

Prayer over the Gifts

Munera, Domine, supplicantis Ecclesiae respice propitius, et huius sacrificii virtute, concede, ut famulum tuum Papam nostrum N., quem sacerdotem magnum tuo gregi praefecisti, in electorum tuorum numero constituas sacerdotum. Per Christum.

Lord, look with kindness on the gifts of your Church as it prays to you. You appointed your servant, our Pope N., as high priest over your flock; through the power of this sacrifice, place him among the number of your chosen priests in heaven. We ask this....

Prayer after Communion

Caritatis tuae, Domine, sumentes sacra subsidia, quaesumus, ut famulus tuus Papa noster N. misericordiam tuam in Sanctorum gloria perpetuo collaudet, qui fidelis exstitit mysteriorum tuorum dispensator in terris. Per Christum.

Lord, as we receive the sacred assistance of your love, we ask that your servant, our Pope N., who proved to be a faithful steward of your mysteries on earth, may praise your mercy forever amid the glory of your saints. We ask this....

MASSES FOR THE DEAD
IV. PRAYERS FOR THE DEAD: #1C, FOR A POPE

Collect

Deus, immortalis pastor animarum, respice populum supplicantem, et praesta, ut famulus tuus Papa noster N., qui Ecclesiae tuae in caritate praefuit, fidelis dispensatoris remunerationem cum grege sibi credito misericorditer consequatur. Per Dominum.

God our Father, eternal shepherd of souls, look upon your people who cry to you. Your servant, our Pope N., lovingly presided over your Church; in your mercy, grant that he, in the company of the flock that was entrusted to him, may attain the reward of his faithful stewardship. We ask this....

Prayer over the Gifts

Oblationem pacificam populi tui, quaesumus, Domine, propitius intuere, qua famulum tuum Papam nostrum N. tuae misericordiae fidenter committimus, et praesta, ut, qui tuae caritatis et pacis in humana familia fuit instrumentum, earum fructu cum Sanctis tuis perpetuo laetari mereatur. Per Christum.

Lord, in your kindness please look upon the offering of reconciliation your people make. By means of it, they trustingly commend your servant, our Pope N., to your mercy. He was the agent of your love and peace amid the human family; grant that, in the company of your saints, he may be privileged to rejoice for ever in the fullness of that love and peace. We ask this....

Prayer after Communion

Ad mensam aeterni accedentes convivii, misericordiam tuam, Domine, pro famulo tuo Papa nostro N. suppliciter imploramus, ut veritatis possessione tandem congaudeat, in qua populum tuum fidenter confirmavit. Per Christum.

Lord, as we come to the table of your eternal banquet, we humbly beg your mercy for your servant, our Pope N., so that he may at last rejoice in the full possession of that truth in which he trustingly strengthened your people's faith. We ask this....

MASSES FOR THE DEAD
IV. PRAYERS FOR THE DEAD: #2A, FOR A DIOCESAN BISHOP

Collect

Da, quaesumus, omnipotens Deus, ut famulus tuus N. episcopus noster, cui familiae tuae curam *tradidisti, cum multiplici laboris fructu gaudia Domini sui ingrediatur aeterna. Per Dominum.*

Almighty God, you entrusted the care of your people to your servant, our bishop N. Please grant that he may receive the manifold reward of his labors, and may enter upon the eternal joys of his Lord. We ask this....

Prayer over the Gifts

Immensam clementiam tuam, Domine, suppliciter imploramus, ut hoc sacrificium, quod famulus tuus N. episcopus noster, dum esset in corpore, maiestati tuae pro salute fidelium obtulit, ipsi nunc prosit ad veniam. Per Christum.

Lord, humbly and earnestly we ask for your boundless mercy. While he was in this life, your servant, our bishop N., offered this sacrifice to your divine majesty on behalf of the eternal welfare of your faithful people. May that sacrifice now help him, in turn, to achieve the forgiveness of his sins. We ask this....

Prayer after Communion

Prosit, quaesumus, Domine, famulo tuo N. episcopo nostro misericordiae tuae implorata clementia, ut Christi, in quo speravit et quem praedicavit, aeternum capiat, his sacrificiis, consortium. Per Christum.

Lord, we beg for your kind mercy and we ask that it may assist your servant and our bishop N. Through this sacrifice, may he attain the eternal companionship of Christ, in whom he hoped and whom he proclaimed. We ask this....

MASSES FOR THE DEAD
IV. PRAYERS FOR THE DEAD: #2B, FOR A BISHOP OTHER THAN THE DIOCESAN BISHOP

Collect

Deus, qui inter apostolicos sacerdotes famulum tuum N. episcopum (vel cardinalem) pontificali fecisti dignitate vigere, praesta, quaesumus, ut eorum quoque perpetuo aggregetur consortio. Per Dominum.

God our Father, among the priests who came after the Apostles, you honored your servant, Bishop (or Cardinal) N., with episcopal rank. Please grant also that he may be added to the company of those Apostles in heaven. We ask this....

Prayer over the Gifts

Suscipe, Domine, quaesumus, pro famulo tuo N. episcopo (vel cardinali) quas tibi offerimus hostias, ut, cui in hoc saeculo pontificale donasti meritum, in caelesti regno Sanctorum tuorum iubeas iungi consortio. Per Christum.

Lord, please receive the offerings we make to you on behalf of your servant, Bishop (or Cardinal) N. While he was in this life, you granted him the dignity of being a bishop; in your heavenly kingdom, bid him join the number of your saints. We ask this....

Prayer after Communion

Quaesumus, omnipotens et misericors Deus, ut famulum tuum N. episcopum (vel cardinalem), quem in terris pro Christo legatione fungi tribuisti, his emundatum sacrificiis, consedere facias in caelestibus cum ipso. Per Christum.

Almighty and merciful God, you gave your servant, Bishop (or Cardinal) N., the privilege of being Christ's delegate on earth. We ask you to cleanse him of his sins by this sacrifice and to seat him in heaven with Christ. We ask this....

MASSES FOR THE DEAD
IV. PRAYERS FOR THE DEAD: #3A, FOR A PRIEST

Collect

Praesta, quaesumus, Domine, ut famulus tuus N. sacerdos, quem in hoc saeculo commorantem sacris muneribus decorasti, in caelesti sede gloriosus semper exsultet. Per Dominum.

Lord, you granted your servant, our priest N., the gift of performing sacred functions while he lived in this world. Please grant that he may ever rejoice in the glory of your heavenly home. We ask this....

Prayer over the Gifts

Concede, quaesumus, omnipotens Deus, ut famulus tuus N. sacerdos, per haec sancta mysteria, conspectu semper claro conspiciat quae hic fideliter ministravit. Per Christum.

Almighty God, through these sacred mysteries, please grant that your servant, our priest N., may behold in unending clarity the mysteries which he served faithfully here on earth. We ask this....

Prayer after Communion

Sumptis salutaribus sacramentis, imploramus, Deus, clementiam tuam, ut famulum tuum N. sacerdotem, quem fecisti mysteriorum tuorum dispensatorem in terris, eorum facias in caelis aperta veritate nutriri. Per Christum.

Lord, we have received your life-giving sacraments, and we earnestly ask for your mercy. You made your servant, our priest N., the steward of your mysteries on earth; please grant that in heaven he may be nourished by those same mysteries, whose truth is now manifest to him. We ask this....

MASSES FOR THE DEAD
IV. PRAYERS FOR THE DEAD: #3B, FOR A PRIEST

Collect

Preces nostras, quaesumus, Domine, quas pro famuli tui N. sacerdotis salute suppliciter deferimus, propitiatus exaudi, ut, qui nomini tuo ministerium fidele dependit, perpetua Sanctorum tuorum societate laetetur. Per Dominum.

Lord, in your forgiving mercy, please hear the prayers we humbly offer for the eternal salvation of your servant and priest N. He spent his days in faithful work for the glory of your name; may he rejoice in the eternal companionship of your saints. We ask this....

Prayer over the Gifts

Quaesumus, Domine, clementiam tuam, ut hoc sacrificium servitutis nostrae, pro famulo tuo N. sacerdote oblatum, ipsi nunc prosit ad veniam, qui illud in Ecclesia devota tibi mente exhibuit. Per Christum.

Lord, we ask for your mercy. May this sacrifice, which marks our loving dedication to you and which we offer for your servant and priest N., obtain the forgiveness of his sins for him who offered this same sacrifice within your Church with his heart intent upon you. We ask this....

Prayer after Communion

Mensae caelestis alimonia refecti, te, Domine, suppliciter exoramus, ut, huius virtute sacramenti, famulus tuus N. sacerdos ante conspectum tuum semper exsultet, qui in Ecclesia tua fideliter ministravit. Per Christum.

Lord, we have been renewed by the banquet of your holy table. We humbly ask that, through the power of this sacrifice, your servant and priest N., who faithfully ministered within your Church, may ever rejoice in your sight. We ask this....

MASSES FOR THE DEAD
IV. PRAYERS FOR THE DEAD: #4, FOR A DEACON

Collect

Concede, quaesumus, misericors Deus, famulo tuo N. diacono felicitatis aeternae consortium, cui donasti in Ecclesia tua consequi ministerium. Per Dominum.

Merciful God, you granted your servant, the deacon N., the gift of an ordained ministery within your Church. Please grant also that he may share in eternal happiness. We ask this....

Prayer over the Gifts

Propitiare, Domine, famulo tuo N. diacono, pro cuius salute hoc tibi sacrificium offerimus, ut, sicut Christo Filio tuo ministravit in carne, cum fidelibus servis exsurgat in gloriam sempiternam. Per Christum....

Lord, be merciful to your servant, the deacon N., for whose eternal salvation we offer this sacrifice to you. Just as he ministered to Christ your Son in this life, so may he rise to eternal glory in the company of your good and faithful servants. We ask this....

Prayer after Communion

Muneribus sacris repleti, te, Domine, humiliter deprecamur, ut per hoc sacrificium famulum tuum N. diaconum, quem inter servos Ecclesiae tuae vocasti, a mortis vinculis absolutum, cum iis qui bene ministraverunt partem recipere et in gaudium tuum intrare benigne concedas. Per Christum.

Lord, we are filled with your sacred gifts. You called your deacon N. to be one of those who serve within your Church; we humbly ask that, through this sacrifice, you will free him from the bonds of death and, in your mercy, will allow him to enter into your joy and share in the reward of those who have served you well. We ask this....

MASSES FOR THE DEAD
IV. PRAYERS FOR THE DEAD: #5, FOR A RELIGIOUS

Collect

Praesta, quaesumus, omnipotens Deus, ut famulus tuus N., qui pro Christi amore perfectae caritatis viam percurrit, in adventu gloriae tuae laetetur, et cum fratribus suis de regni tui beatitudine gaudeat sempiterna. Per Dominum.

Almighty God, please grant that your servant N., who for love of Christ pursued the path of perfect charity, may rejoice at the coming of your glory and, along with his (her) brothers (sisters), enjoy the unending happiness of your kingdom. We ask this....

MASSES FOR THE DEAD
IV. PRAYERS FOR THE DEAD:
#6A, FOR ONE DEAD PERSON

Collect

Deus, apud quem mortui vivunt et in quo sancti tui plena felicitate laetantur, praesta supplicantibus nobis, ut famulus tuus N., qui nunc temporali huius mundi lumine caret, aeternae tuae lucis solatio perfruatur. Per Dominum.

God our Father, the dead live in your presence, and your saints rejoice in perfect happiness in you. Grant our prayer as we cry to you, that your servant N., who is now deprived of the earthly light of this world, may enjoy the consolation of your heavenly splendor. We ask this....

Prayer over the Gifts

Placeat tibi, Domine, sacrificii praesentis oblatio, ut famulus tuus N., peccatorum veniam, quam quaesivit, te miserente inveniens, cum Sanctis tuis semper exsultet, et gloriam tuam in aeternum collaudet. Per Christum.

Lord, may the offering of the sacrifice we bring please you. Through your mercy, may your servant N. find that forgiveness of sins which he (she) has sought; may he (she) ever rejoice with your Saints and praise your glory for ever. We ask this....

Prayer after Communion

Sumentes dona caelestia, gratias tibi, Domine, referimus, humiliter deprecantes, ut famulus tuus N., per Filii tui passionem a peccatorum vinculis absolutus, feliciter valeat ad te pervenire. Per Christum.

Lord, as we receive your heavenly gifts, we thank you and humbly ask that, through the passion of your Son, your servant N. may be freed from the bonds of his (her) sins and be enabled to come joyfully to you. We ask this....

MASSES FOR THE DEAD
IV. PRAYERS FOR THE DEAD:
#6B, FOR ONE DEAD PERSON

Collect

Ascendant ad te, Domine, preces nostrae, et famulum tuum N. gaudia aeterna suscipiant, ut, quem ad imaginem tuam creare dignatus es et adoptionis participem fecisti, iubeas hereditatis tuae esse consortem. Per Dominum.

Lord, may our prayers arise into your presence as we ask that eternal joy await your servant N. You saw fit to create him (her) in your own image and likeness, and you made him (her) your adopted son (daughter); may you also decree that he (she) share in your inheritance. We ask this....

Prayer over the Gifts

Oblationem nostram, quaesumus, Domine, quam pro famulo tuo N. fidenter exhibemus, placatus accipias, ut ei per hoc sacrificium, quod cunctis esse remedium singulare voluisti, salutem tribuas sempiternam. Per Christum.

Lord, be pleased to accept the offering which we bring to you in faith on behalf of your servant N. Through this sacrifice, which you have willed should be the unique remedy for all men and women, may you grant him (her) eternal salvation. We ask this....

Prayer after Communion

Recreati sacri muneris alimonia, quaesumus, Domine, ut frater noster N., mortis vinculis absolutus, resurrectionis Filii tui participatione laetetur. Per Christum.

Lord, we are renewed by the food that is your sacred gift, and we ask that our brother (sister) N. be freed from the bonds of death and rejoice in sharing the resurrection of your Son. We ask this....

MASSES FOR THE DEAD
IV. PRAYERS FOR THE DEAD: #6C, FOR ONE DEAD PERSON

Collect

Inclina, Domine precibus nostris aures tuae pietatis, et famulo tuo N. remissionem omnium tribue peccatorum, ut in resurrectionis die vivat, et in lucis amoenitate requiescat. Per Dominum.

Lord, in your loving faithfulness, hear our prayers, and grant your servant N. the forgiveness of all his (her) sins, so that he (she) may have life on the day of the resurrection and may find peace and delight in your splendor. We ask this....

Prayer over the Gifts

Omnipotens sempiterne Deus, cuius Filius panem vitae nobis praebuit semetipsum, et Sanguinem suum in poculum salutis effudit, miserere famili tui N., ut, quod tibi offerimus, sit illi causa salutis. Per Christum.

Almighty and eternal God, your Son gave himself to us as the bread of life, and he poured out his blood as the cup of our salvation. Have mercy on your servant N. May the sacrifice we offer you be the cause of his (her) attaining salvation. We ask this....

Prayer after Communion

Aeternae pignus vitae capientes, te, Domine, humiliter imploramus pro famulo tuo N., ut, mortalibus nexibus expeditus, redemptorum possit adunari consortio. Per Christum.

Lord, as we receive the pledge of eternal life, we humbly pray to you on behalf of your servant N. Now that he (she) is freed from the bonds of mortality, may he (she) be enabled to join the company of the redeemed. We ask this....

MASSES FOR THE DEAD
IV. PRAYERS FOR THE DEAD: #7, FOR A YOUNG PERSON

Collect

Deus, qui omnium hominum vitam moderaris et tempora, hunc famulum tuum N., quem consummatum in brevi deflemus, tibi humiliter com-

mendamus, ut in beatitudine domus tuae perenni facias iuventute vigere. Per Dominum.

God our Father, you direct the lives and the days of all men and women. We mourn the brevity of the life of your servant N., and we humbly commend him (her) to you, asking that you make him (her) enjoy eternal youth in the happiness of your home. We ask this....

MASSES FOR THE DEAD
IV. PRAYERS FOR THE DEAD:
#8, FOR ONE WHO WORKED IN THE
SERVICE OF THE GOSPEL

Collect

Misericordiam tuam, Domine, pro famulo tuo N. supplices deprecamur, ut, qui pro Evangelio dilatando allaboravit assiduus, ad praemia regni mereatur intrare securus. Per Dominum.

Lord, we humbly ask for your mercy on behalf of your servant N. He (She) labored diligently for the spread of the Gospel; may he (she) be privileged to enter safely into the rewards of your kingdom. We ask this....

MASSES FOR THE DEAD
IV. PRAYERS FOR THE DEAD:
#9, FOR ONE WHO
SUFFERED A LONG ILLNESS

Collect

Deus, qui famulo tuo N. dedisti in aerumnis tibi et infirmitate servire, concede, quaesumus, ut, qui Filii tui secutus est patientiae documentum, eiusdem gloriae consequatur et praemium. Per Dominum.

God our Father, you gave your servant N. the gift of serving you in hardship and in illness. He (She) followed the example of your Son's patience; please grant that he (she) may also receive the reward of sharing in his glory. We ask this....

MASSES FOR THE DEAD
IV. PRAYERS FOR THE DEAD:
#10, FOR ONE
WHO DIED SUDDENLY

Collect

Immensam, Domine, tuae bonitatis ostende virtutem, ut, qui fratrum nostrum N. repentina flemus morte sublatum, ad tuum confidamus transisse consortium. Per Dominum.

Lord, show us the limitless power of your goodness, so that we who mourn the sudden death of our brother (sister) N. may have confidence that he (she) has passed over into your presence. We ask this....

MASSES FOR THE DEAD
IV. PRAYERS FOR THE DEAD: #11A, FOR SEVERAL PERSONS

Collect

Propitiare, Domine, famulis tuis N. et N., ut, quos regenerationis fonte mundasti, ad caelestis vitae beatitudinem facias pervenire. Per Dominum.

Lord, be merciful to your servants N. and N. You cleansed them in the bath of rebirth; grant that they may come to the happiness of eternal life. We ask this....

Prayer over the Gifts

Pro famulis tuis N. et N., Domine, tibi sacrificium offerentes, supplices exoramus, ut ad tuam misericordiam illis conferendam perpetuam dignanter vota nostra perficias. Per Christum.

Lord, as we offer you our sacrifice on behalf of your servants N. and N., we humbly ask that you will make our prayers effective in obtaining your eternal mercy for them. We ask this....

Prayer after Communion

Sumptis, Domine, caelestibus sacramentis, tuam clementiam humiliter deprecamur, ut famuli tui, percipientes hoc munere veniam peccatorum, regnum tuum introire, teque in aeternum mereantur collaudare. Per Christum.

Lord, we have received your heavenly sacraments, and we humbly ask for your mercy. Through this sacrifice, may your servants receive the forgiveness of their sins; may they be privileged to enter your kingdom and praise you for ever. We ask this....

MASSES FOR THE DEAD
IV. PRAYERS FOR THE DEAD: #11B, FOR SEVERAL PERSONS

Collect

Tibi, Domine, commendamus famulos tuos N. et N., ut defuncti saeculo tibi vivant, et quae, per fragilitatem carnis, peccata in mundi conversatione commiserunt, tu venia misericordissimae pietatis absterge. Per Dominum.

Lord, we commend your servants N. and N. to you. They have died to this life; may they live in you. We ask that, with the forgiveness of your most merciful love, you wash away whatever sins they have committed through the weakness of the flesh during their life in this world. We ask this....

Prayer over the Gifts

Propitiare, quaesumus, Domine, famulis tuis N. et N., pro quibus tibi hostias placationis offerimus, et quia in hac vita tibi manserunt fideles, apud te pia illis retributio donetur. Per Christum.

Lord, please be merciful to your servants N. and N., for whom we offer you this sacrifice of atonement. Since they were steadfastly faithful to you in this life, may a loving reward be given them in your home. We ask this....

Prayer after Communion

Praesta, quaesumus, omnipotens Deus, ut famulos tuos, per huius sacramenti virtutem, in congregatione iustorum aeternae beatitudinis iubeas esse consortes. Per Christum.

Almighty God, through the power of this sacrament, please command that your servants share in eternal happiness in the company of the just. We ask this....

MASSES FOR THE DEAD
IV. PRAYERS FOR THE DEAD:
#11C, FOR SEVERAL PERSONS

Collect

Omnipotens sempiterne Deus, cui numquam sine spe misericordiae supplicatur, propitiare famulis tuis N. et N., ut, qui de hac vita in tui nominis confessione discesserunt, Sanctorum tuorum numero facias aggregari. Per Dominum.

Almighty and eternal God, no one ever prays to you without assurance of your mercy. Be gracious to your servants N. and N. Since they left this life as believers in your name, please bring it about that they are added to the number of your Saints. We ask this....

Prayer over the Gifts

Domine Deus, cuius Filius se tibi obtulit hostiam vivam, accipe, quaesumus, Ecclesiae tuae sacrificium, ut famuli tui N. et N., a peccatis omnibus absoluti, ad praemium immortalitatis mereantur pertingere. Per Christum.

Lord our God, your Son offered himself to you as a living victim. Please accept the sacrifice of your Church whereby we ask that your servants N. and N. may be freed from all their sins and be privileged to attain the reward of eternal life. We ask this....

Prayer after Communion

Purificent nos, quaesumus, omnipotens et misericors Deus, sacramenta quae sumpsimus, et praesta, ut hoc sacrificium sit nobis intercessio ad veniam, sit fragilium fortitudo, sit in omnibus firmamentum, sit vivis atque defunctis remissio omnium peccatorum, et pignus redemptionis aeternae. Per Christum.

Almighty and merciful God, we ask that the sacraments we have received may cleanse us. Grant that this sacrifice may be a prayer for our forgiveness, a strength for our weakness, a support in all things; for both the living and the dead, may it be the forgiveness of all sin and the pledge of eternal redemption. We ask this....

MASSES FOR THE DEAD
IV. PRAYERS FOR THE DEAD:
#12, FOR MARRIED PERSONS

Collect

Famulos tuos N., et N., quaesumus, Domine, miseratus absolve, ut, quos coniugalis amor in hac vita fideliter sociavit, in aeterna, tuae caritatis plenitudo coniungat. Per Dominum.

Lord, in your mercy please forgive the sins of your servants N. and N. Married love joined them faithfully together in this life; in eternal life, may the fullness of your own love unite them. We ask this....

Alternate Collect
for One Spouse

Famulum tuum (Famulam tuam) N., quaesumus, Domine, miseratus absolve, et famulam tuam (famulum tuum) N. continua protectione custodi, ut, quos coniugalis amor in hac vita fideliter sociavit, in aeterna, tuae caritatis plenitudo coniungat. Per Dominum.

Lord, in your mercy, please forgive the sins of your servant N., and protect your servant N. his wife (her husband) with your constant and faithful love. Married life joined them faithfully together in this life; in eternal life, may the fullness of your own love unite them. We ask this....

MASSES FOR THE DEAD
IV. PRAYERS FOR THE DEAD:
#13, FOR PARENTS

Collect

Deus, qui nos patrem et matrem honorare praecepisti, miserere clementer patri et matri meae (parentibus nostris) eorumque peccata dimitte, meque (nosque) eos in aeternae claritatis gaudio fac videre. Per Dominum.

God our Father, you have commanded us to honor our father and mother. In your mercy, have pity on my father and mother (our parents), and forgive their sins. Grant that I (we) may see them in the joy of eternal splendor. We ask this....

Prayer over the Gifts

Suscipe sacrificium, Domine, quod tibi pro patre et matre mea (parentibus nostris) offerimus, eisque gaudium sempiternum in regione vivorum concede, meque (nosque) cum illis felicitati Sanctorum coniunge. Per Christum.

Lord, receive the sacrifice which we offer you for my father and mother (our parents). Grant them eternal joy in the land of the living, and unite me (us) with them in the happiness of the Saints. We ask this....

Prayer after Communion

Caelestis participatio sacramenti, quaesumus, Domine, patri et matri meae (parentibus nostris) requiem et lucem obtineat perpetuam, meque (nosque) cum illis gloria tua satiet sempterna. Per Christum.

Lord, we ask that our sharing in your heavenly sacrament may obtain eternal rest and light for my father and mother (our parents), and that your eternal glory may bring both them and me (us) the fullness of happiness. We ask this....

MASSES FOR THE DEAD
IV. PRAYERS FOR THE DEAD:
#14, FOR RELATIVES, FRIENDS, AND BENEFACTORS

Collect

Deus, veniae largitor et humanae salutis amator, quaesumus clementiam tuam, ut nostrae congregationis fratres, propinquos et benefactores, qui ex hoc saeculo transierunt, beata Maria semper Virgine intercedente cum omnibus sanctis tuis, ad perpetuae beatitudinis consortium pervenire concedas. Per Dominum.

God our Father, you grant forgiveness and you strongly desire the salvation of the human race. We seek your mercy, asking that the brothers and sisters, the friends, and the benefactors of our assembly who have gone forth from this world may, by the intercession of the Blessed Mary, ever Virgin, and of all the Saints, come to share in eternal happiness. We ask this....

Prayer over the Gifts

Deus, cuius misericordiae non est numerus, suscipe propitius preces humilitatis nostrae, et animabus fratrum, propinquorum et benefactorum nostrorum, per haec sacramenta salutis nostrae, cunctorum remissionem tribue peccatorum. Per Christum.

God our Father, there is no measure for your mercy. In your kindness, receive our humble prayers, and, through these sacraments of our salvation, grant forgiveness of all sin to the souls of our brothers and sisters, our friends, and our benefactors. We ask this....

Prayer after Communion

Praesta, quaesumus, omnipotens et misericors Deus, ut animae fratrum, propinquorum et benefactorum nostrorum, pro quibus hoc sacrificium laudis tuae obtulimus maiestati, per huius virtutem sacramenti a peccatis omnibus expiatae, lucis perpetuae, te miserante, recipiant beatitudinem. Per Christum.

Almighty and merciful God, by the power of this sacrament please grant that the souls of our brothers and sisters, our friends, and our benefactors, for whom we have offered this sacrifice of praise to your divine majesty, may be freed from all sin and, through your merciful gift, receive the happiness of eternal splendor. We ask this....

MASSES FOR THE DEAD
V. FUNERALS OF CHILDREN: #A1, FOR A BAPTIZED CHILD

Collect

Clementissime Deus, qui sapientiae tuae consiliis hunc parvulum, in ipso vitae limine, ad te vocasti, preces nostras benignus exaudi, et praesta, ut cum ipso, quem baptismatis gratia adoptionis tibi filium effecisti, et in regno tuo iam credimus commorari, nos etiam aeternae vitae tribuas esse aliquando consortes. Per Dominum.

Most merciful God, in the mysterious designs of your wisdom you called this young child, on the threshold of his (her) life, to come to you. You made him (her) your adopted child by the grace of baptism, and we believe that he (she) now lives in your kingdom. In your kindness, hear our prayers and grant that, along with him (her), we too may one day share in eternal life. We ask this....

Prayer over the Gifts

Haec munera tibi, Domine, oblata sanctifica, ut, quem parentes a te donatum tibi reddunt infantem, ipsum laeti in regno tuo mereantur amplecti. Per Christum.

Lord, make holy these gifts we bring to you. This mother and father now return to you the child that they received from you; may they have the joyful privilege of embracing him (her) anew in your kingdom. We ask this....

Prayer after Communion

Corporis, Domine, et Sanguinis Filii tui communione percepta, te fideliter deprecamur, ut, quos in spem vitae aeternae sacris dignatus es nutrire mysteriis, in huius tribuas vitae maeroribus confortari. Per Christum.

Lord, we have received the communion of the Body and Blood of your Son, and we ask in faith that, amidst the sorrows of this life, you will grant strength to those whom you have seen fit to so nourish with your divine mysteries so that they may hope for eternal life. We ask this....

God our Father, be pleased to receive this offering as a sign of our dedication to you. We submit ourselves trustingly to the plans of your divine providence; may we also be aided by the consoling presence of your love. We ask this....

Prayer after Communion

MASSES FOR THE DEAD
V. FUNERALS OF CHILDREN: #A2, OTHER PRAYERS FOR A BAPTIZED CHILD

Collect

Deus, qui maerore scis corda nostra comprimi propter huius infantis excessum, praesta, ut, quem iam hac vita defunctum, te disponente, deflemus, aeternam in caelo sedem credamus adeptum. Per Dominum.

God our Father, you know that our hearts are heavy and sorrowful because of the death of this child. As we now mourn his (her) departure from this life under the circumstances you have chosen, please grant us the firm belief that he (she) has acquired an eternal home in heaven. We ask this....

Prayer over the Gifts

Hanc oblationem, Deus, dignare in nostrae signum devotionis excipere, ut, qui tuae providentiae consiliis submittimur confidentes, tuae quoque pietatis dulcedine sublevemur. Per Christum.

Divino munere satiati, te, Domine, deprecamur, ut, qui hunc infantem ad mensam tribuis regni caelestis accumbere, eandem et nos participare concedas. Per Christum.

Lord, we are filled with your divine gift. You have granted this child the gift of sitting at the banquet of your heavenly kingdom; we ask you to grant that we too may share in that same banquet. We ask this....

MASSES FOR THE DEAD
V. FUNERALS OF CHILDREN: #B, FOR AN UNBAPTIZED CHILD

Collect

Fidelium tuorum, Domine, suscipe vota, ut, quos permittis infantis sibi erepti desiderio deprimi, eosdem concedas in tuae spem miserationis fidenter attolli. Per Dominum.

Lord, receive the prayers of your faithful people. You allow them to be heavy-hearted in their longing for the child that has been taken from them; grant that they may be ever confident and consoled by their hope in your mercy. We ask this....

Alternate Collect

Scrutator cordium, Deus, et piissime consolator, qui horum parentum fidem novisti, praesta, ut infantem suum, quem plorant hac vita defunctum, tuae sentiant divinae pietati commissum. Per Christum.

God our Father, you read the hearts of men and women, and you console them most lovingly. You know the faith of these parents. Grant that they may realize that their child, whose death in this life they mourn, has been entrusted to the care of your divine love. We ask this....

Prayer over the Gifts

Cf. Funeral Mass for a Baptized Child #A2, p.312.

Prayer after Communion

Cf. Funeral Mass for a Baptized Child #A1, p.311.

OREMUS

Speaking with God

in the

Words of the Roman Rite

II

The Sequences

DIES IRAE

THE DAY OF WRATHFUL JUDGMENT

Dies irae, dies illa,
Solvet saeclum in favilla:
Teste David cum Sibylla.

Wrathful judgment our theme this day; • Into ashes grim shall this age pass away: • David so avers, and Sibyl adds her fearsome aye.

Quantus tremor est futurus,
Quando iudex est venturus,
Cuncta stricte discussurus!

Such awesome trembling to come, such terror, such fear, • When that horrific judge so starkly shall appear, • And shall subject all--deeds, things, and souls--to judgment drear!

Tuba mirum spargens sonum
Per sepulcra regionum,
Coget omnes ante thronum.

Lo--the trumpet! In all the world's graves its word, • Its wondrous tones plainly, inescapably heard: • "Come ye all before the throne!"--its mandate clear, no excuse endured.

Mors stupebit, et natura,
Cum resurget creatura,
Judicanti responsura.

Death itself shall gape, as shall nature as well, • When all creation shall rise from threat of hell • To its Creator, its God, its Judge, full account of itself to tell.

Liber scriptus proferetur,
In quo totum continetur,
Unde mundus iudicetur.

Inscribed is the account; forward shall it be brought. • From that fell book shall all be taught • What their judgment shall be: for life--or for naught.

Iudex ergo cum sedebit,
Quidquid latet apparebit:
Nil inultum remanebit.

And thus to the Judge, when He shall assume his throne, • All things, be they hidden, be they shown, shall be ours to own: • Nothing shall remain unavenged, to dread Vindicator unknown.

Quid sum miser tunc dicturus,
Quem patronum rogaturus,
Cum vix iustus sit securus?

Wretched soul that I am, what shall I then plea, • What advocate summon or pray for benefit unto me, • When even the just can scarcely confident be?

Rex tremendae maiestatis,
Qui salvandos salvas gratis,
Salva me, fons pietatis.

King of majesty so awesome, unto me hearken, unto me give ear: • You who save your elect, from so far drawn, from so near, • Choose me as well, save me as well, O giver of love, O banisher of fear.

Recordare, Iesu pie,
Quod sum causa tuae viae:
Ne me perdas illa die.

Be mindful, Jesus so loving, Jesus so rare, • That I am why you chose so lowly a life to dare • To live, lest you end losing me on that day of justice so stern, yet justice so fair.

Quaerens me, sedisti lassus:
Redemisti crucem passus:
Tantus labor non sit cassus.

Seeking me, you sank down, life seeming at loss, death seeming to gain, • Redeeming me, you underwent the Cross, the pain. • Let not such effort, let not such labor, end being in vain.

Iuste iudex ultionis,
Donum fac remissionis
Ante diem rationis.

Just Judge, vengeful-seeming for the sad sin-riven, • Grant unto me the grace of sin forgiven, • Ere come the day when full account must needs to thee be given.

Ingemisco, tamquam reus:
Culpa rubet vultus meus:
Supplicanti parce, Deus.

I blush in shame: full-faulted and sinful do I pine. • Guilt crimsons my face: God divine, • Grant thy suppliant servant that forgiveness which is solely thine.

Qui Mariam absolvisti,
Et latronem exaudisti.
Mihi quoque spem dedisti.

To Mary the sinner you gave pardon, gave sin-cease; • To a thief on a cross did you, in dire anguish, grant happy release: • To me as well have you given hope, joined to faith, joined to peace.

Preces meae non sunt dignae
Sed tu bonus fac benigne,
Ne perenni cremer igne.

Unworthy is my humble prayer. • But in your goodness act in gentle kindness fair, • Lest eternal flame-torment I must needs share.

Inter oves locum praesta,
Et ab haedis me sequestra,
Statuens in parte dextra.

To stand among thy sheep grant me grace; • Far from the goats sequester thou my place, • At thy very right hand grant me to view thy face.

Confutatis maledictis,
Flammis acribus addictis,
Voce me cum benedictis.

Though the condemned be confounded, • And be in flame most harsh impounded: • Yet call thou me into joy unbounded.

Oro supplex, et acclinis,
Cor contritum quasi cinis:
Gere curam mei finis.

Humbly I beg, as suppliant low, in sorrow pleading, • My heart amending, cinderform, sorrow-fire bleeding, • Grant thou care of fate for suppliant me, God-needing.

Lacrimosa dies illa,
Qua resurget ex favilla,
Judicandus homo reus.

Tearful, grief-filled that day • When from ashen flame shall spring the way • Humankind must traverse, to questions dire, dire response to pay.

Huic ergo parce Deus:
Pie Iesu Domine,
Dona eis requiem. Amen.

To one such as me, to one so lowly, • Grant pardon, God, Jesus, who Lord are solely: • To all the dead grant mercy, grant rest most blest and most holy. Amen.

LAUDA SION

SING PRAISE, O SION

Lauda, Sion, Salvatorem, lauda ducem et pastorem in hymnis et canticis. • *Quantum potes, tantum aude: quia maior omni laude, nec laudare sufficis.*

He has atoned for you, O Sion: render him laud. Your leader, your shepherd-king and God: praise him in hymns, praise him in song anew. • How much can you render? So much must you dare. For far further than words can reach spans his love so fair, nor can your praise touch him, e'en with straining reach tend it ever so true.

Laudis thema specialis, panis vivus et vitalis, hodie proponitur. • *Quem, in sacrae mensa caenae, turbae fratrum duodenae datum non ambigitur.*

A theme today most special, of eminence and praise we boldly sing: the bread enquickened, the bread enraptured by our God and King: this our chant this day. • At the holy table, at the sacred meal, gave that God, that King, his flesh full real to apostolic brethren gathered: let none doubt or question, let none dare gainsay.

Sit laus plena, sit sonora, sit iucunda, sit decora mentis iubilatio. • *Dies enim sollemnis agitur, in qua mensae prima recolitur huius institutio.*

Full-throated be our praise, boldly rung: a tune most fair be loudly sung: a joy of mind full fitting let us hear with glad resounding. • For solemn the day we strive to spend, wherein we seek our thoughts to lend to this sacred feast's glad primal and sacred founding.

In hac mensa novi Regis, novum Pascha novae legis Phase vetus terminat. • *Vetustatem novitas, umbram*

At the table of the King new-crowned, a new Passover, of new law most profound, the ancient Pasch fulfilled does prove. • The new puts the old to flight;

fugat veritas, noctem lux eliminat.

shadows flee, vanquished by truth's stern might. Light does night from mind, from heart in holy haste remove.

Quod in caena Christus gessit, faciendum hoc expressit in sui memoriam. • *Docti sacris institutis, panem, vinum in salutis consecramus hostiam.*

What the Lord Christ at his banquet with might did do, He commanded be done by the Apostles, by others too, in memory of his word, his mission, his life. • Thus by mandate taught divine, we too take bread, we too take wine. We consecrate: lo, they are salvation's offering, its victim, atonement-rife.

Dogma datur Christianis, quod in carnem transit panis, et vinum in sanguinem. • *Quod non capis, quod non vides, animosa firmat fides, praeter rerum ordinem.*

A teaching firm and clear we Christians do receive: bread has changed, has flesh become though eye might seem deceived; and in what once was wine are we his blood now given. • You do not understand? You do not perceive? These truths a lively faith will help you boldly to believe, though far outside life's scope and normal rhythm.

Sub diversis speciebus, signis tantum, et non rebus, latent res eximiae. • *Caro cibus, sanguis potus: manet tamen Christus totus, sub utraque specie.*

Thus, under seeming bread hid, under seeming wine--symbols only these, not reality divine--there lie mysteries untold, mysteries sublime. • Flesh is food, blood is drink--yet let none hesitate to think that in each appearance there be the Christ, whole, entire, God divine.

A sumente non concisus, non confractus, non divisus: integer accipitur. • *Sumit unus, sumunt mille: quantum isti, tantum ille: nec sumptus consumitur.*

Do you receive him? His body you do not destroy, nor in dismemb'ring part unto part your strength employ: undivided, whole, entire does he to each receiver come full real. • One receives; receive also do numbers yet untold. No more receive the many than the one, we are bound to hold; nor is the food consumed by being the meal.

Sumunt boni, sumunt mali: sorte tamen inequali, vitae vel interitus. • *Mors est malis, vita bonis: vide paris sumptionis quam sit dispar exitus.*

That the good receive, our senses tell; and receive do sinners as well--but with outcome now fair, now fell: life for the one, for the other hellfire-bearing. • Death the meed for the Satan-souled, life eternal for whoso grasps for heaven's goal. Look ye: an outcome with difference untold, though of the same meal sharing.

Fracto demum sacramento, ne vacilles, sed memento, tantum

Finally, when the sign shall broken lie, waver not: in mind's eye keep clear that under seeming piece doth *esse sub fragmento, quantum toto tegitur.* • *Nulla rei fit scissura, signi tantum fit fractura: qua nec status nec statura signati minuitur.*

lie as much as under the whole: essence full, essence divine. • No dividing of the signified can there be; only a breaking of the sign we see--neither nature nor state therein dare we to lesser plane consign.

Ecce panis angelorum, factus cibus viatorum: vere panis filiorum, non mittendus canibus. • *In figuris praesignatur, cum Isaac immolatur: agnus paschae deputatur: datur manna patribus.*

Lo, bread by angels adored, admired, becomes food of wayfarers weary and tired--in full truth the bread of daughters and sons God-sired: not for dogs and animals provided. • In types and figures clear foretold, when Isaac became the sacrifice of faith full bold, when the lamb of the passover was chosen of old, when toward the ancient ones the manna-dew's fall was guided.

Bone Pastor, panis vere, Iesu, nostri miserere: tu nos pasce, nos tuere: tu nos bona fac videre in terra viventium. • *Tu, qui cuncta scis et vales: qui nos pascis hic mortales: tuos ibi commensales, coheredes et sodales fac sanctorum civium. Amen.*

Shepherd most good, divine bread most true, Jesus God, give unto us that pity whereby you grant us our food, grant us protection anew, grant us that divine reward to view that is found in the land of the saved solely. • All things you ken and can; you nourish on earth mortal woman, mortal man: in the holy place of heav'n's land, make us, by your gracious, loving command, your guests, heirs with you, companions of your friends most holy. Amen.

STABAT MATER DOLOROSA

THE MOTHER STAYED STANDING, IN SORROW RENT

Stabat Mater dolorosa, iuxta crucem lacrimosa, dum pendebat Filius. • *Cuius animam gementem, contristatam et dolentem, pertransivit gladius.*

She stayed standing there, the Mother, in sorrow rent; next to the cross, lo, with bitter tears o'ercome, sadness-bent, while on that rood there hung her Son. • In her grieving spirit, sore afflicted and vast empained, has a slashing, sadding sword of sorrow been soul-blood stained.

O quam tristis et afflicta fuit illa benedicta mater Unigeniti! • *Quae maerebat et dolebat pia mater dum videbat Nati poenas incliti.*

O, how grieved, how sore beset that most holy Mother of the One whom alone saw fit the Father to beget as beloved, sole-born Son. • O, how sad, how heavy of heart that dutiful Mother, who painful gaze must needs impart on the torments of her glorious Son.

Quis est homo qui non fleret, matrem Christi si videret in tanto supplicio? • *Quis non posset contristari, Christi matrem contemplari dolentem cum Filio?*

Who be the man, the woman so cold as not to weep, Christ's mother to behold in straits so awful, in suffering untold? • Who could fail to sorrow in turn, on pondering the mother of the Christic One, as grieves she for her only Son?

Pro peccatis suae gentis vidit Iesum in tormentis et flagellis subditum. • *Vidit suum dulcem Natum moriendo desolatum, dum emisit spiritum.*

For the sins of her own kind and her own race did she her Jesus in torment find, fated fell tortures bravely to embrace. • She gazed on him: beloved Son, in dying undone, as sent He forth his spirit soul.

Eia, Mater, fons amoris, me sentire vim doloris fac ut tecum lugeam. • *Fac ut ardeat cor meum in amando Christum Deum, ut sibi complaceam.*

Lo, O Mother, font of love for us on earth, make me feel sharp sorrow's dearth, that with you I too might grieve. Make it be that soul of mine might blaze in love for Christ divine: so might I, too, be pleasing unto Him.

Sancta Mater, istud agas, Crucifixi fige plagas cordi meo valide. • *Tui nati vulnerati, tam dignati pro me pati, poenas mecum divide.*

Mother most holy, grant this to me your son: the wounds of the Crucified One--stamp them in my heart ineradicably. • Grant to me a share of the sufferings of your Child, wounded, deemed so suited to be so meek, so mild, as to suffer for a sinner like me.

Fac me tecum pie flere, Crucifixo condolere, donec ego vixero. • *Iuxta crucem tecum stare, ac me tibi sociare in planctu desidero.*

Grant me truly to weep, with you bitterly to sigh, to cry: make me sorrow with your Crucified One, till at last I come to die. • Placed next to the cross with you to stand, in grief with you to be yoked: your hand, my hand: for this I long.

Virgo virginum praeclara, mihi iam non sis amara; fac me tecum plangere. • *Fac ut portem Christi mortem; passionis fac consortem et plagas recolere.*

Virgin, of all virgins greatest in renown, turn thou now not to me fierce-wrathed in frown; make me, rather, a sharer in your grief. • To carry that death of Christ, that death accepted so free: to share in his cruel passion grant thou me, and to bear anew his wounds.

Fac me plagis vulnerari, fac me cruce inebriari et cruore Filii. • *Flammis urar ne succensus, per te, Virgo, sim defensus in die iudicii.* • *[Fac me cruce custodiri, morte Christi praemuniri, confoveri gratia.]*

By wounds of his proud marked, may I drink to its dregs that cup of the cross so stark, the blood shed by Him who was and is your Son. • In flames eternal let me not be enfired; through you, O Virgin, may I find the safe harbor I have desired for the dreaded day of judgment divine. • [Make me: by Christ's cross safeguarded, by Christ's death true warded, by his grace be cherished lovingly.]

Christe, cum sit hinc exire, da per Matrem me venire ad palmam victoriae. • *Quando corpus morietur, fac ut animae donetur paradisi gloria. Amen.*

Christ God, when time shall come for me to leave this life and come to Thee, grant that through Mother of Thine I may come to great reward divine. • When this mortal body of mine shall come to sentence of death, grant that to soul of mine may be given the breath of glory eternal in Paradise. Amen.

VENI SANCTE SPIRITUS

COME, MOST HOLY SPIRIT OF LOVE

*Veni, Sancte Spiritus,
et emitte caelitus
lucis tuae radium.*

Come, most holy Spirit of Love; from your bliss'd heaven above send forth the blazing brilliance of your light divine.

*Veni, pater pauperum,
veni, dator munerum,
veni, lumen cordium.*

Come, father of the poor, rich-gifting; come, giver of heaven's boon engracing, uplifting; come, thy light into darksorrowed hearts to shine.

*Consolator optime,
dulcis hospes animae,
dulce refrigerium.*

Comforter whom all must needs exalt, soul-host whom none may dare to fault, Consoler most pleasing, Consoler most benign.

*In labore requies,
in aestu temperies,
in fletu solacium.*

Midst labor you are welcome rest; midst heat of day cool refreshment blest; in time of grief, calm and comfort for sad soul-pine.

*O lux beatissima,
reple cordis intima
tuorum fidelium.*

Light most blessed, light most rare, fill the inmost hearts, calm the stressed care of the faithful people you have created to be thine.

*Sine tuo nomine,
nihil est in homine,
nihil est innoxium.*

Hide thou thy godhead, hide thou thy power: nothing left is there in humans' brief hour, nothing hurtless in bleak life's time.

*Lava quod est sordidum,
riga quod est aridum,
sana quod est saucium.*

Wash thou the blemished, wash thou the soiled; dampen the encrusted, the endusted, the parched-spoiled; heal thou the soul that lies wounded: his, hers, theirs, and mine.

Flecte quod est rigidum,
fove quod est frigidum,
rege quod est devium.

Grant gentle surrender to the harshhearted, grant kindly healing; thy warming love give to the cold, the unfeeling; the struggling straying direct back sagely into heaven-line.

Da tuis fidelibus,
in te confidentibus,
sacrum septenarium.

To thy people, thy name in faith loud-crying, to thy children, in thee full trusting, whole relying, thy gifts: O, of that sacred seven grant them deeply to drink, satefully, gratefully to dine.

Da virtutis meritum,
da salutis exitum,
da perenne gaudium. Amen.

Grant them the reward of an earth life virtue-led; grant them at salvation's table to be heaven-fed; let them drink their fill of eternal life's blest wine. Amen.

VICTIMAE PASCHALI

TO THE PASCHAL VICTIM

Victimae paschali laudes immolent Christiani. Agnus redemit oves: Christus innocens Patri reconciliavit peccatores. Mors et vita duello conflixere mirando: dux vitae mortuus regnat vivus.

To the Passover Victim let Christians render their praise. The Lamb has ransomed the sheep that had strayed: the Anointed One, the Innocent One, has reunited the doers of sin with the Father on High. Death and life have struggled in warfare most wondrous: life's leader, once slain, now reigns alive once more.

Dic nobis, Maria, quid vidisti in via?

Tell us, O Mary: what saw you as you went upon your way?

Sepulcrum Christi viventis: et gloriam vidi resurgentis, angelicos testes, sudarium et vestes.Surrexit Christus spes mea: praecedet vos in Galileam.

The tomb used by the Christ who now lives saw I; and the glory of the Christ who now rises from the dead, the angel witnesses, the cloth once o'er his face, and the wrappings in the tomb did I espy. Christ my hope has arisen: He shall go before you into Galilee.

Scimus Christum surrexisse a mortuis vere: tu nobis, victor Rex, miserere. Amen; Alleluia!

Now we hold certain that Christ has indeed arisen from the dead; may You, who are, lo: King Victorious, take merciful pity upon us. Amen. Alleluia!

OREMUS

Speaking with God

in the

Words of the Roman Rite

III

The Prefaces

LIST OF PREFACES

1. Advent #1	P. 328
2. Advent #2	328
3. Christmas #1	329
4. Christmas #2	329
5. Christmas #3	329
6. Epiphany	330
7. Lent #1	330
8. Lent #2	331
9. Lent #3	331
10. Lent #4	331
11. First Sunday of Lent	332
12. Second Sunday of Lent	332
13. Third Sunday of Lent	333
14. Fourth Sunday in Lent	333
15. Fifth Sunday in Lent	333
16. Passion #1	334
17. Passion #2	334
18. Passion (Palm) Sunday	335
19. Chrism Mass	335
20. Easter #1	336
21. Easter #2	336
22. Easter #3	337
23. Easter #4	337
24. Easter #5	337
25. Ascension #1	338
26. Ascension #2	338
27. Pentecost Sunday	339
28. Most Holy Trinity	339
29. Sacred Heart	340
30. Sundays of the Year #1	340
31. Sundays of the Year #2	341
32. Sundays of the Year #3	341
33. Sundays of the Year #4	342
34. Sundays of the Year #5	342
35. Sundays of the Year #6	342
36. Sundays of the Year #7	343
37. Sundays of the Year #8	343
38. Holy Eucharist #1	344
39. Holy Eucharist #2	344
40. Holy Spirit #1	345
41. Holy Spirit #2	345
42. Blessed Virgin Mary #1	346
43. Blessed Virgin Mary #2	P. 346
44. B.V.M. Mother of the Church	347
45. Angels	347
46. Saint Joseph	348
47. Apostles #1	348
48. Apostles #2	349
49. Saints #1	349
50. Saints #2	350
51. Martyrs	350
52. Pastors	350
53. Holy Virgins and Religious	351
54. Common #1	351
55. Common #2	352
56. Common #3	352
57. Common #4	352
58. Common #5	353
59. Common #6	353
60. Dead #1	353
61. Dead #2	354
62. Dead #3	354
63. Dead #4	355
64. Dead #5	355
65. Immaculate Conception	355
66. Baptism of the Lord	356
67. Presentation of the Lord	356
68. Annunciation	357
69. Saint John the Baptist	357
70. Saints Peter and Paul	358
71. Transfiguration	358
72. Assumption of B.V.M.	359
73. Exaltation of the Holy Cross	359
74. All Saints	360
75. Christ the King	360
76. Dedication of a Church #A	361
77. Dedication of a Church #B	361
78. Dedication of a Church #C	362
79. Dedication of an Altar	362
80. Celebration of Marriage #A	363
81. Celebration of Marriage #B	364
82. Celebration of Marriage #C	364
83. Religious Profession	365
84. Unity of Christians	365

ADVENT PREFACE #1
The Two Comings of Christ

ADVENT PREFACE #2
The Two-Fold Waiting for Christ

(De Duobus Adventibus Christi:) Vere dignum et iustum est, aequum et salutare, nos tibi semper et ubique gratias agere: Domine, sancte Pater, omnipotens aeterne Deus: per Christum Dominum nostrum.

Qui, primo adventu in humilitate carnis assumptae, dispositionis antiquae munus implevit, nobisque salutis perpetuae tramitem reseravit: ut, cum secundo venerit in suae gloria maiestatis, manifesto demum munere capiamus, quod vigilantes nunc audemus exspectare promissum.

Et ideo cum Angelis et Archangelis, cum Thronis et Dominationibus, cumque omni militia caelestis exercitus, hymnum gloriae tuae canimus, sine fine dicentes:

(De Duplici Exspectatione Christi:) Vere dignum et iustum est, aequum et salutare, nos tibi semper et ubique gratias agere: Domine, sancte Pater, omnipotens aeterne Deus: per Christum Dominum nostrum.

Quem praedixerunt cunctorum praeconia prophetarum, Virgo Mater ineffabili dilectione sustinuit, Ioannes cecinit affaturum et adesse monstravit. Qui suae nativitatis mysterium tribuit nos praevenire gaudentes, ut et in oratione pervigiles et in suis inveniat laudibus exsultantes.

Et ideo cum Angelis et Archangelis, cum Thronis et Dominationibus, cumque omni militia caelestis exercitus, hymnum gloriae tuae canimus, sine fine dicentes:

It is, indeed, fitting and right, it is just, it leads to salvation: that at all times and in all places we should render grateful thanks to you, Lord, most holy Father, all-powerful and ageless God, through Christ our Lord.

By his first coming, in lowly human flesh assumed, he fulfilled the task the ancient covenant assigned, and unlocked for us the way of life that leads to eternal salvation: so that, when for a second time he shall come, then in the glory of his divine majesty, we may at last receive the shining gift of that favor for which, as we keep watch, we now but dare to hope, as for a promised boon.

Thus it is that, in company with the Angels, the Archangels, the Thrones, the Dominations, in company with the entire host of the heavenly army, we sing our song of praise to your glory, chanting without ceasing:

It is, indeed, fitting and right, it is just, it leads to salvation: that at all times and in all places we should render grateful thanks to you, Lord, most holy Father, all-powerful and ageless God, through Christ our Lord.

The watchful cries of all the prophets told of him; the Virgin Mother bore him with a love that knew no sound or word. John foretold that he was coming, and proclaimed him after he arrived. He granted us the privilege of joyously awaiting the mystery of his holy birth, so that as he came he might discover us watchful in prayer and joyful at heart as we sing our praises of him.

Thus it is that, in company with the Angels, the Archangels, the Thrones, the Dominations, in company with the entire host of the heavenly army, we sing our song of praise to your glory, chanting without ceasing:

CHRISTMAS PREFACE #1
Christ the Light

(De Christo Luce:) *Vere dignum et iustum est, aequum et salutare, nos tibi semper et ubique gratias agere: Domine, sancte Pater, omnipotens aeterne Deus:*

Quia per incarnati Verbi mysterium nova mentis nostrae oculis lux tuae claritatis infulsit: ut, dum visibiliter Deum cognoscimus, per hunc in invisibilium amorem rapiamur.

Et ideo cum Angelis et Archangelis, cum Thronis et Dominationibus, cumque omni militia caelestis exercitus, hymnum gloriae tuae canimus, sine fine dicentes:

It is, indeed, fitting and right, it is just, it leads to salvation: that at all times and in all places we should render grateful thanks to you, Lord, most holy Father, all-powerful and ageless God:

For, by means of the mystery of your Word enfleshed, a new degree of the radiance of your own splendor has been added to what our mind's eye perceives, so that even as we come to know this God who has become visible, we might through Him be swept up as well into a love of things that are not visible.

Thus it is that, in company with the Angels, the Archangels, the Thrones, the Dominations, in company with the entire host of the heavenly army, we sing our song of praise to your glory, chanting without ceasing:

CHRISTMAS PREFACE #2
*The Restoration of
All Things in the Incarnation*

(De Restauratione Universa in Incarnatione:) *Vere dignum et iustum est, aequum et salutare, nos tibi semper et ubique gratias agere: Domine, sancte Pater, omnipotens aeterne Deus: per Christum Dominum nostrum.*

Qui, in huius venerandi festivitate mysterii, invisibilis in suis, visibilis in nostris apparuit, et ante tempora genitus esse coepit in tempore; ut, in se erigens cuncta deiecta, in integrum restitueret universa, et hominem perditum ad caelestia regna revocaret.

Unde et nos, cum omnibus Angelus, te laudamus, iucunda celebratione clamantes:

It is, indeed, fitting and right, it is just, it leads to salvation: that at all times and in all places we should render grateful thanks to you, Lord, most holy Father, all-powerful and ageless God, through Christ our Lord.

On the feast of this most awesome mystery, it is He who was made manifest: able to be seen in the world where we live, though not--by human eye--in the realm that is His: begotten before the ages began, but now beginning a life bounded by time: all this so that, raising up within himself everything that had been crushed down, he might restore all things to unity, and summon the lost human race back to the kingdom of heaven.

And thus we too, with all the Angel hosts, praise you, singing in happiness and joy:

CHRISTMAS PREFACE #3
*The Holy Exchange Wrought by
the Incarnation of the Word*

(De Commercio in Incarnatione Verbi:) *Vere dignum et iustum est, aequum et salutare, nos tibi semper et ubique gratias agere: Domine, sancte Pater, omnipotens aeterne Deus: per Christum Dominum nostrum.*

Per quem hodie commercium nostrae reparationis effulsit, quia, dum nostra fragilitas a tuo Verbo suscipitur, humana mortalitas non solum in perpetuum transit honorem, sed nos quoque, mirando consortio, reddit aeternos.

Et ideo, choris angelicis sociati, te laudamus in gaudio confitentes:

It is, indeed, fitting and right, it is just, it leads to salvation: that at all times and in all places we should render grateful thanks to you, Lord, most holy Father, all-powerful and ageless God: through Christ our Lord.

Through him the holy exchange that is our ransom from sin is today made clear: as your Word takes unto Himself our sinful weakness, not only is our mortal human nature itself promoted to a state of everlasting honor, but, because of the marvelous unity it now shares with the divine, that human nature renders us deathless as well.

And therefore, joined with choirs of angels, we praise and proclaim you in joy:

EPIPHANY PREFACE
Christ the Light of the Nations

(De Christo Lumine Gentium:) Vere dignum et iustum est, aequum et salutare, nos tibi semper et ubique gratias agere: Domine, sancte Pater, omnipotens aeterne Deus:
Quia ipsum in Christo salutis nostrae mysterium hodie ad lumen gentium revelasti, et, cum in substantia nostrae mortalitatis apparuit, nova nos immortalitatis eius gloria reparasti.
Et ideo cum Angelis et Archangelis, cum Thronis et Dominationibus, cumque omni militia caelestis exercitus, hymnum gloriae tuae canimus, sine fine dicentes:

It is, indeed, fitting and right, it is just, it leads to salvation: that at all times and in all places we should render grateful thanks to you, Lord, most holy Father, all-powerful and ageless God.

For today you have made known the mystery of our redemption in Christ, so that it might be a beacon to the nations; moreover, when He appeared in our nature's mortal frame, then with the new splendor of his own immortality did you restore us to life unending.

Thus it is that, in company with the Angels, the Archangels, the Thrones, the Dominations, in company with the entire host of the heavenly army, we sing our song of praise to your glory, chanting without ceasing:

LENTEN PREFACE #1
The Spiritual Meaning of Lent

(De Spiritali Significatione Quadragesimae:) Vere dignum et iustum est, aequum et salutare, nos tibi semper et ubique gratias agere: Domine, sancte Pater, omnipotens aeterne Deus: per Christum Dominum nostrum.
Quia fidelibus tuis dignanter concedis quotannis paschalia sacramenta in gaudio purificatis mentibus exspectare: ut, pietatis officia et opera caritatis propensius exsequentes, frequentatione mysteriorum, quibus renati sunt, ad gratiae filiorum plenitudinem perducantur.
Et ideo cum Angelis et Archangelis, cum Thronis et Dominationibus, cumque omni militia caelestis exercitus, hymnum gloriae tuae canimus, sine fine dicentes:

It is, indeed, fitting and right, it is just, it leads to salvation: that at all times and in all places we should render grateful thanks to you, Lord, most holy Father, all-powerful and ageless God.

Each year you see fit to grant that your faithful ones should await the paschal mysteries with joyful hope and with cleansed heart: thus, as they perform ever more readily the duties and deeds that a faith-filled charity requires, they may, by their frequent sharing in the mysteries whereby they are reborn, be brought to the fullness of the grace that belongs to them as heirs.

Thus it is that, in company with the Angels, the Archangels, the Thrones, the Dominations, in company with the entire host of the heavenly army, we sing our song of praise to your glory, chanting without ceasing:

LENTEN PREFACE #2
Spiritual Penance

(De Spiritali Paenitentia:) Vere dignum et iustum est, aequum et salutare, nos tibi semper et ubique gratias agere: Domine, sancte Pater, omnipotens aeterne Deus:

Qui filiis tuis, ad reparandam mentium puritatem, tempus praecipuum salubriter statuisti, quo, mente ab inordinatis affectibus expedita, sic incumberent transituris ut rebus potius perpetuis inhaererent.

Et ideo, cum Sanctis et Angelis universis, te collaudamus, sine fine dicentes:

It is, indeed, fitting and right, it is just, it leads to salvation: that at all times and in all places we should render grateful thanks to you, Lord, most holy Father, all-powerful and ageless God.

In concern for the well-being of your children, you have established a special time, so that their cleanness of heart might be restored; this you did so that, during that time, their spirits might be freed from disordered longings, and they would come to make use of passing things in such a way that their attention might rather be fastened upon things that are eternal.

And so, with all the Saints and Angels, we sing your praises, chanting without ceasing:

LENTEN PREFACE #3
The Benefits of Abstinence

(De Fructibus Abstinentiae:) Vere dignum et iustum est, aequum et salutare, nos tibi semper et ubique gratias agere: Domine, sancte Pater, omnipotens aeterne Deus:

Qui nos per abstinentiam tibi gratias referre voluisti, ut ipsa et nos peccatores ab insolentia mitigaret, et, egentium proficiens alimento, imitatores tuae benignitatis efficeret.

Et ideo, cum innumeris Angelis, una te magnificamus laudis voce, dicentes:

It is, indeed, fitting and right, it is just, it leads to salvation: that at all times and in all places we should render grateful thanks to you, Lord, most holy Father, all-powerful and ageless God.

You have willed that we should show our gratitude to you by means of our abstinence, so that abstinence itself might both draw us sinners back from pride's haughty arrogance and, providing as it does the benefit of sustenance for the needy, might cause us to imitate your own kindly generosity.

And so, with uncountable Angels, we glorify you with but a single voice of praise, saying:

LENTEN PREFACE #4
The Benefits of Fasting

(De Fructibus Ieiunii:) Vere dignum et iustum est, aequum et salutare, nos tibi semper et ubique gratias agere: Domine, sancte Pater, omnipotens aeterne Deus:

Qui corporali ieiunio vitia comprimis, mentem elevas, virtutem largiris et praemia: per Christum Dominum nostrum.

Per quem maiestatem tuam laudant Angeli, adorant Dominationes, tremunt Potestates, Caeli caelorumque Virtutes, ac beata Seraphim, socia exsultatione concelebrant. Cum quibus et nostras voces ut admitti iubeas, deprecamur, supplici confessione dicentes:

It is, indeed, fitting and right, it is just, it leads to salvation: that at all times and in all places we should render grateful thanks to you, Lord, most holy Father, all-powerful and ageless God.

By means of bodily fasting you suppress evil deeds, you raise the mind to higher things, you bestow virtuous conduct and its reward: through Christ our Lord.

Through Him the Angels praise your divine majesty, the Dominations adore it, the Powers tremble before it. The Heavens and the Virtues of Heaven, as also the holy Seraphim, give praise to it in shared joy. We ask that you bid our voices to be joined with all these, so as to sing in humble profession of praise:

It is, indeed, fitting and right, it is just, it leads to salvation: that at all times and in all places we should render grateful thanks to you, Lord, most holy Father, all-powerful and ageless God: through Christ our Lord.

Throughout forty days, by not eating earthly food, he established fasting as the way in which this observance was to be kept, and in overcoming all the snares of the ancient serpent, he taught us to conquer the leaven of evil: thus, in observing the paschal mystery with hearts purified and worthy, we might at length come to the paschal feast that has no end.

And so, with hosts of Angels and Saints alike, we sing a hymn of praise to you, chanting without ceasing:

PREFACE FOR THE SECOND SUNDAY IN LENT
The Transfiguration of the Lord

(De Transfiguratione Domini:) Vere dignum et iustum est, aequum et salutare, nos tibi semper et ubique gratias agere: Domine, sancte Pater, omnipotens aeterne Deus: per Christum Dominum nostrum.

Qui, propria morte praenuntiata discipulis, in monte sancto suam eis aperuit claritatem, ut per passionem, etiam lege prophetisque testantibus, ad gloriam resurrectionis perveniri constat.

Et ideo cum caelorum Virtutibus in terris te iugiter celebramus, maiestati tuae sine fine clamantes:

PREFACE FOR THE FIRST SUNDAY IN LENT
The Tempting of the Lord

(De Tentatione Domini:) Vere dignum et iustum est, aequum et salutare, nos tibi semper et ubique gratias agere: Domine, sancte Pater, omnipotens aeterne Deus: per Christum Dominum nostrum.

Qui quadraginta diebus, terrenis abstinens alimentis, formam huius observantiae ieiunio dedicavit, et, omnes evertens antiqui serpentis insidias, fermentum malitiae nos docuit superare, ut, paschale mysterium dignis mentibus celebrantes, ad pascha demum perpetuum transeamus.

Et ideo cum Angelorum atque Sanctorum turba hymnum laudis tibi canimus, sine fine dicentes:

It is, indeed, fitting and right, it is just, it leads to salvation: that at all times and in all places we should render grateful thanks to you, Lord, most holy Father, all-powerful and ageless God, through Christ our Lord.

Once He had told his disciples of the death He himself was to undergo,

He showed them his own divine radiance on the holy mountain, so that it might be clear to them that it was through the passion--as even the Law and the Prophets bore witness--that the way led to the glory of the resurrection.

And so, in union with the Powers of heaven, we on earth sing your ceaseless praises, chanting without end a hymn to your divine majesty:

PREFACE FOR THE THIRD SUNDAY IN LENT
(When the Gospel passage about the Samaritan woman is read)

The Samaritan Woman

(De Samaritana:) Vere dignum et iustum est, aequuum et salutare, nos tibi semper et ubique gratias agere: Domine, sancte Pater, omnipotens aeterne Deus: per Christum Dominum nostrum.

Qui, dum aquae sibi petiit potum a Samaritana praeberi, iam in ea fidei donum ipse creaverat, et ita eius fidem sitire dignatus est, ut ignem in illa divini amoris accenderet.

Unde et nos tibi gratias agimus, et tuas virtutes cum Angelis praedicamus, dicentes:

It is, indeed, fitting and right, it is just, it leads to salvation: that at all times and in all places we should render grateful thanks to you, Lord, most holy Father, all-powerful and ageless God, through Christ our Lord.

Even as He asked that a drink of water be brought to him by the Samaritan woman, He had himself brought forth in her the gift of faith, and He graciously granted that her faith should experience such a thirst that it would awaken within her the fire of divine love.

And so we too give thanks to you, and in company with the Angels we proclaim your mighty works, chanting:

PREFACE FOR THE FOURTH SUNDAY IN LENT
(When the Gospel passage about the man born blind is read)

The Man Born Blind

(De Caeco Nato:) Vere dignum et iustum est, aequuum et salutare, nos tibi semper et ubique gratias agere: Domine, sancte Pater, omnipotens aeterne Deus: per Christum Dominum nostrum.

Qui genus humanum, in tenebris ambulans, ad fidei claritatem per mysterium incarnationis adduxit, et, qui servi peccati veteris nascebantur, per lavacrum regenerationis in filios adoptionis assumpsit.

Propter quod caelestia tibi atque terrestria canticum novum concinunt adorando, et nos, cum omni exercitu Angelorum, proclamamus, sine fine dicentes:

It is, indeed, fitting and right, it is just, it leads to salvation: that at all times and in all places we should render grateful thanks to you, Lord, most holy Father, all-powerful and ageless God, through Christ our Lord.

While men and women walked in darkness and shadow, He led them to the brightness of faith through the mystery of the Incarnation; those who found themselves born as slaves to the ancient sin He promoted to the dignity of heirs by the bath of rebirth.

Because of this, both heaven and earth sing to you a new song in their adoration; we too, with the entire host of the Angels, proclaim you, chanting without ceasing:

PREFACE FOR THE FIFTH SUNDAY IN LENT
(When the Gospel passage about Lazarus is read)

Lazarus

(De Lazaro:) Vere dignum et iustum est, aequuum et salutare, nos tibi semper et ubique

gratias agere: Domine, sancte Pater, omnipotens aeterne Deus: per Christum Dominum nostrum.

Ipse enim verus homo Lazarum flevit amicum, et Deus aeternus e tumulo suscitavit, qui humani generis miseratus, ad novam vitam sacris mysteriis nos adducit.

Per quem maiestatem tuam adorat exercitus Angelorum, ante conspectum tuum in aeternitate laetantium. Cum quibus et nostras voces ut admitti iubeas, deprecamur, socia exsultatione dicentes:

It is, indeed, fitting and right, it is just, it leads to salvation: that at all times and in all places we should render grateful thanks to you, Lord, most holy Father, all-powerful and ageless God, through Christ our Lord.

As one who was completely human, He wept for Lazarus his friend, and as one who was the eternal God he raised him up from the grave; as one who has had mercy on the entire human race, He leads us to newness of life by means of these sacred mysteries.

Through Him the Angel host adores your divine majesty, rejoicing in your sight for ages without end. We ask that you bid our voices to be joined with theirs, so that we may sing as companions in their profession of praise:

PREFACE OF THE LORD'S PASSION #1
The Power of the Cross

(De Virtute Crucis:) Vere dignum et iustum est, aequum et salutare, nos tibi semper et ubique gratias agere: Domine, sancte Pater, omnipotens aeterne Deus:

Quia per Filii tui salutiferam passionem totus mundus sensum confitendae tuae maiestatis accepit, dum ineffabili crucis potentia iudicium mundi et potestas emicat Crucifixi.

Unde et nos, Domine, cum Angelis et Sanctis universis, tibi confitemur, in exsultatione dicentes:

It is, indeed, fitting and right, it is just, it leads to salvation: that at all times and in all places we should render grateful thanks to you, Lord, most holy Father, all-powerful and ageless God:

For by means of the saving suffering of your Son the entire world has come to understand what it means to proclaim your divine majesty, while through the unspeakable force of the Cross it becomes clear what judgment the world deserves, what mighty power the Crucified One wields.

And so we too, Lord, in union with all the Angels and Saints, proclaim you, chanting in joy:

PREFACE OF THE LORD'S PASSION #2
The Victory of the Passion

(De Victoria Passionis:) Vere dignum et iustum est, aequum et salutare, nos tibi semper et ubique gratias agere: Domine, sancte Pater, omnipotens aeterne Deus: per Christum Dominum nostrum.

Cuius salutiferae passionis et gloriosae resurrectionis dies appropinquare noscuntur, quibus et de antiqui hostis superbia triumphatur, et nostrae redemptionis recolitur sacramentum.

Per quem maiestatem tuam adorat exercitus Angelorum, ante conspectum tuum in aeternitate laetantium. Cum quibus et nostras voces ut admitti iubeas, deprecamur, socia exsultatione dicentes:

It is, indeed, fitting and right, it is just, it leads to salvation: that at all times and in all places we should render grateful thanks to you, Lord, most holy Father, all-powerful and ageless God.

We know that the days of his salvation-bringing passion and heavenly resurrection are drawing near; on those days is the haughty pride of the ancient foe overcome, and the sacred mystery of our redemption brought to mind.

Through Him the Angel host adores your divine majesty, rejoicing in your sight for ages without end. We ask that you bid our voices to be joined with all theirs, so that we may sing as companions in their profession of praise:

PREFACE FOR PASSION (PALM) SUNDAY
The Lord's Passion

(De Dominica Passione:) Vere dignum et iustum est, aequum et salutare, nos tibi semper et ubique gratias agere: Domine, sancte Pater, omnipotens aeterne Deus: per Christum Dominum nostrum.

Qui pati pro impiis dignatus est innocens, et pro sceleratis indebite condemnari. Cuius mors delicta nostra detersit, et iustificationem nobis resurrectio comparavit.

Unde et nos cum omnibus Angelis te laudamus, iucunda celebratione clamantes:

It is, indeed, fitting and right, it is just, it leads to salvation: that at all times and in all places we should render grateful thanks to you, Lord, most holy Father, all-powerful and ageless God: through Christ our Lord.

He saw fit to suffer for human guilt, innocent though He was, and to be condemned on behalf of the sin-stained, though no fault was his. His death washed away our sins, and his rising from the dead won justification for us.

And so, in company with all the Angels, we praise you, chanting in joyful celebration:

PREFACE FOR THE CHRISM MASS
Christ's Priesthood and the Ministry of Priests

(De Sacerdotio Christi et de Ministerio Sacerdotum:) Vere dignum et iustum est, aequum et salutare, nos tibi semper et ubique gratias agere: Domine, sancte Pater, omnipotens aeterne Deus:

Qui Unigenitum tuum Sancti Spiritus unctione novi et aeterni testamenti constituisti Pontificem, et ineffabili dignatus es dispositione sancire, ut unicum eius sacerdotium in Ecclesia servaretur. Ipse enim non solum regali sacerdotio populum acquisitionis exornat, sed etiam fraterna homines eligit bonitate, ut sacri sui ministerii fiant manuum impositione participes. Qui sacrificium renovent, eius nomine, redemptionis humanae, tuis apparantes filiis paschale convivium, et plebem tuam sanctam caritate praeveniant, verbo nutriant, reficiant sacramentis. Qui, vitam pro te fratrumque salute tradentes, ad ipsius Christi nitantur imaginem conformari, et constantes tibi fidem amoremque testentur.

Unde et nos, Domine, cum Angelis et Sanctis universis tibi confitemur, in exsultatione dicentes:

It is, indeed, fitting and right, it is just, it leads to salvation: that at all times and in all places we should render grateful thanks to you, Lord, most holy Father, all-powerful and ageless God.

By the anointing of the Holy Spirit, you established your only Son as High Priest of the new and everlasting covenant; and by your ineffable decree you saw fit to ordain that his unique priesthood would remain present in the Church. For not only did He adorn the people He gathered together with a royal priesthood; with a brother's generosity He chose certain ones who, by the imposition of hands, would share in his own sacred ministry. In his name, they would offer anew the sacrifice whereby the human race is redeemed; they would prepare the paschal banquet for your children; they would serve your holy people by their love, would nourish them with your Word, would refresh them with your Sacraments. Surrendering their own lives on your behalf and on behalf of the salvation of their brothers and sisters, they would strive to be formed into the very image of Christ himself, and would give firm testimony to you by their faith and their love.

And so, Lord, in the company of all the Angels and Saints, we praise you, proclaiming in joy:

EASTER PREFACE #1
The Paschal Mystery

(De Mysterio Paschali:) Vere dignum et iustum est, aequum et salutare, Te quidem, Domine, omni tempore confiteri, sed in hac potissimum nocte (die) (sed in hoc potissimum) gloriosius praedicare, cum Pascha nostrum immolatus est Christus.

Ipse enim verus est Agnus qui abstulit peccata mundi. Qui mortem nostram moriendo destruxit, et vitam resurgendo reparavit.

Quapropter, profusis paschalibus gaudiis, totus in orbe terrarum mundus exsultat. Sed et supernae virtutes atque angelicae potestates hymnum gloriae tuae concinunt, sine fine dicentes:

It is, indeed, fitting and right, it is just, it leads to salvation, Father and Lord, to give you thanks at all times, certainly; but it is especially proper (on this night) (on this day) (at this time) to sing your praises even more gloriously than ever, when Christ our Paschal Offering has been sacrificed.

For He is the true Lamb who has taken away the sins of the world. By dying himself He destroyed our death; by rising from the dead, He restored life to us.

And so the entire human race, throughout the whole world, pours out its paschal joy and rejoices. The Virtues on high too, and the Angelic Powers as well, sing a hymn to your glory, chanting without ceasing:

EASTER PREFACE #2
New Life in Christ

(De Vita Nova in Christo:) Vere dignum et iustum est, aequum et salutare, Te quidem, Domine, omni tempore confiteri, sed in hoc potissimum gloriosius praedicare, cum Pascha nostrum immolatus est Christus.

Per quem in aeternam vitam filii lucis oriuntur, et fidelibus regni caelestis atria reserantur. Quia mors nostra est eius morte redempta, et in eius resurrectione vita omnium resurrexit.

Quapropter, profusis paschalibus gaudiis, totus in orbe terrarum mundus exsultat. Sed et supernae virtutes atque angelicae potestates hymnum gloriae tuae concinunt, sine fine dicentes:

It is, indeed, fitting and right, it is just, it leads to salvation, Father and Lord, to give you thanks at all times, certainly; but it is especially proper at this time to sing your praises even more gloriously than ever, when Christ our Paschal Offering has been sacrificed.

Through Him the children of the light rise to eternal life, and for his faithful the halls of the heavenly kingdom are opened wide. For the death we are subject to is ransomed by his death; and in his resurrection the life of everyone has arisen.

And so the entire human race, throughout the whole world, pours out its paschal joy and rejoices. The Virtues on high, too, and the Angelic Powers as well, sing a hymn to your glory, chanting without ceasing:

EASTER PREFACE #3
Christ, Living and Ever Speaking on Our Behalf

(De Christo Vivente et Semper Interpellante pro Nobis:) Vere dignum et iustum est, aequum et salutare, Te quidem, Domine, omni tempore confiteri, sed in hoc potissimum gloriosius praedicare, cum Pascha nostrum immolatus est Christus.

Qui se pro nobis offerre non desinit, nosque apud te perenni advocatione defendit; qui immolatus iam non moritur, sed semper vivit occisus.

Quapropter, profusis paschalibus gaudiis, totus in orbe terrarum mundus exsultat. Sed et supernae virtutes atque angelicae potestates hymnum gloriae tuae concinunt, sine fine dicentes:

It is, indeed, fitting and right, it is just, it leads to salvation, Father and Lord, to give you thanks at all times, certainly; but it is especially proper at this time to sing your praises even more gloriously than ever, when Christ our Paschal Offering has been sacrificed.

Ceaselessly He offers himself for us; in your heavenly tribunal he defends us with advocacy unending. Once offered in sacrifice, He now dies no more; slain, He now lives for ever.

And so the entire human race, throughout the whole world, pours out its paschal joy and rejoices. The Virtues on high too, and the Angelic Powers as well, sing a hymn to your glory, chanting without ceasing:

EASTER PREFACE #4
The Restoration of the Entire World Through the Paschal Mystery

(De Restauratione Universi per Mysterium Paschale:) Vere dignum et iustum est, aequum et salutare, Te quidem, Domine, omni tempore confiteri, sed in hoc potissimum gloriosius praedicare, cum Pascha nostrum immolatus est Christus.

Qui, vetustate destructa, renovantur universa deiecta, et vitae nobis in Christo reparatur integritas.

Quapropter, profusis paschalibus gaudiis, totus in orbe terrarum mundus exsultat. Sed et supernae virtutes atque angelicae potestates hymnum gloriae tuae concinunt, sine fine dicentes:

It is, indeed, fitting and right, it is just, it leads to salvation, Father and Lord, to give you thanks at all times, certainly; but it is especially proper at this time to sing your praises even more gloriously than ever, when Christ our Paschal Offering has been sacrificed.

For what has been from of old is now cast out, and what has been long cast down is now made new; innocence of life is now restored to us once more in Christ.

And so the entire human race, throughout the whole world, pours out its paschal joy and rejoices. The Virtues on high, too, and the Angelic Powers as well, sing a hymn to your glory, chanting without ceasing:

EASTER PREFACE #5
Christ, Both Priest and Sacrificial Victim

(De Christo Sacerdote et Victima:) Vere dignum et iustum est, aequum et salutare, Te quidem, Domine, omni tempore confiteri, sed in hoc potissimum gloriosius praedicare, cum Pascha nostrum immolatus est Christus.

Qui, oblatione corporis sui, antiqua sacrificia in crucis veritate perfecit, et, seipsum tibi pro nostra salute commendans, idem sacerdos, altare, et agnus exhibuit.

Quapropter, profusis paschalibus gaudiis, totus in orbe terrarum mundus exsultat. Sed et supernae virtutes atque angelicae potestates hymnum gloriae tuae concinunt, sine fine dicentes:

It is, indeed, fitting and right, it is just, it leads to salvation, Father and

Lord, to give you thanks at all times, certainly; but it is especially proper at this time to sing your praises even more gloriously than ever, when Christ our Paschal Offering has been sacrificed.

By the offering of his own Body, He brought the ancient sacrifices to fulfillment in the reality that was the Cross; commending himself to you for our salvation, He showed himself to be at once priest, altar, and sacrificial victim.

And so the entire human race, throughout the whole world, pours out its paschal joy and rejoices. The Virtues on high, too, and the Angelic Powers as well, sing a hymn to your glory, chanting without ceasing:

For the Lord Jesus, the King of Glory, in triumphant victory over sin and death, rose (today) to the heights of the heavens, as the Angels looked on in wonder: Mediator between God and the human race, Judge of the World, Lord and Ruler of Powers, He rose not so as to abandon our lowly condition, but rather so that we, his members, might be assured that we would follow Him to the place where He, Head and Source of us all, had gone.

And so the entire human race, throughout the whole world, pours out its paschal joy and rejoices. The Virtues on high, too, and the Angelic Powers as well, sing a hymn to your glory, chanting without ceasing:

PREFACE OF THE ASCENSION #1
The Mystery of the Ascension

(De Mysterio Ascensionis:) *Vere dignum et iustum est, aequum et salutare, nos tibi semper et ubique gratias agere: Domine, sancte Pater, omnipotens aeterne Deus:*

Quia Dominus Iesus, Rex gloriae, peccati triumphator et mortis, mirantibus Angelis, ascendit (hodie) summa caelorum, Mediator Dei et hominum, Iudex mundi Dominusque virtutum; non ut a nostra humilitate discederet, sed ut illuc confideremus, sua membra, nos subsequi quo ipse, caput nostrum principiumque, praecessit.

Quapropter, profusis paschalibus gaudiis, totus in orbe terrarum mundus exsultat. Sed et supernae virtutes atque angelicae potestates hymnum gloriae tuae concinunt, sine fine dicentes:

It is, indeed, fitting and right, it is just, it leads to salvation: that at all times and in all places we should render grateful thanks to you, Lord, most holy Father, all-powerful and ageless God:

PREFACE OF THE ASCENSION #2
The Mystery of the Ascension

(De Mysterio Ascensionis:) *Vere dignum et iustum est, aequum et salutare, nos tibi semper et ubique gratias agere: Domine, sancte Pater, omnipotens aeterne Deus: per Christum Dominum nostrum.*

Qui post resurrectionem suam omnibus discipulis suis manifestus apparuit, et ipsis cernentibus est elevatus in caelum, ut nos divinitatis suae tribueret esse participes.

Quapropter, profusis paschalibus gaudiis, totus in orbe terrarum mundus exsultat. Sed et supernae virtutes atque angelicae potestates hymnum gloriae tuae concinunt, sine fine dicentes:

It is, indeed, fitting and right, it is just, it leads to salvation: that at all times and in all places we should render grateful thanks to you, Lord, most holy Father, all-powerful and ageless God: through Christ our Lord.

After his resurrection, He showed himself clearly to all his disciples; as they looked on, He was taken up into heaven, in order to grant that we might be given a share in his divinity.

And so the entire human race, throughout the whole world, pours out its paschal joy and rejoices. The Virtues on high, too, and the Angelic Powers as well, sing a hymn to your glory, chanting without ceasing:

PREFACE FOR PENTECOST SUNDAY
The Mystery of Pentecost

(De Mysterio Pentecostes:) *Vere dignum et iustum est, aequum et salutare, nos tibi semper et ubique gratias agere: Domine, sancte Pater, omnipotens aeterne Deus.*

Tu enim, sacramentum paschale consummans, quibus, per Unigeniti tui consortium, filios adoptionis esse tribuisti, hodie Spiritum Sanctum es largitus; qui, principio nascentis Ecclesiae, et cunctis gentibus scientiam indidit deitatis, et linguarum diversitatem in unius fidei confessione sociavit.

Quapropter, profusis paschalibus gaudiis, totus in orbe terrarum mundus exsultat. Sed et supernae virtutes atque angelicae potestates hymnum gloriae tuae concinunt, sine fine dicentes:

It is, indeed, fitting and right; it is just, it leads to salvation: that at all times and in all places we should render grateful thanks to you, Lord, most holy Father, all-powerful and ageless God:

For today, as you were bringing the Paschal Mystery to completion, you gave the Holy Spirit to those whom you had made your adopted children through their unity with your only-begotten Son. In turn, at the beginning of the young Church, the Holy Spirit imparted a knowledge of the divinity to all races of people, and gathered together a vast diversity of languages into the profession of but a single faith.

And so the entire human race, throughout the whole world, pours out its paschal joy and rejoices. The Virtues on high, too, and the Angelic Powers as well, sing a hymn to your glory, chanting without ceasing:

PREFACE OF THE HOLY TRINITY
The Mystery of the Most Holy Trinity

(De Mysterio Sanctissimae Trinitatis:) *Vere dignum et iustum est, aequum et salutare, nos tibi semper et ubique gratias agere: Domine, sancte Pater, omnipotens aeterne Deus:*

Qui cum unigenito Filio tuo et Spiritu Sancto unus es Deus, unus es Dominus: non in unius singularitate personae, sed in unius Trinitate substantiae. Quod enim de tua gloria, revelante te, credimus, hoc de Filio tuo, hoc de Spiritu Sancto, sine discretione sentimus. Ut, in confessione verae sempiternaeque Deitatis, et in personis proprietas, et in essentia unitas, et in maiestate adoretur aequalitas.

Quem laudant Angeli atque Archangeli, Cherubim quoque ac Seraphim, qui non cessant clamare cotidie, una voce dicentes:

It is, indeed, fitting and right, it is just, it leads to salvation: that at all times and in all places we should render grateful thanks to you, Lord, most holy Father, all-powerful and ageless God.

With your only-begotten Son and the Holy Spirit you are one God, you are one Lord: not in the uniqueness of a single person, but in the trinity of a single substance. For what we believe about you, because of your own revelation, that we understand to be true of your Son and of the Holy Spirit; no distinction is here to be made. Thus, in our profession of the true and eternal Godhead, we adore a distinctness of persons and a unity in essence, and a parity in majesty as well.

The Angels and Archangels adore you, as do the Cherubim and Seraphim; they cease not in their daily song of praise, chanting with but one voice:

PREFACE OF THE SACRED HEART
The Boundless Love of Christ

(*De Immensa Caritate Christi:*) *Vere dignum et iustum est, aequum et salutare, nos tibi semper et ubique gratias agere: Domine, sancte Pater, omnipotens aeterne Deus: per Christum Dominum nostrum.*

Qui, mira caritate, exaltatus in cruce, pro nobis tradidit semetipsum, atque de transfixo latere sanguinem fudit et aquam, ex quo manarent Ecclesiae sacramenta, ut omnes, ad Cor apertum Salvatoris attracti, iugiter haurirent e fontibus salutis in gaudio.

Et ideo, cum Sanctis et Angelis universis, te collaudamus, sine fine dicentes:

It is, indeed, fitting and right, it is just, it leads to salvation: that at all times and in all places we should render grateful thanks to you, Lord, most holy Father, all-powerful and ageless God: through Christ our Lord.

With love most wondrous, as lifted up on the Cross He hung, He handed himself over on our behalf, and from his pierced side He caused to pour forth blood and water, from whence would flow the sacraments of the Church; thus all people, drawn to the opened heart of the Savior, might ceaselessly drink with joy from the fountain of salvation.

And so, with all the Saints and Angels, we sing your praises, chanting without ceasing:

PREFACE FOR SUNDAYS THROUGHOUT THE YEAR, #1
The Paschal Mystery and the People of God

(*De Mysterio Paschali et de Populo Dei:*) *Vere dignum et iustum est, aequum et salutare, nos tibi semper et ubique gratias agere: Domine, sancte Pater, omnipotens et aeterne Deus: per Christum Dominum nostrum.*

Cuius hoc mirificum fuit opus per paschale mysterium, ut de peccato et mortis iugo ad hanc gloriam vocaremur, qua nunc genus electum, regale sacerdotium, gens sancta et acquisitionis populus diceremur, et tuas annuntiaremus ubique virtutes, qui nos de tenebris ad tuum admirabile lumen vocasti.

Et ideo cum Angelis et Archangelis, cum Thronis et Dominationibus, cumque omni militia caelestis exercitus, hymnum gloriae tuae canimus, sine fine dicentes:

It is, indeed, fitting and right, it is just, it leads to salvation: that at all times and in all places we should render grateful thanks to you, Lord, most holy Father, all-powerful and ageless God.

Through the paschal mystery, it was his marvelous accomplishment to summon us from sin and from the yoke of death to this glorious condition in which we are now termed a chosen race, a royal priesthood, a holy nation, the people of the purchase; and in which we now proclaim everywhere the power that belongs to you, who have called us forth from darkness into your own wondrous light.

Thus it is that, in company with the Angels, the Archangels, the Thrones, the Dominations, in company with the entire host of the heavenly army, we sing our song of praise to your glory, chanting without ceasing:

PREFACE FOR SUNDAYS THROUGHOUT THE YEAR, #2
The Mystery of Salvation

(De Mysterio Salutis:) Vere dignum et iustum est, aequum et salutare, nos tibi semper et ubique gratias agere: Domine, sancte Pater, omnipotens aeterne Deus: per Christum Dominum nostrum.

Qui, humanis miseratus erroribus, de Virgine nasci dignatus est. Qui, crucem passus, a perpetua morte nos liberavit et, a mortuis resurgens, vitam nobis donavit aeternam.

Et ideo cum Angelis et Archangelis, cum Thronis et Dominationibus, cumque omni militia caelestis exercitus, humnum gloriae tuae canimus, sine fine dicentes:

It is, indeed, fitting and right, it is just, it leads to salvation: that at all times and in all places we should render grateful thanks to you, Lord, most holy Father, all-powerful and ageless God, through Christ our Lord.

He took pity on human faults and sins, and saw fit to be born of the Virgin. He endured the Cross, and delivered us from deathless death; rising from the dead, He granted us life eternal.

Thus it is that, in company with the Angels, the Archangels, the Thrones, the Dominations, in company with the entire host of the heavenly army, we sing our song of praise to your glory, chanting without ceasing:

PREFACE FOR SUNDAYS THROUGHOUT THE YEAR, #3
A Human Brings Salvation to Humans

(De Salvatione Hominis per Hominem:) Vere dignum et iustum est, aequum et salutare, nos tibi semper et ubique gratias agere: Domine, sancte Pater, omnipotens aeterne Deus:

Ad cuius immensam gloriam pertinere cognoscimus ut mortalibus tua deitate succurreres; sed et nobis provideres de ipsa mortalitate nostra remedium, et perditos quosque unde perierant, inde salvares, per Christum Dominum nostrum.

Per quem maiestatem tuam adorat exercitus Angelorum, ante conspectum tuum in aeternitate laetantium. Cum quibus et nostras voces ut admitti iubeas, deprecamur, socia exsultatione dicentes:

It is, indeed, fitting and right, it is just, it leads to salvation: that at all times and in all places we should render grateful thanks to you, Lord, most holy Father, all-powerful and ageless God.

We know that it is part of your measureless glory that your godhead would come to the aid of your creatures, and that you would fashion a cure for us out of our own mortality itself; the lost, by exactly the same means whereby they had been lost, you would bring to salvation, through Christ our Lord.

Through Him the Angel host adores your divine majesty, rejoicing in your sight for ages without end. We ask that you bid our voices to be joined with all theirs, so that we may sing as companions in their profession of praise:

PREFACE FOR SUNDAYS THROUGHOUT THE YEAR, #4
The History of Salvation

(*De Historia Salutis:*) *Vere dignum et iustum est, aequum et salutare, nos tibi semper et ubique gratias agere: Domine, sancte Pater, omnipotens aeterne Deus: per Christum Dominum nostrum.*

Ipse enim nascendo vetustatem hominum renovavit, patiendo delevit nostra peccata, aeternae vitae aditum praestitit a mortuis resurgendo, ad te Patrem ascendendo caelestes ianuas reseravit.

Et ideo, cum Angelorum atque Sanctorum turba, hymnum laudis tibi canimus, sine fine dicentes:

It is, indeed, fitting and right, it is just, it leads to salvation: that at all times and in all places we should render grateful thanks to you, Lord, most holy Father, all-powerful and ageless God, through Christ our Lord.

For by his birth, He caused the ancient human condition to be made anew; by his suffering, He took away our sins. He granted us access to eternal life by his resurrection from the dead; and by ascending to you, Father most holy, He flung open wide the gates of heaven.

And so, with hosts of Angels and Saints alike, we sing a hymn of praise to you, chanting without ceasing:

PREFACE FOR SUNDAYS THROUGHOUT THE YEAR, #5
Creation

(*De Creatione:*) *Vere dignum et iustum est, aequum et salutare, nos tibi semper et ubique gratias agere: Domine, sancte Pater, omnipotens aeterne Deus:*

Qui omnia mundi elementa fecisti, et vices disposuisti temporum variari; hominem vero formasti ad imaginem tuam, et rerum ei subiecisti universa miracula, ut vicario munere dominaretur omnibus quae creasti, et in operum tuorum magnalibus iugiter te laudaret, per Christum Dominum nostrum.

Unde et nos cum omnibus Angelis te laudamus, iucunda celebratione clamantes:

It is, indeed, fitting and right, it is just, it leads to salvation: that at all times and in all places we should render grateful thanks to you, Lord, most holy Father, all-powerful and ageless God.

You have brought into being all the things that make up the world, and by your ordinance the seasons and times of the year come and go in turn. Men and women you made in your own image, and to their care you committed all the marvels of your creation, so that in your stead humans might hold sway over all you had made and might give you constant praise in the wonders of your works, through Christ our Lord.

And thus we too, with all the Angel hosts, praise you, singing in happiness and joy:

PREFACE FOR SUNDAYS THROUGHOUT THE YEAR, #6
The Promise of the Eternal Paschal Mystery

(*De Pignore Aeterni Paschatis:*) *Vere dignum et iustum est, aequum et salutare, nos tibi semper et ubique gratias agere: Domine, sancte Pater, omnipotens aeterne Deus:*

In quo vivimus, movemur, et sumus, atque in hoc corpore constituti non solum pietatis tuae cotidianos experimur effectus, sed aeternitatis etiam pignora iam tenemus. Primitias enim Spiritus habentes, per quem suscitasti Iesum a mortuis,

paschale mysterium speramus nobis esse perpetuum.

Unde et nos cum omnibus Angelis te laudamus, iucunda celebratione clamantes:

It is, indeed, fitting and right, it is just, it leads to salvation: that at all times and in all places we should render grateful thanks to you, Lord, most holy Father, all-powerful and ageless God.

In You we live, move, and have our being. Enfleshed as we are in these bodies of ours, not only do we have daily experience of your faithful goodness, but we also, even now, hold the pledge of eternal life. For we possess the first fruits of the Spirit, through Whom you raised Jesus from the dead; and we have hope that the paschal mystery will be an unending one for us.

And thus we too, with all the Angel hosts, praise you, singing in happiness and joy:

PREFACE FOR SUNDAYS THROUGHOUT THE YEAR, #7
Salvation Through the Obedience of Christ

(De Salute per Obedientiam Christi:) Vere dignum et iustum est, aequum et salutare, nos tibi semper et ubique gratias agere: Domine, sancte Pater, omnipotens aeterne Deus:

Quia sic mundum misericorditer dilexisti, ut ipsum nobis mitteres Redemptorem, quem absque peccato in nostra voluisti similitudine conversari, ut amares in nobis quod diligebas in Filio, cuius obedientia sumus ad tua dona reparati, quae per inobedientiam amiseramus peccando.

Unde et nos, Domine, cum Angelis et Sanctis universis tibi confitemur, in exsultatione dicentes:

It is, indeed, fitting and right, it is just, it leads to salvation: that at all times and in all places we should render grateful thanks to you, Lord, most holy Father, all-powerful and ageless God:

For in your mercy You loved the world so much that You sent us the sort of savior who, by your decree, would be kin to us in all ways save sin, so that you might love in us what you cherished in your Son, by whose obedience we are restored to your gifts, which through disobedience we had lost in sin.

And so we too, Lord, in union with all the Angels and Saints, proclaim you, chanting in joy:

PREFACE FOR SUNDAYS THROUGHOUT THE YEAR, #8
The Church, Unified by the Unity of the Trinity

(De Ecclesia Adunata ex Unitate Trinitatis:) Vere dignum et iustum est, aequum et salutare, nos tibi semper et ubique gratias agere: Domine, sancte Pater, omnipotens aeterne Deus:

Quia filios, quos longe peccati crimen abstulerat, per sanguinem Filii tui Spiritusque virtute, in unum ad te denuo congregare voluisti: ut plebs, de unitate Trinitatis adunata, in tuae laudem sapientiae multiformis Christi corpus templumque Spiritus nosceretur Ecclesia.

Et ideo, choris angelicis sociati, te laudamus in gaudio confitentes:

It is, indeed, fitting and right, it is just, it leads to salvation: that at all times and in all places we should render grateful thanks to you, Lord, most holy Father, all-powerful and ageless God:

For by the blood of your Son and the power of your Spirit You willed to gather together unto yourself in unity once more those children of yours whom the stain of sin had scattered far and wide. Thus a people would be made one by means of the unity of the Blessed Trinity, and would, to the praise of your manifold wisdom, be known as the Body of Christ, the Temple of the Holy Spirit: the Church.

And therefore, joined with choirs of Angels, we praise and proclaim you in joy:

his flesh, offered in sacrifice for us, we are strengthened; as we drink his blood, poured out on our behalf, we are washed clean.

Thus it is that, in company with the Angels, the Archangels, the Thrones, the Dominations, in company with the entire host of the heavenly army, we sing our song of praise to your glory, chanting without ceasing:

PREFACE OF THE HOLY EUCHARIST, #1
The Sacrifice and Sacrament of Christ

(De Sacrificio et de Sacramento Christi:) Vere dignum et iustum est, aequum et salutare, nos tibi semper et ubique gratias agere: Domine, sancte Pater, omnipotens aeterne Deus: per Christum Dominum nostrum.

Qui, verus aeternusque Sacerdos, formam sacrificii perennis instituens, hostiam tibi se primus obtulit salutarem, et nos, in sui memoriam, praecepit offerre. Cuius carnem pro nobis immolatam dum sumimus, roboramur, et fusum pro nobis sanguinem dum potamus, abluimur.

Et ideo cum Angelis et Archangelis, cum Thronis et Dominationibus, cumque omni militia caelestis exercitus, hymnum gloriae tuae canimus, sine fine dicentes:

It is, indeed, fitting and right, it is just, it leads to salvation: that at all times and in all places we should render grateful thanks to you, Lord, most holy Father, all-powerful and ageless God, through Christ our Lord.

As true and eternal Priest, He established what sort of lasting sacrifice there would be. First He offered himself to you as a saving victim, and then He commanded us to offer that same sacrifice in memory of Him. As we eat

PREFACE OF THE HOLY EUCHARIST, #2
The Fruits of the Holy Eucharist

(De Fructibus Sanctissimae Eucharistiae:) Vere dignum et iustum est, aequum et salutare, nos tibi semper et ubique gratias agere: Domine, sancte Pater, omnipotens aeterne Deus: per Christum Dominum nostrum.

Qui cum Apostolis suis in novissima cena convescens, salutiferam crucis memoriam prosecuturus in saecula, Agnum sine macula se tibi obtulit, perfectae laudis munus acceptum. Quo venerabili mysterio fideles tuos alendo sanctificas, ut humanum genus, quod continet unus orbis, una fides illuminet, caritas una coniungat. Ad mensam igitur accedimus tam mirabilis sacramenti, ut, gratiae tuae suavitate perfusi, ad caelestis formae imaginem transeamus.

Proper quod caelestia tibi atque terrestria canticum novum concinunt adorando, et nos cum omni exercitu Angelorum proclamamus, sine fine dicentes:

It is, indeed, fitting and right, it is just, it leads to salvation: that at all times and in all places we should render grateful thanks to you, Lord, most holy Father, all-powerful and ageless God: through Christ our Lord.

As He shared the meal with his Apostles at the last supper, He intended to insure that the saving memory of the Cross would be kept in mind for all time; and so He offered himself to you as a Lamb without blemish, the acceptable sacrifice of most perfect praise. It is by nourishing your faithful people with this sacred mystery that you make then holy, so that the human race, already bounded by the one world, might be illumined by one faith, might be joined together by one love. And so we come to the table of this most august sacrament so that, in the midst of the outpouring of your most gracious favor, we might be transformed into the image of heavenly beings.

Because of this, both heaven and earth sing to you a new song of their adoration; we too, with the entire host of the Angels, proclaim you, chanting without ceasing:

PREFACE OF THE HOLY SPIRIT (#1)
The Sending of the Spirit to the Church by the Lord

(De Missione Spiritus a Domino in Ecclesiam:) Vere dignum et iustum est, aequum et salutare, nos tibi semper et ubique gratias agere: Domine, sancte Pater, omnipotens aeterne Deus: per Christum Dominum nostrum.

Qui, ascendens super omnes caelos sedensque ad dexteram tuam, promissum Spiritum Sanctum in filios adoptionis effudit.

Quapropter nunc et usque in saeculum, cum omni militia Angelorum, devota tibi mente concinimus, clamantes atque dicentes:

It is, indeed, fitting and right, it is just, it leads to salvation: that at all times and in all places we should render grateful thanks to you, Lord, most holy Father, all-powerful and ageless God: through Christ our Lord.

As He rose above the highest heavens and took his seat at your right hand, He poured out the Holy Spirit, whom He had promised, upon the children of adoption.

And so, now and for all ages to come, in company with the entire host of Angels and with hearts given over to you, we sing together, crying aloud and chanting:

PREFACE OF THE HOLY SPIRIT #2
The Work of the Spirit in the Church

(De Actione Spiritus in Ecclesia:) Vere dignum et iustum est, aequum et salutare, nos tibi semper et ubique gratias agere: Domine, sancte Pater, omnipotens aeterne Deus:

Qui singulis quibusque temporibus aptanda dispensas, mirisque modis Ecclesiae tuae gubernacula moderaris. Virtute enim Spiritus Sancti ita eam adiuvare non desinis, ut subdito tibi semper affectu nec in tribulatione supplicare deficiat, nec inter gaudia gratias referre desistat, per Christum Dominum nostrum.

Et ideo, choris angelicis sociati, te laudamus in gaudio confitentes:

It is, indeed, fitting and right, it is just, it leads to salvation: that at all times and in all places we should render grateful thanks to you, Lord, most holy Father, all-powerful and ageless God.

You distribute your gifts, to be fitted to every time and every season; and in wondrous ways you guide the helm of your Church. For by the power of the Holy Spirit you unfailingly come to the Church's aid in such a way that, with its heart ever fixed on you, it neither fails to plead for your help in times of tribulation, nor ceases to render you thanks in times of joy, through Christ our Lord.

And therefore, joined with choirs of Angels, we praise and proclaim you in joy:

PREFACE OF THE BLESSED VIRGIN MARY, #1
The Motherhood of the Blessed Virgin Mary

(De Maternitate B. Mariae Virginis:) Vere dignum et iustum est, aequum et salutare, nos tibi semper et ubique gratias agere: Domine, sancte Pater, omnipotens aeterne Deus:

Et te in ... beatae Mariae semper Virginis collaudare, benedicere et praedicare. Quae et Unigenitum tuum Sancti Spiritus obumbratione concepit, et, virginitatis gloria permanente, lumen aeternum mundo effudit, Iesum Christum Dominum nostrum.

Per quem maiestatem tuam laudant Angeli, adorant Dominationes, tremunt Potestates. Caeli caelorumque Virtutes, ac beata Seraphim, socia exsultatione concelebrant. Cum quibus et nostras voces ut admitti iubeas, deprecamur, supplici confessione dicentes:

It is, indeed, fitting and right, it is just, it leads to salvation: that at all times and in all places we should render grateful thanks to you, Lord, most holy Father, all-powerful and ageless God:

As also to praise, bless, and proclaim you (on this feast of the ... of Blessed Mary ever Virgin) (as we pay honor to the ever Blessed Virgin Mary). By the overshadowing of the Holy Spirit she conceived your sole-begotten Son; with her virginal glory unsullied, she brought forth for the world the eternal light, Jesus Christ our Lord.

Through Him the Angels praise your divine majesty, the Dominations adore it, the Powers tremble before it. The Heavens and the Virtues of Heaven, as also the holy Seraphim, give praise to it in shared joy. We ask that you bid our voices to be joined with all these, so as to sing in humble profession of praise:

PREFACE OF THE BLESSED VIRGIN MARY, #2
The Church, in the Words of Mary, Renders Praise to God

(Ecclesia, Verbis Mariae, Laudes Deo Persolvit:) Vere dignum et iustum est, aequum et salutare, in omnium Sanctorum provectu te mirabilem confiteri, et potissimum, beatae Virginis Mariae memoriam recolentes, clementiam tuam ipsius grato magnificare praeconio.

Vere namque in omnes terrae fines magna fecisti, ac tuam in saecula prorogasti misericordiae largitatem, cum, ancillae tuae humilitatem aspiciens, per eam dedisti humanae salutis auctorem, Filium tuum, Iesum Christum, Dominum nostrum.

Per quem maiestatem tuam adorat exercitus Angelorum, ante conspectum tuum in aeternitate laetantium. Cum quibus et nostras voces ut admitti iubeas, deprecamur, socia exsultatione dicentes:

It is, indeed, fitting and right, it is just, it leads to salvation: that we should proclaim your marvels in the honor accorded all your Saints; and most especially, as we call to mind the memory of the Blessed Virgin Mary, that we should extol your merciful kindness with the grateful hymn that she herself once sang.

For the mighty deeds you have performed extend to every boundary of the earth; and you stretched the generous hand of your mercy down through ages to come when you looked upon the lowliness of your handmaid and, through her, gave unto us the author of human salvation: Jesus Christ, your Son, our Lord.

Through Him the Angel host adores your divine majesty, rejoicing in your sight for ages without end. We ask that you bid our voices to be joined with all theirs, so that we may sing as companions in their joyful chant of praise:

PREFACE OF BLESSED MARY, MOTHER OF THE CHURCH
Mary, the Pattern and Mother of the Church

(De Maria, Forma et Matre Ecclesiae:) Vere dignum et iustum est, aequum et salutare, nos tibi semper et ubique gratias agere: Domine, sancte Pater, omnipotens aeterne Deus: Et te in celebratione beatae Mariae Virginis debitis magnificare praeconiis.

Quae Verbum tuum immaculato corde suscipiens virgineo meruit sinu concipere atque, pariens Conditorem, Ecclesiae fovit exordia. Quae iuxta crucem testamentum divinae caritatis accipiens universos homines in filios assumpsit, Christi morte ad supernam vitam generatos. Quae, cum Apostoli Promissum exspectarent tuum, supplicationem suam discipulorum precibus iungens, exemplar exstitit orantis Ecclesiae. Ad gloriam autem evecta caelorum, Ecclesiam peregrinantem materno prosequitur amore eiusque gressus ad patriam tuetur benigna, donec dies Domini gloriosus adveniat.

Et ideo cum Sanctis et Angelis universis te collaudamus, sine fine dicentes:

It is, indeed, fitting and right, it is just, it leads to salvation: that at all times and in all places we should render grateful thanks to you, Lord, most holy Father, all-powerful and ageless God, and that in honoring the Blessed Virgin Mary we should sing of your greatness with fitting hymns of praise.

Receiving your incarnate Word within her immaculate heart, she was made worthy to conceive Him in her Virgin's womb and, giving birth to the very One who had fashioned her, she greeted the beginnings of the Church with love. Standing next to the Cross, she heard expressed the dying wish of divine love and so took all men and women to herself as her children, born to eternal life through the death of Christ. Waiting with the Apostles for the coming of your Promised One, she joined her own petitions to the prayers of the disciples, and so shone forth as the model of the Church at prayer. Finally, taken up to the glory of heaven, she fosters the pilgrim Church with a mother's love, and with kindly care she guards the footsteps that lead it along the way to its heavenly homeland, until that wondrous day, the day of the Lord, shall dawn.

And so, with all the Saints and Angels, we sing your praises, chanting without ceasing:

PREFACE OF THE ANGELS
God Is Given Glory by the Angels

(De Gloria Dei per Angelos:) Vere dignum et iustum est, aequum et salutare, nos tibi semper et ubique gratias agere: Domine, sancte Pater, omnipotens aeterne Deus:

Et in Archangelis Angelisque tuis tua praeconia non tacere, quia ad excellentiam tuam recurrit et gloriam quod angelica creatura tibi probabilis honoretur: et, cum illa sit amplo decore dignissima, tu quam sis immensus et super omnia praeferendus ostenderis, per Christum Dominum nostrum.

Per quem multitudo Angelorum tuam celebrat maiestatem, quibus adorantes in exsultatione coniungimur, una cum eis laudis voce clamantes:

It is, indeed, fitting and right, it is just, it leads to salvation: that at all times and in all places we should render grateful thanks to you, Lord, most holy Father, all-powerful and ageless God;

And that in the case of your Archangels and Angels as well, we should not cease singing our songs of praise to you; for it reflects well upon your own excellence and glory that the class of angelic beings, pleasing to you as they are, should be held in esteem. Since these beings are most worthy of great admiration, it is thereby made clear just how great you yourself are, and how much you are to be preferred to all else: through Christ our Lord.

Through Him the heavenly throng of Angels proclaim your majesty; to them we, offering our adoration in joy, are joined; and so, at one with them, we chant in the voice of praise:

PREFACE OF SAINT JOSEPH
The Mission Given to St. Joseph

(De Missione S. Ioseph:) Vere dignum et iustum est, aequum et salutare, nos tibi semper et ubique gratias agere: Domine, sancte Pater, omnipotens aeterne Deus:

Et te in ... beati Ioseph debitis magnificare praeconiis, benedicere et praedicare. Qui et vir iustus, a te Deiparae Virgini Sponsus est datus, et fidelis servus ac prudens, super Familiam tuam est constitutus, ut Unigenitum tuum, Sancti Spiritus obumbratione conceptum, paterna vice custodiret, Iesum Christum Dominum nostrum.

Per quem maiestatem tuam laudant Angeli, adorant Dominationes, tremunt Potestates. Caeli caelorumque Virtutes, ac beata Seraphim, socia exsultatione concelebrant. Cum quibus et nostras voces ut admitti iubeas, deprecamur, supplici confessione dicentes:

It is, indeed, fitting and right; it is just, it leads to salvation: that at all times and in all places we should render grateful thanks to you, Lord, most holy Father, all-powerful and ageless God:

And also, with hymns that are your due, that we should praise, bless, and proclaim you (on this feast of Saint Joseph) (as we pay honor to Saint Joseph). A just man, he was given by you to the Virgin Mother of God as her husband; a faithful and prudent servant, he was placed at the head of your holy Family, so that in a father's stead he might be the guardian of your sole-begotten one, the one conceived by the overshadowing of the Holy Spirit: Jesus Christ our Lord.

Through him the Angels praise your divine majesty, the Dominations adore it, the Powers tremble before it. The Heavens and the Virtues of Heaven, as also the Holy Seraphim, give praise to it in shared joy. We ask that you bid our voices to be joined with all these, so as to sing in humble profession of praise:

PREFACE OF THE APOSTLES, #1
The Apostles, Shepherds of the People of God

(De Apostolis Pastoribus Populi Dei:) Vere dignum et iustum est, aequum et salutare, nos tibi semper et ubique gratias agere: Domine, sancte Pater, omnipotens aeterne Deus:

Qui gregem tuum, Pastor aeterne, non deseris, sed per beatos Apostolos continua protectione custodis, ut iisdem rectoribus gubernetur, quos Filii tui vicarios eidem contulisti praeesse pastores.

Et ideo cum Angelis et Archangelis, cum Thronis et Dominationibus, cumque omni militia caelestis exercitus, hymnum gloriae tuae canimus, sine fine dicentes:

It is, indeed, fitting and right, it is just, it leads to salvation: that at all times and in all places we should render grateful thanks to you, Lord, most holy Father, all-powerful and ageless God:

As eternal Shepherd, you do not abandon your flock; rather, through your blessed Apostles, you keep watch over it with unfailing protection. And so it is guided by the same rulers whom you provided to have a shepherd's care of it as vicars of your Son.

Thus it is that, in company with the Angels, the Archangels, the Thrones, the Dominations, in company with the entire host of the heavenly army, we sing our song of praise to your glory, chanting without ceasing:

PREFACE OF THE APOSTLES, #2
The Apostolic Foundation and Witness

(De Apostolico Fundamento et Testimonio:) *Vere dignum et iustum est, aequum et salutare, nos tibi semper et ubique gratias agere: Domine, sancte Pater, omnipotens aeterne Deus: per Christum Dominum nostrum.*

Quoniam Ecclesiam tuam in apostolicis tribuisti consistere fundamentis, ut signum sanctitatis tuae in terris maneret ipsa perpetuum, et caelestia praeberet cunctis hominibus documenta.

Quapropter nunc et usque in saeculum cum omni militia Angelorum devota tibi mente concinimus, clamantes atque dicentes:

It is, indeed, fitting and right, it is just, it leads to salvation: that at all times and in all places we should render grateful thanks to you, Lord, most holy Father, all-powerful and ageless God, through Christ our Lord.

For you decreed that your Church was to rest upon the foundation of the Apostles, so that it might remain steadfast on earth as an endless sign of your holiness, and might provide witness to the things of heaven for all men and women.

And so, now and for all ages to come, in company with the entire Angel host, we sing to you with loving hearts, crying out and chanting:

PREFACE OF THE SAINTS, #1
The Glory of the Saints

(De Gloria Sanctorum:) *Vere dignum et iustum est, aequum et salutare, nos tibi semper et ubique gratias agere: Domine, sancte Pater, omnipotens aeterne Deus:*

Qui in Sanctorum concilio celebraris, et, eorum coronando merita, tua dona coronas. Qui nobis eorum conversatione largiris exemplum, et communione consortium, et intercessione subsidium; ut, tantis testibus confirmati, ad propositum certamen curramus invicti et immarcescibilem cum eis coronam gloriae consequamur, per Christum Dominum nostrum.

Et ideo cum Angelis et Archangelis, cumque multiplici congregatione Sanctorum, hymnum laudis tibi canimus, sine fine dicentes:

It is, indeed, fitting and right, it is just, it leads to salvation: that at all times and in all places we should render grateful thanks to you, Lord, most holy Father, all-powerful and ageless God:

Your praises are sung in the Council of the Saints; in honoring their merits, you honor your own gifts. In how they lived you give us their example; in their union with us, you grant us their companionship; in their prayers for us, you provide us with their assistance: all this so that, strengthened by such glorious witnesses, we may hasten invincible to the contest placed before us, and along with them may achieve the unfading crown of glory, through Christ our Lord.

And so with the Angels and Archangels, and with the vast array of all the Saints, we sing to you a hymn of praise, chanting without ceasing:

PREFACE OF THE SAINTS, #2
The Work of the Saints

(De Actione Sanctorum:) Vere dignum et iustum est, aequum et salutare, nos tibi semper et ubique gratias agere: Domine, sancte Pater, omnipotens aeterne Deus: per Christum Dominum nostrum.

Tu enim Sanctorum tuorum confessione mirabili Ecclesiam tuam nova semper virtute fecundas, nobisque certissima praebes tuae dilectionis indicia. Sed etiam, ad mysteria salutis implenda, et ipsorum insigni incitamur exemplo et pia intercessione perpetuo commendamur.

Unde et nos, Domine, cum Angelis et Sanctis universis tibi confitemur, in exsultatione dicentes:

It is, indeed, fitting and right, it is just, it leads to salvation: that at all times and in all places we should render grateful thanks to you, Lord, most holy Father, all-powerful and ageless God: through Christ our Lord.

For by the marvelous profession of your Saints you constantly replenish your Church with new strength, and you extend to us the most clear proofs of your love. Moreover, so that the mystery of salvation might be accomplished, we are inspired by the shining example of the saints and are ever kept in memory in their loving intercession.

And so we too, Lord, in union with all the Angels and Saints, proclaim you, chanting in joy:

PREFACE OF THE HOLY MARTYRS
The Symbol and Example of Martyrdom

(De Signo et Exemplo Martyrii:) Vere dignum et iustum est, aequum et salutare, nos tibi semper et ubique gratias agere: Domine, sancte Pater, omnipotens aeterne Deus:

Quoniam beati martyris N. pro confessione nominis tui, ad imitationem Christi, sanguis effusus tua mirabilia manifestat, quibus perficis in fragilitate virtutem, et vires infirmas ad testimonium roboras, per Christum Dominum nostrum.

Et ideo, cum caelorum Virtutibus, in terris te iugiter celebramus, maiestati tuae sine fine clamantes:

It is, indeed, fitting and right, it is just, it leads to salvation: that at all times and in all places we should render grateful thanks to you, Lord, most holy Father, all-powerful and ageless God:

For, poured out in imitation of Christ in profession of your name, the blood of your holy martyr N. gives shining witness to your wondrous deeds, whereby you make strength perfect in weakness, and you strengthen feeble powers so that they might bear witness to you, through Christ our Lord.

And so, in union with the Powers of heaven, we on earth sing your ceaseless praises, chanting without end a hymn to your divine majesty:

PREFACE OF HOLY PASTORS
The Presence of Saintly Pastors in the Church

(De Praesentia Sanctorum Pastorum in Ecclesia:) Vere dignum et iustum est, aequum et salutare, nos tibi semper et ubique gratias agere: Domine, sancte Pater, omnipotens aeterne Deus: per Christum Dominum nostrum.

Quia sic tribuis Ecclesiam tuam sancti N. festivitate gaudere, ut eam exemplo piae conversationis corrobores, verbo praedicationis erudias, grataque tibi supplicatione tuearis.

Et ideo, cum Angelorum atque Sanctorum turba, hymnum laudis tibi canimus, sine fine dicentes:

It is, indeed, fitting and right, it is just, it leads to salvation: that at all times and in all places we should render grateful thanks to you, Lord, most holy Father, all-powerful and ageless God, through Christ our Lord.

You grant that on this feast of Saint N. your Church should joyfully celebrate in such a way that you strengthen it by the example of the holy life he lived, illumine it by the word he preached, protect it by the prayers he offers that please you so.

And so, with hosts of Angels and Saints alike, we sing a hymn of praise to you, chanting without ceasing:

PREFACE OF HOLY VIRGINS AND RELIGIOUS
The Sign That Is the Life Consecrated to God

(De Signo Vitae Deo Consecratae:) Vere dignum et iustum est, aequum et salutare, nos tibi semper et ubique gratias agere: Domine, sancte Pater, omnipotens aeterne Deus:

In Sanctis enim, qui Christo se dedicaverunt propter regnum caelorum, tuam decet providentiam celebrare mirabilem, qua humanam substantiam et ad primae originis revocas sanctitatem, et ad experienda dona, quae in novo saeculo sunt habenda, perducis.

Et ideo, cum Sanctis et Angelis universis, te collaudamus, sine fine dicentes:

It is, indeed, fitting and right, it is just, it leads to salvation: that at all times and in all places we should render grateful thanks to you, Lord, most holy Father, all-powerful and ageless God:

For when we think of your Saints, who have dedicated their lives to Christ for the sake of the kingdom of heaven, it is fitting to praise your wondrous providence, whereby you summon human nature back once more to the holy state it had when first it was created, and you guide it to a foretaste of the gifts which it is to possess in the new age to come.

And so, with all the Saints and Angels, we sing your praises, chanting without ceasing:

COMMON PREFACE, #1
The Restoration of All Things in Christ

(De Universali Restauratione in Christo:) Vere dignum et iustum est, aequum et salutare, nos tibi semper et ubique gratias agere: Domine, sancte Pater, omnipotens aeterne Deus: per Christum Dominum nostrum.

In quo omnia instaurare tibi complacuit, et de plenitudine eius nos omnes accipere tribuisti. Cum enim in forma Dei esset, exinanivit semetipsum, ac per sanguinem crucis suae pacificavit universa; unde exaltatus est super omnia et omnibus obtemperantibus sibi factus est causa salutis aeternae.

Et ideo cum Angelis et Archangelis, cum Thronis et Dominationibus, cumque omni militia caelestis exercitus, hymnum gloriae tuae canimus, sine fine dicentes:

It is, indeed, fitting and right, it is just, it leads to salvation: that at all times and in all places we should render grateful thanks to you, Lord, most holy Father, all-powerful and ageless God, through Christ our Lord.

It has pleased you to renew all things in Him, and of his fullness you have granted that we should all partake. For although He was divine in nature, He emptied himself, and by means of the blood of his cross he brought peace to the entire world. Thus He has been exalted above all else; all things are under his rule, and He has become the source of eternal salvation.

Thus it is that, in company with the Angels, the Archangels, the Thrones, the Dominations, in company with the entire host of the heavenly army, we sing our song of praise to your glory, chanting without ceasing:

COMMON PREFACE, #2
Salvation Through Christ

(*De Salute per Christum:*) *Vere dignum et iustum est, aequum et salutare, nos tibi semper et ubique gratias agere: Domine, sancte Pater, omnipotens aeterne Deus:*

Qui bonitate hominem condidisti, ac iustitia damnatum misericordia redemisti: per Christum Dominum nostrum.

Per quem maiestatem tuam laudant Angeli, adorant Dominationes, tremunt Potestates. Caeli caelorumque Virtutes, ac beata Seraphim, socia exsultatione concelebrant. Cum quibus et nostras voces ut admitti iubeas, deprecamur, supplici confessione dicentes:

It is, indeed, fitting and right, it is just, it leads to salvation: that at all times and in all places we should render grateful thanks to you, Lord, most holy Father, all-powerful and ageless God.

In your goodness you created the human race and, though it was justly condemned, in your mercy you redeemed it, through Christ our Lord.

Through Him the Angels praise your divine majesty, the Dominations adore it, the Powers tremble before it. The Heavens and the Virtues of Heaven, as also the holy Seraphim, give praise to it in shared joy. We ask that you bid our voices to be joined with all these, so as to sing in humble profession of praise:

COMMON PREFACE, #3
Praise to God for the Creation and Restoration of the Human Race

(*Laudes Deo pro Creatione et Reformatione Hominis:*) *Vere dignum et iustum est, aequum et salutare, nos tibi semper et ubique gratias agere: Domine, sancte Pater, omnipotens aeterne Deus:*

Qui per Filium dilectionis tuae, sicut conditor generis es humani, ita benignissimus reformator. Unde merito tibi cunctae serviunt creaturae, te redempti rite collaudant universi, et uno Sancti tui te corde benedicunt.

Quapropter et nos cum omnibus te Angelis celebramus, iucunda semper confessione dicentes:

It is, indeed, fitting and right, it is just, it leads to salvation: that at all times and in all places we should render grateful thanks to you, Lord, most holy Father, all-powerful and ageless God.

Through your most beloved Son, in great kindliness do you restore the human race, just as you established it in the beginning. Thus it is fitting that all creatures serve you, that all who have been redeemed duly praise you, that your Saints be one at heart in blessing you.

And so we too, with all the Angels, sing your praises, chanting in ever-blessed proclamation:

COMMON PREFACE #4
Praise, the Gift of God

(*De Laude, Dono Dei:*) *Vere dignum et iustum est, aequum et salutare, nos tibi semper et ubique gratias agere: Domine, sancte Pater, omnipotens aeterne Deus:*

Quia, cum nostra laude non egeas, tuum tamen est donum quod tibi grates rependamus, nam te non augent nostra praeconia, sed nobis proficiunt ad salutem, per Christum Dominum nostrum.

Et ideo, choris angelicis sociati, te laudamus in gaudio confitentes:

It is, indeed, fitting and right, it is just, it leads to salvation: that at all times and in all places we should render grateful thanks to you, Lord, most holy Father, all-powerful and ageless God.

Though you have no need of our praise, it is none the less your gracious gift that we should render you grateful thanks. For our songs of gratitude add nothing to your stature; rather, they aid us in attaining salvation, through Christ our Lord.

And therefore, joined with choirs of Angels, we praise and proclaim you in joy:

COMMON PREFACE #5
Proclaiming the Mystery of Christ

(Proclamatio Mysterii Christi:) Vere dignum et iustum est, aequum et salutare, nos tibi semper et ubique gratias agere: Domine, sancte Pater, omnipotens aeterne Deus: per Christum Dominum nostrum.

Cuius mortem in caritate celebramus, resurrectionem fide vivida confitemur, adventum in gloria spe firmissima praestolamur.

Et ideo, cum Sanctis et Angelis universis, te collaudamus, sine fine dicentes:

It is, indeed, fitting and right, it is just, it leads to salvation: that at all times and in all places we should render grateful thanks to you, Lord, most holy Father, all-powerful and ageless God, through Christ our Lord.

With burning love we proclaim his death, with unclouded faith we profess his resurrection, with steadfast hope we await his coming in glory.

And so, with all the Saints and Angels, we sing your praises, chanting without ceasing:

COMMON PREFACE #6
The Mystery of Salvation in Christ

(De Mysterio Salutis in Christo:) Vere dignum et iustum est, aequum et salutare, nos tibi, sancte Pater, semper et ubique gratias agere per Filium dilectionis tuae Iesum Christum, Verbum tuum per quod cuncta fecisti: quem misisti nobis Salvatorem et Redemptorem, incarnatum de Spiritu Sancto et ex Virgine natum. Qui voluntatem tuam adimplens et populum tibi sanctum acquirens extendit manus cum pateretur, ut mortem solveret et resurrectionem manifestaret.

Et ideo cum Angelis et omnibus Sanctis gloriam tuam praedicamus, una voce dicentes:

It is, indeed, fitting and right, it is just, it leads to salvation, O Father most holy, that on every occasion and in every place we should offer you grateful thanks through Jesus Christ, the Son of your love, your Word, through whom you made all that is. He it is whom you sent to us as Savior and Redeemer, enfleshed by the Holy Spirit and of the Virgin born. While fulfilling your command and amassing a people sacred unto you, He stretched forth his hands in suffering, so that he might loose the bonds death had forged and make it clear that we would rise to life once more.

And so with the Angels and all the Saints we proclaim your glory, saying in but one voice:

PREFACE OF THE DEAD, #1
The Hope of Resurrection in Christ

(De Spe Resurrectionis in Christo:) Vere dignum et iustum est, aequum et salutare, nos tibi semper et ubique gratias agere: Domine, sancte Pater, omnipotens aeterne Deus: per Christum Dominum nostrum.

In quo nobis spes beatae resurrectionis effulsit, ut, quos contristat certa moriendi conditio, eosdem consoletur futurae immortalitatis promissio. Tuis enim fidelibus, Domine, vita mutatur, non tollitur, et, dissoluta terrestris huius incolatus domo, aeterna in caelis habitatio comparatur.

Et ideo cum Angelis et Archangelis, cum Thronis et Dominationibus, cumque omni militia caelestis exercitus, hymnum gloriae tuae canimus, sine fine dicentes:

It is, indeed, fitting and right, it is just, it leads to salvation: that at all times and in all places we should render grateful thanks to you, Lord, most holy Father, all-powerful and ageless God, through Christ our Lord.

In Him our hope of a blessed resurrection has shone forth, so that those to whom the human certainty of death brings sorrow might find consolation in the promise of eternal life to come. For, Lord, in the case of your faithful ones, life is but changed; it is not taken away. Although the dwelling place that their earthly body has been is destroyed, a place to live eternally in heaven is made ready for them.

Thus it is that, in company with the Angels, the Archangels, the Thrones, the Dominations, in company with the entire host of the heavenly army, we sing our song of praise to your glory, chanting without ceasing:

PREFACE OF THE DEAD, #2
Christ Died for Our Life

(Christus Mortuus Est pro Vita Nostra:) Vere dignum et iustum est, aequum et salutare, nos tibi semper et ubique gratias agere: Domine, sancte Pater, omnipotens aeterne Deus: per Christum Dominum nostrum.

Ipse enim mortem unus accepit, ne omnes nos moreremur; immo unus mori dignatus est, ut omnes tibi perpetuo viveremus.

Et ideo, choris angelicis sociati, te laudamus in gaudio confitentes:

It is, indeed, fitting and right, it is just, it leads to salvation: that at all times and in all places we should render grateful thanks to you, Lord, most holy Father, all-powerful and ageless God, through Christ our Lord.

One person alone, He accepted death so that all of us would not die; indeed, one person alone, He saw fit to die so that all of us might live forever in you.

And therefore, joined with choirs of Angels, we praise and proclaim you in joy:

PREFACE OF THE DEAD, #3
Christ, Salvation and Life

(Christus, Salus et Vita:) Vere dignum et iustum est, aequum et salutare, nos tibi semper et ubique gratias agere: Domine, sancte Pater, omnipotens aeterne Deus: per Christum Dominum nostrum.

Qui est salus mundi, vita hominum, resurrectio mortuorum.

Per quem maiestatem tuam adorat exercitus Angelorum, ante conspectum tuum in aeternitate laetantium. Cum quibus et nostras voces ut admitti iubeas, deprecamur, socia exsultatione dicentes:

It is, indeed, fitting and right, it is just, it leads to salvation: that at all times and in all places we should render grateful thanks to you, Lord, most holy Father, all-powerful and ageless God, through Christ our Lord.

He is the salvation of the world, the life of the living, the resurrection of the dead.

Through Him the Angel host adores your divine majesty, rejoicing in your sight for ages without end. We ask that you bid our voices to be joined with theirs, so that we may sing as companions in their profession of praise:

PREFACE OF THE DEAD, #4
*Earthly Life
Leading to Heavenly Glory*

(De Vita Terrena ad Gloriam Caelestem:) Vere dignum et iustum est, aequum et salutare, nos tibi semper et ubique gratias agere: Domine, sancte Pater, omnipotens aeterne Deus:

Cuius imperio nascimur, cuius arbitrio regimur, cuius praecepto in terra, de qua sumpti sumus, peccati lege absolvimur. Et, qui per mortem Filii tui redempti sumus, ad ipsius resurrectionis gloriam tuo nutu excitamur.

Et ideo, cum Angelorum atque Sanctorum turba, hymnum laudis tibi canimus, sine fine dicentes:

It is, indeed, fitting and right, it is just, it leads to salvation: that at all times and in all places we should render grateful thanks to you, Lord, most holy Father, all-powerful and ageless God.

By your mandate we are born into life, by your authority the days of our life are governed, by your command we are returned to the earth from which we were taken, in accord with the law that sin imposed. And by your will we who have been redeemed by the death of your Son are raised up to the glory of his resurrection.

And so, with hosts of Angels and Saints alike, we sing a hymn of praise to you, chanting without ceasing:

PREFACE OF THE DEAD, #5
*Our Resurrection, Through
the Victory of Christ*

(De Resurrectione Nostra per Victoriam Christi:) Vere dignum et iustum est, aequum et salutare, nos tibi semper et ubique gratias agere: Domine, sancte Pater, omnipotens aeterne Deus:

Quia, etsi nostri est meriti quod perimus, tuae tamen est pietatis et gratiae quod, pro peccato morte consumpti, per Christi victoriam redempti, cum ipso revocamur ad vitam.

Et ideo, cum caelorum Virtutibus, in terris te iugiter celebramus, maiestati tuae sine fine clamantes:

It is, indeed, fitting and right, it is just, it leads to salvation: that at all times and in all places we should render grateful thanks to you, Lord, most holy Father, all-powerful and ageless God.

For, though it be our just desserts that we die, it is none the less the work of your loving grace that we who have been laid low by death because of sin should be redeemed by the victory of Christ and in company with Him should be summoned back once more unto life.

And so, in union with the Powers of heaven, we on earth sing your ceaseless praises, chanting without end a hymn to your divine majesty:

DECEMBER 8
IMMACULATE CONCEPTION OF THE B.V.M.
*The Mystery of
Mary and the Church*

(De Mysterio Mariae et Ecclesiae:) Vere dignum et iustum est, aequum et salutare, nos tibi semper et ubique gratias agere: Domine, sancte Pater, omnipotens aeterne Deus:

Qui beatissimam Virginem Mariam ab omni originalis culpae labe praeservasti, ut in ea, gratiae tuae plenitudine ditata, dignam Filio tuo Genetricem praeparares, et Sponsae eius Ecclesiae sine ruga vel macula formosae signares exordium. Filium enim erat purissima Virgo datura, qui crimina nostra Agnus innocens aboleret; et ipsam prae omnibus tuo populo disponebas advocatam gratiae et sanctitatis exemplar.

Et ideo, choris angelicis sociati, te laudamus in gaudio confitentes:

It is, indeed, fitting and right, it is just, it leads to salvation: that at all times and in all places we should render grateful thanks to you, Lord, most holy Father, all-powerful and ageless God.

You preserved the most blessed Virgin Mary from all taint of original sin, so that in her, enriched as she was by the fullness of your grace, you might prepare a mother who would be worthy of your Son, and might herald the beginnings of his Spouse, the Church, in a beauty lacking taint of defect or stain. For the most chaste Virgin would bring forth a Son who, as the Lamb without blemish, would wipe away our sins; you established her, far beyond all others, as the intercessor who would obtain grace for your people, and would be the model of the sanctity for which they were to strive.

And therefore, joined with choirs of Angels, we praise and proclaim you in joy:

THE SUNDAY AFTER JANUARY 6:
THE BAPTISM OF THE LORD
The Mystery of the Lord's Baptism

(De Mysterio Baptismatis Domini:) *Vere dignum et iustum est, aequum et salutare, nos tibi semper et ubique gratias agere: Domine, sancte Pater, omnipotens aeterne Deus:*

Qui miris signasti mysteriis novum in Iordane lavacrum, ut, per vocem de caelo delapsam, habitare Verbum tuum inter homines crederetur; et, per Spiritum in columbae specie descendentem, Christus Servus tuus oleo perungi laetitiae ac mitti ad evangelizandum pauperibus nosceretur.

Et ideo cum caelorum virtutibus in terris te iugiter celebramus, maiestati tuae sine fine clamantes:

It is, indeed, fitting and right, it is just, it leads to salvation: that at all times and in all places we should render grateful thanks to you, Lord, most holy Father, all-powerful and ageless God, through Christ our Lord.

By means of your marvelous mysteries you established and marked a new bath of rebirth at the Jordan River. As a result, because of the voice that came down from heaven, it would come to be believed that your Word was living as a human among humans; because of the Spirit that descended in the form of a dove, Christ your Servant Son would be recognized as being anointed with the oil of gladness and sent to proclaim the good news to the poor.

And so, in union with the Powers of heaven, we on earth sing your ceaseless praises, chanting without end a hymn to your divine majesty:

FEBRUARY 2:
THE PRESENTATION OF THE LORD
The Mystery of the Lord's Presentation

(De Mysterio Praesentationis Domini:) *Vere dignum et iustum est, aequum et salutare, nos tibi semper et ubique gratias agere: Domine, sancte Pater, omnipotens aeterne Deus:*

Quia coaeternus hodie in templo tuus Filius praesentatus gloria Israel et lumen gentium a Spiritu declaratur.

Unde et nos, Salutari tuo in gaudiis occurrentes, cum Angelis et Sanctis te laudamus, sine fine dicentes:

It is, indeed, fitting and right, it is just, it leads to salvation: that at all times and in all places we should render grateful thanks to you, Lord, most holy Father, all-powerful and ageless God.

For your Son, co-eternal with you, was today presented in the temple, and was proclaimed by the Spirit as the glory of Israel and the light of the nations.

And so we too, hastening in joy to meet your Salvation as it comes, praise you in the company of the Angels and Saints, chanting without ceasing:

that truth might bring to fulfillment the promises made to the children of Israel, and the desire of the nations might shine forth as now to be fulfilled in a way that no speech could express.

Through Him the Angel host adores your divine majesty, rejoicing in your sight for ages without end. We ask that you bid our voices to be joined with theirs, so that we may sing as companions in their profession of praise:

MARCH 25:
THE ANNUNCIATION
The Mystery of the Incarnation

(De Mysterio Incarnationis:) *Vere dignum et iustum est, aequum et salutare, nos tibi semper et ubique gratias agere: Domine, sancte Pater, omnipotens aeterne Deus: per Christum Dominum nostrum.*

Quem inter homines et propter homines nasciturum, Spiritus Sancti obumbrante virtute, a caelesti nuntio Virgo fidenter audivit et immaculatis visceribus amanter portavit, ut et promissiones filiis Israel perficeret veritas, et gentium exspectatio pateret ineffabiliter adimplenda.

Per quem maiestatem tuam adorat exercitus Angelorum, ante conspectum tuum in aeternitate laetantium. Cum quibus et nostras voces ut admitti iubeas, deprecamur, socia exsultatione dicentes:

It is, indeed, fitting and right, it is just, it leads to salvation: that at all times and in all places we should render grateful thanks to you, Lord, most holy Father, all-powerful and ageless God, through Christ our Lord.

In faith the Virgin heard the words of the heavenly messenger, that by the power of the Holy Spirit coming upon her, Christ would be born among humans and for their sake; in her unsullied womb she lovingly bore Him, so

JUNE 24 AND AUGUST 29:
SAINT JOHN THE BAPTIST
The Mission of the Precursor

(De Missione Praecursoris:) *Vere dignum et iustum est, aequum et salutare, nos tibi semper et ubique gratias agere: Domine, sancte Pater, omnipotens aeterne Deus: per Christum Dominum nostrum.*

In cuius Praecursore beato Ioanne tuam magnificentiam collaudamus, quem inter natos mulierum honore praecipuo consecrasti. Qui cum nascendo multa gaudia praestitisset, et nondum editus exsultasset ad humanae salutis adventum, ipse solus omnium prophetarum Agnum redemptionis ostendit. Sed et sanctificandis etiam aquae fluentis ipsum baptismatis lavit auctorem, et meruit fuso sanguine supremum illi testimonium exhibere.

Et ideo, cum caelorum Virtutibus, in terris te iugiter praedicamus, maiestati tuae sine fine clamantes:

It is, indeed, fitting and right, it is just, it leads to salvation: that at all times and in all places we should render grateful thanks to you, Lord, most holy Father, all-powerful and ageless God: through Christ our Lord.

In Saint John, the one who came before Christ, we praise your great glory; among all the children born of women you anointed him with a unique dignity. For at his birth he occasioned great joy; indeed, even before he was born he rejoiced at the coming of the salvation of the human race. To him alone, of all the prophets, it fell to point out the Lamb who takes away the sin of the world. But more: for the sake of those who were to be made holy, he baptized even the very author of the baptism of living water; and he was found worthy to provide the ultimate witness to Him by the shedding of his blood.

And so, in union with the Powers of heaven, we on earth sing your ceaseless praises, chanting without end a hymn to your divine majesty:

JUNE 29:
STS. PETER AND PAUL
The Two-Fold Mission of Peter and Paul in the Church

(De Duplici Missione Petri et Pauli in Ecclesia:) Vere dignum et iustum est, aequum et salutare, nos tibi semper et ubique gratias agere: Domine, sancte Pater, omnipotens aeterne Deus:

Quia nos beati apostoli Petrus et Paulus tua dispositione laetificant: hic princeps fidei confitendae, ille intellegendae clarus assertor; hic reliquiis Israel instituens Ecclesiam primitivam, ille magister et doctor gentium vocandarum. Sic diverso consilio unam Christi familiam congregantes, par mundo venerabile, una corona sociavit.

Et ideo cum Sanctis et Angelis universis te collaudamus, sine fine dicentes:

It is, indeed, fitting and right, it is just, it leads to salvation: that at all times and in all places we should render grateful thanks to you, Lord, most holy Father, all-powerful and ageless God.

For your holy Apostles Peter and Paul bring us joy by their place in your divine plan: Peter the leader and guide in the faith we are to profess, Paul the defender and teacher of the faith we are to understand; Peter, who fostered the early Church for the remnants of Israel, Paul, who was master and mentor for the gentiles who were to be called. And so the one crown joins together this pair of saints, alike praiseworthy throughout the world, who in different ways gathered into one the single family of Christ.

And so, with all the Saints and Angels, we sing your praises, chanting without ceasing:

AUGUST 6:
THE TRANSFIGURATION
The Mystery of the Transfiguration

(De Mysterio Transfigurationis:) Vere dignum et iustum est, aequum et salutare, nos tibi semper et ubique gratias agere: Domine, sancte Pater, omnipotens aeterne Deus: per Christum Dominum nostrum.

Qui coram electis testibus suam gloriam revelavit, et communem illam cum ceteris corporis formam maximo splendore perfudit, ut de cordibus discipulorum crucis scandalum tolleretur, et in totius Ecclesiae corpore declararet implendum quod eius mirabiliter praefulsit in capite.

Et ideo cum caelorum Virtutibus in terris te iugiter celebramus, maiestati tuae sine fine clamantes:

It is, indeed, fitting and right, it is just, it leads to salvation: that at all times and in all places we should render grateful thanks to you, Lord, most holy Father, all-powerful and ageless God, through Christ our Lord.

To chosen witnesses He revealed his glory; the human body which He had in common with those witnesses, He suffused with supreme brilliance, so that the scandal of the Cross might be lifted from the hearts of the disciples, and so that He might affirm that in the body of the entire Church there would indeed take place that which shone forth so marvelously in its Head.

And so, in union with the Powers of heaven, we on earth sing your ceaseless praises, chanting without end a hymn to your divine majesty:

AUGUST 15:
ASSUMPTION OF THE BLESSED VIRGIN MARY
The Glory of Mary, Who Was Taken up into Heaven

(De Gloria Mariae Assumptae:) Vere dignum et iustum est, aequum et salutare, nos tibi semper et ubique gratias agere: Domine, sancte Pater, omnipotens aeterne Deus: per Christum Dominum nostrum.

Quoniam in caelos hodie Virgo Deipara est assumpta, Ecclesiae tuae consummandae initium et imago, ac populo peregrinanti certae spei et solacii documentum; corruptionem enim sepulcri eam videre merito noluisti, quae Filium tuum, vitae omnis auctorem, ineffabiliter de se genuit incarnatum.

Et ideo, choris angelicis sociati, te laudamus, in gaudio confitentes:

It is, indeed, fitting and right, it is just, it leads to salvation: that at all times and in all places we should render grateful thanks to you, Lord, most holy Father, all-powerful and ageless God: through Christ our Lord.

For today the Virgin, the Godbearer, was taken up into heaven, the first fruits and the type of your Church as it is to be brought to completion, but also the reason for unwavering hope and consolation for your people in their pilgrim journey on earth. Rightly were you unwilling that she should undergo the corruption of the grave, for in a way words cannot express she had borne within herself your incarnate Son, the source of all life.

And therefore, joined with choirs of Angels, we praise and proclaim you in joy:

SEPTEMBER 14:
EXALTATION OF THE HOLY CROSS
The Victory of the Glorified Cross

(De Victoria Crucis Gloriosae:) Vere dignum et iustum est, aequum et salutare, nos tibi semper et ubique gratias agere: Domine, sancte Pater, omnipotens, aeterne Deus:

Qui salutem humani generis in ligno crucis constituisti, ut, unde mors oriebatur, inde vita resurgeret; et, qui in ligno vincebat, in ligno quoque vinceretur: per Christum Dominum nostrum.

Per quem maiestatem tuam laudant Angeli, adorant Dominationes, tremunt Potestates, Caeli caelorumque Virtutes, ac beata Seraphim, socia exsultatione concelebrant. Cum quibus et nostras voces ut admitti iubeas, deprecamur, supplici confessione dicentes:

It is, indeed, fitting and right, it is just, it leads to salvation: that at all times and in all places we should render grateful thanks to you, Lord, most holy Father, all-powerful and ageless God, through Christ our Lord.

You assigned the salvation of the human race to the tree of the Cross, so that life might flourish once more from the very place whence death had arisen, and so that the one who conquered by means of a tree might likewise be conquered by means of a tree, through Christ our Lord.

Through Him the Angels praise your divine majesty, the Dominations adore it, the Powers tremble before it.

The Heavens and the Virtues of Heaven, as also the holy Seraphim, give praise to it in shared joy. We ask that you bid our voices to be joined with all these, so as to sing in humble profession of praise:

NOVEMBER 1
ALL SAINTS
The Glory of Our Mother Jerusalem

(De Gloria Matris Nostrae Ierusalem:) Vere dignum et iustum est, aequum et salutare, nos tibi semper et ubique gratias agere: Domine, sancte Pater, omnipotens aeterne Deus:

Nobis enim hodie civitatem tuam tribuis celebrare, quae mater nostra est, caelestisque Ierusalem, ubi fratrum nostrorum iam te in aeternum corona collaudat. Ad quam peregrini, per fidem accedentes, alacriter festinamus, congaudentes de Ecclesiae sublimium glorificatione membrorum, qua simul fragilitati nostrae adiumenta et exempla concedis.

Et ideo, cum ipsorum Angelorumque frequentia, una te magnificamus, laudis voce clamantes:

It is, indeed, fitting and right, it is just, it leads to salvation: that at all times and in all places we should render grateful thanks to you, Lord, most holy Father, all-powerful and ageless God.

For today you grant that we may celebrate the glory of your city, our own mother, the heavenly Jerusalem, where a vast throng of our brothers and sisters already praises you now and forever. We who are pilgrims on earth draw near through faith; we hasten eagerly toward it and we rejoice in the glorification of the heavenly members of the Church, by which you grant our weak nature at once assistance and exemplar.

And so, with the host of Saints and Angels as well, as one body we proclaim you, crying out with words of praise:

THIRTY-FOURTH SUNDAY OF THE YEAR: CHRIST THE KING
Christ, the King of All

(De Christo Universorum Rege:) Vere dignum et iustum est, aequum et salutare, nos tibi semper et ubique gratias agere: Domine, sancte Pater, omnipotens aeterne Deus:

Qui unigenitum Filium tuum, Dominum nostrum Iesum Christum, Sacerdotem aeternum et universorum Regem, oleo exsultationis unxisti: ut, seipsum in ara crucis hostiam immaculatam et pacificam offerens, redemptionis humanae sacramenta perageret: et, suo subiectis imperio omnibus creaturis, aeternum et universale regnum immensae tuae traderet maiestati: regnum veritatis et vitae, regnum sanctitatis et gratiae; regnum iustitiae, amoris, et pacis.

Et ideo cum Angelis et Archangelis, cum Thronis et Dominationibus, cumque omni militia caelestis exercitus, hymnum gloriae tuae canimus, sine fine dicentes:

It is, indeed, fitting and right, it is just, it leads to salvation: that at all times and in all places we should render grateful thanks to you, Lord, most holy Father, all-powerful and ageless God.

With the oil of jubilation you have anointed your only-begotten Son, our Lord Jesus Christ, as eternal Priest and King of all. In this way, He would offer himself on the altar of the Cross as a spotless offering that would bring about our peace, and would fulfill the solemn promise of human redemption; once all creatures had been rendered subject to his power, He would then hand over to your measureless majesty a kingdom eternal and boundless: a kingdom of truth and life, a kingdom of holiness and grace, a kingdom of justice, of love, of peace.

Thus it is that, in company with the Angels, the Archangels, the Thrones, the Dominations, in company with the entire host of the heavenly army, we sing our song of praise to your glory, chanting without ceasing:

DEDICATION OF A CHURCH
A. WITHIN THE CHURCH TO BE DEDICATED: ON THE DAY OF DEDICATION OR THE ANNIVERSARY
The Mystery of God's Temple, Which Is the Church

(De Mysterio Templi Dei, Quod Est Ecclesia:) Vere dignum et iustum est, aequum et salutare, nos tibi semper et ubique gratias agere: Domine, sancte Pater, omnipotens aeterne Deus: per Christum Dominum nostrum.

Qui in domo visibili, quam nobis exstruere concessisti, ubi familiae in hoc loco ad te peregrinanti favere non desinis, mysterium tuae nobiscum communionis mire figuras et operaris: hic enim tibi templum illud quod nos sumus aedificas, et Ecclesiam per orbem diffusam in dominici compagem corporis facis augeri, in pacis visione complendam, caelesti civitate Ierusalem.

Et ideo, cum multitudine ordinum beatorum, in templo gloriae tuae, te collaudamus, benedicimus et magnificamus, dicentes:

It is, indeed, fitting and right, it is just, it leads to salvation: that at all times and in all places we should render grateful thanks to you, Lord, most holy Father, all-powerful and ageless God, through Christ our Lord.

You have permitted us to construct this visible dwelling place, where you ceaselessly show your favor to your servants as they here make their way to you. Here in wondrous way you labor at fashioning the mystery of your own dwelling among us. For here you construct that temple to yourself which we ourselves are in the depths of our very being; and you cause your Church, spread throughout the whole world, to grow in becoming the edifice of the Lord's body, which it will fully be in the vision of peace, the heavenly city of Jerusalem.

And so, with the many ranks of the heavenly host, we praise you, we bless you, we magnify you within the temple of your glory, chanting:

DEDICATION OF A CHURCH
B. OUTSIDE THE DEDICATED CHURCH: ON THE ANNIVERSARY
The Mystery of the Church, the Bride of Christ and the Temple of the Spirit

(De Mysterio Ecclesiae, Quae Est Sponsa Christi Templumque Spiritus:) Vere dignum et iustum est, aequum et salutare, nos tibi semper et ubique gratias ahere: Domine, sancte Pater, omnipotens aeterne Deus:

Qui domum orationis munificus inhabitare dignaris, ut, gratia tua perpetuis fovente subsidiis, templum Spiritus Sancti ipse nos perficias, acceptabilis vitae splendore coruscans. Sed et visibilibus aedificiis adumbratam, Christi sponsam Ecclesiam perenni operatione sanctificas, ut, innumerabili prole mater exsultans, in gloriam tuam collocetur in caelis.

Et ideo, cum Sanctis et Angelis universis, te collaudamus, sine fine dicentes:

It is, indeed, fitting and right, it is just, it leads to salvation, that at all times and in all places we should render grateful thanks to you, Lord, most holy Father, all-powerful and ageless God:

For in your generosity you have deigned to dwell in this house of prayer; thereby, through the kind influence of your grace's unfailing assistance, you make us into a temple of the Holy Spirit, shining forth with the splendor of a life that is worthy of yourself. By your constant labor you make holy the bride of Christ, the Church, dimly portrayed as it is by buildings that eye can see, so that holy mother Church, rejoicing in offspring beyond count, might find her place amidst your glory in heaven.

And so, with all the Saints and Angels, we sing your praises, chanting without ceasing:

DEDICATION OF A CHURCH: ON THE DAY OF DEDICATION
The Mystery of the Temple of God

(De Mysterio Templi Dei:) *Vere dignum et iustum est, aequum et salutare, nos tibi, sancte Pater, semper et ubique gratias agere.*

Qui templum gloriae tuae universum mundum effecisti, ut nomen tuum ubique clarificaretur, sed et loca divinis apta mysteriis non renuis tibi sacrari: hanc ergo orationis domum, humano exstructam labore, maiestati tuae exsultantes dicamus. Hic veri Templi adumbratur mysterium et caelestis Ierusalem praenotatur imago: corpus enim Filii tui, ex alma Virgine natum, templum effecisti tibi sacratum, in quo habitaret plenitudo divinitatis. Ecclesiam autem sanctam constituisti civitatem, super fundamentum Apostolorum aedificatam, summo angulari labide ipso Christo Iesu; sed electis construendam lapidibus, Spiritu vivificatis, coagmentatis caritate, ubi tu per infinita saecula omnia omnibus eris et Christi lumen fulgebit perenne.

Per quem nos, Domine, cum Angelis et Sanctis universis tibi confitemur, in exsultatione dicentes:

It is, indeed, fitting and right, it is just, it leads to salvation: that at all times and in all places we should render grateful thanks to you, Father most holy.

You have made the entire world to be a place where your glory may dwell, so that the renown of your holy name might everywhere shine forth. But you do not refuse to allow certain chosen places to be made sacred to you for celebrating the divine mysteries. And so we joyfully dedicate this house of prayer, built by human effort, to your divine majesty. Here, the mystery of the true Temple is foreshadowed and the type of the heavenly Jerusalem is seen in advance. For you have made the body of your Son, born of the gracious Virgin, to be a temple sacred to yourself, wherein would dwell the fullness of the divinity. You then established the Church as a holy city, built upon the foundation of the Apostles, with Christ Jesus himself as its supreme cornerstone; it is to be built up with chosen stones, stones given life by the Spirit and joined together by love. In it, for countless ages to come, you will be all things to all people, and the light of Christ will shine without fail.

Through Him, Father and Lord, and in the company of the Angels and all the Saints, we proclaim you, chanting in great joy:

THE DEDICATION OF AN ALTAR
The Altar is Christ Himself

(Altare Ipse Est Christus:) *Vere dignum et iustum est, aequum et salutare, nos tibi semper et ubique gratias agere: Domine, sancte Pater, omnipotens aeterne Deus: per Christum Dominum nostrum.*

Qui verus sacerdos veraque effectus hostia, sacrificii, quod ipse in ara crucis tibi obtulit, memoriale nobis praecepit in perpetuum celebrare. Ideo populus tuus hoc erexit altare, quod tibi, Domine, exsultantes dicamus. Hic est vere locus excelsus, ubi Christi sacrificium in mysterio iugiter offertur, tibi perfecta tribuitur laus nostraque exseritur redemptio. Hic dominica mensa paratur, ad quam filii tui, Christi corpore refecti, in unam sanctamque congregantur Ecclesiam. Hic fideles Spiritum tuum hauriunt de fluminibus a Christo, spiritali petra, manantibus, per quem et ipsi fiunt oblatio sancta, vivum altare.

Unde et nos, Domine, cum Angelis et Sanctis universis, tibi confitemur, in exsultatione dicentes:

It is, indeed, fitting and right, it is just, it leads to salvation: that at all times and in all places we should render grateful thanks to you, Lord, most holy Father, all-powerful and ageless God, through Christ our Lord.

He has become the true priest and the true offering, and has commanded us to celebrate, for all time, the memorial of the sacrifice which He himself offered to you on the altar of the Cross. And so your people have erected this altar, Father and Lord, and dedicate it to you in joy. Here, indeed, is the exalted place where the sacrifice of Christ is continually offered in mystery, where perfect praise is given to you, where our redemption finds its origin. Here the Lord's table is prepared, where your children are renewed with the Body of Christ, and so are gathered together into a Church that is one and holy. Here your faithful people drink deeply of your Spirit from streams coming forth from Christ, the spiritual rock, through whom your people themselves become a holy offering, a living altar.

And so we too, Lord, in union with all the Angels and Saints, proclaim you, chanting in joy:

THE CELEBRATION OF MARRIAGE (A)
The Grandeur of the Marriage Covenant

(De Dignitate Foederis Nuptiarum:) Vere dignum et iustum est, aequum et salutare, nos tibi semper et ubique gratias agere: Domine, sancte Pater, omnipotens aeterne Deus:

Qui foedera nuptiarum blando concordiae iugo et insolubili pacis vinculo nexuisti, ut multiplicandis adoptionum filiis sanctorum connubiorum fecunditas pudica serviret. Tua enim, Domine, providentia, tuaque gratia ineffabilibus modis utrumque dispensas, ut, quod generatio ad mundi produxit ornatum, regeneratio ad Ecclesiae perducat augmentum: per Christum Dominum nostrum.

Per quem, cum Angelis et omnibus Sanctis, hymnum laudis tibi canimus, sine fine dicentes:

It is, indeed, fitting and right, it is just, it leads to salvation: that at all times and in all places we should render grateful thanks to you, Lord, most holy Father, all-powerful and ageless God.

You have bound the marriage covenant together with the pleasant yoke of harmony and the indissoluble bond of peace, so that the chaste fruitfulness of holy marriages might foster an increase in the number of your children of adoption. For, Lord, in your divine providence and by your divine grace, you see to it, in ways words cannot express, that just as birth has brought about the adornment of the world, so rebirth leads to the growth of the Church, through Christ our Lord.

Through Him, in the company of the Angels and all the Saints, we sing a hymn of praise to you, chanting without ceasing:

THE CELEBRATION OF MARRIAGE (B)
The Great Sacrament of Matrimony

(De Magno Sacramento Matrimonii:) Vere dignum et iustum est, aequum et salutare, nos tibi semper et ubique gratias agere: Domine, sancte Pater, omnipotens aeterne Deus: per Christum Dominum nostrum.

Quia novum nexuisti cum tuo populo testamentum, ut, quem mortis et resurrectionis redemisses mysterio, divinae in Christo faceres naturae consortem eiusque in caelis gloriae coheredem. Cuius piissimam gratiae largitatem in viri mulierisque significasti connubio, ut ad ineffabile tui amoris consilium nos revocaret quod agitur sacramentum.

Et ideo, cum Angelis et omnibus Sanctis, te laudamus, sine fine dicentes:

It is, indeed, fitting and right, it is just, it leads to salvation, that at all times and in all places we should render grateful thanks to you, Lord, most holy Father, all-powerful and ageless God, through Christ our Lord.

For you have woven together a new covenant with your people, whereby the man or woman you have redeemed by the mystery of Christ's death and resurrection, you also make a sharer in His divine nature and a co-heir of glory with Him in heaven. His most loving and lavish gift of grace you have signified by the marriage of man and woman, so that the very action of the sacrament itself might summon us back to the unspeakable plan of your divine love.

And so, with the Angels and all the Saints, we sing your praises, chanting without ceasing:

THE CELEBRATION OF MARRIAGE (C)
Marriage as a Sign of Divine Love

(De Matrimonio ut Signum Divinae Caritatis:) Vere dignum et iustum est, aequum et salutare, nos tibi semper et ubique gratias agere: Domine, sancte Pater, omnipotens aeterne Deus:

Qui hominem pietatis tuae dono creatum ad tantam voluisti dignitatem extolli, ut in viri mulierisque consortio veram relinqueres tui amoris imaginem; quem enim ex caritate creasti, eum ad caritatis legem vocare non desinis, ut aeternae tuae caritatis participem esse concedas. Cuius connubii sancti mysterium dum tuae dilectionis signum exsistit, amorem sacrat humanum: per Christum Dominum nostrum.

Per quem, cum Angelis et omnibus Sanctis, hymnum laudis tibi canimus, sine fine dicentes:

It is, indeed, fitting and right, it is just, it leads to salvation, that at all times and in all places we should render grateful thanks to you, Lord, most holy Father, all-powerful and ageless God, through Christ our Lord.

You willed that the people whom you created by the generosity of your faithful love should be raised to such heights of dignity, that in the companionship of a man and a woman you would imprint a true picture of your own love. For the person whom you have created out of love, you do not cease to summon to observance of the law of love, so that you might grant to such a one a share in your eternal love. The mystery of holy marriage, then, shining forth as it does as a sign of your love, renders human love sacred, through Christ our Lord.

Through Him, in the company of the Angels and all the Saints, we sing a hymn of praise to you, chanting without ceasing:

RELIGIOUS PROFESSION
Religious Life as Service of God Through Imitation of Christ

(De Vita Religiosa ut Servitium Dei per Christi Imitationem:) *Vere dignum et iustum est, aequum et salutare, nos tibi semper et ubique gratias agere: Domine, sancte Pater, omnipotens aeterne Deus: per Christum Dominum nostrum.*

Qui, de radice Virginis flos illibatus egressus, mundos corde dixit beatos suaque conversatione docuit castitatis fastigium. Qui tuis semper beneplacitis optavit haerere, et, usque ad mortem pro nobis factus oboediens, hostiam se tibi voluit perfectae suavitatis offerre. Qui omnia propter te relinquentes in terris ad servitium tuae maiestatis dicavit impensius et caelorum confirmavit inventuros esse thesaurum.

Et ideo, cum Angelorum atque Sanctorum turba, hymnum laudis tibi canimus, sine fine dicentes:

It is, indeed, fitting and right, it is just, it leads to salvation: that at all times and in all places we should render grateful thanks to you, Lord, most holy Father, all-powerful and ageless God: through Christ our Lord.

He came forth as a flower unimpaired from the stem that was the Virgin, and proclaimed the clean of heart to be blessed; by his own way of life He showed us the supreme degree of holy purity. He chose to cling always to the things that please you and, becoming obedient even unto death on our behalf, He willed to offer himself to you as an offering that was acceptable in every way. Most profoundly, He consecrated to the service of your divine majesty those who left behind all things on earth for your sake, and promised that they would find treasure in heaven.

And so, with hosts of Angels and Saints alike, we sing a hymn of praise to you, chanting without ceasing:

THE UNITY OF CHRISTIANS
The Unity of the Body of Christ, Which Is the Church

(De Unitate Corporis Christi, Quod Est Ecclesia:) *Vere dignum et iustum est, aequum et salutare, nos tibi semper et ubique gratias agere: Domine, sancte Pater, omnipotens aeterne Deus: per Christum Dominum nostrum.*

Per ipsum enim nos adduxisti ad agnitionem tuae veritatis, ut unius fidei et baptismi vinculo Corpus eius efficeremur; per ipsum in cunctis gentibus largitus es Spiritum Sanctum tuum, qui, in diversitate donorum mirabilis operator et unitatis effector, filios adoptionis inhabitat totamque replet et regit Ecclesiam.

Et ideo, choris angelicis sociati, te laudamus in gaudio confitentes:

It is, indeed, fitting and right, it is just, it leads to salvation: that at all times and in all places we should render grateful thanks to you, Lord, most holy Father, all-powerful and ageless God, through Christ our Lord.

For through Him you have brought us to a knowledge of your truth, so that we might be made into His Body by the bond of one faith and one baptism. Through Him you poured forth your Holy Spirit on all peoples. Through the variety of gifts that He gives, the Spirit does marvelous deeds and brings about unity; dwelling in the children of adoption, the Spirit fills and rules the entire Church.

And therefore, joined with choirs of Angels, we praise and proclaim you in joy:

OREMUS

Speaking with God

in the

Words of the Roman Rite

IV

The Eucharistic Prayers

EUCHARISTIC PRAYER ONE
(The Roman Canon)

80. *Te igitur, clementissime Pater, per Iesum Christum, Filium tuum, Dominum nostrum, supplices rogamus ac petimus, uti accepta habeas et benedicas + haec dona, haec munera, haec sancta sacrificia illibata, in primis, quae tibi offerimus pro Ecclesia tua sancta catholica: quam pacificare, custodire, adunare, et regere digneris toto orbe terrarum: una cum famulo tuo Papa nostro N. et Antistite nostro N. et omnibus orthodoxis atque catholicae et apostolicae fidei cultoribus.*

It is you, then, most merciful Father, whom we ask and implore through Jesus Christ, your Son, our Lord: consider as acceptable and bless + these gifts, these tributes, these hallowed and unblemished sacrifices. We offer them to you especially for your holy Catholic Church; deign to grant it peace, protection, unity, and governance throughout the entire world, in company with your servant, our Pope N., our Bishop(s) N. (and N.), and all who faithfully foster the catholic and apostolic belief.

81. *Memento, Domine, famulorum famularumque tuarum N. et N. et omnium circumstantium, quorum tibi fides cognita est et nota devotio, pro quibus tibi offerimus: vel qui tibi offerunt hoc sacrificium laudis, pro se suisque omnibus: pro redemptione animarum suarum, pro spe salutis et incolumitatis suae: tibique reddunt vota sua aeterno Deo, vivo et vero.*

Father and Lord, bring to mind your sons and daughters N. and N., as also all those who here take their places around this altar. Their faith is well known to you; their dedication to you, an acknowledged fact. On their behalf we offer, or else they themselves offer, this sacrifice of praise to you for themselves and for all who are dear to them. For the redemption of their own souls, for their hope of salvation and safe refuge, they render the offerings they owe to you, ageless God, living God, true God.

82. *Communicantes, et memoriam venerantes, in primis gloriosae semper Virginis Mariae, Genetricis Dei et Domini nostri Iesu Christi: * sed et beati Ioseph, eiusdem Virginis Sponsi, et beatorum Apostolorum ac Martyrum tuorum, Petri et Pauli, Andreae, (Iacobi, Ioannis, Thomae, Iacobi, Philippi, Bartholomaei, Matthaei, Simonis et Thaddaei: Lini, Cleti, Clementis, Xysti, Cornelii, Cypriani, Laurentii, Chrysogoni, Ioannis et Pauli, Cosmae et Damiani) et omnium Sanctorum tuorum; quorum meritis precibusque concedas, ut in omnibus protectionis tuae muniamur auxilio. (Per Christum Dominum nostrum. Amen.)*

In reverential memory, we join ourselves first of all to the company of the glorious and ever Virgin Mary, the Mother of our God and Lord Jesus Christ; then to that of blessed Joseph, Husband of the Virgin, and that of your holy Apostles and Martyrs, Peter and Paul, Andrew, (James, John, Thomas, James, Phillip, Bartholomew, Matthew, Simon, Jude; Linus, Cletus, Clement, Sixtus, Cornelius, Cyprian, Laurence, Chrysogonus, John and Paul, Cosmas and Damian), and all your Saints. Through their merits and prayers, grant that in all dangers we may be defended by the strong rampart of your protection. (We ask this through Christ our Lord. Amen.)

83. {*In Nativitate Domini et per octavam*}: Communicantes, et (noctem sacratissimam) diem sacratissimum celebrantes, (qua) quo beatae Mariae intemerata virginitas huic mundo edidit Salvatorem: sed et memoriam venerantes, in primis eiusdem gloriosae semper Virginis Mariae, Genetricis eiusdem Dei et Domini nostri Iesu Christi: ...

84. {*In Epiphania Domini*}: Communicantes, et diem sacratissimum celebrantes, quo Unigenitus tuus, in tua tecum gloria coaeternus, in veritate carnis nostrae visibiliter corporalis apparuit: sed et memoriam venerantes, in primis gloriosae semper Virginis Mariae, Genetricis eiusdem Dei et Domini nostri Iesu Christi: ...

85. {*A Missa Vigiliae paschalis usque ad dominicam II Paschae*}: Communicantes, et (noctem sacratissimam) diem sacratissimum celebrantes Resurrectionis Domini nostri Iesu Christi secundum carnem: sed et memoriam venerantes, in primis gloriosae semper Virginis Mariae, Genetricis eiusdem Dei et Domini nostri Iesu Christi: ...

86. {*In Ascensione Domini*}: Communicantes, et diem sacratissimum celebrantes, quo Dominus noster, unigenitus Filius tuus, unitam sibi fragilitatis nostrae substantiam in gloriae tuae dextera collocavit: sed et memoriam venerantes, in primis gloriosae semper Virginis Mariae, Genetricis eiusdem Dei et Domini nostri Iesu Christi: ...

87. {*In dominica Pentecostes*}: Communicantes, et diem sacratissimum Pentecostes celebrantes, quo Spiritus Sanctus Apostolis in igneis linguis apparuit: sed et memoriam venerantes, in primis gloriosae semper Virginis Mariae, Genetricis Dei et Domini nostri Iesu Christi: ...

{*Christmas and Throughout the Octave*}: We rejoice in celebration of that most sacred day (night) on which the chaste virginity of the Blessed Mary brought forth a Savior for this world; and in reverential memory we join ourselves first of all to the company of the same glorious and ever Virgin Mary, the Mother of that same Jesus Christ our God and Lord: ...

{*Epiphany*}: We rejoice in celebration of that most sacred day on which your only-begotten Son, albeit sharing with you in your glory from all eternity, nonetheless manifested himself visibly in what was truly our bodily flesh; and in reverential memory we join ourselves first of all to the company of the glorious and ever Virgin Mary, the Mother of that same Jesus Christ our God and Lord: ...

{*From the Easter Vigil until the Second Sunday of Easter*}: We rejoice in celebration of that most sacred day (night) of the Resurrection of our Lord Jesus Christ according to the flesh; and in reverential memory we join ourselves first of all to the company of the glorious and ever Virgin Mary, the Mother of that same Jesus Christ our God and Lord: ...

{*The Ascension*}: We rejoice in celebration of that most sacred day on which our Lord, your only-begotten Son, established a place at the right hand of your glory for our human nature, which he had taken unto Himself in all its frailty; and in reverential memory we join ourselves first of all to the company of the glorious and ever Virgin Mary, the Mother of that same Jesus Christ our God and Lord: ...

{*Pentecost Sunday*}: We rejoice in celebration of that most sacred day of Pentecost, on which the Holy Spirit became visible to the Apostles in the form of tongues of fire; and in reverential memory we join ourselves first of all to the company of the glorious and ever Virgin Mary, the Mother of Jesus Christ, our God and Lord: ...

88. *Hanc igitur oblationem servitutis nostrae, sed et cunctae familiae tuae, quaesumus, Domine, ut placatus accipias: diesque nostros in tua pace disponas, atque ab aeterna damnatione nos eripi et in electorum tuorum iubeas grege numerari. (Per Christum Dominum nostrum. Amen.)*

This offering, then: it arises from our dedicated service to you, but it is also the offering of your entire family: Father and Lord, we ask that it please you and that you accept it. Guide our days in the paths of your peace, save us from eternal condemnation, and command that we be counted among the flock of your chosen ones. (We ask this through Christ our Lord. Amen.)

89. *{A Missa Vigiliae paschalis usque ad dominicam II Paschae}: Hanc igitur oblationem servitutis nostrae, sed et cunctae familiae tuae, quam tibi offerimus pro his quoque, quos regenerare dignatus es ex aqua et Spiritu Sancto, tribuens eis remissionem omnium peccatorum, quaesumus, Domine, ut placatus accipias: diesque nostros in tua pace disponas, atque ab aeterna damnatione nos eripi et in electorum tuorum iubeas grege numerari. (Per Christum Dominum nostrum. Amen.)*

{From the Easter Vigil until the Second Sunday of Easter}: This offering, then, which arises from our dedicated service to you, but which is also the offering of your entire family, and which, moreover, we offer you for those to whom you have been pleased to grant rebirth of water and the Holy Spirit, imparting to them the forgiveness of all their sins: Father and Lord, we ask that it please you and that you accept it. Guide our days in the paths of your peace, save us from eternal condemnation, and command that we be counted among the flock of your chosen ones. (We ask this through Christ our Lord. Amen.)

90. *Quam oblationem tu, Deus, in omnibus, quaesumus, benedictam, adscriptam, ratam, rationabilem, acceptabilemque facere digneris: ut nobis Corpus et Sanguis fiat dilectissimi Filii tui, Domini nostri Iesu Christi.*

God our Father, we ask that you deign to bless this offering, to recognize it as ours, to deem it valid, reasoned, and acceptable in all respects, so that it might become for us the Body and Blood of your most beloved Son, our Lord Jesus Christ.

91. *Qui, pridie quam pateretur, accepit panem in sanctas ac venerabiles manus seas, et elevatis oculis in caelum ad te Deum Patrem suum omnipotentem, tibi gratias agens benedixit, fregit, deditque discipulis suis, dicens: Accipite et manducate ex hoc omnes: hoc est enim Corpus meum, quod pro vobis tradetur.*

The day before He suffered, He took bread into his holy and blessed hands. Raising his eyes heavenward to you, his all-powerful Father and God, and giving thanks to you, he blessed the bread, broke it, and gave it to his disciples, saying: **Take and eat of this, all of you: for this is my Body, which will be handed over on your behalf.**

92. *Simili modo, postquam cenatum est, accipiens et hunc praeclarum calicem in sanctas ac venerabiles manus suas, item tibi gratias agens benedixit, deditque discipulis suis, dicens: Accipite et bibite ex eo omnes: hic est enim calix Sanguinis mei novi et aeterni testamenti, qui*

In like fashion, after the meal was ended, he took this most excellent cup into his holy and blessed hands. Giving thanks to you in the same manner, he blessed the cup and gave it to his disciples, saying: **Take and drink of this, all of you: for this is the cup of my Blood, of the new and everlasting covenant, which will be poured**

pro vobis et pro multis effundetur in remissionem peccatorum. Hoc facite in meam commemorationem.

93. *Mysterium fidei: (a) Mortem tuam annuntiamus, Domine, et tuam resurrectionem confitemur, donec venias. (b) Quotiescumque manducamus panem hunc et calicem bibimus, mortem tuam annuntiamus, Domine, donec venias. (c) Salvator mundi, salva nos, qui per crucem et resurrectionem tuam liberasti nos.*

94. *Unde et memores, Domine, nos servi tui, sed et plebs tua sancta, eiusdem Christi, Filii tui, Domini nostri, tam beatae passionis, necnon et ab inferis resurrectionis, sed et in caelos gloriosae ascensionis: offerimus praeclarae maiestati tuae de tuis donis ac datis hostiam puram, hostiam sanctam, hostiam immaculatam, Panem sanctum vitae aeternae et Calicem salutis perpetuae.*

95. *Supra quae propitio ac sereno vultu respicere digneris: et accepta habere, sicuti accepta habere dignatus es munera pueri tui iusti Abel, et sacrificium Patriarchae nostri Abrahae, et quod tibi obtulit summus sacerdos tuus Melchisedech, sanctum sacrificium, immaculatam hostiam.*

96. *Supplices te rogamus, omnipotens Deus: iube haec perferri per manus sancti Angeli tui in sublime altare tuum, in conspectu divinae maiestatis tuae; ut, quotquot ex hac altaris participatione sacrosanctum Filii tui Corpus et Sanguinem sumpserimus, omni benedictione caelesti et gratia repleamur. (Per Christum Dominum nostrum. Amen.)*

97. *Memento etiam, Domine, famulorum famularumque tuarum N. et N., qui nos praecesserunt cum*

out for you and for countless others so that sins may be forgiven. This must you do as a remembrance of me.

The mystery of faith: (a) We make your death known, O Lord, and we proclaim your resurrection, until you come again. (b) As often as we eat this bread and drink from this cup, O Lord, we make your death known until you come again. (c) Savior of the world, through your cross and resurrection you have given us freedom; bring us to salvation as well.

And so, Father and Lord, we, your servants, and also your entire holy people, are mindful of the holy sufferings of this same Christ, your Son and our Lord, of his resurrection from the dead, and also of his glorious ascension into heaven. From the gifts and blessings you have given us, we offer to your divine majesty a pure offering, a holy offering, a spotless offering: the sacred Bread of life eternal and the Cup of salvation everlasting.

Deign to look down upon these gifts with gracious and tranquil mien, and to consider them acceptable, as in your kindness you considered acceptable the offerings of your righteous servant Abel, the sacrifice of Abraham our Patriarch, and the holy sacrifice, the offering without blemish, which your high priest Melchisedech offered unto you.

God most powerful, we humbly ask you to command that these gifts be carried in the grasp of your holy Angel to your altar on high, in the very sight of your divine majesty, so that all of us who will receive the most sacred Body and Blood of your Son through our sharing in the offering at this earthly altar may be filled with every heavenly blessing and favor as well. (We ask this through Christ our Lord. Amen.)

Father and Lord, bring to mind also those sons and daughters of yours who have gone on ahead

signo fidei, et dormiunt in somno pacis. Ipsis, Domine, et omnibus in Christo quiescentibus, locum refrigerii, lucis et pacis, ut indulgeas, deprecamur. (Per Christum Dominum nostrum. Amen.)

of us bearing the mark of faith, and now repose in tranquil sleep. To them, Father and Lord, and to all who rest in Christ, we pray that you will grant a place of refreshment, of brightness, of serene peace. (We ask this through Christ our Lord. Amen.)

98. Nobis quoque peccatoribus famulis tuis, de multitudine miserationum tuarum sperantibus, partem aliquam et societatem donare digneris cum tuis sanctis Apostolis et Martyribus: cum Ioanne, Stephano, Matthia, Barnaba, (Ignatio, Alexandro, Marcellino, Petro, Felicitate, Perpetua, Agatha, Lucia, Agnete, Caecilia, Anastasia) et omnibus Sanctis tuis: intra quorum nos consortium, non aestimator meriti, sed veniae, quaesumus, largitor admitte. Per Christum Dominum nostrum.

To us as well, sinners, yes, but servants yet of yours, we who place our hope in the countless times you have shown your mercy: we ask that you deign to grant some share in the companionship of your holy Apostles and Martyrs: of John, Stephen, Matthias, Barnabas, (Ignatius, Alexander, Marcellinus, Peter, Felicity, Perpetua, Agatha, Lucy, Agnes, Cecelia, Anastasia), and all your Saints. Grant, we ask, that, bestowing gracious pardon, not reckoning stern balance due, you allow us admittance into their heavenly company. We ask this through Christ our Lord.

99. Per quem haec omnia, Domine, semper bona creas, sanctificas, vivificas, benedicis, et praestas nobis.

O Father and Lord, it is through Christ that ever you bring all these gifts into being, that you make them to be holy, living, and blessed, that you bestow them upon us.

100. Per ipsum, et cum ipso, et in ipso, est tibi Deo Patri omnipotenti, in unitate Spiritus Sancti, omnis honor et gloria per omnia saecula saeculorum. Amen.

God Father Almighty, it is through him, with him, and in him, in unity with the Holy Spirit, that you possess all honor and glory for endless ages to come. Amen.

EUCHARISTIC PRAYER TWO

101. Vere dignum et iustum est, aequum et salutare, nos tibi, sancte Pater, semper et ubique gratias agere per Filium dilectionis tuae Iesum Christum, Verbum tuum per quod cuncta fecisti: quem misisti nobis Salvatorem et Redemptorem, incarnatum de Spiritu Sancto et ex Virgine natum. Qui voluntatem tuam adimplens et populum tibi sanctum acquirens extendit manus cum pateretur, ut mortem solveret et

It is, indeed, fitting and right, it is just, it leads to salvation, O Father most holy, that on every occasion and in every place we should offer you grateful thanks through Jesus Christ, the Son of your love, your Word, through whom you made all that is. He it is whom you sent to us as Savior and Redeemer, enfleshed by the Holy Spirit and of the Virgin born. While fulfilling your command and amassing a people sacred unto you, He stretched forth his hands in suffering, so that

resurrectionem manifestaret. Et ideo cum Angelis et omnibus Sanctis gloriam tuam praedicamus, una voce dicentes: Sanctus, Sanctus, Sanctus Dominus Deus Sabaoth. Pleni sunt caeli et terrae gloria tua. Hosanna in excelsis. Benedictus qui venit in nomine Domini. Hosanna in excelsis.

he might loose the bonds death had forged and make it clear that we would rise to life once more. And so with the Angels and all the Saints we proclaim your glory, saying in but one voice: Holy, Holy, Holy Lord, God of Hosts. Heaven and earth are filled with your glory. Hosanna in the highest! Blessed is the one who comes in the name of the Lord. Hosanna in the highest!

102. *Vere Sanctus es, Domine, fons omnis sanctitatis.*

Truly, you are the Holy One, O Father and Lord; from you all holiness springs.

103. *Haec ergo dona, quaesumus, Spiritus tui rore sanctifica, ut nobis Corpus et Sanguis fiant Domini nostri Iesu Christi.*

These gifts, then: we ask that you make them holy by the gentle coming of your Spirit, so that for our sake they may become the Body and Blood of our Lord Jesus Christ.

104. *Qui cum Passioni voluntarie traderetur, accepit panem et gratias agens fregit, deditque discipulis suis, dicens: Accipite et manducate ex hoc omnes: hoc est enim Corpus meum, quod pro vobis tradetur.*

While of his own will he was being delivered over to his suffering, he took bread, broke it as he gave thanks, and gave it to his disciples, saying: **Take and eat of this, all of you: for this is my Body, which will be handed over on your behalf.**

105. *Simili modo, postquam cenatum est, accipiens et calicem, iterum gratias agens dedit discipulis suis, dicens: Accipite et bibite ex eo omnes: hic est enim calix Sanguinis mei novi et aeterni testamenti, qui pro vobis et pro multis effundetur in remissionem peccatorum. Hoc facite in meam commemorationem.*

In the same way, after the meal was over, he took the chalice and, again giving thanks, gave it to his disciples, saying: **Take and drink of this, all of you: for this is the cup of my Blood, of the new and everlasting covenant, which will be poured out for you and for countless others so that sins may be forgiven. This must you do as a remembrance of me.**

106. *Mysterium fidei:* (a) *Mortem tuam annuntiamus, Domine, et tuam resurrectionem confitemur, donec venias.* (b) *Quotiescumque manducamus panem hunc et calicem bibimus, mortem tuam annuntiamus, Domine, donec venias.* (c) *Salvator*

The mystery of faith: (a) We make your death known, O Lord, and we proclaim your resurrection, until you come again. (b) As often as we eat this bread and drink from this cup, we make your death known, O Lord, until you come again. (c) Savior of the world, through your cross

mundi, salva nos, qui per crucem et resurrectionem tuam liberasti nos.

107. *Memores igitur mortis et resurrectionis eius, tibi, Domine, panem vitae et calicem salutis offerimus, gratias agentes quia nos dignos habuisti astare coram te et tibi ministrare.*

Et supplices deprecamur ut Corporis et Sanguinis Christi participes a Spiritu Sancto congregemur in unum.

Recordare, Domine, Ecclesiae tuae toto orbe diffusae, ut eam in caritate perficias una cum Papa nostro N., et Episcopo N., and universo clero.

(Memento famuli tui [famulae tuae] N., quem [quam] [hodie] ad te ex hoc mundo vocasti. Concede, ut, qui [quae] complantatus [complantata] fuit similitudini mortis Filii tui, simul fiat et resurrectionis ipsius.)

Memento etiam fratrum nostrorum, qui in spe resurrectionis dormierunt, omniumque in tua miseratione defunctorum, et eos in lumen vultis tui admitte.

Omnium nostrum, quaesumus, miserere, ut cum beata Dei Genetrice Virgine Maria, beatis Apostolis et omnibus Sanctis, qui tibi a saeculo placuerunt, aeternae vitae mereamur esse consortes, et te laudemus et glorificemus per Filium tuum Iesum Christum.

108. *Per ipsum, et cum ipso, et in ipso, est tibi Deo Patri omnipotenti, in unitate Spiritus Sancti, omnis honor et gloria per omnia saecula saeculorum. Amen.*

and resurrection you have given us freedom; bring us to salvation as well.

Having in mind, then, his death and resurrection, we offer to you, O Father and Lord, the bread of life and the chalice of salvation, rendering grateful thanks to you because you have considered us worthy to stand in your presence and serve you.

As humble petitioners we beg that we who partake of the Body and Blood of Christ might be gathered into a single flock by the Holy Spirit.

Father and Lord, call to mind your Church, spread out over the entire world, so that you might perfect it in love, along with our Pope N., and our Bishop(s) N. (and N.), and all those in the clerical state.

(Be mindful of your servant N., whom you have summoned out of the world [this day] into your presence. Grant that he [she] who has been placed in the earth in imitation of the death of your Son, may likewise rise in imitation of his resurrection.)

Be mindful also of our brothers and sisters who have gone to rest in the hope of the resurrection. In your mercy be mindful also of all the dead, and grant them admittance to the very light that radiates from your countenance.

We ask that you have mercy on all of us, so that in the company of the Blessed Mother of God, Mary the Virgin, of the blessed Apostles, and of all the Saints who have pleased you down through the ages, we might be made worthy to partake of eternal life, and might praise and glorify you through your Son, Jesus Christ.

God Father Almighty, it is through him, with him, and in him, in unity with the Holy Spirit, that you possess all honor and glory for endless ages to come. Amen.

EUCHARISTIC PRAYER THREE

[109] *Vere Sanctus es, Domine, et merito te laudat omnis a te condita creatura, quia per Filium tuum, Dominum nostrum Iesum Christum, Spiritus Sancti operante virtute, vivificas et sanctificas universa, et populum tibi congregare non desinis, ut a solis ortu usque ad occasum oblatio munda offeratur nomini tuo.*

Truly you are the Holy One, O Father and Lord, and rightly does every creature you have made render praise to you, for through your Son, our Lord, Jesus Christ, and with the power of the Holy Spirit, you give life and holiness to all things. Ceaselessly you gather a people to yourself, so that from the rising of the sun to the setting thereof an oblation pure and undefiled might be offered to your name.

[110] *Supplices ergo te, Domine, deprecamur, ut haec munera, quae tibi sacranda detulimus, eodem Spiritu sanctificare digneris, ut Corpus et + Sanguis fiant Filii tui, Domini nostri Iesu Christi, cuius mandato haec mysteria celebramus.*

In humble prayer, then, O Father and Lord, we ask of you that, through that same Spirit, you would deign to make holy these gifts which we have brought for consecration to you, so that they might become the Body and + Blood of your Son, our Lord Jesus Christ; it is at his command that we celebrate these mysteries.

[111] *Ipse enim in qua nocte tradebatur accepit panem et tibi gratias agens benedixit, fregit, deditque discipulis suis, dicens: Accipite et manducate ex hoc omnes: hoc est enim Corpus meum, quod pro vobis tradetur.*

For on the night he was handed over, he took bread, blessed it as he gave thanks to you, broke it, and gave it to his disciples, saying: **Take and eat of this, all of you: for this is my Body, which will be handed over on your behalf.**

[112] *Simili modo, postquam cenatum est, accipiens calicem, et tibi gratias agens benedixit, deditque discipulis suis, dicens: Accipite et bibite ex eo omnes: hic est enim calix Sanguinis mei novi et aeterni testamenti, qui pro vobis et pro multis effundetur in remissionem peccatorum. Hoc facite in meam commemorationem.*

In the same way, after the meal was over, he took the chalice, blessed it as he gave thanks to you, and gave it to his disciples, saying: **Take and drink of this, all of you: for this is the cup of my Blood, of the new and everlasting covenant, which will be poured out for you and for countless others so that sins may be forgiven. This must you do as a remembrance of me.**

[113] *Mysterium fidei:* (a) *Mortem tuam annuntiamus, Domine, et tuam resurrectionem confitemur, donec venias.* (b) *Quotiescumque manducamus panem hunc et calicem bibimus, mortem tuam annuntiamus, Domine, donec venias.* (c) *Salvator*

The mystery of faith: (a) We make your death known, O Lord, and we proclaim your resurrection, until you come again. (b) As often as we eat this bread and drink from this cup, we make your death known, O Lord, until you come again. (c) Savior of the world, through your cross

mundi, salva nos, qui per crucem et resurrectionem tuam liberasti nos.

and resurrection you have given us freedom; bring us to salvation as well.

[114] *Memores igitur, Domine, eiusdem Filii tui salutiferae passionis necnon mirabilis resurrectionis et ascensionis in caelum, sed et praestolantes alterum eius adventum, offerimus tibi, gratias referentes, hoc sacrificium vivum et sanctum.*

As we remember, then, O Father and Lord, the life-giving passion of this, your Son, as we are mindful of his wondrous resurrection and ascension into heaven, and as we keep watch for when he shall come again, we offer you in thanksgiving this living and sacred sacrifice.

Respice, quaesumus, in oblationem Ecclesiae tuae et, agnoscens Hostiam, cuius voluisti immolatione placari, concede, ut qui Corpore et Sanguine Filii tui reficimur, Spiritu eius Sancto repleti, unum corpus et unus spiritus inveniamur in Christo.

We ask that you look upon the offering of your Church, and recognize the Victim by whose offering of himself you have decreed that you would be appeased. Grant that we who are made new by the Body and Blood of your Son may, when filled with his Holy Spirit, be found to be one body and one spirit in Christ.

Ipse nos tibi perficiat munus aeternum, ut cum electis tuis hereditatem consequi valeamus, in primis cum beatissima Virgine, Dei Genetrice, Maria, cum beatis Apostolis tuis et gloriosis Martyribus, (cum Sancto N.,) et omnibus Sanctis, quorum intercessione perpetuo apud te confidimus adiuvari.

May he make of us an eternal offering to you, so that in the company of your chosen ones we might be enabled to attain an eternal inheritance, especially with the Blessed Virgin, Mary, the Mother of God, with your holy Apostles and glorious Martyrs, (with Saint N.,) and with all the Saints, through whose prayers we trust that we will find unceasing intercession in your presence.

Haec Hostia nostrae reconciliationis proficiat, quaesumus, Domine, ad totius mundi pacem atque salutem. Ecclesiam tuam, peregrinantem in terra, in fide et caritate firmare digneris cum famulo tuo Papa nostro N. et Episcopo nostro N., cum episcopali ordine et universo clero et omni populo acquisitionis tuae. Votis huius familiae, quam tibi astare voluisti, adesto propitius. Omnes filios tuos ubique dispersos tibi, clemens Pater, miseratus coniunge.

Lord, we ask that this Sacrifice, which has reconciled us to you, may enable the entire world to come ever closer to peace and salvation. Your Church, too, in its pilgrim state on earth: deign to strengthen it in faith and love, along with your servant, our Pope N., with our Bishop(s) N. (and N.), with the entire college of bishops, with all who are clerics, and with all the people you have gathered to yourself. In your kindness, be attentive to the prayers of this family of yours which you have willed should stand here in your presence. Merciful Father, in your kind pity join to yourself all your children who are scattered throughout the world.

***Fratres nostros defunctos et omnes qui, tibi placentes, ex hoc saeculo transierunt, in regnum tuum*

**In your abundant kindnesss, grant to all our deceased brothers and sisters, and to all who have been pleasing to you as they have gone

benignus admitte, ubi fore speramus, ut simul gloria tua perenniter satiemur, per Christum Dominum nostrum, per quem mundo bona cuncta largiris.

[115] Per ipsum, et cum ipso, et in ipso, est tibi Deo Patri omnipotenti, in unitate Spiritus sancti, omnis honor et gloria per omnia saecula saeculorum. Amen.

(**[116] Memento famuli tui (famulae tuae) N., quem (quam) (hodie) ad te ex hoc mundo vocasti. Concede, ut, qui (quae) complantatus (complantata) fuit similitudini mortis Filii tui, simul fiat et resurrectionis ipsius, quando mortuos suscitabit in carne de terra et corpus humilitatis nostrae configurabit corpori claritatis suae. Sed et fratres nostros defunctos, et omnes qui, tibi placentes, ex hoc saeculo transierunt, in regnum tuum benignus admitte, ubi fore speramus, ut simul gloria tua perenniter satiemur, quando omnem lacrimam absterges ab oculis nostris, quia te, sicuti es, Deum nostrum videntes, tibi similes erimus cuncta per saecula, et te sine fine laudabimus, per Christum Dominum nostrum, per quem mundo bona cuncta largiris.)

forth from this world, admittance into your kingdom, where we hope that in their company we too will perpetually be filled with the vision of your glory, through Christ our Lord, through whom you give every blessing to the world.

God Father Almighty, it is through him, with him, and in him, in unity with the Holy Spirit, that you possess all honor and glory for endless ages to come.

(**Be mindful of your servant N., whom you have summoned out of the world (this day) into your presence. Grant that, as he (she) is placed in the earth in imitation of the death of your Son, so may he (she) likewise rise in imitation of his resurrection, when he will raise the dead from the earth in their flesh and will refashion our lowly body after the pattern of his glorified one. In your abundant kindnesss, grant to all our deceased brothers and sisters, and to all who have been pleasing to you as they have gone forth from this world, admittance into your kingdom, where we hope that in their company we too will perpetually be filled with the vision of your glory, when you will wipe away every tear from our eyes because, gazing at you, our God, as you are, we shall be like you for all ages to come, and we shall praise you without ceasing through Christ our Lord, through whom you give every blessing to the world.)

EUCHARISTIC PRAYER FOUR

[117] *Vere dignum est tibi gratias agere, vere iustum est te glorificare, Pater sancte, quia unus es Deus vivus et verus, qui es ante saecula et permanes in aeternum, inaccessibilem lucem inhabitans; sed et qui unus bonus atque fons vitae cuncta fecisti, ut creaturas tuas benedictionibus adimpleres multasque laetificares tui luminis claritate. Et ideo coram te innumerae astant turbae angelorum, qui die ac nocte serviunt tibi et, vultus tui gloriam contemplantes, te incessanter glorificant. Cum quibus et nos et, per nostram vocem, omnis quae sub caelo est creatura nomen tuum in exsultatione confitemur, canentes: Sanctus, Sanctus, Sanctus Dominus Deus sabaoth. Pleni sunt caeli et terra gloria tua. Hosanna in excelsis. Benedictus qui venit in nomine Domini. Hosanna in excelsis.*

Truly it is proper to give you thanks, truly it is right to render you honor, Father most holy, for you alone are the living and true God: you were before the ages began and you will be for all eternity, dwelling in a splendor whereto none may draw near. You alone are good, alone the fountain of life: you have brought all things into being, so that you might fill your creatures to the fullest with your blessings and make many of them joyful with the magnificence of your own light. And so angel hosts without number stand in your presence and serve you day and night; gazing upon the loveliness of your countenance, they render you honor without ceasing. In their company we too and, through our voice, every creature that lives beneath heaven's dome proclaim your name with joy unbounded as we sing: Holy, holy, holy Lord, God of Hosts. Heaven and earth are filled with your glory. Hosanna in the highest! Blessed is the one who comes in the name of the Lord. Hosanna in the highest!

[118] *Confitemur tibi, Pater sancte, quia magnus es et omnia opera tua in sapientia et caritate fecisti. Hominem ad tuam imaginem condidisti eique commisisti mundi curam universi, ut, tibi soli Creatori serviens, creaturis omnibus imperaret. Et cum amicitiam tuam, non oboediens, amisisset, non eum dereliquisti in mortis imperio. Omnibus enim misericorditer subvenisti, ut te quaerentes invenirent. Sed et foedera pluries hominibus obtulisti eosque per prophetas erudisti in exspectatione salutis. Et sic, Pater sancte, mundum dilexisti, ut, completa plenitudine temporum, Unigenitum tuum nobis mitteres Salvatorem. Qui, incarnatus de Spiritu Sancto et natus ex Maria Virgine, in nostra condicionis forma est conversatus per omnia absque peccato; salutem evangelizavit pauperibus, redemptionem*

We proclaim you, Father most holy, for you are great: you have performed all your works with wisdom and love. Human beings you formed in your own likeness, and to them entrusted the care of the entire world, so that, in submission and service to you alone, their Creator, they might hold sway over all other creatures. And when in disobedience they rejected your friendship, you did not abandon them to death's rule, for in your great mercy you came to the aid of every one of them, so that those who sought you might find you. Repeatedly, you offered covenants to them, and through the prophets you taught them how they should await salvation's coming. Father most holy, your love for the world was so great that, when the fullness of time had come, you sent your only-begotten one to us as Savior of the World. Enfleshed by the Holy Spirit, born of Mary the Virgin, He was transformed into our human condition in all

captivis, maestis corde laetitiam. Ut tuam vero dispensationem impleret, in mortem tradidit semetipsum ac, resurgens a mortuis, mortem destruxit vitamque renovavit. Et, ut non amplius nobismetipsis viveremus, sed sibi qui pro nobis mortuus est atque surrexit, a te, Pater, misit Spiritum Sanctum primitias credentibus, qui, opus suum in mundo perficiens, omnem sanctificationem compleret.

respects save sin. He proclaimed the good news of salvation to the poor, freedom to prisoners, joy to the stricken of heart. But so that he might fulfill what you had decreed, he handed himself over to death and, in rising from the dead, destroyed death and restored life. Furthermore, so that we might no longer live self-centeredly, but rather might spend our lives for him who died and rose for us, he sent from you, Father, the Holy Spirit as the first fruits of redemption for those who believed in him; it was the Spirit who would bring his work to perfection in the world and so bring to full measure the entire work of sanctification.

[119] Quaesumus igitur, Domine, ut idem Spiritus Sanctus haec munera sanctificare dignetur, ut Corpus et + Sanguis fiant Domini nostri Iesu Christi ad hoc magnum mysterium celebrandum, quod ipse nobis reliquit in foedus aeternum.

Therefore we ask, Father and Lord, that this same Holy Spirit deign to make these gifts holy, so that they might become the Body and + Blood of our Lord Jesus Christ, in celebration of this great mystery which he himself left us as an eternal covenant.

[120] Ipse enim, cum hora venisset ut glorificaretur a te, Pater sancte, ac dilexisset suos qui erant in mundo, in finem dilexit eos: et cenantibus illis, accepit panem, benedixit ac fregit, deditque discipulis suis, dicens: Accipite et manducate ex hoc omnes: hoc est enim Corpus meum, quod pro vobis tradetur.

Since the appointed hour had arrived when he was to receive glory from you, Father most holy, and since he had loved those who were his own in the world, he continued that love to the very end. While they were at table, he took bread, blessed it, broke it, and gave it to his disciples, saying: **Take and eat of this, all of you: for this is my Body, which will be handed over on your behalf.**

[121] Simili modo accipiens calicem, ex genimine vitis repletum, gratias egit, deditque discipulis suis, dicens: Accipite et bibite ex eo omnes: hic est enim calix Sanguinis mei novi et aeterni testamenti, qui pro vobis et pro multis effundetur in remissionem peccatorum. Hoc facite in meam commemorationem.

In the same way, he took the cup, brimming with the fruit of the vine. He offered thanks, and gave the cup to his disciples, saying: **Take and drink of this, all of you: for this is the cup of my Blood, of the new and everlasting covenant, which will be poured out for you and for countless others so that sins may be forgiven. This must you do as a remembrance of me.**

[122] Mysterium fidei: (a) Mortem tuam annuntiamus, Domine, et tuam resurrectionem confitemur, donec venias. (b) Quotiescumque manducamus panem hunc et calicem

The mystery of faith: (a) We make your death known, O Lord, and we proclaim your resurrection, until you come again. (b) As often as we eat this bread and drink from this cup, we make

bibimus, mortem tuam annuntiamus, Domine, donec venias. (c) Salvator mundi, salva nos, qui per crucem et resurrectionem tuam liberasti nos.

[123] *Unde et nos, Domine, redemptionis nostrae memoriale nunc celebrantes, mortem Christi eiusque descensum ad inferos recolimus, eius resurrectionem et ascensionem ad tuam dexteram profitemur, et, exspectantes ipsius adventum in gloria, offerimus tibi eius Corpus et Sanguinem, sacrificium tibi acceptabile et toti mundo salutare. Respice, Domine, in Hostiam, quam Ecclesiae tuae ipse parasti, et concede benignus omnibus qui ex hoc uno pane participabunt et calice, ut, in unum corpus a Sancto Spiritu congregati, in Christo hostia viva perficiantur, ad laudem gloriae tuae. Nunc ergo, Domine, omnium recordare, pro quibus tibi hanc oblationem offerimus: in primis famuli tui, Papae nostri N., Episcopi nostri N., et Episcoporum ordinis universi, sed et totius cleri, et offerentium, et circumstantium, et cuncti populi tui, et omnium, qui te quaerunt corde sincero. Memento etiam illorum, qui obierunt in pace Christi tui, et omnium defunctorum, quorum fidem tu solus cognovisti. Nobis omnibus, filiis tuis, clemens Pater, concede, ut caelestem hereditatem consequi valeamus cum beata Virgine, Dei Genetrice, Maria, cum Apostolis et Sanctis tuis in regno tuo, ubi cum universa creatura, a corruptione peccati et mortis liberata, te glorificemus per Christum Dominum nostrum, per quem mundo bona cuncta largiris.*

[124] *Per ipsum, et cum ipso, et in ipso, est tibi Deo Patri omnipotenti, in unitate Spiritus Sancti, omnia honor et gloria per omnia saecula saeculorum.*

your death known, O Lord, until you come again. (c) Savior of the world, through your cross and resurrection you have given us freedom; bring us to salvation as well.

And so, Father and Lord, as we celebrate this memorial of our redemption, we also call to mind the death of Christ and his descent to the lower world; and we proclaim his resurrection and ascension to your right hand. As we await his return in glory, we offer you his Body and Blood, a sacrifice acceptable to you and life-bringing for the entire world. Lord, look upon this offering which you yourself have prepared for your Church; in your kindly mercy grant to all who will share in this one bread and one cup this favor: gathered together into one body by the Holy Spirit, may they be made into a living sacrifice in Christ, to the praise of your divine glory. Lord, be mindful also of all those for whom we bring this offering to you, especially your servant, our Pope N., our Bishop(s) N(N)., the entire college of Bishops, those in the clerical state, those who offer this sacrifice, those who are present here, the whole of those who are your people, and all who seek you with a sincere heart. Be mindful too of those who have died in the peace of your Anointed One, and of all the dead whose faith you alone have known. To all of us, your children, merciful Father, grant the favor of being able to attain a heavenly inheritance in your kingdom in the company of the Blessed Virgin, Mary, the Mother of God, of the Apostles, and of your Saints. In that kingdom, along with the whole of creation, freed as it will then be from the contagion of sin and death, may we sing your praises through Christ our Lord, through whom you give every blessing to the world.

God Father Almighty, it is through him, with him, and in him, in unity with the Holy Spirit, that you possess all honor and glory for endless ages to come. Amen.

OREMUS

Speaking with God

in the

Words of the Roman Rite

V

Index

INDEX

SIGLA: A = Apostle; AB = Abbot; B = Bishop; D = Doctor; M = Martyr; M&P = Mass(es) and Prayers; P = Pope; PR = Priest; R = Religious; V = Virgin

-A-

Abbot or Abbess, *Blessing of, p.230* | Achilleus and Nereus (MM), *12 May, p.122* | Advent, Dec 17-24, *p.14* | Advent, *Prefaces #1 and #2, p.328* | Advent, Season of, *p.7* | Advent, Sundays in, *p.9* | | Advent, Weekdays Before Dec 16, *p.11* | Agatha (V-M), *05 Feb, p.109* | Agnes (V-M), *21 Jan, p.105* | Alacoque, Margaret Mary (V), *16 Oct, p.163* | Albert the Great (B-D), *15 Nov, p.171* | All Saints, *01 Nov, p.167* | All Saints, *Preface, p.360* | All Souls, *02 Nov, p.167* | All the Saints, *Votive Mass of, p.287* | Aloysius Gonzaga (R), *21 Jun, p.130* | Alphonsus Liguori (B-D), *01 Aug, p.142* | Altar, Dedication of, *Preface, p.362* | Ambrose (B-D), *07 Dec, p.176* | Andrew (A), *30 Nov, p.174* | Angela Merici (V), *27 Jan, p.107* | Angels, Holy, *Votive Mass of, p.284* | Angels, Holy Guardian, *02 Oct, p.160* | Angels, *Preface of, p.347* | Ann and Joachim, *Parents of the BVM, 26 Jul, p.140* | Anniversaries of Marriage, *p.229* | Anniversary Masses for the Dead, *p.293* | Annunciation, *25 Mar, p.115* | Annunciation, *Preface, p.357* | Anselm (B-D), *21 Apr, p.118* | Ansgar (B), *03 Feb, p.109* | Anthony (AB), *17 Jan, p.104* | Anthony Mary Claret (PR), *24 Oct, p.166* | Anthony Mary Zaccaria (PR), *05 Jul, p.135* | Anthony of Padua (PR-D), *13 Jun, p.129* | Any Need, Masses in Time of, *p.270* | Apostles, All, *Votive Mass of, p.285* | Apostles, Prefaces #1 and #2, *pp.348-349* | Aquinas, Thomas (P-D), *28 Jan, p.107* | Ascension, *p.70* | Ascension, *Prefaces #1 and #2, p.338* | Ash Wednesday, *p.33* | Ash Wednesday, *Weekdays after, p.34* | Assumption of the BVM, *15 Aug, p.146* | Assumption, *Preface, p.359* | Athanasius (B-D), *02 May, p.121* | Augustine (B-D), *28 Aug, p.151* | Augustine of Canterbury (B), *27 May, p.125*.

-B-

BVM, Birth of, *08 Sep, p.153* | BVM, Common of, *p.186* | BVM Mother of God, *01 Jan, p.25* | Blessed Virgin Mary, Mother of the Church, *Preface, p.347* | BVM of Lourdes, *11 Feb, p.111* | BVM, *Prefaces #1 and #2, p.346* | BVM, Presentation of, *21 Nov, p.173* | BVM, *Votive Masses of, p.283* | Baptism of the Lord, *p.26* | Baptism of the Lord, *Preface, p.356* | Barnabas (A), *11 Jun, p.129* | Bartholomew (A), *24 Aug, p.150* | Basil and Gregory (BB-DD), *02 Jan, p.103* | Basilica of St. Mary Major, *Dedication of, 05 Aug, p.143* | Becket, Thomas (B-M), *29 Dec, p.181* | Bede, Venerable (P-D), *25 May, p.124* | Beginning of Civil Year, *M&P for, p.261* | Beheading of John the Baptist, *29 Aug, p.151* | Bellarmine, Robert (B-D), *17 Sep, p.155* | Benedict (AB), *11 Jul, p.136* | Bernadine of Sienna (PR), *20 May, p.123* | Bernard (AB), *20 Aug, p.148* | Birth of John the Baptist, *24 Jun, p.132* | Birth of the BVM, *08 Sep, p.153* | Bishop, *M&P for, p.243* | Bishop, Diocesan, *M&P for a Deceased, p.301* | Bishop, Non-diocesan, *M&P for a Deceased, p.302* | Blase (B-M), *03 Feb, p.109* | Blessing of Abbot or Abbess, *p.230* | Bonaventure (B-D), *15 Jul, p.137* | Boniface (B-M), *05 Jun, p.128* | Borromeo, Charles (B), *04 Nov, p.169* | Bosco, John (P), *31 Jan, p.107* | Brebeuf, John de, Isaac Jogues, and Companions (MM), *19 Oct, p.165* | Bridget (R), *23 Jul, p.139* | Bruno (PR), *06 Oct, p.161*.

-C-

Cajetan (PR), *07 Aug, p.144* | Calasanz, Joseph (P), *25 Aug, p.150* | Callistus I (P-M), *14 Oct, p.162* | Camillus de Lellis (PR), *14 Jul, p.137* | Canisius, Peter (P-D), *21 Dec, p.179* | Captives, *M&P for, p.266* | Casimir,

385

04 Mar, p.113 | Catherine of Sienna (V-D), 29 Apr, p.120 | Cecelia (V-M), 22 Nov, p.173 | Celebration of Marriage, *Prefaces #A-#C, pp.363-364* | Certain Particular Needs, *M&P for, p.272* | Chair of St. Peter, 22 Feb, p.112 | Chanel, Peter (P-M), 28 Apr, p.119 | Charity, *M&P to Ask for, p.273* | Charles Borromeo (B), 04 Nov, p.169 | Charles Lwanga and Companions (MM), 03 Jun, p.127 | Children, *Funerals of, p.311* | Chrism Mass, p.54 | Chrism Mass, *Preface, p.335* | Christ the King *(34th Sunday in Ordinary Time), p.97* | Christ the King, *Preface, p.360* | Christian Initiation, *Ritual Masses of, p.219* | Christians Undergoing Persecution, *M&P for, p.255* | Christians, Unity of, *Preface, p.365* | Christmas Day, 25 Dec, p.21 | Christmas, *Masses During the Octave, p.24* | Christmas, *Prefaces #1-#3, p.329* | Christmas, *Season of, p.19* | Christmastime, *Weekdays of, p.27* | Chrysologus, Peter (B-D), 30 Jul, p.141 | Chrysostom, John (B-D), 13 Sep, p.153 | Church, Dedication of, *Prefaces #A-#C, pp.361-362* | Church, *M&P for, p.239* | Civil Year, *M&P at the Beginning of, p.261* | Clare (V), 11 Aug, p.145 | Clement I (P-M), 23 Nov, p.174 | Columban (AB), 23 Nov, p.174 | Come, Most Holy Spirit of Love, *Sequence, p.323* | Common of BVM, *p.186* | Common of Dedication of a Church, *p.185* | Common of Doctors of the Church, *p.205* | Common of Holy Men and Women, *p.208* | Common of Martyrs, *p.190* | Common of Pastors, *p.198* | Common of Virgins, *p.206* | Commons, *p.183* | Common Prefaces #1-#6, *pp.351-353* | Consecration to a Life of Virginity, *p.231* | Conversion of St. Paul the Apostle, 25 Jan, p.106 | Cornelius and Cyprian (MM), 16 Sep, p.155 | Corpus Christi, *p.99* | Cosmas and Damian (MM), 26 Sep, p.157 | Council or Synod, *M&P for, p.245* | Cyril and Methodius (BB), 14 Feb, p.111 | Cyril of Alexandria (B-D), 27 Jun, p.132 | Cyril of Jerusalem (B-D), 18 Mar, p.114.

-D-

Damascene, John (P-D), 04 Dec, p.176 | Damasus I (P), 11 Dec, p.177 | Damian and Cosmas (MM), 26 Sep, p.157 | Damian, Peter (B-D), 21 Feb, p.112 | Day of Wrathful Judgment, *Sequence, p.317* | Deacon, *M&P for a Deceased, p.304* | Dead, *Masses for the, p.289* | Dead, *Prefaces for the, #1-#5, pp.353-355* | Death, Happy, *M&P to Seek the Grace of, p.276* | Dedication of an Altar, *Preface, p.362* | Dedication of a Church, *Common of, p.185* | Dedication of a Church, *Prefaces #A-#C, pp.361-362* | Dedication of a Church, *Ritual Masses for, p.235* | Dedication of Churches of Saints Peter and Paul, 18 Nov, p.173 | Dedication of Saint Mary Major, 05 Aug, p.143 | de la Salle, John Baptist (P), 07 Apr, p.117 | Denis and Companions (MM), 09 Oct, p.161 | Development of Nations, *M&P for, p.257* | Dies Irae, *Sequence, p.317* | Doctors of the Church, *Common of, p.205* | Dominic (PR), 08 Aug, p.144 | Dying, *M&P for the, p.268.*

-E-

Earthquake, *M&P in Time of, p.269* | Easter, *Prefaces of #1-#5, p.336-337* | Easter Sunday, p.65 | Easter Week, *Weekdays of, p.65* | Easter, *Season of, p.59* | Election of a Pope or Bishop, *M&P for, p.244* | Elizabeth of Hungary (R), 17 Nov., p.172 | Elizabeth of Portugal, 04 Jul, p.135 | Emiliani, Jerome, 09 Feb, p.110 | Epiphany, p.26 | Epiphany, *Preface, p.330* | Ephraem (Deacon-D), 09 Jun, p.128 | Epiphany, p.27 | Eucharist, Holy, *Prefaces #1 and #2, p.344* | Eucharist, Holy, *Votive Mass of the, p.279* | Eusebius of Vercelli (B), 02 Aug, p.142 | Eucharistic Prayers, *p.367* | Eucharistic Prayers: One, p.369; Two, p.373; Three, p.376; Four, p.379 | Eudes, John (P), 19 Aug, p.147 | Exaltation of the Holy Cross, 14 Sep, p.154 | Exaltation of the Holy Cross, *Preface, p.359* | Exiles and Fugitives, *M&P for, p.265.*

-F-

Fabian and Sebastian (MM), 20 Jan, p.104 | Family, *M&P for, p.274* | Famine, *M&P for Those Suffering from, p. 264* | Famine, *M&P in Time of, p.264* | Felicity and Perpetua (MM), 07 Mar, p.113 | Ferrer, Vincent (P), 05 Apr, p.117 | Fidelis of Sigmaringen (PR-

M), 24 *Apr, p.119* | Fifth Sunday of Easter, *p.69* | First Martyrs of Rome, 30 *Jun, p.134* | First Sunday of Advent, *p.9* | Forgiveness of Sins, *M&P for, p.272* | Fourth Sunday of Advent, *p.10* | Fourth Sunday of Easter, *p.69* | Frances of Rome (R), *09 Mar, p.114* | Francis Xavier (PR), *03 Dec, p.175* | Francis de Sales (B-D), 24 *Jan, p.105* | Francis of Assisi (R), 04 *Oct, p.160* | Francis of Paola (Hermit), 02 *Apr, p.116* | Friends and Relatives, *M&P for, p.274* | Fugitives and Exiles, *M&P for, p.265* | Funeral Masses, *p.291*.

-G-
Gabriel, Michael, Raphael, *Archangels,* 29 Sep, *p.158* | George (M), 23 *Apr, p.118* | Gertrude (V), 16 *Nov, p.172* | Gonzaga, Aloysius (R), 21 *Jun, p.130* | Good Friday, *p.55* | Good Weather, *M&P for, p.269* | Goretti, Maria (V-M), *06 Jul, p.136* | Gospel, *M&P for the Spread of, p.253* | Gregory Nazienzen and Basil the Great (BB-DD), 02 *Jan, p.103* | Gregory VII (P), 25 *May, p.124* | Gregory the Great (P-D), 03 *Sep, p.152* | Guardian Angels, Holy, 02 *Oct, p.160*.

-H-
Happy Death, *M&P to Seek the Grace of, p.276* | Harmony, *M&P to Foster, p.273* | Harvest, *M&P after, p.264* | Head of State, *M&P for, p.257* | Hedwig (R), 16 *Oct, p.163* | Henry, 13 *Jul, p.137* | Hilary (B-D), 13 *Jan, p.103* | Hippolytus and Pontian (MM), 13 *Aug, p.146* | Holy Angels, *Votive Mass of, p.284* | Holy Apostles, *Votive Mass of All, p.285* | Holy Cross, Exaltation (Triumph) of, 14 *Sep, p.154* | Holy Cross, Exaltation (Triumph) of, *Preface, p.359* | Holy Cross, Mystery of, *Votive Mass, p.279* | Holy Eucharist, *Votive Mass of, p.279* | Holy Eucharist, *Preface of #1 and #2, p.344* | Holy Family, *p.23* | Holy Guardian Angels, 02 *Oct, p.160* | Holy Innocents (MM), 28 *Dec, p.180* | Holy Men and Women, *Common of, p.208* | Holy Name of Jesus, *Votive Mass of, p.280* | Holy Name of Mary, *Votive Mass of, p.284* | Holy Saturday, *p.61* | Holy Spirit, *Votive Mass of, p.282* | Holy Spirit, *Prefaces #1 and #2, p.345* | Holy Thursday, *p.54* | Holy Trinity, *preface, p.339* | Holy Trinity, *Votive Mass of, p.279* | Holy Virgins and Religious, *Preface, p.351* | Holy Week, *Weekdays of, p.52* | Human Work, *M&P for Sanctification of, p.262*.

-I-
Ignatius of Antioch (B-M), 17 *Oct, p.163* | Ignatius of Loyola (PR), 31 *Jul, p.141* | Immaculate Conception of the BVM, 08 *Dec, p.177* | Immaculate Conception, *Preface, p.355* | Immaculate Heart of Mary, *Saturday after Second Sunday after Pentecost, p.126* | Injurers, *M&P for, p.275* | Innocents, Holy (MM), 28 *Dec, p.180* | Irenaeus (B-M), 28 *Jun, p.133* | Isaac Jogues, John de Brebeuf, and Companions (MM), 19 *Oct, p.165* | Isidore (B-D), 04 *Apr, p.116*.

-J-
James (A), 25 *Jul, p.139* | James and Philip (AA), 03 *May, p.122* | Jane Frances de Chantal (R), 12 *Dec, p.178* | Januarius (B-M), 19 *Sep, p.156* | Jerome (PR-D), 30 *Sep, p.158* | Jerome Emiliani, 09 *Feb, p.110* | Joachim and Ann, *Parents of the BVM,* 26 *Jul, p.140* | Jogues, Isaac, John de Brebeuf, and Companions (MM), 19 *Oct, p.165* | John the Baptist, *Beheading of,* 29 *Aug, p.151* | John the Baptist, *Birth of,* 24 *Jun, p.132* | John the Baptist, *Preface, p.357* | John Baptist de la Salle (PR), 07 *Apr, p.117* | John Bosco (PR), 31 *Jan, p.107* | John Chrysostom (B-D), 13 *Sep, p.153* | John Damascene (PR-D), 04 *Dec, p.176* | John Eudes (PR), 19 *Aug, p.147* | John Fisher and Thomas More (MM), 22 *Jun, p.131* | John I (P-M), 18 *May, p.123* | John Leonard (PR), 09 *Oct, p.161* | John Mary Vianney (PR), 04 *Aug, p.142* | John de Brebeuf, Isaac Jogues, and Companions (MM), 19 *Oct, p.165* | John of Capistrano (PR), 23 *Oct, p.166* | John of God (R), 08 *Mar, p.113* | John of Kanty (PR), 23 *Dec, p.179* | John of the Cross (PR-D), 14 *Dec, p.178* | John the Evangelist (A), 27 *Dec, p.180* | Joseph Calascanz (PR), 25 *Aug, p.150* | Joseph the Husband of Mary, 19 *Mar, p.115* | Joseph the Worker, 01 *May, p.121* | Joseph, Saint, *Votive Mass of, p.285* |

Joseph, *Preface, p.348* | Josephat (B-M), *12 Nov, p.171* | Jude and Simon (AA), *28 Oct, p.166* | Justin (M), *01 Jun, p.126.*

-K-

-L-

Laity, *M&P for, p.250* | Lauda Sion, *Sequence, p.319* | Lawrence (Deacon-M), *10 Aug, p.145* | Lawrence of Brindisi (PR-D), *17 Jul, p.138* | Lent: *Season of, p.31; First Week, p.35; Second Week, p.38; Third Week, p.41; Fourth Week, p.45; Fifth Week, p.48; Prefaces #1-#4, p.330-331, Prefaces for First, Second, Third, Fourth, and Fifth Sundays in, pp.332-333* | Leo the Great (P-D), *10 Nov, p.170* | Leonard, John (P), *09 Oct, p.161* | Life of Virginity, *Consecration to, p.231* | Liguori, Alphonsus (B-D), *01 Aug, p.142* | Local Church, *M&P for, p.241* | Louis of France, *25 Aug, p.150* | Lucy (V-M), *13 Dec, p.178* | Lourdes, Our Lady of, *11 Feb, p.111* | Loyola, Ignatius (P), *31 Jul, p.141* | Luke, Evangelist, *18 Oct, p.164* | Lwanga, Charles, and Companions (MM), *03 Jun, p.127.*

-M-

Marcellinus and Peter (MM), *02 Jun, p.127* | Margaret Mary Alacoque (V), *16 Oct, p.163* | Margaret of Scotland, *16 Nov, p.172* | Maria Goretti (V-M), *06 Jul, p.136* | Mark, Evangelist, *25 Apr, p.119* | Marriage, Celebration of, *Prefaces #A-#C, pp.363-364* | Married Persons, *M&P for Deceased, p.309* | Martha, *29 Jul, p.140* | Martin I (P-M), *13 Apr, p.118* | Martin de Porres (R), *03 Nov, p.169* | Martin of Tours (B), *11 Nov, p.170* | Martyrs, *Common of, p.190* | Martyrs, *Preface, p.350* | Mary Magdalene, *22 Jul, p.138* | Mary Magdalene de Pazzi (V), *25 May, p.124* | Mary Mother of the Church, *Votive Mass of, p.283* | Mary Mother of the Church, *Preface, p.347* | Mary, Blessed Virgin, *Prefaces #1 and #2, p.346* | Masses and Prayers for Certain Particular Needs, *p.272* | Masses and Prayers for Public Needs, *p.256* | Masses and Prayers for Various Needs, *p.237* | Masses and Prayers for Various Public Concerns, *p.261* | Masses for the Dead, *p.289* | Matthew, Apostle and Evangelist, *21 Sep, p.156* | Matthias (A), *14 May, p.123* | Meeting of National Leaders, *M&P for, p.257* | Methodius and Cyril (BB), *14 Feb, p.111* | Michael, Gabriel, and Raphael, *Archangels, 29 Sep, p.158* | Miki, Paul, and Companions (MM), *06 Feb, p.110* | Ministers of the Church, *M&P for, p.248* | Monica, *27 Aug, p.151* | Mount Carmel, Our Lady of, *16 Jul, p.138* | Mystery of the Holy Cross, *Votive Mass of, p.279.*

-N-

Nation or State, *M&P for, p.256* | National Leaders, *Meeting of, M&P for, p.257* | Nations, Development of, *M&P for, p.257* | Need, Any, *M&P for, p.270* | Nereus and Achilleus (MM), *12 May, p.122* | Neri, Philip (P), *26 May, p.125* | Nicholas (B), *06 Dec, p.176* | Norbert (B), *06 Jun, p.128.*

-O-

Octave of Christmas, *p.23* | One Apostle, *Votive Mass of, p. 287* | One Deceased Person, *M&P for, p.296 and p.305* | One Who Died Suddenly, *M&P for, p.307* | One Who Suffered a Long Illness, *M&P for, p.307* | One Who Worked in the Service of the Gospel, *M&P for a Deceased, p.307* | Ordinary Time, *p.81* | Our Lady of Lourdes, *11 Feb, p.111* | Our Lady of Mount Carmel, *16 Jul, p.138* | Our Lady of Sorrows, *15 Sep, p.154* | Our Lady of the Rosary, *07 Oct, p.161.*

-P-

Palm (Passion) Sunday, *p.51* | Pancratius (M), *12 May, p.122* | Parents, *M&P for Deceased, p.310* | Passion (Palm) Sunday, *p.51* | Passion (Palm) Sunday, *Preface, p.335* | Passion, *Preface #1 and #2, p.334* | Pastoral or Spiritual Meetings, *M&P for, p.255* | Pastors, *Common of, p.198* | Pastors, *Preface, p.350* | Patrick (B), *17 Mar, p.114* | Paul Miki and Companions (MM), *06 Feb, p.110* | Paul of the Cross (PR), *19 Oct, p.165* | Paul the Apostle, *Conversion of, 25 Jan, p.106* | Paul, *Votive Mass of, p.286* | Paulinus of Nola (B), *22 Jun, p.131* | Peace and Justice, *M&P for Preserving, p.258* | Peace, *M&P for,* p.259 | Pentecost, p.71 | Pentecost, *Preface*, p.339 | Perpetua and Felicity (MM), 07 Mar, p.113 | Persecuted Christians, *M&P for*, p.255 | Peter, Chair of, 22 Feb, p.112 | Peter Chanel (PR-M), 28 Apr, p.119 | Peter Canisius (PR-D), 21 Dec, p.179 | Peter Chrysologus (B-D), 30 Jul, p.141 | Peter Damien (B-D), 21 Feb, p.112 | Peter and Marcellinus (MM), 02 Jan, p.127 | Peter and Paul (AA), 29 Jun, p.134 | Peter and Paul, *Vigil of*, 28 Jun, p.133 | Peter and Paul, *Votive Mass of*, p.286 | Peter and Paul, *Preface*, p.358 | Peter, *Votive Mass of*, p.286 | Philip Neri (PR), 26 May, p.125 | Philip and James (AA), 03 May, p.122 | Pius V (P), 30 Apr, p.120 | Pius X (P), 21 Aug, p.148 | *Planting Time*, M&P for, p.262 | Polycarp (B-M), 23 Feb, p.112 | Pontian and Hippolytus (MM), 13 Aug, p.146 | Pope or Bishop, *M&P for Election of*, p.244 | Pope, *M&P for a Deceased*, p.300 | Pope, *M&P for*, p.242 | Precious Blood, *Votive Mass of*, p.280 | Prefaces, p.325 | Presentation of the BVM, 21 Nov, p.173 | Presentation of the Lord, 02 Feb, p.108 | Presentation of the Lord, *Preface*, p.356 | Preserving Peace and Justice, *M&P for*, p.258 | Priest, *M&P for a Deceased*, p.303 | Priesthood, *M&P for Vocations to*, p.248 | Priests, *M&P for*, p.245 | Prisoners, *M&P for*, p.267 | Profession, Religious, Ritual Mass for, p.231 | Religious Profession, *Preface*, p.365 | Proper of the Saints, p.101 | Public Needs, *M&P for*, p.256.

-Q-
Queenship of Mary, 22 Aug, p.149.

-R-
Rain, *M&P for*, p.269 | Raphael, Michael, Gabriel, *Archangels*, 29 Sep, p.158 | Raymond of Pentafort (PR), 07 Jan, p.103 | Reconciliation, *M&P for*, p.259 | Relatives and Friends, *M&P for*, p.274 | Relatives, Friends, and Benefactors, *Deceased*, *M&P for*, p.310 | Religious and Holy Virgins, *Preface*, p.351 | Religious Profession, *Preface*, p.365 | Religious Profession, *Ritual Masses for*, p.231 | Religious Vocations, *M&P for*, p.250 | Religious, *M&P for*, p.249 | Religious, *and Holy Virgins*, *Preface*, p.351) | Religious, *M&P for a Deceased*, p.304 | Revolution or War, *M&P in Time of*, p.260 | Ritual Masses, p.217 | Robert Bellarmine (B-D), 17 Sep, p.155 | Romuald (AB), 19 Jun, p.130 | Rose of Lima (V), 23 Aug, p.149.

-S-
Sacred Heart, p.100 | Sacred Heart, *Preface*, p.340 | Sacred Heart, *Votive Mass of*, p.281 | Saints, All, *Votive Mass of*, p.287 | Saints, All, 01 Nov, p.167 | Saints, All, *Preface*, p.360 | Saints, *Prefaces #1 and #2*, pp.349-350 | Saints, *Proper of*, p.101 | Sanctification of Human Work, *M&P for*, p.261 | Scholastica (V), 10 Feb, p.110 | Sebastian and Fabian (MM), 20 Jan, p.104 | Second Sunday after Christmas, p.25 | Second Sunday of Advent, p.9 | Second Sunday of Easter, p.68 | Sequences, p.315 | Seven Holy Founders of Servites, Feb 17, p.111 | Seventh Sunday of Easter, p.70 | Seventh Week of Easter, p.78 | Several Deceased Persons, *M&P for*, p.297 and p.308 | Sick, *M&P for the*, p.267 | Sing Praise, O Sion, *Sequence*, p.319 | Simon and Jude (AA), 28 Oct, p.166 | Sins, *the Forgiveness of*, *M&P for*, p.272 | Sixth Sunday of Easter, p.69 | Sixtus II and Companions (MM), 07 Aug, p.144 | Sorrows, Our Lady of, 15 Sep, p.154 | Souls, All, 02 Nov, p.167 | Spirit, Holy, *Prefaces #1 and #2*, p.345 | Spread of the Gospel, *M&P for*, p.253 | Stabat Mater Dolorosa, *Sequence*, p.321 | Stanislaus (B-M), 11 Apr, p.117 | Start of the Civil Year, *M&P at the*, p.261 | State or Nation, *M&P for*, p.256 | State, Head of, *M&P for*, p.257 | Stephen of Hungary, 16 Aug, p.147 | Stephen the Protomartyr, 26 Dec, p.179 | Storms, *M&P to ward off*, p.270 | Sundays in Advent, p.9 | Sundays in Lent, *Prefaces*, pp.332-333 | Sundays in Ordinary Time #1 - #33, p.83 | Sundays of the Year, *Prefaces, #1-#8*, pp.340-343 | Sylvester I (P), 31 Dec, p.181 | Synod or Council, *M&P for*, p.245.

-T-
Teresa of Avila (V-D), 15 Oct, p.162 | Thanksgiving to God, *M&P for*, p.271 | The

Mother Stayed Standing, in Sorrow Rent, *Sequence, p.321* | Theresa of the Child Jesus (V), *01 Oct, p.159* | Third Sunday of Advent, *p.10* | Third Sunday of Easter, *p.68* | Thomas (A), *03 Jul, p.135* | Thomas Aquinas (PR-D), *28 Jan, p.107* | Thomas Becket (B-M), *29 Dec, p.181* | Thomas More and John Fisher (MM), *22 Jun, p.131* | Those Who Govern the State, *M&P for, p.256* | Time of War or Revolution, *M&P in, p.260* | Timothy and Titus (BB), *26 Jan, p.106* | To the Paschal Victim, *Sequence, p.324* | Transfiguration, *06 Aug, p.143* | Transfiguration, *Preface, p.358* | Trinity, *Preface of the Most Holy, p.339* | Trinity Sunday, *p.99* | Trinity, *Votive Mass of the Holy, p.279* | Triumph of the Holy Cross, *14 Sep, p.154* | Turibius of Mongrovejo (B), *23 Mar, p.115*.

-U-

Unity of Christians, *M&P for the, p.251* | Unity of Christians, *Preface, p.365* | Universal Church, *M&P for the, p.239*.

-V-

Various Commemorations for the Dead, *p.296* | Various Needs, *M&P for, p.237* | Various Public Concerns, *M&P for, p.261* | Venerable Bede (PR-D), *25 May, p.124* | Veni, Sancte Spiritus, *Sequence, p.323* | Vianney, John Mary (P), *04 Aug, p.142* | Viaticum, *Ritual Mass for, p.224* | Victimae Paschali, *Sequence, p.324* | Vigil of John the Baptist, *23 Jun, p.131* | Vigil of Peter and Paul, *28 Jun, p.133* | Vigil of the Assumption, *14 Aug, p.146* | Vincent (Deacon-M), *22 Jan, p.105* | Vincent Ferrer (PR), *05 Apr, p.117* | Vincent de Paul (PR), *27 Sep, p.157* | Virginity, *Consecration to a Life of, p.231* | Virgins, *Common of, p.206* | Virgins, Holy, and Religious, *Preface, p.351* | Visitation, *31 May, p.125* | Vocations to the Religious Life, *M&P for, p.250* | Vocations to the Priesthood, *M&P for, p.248* | Votive Masses, *p.277*.

-W-

War or Revolution, *M&P in Time of, p.260* | Wedding Masses, *p.224* | Weekdays *after 2nd, 4th, and 6th Sundays of Easter, p.72* | Weekdays *after 3rd and 5th Sundays of Easter, p.76* | Weekdays *after 7th Sunday of Easter, p.78* | Weekdays *after Ash Wednesday, p.34* | Weekdays *from 02 Jan to the Baptism of the Lord, p.27* | Weekdays *of the 34th Week in Ordinary Time, p.98* | Weekdays *of Advent Before 16 Dec, p.11* | Weekdays *of Easter Week, p.65* | Weekdays *of Holy Week, p.52* | Wenceslaus (M), *28 Sep, p.158* | Work, *M&P for the Sanctification of Human, p.262*.

-X-

Xavier, Francis (P), *03 Dec, p.175*.

-Y-

Year, Sundays of the, *Prefaces #1-#8, pp.340-343* | Young Person, *M&P for a Deceased, p.306*.

-Z-

Zaccaria, Anthony Mary (P), *05 Jul, p.135*.